Library of Congress Cataloging-in-Publication Data

Cords, Sarah Statz, 1974-
   The inside scoop : a guide to nonfiction investigative writing and exposés / Sarah Statz Cords.
      p. cm. — (Real stories)
   Includes bibliographical references and index.
   ISBN 978-1-59158-650-0 (alk. paper)
   1. Investigative reporting—Bibliography. I. Title.
   Z6944.I58C67 2009
   [PN4781]
   016.813'54—dc22   2008038278
British Library Cataloguing in Publication Data is available.

Library of Congress Catalog Card Number: 2008038278
ISBN: 978-1-59158-650-0

First published in 2009

Libraries Unlimited, 88 Post Road West, Westport, CT 06881
A Member of the Greenwood Publishing Group, Inc.
www.lu.com

Printed in the United States of America

The paper used in this book complies with the
Permanent Paper Standard issued by the National
Information Standards Organization (Z39.48–1984).

10   9   8   7   6   5   4   3   2   1

For Barbara and Laura

Contents

Series Foreword ix
Acknowledgments...xi
Introduction...xiii

Chapter 1—In-Depth Reporting 1
    Definition of In-Depth Reporting...1
    Appeal of In-Depth Reporting...4
    Organization of the Chapter 4
    Feature Stories: Human Interest 5
    Feature Stories: On Location...21
    Historical Perspectives 27
    Historical Perspectives: Oral Histories...35
    Science Reporting 40
    Sports Reporting..48
    True Crime Investigations 57
    War Reporting 65
    Cultural Criticism..74
    Fiction Read-Alikes...79
    Further Reading...80
    References 81

Chapter 2—Exposés...83
    Definition of Exposés...83
    Appeal of Exposés..85
    Organization of the Chapter 86
    Government Exposés...86
    Corporate Exposés...95
    Social Exposés...113
    International Exposés 133
    Fiction Read-Alikes...144
    Further Reading...145
    References 146

Chapter 3—Immersion Journalism 147
    Definition of Immersion Journalism 147
    Appeal of Immersion Journalism 148
    Organization of the Chapter 149
    Personal Journeys..149
    The Work World 160
    Community Life and Society 170
    International Affairs 181

Fiction Read-Alikes 188
Further Reading 189
References 189

Chapter 4—Character Profiles 191
Definition of Character Profiles 191
Appeal of Character Profiles 192
Organization of the Chapter 193
Character Portraits 193
Ordinary People, Extraordinary Stories 201
Shared Experiences 207
Group Portraits 214
Fiction Read-Alikes 223
Further Reading 225
References 225

Chapter 5—Political Reporting 227
Definition of Political Reporting 227
Appeal of Political Reporting 228
Organization of the Chapter 229
Political Commentary: Right 230
Political Commentary: Left 241
Hot-Button Issues 257
Politics in Practice 270
Politicos 276
Fiction Read-Alikes 283
Further Reading 284
References 284

Chapter 6—Business Reporting 285
Definition of Business Reporting 285
Appeal of Business Reporting 286
Organization of the Chapter 287
Business Histories and Profiles 287
Business Trends 297
Biz Crit 307
Success Guides 320
Fiction Read-Alikes 328
Further Reading 329
References 329

Appendix A: Investigative Writing Book Awards 331
Appendix B: Documentary Films 337
Appendix C: Internet Resources 347
Appendix D: Magazines Offering Investigative Writing and Authors 353
Author/Title Index 359
Subject Index 399

Series Foreword

In my foreword to Sarah Statz Cords's *The Real Story: A Guide to Nonfiction Reading Interests,* I noted that her book provided a much-needed map to "the rich and varied world of nonfiction."

The titles in the <u>Real Stories</u> series flesh out the map that Sarah drew and take us even deeper into the exciting worlds of nonfiction genres—Investigative Writing, Biography, Autobiography and Memoir, Women's Nonfiction, True Adventure, Travel Literature, Environmental Writing, True Crime, Sports Stories, and many others.

The titles in this series are designed to assist librarians and other professionals who work with readers in identifying nonfiction books that their patrons or customers will enjoy reading. The titles in the series will also help libraries evaluate and build their collections in the various nonfiction genres.

Similar to the titles in Libraries Unlimited's <u>Genreflecting</u> series, each of the volumes in the Real Stories series focuses on a popular genre in the nonfiction arena. Individual guides organize and describe hundreds of books each and include definitions of each genre and its subgenres, as well as a discussion of the appeal of the genre and its subgenres. Because readers' advisory is ultimately about making connections, recommendations of other nonfiction books and fiction read-alikes are also provided for each book highlighted.

With *The Real Story,* nonfiction lovers gained the equivalent of general guidebooks to fiction genres, such as *Genreflecting* or Saricks' *Readers' Advisory Guide to Genre Fiction.* With the titles in the <u>Real Stories</u> series, we now have even more specific guidebooks, similar to the fiction guides, *Make Mine a Mystery* and *Hooked on Horror.*

God, as 20th-century architect Mies van der Rohe reminded us, is in the details. The titles in the <u>Real Stories</u> series help us to better understand the details of nonfiction and thereby to better serve our users who read nonfiction for pleasure.

—Robert Burgin

Acknowledgments

I'd like to open with a big shout-out and thanks to Libraries Unlimited, not only for letting me write this latest volume but also for continuing to publish readers' guides of all sorts; and I am also eternally grateful for their helpful and friendly staff.

Thank you to Elizabeth Budd, for the copyediting of this book; and particular thanks to Diana Tixier Herald and Nancy Pearl, on whose <u>Genreflecting</u> and <u>Now Read This</u> titles this book was modeled. Without the unceasing help and invaluable guidance of both Robert Burgin and Barbara Ittner, this book would not exist. Thanks also to Laura Calderone and her work on the Readers' Advisor Online database.

For countless book recommendations and conversations, I must say thanks to many librarians who I am also fortunate enough to call friends: Lisa Bitney, Katharine Clark, Katie Hanson, Roberta Johnson, Jane Jorgenson, Lee Konrad, Barbara Lundt, Sarah Nagle, Maureen O'Connor, Cynthia Orr, Rick Roche, Joyce Saricks, Richard Schwartz, Venta Silins, Kori Wex, Neal Wyatt, and Jessica Zellers. Can you all move closer to me so we can start our own book club?

I will never be able to thank my parents and my siblings enough, for everything they do for me and their acceptance of my annoying habit of hiding behind a book whenever possible. And thank you, thank you, thank you, to Kevin Cords. I knew when I first saw you reading your Norton anthology you were the one for me, and I'm still just grateful you agreed.

Introduction

Oscar Wilde once said, "The difference between literature and journalism is that journalism is unreadable and literature is not read." Wilde got a lot right, but I'd like to believe he got both parts of that particular witticism wrong; unreadable journalism may be available, but the vast majority of today's investigative and journalistic writing is skillfully done and engrossing to read. Likewise, alarming studies such as the 2004 report *Reading at Risk,* in which it was loudly proclaimed that "less than half of the adult American population now reads literature" (National Education Association 2004, ix) aside, many readers out there are still reading and enjoying literature of all types. Before I try and prove Wilde wrong (although I would never try to argue that he wasn't witty) and discuss why and how a reader's guide devoted to Investigative Writing and journalistic book-length works might be used, it might be a good idea to experience some déjà vu all over again (so said Yogi Berra; you can see I'm bringing in all the heavy hitters for this introduction) and consider the resurgence in popularity of both reading and advising readers on nonfiction books in general. A description and consideration of nonfiction Investigative Writing follows immediately thereafter.

Why Nonfiction Readers' Guides Are Needed: The Rise of the Real

In *The Real Story: A Reading Guide to Nonfiction Reading Interests,* I shared a quote from essayist Chuck Klosterman (several of whose titles appear in this volume), in which he opined, "it has come to my attention that there is a burgeoning generation of Americans who are suddenly and deeply engrossed with the consumption of nonfiction. I like to refer to these people as the Suddenly and Deeply Engrossed with Nonfiction Generation" (Klosterman 2004, 194). Klosterman was being facetious, as Klosterman so often is, but there can be no doubt that readers continue to be interested in nonfiction of all types. Americans are continuing to spend money on reading materials; in 2000, Americans spent $33.7 billion on "books and maps"; in 2005, that number was up to $42.2 billion. Spending on "magazines, newspapers, and sheet music" increased from $35 billion in 2000 to $43.8 billion in 2005, and I refuse to believe that sheet music alone was responsible for that increase (*Statistical Abstract* 2007, 755). In the winter and spring of 2008, reality television programs ruled (*American Idol, The Biggest Loser, Survivor*)—largely because of the unfortunate writers' strike during that time but also because viewers love them. "News" programs spoofing the news, notably *The Daily Show* with Jon Stewart and *The Colbert Report* with Stephen Colbert, not to mention the granddaddy of them all, the *Onion* newspaper and online broadcasts, continue to grow in popularity and also happen to feature nonfiction author interviews and promote reading. Of the top ten titles in Amazon's Top 100 list (updated hourly, the number cited reflects my findings the day I accessed the site) early in 2008, six were nonfiction and were holding their own against John Grisham's and Stephen King's new releases. Nonfiction, both informational (how-to, self-help, cookbooks, etc.) and more story-driven, is clearly here to stay, at least as a popular choice among readers.

It took time for the view to come back into favor that readers of nonfiction, in addition to fiction readers, might also be worthy of receiving help from librarians and other readers' advisors. In the 1987 first edition and the 1997 second edition of their reference book *Readers' Advisory Service in the Public Library*, Joyce Saricks and Nancy Brown stated that "readers' advisory service, as discussed in this book, is a patron-oriented library service for adult fiction readers" (Saricks and Brown 1997, 1); it was not until the third edition, published in 2005, that Saricks updated that definition to include the more general phrase of "adult leisure readers," (Saricks 2005, 1) to open the door to nonfiction. Although Robert Burgin had long been an advocate for nonfiction advising, most notably in his essay titled "Readers' Advisory and Nonfiction" (which appeared in the collection *The Readers' Advisor's Companion*, which he coedited with Kenneth Shearer and published in 2001), it was not until 2004 that an entire volume (*Nonfiction Readers' Advisory*, again edited by Burgin), was dedicated to issues surrounding reading and publicizing nonfiction collections. Neal Wyatt, collection development librarian extraordinaire and editor of *Library Journal*'s "Reader's Shelf" column (not to mention, among many other awards, a *Library Journal* magazine "mover and shaker" and winner of the Smart Bitches and Trashy Books Web site's "I-Just-Invented-It Award for Asskickingly Non-Condescending Description of Romance" award) also gave nonfiction books and readers a valuable resource when she published *The Readers' Advisory Guide to Nonfiction* in 2007. More readers' guides will soon be appearing for various nonfiction genres and subjects, including volumes on biographies, memoirs, and women's nonfiction, and this reader, at least, has only two words to say to that: please hurry. Nonfiction books, even in the midst of the information glut of our increasingly connected society and in a world where "everything is miscellaneous" and supposedly available online, are increasingly where it's at for many readers.

Readers' guides for nonfiction books (to supplement those already being published for mainstream and genre fiction titles) can also be used not only to stimulate our own reading choices but to perform better and broader advising work with patrons. Readers and those who advise them are also becoming increasingly aware that there are many connections to be made—not only between titles in the same fiction and nonfiction genres, but across those genres and classifications as well. The metaphor often used to illustrate this phenomenon is handily available in many of our libraries; with the majority of our collections separated into fiction and nonfiction, it is very easy to see that advisors who only read or prepare for fiction questions are quite literally cutting themselves off from all the riches of literature on the nonfiction side (and vice versa). Many readers of fiction can also appreciate a wide variety of nonfiction titles; likewise, many hardcore fans of nonfiction (myself included) are not averse to listening to and following up recommendations of fiction titles. They are not interchangeable, of course, and each type of reading has something to offer the reader, but Catherine Ross's study of adult pleasure readers, outlined in her essay "Reading Nonfiction for Pleasure: What Motivates Readers?" offers her assertions that "a great many readers read both" and "an interest in a particular subject can trump the distinction between fiction and nonfiction" (Ross 2004, 107). Abby Alpert also made a strong argument for incorporating nonfiction, especially narrative nonfiction (as she defines it, "a style that encompasses any nonfiction genre or topic that emphasizes story, including biography, memoir, and essays") in her *Reference and User Services Quarterly* article titled "Incorporating Nonfiction into Readers' Advisory Services" (Alpert 2006, 26). But where to begin when working with fiction readers who might consider nonfiction, and vice versa? Perhaps the best place to start might be a quick consideration of the differences and similarities between the two.

Fiction and Nonfiction: Why Can't These Two Kids Just Get Along?

Well, the answer to that, of course, is that they can and do. In the course of a normal day, I can switch quite happily between nonfiction books and novels, depending on where I am and what kind of reading I feel like at that very moment. And I know I am not unique in this. I know that from the literature on the subject, including Catherine Ross's already mentioned "Reading Nonfiction for Pleasure" article and Neal Wyatt's *The Readers' Advisory Guide to Nonfiction*, in which she suggests that "not only can nonfiction be a suggestion in and of itself, but nonfiction can also be a support to fiction reading, expanding the world of the book beyond the limits of its bound pages" (Wyatt 2007, 35). I also know it from seven years of working behind a circulation desk. Sure, a number of patrons simply check out the very newest best sellers, novels, or movies. But a lot of them also check out a mix of materials: novels, biographies, political titles, cookbooks, magazines, and movies, to name just a few. Think of all the people you see in lines, on planes, and waiting in the doctor's office reading magazines. Do those readers turn their noses up at such materials because they're nonfiction? Will those same magazine browsers refuse to touch a novel when they get home? Of course not.

But if it is wrong to assume that fiction and nonfiction materials—and by extension, readers—are completely different, it is also wrong to assume that there are no differences between them. Nonfiction, for starters, is the only literary style defined by what it is not: it is *not* an invented story (Merriam-Webster); it is *not* fiction. It is not made up. (This contention will become very important later on, as we more carefully examine the style of investigative writing in particular.) When offering nonfiction books to readers, it is always very important to keep in mind that the events and characters described therein are real; *The Kite Runner*, a best-selling novel about war and Afghanistan, might be read and enjoyed by a patron, but that is no guarantee that the same patron will take to Åsne Seierstad's Immersion Journalism classic, *The Bookseller of Kabul*, and the very real and therefore flawed individuals she describes.

Nonfiction also differs from (particularly genre) fiction in the time its authors take to research and write it. Whereas fans of James Patterson and Alexander McCall Smith can reliably depend on at least one new title a year (or two, or three), many authors of nonfiction indulge, by necessity, in longer periods between books. This is necessary, especially when reporting on complex stories and unique individuals (Adrian Nicole LeBlanc, for example, spent a decade researching her title *Random Family*), but it does pose a problem for the dedicated nonfiction reader who can't wait for his favorite author's next book. If it poses a challenge for the reader, you can bet it poses a problem for that reader's advisor; where do you send the person who loved LeBlanc's work, when another title by that author isn't even on the horizon? Along with its longer production times, nonfiction often (not always) can take longer to read than do novels, particularly novels that are quickly paced or meant to be page-turners. Again, this feature poses challenges for both readers and their advisors: readers who know they'll be spending some time with their nonfiction titles, want to find good ones; likewise, advisors wanting to find those "good ones" in advance might be stymied in their attempts to quickly skim as many nonfiction books as they can fiction books. Nonfiction also rarely appears in series, making each nonfiction author's new outing less predictable than those of series authors. Readers who enjoy Sue Grafton can be reasonably assured that *T Is for Trespass* won't be all that different from *A Is for Alibi*, and that is part of the appeal. Fans of, say, Joan Didion, have no such assurance. Will her new book be a book of essays, like *Slouching toward Bethlehem*? Or a memoir, like her *The Year of Magical Thinking*? Or a wonderful mix of both, as in *Where I Was From*? This is both the glory and the difficulty of following and recommending nonfiction titles.

Nonfiction also poses difficulties in that we rarely arrange it, in libraries, according to the genre or style conventions that can be so useful when offering and promoting fiction collections such as mysteries and romances. Although some libraries are cataloging or displaying their nonfiction in popular interest categories that mimic those in bookstores, including Self-Help, Pop Culture, and Nature, we are still largely bound to organization by subject, as dictated by the Dewey Decimal and Library of Congress classification systems. This is very handy when we want to help a patron quickly locate all of our titles on Ayurvedic massage, feng shui, or knitting. It is not nearly as useful when we have a patron who's in the mood for something adventurous, maybe a bit like Sebastian Junger's *The Perfect Storm* or Robert Kurson's *Shadow Divers*, and who doesn't much care if the adventure takes place on top of a mountain or in the middle of the ocean. Then we are largely on our own. We also don't have a whole lot of tools at our disposal to determine the tone or mood of a certain book; to determine what level of sex, violence, or profanity is involved; or to tell if it's a more scholarly and heavily researched book or if it's, for lack of a better term, a work of more "popular" history. (We have these problems with fiction, too, I realize.) As I type, all sorts of social cataloguing and networking online sites and services are attempting to address this issue by allowing readers to assign "tags" to certain books; this is a helpful step, but it is hampered by the lack of consistency among tags. One person's "sexy" tag might be someone else's "spicy" tag (I myself, a *Simpsons* fan, might have to indulge in an inside joke from that show, with an elderly lady watching her soap opera stories, and tag such books in my library as "filthy, but genuinely arousing"). It is the point of this readers' guide and guides like it to provide some of those clues for us, by offering such subjects and tags of our own as "Profanity" and "Gentle Reads." The point is, this is another dimension of nonfiction books that must be taken into account. It's important in fiction too, but when the profanity, sex, and violence are real, the chances are greater that readers will have a stronger reaction to them.

Of course, although the differences are many, these are still all books we're talking about, and there are many similarities between fiction and nonfiction as well. Fiction often lends itself to genres, the books that Diana Tixier Herald says "share multiple characteristics and features" (Herald 2006, 31); although it is not as common for nonfiction books to be defined and grouped according to their shared characteristics, it is common to think of some titles as True Adventure titles, or Travel books, or sharing the same style of Investigative Writing. Likewise, nonfiction books can offer many of the same appeal factors as do novels; in Nancy Pearl's readers' guides to mainstream and literary fiction, the appeal factors of setting, story, character, and language were used to organize novels together by style rather than subject, author, or genre. Joyce Saricks's appeal factors vary from those slightly, as she lists pacing, characterization, story line, and frame (Saricks 2005, 44–65). The vocabulary is not really what's important here, because every readers' advisor will tend to take in all of these labels and silently apply them as necessary while providing advisory help rather than sharing their definitions with patrons; what is important is recognizing that nonfiction can be every bit as story-driven, every bit as quickly (or leisurely) paced, every bit as chock-full of unique characters. Neal Wyatt provides a particularly helpful overview of this phenomenon in her chapter "A Reader's Advisory Approach to Nonfiction," when she considers appeal factors such as pacing, detail, and tone (among others) and places them in context alongside specialized appeal factors in nonfiction, such as learning and experiencing, stating both that it is a "notable part of nonfiction that many authors set out to teach readers and many readers pick up books to learn," as well as that "books that do not intend to teach usually intend to share an experience or explain a particular feeling or event" (Wyatt 2007, 19–20). Wyatt also notes the importance of subject to nonfiction readers and defines various types of nonfiction as well, including memoirs, essays, biographies, and others.

When considering the plots and story types found in many fiction narratives, it is important also to note that many of those same plots can be found in nonfiction as well. One of the most informative and liveliest books on this subject, Christopher Booker's *The Seven Basic Plots,* offers only novels (as well as a few poetic epics and dramatic classics, including plays by Shakespeare) as examples, but it's not hard to extrapolate from his fiction categories to nonfiction narratives. Among the types of plots he lists are "overcoming the monster," "rags to riches," "voyage and return," as well as "comedy" and "tragedy" (Booker 2005). One of my favorite descriptions of his is that of the movie *Star Wars,* in which "the story is set in the distant future, when the many planetary worlds of our galaxy are ruled by one [benevolent] government.... But the government has now been seized by a conspiracy of power-crazed politicians" (Booker 2005, 42). You would not have to read many of the titles listed in the "Political Reporting" chapter of this book to find that they largely follow that same plot, no matter who is in the White House. Another stunning similarity can be found between stories and nonfiction narratives offering rags to riches themes. Booker provides the example of the myth of King Arthur: "anyone who can pull out the sword [from the stone in St. Paul's churchyard] shall be king. All the great men of the nation try and fail. But to everyone's astonishment the unknown young squire steps forward and removes the sword effortlessly. He becomes King Arthur" (Booker 2005, 51). Ron Suskind's character profile *A Hope in the Unseen: An American Odyssey from the Inner City to the Ivy League,* set in a different century and very different place, relates nearly the same story: that of inner-city youth Cedric Jennings, who attends high school in a crime-ridden neighborhood in Washington, D.C., but who has applied and then gains admittance to the Ivy League Brown University. If one but looks, nonfiction stories following fiction plots can be found everywhere.

So, there are similarities. There are also differences. But the biggest similarity of all may be the need that supercedes the needs of fiction readers or nonfiction readers; that is the need of each individual reader to be matched with his or her book. It is to answer that need that we have to gain familiarity not only with a wide variety of fiction and nonfiction authors, titles, publishers but also with appeal factors ranging from story to language to tone, and with even more specific questions of type, genre, and style. It is for that reason that now may be a good time to examine exactly which types of books and stories can be considered examples of Investigative Writing.

The Problem of What to Call It

Why a readers' guide for, of all things, Investigative Writing?

It is not, after all, a genre or subject matter that patrons and readers are liable to march up to our help desks and demand. It is not a heading we will easily find in our public catalogs and other review resources (unless we happen to chance across its closely related heading "journalism"), and it is not even a category that you will find in any self-respecting Borders or Barnes and Noble. William Langewiesche, a notable writer of the style and one of my particular favorites, describes how the style offers booksellers, librarians, and readers a unique problem: "in truth it doesn't really have a label—which is why you can never find the stuff in a bookstore. They don't know where to put it, so they try to force it into existing categories" (Boynton 2005, 225). For booksellers, the problem of where to put these books so that customers will find and buy them is the problem; for librarians, the problem of placement where nonfiction is concerned is typically answered for us by the collection management and cataloguing staffs. For readers' advisors, the problem is not so often where to put something, but more frequently remembering that, sandwiched between all those informational books falling neatly into their Dewey and Library of Congress subject classifications, all those medical reference books and cookbooks and annual travel guides, are wonderfully narrative, character-driven, and richly styled nonfiction titles that are recreational reading treasures in their own right.

Langewiesche still raises an important point. The only things seemingly more numerous than quality investigative books are the labels that have been devised to group them together. What should we be calling it? One of the earliest entries in the label game was Tom Wolfe's "new journalism," a heading that he attributes, variously, to both Seymour Krim and Pete Hamill (Wolfe 1973, 23) and that is the title he used for his *The New Journalism*, an early anthology of such journalistic pieces. Of course editor Robert Boynton had to then come along and top that with his anthology, *The New New Journalism*, published in 2005. I can't imagine it will be long before a title such as *The Newest Journalism of All, Now, We Mean It, This Is as New as It Gets* comes out. Lee Gutkind threw his hat in the naming ring when he promoted the title "creative nonfiction," a concept that, according to him, "offers great flexibility and freedom, while adhering to the basic tenets of nonfiction writing and/or reporting.... Creative nonfiction writers are encouraged to utilize fictional (literary) techniques in their prose—from scene to dialogue to description to point of view—and to be cinematic at the same time" (Gutkind 1998, 3). But what does "creative" really mean? Does it mean that the author has taken liberties with some of the facts and the details? Has he or she invented dialogue? No matter how stridently Gutkind (often considered the godfather of creative nonfiction and the founder of the journal *Creative Nonfiction*) protests that the one thing creative nonfiction writers can't do is make up stuff, describing nonfiction as "creative" is a sure way to keep readers wondering what such nonfiction authors are creating out of their own imaginations. Gutkind also goes on, in the same introduction, to divide creative nonfiction further into autobiography and "documentary drama." He also, in his definition, inadvertently lists another label often ascribed to this type of writing: "literary nonfiction" or "literary journalism." To my mind, the difficulty with that description is the same one that the loaded term "literary" brings to "literary fiction." It does give the reader and advisor an idea of the book's style and quality, but it is hard to define and even harder to judge or categorize. Are novels by Jodi Picoult "literary fiction"? Talk to five different readers, and you'll probably get five different opinions on that question. Can Malcolm Gladwell's popular nonfiction title be called "literary" nonfiction? If so, what makes it "literary"? On that particular moniker, I am in complete agreement with radio producer and host Ira Glass, who had this to say on that subject: "I'm a snob when it comes to that phrase. I think it's for losers. It's pretentious, for one thing, and it's a bore. Which is to say, it's exactly the opposite of the writing it's trying to describe. Calling a piece of writing 'literary nonfiction' is like daring you to read it" (Glass 2007, 12).

The same problems, magnified, go along with the term "narrative nonfiction," which seems to be gaining in vogue among literary theorists and readers' advisors alike. It is not a label with which I am fully comfortable, however, because it seems to exclude any nonfiction titles that do not tell a story. Do Malcolm Gladwell's titles *The Tipping Point* or *Blink* really tell cohesive stories? Do books such as Brian Greene's *The Elegant Universe*? If "narrative nonfiction" is too narrow, then "general nonfiction" is too broad. Wyatt offered a category of "general nonfiction" in her 2007 title *The Readers' Advisory Guide to Nonfiction,* including such titles as Nicholas Basbanes's *A Gentle Madness* (Arts, Literature, and Philosophy), *The Art of Travel* by Alain de Botton (Essays), and Chris Anderson's *The Long Tail* (Economics); she also lists titles in various subject chapters such as "Food and Cooking" and "True Crime" as "reporting" titles, which might work for "a reader who wants insider looks at different subjects" (Wyatt 2007, 9). And the labels only get more complicated from there; Robert Boynton, in addition to differentiating between new journalism and new new journalism, calls it "reportorially based, narrative-driven long-form nonfiction" (Boynton 2005, xi). There is nothing really wrong with any of these categories and headings, but I defy you to try fitting them in on snappy library signs or bookmarks.

Likewise, headings such as "Current Affairs" raise more difficulties than they solve: what does "affairs" really mean? And in a world where everything moves so fast that books and stories are often obsolete before they can be adequately proofread and edited, much less published and sold, what makes an affair "current"? In libraries and recreational reading collections, where we are luckily not bound to keeping only those books that sell and then guaranteeing them shelf space only six months or a year before they are remaindered, the "current" label loses even more in the way of practicality. Current Affairs, Politics, Sociology, Business—none of these interest categories adequately or wholly explain this style of books.

So why Investigative Writing? It doesn't readily roll off the tongue or lend itself to signs or displays, I'll admit. Among the reasons I chose the heading was because of its descriptive nature and because it is at least a little familiar: if nothing else, we've all heard the *Dateline* and other news programs headlines: "And now, an investigative report from.. . ." The stories and the people and the events in these books were, first and foremost, investigated. For the vast majority of these titles, although in differing degrees, there are two certainties: research was done, and someone was talked to. This is the crux of what makes Investigative Writing hang together as a style. The former journalism major in me has to apologize for burying this key information in the middle of the introduction; in journalistic circles, opening with secondary information and revealing the true heart of the story later is known as "burying the lede" (and yes; it is "lede," a throwback to the times when writers had to distinguish their opening sentence, the lede, from the lead type used to set their stories).

Speaking of journalists, there's no denying that what I term Investigative Writing is very close in style and tone to journalism, whether it is of the daily newspaper variety or that found in books. Many of the authors found in this book either were or are working journalists, and the developmental history of this writing style closely resembles the history of journalism, particularly in its traditional reporting and muckraking forms. Some of these books even started out as journalism, as essays and articles in newspapers, magazines, and online journals and blogs. Many of the titles in this book share the hallmarks of journalism, which George Kennedy and Daryl Moen so eloquently list in their book *What Good Is Journalism?*: "Journalism tells us most of what we know about the world beyond our own experience. Journalism goes where its audience cannot or will not.. . . Journalism tells stories of heartbreak and heroism, of triumph and disaster, of the endless fascinations in ordinary life. Journalism is the glue of information that holds a complex nation together" (Kennedy and Moen 2007, 1).

So why not just call this volume *Journalism* and be done with it? Because, as closely related as the journalistic and investigative styles are, they are not the same thing. The term "journalism," for one thing, is too closely linked to the daily and the ephemeral, in print and online, to truly and comfortably be applied to book-length works of nonfiction. Journalism has also popularly been called, in a phrase often attributed to Philip Graham, infamous editor of the *Washington Post*, "the first draft of history." That is a memorable turn of phrase, and one that fairly accurately gets at the appeal and immediacy of most serial journalism, but it is not really accurate or appropriate when it comes to many of these books, many of which took shape over the course of years of careful and dedicated research and investigation and then were written with more care than the term "first draft" would imply. With its emphasis on immediacy and notoriety, the term journalism also does not adequately describe many of the subgenres (or types or substyles, if you prefer) outlined in this book; are character profiles of individuals who aren't famous really journalism? Are Immersion Journalism stories, in which authors go undercover to live the stories on which they're reporting, typically found in daily newspapers? Even if a case could be made that they are, the word journalism just doesn't seem big enough to encompass them. With respect for and belief in the mass media and its practitioners also riding at an all-time low, now is also a particularly tricky time to label a work journalism and earn it any respect.

So, Investigative Writing it is—at least in this volume (as it was in *The Real Story*). As with all genre and style types, as well as appeal factors, you are welcome to refer to it in any way that feels natural to you. The more important thing, rather than its heading, is to recall that when readers come to you looking for books or nonfiction in particular that are based in facts and research and interviews, or that tell stories of unique individuals, or that offer an inside look at a subject, or the untold story, they might really be asking you for Investigative Writing books.

The Characteristics of Investigative Writing

The Big Idea

Investigative Writing books, like many other nonfiction titles, have much to offer readers of all types; there are titles here for readers who love action-packed, dramatic stories; unique and empathetically described and fascinating characters; exotic settings and smooth and literary prose styles galore. But Investigative Writing offers yet another appeal factor beyond all of those, and even beyond subject, tone, and mood; another hard-to-describe appeal factor of these books is, to put it simply, the "idea." (Authors of some of the more sweeping and historical titles might call it the "big idea.") It is hard to write about ideas, as NPR commentator Ira Glass points out: "Usually the plot is the easy part. You do whatever research you can, you talk to lots of people, and you figure out what happened. It's the ideas that kill you. What's the story mean? What bigger truth about all of us does it point to?" (Glass 2007, 8). Ideas are often linked to the subject matters of authors' books, but they are not the subjects themselves. They are the intangibles. And, perfectly, wonderfully, or exasperatingly (depending on how you choose to look at it), the ideas that different readers can take away from the same book vary as often as do the other such intangibles as mood. In this respect, this is an appeal factor that makes the divisions between good fiction and good nonfiction even hazier; just as two readers can get totally different things out of the same novel (I thought Anne Tyler's novel *The Clock Winder* had a happy ending; the author herself is on record saying she thought it was a depressing ending), so, too, can readers get very different ideas out of the same work of nonfiction. One reader of Elizabeth Gilbert's Character Profile *The Last American Man* might find Eustace Conway, her protagonist, a back-to-the-land hero; another may find him an obnoxious eccentric. Likewise, one reader might find Stefan Fatsis's Immersion title *Word Freak* a fun and funny diversion; another reader might find it a slightly darker tale of a hobby that turns into an unhealthy obsession.

The Search for Truth

One of the biggest and most amorphous of ideas in all of Investigative Writing is the idea of truth, and the processes by which it is discovered. This is such a central concern and tenet of the style that in Robert Boynton's collection *The New New Journalism,* which consists largely of interviews with "new new" journalists (William Langewiesche, Adrian Nicole LeBlanc, Michael Lewis, are just a few examples), Boynton poses the question of what the authors think is meant by the word truth, and how they seek to investigate it. The answers are as varied as the writers and their topics themselves: Leon Dash says, "there is no such thing as absolute truth.. . . What I am seeking to do in my writing is to get as close as I can to the whole truth about someone's motivations as I can" (Boynton 2005, 71), and Gay Talese opines that "there is no such thing as absolute truth. Reporters can find anything they want to find. Every reporter brings the totality of his battle scars to the event" (Boynton 2005, 377). Investigative Writing authors are fact finders who engage in copious amounts of research (using primary sources, archives, photographic evidence, and any other information they can get their hands on), interview anyone with a connection to their story they can find, and sometimes even immerse themselves in their own stories and live the subjects they are writing about.

Are Investigative Writing Books "Objective"?

Closely related to the idea of truth is the hallowed concept of journalistic objectivity. Although early journalistic writing in America was anything but objective (many newspapers during the Federalist period, for example, declared themselves openly to be for one political party or another), the idea gained popularity in the twentieth century that journalists and news authors had a responsibility to their readers to be completely objective, without opinions themselves; or, if they did have opinions, they had to make sure those opinions never found their way into their reporting. The development of the inverted pyramid format for reporting the news encouraged journalists to leave out description and impressions and state, in the first paragraph of their reports, the who, why, what, where, and when of events, only adding less important details further down in their narratives, was a direct result of the idea that the journalist's voice and writing style should be secondary to the content. Again, this is an easier concept to accept if you are not actually a reader of investigative nonfiction. Although many nonfiction investigative writers still carefully keep themselves out of their stories, many also now share indications of their worldviews with their readers, and many actively immerse themselves in their stories. There can be no doubt how Barbara Ehrenreich, when she worked service and maid jobs in her Immersion classic *Nickel and Dimed*, felt about the economic situations in which such workers find themselves. Likewise, the authors of most Business and Political Reporting books clearly make their alliances known: you don't have to read very many pages of books by either Michael Moore or Ann Coulter to know where they stand on political and cultural issues. Have no fear that the books included in this volume consist only of fact-bound, nondescriptive, purely objective works in which the author's voice or beliefs are impossible to discern. The practitioners of Investigative Writing themselves often admit that the heralded idea of objectivity is nearly impossible to achieve in practice. Rebecca Solnit has confessed that "I did much better with professors like Ben Bagdikian [himself a well-known journalist and author], who said that there's no such thing as objectivity but there is fairness" (Terzian 2007, 52). Michael Lewis takes it a step further when he declares, "I reject the idea of the 'objective journalist.' The notion that you can be so detached that who you are doesn't affect how you see things is worse than bad.... The best I can do is to purify my vision and then leave it to the reader to decide what it is worth" (Boynton 2005, 268).

Although we have now jettisoned the idea that investigative writers must have no opinions of their own, Lewis's quote is still instructive in his focus on the reader. Although many of the writers in this volume violate what journalism professors would define as strict objectivity, they do not typically seek to enforce their version of and understanding of events on their readers. This small but important difference is what makes the titles in this volume stylistically different from nonfiction books that I have referred to as part of the "Making Sense . . ." genre in the past: those "books are characterized by their author's neologisms, theorizing, and subject synthesis" (Cords 2006, 300). Malcolm Gladwell not only provides information on his investigations of cause and effect in *The Tipping Point*; he goes one step further and calls some people "Early

Adopters" and others "Influencers." Steven Johnson, in his book *Everything Bad Is Good for You,* not only cites facts and figures about young people and their use of video games, but makes the strident case that those video games are really making today's youth smarter. Making Sense. . . authors, many of them fine writers and journalists in their own rights, nonetheless put the emphasis not on the stories they're investigating but on the conclusions that they themselves draw from those stories. Investigative authors, particularly those who write on subjects other than politics and business, don't do that. As noted by Michael Lewis, they tend to present their characters and their stories and then trust their readers to draw their own conclusions. Elizabeth Gilbert profiled a fascinating and individualistic man, Eustace Conway, in her Character Profile *The Last American Man*; although she shared her personal opinions about his quest to live a more authentic life in the Appalachian Mountains, she did not heartily endorse his way of life as one her readers should emulate. Adrian Nicole LeBlanc told the stories of women and families trapped in urban poverty and crime but did not advance her own recommendations to ameliorate such a situation.

The Appeal of Investigative Writing

All of the characteristics just described, from strong storylines and empathetically drawn characters, to the larger ideas (truth and objectivity or impartiality among them, as well as concepts such as justice, heroism, and love, to name a few others) combine to form one cohesive style. The subjects in this collection vary from business to politics, sports to crime, social policy to personal obsessions, and back again. The stories these authors cover also often represent stories that have been ignored, inadequately told or explored, or misrepresented in other, more immediate venues, including the broadcast and print news media and blogs and other Internet sources, which also adds to their appeal, particularly to curious readers who want to know the "whole story" or the "real story." But they also share one very important attribute, and that is their genesis in their authors' abiding curiosity about the world and the people around them, and those authors' desire to find things out for themselves. They offer the further appeal of their authors' presenting the stories and trusting their readers to draw their own conclusions regarding the situations they have described.

Above all, these books will appeal to readers who approach their favorite books as a way to have conversations with the authors and with those individuals whose stories are being told. There are no easy answers in these books. But there is the trust that between the writers' presentation of the facts and stories, and their readers' experience of learning about them, knowledge and understanding will be increased on all sides. In the foreword to a collection of investigative journalism by Mike Sager, journalism professor Walt Harrington described Sager's (and, by extension, all investigative authors') craft by describing exactly what he did: "Anything to reach readers where they lived. Anything to take readers where *other* people lived" (Sager 2007, xiii).

Investigative Writing and the Reader: Connections to Other Nonfiction and Fiction Genres

As all readers' advisors know, being familiar with the titles and authors in particular genres and styles, and knowing a little something about how such titles relate to one another and to titles in other genres and subgenres, is only half the job. The majority of our book and reading knowledge is often acquired to better manage and organize our library collections, make purchase decisions among the huge variety of new titles and authors published every month, and to work with readers to determine where their reading tastes and inclinations may take them on any given day. Increasingly I think we are becoming aware that it is not enough to simply ascertain what was the last book a patron read, and then give that reader everything else in your collection that is "just like" that prior book. That may indeed be what some patrons want. But we may also encounter readers who just finished a serious literary novel and are now in the mood for "something lighter"; likewise, the reader who just finished that long presidential candidate biography may be ready for some more quickly paced novels. As a reader, I will always consider a memoir that someone wants to suggest, but I'll admit I'm usually more amenable to those suggestions if I haven't just finished reading multiple memoirs. (This is a very real occurrence, in our age of plentiful memoirs.)

Investigative Writing, as a cohesive nonfiction style, has much to offer in its lack of cohesive subject matters or genre conventions. Because these writers write books that span the full range of possible subjects and human foibles, from scientific advances to business histories, corrupt individuals to the incorruptible, connections can be made between these titles and a wide range of nonfiction genres, subgenres, and titles. Readers who enjoy one reporter's take on the individuals who clean up crime scenes (Gil Reavill's *Aftermath, Inc.*) might also consider True Crime narratives by authors such as Ann Rule or Harold Schechter. Fans of an environmental exposé such as Elizabeth Kolbert's *Field Notes from a Catastrophe: Man, Nature, and Climate Change*, might also consider more reflective Environmental Writing titles such as Annie Dillard's *Pilgrim at Tinker Creek* or even Henry David Thoreau's *Walden*. Fans of Political Reporting books might be enthralled by a good political biography; Business Reporting readers might enjoy the insights to be found in many a Working Life memoir. The combinations are endless and are not restricted solely to nonfiction books. Fans of In-Depth Reporting titles, in which authors often function as investigators out to track down the truth, might find themselves drawn to mystery and thriller titles in which the protagonists also function as investigators seeking to unravel secrets and complicated plots. Many of the Character Profile titles in this collection feature touching and intense love stories; mainstream, historical, and romance fiction titles that also feature love stories might also hold some interest for such readers.

Investigative Writing is also related, as noted earlier, to the nonfiction style I like to call "Making Sense. . . ." Between these two styles of nonfiction writing, however, there is one very important difference, and that is one of direction: inveterately curious, investigative writers want to get to the bottom of the story and then let their reader decide what to do with that information, whereas Making Sense. . . writers are also interested in getting and telling the story but are more interested in telling their readers what they themselves think it means. Although not all investigative authors are impartial (a great many of them, in fact, particularly in the Exposés and Political Reporting chapters, are very partial indeed), they do tend to direct their readers a little less obviously. Authors such as Malcolm Gladwell and Jared Diamond do the research and tell the stories, but they often take that next step and extrapolate conclusions, describing why things might be the way they are; investigative authors such as Eric Schlosser and Jonathan Kozol direct the bulk of their energy to simply exposing how things are now. This emphasis on the present makes Investigative Writing titles more immediately affecting narratives, but there is no denying that many curious and engaged readers who enjoy investigative titles might also find much to like in more analytical "Making Sense. . ." books—particularly those that correspond to their favorite and pet subjects —but they should also be aware that such books are typically more slowly paced and more scholarly in tone than most titles found in *The Inside Scoop*.

The Selection Process

So how does a reader looking for Investigative Writing titles find them?

This reader tried to look in a variety of places. When selecting titles for inclusion in this volume, I started once again with my periodical bible of the book publishing world, *Publisher's Weekly*, and considered reviews for the last several years' worth of nonfiction titles. Other review publications including *Library Journal* and *Booklist* provided titles, as did the glossier magazine *Bookmarks*. Browsing the "Current Affairs," "Cultural Studies," "Journalism," and "Sociology" shelves at bookstores was also informative and helpful, as was browsing my own library system's catalog under what similar subject headings I could find. As when selecting nonfiction titles for *The Real Story*, I also chose and annotated as many titles as fit the Investigative Writing genre from various award lists, including the prior decade's ALA Notable Books, New York Times Notable Books, and winners of the National Book Award, National Book Critics Circle Award, and the Pulitzer Prize. Although a frustratingly low number of books in translation or books published first in other countries are available to us in the United States, I included as many as I could find (and listed "Books in Translation" as one of their subjects); likewise, most of the publishers represented in this volume are major ones and therefore owned by the same few conglomerates, but an effort was made to include titles by smaller, independent publishers, including Soft Skull Press and Chelsea Green Publishing. When I could find university press titles that I felt conformed to the Investigative Writing style, I included them; because those titles tend to be more scholarly and analytical than truly investigative in nature, however, university presses are not heavily represented in this volume.

Many authors found throughout this collection can also be found writing more ephemeral journalism pieces for daily newspapers and magazines; whenever possible, information has been added to the title annotations and the "Now Try" read-alike suggestions to provide information on an authors' reporting background. Because blogs have become an increasingly important part of our daily mass media mix, I also searched among them for possible authors and titles. For example, Arianna Huffington, of the online publication *The Huffington Post*, is not only a political author in her own right but features writings by many other journalists who have also written books.

I also chose and annotated books based on their subject matters, choosing the titles I thought would have the broadest appeal and were some of the best examples of the investigative style in their subgenres and on their subjects; when similar books were available, even if I haven't annotated all of them, I did try to make reference to them in the "Now Try" sections of reading suggestions following each annotated title. Because Investigative Writing is also a nonfiction genre that trades at least partially on its currency, the vast majority of titles included in this volume were published within the past decade (many titles in the Political and Business Reporting chapters, specifically, were published within the past five years). Although a certain number of perennially popular and widely read "classics" were included, some of which boast publishing dates from the early half of the twentieth century, the emphasis in this volume has been selecting and organizing more current books.

As in *The Real Story*, it should be noted that this volume of Investigative Writing books is emphatically not comprehensive. Thousands of Business Reporting books alone are published each year, not to mention all of the titles from the other subgenres (Exposés and Political Reporting, as well as general works of In-Depth Reporting, are also large nonfiction publishing areas). This guide, as with most readers' guides, is meant to be used as a starting point, and as a tool for further thinking about and engaging in (particularly nonfiction, although fiction should never be forgotten) readers' advisory practice. This collection contains annotations and specific read-alike suggestions for more than five hundred nonfiction titles; many of the titles that were first included in the Investigative Writing chapter of *The Real Story* are also included here (comprising less than 10 percent of the titles in this guide) but have been updated to reflect more specific subgenre placements, as well as to include, whenever possible, more current fiction and nonfiction titles in their "Now Try" read-alike sections.

Organization of the Chapters

I have divided the broad category of Investigative Writing into six distinct subcategories, or subgenres, largely based on their different styles, appeals, and sometimes even, yes, subject matter (although subject matter is not the only reason people choose and enjoy specific nonfiction books, it remains an important part of their appeal and categorization). The first and longest chapter features works of In-Depth Reporting, which are books generally written by investigative authors doing what they do best: getting out there and investigating a story, performing research, or interviewing people they think can give them a deeper understanding of their chosen subject, topic, theme, or current obsession. It is within this first chapter that the largest number and widest array of appeal factors can be found; In-Depth Reporting titles often feature great stories, compelling characters, particular settings or journeys, or unique and sometimes even experimental writing styles and language. Because these are nonfiction titles, they also offer a great deal of quantitative information that can help readers experience or learn more about subjects of interest or generally interesting stories; further, because they often involve multiple viewpoints and many investigative authors seek the truth, not as an absolute, but as an ever-shifting construct, they can also offer a wealth of qualitative information and stories as well. Because they are often the most accessible and popular of the Investigative Writing genre, they have been placed front and center.

The In-Depth Reporting subgenre is followed by a section of Exposés, which are distinctive in their authors' relentless pursuits of their stories, as well as in their tones of discovery and the revelation of secrets. These are truly the stories that have slipped through the cracks and were simply awaiting an intrepid investigative author's interest and research; some of the most popular phrases found in the subtitles of these books are "the true story," "the secret history," "the inside story," "the untold story," "lost history," and "dark side"; popular subtitle words include "subversion," "betrayal," "deadly," and "changing." They're scary words, but they also evoke a thrill, even if it's a worried one. These books tend largely to be story-driven page-turners that might appeal to a wide variety of nonfiction and fiction readers who are in search of a good old-fashioned start-to-finish narrative (although it should be noted that these books do not always have a happy ending). Many Exposés also rely heavily on the appeal of setting, because many of their stories are set in very distinctly described regions and locations, most of which are part of the larger narrative.

In the third chapter, you'll find Immersion Journalism titles, the defining feature of which is their authors' willingness to immerse themselves in their stories and relate their experiences. Although the heading of "Immersion Journalism" is one that is heard with frequency only in MFA writing and graduate journalism programs and literary criticism, the practitioners of this subgenre are some of the most well known in the entire guide. There you will find Barbara Ehrenreich, Ted Conover, A. J. Jacobs, Bill Buford, John McPhee, George Plimpton, and countless others. These titles offer not only fascinating stories, but also unique characters—not only those individuals the authors interview and get to know, but also the authors themselves, who share their own thoughts, impressions, and experiences as freely as the most personal of memoirists.

The shift to strongly drawn characters in Immersion Journalism propels us toward the subgenre that follows it: Character Profiles. For readers who are interested in people, not to mention their personalities, foibles, and relationships, these are the investigative books to suggest. Although the authors of these titles investigate their subjects' lives very closely, these are not typically the characters of which you might think when you hear the phrase "character profiles." There are very few puff pieces about Brad Pitt and Angelina Jolie or George Clooney here (although many authors of profiles, such as Gay Talese, have in fact written celebrity profiles for a wide variety of magazines and other publications); for the most part, these books feature stories of very ordinary people going about their interests, their work, and their lives as they have always done. Their extraordinariness in these books has largely been bestowed upon them by the authors, who, in dedicating years of their lives to such "ordinary" subjects as employees, spouses, parents, friends, card players, and many others, indicate their beliefs that even the most common of lives is worthy of consideration.

The final two chapters, Political Reporting and Business Reporting, again offer a variety of appeal factors to their readers (including, as they do, narratives about business and political deals, as well as character profiles and stories by and about notables in both fields). It is true that the titles included in these chapters are there largely because of their subject matter. But to assume that all political and business books are the same in coverage, style, and tone would be to underestimate woefully their authors' talents and investigative and prose skills. One of the finest literary journalism practitioners of the last decade, Michael Lewis, started his career as, and largely remains, a "business writer," although his latest book *The Blind Side* not only tackled the business end of collegiate football but also the characters of the family he described. Richard Ben Cramer, Seymour Hersh, Lawrence Wright, and David Halberstam, all well-respected journalists and historians, appear in the political chapter. Just because these titles can be sorted by subject does not mean that they can't be further subdivided into distinct literary styles and subgenres as well.

A Word about the "Subjects"

Each annotated title in this collection includes not only a description and a list of related reading and read-alike title suggestions, but also a list of "subjects" that are used to describe the books. For the most part, these "tags" (as we are starting to think of them; social software vocabulary terms are starting to slip in everywhere) are meant to act as stereotypical subject headings, listing subjects, locations, historical characters, and time periods. However, an effort has been made to include tags that are more esoteric in nature, including headings such as "Quick Reads" (which, for the most part, refer to narratives less than 250 pages in length), "Classics" (meant to single out books which have proven their popularity and continued currency over the course of many years), and "Humor" (used not only when a book is catalogued or published as a "humor book" but also when an author's lightness of tone or skill with words and anecdotes lends it a funny "feel"). We have also started to make an effort to use tags that readers might not find in stereotypical library catalogs (or even at Amazon.com) but that more closely mirror natural language; an example of one such tag is "Year in the Life," which is used frequently throughout this volume to denote books in which authors literally spent some predetermined amount of time living or researching their stories (often a year, but not always). All of these subject tags are indexed in the Subject Index at the conclusion of this collection, meaning that readers who enjoy Quick Reads, Essays, books of Humor (and many others) might easily find them by starting their search there.

Conclusion

In many ways, the desire to pull together the collection of books that follows is what preceded and prodded my desire to write a book about nonfiction reading choices and advisory. When I started *The Real Story*, the first titles I gathered for a sample chapter were the ones I thought were being ignored by readers' advisors who were largely focusing on fiction; why not provide a guide of nonfiction books that provided the inside look behind the scenes of everyday occurrences (including, notably, books as widely varied as Ted Conover's *Newjack: Guarding Sing Sing* and Debra Ginsberg's very personal memoir *Waiting: The True Confessions of a Waitress*)? At the time, I had nowhere to look for other similar books that I referred to, in my own mind, as "behind the scenes" or "inside story" books, and largely stumbled across them serendipitously. I had the same problem with "year in the life" books, in which writers followed other people and their lives for set periods of time, to better understand and portray their circumstances; or "immersion" books, in which authors themselves tried to live the experiences of those whose lives they were chronicling, and "exposés" that exposed topics outside of the normal realm of politics and "current affairs." The world of nonfiction is so much broader than mere subject matters or even genres can describe; this book is nothing more than an attempt to provide another way to access that world and to become engaged with and by its offerings. Only someone who has worked as a librarian could probably ever consider something as prosaic as a reference book to constitute a love letter, but that is what this collection felt like as I wrote it.

Infamous journalist and war correspondent Martha Gellhorn wrote her own love letter to the form when she described her six-decade career, during which she produced war reporting titles, memoirs, and travel narratives: "A writer publishes to be read; then hopes the readers are affected by the words, hopes that their opinions are changed or strengthened or enlarged, or that readers are pushed to notice something they had not stopped to notice before. All my reporting life, I have thrown small pebbles into a very large pond, and have no way of knowing whether any pebble caused the slightest ripple. I don't need to worry about that. My responsibility was the effort" (Gellhorn 1987, 9). We, too, have a responsibility to make an effort—the effort to read and be aware of these titles and to share them with readers who might enjoy them or find them enlightening.

References

Alpert, Abby. 2006. "Incorporating Nonfiction into Readers' Advisory Services." *Reference & User Services Quarterly* Volume 46, no. 1 (Autumn): 25–32.

Booker, Christopher. 2004. *The Seven Basic Plots*. New York: Continuum.

Boynton, Robert, ed. 2005. *The New New Journalism: Conversations with America's Best Nonfiction Writers on Their Craft*. New York: Vintage.

Burgin, Robert, ed. 2004. *Nonfiction Readers' Advisory*. Westport, CT: Libraries Unlimited.

Cords, Sarah Statz, and Robert Burgin (ed.). 2006. *The Real Story: A Guide to Nonfiction Reading Interests*. Westport, CT: Libraries Unlimited.

Gellhorn, Martha. 1987. *The View from the Ground*. New York: Atlantic Monthly Press.

Glass, Ira, ed. 2007. *The New Kings of Nonfiction*. New York: Riverhead.

Gutkind, Lee. 1998. *The Essayist at Work*. Portsmouth, NH: Heinemann.

Herald, Diana Tixier. 2006. *Genreflecting: A Guide to Popular Reading Interests*. 6th ed. Westport, CT: Libraries Unlimited.

Kennedy, George, and Daryl Moen. 2007. *What Good Is Journalism? How Reporters and Editors Are Saving America's Way of Life*. Columbia: University of Missouri Press.

Klosterman, Chuck. December 2004. "The Rise of the Real." *Esquire* 142, no. 6: 194–95; 236.

Langewiesche, William. 2005. "William Langewiesche" in *The New New Journalism*, edited by Robert Boynton. New York: Vintage.

National Education Association. 2004. *Reading at Risk*. Accessed at http://www.nea.gov/pub/ReadingAtRisk.pdf (11 March 2008).

Ross, Catherine. 2004. "Reading Nonfiction for Pleasure: What Motivates Readers?" in *Nonfiction Readers' Advisory*, edited by Robert Burgin. Westport, CT: Libraries Unlimited. pp. 105–120.

Sager, Mike. 2007. *Revenge of the Donut Boys: True Stories of Lust, Fame, Survival, and Multiple Personality*. New York: Thunder's Mouth Press.

Saricks, Joyce G. 2005. *Readers' Advisory Service in the Public Library*. 3rd ed. Chicago: American Library Association.

Saricks, Joyce G., and Nancy Brown. 1997. *Readers' Advisory Service in the Public Library*. 2nd ed. Chicago: American Library Association.

Shearer, Kenneth D., and Robert Burgin. 2001. *The Readers' Advisor's Companion*. Englewood, CO: Libraries Unlimited.

Statistical Abstract of the United States 2007. Accessed at http://www.census.gov/prod/2007pubs/08abstract/arts.pdf (9 March 2008).

Talese, Gay. 2005. "Gay Talese" in *The New New Journalism*, edited by Robert Boynton. New York: Vintage.

Terzian, Peter. 2007. "Room to Roam: Rebecca Solnit's Peripatetic Education." *Columbia Journalism Review* (July/August): 52.

Wolfe, Tom, and E. W. Johnson. 1973. *The New Journalism*. New York: Harper & Row.

Wyatt, Neal. 2007. *The Readers' Advisory Guide to Nonfiction*. Chicago: American Library Association.

Chapter 1

In-Depth Reporting

Definition of In-Depth Reporting

In some ways the history of In-Depth Reporting is the easiest history in this book to write. This is largely because it is easy to draw parallels between it and the larger tradition of journalistic writing in newspapers and magazines, and histories of American journalism are widely available (although it should be noted that journalists, fonder of writing about their subjects than themselves, have not been hugely prolific in this area). Those types of books, listed at the end of this chapter, are the source for most of this brief historical overview of American journalistic writing. The broader history of investigative writing throughout the world, because it is a subject that is too broad and not as germane to a reference book consisting primarily of books published in the United States, I will leave unexplored, except to note that those with an interest in the subject should consider reading Mitchell Stephens's *A History of News: From the Drum to the Satellite,* which includes all sorts of interesting information about the dissemination of news throughout global history, starting with societies with largely oral traditions, through Asia and Europe, up through the modern day (well, as modern as the book's 1988 copyright date allows).

Although Thomas Jefferson commented, famously, "were it left to me to decide whether we should have a government without newspapers, or newspapers without a government, I should not hesitate a moment to prefer the latter," the first fifty years of news publishing in America, dating from 1689, saw largely news and newspapers that were "published by authority" (Tebbel 1969, 11). One notable exception was what John Tebbel has noted was the first American newspaper, Benjamin Harris's *Publick Occurrences Both Foreign and Domestick,* first published in a six by nine-and-a-half–inch format in 1690, which he published without first applying for a license. In addition to its very modern avoidance of licensing restrictions, Harris's paper also displayed a fascinating similarity to such interactive media as the blogs and reader comment sections of today: it was published with a "fourth page blank so that readers could add their own news in longhand before they forwarded it to friends who lived elsewhere" (Tebbel 1969, 13).

By comparison, Boston's John Campbell did seek the approval of authorities before publishing his Boston *News-Letter* in 1704, which offered news and a style of dissemination so dull that Tebbel speculates it hardly needed to advertise that it was published by authority. During this era, printers often doubled as publishers, and

James Franklin (along with his younger brother Benjamin) were no exceptions. They entered the field in 1721 with the *New England Courant*, and Benjamin Franklin would go on to found the *Pennsylvania Gazette* in 1729. Eventually John Peter Zenger, publishing his paper in New York, would take a stand in print against the corrupt activities of New York governor William Cosby; he published what could be considered early examples of investigative stories of corruption and was charged with criminal libel for his trouble. His case ended in a fantastic trial in which his attorney admitted his client's guilt at the start of the trial—that he had indeed printed the papers in question—but that such stories must be false to make them truly libelous, and after appealing to the jury to make an end-run around the law because the truth of Zenger's reporting was backed up with facts and proof, the jury went along and found Zenger not guilty. A tradition of reporting and investigative writing as the search for and revelation of truth(s) was born.

Newspapers continued to be important instruments of community and political life during the events of the American Revolution, although the journalistic ideal of "objective" reporting (that is, reporting and writing stories without the journalist sharing their personal opinions and striving to present just the facts) still lay ahead and many papers and pamphlets were quite obviously the tools of one political faction or another; an example of such partisanship is the case of Isaiah Thomas, founder of the Boston *Massachusetts Spy*, who offered the slogan "A Weekly Political and Commercial Paper—Open to All Parties, but influenced by None," but was himself personally involved with Paul Revere's famous ride (Tebbel 1969, 40). Thomas was also notable for being the printer of several newspapers and hundreds of books, showing clearly the links, even then, between the publishing of daily journalism and the publishing of books.

In the years following the American Revolution, papers would increasingly become driven by technological advances (particularly advances in printing and typography practices in the first half of the nineteenth century) and the personalities of the owners and editors who ran them. New York City in particular would become a hotbed of news publishing, from James Gordon Bennett's New York *Herald* (founded in 1835 and selling for a penny a paper) to Horace Greeley's hugely influential, from coast to coast, New York *Tribune*, founded in 1841; the *New York Times* would arrive on the scene in 1851 (Tebbel 1969, 105.) This is not only a story of newspapers; magazines were also appearing by this time. Many hugely popular women's periodicals, including *Godey's Lady's Book*, started publishing in the mid-nineteenth century and would continue to be popular for many years to come. Again, the close relationship between periodical publishing and the publishing of books is evident; *Harper's Monthly*, which was first published in 1850, was started largely to support the book-publishing business of the Harper Brothers; the brothers placed ads for the books they were publishing in their magazine, a lucrative and self-fulfilling cycle (Tebbel 1974, 232). *Harper's Monthly* would go on to become the most successful magazine in America. Through the early part of the twentieth century, magazines would become home to social activist authors, as well as the stories of literary greats and literary and personal essayists and humorists such as Robert Benchley, James Thurber, and Dorothy Parker (particularly in the venerable pages of *The New Yorker*, which has continued to provide a valuable forum for writers of investigative nonfiction).

The tradition of journalistic writing continued apace, in both newspapers (including the first "national" newspaper, *USA Today*, which was founded in 1982 by Allen Neuharth) and magazines, as well as in online news forums and magazines, including *Slate* and *Salon*. Although increasingly there is the sense that traditional newspapers are failing, as both an information source and a business proposition, there is currently no reason to suppose that they will disappear tomorrow (for a fascinating discussion of newspapers' past and future, please consider *30: The Collapse of the Great American Newspaper*, edited by Charles Madigan). The same tenet is true for In-Depth Reporting books; many of the titles in this chapter have been written by people who have worked or currently work for some type of mass media outlet. They have been written because not all news and feature stories lend themselves to the daily deadline writing of the more ephemeral media (newspapers, blogs, magazines, online journals, and television among them). Journalist James Fallows best explains the process of creating these reconstructions of stories and events, describing the authors' process of "pulling together details, comparing accounts, answering leftover questions, and ultimately retelling a story that was misexplained or only half explained before" (Fallows 2006, ix).

The In-Depth Reporting titles in this chapter differ widely in subject, but they all offer the best in lively and thoughtful investigative writing. These are the books in which the authors straightforwardly announce to their readers and their subjects what they are researching, and they are often written in that same straightforward style. Whether their authors are sharing feature or human-interest stories, or news about true crime cases or wars, they remain dedicated to reporting what they believe, after their research and interviewing, is the truth. They offer the who, what, where, when, and why of their stories, but they do so with idiosyncratic writing styles. Much like nonfiction as a whole, they can almost be best defined by what they are not: they are not as explosive as Exposés, as person-centric as Character Profiles, or as stylized and intensely personal as Immersion Journalism. They are cracking good stories, told straight up.

> Works of In-Depth Reporting are works in which their authors strive to fully research their topic, observe details surrounding their story, and interview the individuals involved. They then combine their research, observations, and interview responses into (primarily) third-person accounts that are crisply and evocatively written. Authors in this subgenre rarely offer personal asides or incendiary calls to action. These are informational works, designed to impart a lot of information in about three hundred or fewer pages (although some, particularly works featuring extensive interview material, are longer).

Appeal of In-Depth Reporting

Just because reporting or writing is in-depth doesn't mean that it has to be dull or that this type of writing can only be done in the absence of the writer's personality or opinions, although that has been the tradition most frequently taught in journalism schools around the nation. Ira Glass explains the continuing appeal of the idea of objectivity in the introduction to his collection *The New Kings of Nonfiction* by saying that "as if being interesting and expressing any trace of a human personality would somehow detract from the nonstop flow of facts she assumed her listeners were craving. There's a whole class of reporters . . . who have a strange kind of religious conviction about this" (Glass 2007, 3). The titles in this chapter, although many of them spring from the journalistic tradition and have been written by professionals working as journalists, turn the idea of objectivity on its head; the authors write their stories from their very subjective points of view.

The primary appeal of these straightforward titles tends to be their stories, but not in the sense that they portray chronologically ordered and discrete narratives. Unlike other story-driven nonfiction genres such as True Adventure or True Crime, the writers of these books don't always pick one unique event or time period to explore; rather, the "story" is created and organized in their writing approach. This is most obvious in Feature Stories; there is no real "story" in Steve Almond's *Candyfreak,* in which he describes his journey around candy-making factories in the United States, other than his actual traveling around to write that story. Because these stories are constructed by their writers out of their experiences, interviews, and research makes them no less compelling, however. This is true, to some extent, for all the subgenres of In-Depth Reporting; more so than telling any one sports story or the story of one particular scientific advance, these authors create stories out of their investigating those sports or science (or historical, or true crime, or war) events.

This is also why these titles can be enjoyed for so many different reasons. Although characters are not the primary appeal of these books (as they are in the Character Profiles subgenre), these authors often meet and talk with a wide variety of fascinating people in the process of researching their narratives. They also travel to get their stories and are set across America and the world; further, they have to display writing talent and prose styling to organize their research and participation into cohesive storylines. More so than any other chapter in this book, there really is something here for everyone.

Organization of the Chapter

Feature Stories, almost equally divided between **Human Interest** narratives and **On Location** titles, are listed at the beginning of the chapter and offer a wide array of subjects, as well as appeal factors (touching on character, story, and setting, not to mention language and the use of style and humor). They are listed first because of their popularity and their accessibility; readers looking to branch out from other fiction and nonfiction reading interests might want to start with those titles. Subsequent subgenres might be described as further variations of Feature Stories, in that they are not really news in the sense that daily journalism is news; but neither do they belong to any other nonfiction genre, given their authors' investigative writing styles. Because they vary more in subject matter than in style, they are simply listed alphabetically: *Historical Perspectives*, *Science Reporting*, *Sports Reporting*, *True Crime Reporting*, and *War Reporting*. A final section offering books of *Cultural Criticism* rely more heavily on their authors' subject expertise, personalities, and notoriety as critics, journalists, and writers; although the titles in that subgenre do not seem to feature the same "in the field" investigations and personal interviews, they do offer in-depth considerations of the literature, art forms, and social norms that make up our culture.

Feature Stories

Human Interest

Newspapers, magazines, and books are only as good as the authors and reporters producing them. Throughout human history, there have always been certain members of the population who have stood aside and reported on the activities of the other part of the population; these individuals are the ones we have to thank for most of our investigative writing books. Although, again, numerous definitions and ideas exist on what constitutes "reporting," the one we will use as a starting point is Stephens's: "Reporting—embarking into the field in search of news—is an act of deference toward facts, an acknowledgment of the limitations of one's own deductive or creative powers" (Stephens 1988, 228). Investigative writers emphatically do not have all the answers. But they consistently get up from behind their desks and their computers and embark into the field to gather what answers they can on the subjects that interest them. When what interests journalists, news writers, and authors is the actual news, what they end up writing is journalism of the daily paper or online edition variety; those daily journalistic pieces can be very well written and entertaining indeed, but they are outside the scope of this book.

However, when what interests reporters and writers are subjects and stories outside the norm, they become what I have termed Feature Stories. The questions these writers set out to answer, although approached every bit as professionally and with as much of a desire to report the truth, are not typically the questions of life and death. Instead, these authors answer questions such as the following: Where are candy bars made, and how? What are the alternatives for people who don't want a stereotypical funeral when they die? How are flowers grown and marketed as commodities? Brendan Hennessy, a journalist and author of how-to books for journalists, defines a feature story as one that "aims to inform, but it may also narrate, describe, explain, persuade, or entertain, and sometimes all five" (Hennessy 2006, 17).

In Human Interest Feature Stories, the emphasis is on the characters with whom these authors meet and interact in the course of reporting their stories. Although not all the characters are always sympathetic, they are always interesting, and although they may not be celebrities, the individuals featured in these tales are definitely the largest part of what makes the titles unique. There is no real consistency among the following titles in subject, but they often include elements of the very personal, the humorous, and the quirky.

Readers who enjoy these books are most likely curious individuals who enjoy both the learning and the experiencing aspects of reading nonfiction; as such, they might also consider a wide variety of other nonfiction titles and genres, from Travel writing to Immersion Journalism to character-driven Memoirs and Biographies. Likewise, well-told genre fiction stories and lively mainstream fiction with unique characters and offbeat stories might also be of some interest to them.

> Human Interest Feature Stories cover a wide variety of subjects, and are written in a lively journalistic style, filled with interviews and anecdotes, as well as interesting bits of research and trivia. They offer very distinctive characters, whom the authors have chosen as the best possible candidates to help them tell the stories about which they are so curious.

Alexander, Brian

America Unzipped: In Search of Sex and Satisfaction. Harmony Books. 2008. 304 pp. ISBN 9780307351326.

Author of the "Sexploration" column for MSNBC.com, Alexander was stunned to learn the type and variety of questions about sex that he regularly received from readers, so he decided to try and set out to discover the current state of sexual affairs in America. What he learned, by shadowing producers of instructional sex videos, a Christian preacher who teaches seminars on the joys of sex in marriage, employees in a "romance superstore," and dominatrixes (among others) is that Americans increasingly view all their sexual proclivities and choices more as personal issues than as the domain of any cultural, political, or religious ideologies.

Subjects: Explicit Sexuality, Pop Culture, Pornography, Sexuality, Society, Travel

Now Try: Gay Talese's Immersion Journalism classic *Thy Neighbor's Wife*, in which Talese himself engaged in the sexual goings-on, might appeal to these readers, as might a wide variety of forthright sexuality memoirs, including the anonymously penned *Secret Diary of a Call Girl*, Diablo Cody's *Candy Girl* (about her work as a stripper), Chelsea Handler's *My Horizontal Life*, or Catherine Millet's *The Sexual Life of Catherine M.* Another entertaining investigation into the subject is Mary Roach's *Bonk: The Curious Coupling of and Science and Sex*, and other investigative works like Sheri Caudron's *Who Are You People?* and Lisa Takeuchi Cullen's *Remember Me* might also hold some appeal. The author also makes a reference to Jenna Jameson's best-selling memoir, *How to Make Love Like a Porn Star*.

Almond, Steve

Candyfreak: A Journey through the Chocolate Underbelly of America. Algonquin Books of Chapel Hill. 2004. 266 pp. ISBN 9781565124219.

Short story author and essayist Almond gave in to the power of his sweet tooth and set out across the nation to track the availability and manufacturing processes of some of the world's best- and least-known candies, including Peanut Chews (Philadelphia), the Goo Goo Cluster (Nashville), and the Twin Bing (Sioux City, Iowa). In addition to taking factory tours, interviewing candy creators and hobbyists (including candy wrapper collectors and attendees at chocolate conventions), and researching the history and development of America's regional tastes, Almond also took one for the team and, yes, ate copious amounts of candy. All of his exploits are shared with Almond's trademark humor and obsession with his subject matter (by his own confession, he has at least "three to seven pounds" of candy in his own house at any given time).

Subjects: American History, Business, Chocolate, Essays, Food, Humor, Travel

Now Try: Almond is a popular humorist and has written another essay collection titled *(Not That You Asked): Rants, Exploits, and Obsessions,* as well as the short story collection *The Evil B. B. Chow* and the novel (with Julianna Baggott) *Which Brings Me to You.* Titles by other humorists including David Rakoff, David Sedaris, and Calvin Trillin (particularly Trillin's *Feeding a Yen*) might be offered, while humorous travel books by British author Tony Hawks (*Round Ireland with a Fridge* and *Playing the Moldovans at Tennis*) might appeal, as might other "inside looks" at industries not much explored, such as Amy Stewart's *Flower Confidential* or Steve Ettlinger's *Twinkie, Deconstructed.* Advisors might also consider offering books meant to appeal to "foodies," such as titles by Ruth Reichl, Anthony Bourdain (whose bold humor might particularly appeal to Almond's readers), or Michael Ruhlman.

Barron, James C.

Piano: The Making of a Steinway Concert Grand. Times Books. 2006. 280 pp. ISBN 9780805078787.

The Steinway piano company is the only remaining manufacturer who crafts its grand concert pianos largely by hand, giving each one its own attributes, both strengths and weaknesses. In this slim volume, Barron follows the progress of one particular piano (known only as K0862) through the manufacturing process and each individual craftperson's hands and area of expertise. It takes a full eleven months to build, tune, and become familiar with such an instrument, and in addition to illuminating the instrument's manufacture, Barron also periodically digresses into the history of New York City, the Steinway company, industry, and workplace dynamics in general (including such telling details as the fact that Fridays used to be the day when the youngest worker was sent to the saloon down the street to bring back buckets of beer). Although the main character in this title is, in all honesty, an inanimate object, Barron nonetheless gives K0862 a life and personality all its own.

Subjects: Business Histories, Labor History, Music and Musicians, New York City, Pianos, Professions, Work Relationships

Now Try: Readers intrigued by this fascinating inside look at pianos and craftsmanship might also consider Thad Carhart's *The Piano Shop on the Left Bank: Discovering a Forgotten Passion in a Paris Atelier* or Charles Rosen's *Piano Notes: The World of the Pianist.* Other books that focus on the particular delight taken by individuals who make things include Tracy Kidder's *The Soul of a New Machine,* Michael Ruhlman's *The Making of a Chef,* or David McCullough's *The Great Bridge: The Epic Story of the Building of the Brooklyn Bridge.* Fiction titles in which music and a love of music might also be offered, such as Anne Tyler's *Searching for Caleb,* Marcia Preston's *The Piano*

Man, or Mark Salzman's *The Soloist*; biographies of composers and musicians might also be offered (such as Benita Eisler's *Chopin's Funeral*, among many others).

Bowden, Mark

Road Work: Among Tyrants, Heroes, Rogues, and Beasts. Atlantic Monthly Press. 2004. 467 pp. ISBN 9780871138767.

Bowden was a staff writer for the *Philadelphia Inquirer* for twenty-four years, and this book is a collection of his pieces from that time. The subjects range from politics and foreign relations to sports and true crime; the book even includes profiles of such individuals as Al Sharpton and Norman Mailer. Each piece is dated and has an introduction written by Bowden, and the writing is a bit more evocative than much fact-driven reporting: "Now, some say there is no more than a hair's difference between minor league baseball and the bigs. Most who say so, admittedly, are minor-leaguers, whose dreams often dine at the table of delusion."

> **Subjects:** Afghanistan, Character Profiles, Essays, History, Saddam Hussein, Journalism, Norman Mailer, Politics, Sports, True Crime, War Reporting

> **Now Try:** Another journalist well known for his time spent reporting at the *Philadelphia Inquirer*, Pete Dexter, has published a collection of his searingly honest columns from that paper, titled *Paper Trails*; he is also an award-winning novelist (he won the National Book Award for *Paris Trout* and both that novel and *The Paperboy* were ALA Notable books). Bowden is a detailed and dedicated journalist (he is also the author of the bestselling titles *Black Hawk Down* and *Guests of the Ayatollah*); other such "old-school" reporters and their works who might appeal to his readers include William Langewiesche (*American Ground* and *The Outlaw Sea*), George Packer (*The Assassins' Gate: America in Iraq*), and George Jonas (*Vengeance: The True Story of an Israeli Counter-Terrorist Team*). He often covers political and historical subjects; his readers might consider titles from the Political Reporting chapter.

Brooks, Geraldine

Nine Parts of Desire: The Hidden World of Islamic Women. Anchor Books. 1995. 255 pp. ISBN 9780385475761.

Brooks spent two years as a news correspondent in the Middle East, covering events such as the death of the Ayatollah Khomeini, and also developed an interest in the lives of Islamic women and how they themselves viewed their place in society. Brooks is well versed in both the complex history of the region and in Islamic faith and practices, and she brings that contextual knowledge to her interviews with and exposition of the lives of Islamic women. Although she makes no secret of the fact that she herself is a secular feminist, she interviews a wide variety of women and straightforwardly reports their responses on a number of issues including female genital mutilation, education, legal issues, wearing the veil, and relationships.

> **Subjects:** Book Groups, Family Relationships, Female Genital Mutilation, Gender, Islam, Middle East, Multicultural Issues, Muslims, Religion, Society, Women's Nonfiction

> **Awards:** ALA Notable

> **Now Try:** Brooks is also a hugely popular novelist who frequently tackles historical and sociological issues in her fiction; her readers might enjoy her novels *Year of Wonders* or *People of the Book*. There is also no shortage of quality nonfiction titles exploring the experiences of Muslim women; these include Judith Miller's *God Has*

Ninety-Nine Names, Åsne Seierstad's *The Bookseller of Kabul*, Deborah Rodriguez's *Kabul Beauty School*, Azar Nafisi's *Reading Lolita in Tehran*, or Ayaan Hirsi Ali's *Infidel*. Fiction titles that might appeal include *A Thousand Splendid Suns* by Khaled Hosseini, *Brick Lane* by Monica Ali, or *White Teeth* by Zadie Smith. (Interestingly enough, Brooks is the spouse of journalist and writer Tony Horwitz, whose investigative titles *Confederates in the Attic* or *Baghdad without a Map* might also appeal to these readers.)

Caudron, Shari

Who Are You People?: A Personal Journey into the Heart of Fanatical Passion in America. Barricade Books. 2006. 285 pp. ISBN 9781569803042.

Intrigued by people and their seemingly fanatical interests and passions, Caudron set out over the course of three years not only to explore the world of fandom and obsession but also, hopefully, to discover why she doesn't care about anything as much as her subjects care about their very specific areas of interest. Along the way she attends conventions, conferences, sporting events, and concerts; she also interviews Barbie collectors, Grobanites (rabid fans of pop star Josh Groban), ice fishers, "furries," and Lego Club members. The result is a fascinating but lighthearted take on what it means to love something more than you probably should; Caudron's writing is detailed and often very funny but always very accepting and empathetic as well.

> **Subjects:** Character Profiles, Fandom, Hobbies, Humor, Pop Culture, Small Press, Travel
>
> **Now Try:** Readers who try this title from independent publisher Barricade Books might also be up for other delightful and offbeat investigative and travel titles such as Amy Stewart's *Flower Confidential*, Mark Singer's *Character Studies*, Lisa Takeuchi Cullen's *Remember Me: A Lively Tour of the New American Way of Death*, Paul Bibeau's *Sundays with Vlad* (about his adventures exploring the subculture of vampire fans), Michael Beaumier's *I Know You're Out There: Private Longings, Public Humiliations, and Other Tales from the Personals* or David Rose's *They Call Me Naughty Lola* (a collection of personal ads from the *London Review of Books*), or even John McPhee's *Uncommon Carriers*. Other nonfiction titles with the subject of "Year in the Life," from the Character Profiles chapter might be offered, as might quirky, character-driven mainstream fiction titles such as Katherine Dunn's *Geek Love* or John Irving's *A Prayer for Owen Meany*.

Cullen, Lisa Takeuchi

Remember Me: A Lively Tour of the New American Way of Death. Collins. 2006. 218 pp. ISBN 9780060766832.

Cullen, a staff writer for *Time* magazine, did not set out to expose the hucksterism of American funeral directors and their industry, as Jessica Mitford had four decades previously (in her book *The American Way of Death*). Cullen attended funeral industry conventions, met with the founders of a "green" cemetery, interviewed families who chose to have the cremated remains (cremains) of their loved ones turned into diamonds, traveled to the Frozen Dead Guy Days festival in Colorado, and noted the cultural differences among a stereotypical American funeral, a

Hmong funeral, and the funeral of her own Japanese grandfather in Tokyo. She provides both facts (in 2003, 25 percent of Americans who died were cremated; by 2025, it'll be 48 percent) and character portraits ("Peggy greets me politely, if guardedly. She is tiny, bespectacled, and dressed in a black turtleneck and long black skirt. She embodies my image of a Broadway voice teacher, which is what she is . . ."), and provides a unique and gentle insight into the ways people choose to be remembered and to remember their loved ones.

Subjects: Business, Death and Dying, Humor, Pop Culture, Society, Travel

Now Try: Although readers intrigued by this title will most likely have already read the classic in the field, Jessica Mitford's *The American Way of Death Revisited*, as well as Mary Roach's *Stiff: The Curious Lives of Human Cadavers*, it never hurts to suggest them. Other offbeat, inside looks at other not-often described industries, such as Steve Almond's *Candyfreak*, Amy Stewart's *Flower Confidential*, or even memoirs like Alison Bechdel's graphic novel *Fun Home: A Family Tragicomic* (about her family's funeral home), or work memoirs like Caroline Burau's *Answering 911: Life in the Hot Seat* or Michael Perry's *Population 485: Meeting Your Neighbors One Siren at a Time* might also be offered.

Dexter, Pete

Paper Trails: True Stories of Confusion, Mindless Violence, and Forbidden Desires, a Surprising Number of Which Are Not about Marriage. Ecco. 2007. 289 pp. ISBN 9780061189357.

Dexter's ability to be personal, and to provoke a personal reaction, is what makes his writing so noteworthy. In this collection of newspaper columns from sources including the *Sacramento Bee*, the *Philadelphia Daily News*, and *Esquire*, Dexter offers stories as wild and characters as varied as you'd think only the most imaginative fiction could produce. He not only knows people with names such as Low Gear and Minus, but they know him, and tell him their stories of road trips gone wrong and other escapades. Dexter also isn't afraid to tell the more personal stories, even those featuring the intrepid Mrs. Dexter, or those which include more criminal elements (at one point in his career he was beaten so savagely by individuals about whom he had written that he suffered a broken back).

Subjects: Character Profiles, Essays, Family Relationships, Humor, Journalism, Pennsylvania, Philadelphia, True Crime

Now Try: Another collection of stories that should by all means be offered to Dexter's readers is *Rocky Stories: Tales of Love, Hope, and Happiness at America's Most Famous Steps* by Michael Vitez and Tom Gralish; Dexter's fiction might also appeal, including *Paris Trout*, *The Paperboy*, and *Dead Wood*. Books by other well-known reporters such as Mark Bowden and classic authors such as Joseph Mitchell and E. B. White might also be suggested, as might former police beat reporter Michael Connelly (both his nonfiction and his novels). Fiction by Carl Hiaasen, with his trademark dark humor, might provide a good read-alike to Dexter's collection (Jim Knipfel's dark humor, evident in his *Slackjaw* and *Ruining It for Everybody* might also be similar in tone).

Fadiman, Anne

🏆 *The Spirit Catches You and You Fall Down: A Hmong Child, Her American Doctors, and the Collision of Two Cultures.* Farrar, Straus & Giroux. 1997. 341 pp. ISBN 9780374267810.

Fadiman recounts the tale of Hmong couple Foua Yang and Nao Kao, whose youngest daughter (and the only one born in the United States), Lia Lee, suffered from epilepsy, and their struggle to understand and comply with their American doctors' recommendations and treatments. Fadiman explores the cultural gap between the Hmong family's more spiritual approach to bodily health (Lia's parents ascribed her illness to a "spirit entering her" and causing her seizures) and the doctors' physical approach, which the family did not understand because of both poor explanations and language difficulties. Based on Fadiman's interviews with individuals on both sides, the story is told with admirable objectivity and skillful pacing.

Subjects: Book Groups, Classics, Culture Clash, Family Relationships, Health Issues, Medicine, Multicultural Issues

Awards: National Book Critics Circle

Now Try: Barron Lerner's ALA Notable Book *The Breast Cancer Wars: Hope, Fear, and the Pursuit of a Cure in Twentieth-Century America* is also a compellingly quick medical read and presents the different opinions of men (mainly cast as the doctors, particularly in the 1950s) and women (primarily the patients) regarding such different radical treatments as complete mastectomies and chemotherapies, as well as the controversies surrounding the need for yearly mammograms. Abraham Verghese relates his experiences treating victims of AIDS in a small community in Tennessee in the 1980s, in his quiet and even-handed *My Own Country: A Doctor's Story*. Another story of the history of controversial medical issues is told in Cynthia Gorney's ALA Notable book *Articles of Faith: A Frontline History of the Abortion Wars*. Jerome Groopman's informative *How Doctors Think* might also be offered, as might Pauline Chen's *Final Exam* or Atul Gawande's memoir about being a surgeon (*Complications*).

Fagone, Jason

Horsemen of the Esophagus: Competitive Eating and the Big Fat American Dream. Crown. 2006. 303 pp. ISBN 9780307237385.

Journalist Fagone spent months attending eating contests, spending time with contestants, meeting many-time champion hot-dog eater Takeru Kobayashi, and trying to understand how gluttony and excess play a part in the American dream. In addition to interviewing some of the biggest names in the "sport," including Dave "Coondog" O'Karma, "Hungry" Charles Hardy, Ed "Cookie" Jarvis, and Joey "Jaws" Chestnut, Fagone also speaks with promoters of the sport like the infamous George Shea, widely considered the P. T. Barnum of the sport. He also shares the details of twenty-seven different eating contests, many of them sponsored by the IFOCE (International Federation of Competitive Eating), as well as the logistical details of his travels around the circuit (the "Wing Bowl" in Philadelphia presented unique transportation nightmares) and the competitors' training for the contests. Although packed with telling story and character details, Fagone's writing is quickly paced, and the topic is one that is as strangely fascinating as it is vaguely repellant.

Subjects: Character Profiles, Food, Hobbies, Humor, Japan, Pop Culture, Sports, Travel

Now Try: Fagone went all out, traveling with and interviewing his subjects for this book; other Character Profile titles might also be suggested, such as Elizabeth Gilbert's *The Last American Man* (about a man seeking to live on his own terms in the Appalachian Mountains), Susan Orlean's *The Orchid Thief* or *Saturday Night*, or Tom Gralish's and Michael Vitez's *Rocky Stories* (also set in Philadelphia, where some of Fagone's narrative is set). Other travel and obsession narratives might also be offered, particularly Calvin Trillin's *Feeding a Yen* (also about food), Stefan Fatsis's *Word Freak* (about the world of competitive Scrabble), Jay Greenspan's *Hunting Fish*, or James McManus's *Positively Fifth Street* (about gambling).

Goodnough, Abby

Ms. Moffett's First Year: Becoming a Teacher in America. PublicAffairs. 2004. 258 pp. ISBN 9781586482596.

When the New York State education department implemented a program titled "New York City Teaching Fellows," seeking "talented professionals" with little or no previous teaching experience to swell the ranks of entry-level teachers, no one was expecting it to draw the 2,300 applicants that it did. One of the 350 professionals accepted was Donna Moffett, a middle-aged legal secretary who had long had an interest in switching careers. The author's fair handling of all individuals affected by the program, from Ms. Moffett to her school administrators to her first-grade pupils and their parents provides a journalistically objective portrait of an unprecedented educational experiment and also manages to place it in the greater current milieu of the state of education, especially after the No Child Left Behind legislative act.

> **Subjects:** Community Life, Education, Government, New York City, Professions, Quick Reads, Women's Nonfiction, Work Relationships

> **Now Try:** Also set in New York City, Anemona Hartocollis's story of a young Finnish music teacher who sought to bond with her students through gospel music in *Seven Days of Possibilities: One Teacher, 24 Kids, and the Music that Changed Their Lives Forever* examines one specific teacher's experiences within the social and political structure of a public school over the course of one year. Sam Swope's curmudgeonly but still subtly humorous *I Am a Pencil: A Teacher, His Kids, and Their Worlds of Stories* also follows a volunteer writing teacher's unforgettable experiences in the world of the classroom. Frank McCourt's memoir of his time spent teaching in New York, *Teacher Man*, might also appeal to these readers, as might Tracy Kidder's classic *Among Schoolchildren*.

Halpern, Jake

Fame Junkies: The Hidden Truths Behind America's Favorite Addiction. Houghton Mifflin. 2007. 226 pp. ISBN 9780618453696.

Who better to write an investigation into the American obsession with fame and all famous people than a Hollywood reporter who's worked for NPR? Taking as his starting point questions like, why do more people watch *American Idol* than all three of the nightly news programs combined? What is the fascination with Paris Hilton? Why does the wish at the top of many ordinary people's lists include a desire to be famous? Halpern seeks to provide answers to these questions and many more by interviewing aspiring stars, consultants who work in the entertainment and talent conference businesses, and even celebrities themselves (among them, Rod Stewart and The Edge of U2). Combining issues of psychology, technology, and pop culture, the result is a nuanced look at why our society is so fascinated by the glitterati.

Subjects: California, Character Profiles, Fame, Fandom, Film, Mass Media, Pop Culture, Society

Now Try: Two other interesting books about obsessions, Shari Caudron's *Who Are You People? A Personal Journey into the Heart of Fanatical Passion in America* and Mark Singer's *Character Studies* might also be offered to these readers. Other authors who frequently comment on pop culture and society might also appeal; these include Chuck Klosterman, Steve Almond, Toby Young, A. J. Jacobs, and Charlie LeDuff; British author Jon Ronson's investigative works, which tend to be a bit darker in tone, might also be enjoyed (*Them: Adventures with Extremists* and *The Men Who Stare at Goats*).

Heller, Peter

The Whale Warriors: The Battle at the Bottom of the World to Save the Planet's Largest Mammals. Free Press. 2007. 288 pp. ISBN 9781416532460.

Author Heller tagged along for a two-month season of eco-piracy with the crew of the ship *The Farley Mowat,* whose mission it is to patrol the waters around Antarctica and either scare away or sink Japanese vessels that are engaged in illegal whaling. In addition to the story-driven and adventure-rich aspects of the ship's navigation and anti-whaling-vessel activities (including the not-very-subtle practice of ramming them and leaving them to sink if necessary), Heller also provides in-depth character portraits of the vessel's captain, Paul Watson, who refers to himself as the head of the "Sea Shepherd Conservation Society," and the other members of his crew who staff the ship (which is also vegan in its eating practice). Also included is a consideration of the illegal fishing and whaling business worldwide, as well as information about the crew's ideological and political differences with the Greenpeace organization.

Subjects: Antarctica, Character Profiles, Environmental Writing, Immersion Journalism, Maritime Disasters, Nature, Oceans, Politics, True Adventure, Whales, Year in the Life

Now Try: Heller has also written a True Adventure book titled *Hell or High Water*; other books from the True Adventure nonfiction genre might also appeal (particularly maritime titles such as Todd Lewan's *The Last Run* or Sebastian Junger's *The Perfect Storm*). Environmental Writing narratives, particularly with a political bent, might also be offered; these include Edward Abbey's *Desert Solitaire*, Farley Mowat's *Never Cry Wolf*, Tim Flannery's *The Weather Makers*, or Bill McKibben's *The End of Nature*. Books related in subject and tone, including William Langewiesche's *The Outlaw Sea*, Charles Wohlforth's *The Whale and the Supercomputer*, and Robert Sullivan's *A Whale Hunt* might provide a similar reading experience as well.

Kamp, David

The United States of Arugula: How We Became a Gourmet Nation. Broadway Books. 2006. 392 pp. ISBN 9780767915793.

Kamp takes his reader on a lively tour through a brave new world of . . . gourmet foods? Wondering exactly when "macaroni" became "pasta" and Wonder Bread was replaced by organic wheat bread, Kamp set out to chronicle the rise of gourmet food shopping, preparing, and eating in the

United States. Along the way, he describes those individuals who he believes had the biggest effect on the way America eats: infamous chef and food lover James Beard, television and cookbook favorite Julia Child, and *New York Times* food critic Craig Claiborne. Kamp also includes interviews with Alice Waters, Wolfgang Puck, Emeril Lagasse, and numerous other food-world notables on his quest to uncover the roots of America's "foodie" phenomenon.

> **Subjects:** James Beard, Business, Julia Child, Craig Claiborne, Food, Foodies, Society
>
> **Awards:** New York Times Notable
>
> **Now Try:** Kamp provides a ready-made read-alike guide in his introduction, when he cites an impressive list of cookbook and other food authors, including but not limited to: Rachael Ray, Charlie Trotter, Mollie Katzen, Ruth Reichl, Calvin Trillin, and Anthony Bourdain. Other authors who might appeal include Michael Ruhlman; other business histories featuring restaurants such as Thomas McNamee's *Alice Waters & Chez Panisse* or Taylor Clark's *Starbucked* might also be offered. Also of interest might be more political foodie authors such as Marion Nestle (*What to Eat*) or Frances Moore Lappe; biographies of food-world notables including Julia Child (*Appetite for Life*) and James Beard (*The Solace of Food*); or inside looks at other industries, such as Rebecca Mead's *One Perfect Day* or Amy Stewart's *Flower Confidential*.

Kidder, Tracy

Among Schoolchildren. Houghton Mifflin. 1989. 340 pp. ISBN 9780395475911.

When author Kidder decided he wanted to know what really went on among schoolchildren, he went right to the source and spent nine months in a classroom in an economically depressed section of the community of Holyoke, Massachusetts. Although Kidder does offer sympathetic and nuanced portraits of many of the fifth-grade students themselves (describing them only under first names), including students like Clarence, who offered his teacher disciplinary challenges, and Judith, who stood out as one of the brightest pupils in the class, he focuses primarily on their teacher, Mrs. Zajac. Following both her struggles and her triumphs, including the challenges of working with a diverse population of students, many of whom also come from disadvantaged households, Kidder's narrative is organized starting with the first school month and ending with the last day of school. He excels at giving his narrative a novelistic feel, but his characterizations and storytelling are strongly grounded in his lengthy observation and numerous interviews.

> **Subjects:** Character Profiles, Classics, Education, Massachusetts, Multicultural Issues, Poverty, Society, Sociology
>
> **Now Try:** Kidder's beautifully written work offers compelling portraits of students and teachers alike; his fans might consider similarly toned books on education including Abby Goodnough's *Ms. Moffett's First Year: Becoming a Teacher in America*, Sam Swopes's *I Am a Pencil*, Jonathan Kozol's *Savage Inequalities* or *Letters to a Young Teacher*, Alex Kotlowitz's *There Are No Children Here*, or Ron Suskind's *A Hope in the Unseen*. Other works by Kidder might be offered, particularly his character-driven titles *The Soul of a New Machine* and *Mountains Beyond Mountains* (about Dr. Paul Farmer, who has practiced medicine in some of the poorest regions of the world, including Haiti and Russia). Kidder's writing is richly novelistic, and a wide variety of character-driven Mainstream Fiction titles might also be offered to his readers. Books on class matters and issues of poverty, including David Shipler's *The Working Poor* or Joe Bageant's *Deer Hunting with Jesus* might also appeal.

Kidder, Tracy

🏵 *The Soul of a New Machine*. Little, Brown. 1981. 293 pp. ISBN 9780316491709.

Kidder got in on the ground floor of reporting about the personal computer revolution when he wrote this classic of investigative journalism in the early 1980s. Although admitting his total lack of comprehension when it comes to the technological side of computer building, Kidder's year spent following the managers and software engineers of the Data General Corporation in their rush to build a 32-bit mini-computer helped him provide a nuanced picture of individuals whose intelligence and drive, including long working hours and an obsession with the technology and its possibilities, would eventually play a part in the explosion in popularity and ubiquity of the personal computer. As always, Kidder is the narrator of a story rich in achievements, as well as in personalities, but he manages to very nearly and completely leave himself and his own judgments out of the narrative, although his admiration for his subjects' dedication is abundantly clear.

Subjects: 1970s, Business, Character Profiles, Classics, Computers, Engineering, Professions, Technology, Work Relationships

Awards: National Book Award, Pulitzer Prize

Now Try: This is one of Kidder's most well-known works; readers who come across it might also consider his more recent titles, including *Mountains Beyond Mountains: The Quest of Dr. Paul Farmer*, or even his Vietnam War memoir *My Detachment*. A more recent telling of the continuing story of technology is Scott Rosenberg's *Dreaming in Code*, David Weinberger's *Everything Is Miscellaneous*, Philip Evans's and Thomas Wurster's *Blown to Bits: How the New Economics of Information Transforms Strategy*, or Henry Petroski's *Pushing the Limits: New Adventures in Engineering*. This is also an intimate look at the development of a company; other Business Histories (from the Business Reporting chapter) such as Kurt Eichenwald's *Conspiracy of Fools* or John Newhouse's *Boeing vs. Airbus* might also be offered. These readers might also try Character-driven fiction by such authors as John Irving, Richard Russo, Richard Ford, and John Updike.

Lee, Jennifer 8

The Fortune Cookie Chronicles: Adventures in the World of Chinese Food. Twelve. 2008. 307 pp. ISBN 9780446580076.

Journalist Lee set out to chronicle the history of the Chinese American experience by exploring the ubiquitous nature of Chinese food in American culture. Lee exposes the fact that there are more Chinese restaurants in America than McDonalds, Burger Kings, and Wendy's combined; in addition to investigating the working lives of the chefs, many of them illegal immigrants, Lee also explains such connections as those between Jewish people and Chinese food, the nutritional value of most Chinese cuisine produced and delivered in America, and her own history and experiences with Chinese cooking as well.

Subjects: Business, Food, Globalization, Immigrants, Micro-histories, Society

Now Try: Fans of Lee's investigative writing might also consider other books that feature the topic of food and a similar style of writing, including Sasha Issenberg's *The Sushi Economy*, Bill Buford's *Heat*, Kathleen Flinn's *The Sharper Your Knife*, or Barbara Kingsolver's *Animal, Vegetable, Miracle*; other food-related micro-histories might also be suggested, including Mark Kurlansky's *Salt* or *Cod*, Dan Koeppel's *Banana: The Fate of the Fruit that Changed the World*, Patricia Rain's *Vanilla*, or Jack Turner's *Spice*. Lee's book was published by new and unique publisher Twelve; they only publish twelve books a year, and many of their other sociological titles might appeal to these readers, such as Eric Weiner's *The Geography of Bliss*, Bryan Christy's *The Lizard King*, and Sheena Iyengar's *How We Choose*.

McPhee, John A.

🌳 *Uncommon Carriers*. Farrar, Straus & Giroux. 2006. 248 pp. ISBN 9780374280390.

It's a simple premise: McPhee wanted to find out who and what travels along the highways, railways, and waterways in America, and so he sets out to travel along with those individuals who drive, carry, and haul things for a living. Along the way he travels with chemical tanker driver Don Ainsworth, in the cabs of coal trains, and in a canoe on the Merrimack River; he also investigates such little-seen locations as inside an Illinois River towboat and the sorting and distribution hub for UPS at the Louisville International Airport.

Subjects: Classics, Essays, Professions, Quick Reads, Transportation, Travel

Awards: New York Times Notable

Now Try: McPhee is an institution in the field of nonfiction writing; his readers might consider titles by other iconic nonfiction authors including Joseph Mitchell, E. B. White, Studs Terkel, Calvin Trillin, and Gay Talese. Titles by William Langewiesche, a writer who also tackles diverse subjects, might be offered; likewise, readers enthralled with McPhee's journey on the Merrimack River might consider classic works by Henry David Thoreau, who traversed the same river. Offbeat travel authors including Paul Theroux (*The Old Patagonian Express*) and Christopher Wren (*Walking to Connecticut*) might appeal to these readers, as might novels featuring "working-class" heroes by such authors as Richard Russo or John Irving.

Rosenberg, Scott

Dreaming in Code: Two Dozen Programmers, Three Years, 4,732 Bugs, and One Quest for Transcendent Software. Crown. 2007. 400 pp. ISBN 9781400082469.

Whenever you're frustrated by your computer, do you ever wish you were one of those programmer or tech types who always know just what's going on with software? In this illuminating investigative work, Rosenberg observed a group of programmers working on a very specific software program, a "personal information manager" named Chandler. Along the way he learned that creating software is a manufacturing challenge like no other (for example, it doesn't abide by normal work power rules such as adding more people to a project making the work go faster) and that many experts in the field readily admit they sometimes don't understand what's going on with software and the bugs that might creep up. Rosenberg also illuminates issues of technology, business issues, open source collaboration, and work relationships (particularly those between Mitchell Kapor, the boss on the Chandler project, and his subordinates).

Subjects: Computers, Professions, Science, Software, Technology, Work Relationships, Year in the Life

Now Try: Other books on the brave new world of technological advances and issues might be offered to fans of Rosenberg's book; these include Lawrence Lessig's *Free Culture*, David Weinberger's *Everything Is Miscellaneous*, or even Chris Anderson's *The Long Tail*; Tracy Kidder's classic *The Soul of a New Machine* might also appeal. Rosenberg mentions fellow authors Ray Kurzweil and Steve Lohr frequently in his text, and books offering inside looks into a variety of professions and work relationships might appeal to these readers, including William Langewiesche's *The Outlaw Sea*, Bill Buford's *Heat*, or Richard Yancey's *Confessions of a Tax Collector*.

Sager, Mike

Revenge of the Donut Boys: True Stories of Lust, Fame, Survival, and Multiple Personality. Thunder's Mouth Press. 2007. 331 pp. ISBN 9781568583501.

Sager has been called a successor to such well-known "gonzo journalists" as Hunter S. Thompson and Tom Wolfe; although he does not immerse himself in his stories as fully as Thompson, he does provide a true inside look at the stories he pursues, many of which flirt with the darker side of American personalities and culture. In this collection he provides character portraits of Roseanne Barr, renowned beauty Brooke Burke, dot-com billionaire Mark Cuban, and others; he also provides the stories told to him by survivors of California wildfires, fans of the band Slayer, and a family striving to make ends meet in San Diego in the aftermath of a lost job.

Subjects: California, Character Profiles, Essays, Gonzo Journalism, Journalism, Pop Culture, Profanity

Now Try: Sager is also the author of an earlier collection of journalistic pieces titled *Scary Monsters and Super Freaks*. Sager's fans might also consider classic works by Hunter S. Thompson (*Hell's Angels* and *Fear and Loathing in Las Vegas*), Tom Wolfe (*The Right Stuff*), or Pete Dexter (*Paper Trails*). Sager is a longtime contributor to *Esquire* magazine; another well-known contributor to that publication, Chuck Klosterman, might also appeal to these readers (particularly Klosterman's titles *Fargo Rock City* and *Sex, Drugs, and Cocoa Puffs*). Fiction by such authors as Nick Hornby, Richard Russo, and John Irving might also appeal to Sager's fans.

Scott, Aurelia C.

Otherwise Normal People: Inside the Thorny World of Competitive Rose Gardening. Algonquin Books of Chapel Hill. 2007. 235 pp. ISBN 9781565124646.

Scott immerses herself in a world where doctors, teachers, mechanics, and people from all other walks of life indulge in their true passion: gardening, and, more specifically, breeding and growing prize-winning roses. Referring to her subjects as "Roseaholics," the author interviews them and joins them in their gardens, greenhouses, and twice-yearly rose shows, where all bets are off and formerly congenial gardeners contend like gladiators for the highest honor possible: Queen of Show.

Subjects: Character Profiles, Flowers, Gardening, Quick Reads, Year in the Life

Now Try: All types of books about gardening and flowers might appeal to these readers, such as Amy Stewart's *From the Ground Up* or *Flower Confidential*, Susan Warren's *Backyard Giants* (about pumpkins), Susan Orlean's *The Orchid Thief: A True Story of Beauty and Obsession*, Jim Nollman's *Why We Garden*, or even Michael Pollan's *The Botany of Desire*. Other books about people with consuming hobbies might also be offered; these include Stephen Fatsis's *Word Freak* or Shari Caudron's *Who Are You People?*

Stewart, Amy

Flower Confidential: The Good, the Bad, and the Beautiful in the Business of Flowers. Algonquin Books of Chapel Hill. 2007. 306 pp. ISBN 9781565124387.

In this book, Stewart lays bare a $40 billion industry that is not often thought of as an industry. The book is split into three main segments: "Breeding," "Growing," and "Selling"; in the chapters on breeding, Stewart visits California's Sun Valley Floral Farms and explores the uneasy past relationship of the owners of that enterprise and Leslie Woodriff, a well-known but not business-savvy lily breeder. When examining how flowers are now grown, she travels from California to Holland to Ecuador, learning about very different methods of production in each location. Finally, she ends up on the wholesale and retail side of the equation and interviews those who inspect flowers shipped to the United States from other countries; the woman in charge of public relations at Bloemenveiling Aalsmeer, the Dutch flower auction; and the owner of a small flower shop/kiosk in Santa Cruz, California. It's a whirlwind tour, and it seems only appropriate that Stewart didn't have much time to stop and smell the flowers, as she notes that most modern varieties have been bred for shipping-and-handling hardiness, and not for fragrance. The result is a thoughtful book touching on issues of botany, beauty, business, with a dash of travel and personal relationship issues thrown in for good measure.

Subjects: Agriculture, Book Groups, Business, Economics, Environmental Writing, Flowers, Globalization, Travel

Now Try: Stewart has written other books on earthy topics; they include *From the Ground Up* and *The Earth Moved*. Other authors who might appeal to her fans include Bill McKibben (*Deep Economy*), Barbara Kingsolver (*Animal, Vegetable, Miracle*), Wendell Berry (*The Long-Legged House*), Elizabeth Gilbert (*Eat, Pray, Love*), or Michael Pollan (*The Omnivore's Dilemma*). Business Reporting books with the subject of globalization might be offered (such as John Bowe's *Nobodies*), as might "inside looks" at other industries and professions, such as Lisa Takeuchi Cullen's *Remember Me* (about the funeral industry), Anthony Bourdain's *Kitchen Confidential* (about the restaurant business), or Reg Theriault's *How to Tell When You're Tired*.

Torgovnick, Kate

Cheer! Three Teams on a Quest for College Cheerleading's Ultimate Prize. Simon & Schuster. 2008. 355 pp. ISBN 9781416535966.

Torgovnick tells a story-driven and character-rich narrative of competitive cheerleading, following the training and competitive events undertaken by three cheer squads. Told over the course of a year, the story concludes at Nationals, the national and annual championship of the sport; along the way Torgovnick describes the risks and demands of the sport, the very different personalities of the athletes involved, and the cultural beliefs and attitudes toward cheerleaders and their place in the American culture.

> **Subjects:** Cheerleading, Friendships, Pop Culture, Sports, Women's Nonfiction, Year in the Life

> **Now Try:** Other books in which journalists have strived to illuminate the world of particular sports might be offered to fans of this book, including H. G. Bissinger's *Friday Night Lights*, John Feinstein's *Next Man Up: A Year behind the Lines in Today's NFL* or *Tales from Q School: Inside Golf's Fifth Major*, Gene Wojciechowski's *Cubs Nation*, or even George Plimpton's classic *Paper Lion*. Other books in which authors follow individuals obsessed with hobbies, interests, or other competitions might also be suggested, such as Jason Fagone's *Horsemen of the Esophagus* (about competitive eating), Michael Weinreb's *The Kings of New York* (about chess), or Steve Almond's *Candyfreak* (about regional candy production); Immersion Journalism titles might also be of some appeal.

Warren, Susan

Backyard Giants: The Passionate, Heartbreaking, and Glorious Quest to Grow the Biggest Pumpkin Ever. Bloomsbury. 2007. 245 pp. ISBN 9781596912786.

What kind of people try to grow and nurture pumpkins into 1,500-pound, prize-winning behemoths? This is the question *Wall Street Journal* reporter and intrepid pumpkin-grower herself Susan Warren set out to answer by observing and interviewing a number of individuals who compete each growing season in a close-knit community of hobbyists to grow the biggest pumpkin in the world. Warren spends most of her investigative time with father-and-son duo Dick and Ron Wallace and illuminates for her readers the process from seed to pumpkin, giving details about fertilizers, growing tricks, superstitions, and county fair and weigh-off competitions across the country.

> **Subjects:** Character Profiles, Gardening, Hobbies, Year in the Life

> **Now Try:** Books about gardening or hobbies (or obsessions?) might be equally good as read-alikes to this title; consider Hannah Holmes's *Suburban Safari*, Aurelia C. Scott's *Otherwise Normal People*, Stephen Fatsis's *Word Freak*, or Shari Caudron's *Who Are You People?* Lighthearted travel narratives, such as those written by Calvin Trillin (*Feeding a Yen*), Bill Bryson (*A Walk in the Woods*), Tony Horwitz (*Confederates in the Attic*), or Hank Stuever (*Off Ramp*) might also appeal.

Weiss, Mike

A Very Good Year: The Journey of a California Wine from Vine to Table. Gotham Books. 2005. 278 pp. ISBN 9781592401291.

Although this story was originally published as a features article in the *San Francisco Chronicle,* author Weiss expanded it by gaining access to the Ferrari-Carano Vineyards in California and following its yearlong development of a new vintage of wine, a special fumé blanc (a kind of sauvignon blanc). Over the course of the year (2002), Weiss interviewed the vineyard owners, its workers, and reviewers, and also got an in-depth education on viticulture and the process of making wine, all to provide this "biography of a wine." Although the vintage itself did not garner the reviews its creators hoped it would, Weiss provides a valuable inside look into the world of grape harvesting and fermentation, wine creation, and the business and marketing sides of the wine culture.

> **Subjects:** Agriculture, Business, California, Character Profiles, Foodies, Wine, Year in the Life
>
> **Now Try:** Recent interest in foodie books of all kinds have led to a boom in the publishing of books about wine; these include Lawrence Osborne's *The Accidental Connoisseur: An Irreverent Journey through the Wine World*, William Echikson's *Noble Rot: A Bordeaux Wine Revolution*, Julia Flynn Siler's *The House of Mondavi: The Rise and Fall of an American Wine Dynasty*, Benjamin Wallace's *The Billionaire's Vinegar*, and Eric Arnold's *First Big Crush*. Other books with the subject of "Year in the Life" might also be offered, such as Bill Buford's memoir *Heat* or Elizabeth Gilbert's *Eat, Pray, Love*.

Whynott, Douglas

A Country Practice: Scenes from the Veterinary Life. North Point Press. 2004. 289 pp. ISBN 9780865476479.

Although Whynott leaves himself out of the narrative, this extremely readable and personal account of many days in the lives of veterinary practitioners in rural New Hampshire is anything but hands-off. The character-driven narrative revolves around Chuck Shaw, the owner of the practice; Roger Osinchuk, his associate who specializes in horse treatment; and the newly graduated Erika Bruner, their latest addition to the firm. All are portrayed honestly but with sympathy for the many challenges facing modern-day vets: long hours, industrialized farming techniques that focus on animal productivity rather than animal husbandry, and the difficulty of recruiting and keeping well-educated and young staff members in rural settings.

> **Subjects:** Animals, Character Profiles, Community Life, Professions, Rural Life, Work Relationships, Year in the Life
>
> **Now Try:** Susan Nusser's in-depth study of racehorses and the grooms who care for them, *In Service to the Horse: Chronicles of a Labor of Love*, is set against the backdrop of their owners, stables, and competitive world and is similar to Whynott's work for its unapologetic examination of a very unique world. Likewise, any of James Herriot's books about his veterinary practice, which are set in post–World War II England, will provide complementary (but even gentler) reads to Whynott's story; Herriot's series includes *All Creatures Great and Small, All Things Bright and Beautiful, All Things Wise and Wonderful*, and *The Lord God Made Them All*. Lee Gutkind's literary nonfiction classic on the veterinary profession, *The Veterinarian's Touch*, might also prove to be a good related read.

Winerip, Michael

🏵 *9 Highland Road: Sane Living for the Mentally Ill.* Pantheon Books. 1994. 454 pp. ISBN 9780679407249.

Winerip details a large chunk of the history behind the "group home" concept of supervised but independent living for individuals suffering from mental illnesses, but the majority of his narrative rests on his own experiences, over the course of two years, of visiting and observing the multiple residents of 9 Highland Road in Glen Cove, New York. In addition to providing a journalistically sound account of the opening of the house and the community's protests about it, Winerip also provides a number of complex and sympathetic character portraits of several of the home's more troubled occupants, including a woman whose multiple personality disorder wasn't diagnosed until some time after she moved in, and a schizophrenic man, both struggling to prove that they could function in society.

Subjects: Character Profiles, Community Life, Health Issues, Mental Health, New York

Awards: ALA Notable

Now Try: Alex Beam's history of a famous mental health institution, McLean Hospital, is provided in his book *Gracefully Insane: The Rise and Fall of America's Premier Mental Hospital* and provides another perspective on the treatment of mental diseases in America. More personal narratives regarding mental health might also be offered, such as Susanna Kaysen's *Girl, Interrupted*; Debra Ginsberg's *Raising Blaze*; or Pete Earley's *Crazy: A Father's Search through America's Mental Health Madness.* Matt Ruff's novel, *Set This House in Order*, revolves around the multiple personalities of its main characters, and may appeal to readers who are fascinated by the story of 9 Highland Road's residents.

Feature Stories

On Location

On Location Feature Stories, in which the authors focus more attention on the locations of the stories than on the people involved, can be grouped together according to their primary appeal factor of setting. Although these titles are very similar in tone and style to Human Interest Feature Stories, they can often be easily detected by their titles; in Human Interest stories, the characters involved are mentioned ("Otherwise Normal People," "Among Schoolchildren," etc.), whereas the proper nouns in On Location books more often refer to places: Kruger National Park, New York, The New Daleville Real Estate Development. (Even when they're not proper nouns, these titles still refer to definite places: the suburban lawn; the "outlaw sea.") These books often include slightly fewer personal interviews; making up for the loss of dialogue with a more reflective and thoughtful style, and their authors often travel to the site of the story they're covering and let the humans involved come to them there.

Although readers of these books might also like a wide variety of Human Interest stories and other types of In-Depth reporting subgenres, they might also consider a wide variety of other nonfiction titles that feature locations and settings as their primary appeal, including Travel Writing and Environmental Writing of all types. Also of interest to these readers might be Immersion Journalism titles, in which authors also travel to definite locations or surroundings and then proceed to live their own lives there; also of interest might be setting-driven mainstream fiction titles.

On Location Feature Stories cover a wide variety of subjects, and are written in a lively journalistic style, filled with interviews and anecdotes, as well as interesting bits of research and trivia. They offer very distinctive settings, to which their authors have traveled or researched because the settings so heavily influence the stories. Like Human Interest stories, they also feature unique characters, although characterization is not the primary appeal of these books.

Frump, Robert

The Man-Eaters of Eden: Life and Death in Kruger National Park. Lyons Press. 2006. 216 pp. ISBN 9781592288922.

Although we are used to thinking of humans as being at the top of the food chain, Frump journeys to a place where that kind of thinking can easily get you killed. In South Africa's Kruger National Park, more humans than ever before are being attacked and devoured by lions; this dangerous state of affairs is exacerbated by the flood of Mozambican refugees trying to cross the park on foot. In July 2002, Frump flew to South Africa with the idea of joining the refugees on their trek (effectively "becoming prey" himself) but had to content himself with interviewing them, as well as park rangers, field biologists, and safari guides, who candidly discussed their problem and its history with him. In addition to exploring the present-day problems of striking a balance between conservation and safety, Frump also relates the tale of park ranger Harry Wolhuter, who survived a harrowing lion attack in 1902. The book, which originally ran in the magazine *Men's Journal*, is a mix of animal stories, true adventure, history, and an investigation of troubling issues of economics, politics, and environmentalism in today's Africa.

> **Subjects:** Africa, Animals, Ecology, Environmental Writing, Mozambique, Travel, True Adventure

> **Now Try:** Frump's readers might consider a wide variety of other nonfiction narratives featuring animals, such as Philip Caputo's book about lions in Kenya (*Ghosts of Tsavo*), David Quammen's *Monster of God*, Dian Fossey's *Gorillas in the Mist*, or Farley Mowat's *Never Cry Wolf* (Seamus Heaney's new translation of the literary classic *Beowulf* might also appeal, although it features a "monster" more so than an animal). A wide variety of travel narratives, particularly those about Africa, might also be offered; these include Graham Greene's *Journey without Maps*, Tahir Shah's *In Search of King Solomon's Mines*, and memoirs such as Alexandra Fuller's *Don't Let's Go to the Dogs Tonight*, and Joy Adamson's *Born Free: A Lioness of Two Worlds*.

Goldberger, Paul

🎗 *Up from Zero: Politics, Architecture, and the Rebuilding of New York.* Random House. 2004. 273 pp. ISBN 9781400060177.

Architecture critic and *New Yorker* writer Goldberg provides a fascinating and refreshingly objective tale of the process of rebuilding at the World Trade Center Ground Zero site and relates the intimate details of the machinations among many of the key players with a stake in the new structure: businesspeople, politicians, architects, government agencies, and victims' families and community groups.

> **Subjects:** 9/11, Architecture, Business, Community Life, Government, New York City, Politics

Awards: New York Times Notable

Now Try: Readers interested in the engineering and architectural challenges of the World Trade Center site might backtrack and read William Langewiesche's quietly elegiac *American Ground: Unbuilding the World Trade Center.* Neal Bascomb's *Higher: A Historic Race to the Sky and the Making of a City* tells an earlier tale of the characters and methods involved with building New York's Chrysler and Empire State buildings, and James Traub's comprehensive (although not as compelling) discussion of another New York City institution in *The Devil's Playground: A Century of Pleasure and Profit in Times Square* might appeal to readers who are particularly interested in recent developments (such as "Disneyfication") in urban renewal and planning. Although set on a different continent, John Berendt's *The City of Falling Angels,* as an in-depth look at architectural conservation and community policy-setting in Venice, might also appeal to these readers.

Holmes, Hannah

Suburban Safari: A Year on the Lawn. Bloomsbury. 2005. 262 pp. ISBN 9781582344799.

Science journalist Holmes decided to turn her powers of observation to a bit smaller and closer-to-home turf than she had previously: the .2-acre patch of land she called her own backyard in suburban Portland, Maine. Over the course of a year, she went from viewing her yard as a piece of land that she should keep busy fertilizing and mowing to seeing it for the diverse ecosystem that it really was, supporting a wide variety of bird, mammal, and insect life. Holmes also touches on issues of urban design, our dependence on chemicals, and the drive for perfection, even in our lawns, that is not only bad for the planet but also is an impossible pursuit to maintain.

Subjects: Environmental Writing, Gardening, Homes, Maine, Nature, Suburbs, Year in the Life

Now Try: Interestingly enough, another book about the American lawn is available (Ted Steinberg's *American Green: The Obsessive Quest for the Perfect Lawn*); gardening books might also appeal, such as Amy Stewart's *From the Ground Up* and *The Earth Moved,* Susan Warren's *Backyard Giants: The Passionate, Heartbreaking, and Glorious Quest to Grow the Biggest Pumpkin Ever,* Michael Pollan's *A Botany of Desire,* and Jim Nollman's *Why We Garden.* Books by environmental and reflective authors, such as Rachel Carson, Annie Dillard, and Jane Brox might be enjoyed, as might books about urban and suburban planning by Witold Rybczynski (*City Life* and *A Clearing in the Distance*) or James Kunstler.

Kennedy, Randy

Subwayland: Adventures in the World beneath New York. St. Martin's Griffin. 2004. 226 pp. ISBN 9780312324346.

A compilation of *New York Times* reporter Kennedy's "Tunnel Vision" columns, this rider's view of the city's subway system is both dryly sardonic and warmly descriptive. Written in the true reporter's style (in which the reporter is invisible), each short column provides a perfect thumbnail sketch in words of both the system's mechanical workings and its more memorable employees, fans, and customers.

> **Subjects:** Essays, Humor, New York City, Quick Reads, Transportation

> **Now Try:** Phillip Lopate chose to document a different part of New York City's unique geography and transportation system in his *Waterfront: A Journey around Manhattan*. Charlie LeDuff's book of *New York Times* columns, *Work and Other Sins: Life in New York City and Thereabouts*, sometimes wanders further afield than the city for its subjects, but is much the same in honest and absentee narrator form.

Kidder, Tracy

Home Town. Random House. 1999. 349 pp. ISBN 9780679455882.

Kidder brings his keen powers of observation, his imagination, and, as always, his empathy for a wide variety of characters to this in-depth examination of the town of Northampton, Massachusetts. At first glance, the town seems like any other of countless such towns in America, but Kidder knows better; he interviews people and tells their stories until he reveals the complexity and the richness of even the most ordinary lives in the most ordinary town. These friends and neighbors might not always love each other, but at the end of the day Kidder illustrates how very different people—cops and single mothers, judges and criminals, and a wide variety of others—contribute to the creation of a community. Although the book is based on interviews and research, Kidder also readily admits that he has ascribed thoughts to his subjects but maintains that as those thoughts were "plausibly described to me," the work remains one of unabashed nonfiction.

> **Subjects:** Character Profiles, Community Life, Massachusetts, Society, Sociology, Urban Life

> **Now Try:** In Kidder's bibliography, he suggests other classics of urban design and living nonfiction by Jane Jacobs (*The Death and Life of Great American Cities*) and Lewis Mumford (*The City in History*); nonfiction Relationships titles about Community Life might also appeal—these include Michael Perry's *Population 485: Meeting Your Neighbor One Siren at a Time* and Heather Lende's *If You Lived Here, I'd Know Your Name*—as well as more Investigative titles like Michelle Slatalla's *The Town on Beaver Creek*, Stephen G. Bloom's *Postville: A Clash of Cultures in Heartland America*, and memoirs like Roger Welsch's *Forty Acres and a Fool* or even Wendell Berry's community-life novel *Jayber Crow*. Of course, Kidder has written on a variety of other subjects and readers might want to check out the rest of his titles as well.

Langewiesche, William

American Ground: Unbuilding the World Trade Center. North Point Press. 2002. 205 pp. ISBN 9780865475823.

In the aftermath of 9/11, when the work of cleaning up the site of the fallen World Trade Center had commenced in earnest, then-*Atlantic Monthly* correspondent Langewiesche was the only journalist granted unrestricted and around-the-clock access to the site and the many government officials, contractors, workers, and other individuals who coordinated the massive and highly dangerous efforts to both remove the massive amounts of rubble, secure the unstable tunnels and retaining walls underneath the rubble, and make the site ready for rebuilding efforts. Langewiesche balances interview material and character portraits of many of the individuals who stepped into roles of responsibility with an engineer's eye for structural and scientific details (all of which he makes understandable for all general readers). Although there was controversy at the time of the book's publication regarding the author's inclusion of reports of looting by fire department and other personnel, both the *Atlantic Monthly* and the author's publisher stood behind his account and offered proof of their fact-checking.

Subjects: 9/11, Architecture, Government, New York City, Politics, Professions, Quick Reads, Terrorism, Work Relationships

Now Try: Langewiesche is not a prolific writer, but he has written on a variety of topics; his books include *Sahara Unveiled, Cutting for Sign, The Outlaw Sea*, and *The Atomic Bazaar*. Readers fascinated by this behind-the-scenes look at New York City politics and procedures might also consider Paul Goldberger's *Up from Zero* or Jim Dwyer's and Kevin Flynn's dramatic *102 Minutes: The Untold Story of the Fight to Survive inside the Twin Towers*. Books exploring the scientific nitty-gritty of our city environments and infrastructure might also consider Alan Weisman's *The World without Us* or Mark Eberhart's *Why Things Break: Understanding the World by the Way It Comes Apart*; authors including Henry Petroski, Len Fisher, and John McPhee might also appeal.

Langewiesche, William

🏵 *The Outlaw Sea: A World of Freedom, Chaos, and Crime*. North Point Press. 2004. 239 pp. ISBN 9780865475816.

Atlantic Monthly correspondent Langewiesche investigates the largest yet least examined part of the globe: the ocean, those who live and work on it, and those individuals and governments who try to regulate it. The 1994 sinking of the ferry ship *Estonia* in the Baltic Sea, at the cost of 852 lives, anchors the book's examination of the wild and fundamentally uncontrollable nature of the sea. Langewiesche's writing is often described as "lyrical," and he tells these compelling stories with a reporter's attention to detail and characterization.

Subjects: Business, Government, Maritime Disasters, Oceans, Professions, Quick Reads

Awards: New York Times Notable

Now Try: Richard Pollak spent five weeks aboard the container ship the *Colombo Bay* and combines stories of his experiences there with other tales of adventure and piracy in the present world of worldwide shipping and ocean navigation in *The Colombo Bay*, which is less quietly lyrical than Langewiesche's book but is similarly disquieting and even more suspenseful. Those readers who wouldn't mind a dose of history with their sea adventure might also find Laurence Bergreen's *Over the Edge of the World: Magellan's Terrifying Circumnavigation of the Globe* a compelling nautical read. Other books by William Langewiesche might be offered, as might works by other dedicated reporters such as Alex Kotlowitz, Michael Lewis, or Mark Bowden.

Rybczynski, Witold.

Last Harvest: How a Cornfield Became New Daleville Real Estate Development in America from George Washington to the Builders of the

Twenty-first Century, and Why We Live in Houses Anyway. Scribner. 2007. 309 pp. ISBN 9780743235969.

Architectural and micro-history writer Rybczynski follows the development of a new American residential subdivision from conception and planning to completion and the moving in of the new homes' owners and residents. When the author first heard about New Daleville, in rural Pennsylvania, he got to know the area's community leaders and the developer's planners so that he could learn about the building of a community from the ground up. In addition to clearly explaining local building codes and ordinances, as well as the nitty-gritty details of the building trades, he also illustrates the changing American ideal of community and residential traditions, seeking to reconcile ideas of sustainability with building trends that continually emphasize larger bathrooms and homes in general.

> **Subjects:** Architecture, Business, Community Life, Economics, Environmental Writing, Homes, Suburbs, Urban Life
>
> **Now Try:** Rybczynski is able to weave architectural and historical detail into very compelling narratives; readers of this book might consider his other titles, including *Home: A Short History of an Idea, City Life*, or *A Clearing in the Distance*. Other authors who can make their descriptions of their surroundings fascinating include Robert Sullivan (*Rats*), Tracy Kidder (*Home Town*), James Howard Kunstler (*The Geography of Nowhere* and *The Long Emergency*), and even one of the masters of the environmental essay form, Henry David Thoreau. Also of interest might be books with sociology or community life as subjects; these include Robert Putnam's *Bowling Alone* or Alain De Botton's *Status Anxiety*. Many critics have also compared Rybczynski favorably with such other popular authors as Malcolm Gladwell and John McPhee.

Steinberg, Ted

American Green: The Obsessive Quest for the Perfect Lawn. W. W. Norton. 2006. 295 pp. ISBN 9780393060843.

In this thoroughly amusing, rollicking little investigation into the love affair between Americans and their lawns, Steinberg investigates all botanical, cultural, and suburban design aspects of the lawn, which is now one of America's leading crops (there are twice as many acres of lawn in this country as there are acres of cotton). Although the author offers a good dose of history on the phenomenon of the perfect lawn (beginning with its origins in the post–World War II community of Levittown), he also investigates current trends in lawn care including leaf blowers, riding mowers, and even something called turf colorants, as well as interviewing individuals and yard workers regarding their love for the green stuff and their hate for its demanding upkeep.

> **Subjects:** American History, Biology, Botany, Chemistry, Gardening, Homes, Illustrated Books, Micro-histories
>
> **Now Try:** Other books in which authors discover natural wonders in their own backyards might appeal, such as Hannah Holmes's *Suburban Safari: A Year on the Lawn*, Amy Stewart's *From the Ground Up*, or Robert Sullivan's *Rats* (although in Sullivan's book his "backyard" was actually an alley in New York City). These readers might also enjoy a selection of micro-histories such as Mark Kurlansky's *Salt* or *Cod*, Gavin Pretor-Pinney's *The Cloudspotter's Guide*, or Tristram Stuart's *Bloodless Revolution*. Also of interest might be the architectural writer Witold Rybczynski.

Historical Perspectives

Many journalistic reports and stories are written about events that just happened or are happening; this is how journalism has earned its reputation as the rough draft of history. However, there are many investigative writers who are every bit as keen to investigate further and report on historical events (or events that will become part of history) as others are to get the freshest scoop on the newest story. In these Historical Perspectives, writers seek to uncover truths and discover facts and human perspectives that were not uncovered in previous investigations. As such, they blend the stylistic immediacy of In-Depth Reporting with the thoughtfulness and reflective language, as well as a larger emphasis on research and interviews, of history narratives. These books are the ones that occupy the uneasy middle ground between Current Affairs and History; when will books on Hurricane Katrina become part of the History section? In a book like Mark Levine's *F5*, the events may already be history (a day of horrific tornados in 1978), but the telling of the story is done with such investigative immediacy that the book can still be seen as a work of story-driven journalism.

Readers who enjoy these titles might, of course, be particularly drawn to History nonfiction as well, particularly narratives that are story-driven and relate interviews with firsthand witnesses, survivors, and actors in history's stories. Many of these titles are quickly paced and appeal because of their story; as such, their readers might like True Adventure nonfiction books as well (Robert Kurson's very popular *Shadow Divers* comes to mind). Fiction thrillers, particularly those that offer similar subjects (storms, disasters, crime, government corruption or incompetence) might also be suggested.

> The authors of Historical Perspectives investigative titles typically turn their reporting skills and writing styles to events that happened in the past or which will long retain historical significance. Because these narratives most often feature important or traumatic events, they can be quite story-driven. In addition to their quicker pace, these titles still feature interview quotes and the extensive research and factual aggregation for which the entire Investigative Writing style is known.

Bergal, Jenni

City Adrift: New Orleans Before and After Katrina. Louisiana State University Press. 2007. 168 pp. ISBN 9780807132845.

In this collection of journalistic pieces written in the aftermath of Hurricane Katrina, multiple authors examine various aspects of the problem, starting with the storm itself, the levee system, the federal disaster response (or the failure thereof), the state of social services in New Orleans, health care, politics, and the state of housing in the area even years after the storm. Each piece is thoroughly researched and immediately reported, making this a quickly paced, if horrifying, read. Also included are two sections of photographs.

Subjects: Disasters, Government, Health Care, Hurricane Katrina, Hurricanes, Louisiana, New Orleans, Politics, Poverty, Race Relations, Small Press

Now Try: Other books about Hurricane Katrina and its aftermath in Louisiana might serve as related reads for this title; they include Thomas Brinkley's *The Great Deluge*, Jed Horne's *Breach of Faith*, or even Andrei Codrescu's collection of essays about the tragedy, *New Orleans, Mon Amour*. Other Survival and Disaster nonfiction narratives, such as *The Perfect Storm* by Sebastian Junger, might appeal, as might other books about natural disasters, such as Erik Larson's *Isaac's Storm* or Ashley Shelby's *Red River Rising*. Other books by contributors to this volume, including Curtis Wilkie's *Dixie: A Personal Odyssey through Events That Shaped the Modern South* and John McQuaid's *Path of Destruction* might also appeal.

Brinkley, Douglas

🏵 *The Great Deluge: Katrina, New Orleans, and the Mississippi Gulf Coast.* Morrow. 2006. 716 pp. ISBN 9780061124235.

Historian Brinkley, a professor at Tulane University, lived through Hurricane Katrina and has written a masterful account of the storm, its devastating aftermath, and the failure of agencies charged with protecting the citizens of New Orleans. Telling the story by interweaving the narrative with the experiences of those who were there, he lends an immediacy to the tale of this shocking and terrible disaster.

Subjects: American History, Book Groups, Hurricane Katrina, Hurricanes, Louisiana, Natural Disasters, New Orleans, Politics, Survival Stories, Weather

Awards: New York Times Notable

Now Try: Other books on Hurricane Katrina and its aftermath might be suggested, including Jed Horne's *Breach of Faith*, Christopher Cooper's *Disaster*, Frank Rich's *The Greatest Story Ever Sold*, Jenni Bergal's *City Adrift*, or Andrei Codrescu's *New Orleans, Mon Amour*. Other nonfiction titles considered to be Disaster and Survival narratives might be suggested, such as Sebastian Junger's *The Perfect Storm*, Erik Larson's *Isaac's Storm*, Ashley Shelby's *Red River Rising*, or Mark Levine's *F5*, as might a variety of American history titles, such as Simon Winchester's *A Crack in the World: America and the Great California Earthquake of 1906*, or other fiction storm thrillers such as J. G. Ballard's *The Drowned World* or John Barnes's *Mother of Storms*.

Caputo, Philip

13 Seconds: A Look Back at the Kent State Shootings. Chamberlain Bros. 2005. 198 pp. ISBN 9781596090804.

Pulitzer Prize–winning journalist Caputo was one of the first reporters on the scene at Kent State (Ohio) University after the May 4, 1970, incident in which National Guard soldiers opened fire on and killed four students (and wounded several others). Caputo originally reported on the story for the *Chicago Tribune*; in this book, he mixes reporting, history, and memoir by looking back at the situation, his own personal reaction to it, and the lessons that can still be learned from the tragedy in cases of contemporary protests and governmental actions. Most of all, he presents a time-tempered and nuanced picture of the time, offering details regarding Richard Nixon's decision to invade Cambodia, the militaristic actions of the ultra-leftist group the Weathermen, and such statements as Ronald Reagan's (spoken when he was governor of California, and three weeks before the shootings): "If it takes a bloodbath, let's get it over with." The book is short but augmented by newspaper and other clippings from the time, as well as a timeline and transcripts of contemporary reports on the incident.

> **Subjects:** 1970s, American History, Death and Dying, Government, Journalism, Law Enforcement, Ohio, Quick Reads, Vietnam War, Violence, War Reporting

> **Now Try:** Other classic perspectives on the Vietnam War might be offered to these readers, including David Maraniss's *They Marched into Sunlight*, Norman Mailer's *The Armies of the Night*, Michael Herr's *Dispatches*, Tom Bissell's history/memoir *The Father of All Things*, Stanley Karnow's comprehensive history *Vietnam: A History*, or Tim O'Brien's novels *The Things They Carried* or *Going after Cacciato*. Caputo himself is a prolific essayist and novelist; his readers might also consider his titles *A Rumor of War*, *Means of Escape*, and the novels *Horn of Africa* and *DelCorso's Gallery*.

Dwyer, Jim, and Kevin Flynn

🌻 *102 Minutes: The Untold Story of the Fight to Survive inside the Twin Towers.* Times Books. 2005. 322 pp. ISBN 9780805076820.

> *New York Times* reporters Dwyer and Flynn take as the starting point for their compelling narrative 8:46 A.M. on Tuesday morning, September 11, 2001, when 14,000 people were starting their day of work in New York City's World Trade Center. Although there are a seemingly infinite number of books written on the subject of 9/11, this one stands apart in its authors' synthesis of oral history interviews; phone, e-mail, and emergency radio transcripts; and old-fashioned and detail-oriented investigative journalism. Of particular note are the many personal and heroic stories of ordinary individuals going to extraordinary lengths to save themselves and others. In addition to their riveting account of the 102 minutes between the impact of the planes and the collapse of the first tower, the authors also raise questions about building safety and the emergency response system in New York City.

> **Subjects:** 21st Century, 9/11, American History, Architecture, Character Profiles, New York City, Terrorism

> **Awards:** New York Times Notable

> **Now Try:** Related books, subject-wise, including William Langewiesche's *American Ground: Unbuilding the World Trade Center* and Paul Goldberger's *Up from Zero*, as well as Art Spiegelman's graphic novel memoir *In the Shadow of No Towers*, might also be suggested. Other works by family members of 9/11 victims might also appeal; these include Kristen Breitweiser's *Wake-Up Call: The Political Education of a 9/11 Widow* or Marian Fontana's *A Widow's Walk: A Memoir of 9/11*, as well as novels like Jay McInerney's *The Good Life*, Don DeLillo's *Falling Man*, or Robert Baer's *Blow the House Down*.

Friedman, Thomas L.

🌻 *From Beirut to Jerusalem.* Farrar, Straus & Giroux. 1989. 525 pp. ISBN 9780374158941.

> First published in 1990, this collection of sociopolitical pieces was written during Friedman's time as an international correspondent in Lebanon and

Israel. In addition to offering detailed descriptions of the people, the land, and the complex historical and social forces at work in the Middle East, Friedman makes a plea for greater understanding for the complex issues and history of the region. The essays are organized into three parts, by geographic region: Beirut, Jerusalem, and Washington, D.C.; also included is a Middle East timeline.

> **Subjects:** 1970s, 1980s, Arab-Israeli Conflict, Classics, Essays, Government, Israel, Journalism, Lebanon, Middle East, Multicultural Issues, Politics, Travel, World History
>
> **Awards:** National Book Award
>
> **Now Try:** Friedman is a favored author among readers with a more politically conservative bent (largely because of his subsequent books *The Lexus and the Olive Tree* and *The World Is Flat*); his readers might consider other titles such as Mark Bowden's *Guests of the Ayatollah*, David Brooks's *Bobos in Paradise*, or Zev Chafets's *A Match Made in Heaven*. Other books on the complex history of the region, including Robert Fisk's *Pity the Nation: The Abduction of Lebanon* or David Shipler's *Arab and Jew*, might also be offered.

Gorney, Cynthia

🦋 *Articles of Faith: A Frontline History of the Abortion Wars.* Simon & Schuster. 1998. 575 pp. ISBN 9780684809045.

Gorney relates the long history of the impassioned debate about abortion rights, relating personal stories and anecdotes from individuals who both support the legality of abortion and those who oppose it. Covering a time period of more than twenty-five years, from before the 1973 *Roe v. Wade* ruling that made the procedure legal through the 1990s, Gorney provides not only a very personal history of both sides of the debate but also focuses on specific court cases in both state and federal courts that had an impact on the Supreme Court ruling and the status of reproductive rights in the United States.

> **Subjects:** 1970s, 1980s, 1990s, Abortion, American History, Law and Lawyers, Oral Histories, Society, Supreme Court, Women's Nonfiction, Women's Rights
>
> **Awards:** ALA Notable
>
> **Now Try:** Other nonfiction narratives about health issues might be offered, such as Barron Lerner's *The Breast Cancer Wars* or Anne Fadiman's *The Spirit Catches You and You Fall Down*. Also of interest to these readers might be other books that explore legal and court issues, such as Jonathan Harr's *A Civil Action*, Steve Bogira's *Courtroom 302*, Edward Humes's *No Matter How Loud I Shout*, or William Mishler's *A Measure of Endurance* (not to mention legal novels such as those by Lisa Scottoline, John Grisham, or Phillip Margolin).

Krosney, Herbert

The Lost Gospel: The Quest for the Gospel of Judas Iscariot. National Geographic. 2006. 309 pp. ISBN 9781426200410.

Krosney weaves an archaeological tale of discovery and intrigue as he traces the discovery of the lost Gospel of Judas from its unearthing through its handling by various antiquities dealers, and its eventual acquisition and study of by an educational institution and biblical scholars.

> **Subjects:** Ancient History, Antiquities, Archaeology, Bible, Christianity, Jesus Christ, Judas Iscariot, Religion, Travel, True Adventure

Now Try: Fans of this book might want to consider another title published by the National Geographic Society in the same year: *The Gospel of Judas*, edited by Rodolphe Kasser, which is a more literal translation of the lost gospel (or even Simon Mawer's novel *The Gospel of Judas*). These readers might also be intrigued by other antiquities and art investigative stories, including *The Lost Painting* by Jonathan Harr, *The Irish Game* by Matthew Hart, or even the fiction thriller *The Flanders Panel* by Arturo Pérez-Reverte. Noted religious scholar Bart Ehrman wrote the foreword for this book; these readers might also consider his bestselling title *Misquoting Jesus*, as well as books on similar subjects, such as Elaine Pagels's *Reading Judas*, David Damrosch's *The Buried Book*, or Reviel Netz's and William Noel's *The Archimedes Codex*.

Levine, Mark

F5: Devastation, Survival, and the Most Violent Tornado Outbreak of the 20th Century. Miramax Books. 2007. 307 pp. ISBN 9781401352202.

Over a sixteen-hour period on April 3, 1974, a series of 148 separate tornados (sixty-four of them were classified as F5, or "incredible tornados") ripped across a large part of the United States from Michigan to Mississippi and Alabama; journalist Levine recreates the horrifying events of that day by telling the stories of the storms' victims. Hundreds of people were killed in the storms, and many others were injured, including a teenage couple who were caught by a tornado while driving in their car and a sheriff who found himself facing two cyclones. Also included are broader historical stories and cultural context including anecdotes regarding Hank Aaron, Patty Hearst, Richard Nixon, and George Wallace, as well as an introduction to an eccentric scientist and weather expert known widely as "Mr. Tornado."

> **Subjects:** 1970s, Alabama, American History, American South, Death and Dying, Family Relationships, Survival Stories, Tornadoes, True Adventure, Weather
>
> **Now Try:** Other survival and disaster True Adventure narratives might be offered to these readers, such as Sebastian Junger's *The Perfect Storm*, Erik Larson's *Isaac's Storm*, Robert Kurson's *Shadow Divers*, or R. A. Scotti's *Sudden Sea: The Great Hurricane of 1938*. Other books about natural phenomena might also appeal, such as Jan DeBlieu's *Wind*, Scott Huler's *Defining the Wind*, and David Ulin's *The Myth of Solid Ground*.

Moats, David

🔖 *Civil Wars: A Battle for Gay Marriage.* Harcourt. 2004. 288 pp. ISBN 9780151010172.

Part history, part Pulitzer Award–winning investigative writing and commentary, in this book Moats relates the history of the grassroots movement in the state of Vermont (also the first state in the Union to abolish slavery) to make civil unions for homosexual couples legal; the court battle was won in 2000 when state law allowing such unions was passed. Moats also relates the stories of those lawmakers involved in the process (as well as political player Howard Dean, who had wider political ambitions of his own) and the citizens of Vermont who weigh in throughout the text with their opinions on the matter.

Subjects: 20th Century, Civil Rights, Community Life, Family Relationships, GLBTQ, Government, Politics, Vermont

Awards: ALA Notable

Now Try: Fans of this book might consider other works with GLBTQ viewpoints, including Dan Savage's *The Commitment* (although Savage's writing is a bit more informal than Moats's), Gean Harwood's *The Oldest Gay Couple in America*, or Randy Shilts's classic *And the Band Played On*. Also of interest might be other books exploring legislation and how it is created and interpreted, including Cynthia Gorney's *Articles of Faith: A Frontline History of the Abortion Wars* (also an ALA Notable book) or Jeffrey Toobin's *The Nine: Inside the Secret World of the Supreme Court*. A number of titles from the Political Reporting chapter might also be offered to these readers, particularly those by authors such as Chris Hedges or Lewis Lapham.

Packer, George

🎗 *The Assassins' Gate: America In Iraq.* Farrar, Straus & Giroux. 2005. 467 pp. ISBN 9780374299637.

Staff writer for *The New Yorker* and memoirist, Packer offers a densely written but extensively researched title exploring America's involvement in the 2003 Iraq War (and earlier Gulf War), as well as Iraq's history and current political situation. In later chapters, he interviews such individuals as Drew Erdmann, a U.S. State Department employee; Dr. Baher Butti, an Iraqi psychiatrist; Meghan O'Sullivan, another CPA employee who worked under both Jay Garner and Paul Bremer; and Captain John Prior, a rifle company commander in charge of small reconstruction projects in postwar Baghdad. He also interviews many Iraqis on their impressions of Americans. The result is a complex but well-told combination of history, current affairs, political commentary, and investigative reporting.

Subjects: George W. Bush, Government, Iraq, Iraq War (2003), Middle East, Multicultural Issues, Politics, World History

Awards: ALA Notable, New York Times Notable

Now Try: Those readers most interested in Packer's subject matter might consider related titles such as Michael Gordon's *Cobra II: The Inside Story of the Invasion and Occupation of Iraq*, Thomas Ricks's *Fiasco: The American Military Adventure in Iraq*, Anthony Shadid's *Night Draws Near: Iraq's People in the Shadow of America's War*, or James Risen's *State of War*. Authors Christopher Hitchens and Samantha Powers provided blurbs for this book; their respective books, *A Long Short War* and *"A Problem from Hell": America and the Age of Genocide*, might also be offered, as might other authors known for their exhaustive research and storytelling, including Mark Bowden, William Langewiesche, or Ron Suskind.

Shelby, Ashley

Red River Rising: The Anatomy of a Flood and the Survival of an American City. Borealis Books. 2003. 265 pp. ISBN 9780873515009.

Shelby illustrates a national disaster that predated Katrina by nearly a decade: the 1997 flooding of the Red River at Grand Forks, North Dakota. The author provides a history of Great Plains weather, national weather service measurement and prediction techniques, how the flood destroyed the better part of the city, and how the city's residents sought to rebuild their city, even though many of them were less than pleased with ways sought by the city to rebuild their homes and businesses in safer locations and away from the floodplain.

Subjects: 1990s, Community Life, Disasters, Engineering, Floods, Natural Disasters, North Dakota, Rivers, Science, Small Press, Survival Stories, Weather

Now Try: Books about other natural disasters and phenomena include Erik Larson's *Isaac's Storm*, Mark Levine's *F5*, Michelle Slatalla's *The Town on Beaver Creek* (about a town which experienced frequent floods), or David Ulin's *The Myth of Solid Ground*. Books about weather might also appeal, such as Tim Flannery's *The Weather Makers*, Charles Wohlforth's *The Whale and the Supercomputer*, or Douglas Brinkley's *The Great Deluge* (about Hurricane Katrina); also consider novels featuring storms such as J. G. Ballard's *The Drowned World* or John Barnes's *Mother of Storms*. Books about closely knit communities might also be suggested, such as Michael Perry's *Population 485* or Heather Lende's *If You Lived Here, I'd Know Your Name*.

Spencer, Lynn

Touching History: The Untold Story of the Drama That Unfolded in the Skies Over America on 9/11. Free Press. 2008. 309 pp. ISBN 9781416559252.

Author Spencer tells the story of the terrorist attacks on New York City and Washington, D.C., on 9/11 from a different perspective: that of the air-traffic controllers and the staff of America's national air-defense systems. Using tape archives, interviews, and extensive research, Spencer recreates each minute of that day and uses her expertise as a flight instructor to make her sometimes technical wealth of information and detail accessible to the common reader.

Subjects: 9/11, American History, Aviation, Flight, Military, Terrorism

Now Try: Other perspectives from that day in American history might be suggested to these readers, including Jim Dwyer's *102 Minutes: The Untold Story of the Fight to Survive inside the Twin Towers*, William Langewiesche's *American Ground: Unbuilding the World Trade Center*, or Marian Fontana's *A Widow's Walk: A Memoir of 9/11*. Other historical accounts of seminal moments in American history might also hold some appeal to these readers, including David McCullough's *1776*, Margaret Macmillan's *Nixon and Mao: The Week That Changed the World*, or Gordon Prange's classic *At Dawn We Slept: The Untold Story of Pearl Harbor*.

Talese, Gay

The Kingdom and the Power: The Story of the Men Who Influence the Institution That Influences the World. World. 1969. 555 pp. ISBN 9780385144049.

Although becoming more a work of history every year, Talese's intensive history of the newspaper of record, the *New York Times*, and its management under the Adolph Ochs family and eventually his descendant Arthur Sulzberger, remains a classic in the field of journalistic investigation and reporting. Talese relates some of the biggest news stories of the twentieth century (particularly during the 1960s), all told from the perspective of those journalists, editors, and publishers who wrote and ran the stories, many of whom Talese interviewed not only to get a feel for the events but also to learn how the individuals in question responded to those events. Also on display are the very complex interpersonal and work relationships that governed work at the *Times* for decades.

Subjects: 1960s, Business Histories, Classics, Journalism, Mass Media, Work Relationships

Now Try: Seth Mnookin's more recent book, *Hard News*, about the struggles of the *New York Times* to remain relevant might be enjoyed by these readers. Gay Talese has written on a variety of topics; his readers might consider his other titles such as *Thy Neighbor's Wife* and his autobiography *A Writer's Life*, as well as other titles about the 1960s, such as Robert Stone's *Prime Green*, Tom Brokaw's *Boom!*, or Mark Kurlansky's *1968*. Katharine Graham's seminal memoir of her work as editor of the *Washington Post*, *Personal History*, might also be suggested.

Tolan, Sandy

The Lemon Tree: An Arab, a Jew, and the Heart of the Middle East. Bloomsbury. 2006. 362 pp. ISBN 9781582343433.

Tolan's nuanced and beautifully written exploration of the Arab-Israeli conflict as experienced by two people, Palestinian Bashir Al-Khairi and Israeli Dalia Eshkenazi, is equal parts journalistic investigation, history, and character portrait. In 1967, Bashir set out to visit what had been his family's home twenty years earlier; Dalia, whose family lived there, opened the door to him when he arrived. The narrative unfolds with alternating chapters on the histories of the Khairi and Eshkenazi families, opening in 1967, flashing back to the building of the house and the planting of the lemon tree in 1936, Dalia's parents' escape from certain death in 1943, and then moving through other times and events such as the expulsion of Bashir's family from their home and Dalia's family's arrival to it. Over the course of the years the friendship between Bashir and Dalia would be severely tested, although they eventually reconciled and converted the house in Ramla into a day-care center for Arab and Jewish children. It is a uniquely told and engaging story and hinges on Dalia's eventual realization that "I cannot afford to fight one wrong with another wrong. It doesn't lead *anywhere*!"

Subjects: Arab-Israeli Conflict, Book Groups, Friendships, Homes, Israel, Middle East, Multicultural Issues, Palestine, Politics, World History

Now Try: In addition to the good writing throughout this book, Tolan has also provided a list of spectacular read-alikes for his readers in his book's bibliography, suggesting such authors as Bruce Feiler and Joe Sacco; other authors who might appeal to these readers include Karen Armstrong (particularly her title *Jerusalem*), George Packer (*The Assassins' Gate: America in Iraq*), or Azar Nafisi (*Reading Lolita in Tehran*). Tolan does an admirable job of trying to present both sides of the conflict; therefore, advocate for Palestinian rights author Edward Said might be considered, as might Holocaust survivor Elie Wiesel.

Venkatesh, Sudhir Alladi

American Project: The Rise and Fall of a Modern Ghetto. Harvard University Press. 2000. 332 pp. ISBN 9780674008304.

In this somewhat scholarly but still highly readable and compelling social history, Venkatesh reports on his near-decade of fieldwork spent researching and interviewing inhabitants of Chicago's Robert Taylor Homes, which opened with 4,500 units in 1962 and was demolished in the late 1990s. Although such "projects" as the Robert Taylor Homes were begun in an effort to provide inexpensive housing for America's urban populations, they quickly fell into various states of disrepair and became synonymous with the urban poor, as well as with overcrowding and drug, gangs, and violence problems. In addition to providing a comprehensive history of the projects from the 1960s through the 1970s and '80s, Venkatesh also offers a variety of sympathetic character portraits of individuals seeking tirelessly to better their neighborhoods from the inside out, sometimes even asking for help from gang members and creating their own version of community watches and barter and trade economies.

> **Subjects:** Chicago, Community Life, Homes, Illinois, Poverty, Race Relations, Scholarly, Small Press, True Crime, Urban Life

> **Now Try:** These readers might also enjoy Venkatesh's other titles, *Off the Books: The Underground Economy of the Urban Poor* and *Gang Leader for a Day: A Rogue Sociologist Takes to the Streets*. Other thoughtful nonfiction titles on urban life and poverty might appeal to these readers, such as David Shipler's *The Working Poor*, Adrian Nicole LeBlanc's classic *Random Family*, Buzz Bissinger's *A Prayer for the City*, Alex Kotlowitz's *There Are No Children Here*, Ron Suskind's *A Hope in the Unseen*, Thomas L. Webber's *Flying Over 96th Street: Memoir of an East Harlem White Boy*, E. Vernon Jordan's *Jordan Can Read!*, Tracy Kidder's *Among Schoolchildren*, Stephen G. Bloom's *Postville: A Clash of Cultures in Heartland America*, or Jennifer Gonnerman's *Life on the Outside*.

Weschler, Lawrence

A Miracle, a Universe: Settling Accounts with Torturers. Pantheon Books. 1990. 293 pp. ISBN 9780394582078.

> Weschler examines two case studies of countries where brutal military political regimes, which had engaged in the torture of their political enemies and their citizens, were toppled, and how residents of those countries sought to avenge themselves. In the first half of the book Weschler describes Brazil in the 1980s and that country's citizens' publication of the book *Torture in Brazil*, which provided a "shocking report on the pervasive use of torture by Brazilian military governments, 1964–1979"; in the second half he travels to Uruguay and examines the citizens' responses to their former regime's use of torture. Weschler's writing is immediate, and his travels and interviews in both countries lend this book, even though it was published two decades ago, a feel of authority.

> **Subjects:** 1970s, 1980s, 20th Century, Brazil, Classics, Government, Politics, Torture, Uruguay, World History

> **Now Try:** Although it is not an easy subject, other compelling books on torture might be offered to Weschler's readers, such as *Unspeakable Acts, Ordinary People*, by John Conroy; *Brainwash*, by Dominic Streatfeild; or *The Men Who Stare at Goats*, by Jon Ronson. Books about Abu Ghraib or Guantanamo Bay atrocities might provide similar read-alikes (Joseph Margulies's *Guantánamo and the Abuse of Presidential Power* or Mark Danner's *Torture and Truth*), as might other books about Central and South American politics, such as *Salvador* by Joan Didion or John Perkins's *Confessions of an Economic Hit Man*.

Historical Perspectives: Oral Histories

Oral Histories are quite literally in a class all their own. Very rarely, I'll admit, do readers ask me for a good work of oral history. And yet authors and journalists like Studs Terkel have made a career out of getting out of the way of their subjects and letting them tell their own stories, which is really what this subgenre is all about. Although these titles may seem too dependent on one source of information—the personal interviews that are transcribed—to be truly investigative works, they are the icebergs of the journalism world. These books are the ultimate in "hands-off" reporting, in that journalists find their subjects and let them tell their own stories, leaving their readers to draw their own conclusions and beliefs from their stories; what the reader doesn't typically see is the authors' often deep backgrounds in researching, studying, and writing in other sources about their chosen subjects. John Bowe, the editor of the volume *Gig*, has been reporting on workplace stories and working conditions for years; Svetlana Alexievich made a journalism career out of talking to citizens throughout the Ukraine and Belarus long before she compiled *Voices from Chernobyl*.

Although the reporter is there to document the interview and the responses, the telling of the story is left to the person who experienced it, which lends these narratives a feel of immediacy and truth (as subjective as that concept is) that is hard to match, even in other very immediate and interview-heavy titles. These titles are called histories because, even when they pertain to subjects in the current day (as did Terkel's *Working*, when it was first published), they eventually become even more valuable as historical resources and evidence. In some books, the people speaking are remembering events that did happen to them in the past, but they are often speaking to a reporter or an author in the present day, seeking to make sense or simply come to terms with past events. This method of gathering firsthand accounts is what still places these books firmly in the broader investigative writing category.

Oral Histories are truly in a class of their own. Although they are often written by journalists who travel widely and interview numerous people so that they can let them tell their stories (and history) in their own words (which can be extremely evocative), they offer both current perspectives on issues as well as the historical perspective on ways of life and surroundings for generations to come. They do not offer stories as such, but they often feature a wide variety of voices on different but related subjects and can be read piecemeal. Although they do not often contain more stereotypical factoids from research, their authors nonetheless have to research their subjects well to find their interview subjects and know what questions to ask of them.

Bowe, John, Marisa Bowe, and Sabin C. Streeter

Gig: Americans Talk about Their Jobs at the Turn of the Millennium. Crown. 2000. 548 pp. ISBN 9780609605882.

This series of interviews creates a comprehensive work of oral history about people, their jobs and professions, and how they feel about those professions at the turn of the twenty-first century. The editors have made a good effort to represent a wide range of professions and pay ranges; interviewees include waitresses, funeral home directors, CEOs, clutter consultants, and porn stars (to name a very few). Organized into fourteen sections by industry sector such as "goods and services," "transportation," "workers and managers," "children and teachers," and so on, the result is an in-depth look into what work looked like at this time in history.

Subjects: Business, Oral Histories, Professions, Work Relationships

Now Try: Studs Terkel's classic *Working* is the original model for this book; readers might enjoy Terkel's subjects' candor and the more historical aspects of his much earlier title. Bowe's more recent book about modern-day slavery and globalization, *Nobodies*, might be suggested to these readers, as might Immersion Journalism classics like Barbara Ehrenreich's *Nickel and Dimed* or Ted Conover's *Newjack: Guarding Sing Sing*, as well as Working Life Memoirs like Debra Ginsberg's *Waiting: The True Confessions of a Waitress*, Pete Jordan's *Dishwasher*, or Iain Levison's *A Working Stiff's Manifesto*.

Gates, Henry Louis, Jr.

America Behind the Color Line: Dialogues with African Americans. Warner Books. 2004. 448 pp. ISBN 9780446532730.

In conjunction with the production of the PBS documentary *America behind the Color Line*, Gates spoke with numerous individuals to provide both a nuanced and a broadly based oral history of the African American experience in America during the latter half of the twentieth century (after the assassination of Martin Luther King, Jr.). Among the cultural groups upon which Gates focuses are "Black Hollywood," the "Black Elite," "The Ghetto," and the "New South."

Subjects: African American Authors, American History, Civil Rights, Oral Histories, Race Relations, Racism, Society

Now Try: Henry Louis Gates, Jr. is a prolific and well-reviewed author; his other books might also be suggested, including *Thirteen Ways of Looking at a Black Man*, *The Future of the Race*, and the memoir *Colored People*. Other titles that may be of interest to these readers are Charles Barkley's *Who's Afraid of a Large Black Man?*, Nelson George's *Post-Soul Nation*, Larry Tye's *Rising from the Rails: Pullman Porters and the Making of the Black Middle Class*, or the memoirs *Warriors Don't Cry* by Melba Pattillo Beals or *The Color of Water* by James McBride.

Hatzfeld, Jean, and Linda Coverdale

Machete Season: The Killers in Rwanda Speak. Farrar, Straus & Giroux. 2005. 253 pp. ISBN 9780374280826.

Over the course of 100 days in the spring of 1994, 800,000 people in the tiny African country of Rwanda were hacked to death by their machete-wielding neighbors. Six years after the genocide took place, Hatzfeld, a French journalist, met with and interviewed ten Hutu men who had been convicted for their roles in the killing and were incarcerated in a Rwandan prison. All ten men were childhood friends and neighbors and completed their work during the slaughter as a self-described "gang." The interviews are arranged into thematic chapters, covering a variety of horrific topics: how the killing was organized, where it took place, how each man felt about the first time they killed someone, their family and neighborhood histories, and how their hatred toward the Tutsis developed. The result is an immediate and disturbing firsthand account of the genocide; also included is a foreword by Susan Sontag and an epilogue describing where the ten Hutu men are now.

> **Subjects:** 1990s, 20th Century, Africa, Atrocities, Books in Translation, Explicit Violence, Genocide, Hutu, Multicultural Issues, Oral Histories, Rwanda, Tutsi

> **Now Try:** Hatzfeld and his translator Coverdale have produced a second volume in this series, in which they provide the stories of Tutsi survivors of the genocide, called *Life Laid Bare*, which is every bit as heartbreaking and compelling as this first volume. Philip Gourevitch's *We Wish to Inform You That Tomorrow We Will Be Killed with Our Families* might also appeal, as might a variety of nonfiction (*A Long Way Gone* by Ishmael Beah or *Sahara Unveiled* by William Langewiesche) and fiction (*What Is the What* by Dave Eggers or *Things Fall Apart* by Chinua Achebe).

Holthaus, Gary H.

From the Farm to the Table: What All Americans Need to Know about Agriculture. University Press of Kentucky. 2006. 363 pp. ISBN 9780813124193.

Author Holthaus interviewed more than forty American farm families to hear their opinions on those still making a living in agriculture, as well as about the practices and values that related to their land, work, and communities. Although these families put a strong personal touch on the narrative, the author also illustrates how economic, governmental, regulatory, and local governance issues affect these individuals and their livelihoods. Among the more controversial subjects discussed are genetically modified crops, pesticide and chemical use, and the formation and dominance of huge agricultural conglomerates. The book is published by a university press but is very readable and based largely on interviews rather than on academic research or sources.

> **Subjects:** Agriculture, Community Life, Economics, Food, Government, Oral Histories, Scholarly, Small Press, Sustainability, Technology

> **Now Try:** Other nonfiction titles on food production and modern agribusiness (and there are a lot of them) might also appeal to these authors, such as Michael Pollan's *In Defense of Food* or *The Omnivore's Dilemma* or Mark Winne's more scholarly *Closing the Food Gap*; books on migrant labor such as John Bowe's *Nobodies* or the illustrated book *Communities without Borders* might also be offered. Other authors who write books on similar subjects include Wendell Berry, Ben Logan (novels), Wes Jackson, Anna Lappé and Frances Moore Lappé, Eric Schlosser, Marion Nestle, Nina Planck, and Scott Russell Sanders.

Stone, Pamela

Opting Out?: Why Women Really Quit Careers and Head Home. University of California Press. 2007. 295 pp. ISBN 9780520244351.

Stone offers a compilation of her in-depth interviews with women who returned home to raise their families full time, leaving their various jobs as doctors, lawyers, bankers, scientists, and many others. This phenomenon, which has been widely referred to in the media as women "opting out" of their careers when they become parents, is complex in both its many causes and its effects. Stone's candidly reported interviews reveal what women who have followed this course of action actually think and feel about other players in the situation, including their colleagues, spouses, and the children themselves; her conclusions point more in the direction of women being pushed out of their careers rather than voluntarily "opting out" of them without remorse or regret. The author also explores ways in which the modern workplace might become more flexible to the needs of parents of both genders.

> **Subjects:** Business, Feminism, Oral Histories, Parenting, Professions, Psychology, Small Press, Society, Women's Contributions, Women's Nonfiction, Work Relationships

> **Now Try:** A wide variety of authors who have written on issues concerning women's rights and lifestyles at the beginning of the twenty-first century include (of course) Betty Friedan (*The Feminine Mystique*), Leslie Bennetts (*The Feminist Mistake*), or Susan Douglas (*The Mommy Myth*). Authors referred to in the notes of Stone's book might also be offered; these include Linda Hirshman, Susan Faludi, and Juliet Schor. Another book based on interviews, Peggy Orenstein's *Flux: Women on Sex, Work, Love, Kids, and Life in a Half-Changed World*, might also appeal.

Terkel, Studs

Working: People Talk about What They Do All Day and How They Feel about What They Do. Pantheon Books. 1974. 589 pp. ISBN 9780394478845.

Although it was first published in 1972, there is something universal about Terkel's unobtrusive interviews with all members of the working classes, including professions from "hooker" to "executive" to "janitor" to "department store salesman." Although the majority of the narrative is told by the interviewees, in their own distinctive voices, Terkel introduces each of his subjects with an evocative introductory description, and his own questions sprinkled throughout the interviews are informal but always manage to advance the stories in unexpected and fascinating ways.

> **Subjects:** Classics, Oral Histories, Professions, Work Relationships

> **Now Try:** Although not as poignant as Terkel's volume, readers looking for a more current view of the work world might enjoy *Gig: Americans Talk about Their Jobs at the Turn of the Millennium*, edited by John Bowe, Marissa Bowe, and Sabin Streeter. Terkel is, of course, a master in the production of oral histories; his other volumes include *Hard Times: An Oral History of the Great Depression*, *American Dreams: Lost and Found*, and *Race*. Other books about professions and work relationships might also appeal, such as Reg Theriault's *How to Tell When You're Tired* and *Punching In* by Alex Frankel.

Vollmann, William T.

Poor People. Ecco. 2007. 314 pp. ISBN 9780060878825.

Vollmann traveled the globe in search of answers to his one question, "Why are you poor?" The range of answers, from "because I was bad in my last life," to "because the rich do nothing for the poor" offer a glimpse into the complex issues surrounding poverty with all its attendant issues of homelessness, sickness, violence, and misery. Vollmann is less an investigative reporter than a recorder of conversational snippets and an arranger of vignettes; he disappears nearly completely in his own narrative to allow the poor to speak for themselves. Also included are more than one hundred black-and-white and sometimes graphic photographs, taken by the author, showing his subjects in their respective environments.

Subjects: Economics, Illustrated Books, Oral Histories, Poverty, Religion, Travel, Underdogs

Now Try: Vollmann's literary style is very unique; a combination of stream-of-consciousness observations with very stylized prose. Readers who enjoy this title might enjoy his other works, such as *The Atlas* and *Rising Up and Rising Down: Some Thoughts on Violence, Freedom, and Urgent Means* (as well as his novels *Europe Central* or *The Royal Family*). A similar book, albeit eighty years older, is James Agee's *Let Us Now Praise Famous Men*; other literary stylists and novelists might also be offered, such as Kurt Vonnegut, Jose Saramago, Thomas Pynchon, or Don DeLillo.

Science Reporting

Science reporting has been around for at least as long as newspapers, which seems about right, considering that scientists began to organize themselves into groups for the sharing of information and communicating with one another in the mid-seventeenth century (England's Royal Society, one of the most well known of such groups, was founded in 1660). While scientists took steps to further communication among one another, it only made sense that they would also be interested in sharing more news with the public, and news publications, particularly early periodicals, were soon founded for this purpose, including the French journal *Journal des savants* (founded in 1665) and England's Royal Society's *Philosophical Transactions* (also starting in 1665 with monthly publication). Other journals in other cities followed, and soon "news of science was spreading faster, farther and with more accuracy than ever before" (Stephens 1988, 177).

Science Reporting tends to be a marriage between the most fascinating scientific developments and the most skillful journalistic writing; the authors in this category know they have to be clear and engaging to make their topics understandable and compelling to readers who may or may not have extensive scientific knowledge or backgrounds. Although these books tend to be about very specific subjects, the subject is not always the sole appeal, and readers who enjoy other in-depth works on a variety of subjects might be just as ready to consider a book on germs, or robots, or diamonds. Depending on their backgrounds and interests, these readers might also consider a wide variety of more traditional Science and Math books, particularly by such popular authors as Dava Sobel, Richard Dawkins, Timothy Ferris, Henry Petroski, or Oliver Sacks. These readers might also consider a wide variety of Thrillers, including Bio Thrillers and Medical Thrillers, as well as Ecological Horror.

> Science Reporting books feature stories of fascinating developments and discoveries, offered by science journalists who can make the information accessible to general readers. They tend to be very clearly written, cover a wide variety of scientific topics and subjects, and often feature lively pacing and compelling story-driven narratives.

Ettlinger, Steve

Twinkie, Deconstructed: My Journey to Discover How the Ingredients Found in Processed Foods Are Grown, Mined (Yes, Mined), and Manipulated into What America Eats. Hudson Street Press. 2007. 282 pp. ISBN 9781594630187.

When Ettlinger's daughter used her new reading skills to read ingredient lists on the food their family was eating, one of her first questions was "Daddy, what's polysorbate 60?" Disturbed by the question (at least in part because he didn't know the answer and they were all eating it), the author set out to track down the details of all the ingredients listed for one of America's favorite snack foods: the Twinkie. Each chapter in his narrative provides a detailed description of each ingredient, which Ettlinger learned about through research and by interviewing individuals in the industry. As a result, the book includes information about cornfields in Iowa, the vanilla harvest in Madagascar, phosphate mines in Idaho, and even gypsum mines in Oklahoma. Although humorous at times, the book as a whole is a serious consideration of how little we know about all the processed foods we ingest every single day.

> **Subjects:** Agriculture, Companies, Engineering, Food, Pop Culture, Science
>
> **Now Try:** Readers of this inside look at food production might also enjoy Vince Staten's *Can You Trust a Tomato in January?*, Steve Almond's *Candyfreak*, or Mark Kurlansky's micro-history *Salt*. They might also consider other works about food and agriculture, ranging from Eric Schlosser's *Fast Food Nation* and Michael Pollan's *The Omnivore's Dilemma* to Barbara Kingsolver's *Animal, Vegetable, Miracle: A Year of Food Life* or Thomas Pawlick's exposé *The End of Food*. Other micro-histories and micro-science books might appeal, as might books by cultural critics including Wendell Berry, Bill McKibben, or Jonathan Schell.

Garrett, Laurie

The Coming Plague: Newly Emerging Diseases in a World Out of Balance. Farrar, Straus & Giroux. 1994. 750 pp. ISBN 9780374126469.

This may indeed be more than any one reader wants to know about diseases and plagues, and how they might blossom into epidemics, but it is also an extremely comprehensive and scientific investigation into the symptoms and transmission of such diseases as Bolivian hemorrhagic fever, the Marburg virus, Lassa fever, Ebola, swine flu, genetic engineering, sexually transmitted diseases, and hantaviruses. Garrett's text is dense and scientific, but in addition to describing these diseases and their spread, she also reports on how governments are (or are not) prepared for possible epidemic risks and the ways in which they might deal with such outbreaks as they occur. The author is also a Pulitzer Prize–winning journalist who has written extensively on public health issues.

> **Subjects:** Diseases, Epic Reads, Epidemiology, Health Issues, Medicine, Scholarly, Science
>
> **Now Try:** Other books by virtuoso science reporters and writers might appeal to these readers, such as those by Richard Preston (*The Demon in the Freezer* and *The Hot Zone*), Judith Miller and William Broad (*Germs: Biological*

Weapons and America's Secret War), Jonathan Weiner, Alan Weisman, or William Wright. Robert Morris's intriguing *The Blue Death: Disease, Disaster, and the Water We Drink* as well as Steven Johnson's more historical *The Ghost Map: The Story of London's Most Terrifying Epidemic* might be offered, as might other books with the subject "History of Medicine," or even Garrett's own title *Betrayal of Trust: The Collapse of Global Public Health*.

Gutkind, Lee

Almost Human: Making Robots Think. W. W. Norton. 2006. 284 pp. ISBN 9780393058673.

Often referred to as the godfather of creative nonfiction, Gutkind has long been an author of compelling "inside look" narratives, beginning with *The Best Seat in Baseball* and *Many Sleepless Nights: The World of Organ Transplantation*. In this 2006 title, he immerses himself in scientists' quests for robot autonomy and the world of the robotic subculture at such institutions as the Robotics Institute at Carnegie Mellon University and NASA. Along the way, he met not only dozens of "cavorting mechanical creatures" and Segways learning to play soccer, but also the (primarily) young men behind their creations, controlling their robots through remote controls and laptops and bringing a fierce intensity to their research.

Subjects: Artificial Intelligence, Professions, Robotics, Science, Technology

Now Try: Tracy Kidder was one of the earliest writers to tell the personal stories of those individuals in love with technology, in his classic The *Soul of a New Machine*, while Scott Rosenberg wrote a similar book called *Dreaming in Code* about a driven group of computer programmers. Other futurist and science books might be offered to these readers, including titles by Ray Kurzweil, Alvin Toffler, and John Brockman. Gutkind, also known as the "godfather of creative nonfiction" has many other titles to his credit, including *Many Sleepless Nights* (about organ transplantation) and *Forever Fat* (a collection of essays).

Gutkind, Lee

Many Sleepless Nights: The World of Organ Transplantation. W. W. Norton. 1988. 368 pp. ISBN 9780393025200.

In this, an early example of book-length investigative writing, creative nonfiction guru Gutkind immersed himself in the world of those surgeons and medical professionals working in the world of organ transplantation. Participants in that world whom Gutkind profiled include Thomas Starzl, chief transplant surgeon at the Pittsburgh Presbyterian-University Hospital; the fifteen-year-old donor Richie Becker; patients' agonized waiting for donated organs; as well as the actual physical procedure and recovery. Although much of the medical information is by now most likely outdated, it is still an important glimpse inside this highly specialized medical world, and the human sides of the equation remain much the same now as they stood in the 1980s. Gutkind has long been a vocal proponent of the creative nonfiction form and has always been adamant that true nonfiction writers do not make up stuff; this book is an admirably straightforward and impressively documented investigation.

Subjects: Character Profiles, Classics, Health Issues, Medicine, Science

Now Try: Gutkind has written many classics in the investigative writing field, including *The Veterinarian's Touch* and many nonfiction collections, including *In Fact: The Best of Creative Nonfiction* and *The Best Creative Nonfiction*. Readers who find this classic might also consider more recent titles on medicine and medical break-throughs, including such books as Jerome Groopman's *How Doctors Think* or Atul Gawande's *Complications*; investigative works like Michael McCarthy's *The Sun Farmer* or Anne Fadiman's *The Spirit Catches You and You Fall Down*; or history of medicine titles like Arthur Allen's *Vaccine*, David Oshinsky's *Polio*, or John Barry's *The Great Influenza*. Other narratives and memoirs about professions might also appeal, such as Edward Conlon's *Blue Blood*, Ted Conover's *Newjack: Guarding Sing Sing*, or Thomas Edward Gass's *Nobody's Home: Candid Reflections of a Nursing Home Aide*.

Hart, Matthew

Diamond: A Journey to the Heart of an Obsession. Walker & Company. 2001. 276 pp. ISBN 9780802713681.

Journalist Matthew Hart (and former editor of the industry magazine "Rapaport Diamond Report") leaves no stone unturned (literally) in his investigative quest to discover how these most precious of jewels are found, mined, advertised, often sold to finance revolutions, and moved around the world as both the centerpiece of much jewelry and a highly useful industrial tool. His writing is crisp and detailed, and he interviews many of the people involved in many of the aspects of diamond discovery and marketing.

Subjects: Business, Diamonds, Geology, Quick Reads, Science, World Travel

Now Try: Matthew Hart is one of those great nonfiction authors who just hasn't written enough books yet. His most recent title, *The Irish Game: A True Story of Crime and Art*, is a quickly paced introduction to some of the most recent and spectacular international art heists. Hart's style, journalistic but styled, personal but not sentimental, seems vaguely reminiscent of *Atlantic Monthly* correspondent William Langewiesche's, and fans of this book may also want to check out some of his titles, including *The Outlaw Sea: A World of Freedom, Chaos, and Crime* or *American Ground: Unbuilding the World Trade Center*. Other books on the diamond trade, legal and illegal, are also available; these include Greg Campbell's *Blood Diamonds* and Tom Zoellner's *The Heartless Stone*.

Kessler, Andy

The End of Medicine: How Silicon Valley (and Naked Mice) Will Reboot Your Doctor. Collins. 2006. 354 pp. ISBN 9780061130298.

Kessler, who has written other books about his experiences in the worlds of high finance and technology, turns his questioning glance to the health care industry, and, specifically, high-tech advances in radiology and diagnostics. Told primarily in a series of anecdotes, Kessler interviews health care professionals and tries to understand why, in his opinion, such wonderful diagnostic technology is available but rarely employed in time to help people prevent rather than react to heart attacks, strokes, and cancer. Kessler also puts his money where his mouth is by offering himself as a guinea pig for a wide variety of health tests himself, including CT scans and other procedures.

Subjects: Genetics, Health Issues, Humor, Medicine, Memoirs, Pharmacology, Physicians, Quick Reads, Science, Technology

Now Try: Kessler has written many other books, primarily about finance and technology; these include *How We Got Here*, *Running Money*, and *Wall Street Meat*. Other books by reporters with a keen sense of humor might be offered, such as Mary Roach (*Stiff*), Richard Schweid (*The Cockroach Papers*), and Jessica Mitford (*The American Way of Death Revisited*), as might more serious books about health care issues, such as Anne Fadiman's *The Spirit Catches You and You Fall Down* or Jonathan Cohn's exposé *Sick: The Untold Story of America's Health Care Crisis*. Also of some interest might be nonfiction titles by Immersion journalists including Barbara Ehrenreich, Ted Conover, or A. J. Jacobs.

Kolbert, Elizabeth

🐾 *Field Notes from a Catastrophe: Man, Nature, and Climate Change.* Bloomsbury. 2006. 210 pp. ISBN 9781596911253.

Kolbert organizes her treatise on global warming and the environment into two very important sections: "nature" and "man." Recognizing that there are no easy ways to categorize massive climate change and that there are numerous controversial ways to discuss it, although she "seeks to convey, as vividly as possible, the reality of global warming," she also strives to present her and others' experiences of it in such varied locations as Alaska, the countryside surrounding Reykjavík, the Greenland ice sheet, and Great Britain (although she points out that the global effect of the warming is so widespread, she could have researched it from hundreds of other locations). In the second half of her book, she examines how humans study climate change using research and computer modeling, and also how we both affect and respond to it through water management, emissions controls, and treaties such as the Kyoto Protocol. The result is a straightforward book on a complex subject that can be read quickly and with greater understanding. The book, which was first published as a series of three articles in *The New Yorker*, also includes a helpful chronology and bibliography.

Subjects: Alaska, Arctic, Book Groups, Climate, Environmental Writing, Politics, Quick Reads, Science, Travel, Vermont

Awards: ALA Notable, New York Times Notable

Now Try: A number of other popular environmental titles might be offered to these readers, including Al Gore's *An Inconvenient Truth*, Charles Wohlforth's *The Whale and the Supercomputer*, Rachel Carson's *Silent Spring* (some reviewers referred to this book as the "Silent Spring" of our time), Gretel Ehrlich's *This Cold Heaven*, or Bill McKibben's *The End of Nature*. A wide variety of authors provided blurbs for Kolbert's book, including novelist T. C. Boyle, Jonathan Franzen, and nonfiction writers Jonathan Weiner and Sylvia Nasar.

McCarthy, Michael

The Sun Farmer: The Story of a Shocking Accident, a Medical Miracle and a Family's Life and Death Decision. Ivan R. Dee. 2007. 216 pp. ISBN 9781566637008.

McCarthy relates the story of farmer Ted Fink, who was in a propane explosion accident on the farm in 1999 that resulted in horrible burns over 93 percent of his body. After being taken to the University of Wisconsin Hospital in Madison, his wife Rhoda was asked to approve a risky plan to replace his burned skin with an artificial skin developed by Ioannis Yannas at the Massachusetts Institute of Technology. Although Ted was eventually released from the hospital and returned to the farm to work, he would be plagued by a wide variety of health problems and the frustration of not being able to work up to his previous capacity until his death in 2005. The story is told compassionately by journalist McCarthy and rests largely on Rhoda's diaries from the time and her interviews with the author.

> **Subjects:** Accidents, Agriculture, Health Issues, Illinois, Medicine, Quick Reads, Rural Life, Science, Survival Stories, Wisconsin

> **Now Try:** This book combines an incredible human story with equally incredible details of medical advances; books similar in tone and subject include William Mishler's *A Measure of Endurance*, John Colapinto's *As Nature Made Him*, Brian Fies's graphic novel *Mom's Cancer*, Robert Kurson's *Crashing Through*, and Oliver Sacks's *The Man Who Mistook His Wife for a Hat*. Fiction titles involving health issues might also be offered, such as John Irving's *The Cider House Rules*, Jodi Picoult's *Her Sister's Keeper*, and Chris Bohjalian's *Midwives*.

Miller, Judith, Stephen Engelberg, and William J. Broad

Germs: Biological Weapons and America's Secret War. Simon & Schuster. 2001. 382 pp. ISBN 9780684871585.

A team of *New York Times* journalists explore the history of germ warfare and the possibilities, both in America and abroad, of biological and chemical weapons development. Although the United States and other nations pledged in 1972 to halt development of such weapons (at the Biological and Toxin Weapons Convention), the authors tell intense stories of the continuing research on and production of biological weapon agents in the U.S., the former Soviet Union, and worldwide.

> **Subjects:** Biology, Germs, Science, Terrorism, Weapons

> **Now Try:** Richard Preston's unsettling nonfiction accounts, *The Demon in the Freezer* and *The Hot Zone*, might be suggested to these readers, as might histories of medicine such as Arthur Allen's *Vaccine*, Eric Lax's *The Mold in Dr. Florey's Coat*, and John Barry's *The Great Influenza*. Other histories of weapons, such as Richard Rhodes's *The Making of the Atomic Bomb* or William Langewiesche's *The Atomic Bazaar* might be offered, as might fiction thrillers by Robin Cook or Michael Crichton.

Moir, John S.

Return of the Condor: The Race to Save Our Largest Bird from Extinction. Lyons Press. 2006. 223 pp. ISBN 9781592289493.

Moir tells a quickly paced story of the dramatic race to save the condor, a dangerously endangered bird in America. As of 1987, only twenty-seven condors were left in California; what followed and what Moir describes is a concerted effort by both scientists and conservationists to bring attention to the birds' plight, to rescue the birds they could and encourage their breeding, and to re-release as many as possible into the wild. As a result, although the struggle to increase their numbers continues, the birds are much more numerous today and the outlook for their survival is more positive.

> **Subjects:** Animals, Birds, Condors, Environmental Writing, Nature, Science

Now Try: A wide variety of books on environmental topics might appeal to these readers: Rachel Carson's *Silent Spring*, Dian Fossey's *Gorillas in the Mist*, Farley Mowat's *Never Cry Wolf*, Bernd Heinrich's *Mind of the Raven*, or Peter Matthiessen's *Tigers in the Snow*. Books by authors with environmental interests might also be offered; these include Bill McKibben, Elizabeth Kolbert, and Jonathan Schell.

Preston, Richard

First Light: The Search for the Edge of the Universe. Atlantic Monthly Press. 1987. 263 pp. ISBN 9780871132000.

Preston writes a nonfiction account of the Hale Telescope and the work and lives of astronomers and scientists that reads more like a character-driven and detail-rich novel than high-tech science reporting. Although he describes the work and genius of such scientists as James Gunn and the rest of his team, the main character in the book is the seven-story-tall telescope itself, which Preston spent much of his reporting time climbing in and around and which was used primarily to see into the very farthest depths of space; Preston also does an able job of describing the scientific principles involved ("Astronomers refer to the depth of astronomical vision as lookback time. Seeing outward is equivalent to looking backward in time, because the telescope's mirror is capturing primeval light," p. 25).

Subjects: Astronomy, Classics, Science, Space, Technology

Now Try: A number of science-writing notables provided blurbs for Preston's title; they include Alan Lightman (novels *Einstein's Dream* and *Ghost*; nonfiction *A Sense of the Mysterious*), Richard Rhodes (*The Making of the Atomic Bomb* and *Arsenals of Folly*), Robert Kanigel, Freeman Dyson, and Dennis Overbye. Other books by Preston, particularly his hugely popular *The Demon in the Freezer* and *The Hot Zone*, might also be offered, as might other classics about space exploration, including Jeffrey Kluger's *Journey beyond Selene*, Carl Sagan's *Cosmos*, Dava Sobel's *The Planets*, and Timothy Ferris's *Coming of Age in the Milky Way*.

Roach, Mary

Bonk: The Curious Coupling of Science and Sex. Norton. 2008. 319 pp. ISBN 9780393064643.

Roach employs her trademark voracious research skills, personal interviews, great sense of humor, and flair with educational footnotes in this investigation of the history of sexual investigations. Along the way she shares information about the studies done by Alfred Kinsey, Masters and Johnson, and many other researchers; interviews workers who first stimulate and then artificially inseminate sows to increase the chances of successful breeding; relates the story of Princess Marie Bonaparte, who undertook during the early twentieth century to have her clitoris moved for increased sexual pleasure; considers treatments for impotence; and travels down many other roads of sexual inquiry.

Subjects: Biology, Explicit Sexuality, Fertility, Health Issues, Humor, Science, Sexuality

Now Try: Roach has mastered her particular variety of highly personal science reporting, and fans of this provocatively titled book might enjoy her other titles, *Stiff: The Curious Lives of Human Cadavers* and *Spook: Science Tackles the Afterlife*. Other authors who have tackled aspects of human sexuality stories include Gay Talese (*Thy Neighbor's Wife*), Brian Alexander (*America Unzipped*), and Pagan Kennedy (*The First*

Man-Made Man); similarly written books such as Amy Stewart's *Flower Confidential* or Lisa Takeuchi Cullen's *Remember Me*, although not on salacious subjects, might also be offered. Readers might also enjoy engagingly written science books by authors such as Natalie Angier (*Woman: An Intimate Geography* or *Canon: A Whirligig Tour of the Beautiful Basics of Science*) or Carl Zimmer (*Parasite Rex* and *Microcosm: E. Coli and the New Science of Life*).

Roach, Mary

Stiff: The Curious Lives of Human Cadavers. W. W. Norton. 2003. 303 pp. ISBN 9780393050936.

Roach offers an unstinting amount of research, interviews, and dark humor in her attempt to study the life of our bodies after death. Organized thematically, she describes her visits to morgues, crematoriums, and research farms where bodies are left to decay in the elements to aid forensic science, and laboratories and classrooms with equal aplomb, introducing a wide array of professionals employed in those situations along the way. Not for the squeamish, Roach's quick prose, often self-effacingly humorous asides, and use of dialogue make this an ironically lively read.

Subjects: Book Groups, Classics, Death and Dying, Forensic Science, Humor, Professions, YA

Now Try: Roach's more recent titles, *Spook: Science Tackles the Afterlife* and *Bonk: The Curious Coupling of Science and Sex*, are written in the same light but still rigorously investigated style and might also appeal to her fans. Also of some interest might be Jessica Mitford's infamous tell-all about the funeral industry, *The American Way of Death* (which is extremely similar to this title in both subject matter and darkly humorous tone, although Mitford's conclusion that the funeral industry is one that's on the make is refuted by Gary Laderman in his more scholarly *Rest in Peace: A Cultural History of Death and the Funeral Home in Twentieth-Century America*). Those readers more interested in the science surrounding bodily remains or their preservation might also include the slightly drier (no pun intended) book *The Mummy Congress: Science, Obsession, and the Everlasting Dead* by Heather Pringle. Fiction readers of the unsqueamish variety might also be drawn to Jim Crace's fascinating novel *Being Dead*, in which the life story of a murdered couple is told against the backdrop of the decay of their bodies, or even Sean Doolittle's crime novel *Dirt*, which is set in a funeral home.

Sachs, Jessica Snyder

Good Germs, Bad Germs: Health and Survival in a Bacterial World. Hill and Wang. 2007. 290 pp. ISBN 9780809050635.

Although arguably more a scientific title than an investigative one, Sachs's status as a science journalist and her skillful weaving together of scientific information, historical stories, and suggestions for future approaches to the use of antibiotics and other health issues makes this a broadly informed book with a reporter's attention to detail and use of personal interviews. In various chapters Sachs relates the statistics regarding disease and health trends in America's children (including a rise in inflammatory and bowel diseases, as well as allergies), the development and history of the (over)use of antibiotics in combating infections and in the agricultural production of animals, and thoughts about the future of the interaction between humans and their bacterial co-residents on earth.

Subjects: Diseases, Germs, Health Issues, Pharmacology, Science

Now Try: Other books on the history of disease and epidemiology might be offered, such as Steven Johnson's best seller *The Ghost Map* or Robert Morris's *The Blue Death*. Other investigative works and exposés about health issues might also appeal, such as Randall Fitzgerald's *The Hundred-Year Lie*, Peter Rost's *The Whistleblower*, Jonathan Cohn's *Sick: The Untold Story of America's Health Care Crisis*, or Mark Schapiro's *Exposed: The Toxic Chemistry of Everyday Products and What's at Stake for American Power*. Nonfiction by respected science authors including Jonathan Weiner, Diane Ackerman, Rachel Carson, Richard Dawkins, and Sherwin Nuland might also appeal.

Slade, Giles

Made to Break: Technology and Obsolescence in America. Harvard University Press. 2006. 330 pp. ISBN 9780674022034.

Slade seeks to explain the brave new world of "planned obsolescence"—the newest trend in technology, in which higher-tech gadgets and tools are designed to last for a shorter amount of time than the items you're replacing. Also within Slade's investigation of the shorter lives of technologies such as computers, cell phones, televisions, and cameras is an underlying investigation of how Americans' cultural rejection of tradition and our ready acceptance of change led us to develop and perfect the very concept of disposability, particularly where the items that we consume are concerned. Also investigated are such inventions as branding, packaging, and advertising, as well as a wide variety of other business practices and profit models (explored through case studies such as the struggle for market dominance between GM and Ford).

Subjects: 20th Century, American History, Business, Communications, Garbage, Industry, Making Sense . . ., Scholarly, Science, Small Press, Technology

Now Try: Other books on our consumption habits might also be offered to these readers, including Elizabeth Royte's *Garbage Land: On the Secret Trail of Trash*, Judith Levine's memoir *Not Buying It*, Naomi Klein's *No Logo*, Juliet Schor's *The Overspent American*, or even Paco Underhill's *Why We Buy*. Other books offering a mix of sociology and history, such as Stephanie Coontz's *The Way We Never Were: American Families and the Nostalgia Trap*, Christopher Lasch's *The Age of Narcissism*, and Alain de Botton's *Status Anxiety* might be offered, as might titles from the Business Reporting chapter dealing with manufacturing and globalization.

Sports Reporting

Another popular category of In-Depth Reporting titles are those that feature sports stories. Sportswriting has a long and proud tradition, from early practitioners including baseball reporters Ring Lardner and E. B. White through the present day and the many fine writers employed by such publications as *Sports Illustrated*, *ESPN Magazine*, and *Outside* (among many others). In an age when many sports fans can access instant scores and sports news from online sources, what further information can sports fans be seeking from sportswriters? Well, it turns out, lots of things. Readers still want to know more about their favorite teams and athletes. They want to know the sports stories behind the sports contests. And they're not afraid to hear commentary with a bit of opinion thrown in; in an article in the *Columbia Journalism Review*, the author commented on the popularity of sports blogs and the fact that "sports fans have an appetite for strongly opinionated takes on virtually every facet of their team" (Weintraub 2007, 16). The authors in this section offer not only those sorts of opinionated takes, but also scintillating narratives and character profiles that, as often as not, are about some of the most compelling character types available, from the sympathetic underdogs to the most driven of competitors and heroes.

Readers who enjoy these "inside looks" at sports might be particularly drawn to True Adventure nonfiction titles, also about sports contests and athletes (Laura Hillenbrand's classic *Seabiscuit* and Wayne Coffey's *The Boys of Winter* among them) as well as Biographies, Autobiographies, and Memoirs by and about athletes, such as David Remnick's *King of the World* (about Muhammad Ali) or Lance Armstrong's *It's Not about the Bike*. Many of these books offer a "year in the life" topic matter, in which their reporter authors spend a season or a year or any set unit of time following a certain team; many Immersion Journalism titles also follow that format and may appeal to these readers (such as Ted Conover's *Newjack: Guarding Sing Sing* or A. J. Jacobs's *The Year of Living Biblically*). Because these books are often quite thrilling and quickly paced, adventure fiction by authors such as Clive Cussler, Dale Brown, or John Nance might also be suggested.

Sports Reporting books are written by journalists who typically cover events in the sporting world. Because sporting events can be rousing contests and boast participants who eventually become winners and losers, champions and nearly-rans, these are often lively narratives written by authors who know their fields and have opinions about them. They also feature both sympathetic and unsympathetic characters, and they are linked together most obviously by their shared subject matters and journalistic style.

Angell, Roger

The Summer Game. Viking Press. 1972. 303 pp. ISBN 9780670681648.

This collection of essays written over the course of ten years and from a fan's point of view (although the fan eventually worked up the courage to interview some players and staff), includes six sections, including "the rustle of spring" and "the future." The focus in these essays is not the actual play-by-play action of the game, but rather thoughtful ruminations on the culture of the game, the characters of the players and the coaches, and the business of the game's business.

Subjects: American History, Baseball, Classics, Essays, Sports

Now Try: Angell's father was E. B. White, one of the quintessential essay and *New Yorker* writers of the twentieth century; any of his collections might be offered to these readers, as might collections and short stories by Ring Lardner, another classic baseball writer from the early part of the twentieth century. Other classic sports writers such as Michael Lewis, John Feinstein, Frank

Deford, and John Schulian might be suggested, as might other *New Yorker* writers including Joseph Mitchell or A. J. Liebling.

Bissinger, H. G.

Friday Night Lights: A Town, a Team, and a Dream. Addison-Wesley. 1990. 357 pp. ISBN 9780201196771.

Bissinger's classic of sports reporting is set in Odessa, Texas, a city that takes its high school football team very seriously. They do so with good reason; their team, the Permian High Panthers, compiled the winningest record in state annals, and the entire team, its coaches, and its community support feel the shared glory of their every win. The author is a Pulitzer Prize–winning journalist who moved his entire family to Odessa for a year to follow the football team's 1988 season. In addition to chronicling their wins, he raises important questions like the priorities of the school's administrators and teachers, as well as some of the parents. An epilogue in more recent editions of this title also explores the anger that was directed at Bissinger by the town's residents when the book was published.

> **Subjects:** 20th Century, Book Groups, Classics, Community Life, Football, Immersion Journalism, Sports, Texas, YA, Year in the Life

> **Now Try:** Bissinger's book is a classic of both sports reporting and community life nonfiction; his readers might enjoy other sports- and character-driven works such as Michael Lewis's *The Blind Side*, Michael Sokolove's *The Ticket Out*, Madeleine Blais's *In These Girls, Hope Is a Muscle* (about a girls' high school basketball team in Massachusetts), Laura Hillenbrand's classic *Seabiscuit*, or George Plimpton's *Paper Lion*; books about what makes communities cohesive might also appeal, such as Michael Perry's *Population 485* or Heather Lende's *If You Lived Here, I'd Know Your Name*. Novels in which sports play a role might also be offered, such as Harlan Coben's Myron Bolitar series (starting with *Deal Breaker*); other quickly paced Adventure fiction (Robert Ludlum, Tom Clancy) and True Adventure nonfiction titles (Jon Krakauer, Ben Mezrich) might also appeal.

Bissinger, H. G.

Three Nights in August: Strategy, Heartbreak, and Joy inside the Mind of a Manager. Houghton Mifflin. 2005. 280 pp. ISBN 9780618405442.

Bissinger, best known for his book detailing an entire high school football season in *Friday Night Lights*, here narrows his focus and carefully examines the events over the course of a three-night baseball series in August, when the Saint Louis Cardinals played the Chicago Cubs. The author had full access to both staff and players in the Cardinals organization, but even more important, he had the full access to and cooperation of Cardinal manager Tony La Russa, who provides both Bissinger and his readers with a unique inside look into the game, complemented by his experience and nuanced knowledge of baseball. This book will of course be of most interest to hardcore baseball fans, but Bissinger's writing is punchy and descriptive enough to hook any reader who enjoys behind-the-scenes sports books of any type.

> **Subjects:** Baseball, Character Profiles, Tony La Russa, Sports, YA

> **Now Try:** Although Bissinger's writing is always quickly paced and story-driven, in this book he very much focuses on the character of Coach La Russa. Similarly character-driven sports nonfiction titles should be offered, such as Michael Lewis's *Moneyball* or *The Blind Side*, David Halberstam's *The Education of a Coach*, Mark

Kriegel's *Pistol: The Life of Pete Maravich* or *Namath*; books about baseball might particularly appeal, such as Jonathan Eig's *Opening Day*, Seth Mnookin's *Feeding the Monster*, or Mark Fainaru-Wada's *Game of Shadows*; fiction in which baseball plays a role might also be enjoyed, such as W. P. Kinsella's classic *Shoeless Joe* or Pete Hamill's *Snow in August*.

Black, George

Casting a Spell: The Bamboo Fly Rod and the American Pursuit of Perfection. Random House. 2006. 244 pp. ISBN 9781400063963.

Black's topic is the design and crafting of bamboo fly-fishing rods in America, but his subtext is really more about what he calls the "American pursuit of perfection." Based on his own interest in and experiences with fly-fishing, the author sets off to explore how bamboo is grown and how rods are engineered. He further describes how craftspeople became masters in the art of crafting rods and also examines more intangible aspects of the art including a love of solitude (including allusions to Henry David Thoreau) and mysticism (as first explored in Norman Maclean's classic *A River Runs through It*). Although Black takes his reporting and travel duties seriously, his tone is light and even self- (and other!) deprecating, as shown in such quotes as "I should say right away that I've never been one of those who believe that fly-fishing elevates the practitioner to some higher order of humanity—I mean, Dick Cheney is a fly fisherman, for heaven's sake, and is even reputed to favor bamboo rods."

> **Subjects:** American History, Fishing, Fly Fishing, Humor, Micro-histories, Nature, Rivers, Sports, Technology, Travel
>
> **Now Try:** Of course, any book about fly-fishing will draw comparisons to Norman Maclean's classic novel/memoir *A River Runs through It*; other light-hearted travel narratives in which the authors follow their Zen might also be offered, such as John McPhee's *Uncommon Carriers*, Calvin Trillin's *Alice, Let's Eat* and *Feeding a Yen*, Christopher Wren's *Walking to Vermont*, and Nathaniel Stone's *On the Water: Discovering America in a Rowboat*. Other micro-histories and books in which craftsmanship is celebrated as an art form might also appeal; these include James Barron's *Piano: The Making of a Steinway Concert Grand*, Michael Ruhlman's *The Making of a Chef*, and Henry Petroski's *The Evolution of Useful Things*.

Bowden, Mark

Bringing the Heat: A Pro Football Team's Quest for Glory, Fame, Immortality, and a Bigger Piece of the Action. Knopf. 1994. 482 pp. ISBN 9780679428411.

In 1992 *Philadelphia Inquirer* staff writer Bowden followed the Philadelphia Eagles football team through their season. Although they had been on the brink of greatness for years, the Eagles of 1992 found themselves struggling both to take their performance to another level and to deal with the aftermath of the death of their teammate Jerome Brown (who had been killed in a car accident before the start of the season). Bowden structures his narrative around various games from that season and offers character portraits of such players as the quarterback Randall Cunningham, Seth Joyner, and Reggie White, as well as of coach Richie Cotite; he also includes game highlights, press accounts of the team and their record, and even, in the final chapter, a thrilling play-by-play account of one of the seminal games of the team's 11–5 season.

> **Subjects:** 1990s, Character Profiles, Classics, Football, Pennsylvania, Philadelphia, Professions, Sports, Work Relationships, YA, Year in the Life
>
> **Now Try:** Although Bowden's book is aging, it is still a compelling and timeless record of a football team's season; the first titles to offer might be other football classics, such as George Plimpton's *Paper Lion*, Mark Kriegel's *Namath*, or Tony Dungy's *Quiet Strength* (John Grisham's novel *Playing for Pizza* even centers on football). Other sports reporting titles might also appeal, such as Michael Sokolove's *The Ticket Out*, Wayne Coffey's *The Boys of Winter*, or John Feinstein's *Last Dance* or *A Season on the Brink*. This book also offers the flavor of the city of Philadelphia; a number of fantastic books about that city have been written, including Michael Vitez's *Rocky Stories*, Buzz Bissinger's *A Prayer for the City*, and Pete Dexter's collection of newspaper columns (many from the *Philadelphia Inquirer*), *Paper Trails*.

Bryant, Howard

Juicing the Game: Drugs, Power, and the Fight for the Soul of Major League Baseball. Viking. 2005. 439 pp. ISBN 9780670034451.

Less of an exposé than a thoroughly researched treatise on the use of steroids by athletes in major league baseball, Bryant's narrative gives a history of the development of steroids and their chemical properties, the BALCO scandal (referring to such players as Mark McGwire, Jose Canseco, and Barry Bonds), and other issues, while examining the complex interplay of such factors as labor disputes (the book takes as its starting point the disastrous 1994 players' strike), baseball economics, fans' demands and the rise of home-run hitting, and the trajectories of baseball players' careers as contributing factors to steroid abuse. The author is a sports columnist for the *Boston Herald* and author of a previous book on baseball titled *Shut Out*.

> **Subjects:** Baseball, Business, Chemicals, Drugs, Exposés, Sports
>
> **Now Try:** Other books on this subject might also be offered, if the reader can stand any more of them: suggest Mark Fainaru-Wada's *Game of Shadows* or even Jose Canseco's memoir *Juiced*. Bryant also suggests a number of well-known and respected baseball writers in his bibliography: Roger Angell, Mike Lupica, and Fay Vincent; additionally, other exposés might be offered, especially those exposing business corruption, such as Stephen Klaidman's *Coronary: A True Story of Medicine Gone Awry*, Michael Lewis's *Liar's Poker* (or his baseball title *Moneyball*), Jeremy Scahill's *Blackwater*, or Kurt Eichenwald's *Conspiracy of Fools*.

Drape, Joe

The Race for the Triple Crown: Horses, High Stakes, and Eternal Hope. Atlantic Monthly Press. 2001. 261 pp. ISBN 9780871137852.

One of the most famous and historically rich series of contests in sports, horse racing's Triple Crown is won by horses and their riders who prevail at the season's three biggest races: the Kentucky Derby, run the first Saturday in May; Pimlico, run in Baltimore; and the Preakness Stakes, run at Belmont. Drape, a sportswriter for the *New York Times*, explores the full drama and pathos of the sport, interviewing owners, trainers, and jockeys and telling the individual stories of some of the horses whose fortunes he follows, the uniquely named More than Ready, Charismatic, and Fusaichi Pegasus.

Subjects: Animals, Horses, Sports, True Adventure, Year in the Life

Now Try: At least two horse-racing classics might be suggested to these readers: Laura Hillenbrand's historical *Seabiscuit* and Jane Smiley's *Horse Heaven*. Other "Year in the Life" sports books might also appeal to readers who enjoy the behind-the-scenes look at the racing world; consider offering John Feinstein's *Next Man Up* or *Tales from Q School*, David Halberstam's *Summer of '49* or *October 1964*, or even George Plimpton's sports immersion classics, such as *Paper Lion* or *Out of My League*. Fiction novels by Dick Francis, who set his mysteries in the horse-racing world, might also make for fun related reads.

Feinstein, John

Next Man Up: A Year behind the Lines in Today's NFL. Little, Brown, 2005. 502 pp. ISBN 9780316009645.

Feinstein goes behind the scenes of one of America's more secretive sports and leagues—the National Football League (NFL)—to provide his readers with a better picture of the ups and downs of the football season, from overheated training camps to frigid January games. Feinstein more particularly investigates the Baltimore Ravens football team, an expansion team created in 1996 that won its first Super Bowl in 2001 against huge odds, including losing a number of their players to both injuries and criminal indictments. Following the team from draft to camp to game days in 2004, Feinstein also offers insight into the personalities of the players, their owner Steve Bisciotti, and their coach Brian Billick.

Subjects: Baltimore, Football, Sports, True Adventure, Underdogs, YA, Year in the Life

Now Try: Feinstein is a venerable sports journalist and has a wide variety of other titles that might appeal to these readers, including *Tales from Q School*, *Last Dance*, *Season on the Brink*, and *Living on the Black* (as well as the sports novels *Cover-Up: Mystery at the Super Bowl* or *Last Shot: A Final Four Mystery*). Books by other sports journalists might also be suggested: George Plimpton, David Halberstam, or Frank Deford.

Feinstein, John

Tales from Q School: Inside Golf's Fifth Major. Little, Brown. 2007. 343 pp. ISBN 9780316014304.

Golf pros needing a bit of remedial work and those less established in the sport compete annually at the PGA Tour Qualifying Tournament, a grueling endurance contest of golf culminating in a six-day round of finals. Known more popularly as "Q School," the tournament is one of the more storied parts of the world of professional golf. Sports journalist and author Feinstein goes behind the scenes and gets to know a number of the 973 players who took part in the 2005 competition, mixing sympathetic character profiles with some of the most daunting numbers in sports. As Feinstein states in his introduction: "There are more than 30 million golfers in the US. Perhaps 2,000 can legitimately think about trying to make a living playing the game."

Subjects: Character Profiles, Golf, Sports, True Adventure, Underdogs, YA

Now Try: Feinstein has made a career out of taking readers behind the scenes at lesser-known sporting events; his earlier books include *Open: Inside the Ropes at Bethpage Black* (also golf) and *Last Dance: Behind the Scenes at the Final Four* (basketball). Readers who enjoy his crisp sports narratives and biographies might also consider George Plimpton's "insider" sports tales, including *Paper Lion: Confessions of a Last-String Quarterback, Out of My League,* or *The Bogey Man: A Month on the PGA Tour;* Mark Kriegel's quickly paced sports biographies *Namath* and *Pistol: The Life of Pete Maravich,* or even Wayne Coffey's *The Boys of Winter* or Laura Hillenbrand's classic tale of the quintessential underdog, *Seabiscuit.*

Halberstam, David

The Breaks of the Game. Knopf. 1981. 362 pp. ISBN 9780394513096.

Reporter extraordinaire Halberstam followed the professional basketball team the Portland Trail Blazers for the entirety of their 1979–1980 season, writing about the coaches and the owners, the players, as well as about their fans and media coverage. Although the book is more than two decades old, it is a classic example of the ever-popular "season in the life of . . ." subgenre of sports books, and although many things about the world in general, and sports and professional basketball in specific, have changed, Halberstam still tells a powerful story with the mythos and characterization that sports books often offer so well, and readers might enjoy this work now for its historical value as well as for its narrative.

Subjects: Basketball, Classics, Oregon, Sports, YA, Year in the Life

Now Try: Other books on basketball, of course, might provide solid related reads, including John Feinstein's *Last Dance* or *A Season on the Brink,* Mark Kriegel's haunting biography *Pistol: The Life of Pete Maravich,* Darcy Frey's *Last Shot* (an ALA Notable Book) or fiction titles by Harlan Coben. Other sports classics by Halberstam might appeal, including *The Education of a Coach* or *The Amateurs,* as might similar "season in the life" sports books such as Buzz Bissinger's *Friday Night Lights,* Adrian Wojnarowski's *The Miracle of St. Anthony: A Season with Coach Bob Hurley and Basketball's Most Improbable Dynasty,* Mark Bowden's *Bringing the Heat: A Pro Football Team's Quest for Glory, Fame, Immortality, and a Bigger Piece of the Action,* or Gene Wojciechowski's *Cubs Nation: 162 Games. 162 Stories. 1 Addiction.*

Lewis, Michael D.

Moneyball: The Art of Winning an Unfair Game. W. W. Norton. 2003. 288 pp. ISBN 9780393057652.

Lewis himself explains that he came to write this book because he fell in love with a story, a story that "concerned a small group of undervalued professional baseball players and executives, many of whom had been rejected as unfit for the big leagues, who had turned themselves into one of the most successful franchises in major league baseball." Lewis, long known for his financial writing in the classic Wall Street tale *Liar's Poker,* explores how the Oakland A's, a team with one of the league's smallest payrolls, used smart scouting and extreme number-crunching to go on to beat some of the most richly funded teams in baseball. The book also doubles as a character profile of the A's manager, Billy Beane, who presided over his team's ascent in the league, and offers chapters on scouting, the mental aspect of the game, the statistical analyses of the game by a man named Bill James, and a variety of other players' stories and triumphs.

Subjects: Baseball, Billy Beane, Book Groups, Business, California, Character Profiles, Classics, Mathematics, Sports, Statistics, Underdogs

Awards: New York Times Notable

Now Try: A wide variety of baseball books (especially the classics) might be suggested for these readers, including David Maraniss's *Clemente*, Hank Aaron's *I Had a Hammer*, Michael Sokolove's *The Ticket Out*, or Buzz Bissinger's *Three Nights in August*, as well as other books by Michael Lewis, including his financial memoir *Liar's Poker* and his other sports title *The Blind Side: Evolution of a Game*. Other books about the strange properties of numbers and statistics might appeal, including Nassim Nicholas Taleb's *Fooled by Randomness* or Ian Ayres's *Super Crunchers*.

McGuane, Thomas

An Outside Chance: Classic & New Essays on Sport. Farrar, Straus & Giroux. 1980. 243 pp. ISBN 9780374104726.

In this collection of short (few are longer than ten pages), action- and story-driven essays, McGuane relates his stories of indulging in such sports as fishing, bird dogging, and rodeos; along the way, he travels across the country, from Michigan to Montana to Florida.

Subjects: Classics, Essays, Memoirs, Sports, Travel

Now Try: McGuane is also a novelist; his readers might consider his titles *The Cadence of Grass* or *Nothing but Blue Skies*. Other titles from this Sports Reporting subgenre might be offered, including George Black's *Casting a Spell: The Bamboo Fly Rod and the American Pursuit of Perfection* and John Schulian's *Twilight of the Long-ball Gods: Dispatches from the Disappearing Heart of Baseball*, as might novels by such authors as Richard Russo, John Irving, Jim Harrison, Richard Ford, or Kent Haruf. He has also been compared to such authors as William Faulkner, F. Scott Fitzgerald, and Ernest Hemingway.

Mnookin, Seth

Feeding the Monster: How Money, Smarts, and Nerve Took a Team to the Top. Simon & Schuster. 2006. 433 pp. ISBN 9780743286817.

Vanity Fair contributing editor Mnookin has written a behemoth of a book examining not only the curse-ending 2004 Boston Red Sox triumph at the World Series, but also their history as a team and their place within Boston's cultural society. Mnookin, who was offered unprecedented access to the team during the 2005 season, also offers character portraits of the team's owners, including John Henry, Tom Werner, and Larry Lucchino.

Subjects: Baseball, Boston, Boston Red Sox, Character Profiles, Community Life, Fandom, Massachusetts, Sports, YA

Now Try: Fans of Mnookin's Red Sox extravaganza might enjoy other popular baseball books, including *Moneyball* by Michael Lewis, *Feeding the Green Monster* by Rob Neyer, *Ted Williams* by Leigh Montville, *Summer of '49* by David Halberstam, *The Ticket Out* by Michael Sokolove, *Jackie Robinson* by Rachel Robinson, or *The Last Best League* by Jim Collins. Baseball novels might also make good related reads, such as *Shoeless Joe* by W. P. Kinsella, *Last Days of Summer* by Steve Kluger, or *Brooklyn Boy* by Alan Lelchuk.

Schulian, John

Twilight of the Long-ball Gods: Dispatches from the Disappearing Heart of Baseball. University of Nebraska Press. 2005. 184 pp. ISBN 9780803293274.

In a book for the true fan, Schulian relates tales of life and play in baseball's minor leagues. A former columnist for the *Chicago Sun-Times* and a contributor to *Sports Illustrated*, Schulian mixes character profiles of individuals such as Rocky Bridges, a minor-league manager, and Josh Gibson, star of the Negro League with descriptive writing and stories designed to make you taste the ballpark peanuts and hear the crack of the bat.

Subjects: Baseball, Essays, Journalism, Quick Reads, Small Press, Sports

Now Try: Of course, anything relating to baseball will probably appeal to these readers, including such classics as Roger Angell's *The Summer Game*, Michael Lewis's *Moneyball*, David Halberstam's *Summer of '49* or *The Teammates*, Hank Aaron's *I Had a Hammer*, Al Stump's *Cobb*, or Michael Sokolove's *The Ticket Out*. Books by other well-reviewed sportswriters might also be suggested, including those by Fred Lieb, Gary Smith, and Jerry Kramer. Other investigative writing books focusing on characters and lost ways of life, including Elizabeth Gilbert's *The Last American Man*, H. G. Bissinger's *A Prayer for the City*, or Susan Orlean's *Saturday Night* may appeal.

Wojciechowski, Gene

Cubs Nation: 162 Games. 162 Stories. 1 Addiction. Doubleday. 2005. 417 pp. ISBN 9780385513005.

Diehard Chicago Cubs fans will recognize Wojciechowski as one of their own over the course of this intense "year in the life" narrative following his team, in which the author attends every single one of the Cubs' 162 games (home *and* away, lending the book a bit of a travel narrative feel as well) during the 2004 season. In addition to providing the highlights of each and every game, the author also offers interviews with and character profiles of such notables as manager Dusty Baker and home-run hitter Sammy Sosa, as well as a wide variety of other players, stadium staff members, and dedicated fans who love their team with a love as boundless as the Cubs' own seemingly infinite capacity for losing.

Subjects: Baseball, Chicago, Chicago Cubs, Fandom, Sports, Underdogs, YA, Year in the Life

Now Try: A wide variety of baseball books (especially the classics) might be suggested for these readers, including Michael Lewis's *Moneyball*, Jonathan Eig's *Opening Day*, Michael Sokolove's *The Ticket Out*, Buzz Bissinger's *Three Nights in August*, Seth Mnookin's *Feeding the Monster*, or Sam Walker's *Fantasyland*. Other books about fans and other enthusiastic hobbyists might also appeal, such as Warren St. John's *Rammer, Jammer, Yellow, Hammer* or Shari Caudron's *Who Are You People?*

Wojnarowski, Adrian

The Miracle of St. Anthony: A Season with Coach Bob Hurley and Basketball's Most Improbable Dynasty. Gotham Books. 2005. 382 pp. ISBN 9781592401024.

High school basketball coach Bob Hurley, an institution himself at the institution of St. Anthony High School in Jersey City, has taken his team to and won the state championship twenty-two times over the course of his thirty-one-year career. What is more impressive is that each year he manages to forge a national-caliber

team out of the tiny school's student body of two hundred students and has also managed to see all of his players, with one exception, go on to attend college. In addition to relating the exciting basketball action of the school's 2003–2004 season, sportswriter Wojnarowski also tells the story of the coach (and his son Bobby, who went on to play college ball for Duke), the school, and its Franciscan nun administrators and teachers who strive to hold the school together and help their students, many from backgrounds of poverty, go on to higher education and brighter futures.

> **Subjects:** Basketball, Character Profiles, Education, Bob Hurley, New Jersey, Sports, YA, Year in the Life
>
> **Now Try:** Other "year in the season" sports books might appeal, such as Darcy Frey's *Last Shot*, David Halberstam's *The Breaks of the Game*, or Mark Bowden's *Bringing the Heat*. Character-driven sports narratives such as Mark Kriegel's *Pistol: The Life of Pete Maravich* or *Namath*, Wayne Coffey's *The Boys of Winter*, or Michael Sokolove's *The Ticket Out* might be suggested, as might other books about education, such as Tracy Kidder's *Among Schoolchildren* or Ron Suskind's *A Hope in the Unseen*.

True Crime Investigations

Of course the True Crime genre is one of the larger and more popular of all the nonfiction genres (even if it doesn't get a lot of press in the popular literature). So how does True Crime differ from True Crime Investigations? The most obvious difference between the two types of writing is to examine the authors of the different works; many True Crime writers write exclusively True Crime books, whereas True Crime Investigations authors tend to be reporters and journalists who have written on a wide variety of subjects other than crime. The tone and the scope of these Investigations stories also help to set these books apart from more traditional True Crime books; most of the titles in this category do not include as many graphic details as do their True Crime counterparts, and most focus less on one particularly heinous crime or criminal than they do on criminal justice systems and processes, as well as on a broader category of crimes or the crimes in their social, political, or historical context. These narratives are the direct descendants of the crime reporting and the police beats of the early nineteenth century, when New York newspapers "began to find a regular source of local news in the city's police courts" (Stephens 1988, 239). The authors who write these books tend to combine their research and interviews with a slightly more dispassionate tone (and usually, fewer pictures) to produce books that are darkly fascinating but not quite as deliberately shocking.

Fans of these titles might still, of course, enjoy titles from more traditional True Crime categories, including classics like Truman Capote's *In Cold Blood* or titles by Ann Rule, a popular author and herself a former reporter. These readers might also consider Immersion Journalism books (particularly titles related by subject, like Ted Conover's *Newjack: Guarding Sing Sing*), or memoirs in which authors discuss their Working Lives, as many of these authors provide an inside look at law enforcement jobs (Edward Conlon's *Blue Blood*, for instance, might strongly appeal to those readers who enjoy Michael Connelly's investigative *Crime Beat*). Fiction thrillers and crime novels might also be suggested to these readers, particularly books by authors such as Michael Connelly (who writes fiction and nonfiction), Patricia Cornwell, Kathy Reichs, Ian Rankin, Jeffery Deaver, Jonathan Kellerman, or Margaret Maron (particularly her Sigrid Harald series).

True Crime Investigations titles feature inside stories about crime and punishment, as well as investigations into past crimes. These are less sensationalistic than most True Crime nonfiction classics, because their authors tend not to dwell on bloody details but rather offer systematic stories written in a journalistic style and focusing on those who investigate and analyze crimes rather than on those who commit or suffer them.

Bogira, Steve

Courtroom 302: A Year behind the Scenes in an American Criminal Courthouse. Knopf. 2005. 404 pp. ISBN 9780679432524.

> *Chicago Reader* journalist Bogira faithfully chronicles a year in the life of a criminal court in Illinois's Cook County. In addition to describing the jail attached to the courthouse and the legal proceedings within, he tells the many more personal stories of both those being charged with crimes (from daily drug offenses to more high-profile murder cases) as well as those dispensing justice.
>
> **Subjects:** Chicago, Law and Lawyers, Prisons, Professions, True Crime, Year in the Life
>
> **Now Try:** Pulitzer Prize winner Edward Humes provides an even more evocative report on the juvenile prison and court system in *No Matter How Loud I Shout: A Year in the Life of Juvenile Court*. Another "insider's look" at a related part of the criminal justice system can be found in Edward Conlon's memoir about his life as a New York City police officer, *Blue Blood*; Stacy Horn's *The Restless Sleep: Inside New York City's Cold Case Squad* might also be offered.

Bowden, Charles

🕮 *Down By the River: Drugs, Money, Murder, and Family.* Simon & Schuster. 2002. 433 pp. ISBN 9780684853437.

> Bowden relates the story of a 1995 homicide in El Paso, Texas, where a man named Lionel Jordan was shot and killed; eventually, a thirteen-year-old Mexican boy was investigated and convicted of the crime. Jordan's brother, an agent with the Drug Enforcement Administration, suspected all along that the murder had something to do with his own work; Bowden explores the complicated state of border politics, immigration issues, crime investigation, and drug trafficking (and Mexican drug lord Amado Carrillo) in this complex but quickly paced and well-researched book.
>
> **Subjects:** Corruption, Drugs, Family Relationships, Government, Homicides, Immigration, Law Enforcement, Mexico, Multicultural Issues, Texas, True Crime
>
> **Awards:** New York Times Notable
>
> **Now Try:** Readers of this book might find another distressing true crime book about the border a good companion read: *The Daughters of Juarez: A True Story of Serial Murder South of the Border* by Teresa Rodriguez. Mark Bowden's tale of Colombian

drug lord Pablo Escobar, *Killing Pablo*, might also be a good related read, as might Alex Kotlowitz's *The Other Side of the River*. Other books about immigrants and immigration might also be suggested, such as William Langewiesche's *Cutting for Sign* or Ruben Martinez's *Crossing Over*.

Bowden, Mark

Killing Pablo: The Hunt for the World's Greatest Outlaw. Atlantic Monthly Press. 2001. 296 pp. ISBN 9780871137838.

Journalist Bowden recounts the story of Colombian drug (specifically, cocaine) cartel leader Pablo Escobar, who escaped from prison in Colombia while being transferred to another facility in 1992, setting off the world's largest manhunt ever. With the same skill he displayed weaving together complex and numerous story lines in the war classic *Black Hawk Down*, Bowden again combines the firsthand accounts and stories of police, politicians, U.S. military personnel, Drug Enforcement Administration agents, and even the private vigilante squads known as "Los Pepes"; his account culminates with the location of Escobar and the shoot-out that resulted in his death. As always, Bowden's writing is detailed but propelled forward by its strong story line, and in addition to describing the manhunt, the author also provides the story of Escobar's rise to prominence, his family and business relationships, and the aftermath of his capture.

> **Subjects:** Adventure, Biographies, Cocaine, Colombia, Drugs, Pablo Escobar, Explicit Violence, Family Relationships, Foreign Relations, Law Enforcement, South America, True Crime

> **Now Try:** Other investigative titles by Bowden might appeal to these readers, particularly *Finders Keepers* or *Black Hawk Down*; other True Crime books about families cooperating in crime might also be suggested: Donnie Brasco's *The Way of the Wise Guy*, Bryan Burrough's history *Public Enemies*, Robert Friedman's *Red Mafiya*, or Peter Maas's *Underboss*. Related reads might also include books about American foreign policy and interactions with other nations, such as Joan Didion's *Salvador*, Tom Hart Dyke's and Paul Winder's *The Cloud Garden*, or John Perkins's *Confessions of an Economic Hit Man*. Tom Clancy's novel, *Clear and Present Danger*, is also said to be based on this story.

Breslin, Jimmy

Good Rat: A True Story. Ecco. 2008. 270 pp. ISBN 9780060856663.

Breslin, a Pulitzer Prize–winning journalist and stalwart of the "new journalism" style (in which authors write true stories using novelistic conventions such as dialogue and scenes), offers a biography of Burton Kaplan, a mafia informant who testified in the 2006 case in New York City in which two NYPD detectives were charged with working for and committing murders for mob bosses. Breslin also relates classic mafia stories from the last half-century, illuminating the mob way of life, family relationships, and the history and development of their criminal activities in New York.

> **Subjects:** Burton Kaplan, Mafia, New York City, Organized Crime, Quick Reads, Trials, True Crime

> **Now Try:** Jimmy Breslin has also written a classic mafia novel, *The Gang That Couldn't Shoot Straight*, as well as nonfiction accounts *How the Good Guys*

Finally Won and *The World According to Breslin*. Other Mafia Crime nonfiction titles might appeal, such as Donnie Brasco's *The Way of the Wise Guy* or Peter Maas's *Underboss: Sammy the Bull Gravano's Story of Life in the Mafia*; Mario Puzo's classic mob novels, starting with *The Godfather*, might also appeal. Breslin is one of the founders of the "new journalism"; other authors from that tradition who these readers might enjoy include Norman Mailer, Gay Talese, Joan Didion, and Tom Wolfe; authors who provided blurbs for this title, including Nicholas Pileggi and Pete Dexter, might also be of interest.

Connelly, Michael

Crime Beat: A Decade of Covering Cops and Killers. Little, Brown. 2006. 375 pp. ISBN 9780316153775.

Before becoming a popular and bestselling crime novelist (best known for his Harry Bosch series, starting with 1992's *The Black Echo*), Connelly was a journalist working the crime beat in Florida and Los Angeles. Each chapter starts with a headline and story from Connelly's beat, which he then expands on by providing the "inside story" of the crimes, how they were investigated, and how he researched them. Written in a highly immediate style and including numerous quotes from interviews conducted by the author, this is a quickly paced but sometimes graphic crime narrative.

Subjects: Crime, Florida, Homicides, Journalism, Law Enforcement, Los Angeles, Quick Reads, True Crime

Now Try: Connelly is also a mystery/thriller novelist; these readers might consider his Harry Bosch series, starting with *The Black Echo* and *The Black Ice*. Other thriller and classic noir authors might be suggested, including Raymond Chandler, James Ellroy, Robert Park, Walter Mosley, or Lawrence Sanders. Likewise, True Crime nonfiction which focuses on the law enforcement side might also appeal, such as Edward Conlon's memoir *Blue Blood*, Philip Gourevitch's *A Cold Case*, or Ann Rule's *Green River, Running Red*.

Denfeld, Rene

All God's Children: Inside the Dark and Violent World of Street Families. PublicAffairs. 2007. 306 pp. ISBN 9781586483098.

In 1992 a teenager named James Daniel Nelson ran away from home and joined a group of other runaways and street kids who lived together under a Portland, Oregon, bridge; within months, numerous members of this "street family" would be arrested for a series of violent murders. Although Nelson was convicted and sent to prison, he was released in 2003 and immediately went back to Portland, where he created a new family (they were known as the "Thantos family") and again committed murder. Author Denfeld spent over a decade researching and tracking the evolution of street family culture, including getting to know many teenaged members of such families and Nelson in particular. The result is a thoroughly chilling and in-depth picture of life on the streets, which, contrary to popular belief, is populated largely by young adults who have left financially secure and stable middle-class homes; of particular note are the rules to which all members of street families religiously adhere: no snitching, respect the Old-Timers, and never talk to a cop.

Subjects: Character Profiles, Explicit Violence, Family Relationships, Homelessness, Homicides, True Crime, Urban Life

Now Try: Other books that explore ties among families, poverty, and crime might be offered: Don Lattin's equally dark *Jesus Freaks: A True Story of Murder and Madness on the Evangelical Edge*, Adrian Nicole LeBlanc's *Random Family*, Leon Dash's *Rosa Lee*, or Joanna Lipper's *Growing Up Fast*. This non-fiction book offers an unsettling view of urban life; these readers might also consider Bleak Future or Dystopia science fiction and fantasy books by authors including Margaret Atwood, William Gibson, J. G. Ballard, Chuck Palahniuk (whose novel *Fight Club* might particularly appeal), Anthony Burgess, and Octavia Butler.

Dunne, Dominick

Justice: Crimes, Trials, and Punishments. Crown. 2001. 337 pp. ISBN 9780609608739.

Dunne was a Hollywood producer who was impelled into journalism when his daughter, Dominique Dunne, was murdered in 1982; her accused killer, John Sweeney, was eventually convicted but was sentenced to only six-and-a-half years in prison (of which he only served two and a half). Dunne was so shocked and appalled by the travesty of the trial and what he considered the showboating of the presiding judge that he wrote the stunning and heartbreaking journalistic piece "Justice," which is the piece that opens this book. The rest of the book comprises Dunne's essays about other true crime subjects, including the Menendez brothers, Claus von Bulow, O. J. Simpson, and such cases as the murder of Martha Moxley. Most of these essays were first published in the magazine *Vanity Fair*, and Dunne writes with clarity and great attention to details, particularly regarding the complex workings of the American justice system and the wide variety of characters who find themselves either victims of or implicated in serious crimes.

Subjects: Character Profiles, Classics, Essays, Family Relationships, Homicides, Law and Lawyers, Law Enforcement, Trials, True Crime

Now Try: Dunne's accused murderer was her boyfriend; other True Crime books in which crimes are perpetrated by the victims' family or loved ones might be offered, such as Janine Latus's *If I Am Missing or Dead*, John Berendt's *Midnight in the Garden of Good and Evil*, Ann Rule's *Bitter Harvest*, Joe McGinniss's *Fatal Vision*, or Gary Provost's *Without Mercy*. Dunne is also somewhat of a high society reporter; his readers might also consider books that combine stories of true crime and celebrity, such as *If I Did It* by the Goldman family (about O. J. Simpson) or *Tearing Down the Wall of Sound: The Rise and Fall of Phil Spector* by Mick Browne; books about simply the upper crust alone (without the crime) might also be offered, such as Ronald Kessler's *The Season: Inside Palm Beach* or novels by Danielle Steel, Judith Krantz, or Sidney Sheldon.

Horn, Stacy

The Restless Sleep: Inside New York City's Cold Case Squad. Viking. 2005. 320 pp. ISBN 9780670034192.

In Horn's detailed but still empathetic investigative look into horrific criminal cases gone cold, she relates the stories of four crimes (the murder of parents in front of their children, the murder of an off-duty cop who interrupted a robbery, a sex crime turned fatal, and a fetishistic strangling) and the stories of the detectives laboring through evidence and testimony to bring some sort of justice or closure to the files. Horn does not provide any more sensationalistic details than are necessary but rather offers solid science and police-beat reporting, as well as poignant character profiles of both the victims and the investigators.

Subjects: Explicit Violence, Law Enforcement, New York City, Professions, True Crime

Now Try: Horn's book did not receive the review or sales attention that it deserved; other similarly "under the radar" crime titles include Philip Gourevitch's *A Cold Case*, Gil Reavill's *Aftermath, Inc.: Cleaning Up after CSI Goes Home*, Steven Koehler's *Postmortem*, or A. M. Rosenthal's *Thirty-Eight Witnesses: The Kitty Genovese Case* might be offered, as well as law enforcement memoirs such as Edward Conlon's *Blue Blood*, Michael Connelly's *Crime Beat*, or Edward Humes's *No Matter How Loud I Shout*; Alex Kotlowitz's empathetic *There Are No Children Here* or *The Other Side of the River* are two other classics that might be offered.

Humes, Edward

Mean Justice: A Town's Terror, a Prosecutor's Power, a Betrayal of Innocence. Simon & Schuster. 1999. 491 pp. ISBN 9780684831749.

Humes tells the story of Pat Dunn, a man convicted of killing his wife (and who protested his innocence throughout his trial) with what Humes contends was a disturbing lack of actual evidence linking him to the crime. Rather, Humes argues, the conviction was politically motivated; Bakersfield, California, had a reputation as a community that was hard on crime and a place where prosecutors and judges would do anything to further that reputation and secure convictions (including making false accusations and indulging in other corruption).

Subjects: Bakersfield, California; Corruption; Patrick Dunn; Homicides; Law and Lawyers; Trials

Now Try: Humes is a well-known investigative author who often writes about trials and the justice system; his other titles include *Mississippi Mud, Monkey Girl: Evolution, Education, Religion, and the Battle for America's Soul* and the more contemplative *No Matter How Loud I Shout: A Year in the Life of Juvenile Court*. Other nonfiction and True Crime titles focusing on trials and less-than-forthright methods of investigating crimes might consider Jeanine Cummins's *A Rip in Heaven*, Lawrence Schiller's *Perfect Murder, Perfect Town*, or Mark Arax's *In My Father's Name: A Family, a Town, a Murder*. Legal thrillers by authors including John Grisham, John Lescroart, or Phillip Margolin might also appeal.

Humes, Edward

No Matter How Loud I Shout: A Year in the Life of Juvenile Court. Simon & Schuster. 1996. 399 pp. ISBN 9780684811949.

Humes observed the juvenile justice system of Los Angeles for a year to understand how the lives of children are affected by their day in court. Organized in three parts, the book offers details of the flooded juvenile justice system, how such cases might be settled more beneficially to the children and adults involved, and how their experiences affect the children in question. Telling stories of individual children, families, and court professionals, Humes makes a direct link between the system's handling (or mishandling) of children and their propensity to engage in crime as adults. Humes is a Pulitzer Prize–winning journalist, and this book was a finalist for the 1997 Edgar Award in Fact Crime writing.

> **Subjects:** California, Character Profiles, Law and Lawyers, Law Enforcement, Trials, True Crime, Year in the Life
>
> **Now Try:** Steve Bogira's *Courtroom 302* also offers an inside look into the legal system, as do Marissa Batt's *"Ready for the People,"* Kevin Flynn's *Relentless Pursuit*, David Feige's *Indefensible*, Jonathan Harr's *A Civil Action*, or Jennifer Wynn's *Inside Rikers*. Books about children who suffer through poverty and crime, such as Tracy Kidder's *Among Schoolchildren*, Alex Kotlowitz's *There Are No Children Here* and *The Other Side of the River*, Adrian Nicole LeBlanc's *Random Family*, and Jonathan Kozol's *Savage Inequalities* might also make good read-alikes.

Kotlowitz, Alex

The Other Side of the River: A Story of Two Towns, a Death and America's Dilemma. Nan A. Talese. 1998. 317 pp. ISBN 9780385477208.

In this immediate and heartfelt investigation of both a murder and inequality, Kotlowitz relates the story of the investigation into the death of African American teenager Eric McGinnis, who was found dead in the river separating the Michigan cities of St. Joseph and Benton Harbor in 1991. In chapters exploring the investigation into McGinnis's death, Kotlowitz also tells the story of the two vastly different cities; the relatively affluent St. Joseph, with a 95 percent white population, and the impoverished city of Benton Harbor, with its 92 percent black population. Through interviews with McGinnis's family members, police investigators, and other individuals from both communities, the author relates the tragic tale of two towns linked geographically but miles apart in terms of economic and social prosperity; to this day, the crime remains unsolved and the tension between the cities still readily apparent.

> **Subjects:** Classics, Community Life, Homicides, Law Enforcement, Michigan, Poverty, Race Relations, Racism, True Crime, Urban Life
>
> **Now Try:** Kotlowitz himself shares with his reader the books he read while researching this book; they include Tim O'Brien's novel *In the Lake of the Woods*, Sherwood Anderson's classic *Winesburg, Ohio*, and Rian Malan's *My Traitor's Heart*. Books by other intensive researchers and social journalists might also appeal (in tone and in subject); these include Jonathan Kozol, Tracy Kidder, Adrian Nicole LeBlanc, Sudhir Venkatesh, Barbara Ehrenreich, and Leon Dash.

Krakauer, Jon

Under the Banner of Heaven: A Story of Violent Faith. Doubleday. 2003. 372 pp. ISBN 9780385509510.

Krakauer brings his trademark action-oriented and story-driven prose style to the tragic story of the murders of their sister-in-law and her infant by Don and Ron Lafferty, who later claimed they were told to execute the crimes by God. Krakauer reveals not only the details of the crimes and the family relationships between Ron, Don, and their younger brother Allen but also relates the history of the Mormon church in America, focusing primarily on its more fundamentalist principles and adherents. Including interviews which Krakauer conducted with Don Lafferty while he was serving his sentence, this is a chilling look at both cultlike religious beliefs and practices and a murderer's continuing belief that he did the right thing.

Subjects: Book Groups, Classics, Cults, Family Relationships, Fundamentalism, Homicides, Mormonism, Radicalism, Religion, True Crime, Utah

Awards: ALA Notable, New York Times Notable

Now Try: Krakauer is most well known for his True Adventure and disaster narratives *Into Thin Air* and *Into the Wild*. Other books on crime and family relationships, including Mikal Gilmore's superlative *Shot in the Heart* (also about Mormonism), Joe McGinniss's classic *Fatal Vision*, Jack Olsen's *Salt of the Earth*, and Ann Rule's *Bitter Harvest* might be offered, as might Truman Capote's novelistic classic *In Cold Blood*. Another nonfiction account of Mormonism can be found in Carolyn Jessop's memoir *Escape*. Novels featuring themes of religious fundamentalism include Sheri Reynolds's *The Rapture of Canaan*, A. Manette Ansay's *Vinegar Hill*, and Paula Sharp's *I Loved You All* might appeal, as well as nonfiction memoirs such as Kim Barnes's *In the Wilderness* or Sonsyrea Tate's *Do Me Twice: My Life after Islam*.

Playboy Enterprises

The Playboy Book of True Crime. Playboy Press. 2007. 368 pp. ISBN 9781586421274.

This wide-ranging and fascinating compilation of crime reporting from the pages of *Playboy* magazine opens with a piece about the Mafia, first published in 1970; follows that with an author's personal report of being mugged in New York City; moves swiftly into an interview with Jimmy Hoffa; and never slows down from there. Each piece contains the date it first appeared in print, and the book also contains interviews that the magazine ran with convicted murderer Gary Gilmore, as well as with true crime reporter Lawrence Schiller.

Subjects: Essays, Homicides, Journalism, Mafia, True Crime

Now Try: Books about and by convicted felons and authors discussed in this book might be suggested, including classics about Gary Gilmore, such as his brother Mikal Gilmore's *Shot through the Heart* or Norman Mailer's classic about the case, *The Executioner's Song*. Books by Lawrence Schiller might appeal, and, because there is a decided emphasis on Mafia and mob crime in this volume, titles from the True Crime subgenre of Mafia Crime, including Donnie Brasco's *The Way of the Wise Guy*, Peter Maas's *Underboss*, or Roberto Saviano's international title *Gomorrah: A Personal Journey into the Violent International Empire of Naples' Organized Crime System* might all be suggested as read-alikes.

Wright, Lawrence

Remembering Satan: A Case of Recovered Memory and the Shattering of an American Family. Knopf. 1994. 205 pp. ISBN 9780679431558.

In this unflinchingly detailed account, Wright relates the story of Paul Ingram, a married father of five, deputy sheriff, and local Republican party notable, who was accused of sexual abuse and participation in satanic rituals by two of his daughters, who brought charges against him based on recovered memories. Although Ingram initially said he could not remember any such incidents, he also recovered memories under interrogation and hypnosis and eventually pleaded guilty to and was convicted of the crimes. Wright examines subjects of the family's dynamic, what it means to "recover" memories, and how the criminal justice system often relies on such testimonies.

Subjects: Abuse, Classics, Explicit Sexuality, Explicit Violence, Hypnotism, Law Enforcement, Psychology, True Crime

Now Try: Other books in which the difficulties of investigating crimes and determining what really happened might also be offered; these include Lawrence Schiller's *Perfect Murder, Perfect Town*, Jeanine Cummins's *A Rip in Heaven*, Sebastian Junger's *A Death in Belmont*, Mark Arax's *In My Father's Name*, John Berendt's *Midnight in the Garden of Good and Evil*, and Mark Olshaker's *The Cases That Haunt Us*. Wright is also considered one of the foremost practitioners of the "new new journalism"; his other books might appeal to readers (*The Looming Tower* and *Twins*), as might books by similar authors such as William Langewiesche, Leon Dash, and Lawrence Weschler.

War Reporting

The American tradition of war reporting is firmly rooted in the newspaper, magazine, and book publishing practices during the American Revolution and the Civil War. During the American Revolution, the emphasis was not as much on the day-to-day reporting of military actions and troop movements but more so on the publishing of pamphlets and newspapers that were obviously aligned with either the Revolutionary or Royalist sides. This made for admirably clear boundaries when deciding what to read but also led to incidents in which editors who tried to present multiple viewpoints in their papers were threatened by mobs who demanded they then repudiate, in print, stories with which they didn't agree. For example, in 1777 Baltimore, editor Charles Goddard was forced, "under pistol point," to write and publish a repudiation of one of his writers' articles that painted General George Washington in a less than complimentary light (Tebbel 1969, 52). For the two decades following the Revolution, the newspapers would descend into what journalism historians refer to as the "dark ages" of the American newspaper, with partisan divisions and propaganda rife on all sides between the Federalists and the Republicans.

There was also international participation in the profession of war reporting; Phillip Knightley credits Irishman William Howard Russell for being one of the earliest war correspondents, for his reports filed during the Crimean War. Even at that early stage, and with only a small number of writers working in the same arena, there were two different schools of reporting; Russell tried to give the big picture of troop movements and tactics, whereas another correspondent, Edwin Lawrence Godkin, strove to illustrate the plights of individual soldiers. Both correspondents, it should be noted, were critical of the British army's "blunders" and their reports would prove popular with the British reading public hungry for news (Knightley 1975, 4–17). Knightley also notes that the floodgates of war reporters would be opened during the American Civil War; when it "broke out, five years later, 500 of them turned out to report the conflict on the Northern side alone" (Knightley 1975, 17).

There is no question that these narratives may prove difficult to read because they include details of human suffering and cruelty; but it is also no great secret that many war reporters are drawn to their jobs because they seek to learn about (and report) what is basic and elemental about human nature. Gay Talese described writers such as these in his massive history of the *New York Times* newspaper, titled *The Kingdom and the Power*: "Most journalists are restless voyeurs who see the warts on the world, the imperfections in people and places. The sane scene that is much of life, the great portion of the planet unmarked by madness, does not lure them like riots and raids, crumbling countries and sinking ships . . . gloom is their game, the spectacle their passion, normality their nemesis" (Talese 1969, 1). So, too, do the readers of these books want to have their eyes opened to those great portions of the planet torn by wartime events and the aftermaths of conflicts.

Titles in the War Reporting category differ from War Stories that are considered True Adventure nonfiction in that they are written by individuals whose charge is not ideological or personal (many True Adventure war stories are written by those fighting in or being held as prisoners of wars) but informational: war correspondents cover war stories to disseminate them to a public not involved with or able to witness the battles firsthand. They often have a tone of immediacy because they are written shortly after the authors witness the events about which they're writing; they can be ideological but more often tend to focus on character details of those fighting the wars or suffering from their proximity. Those titles with more of a political or personal opinion about the events can be found in the Exposés chapter (in the Government Exposés category), and books about military history and True Adventure War Stories or Intrigue and Espionage (David Howarth's *We Die Alone* or Pete Earley's *Family of Spies*) might also appeal, as might fiction in which battles (historical or otherwise) take center stage, such as titles by Bernard Cornwell (the Richard Sharpe series), W. E. B. Griffin, James Brady, or William P. Mack.

War Reporting titles are often written by war reporters and correspondents whose primary aim is not to craft a quickly paced adventure story but rather to disseminate information and sensory impressions to general readers. Although they can be very immediate and affecting in tone and the authors often relate stories that they experienced firsthand, they do not tend to dwell on gory details but rather offer human interest and personal stories in the larger context of civil unrest and war. Set in varying locations throughout the world, these narratives may also appeal to readers with an interest in multicultural issues and faraway settings.

Bortolotti, Dan

Hope in Hell: Inside the World of Doctors Without Borders. Firefly Books. 2004. 303 pp. ISBN 9781552978658.

This beautifully produced and photographed book provides a biography of Médicins Sans Frontières (Doctors Without Borders) from its genesis in 1968, to its official founding in Paris in 1971, to its current struggle to remain a completely neutral human rights organization as opposed to a political human rights organization. The group's history is not devoid of controversy, and many of its members are compellingly described here in the context of both their humanitarian work and their differing viewpoints regarding the organization's mission to provide aid without judging the rightness of any one group's claims or conflicts.

> **Subjects:** Africa, France, Health Issues, Human Rights, Illustrated Books, Medicine, Multicultural Issues, Small Press, War Reporting, Work Relationships

> **Now Try:** Tracy Kidder's story of Dr. Paul Farmer and his struggle to make the best health care possible to all Haitians, as told in *Mountains beyond Mountains: The Quest of Dr. Paul Farmer, a Man Who Would Cure the World*, is also a compelling and quickly paced history. The extremely personal collection of stories told in *Another Day in Paradise: International Humanitarian Workers Tell Their Stories*, edited by Carol Bergman, also provides an evocative picture of the struggles and triumphs of medical and other humanitarian aid workers worldwide.

Burke, Jason

On the Road to Kandahar: Travels through Conflict in the Islamic World. Thomas Dunne Books. 2006. 297 pp. ISBN 9780312366223.

In the early 1990s, Burke, then a university student, traveled to northern Iraq to join Kurdish guerrillas in their fight against Saddam Hussein. With such a background, it is only natural that he returned to report on the current state of the Middle East, the influence of al-Qaeda, and the observance of Islam by traveling from the Sahara to the Himalayas, meeting with refugees, soldiers, mujahideen, government officials, and many other individuals involved, from the other side, with the "war on terrorism." Burke provides valuable insight into Islamic radicalism and how the West might choose to respond to it, postulating that extremist violence eventually alienates those caught in the middle of it. His first-person narration and attention to landscape and personal details make this a quick read, sure to appeal to fans of travel nonfiction, and he concludes that "there was no general theory that could explain the Islamic world and that to search for one was not only futile but in fact counter-productive."

> **Subjects:** Afghanistan, Iraq, Islam, Middle East, Multicultural Issues, Pakistan, Travel, True Adventure, War Reporting

> **Now Try:** Other intrepid authors who have traveled through war-torn and desolate regions include Tom Bissell (*Chasing the Sea: Lost among the Ghosts of Empire in Central Asia*), Redmond O'Hanlon (*Into the Heart of Borneo*), and William Langewiesche (*Sahara Unveiled*). Books about the effects of war and culture clash might also appeal; these include *Three Cups of Tea* by Greg Mortenson, *Uncivilized Beasts and Shameless Hellions* by John Burnett, *Emergency Sex and Other Measures* by Kenneth Cain, *Mirrors of the Unseen: Journeys in Iran* and *An Unexpected Light* by Jason Elliot, Rob Ferguson's *The Devil and the Disappearing Sea*, or Chris Hedges's *War Is a Force That Gives Us Meaning*. Fiction and nonfiction set in Afghanistan, particularly titles by Khaled Hosseini (*The Kite Runner* or *A Thousand Splendid Suns*), might also make good read-alikes, as might books about the Middle East such as Geraldine Brooks's *Nine Parts of Desire*, Ian Buruma's *Occidentalism*, or Lawrence Wright's *The Looming Tower*.

Burnett, John F.

Uncivilized Beasts and Shameless Hellions: Travels with an NPR Correspondent. Rodale. 2006. 239 pp. ISBN 9781594863042.

As a journalist with NPR, Burnett has traveled to some of the most war-torn and remote places on Earth. Here he relates his experiences reporting in the midst of conflicts from Kosovo, Iraq, Afghanistan, Pakistan, and even from natural disaster sites such as New Orleans after Hurricane Katrina. The title refers to a sign Burnett saw held up in Pakistan, referring to journalists as "uncivilized beasts and shameless hellions," and throughout he tells not only human-interest, current affairs, and war stories with empathy but also examines journalists' difficult roles as people who may want to stop reporting long enough to help those struggling around them but who feel the greater good is served by their reporting the story worldwide. As a radio reporter, Burnett is used to telling his stories, and that strong storytelling skill is evident in these short chapters and pieces; the book concludes with a number of character profiles of individuals the author refers to as "rogues and heroes."

> **Subjects:** Afghanistan, Character Profiles, Guatemala, Hurricane Katrina, Iraq, Journalism, Kosovo, Mass Media, Multicultural Issues, Pakistan, Travel, War Reporting

> **Now Try:** At one point in his narrative, Burnett mentions Ernie Pyle, one of the best-known war correspondents of all time; books by and about him (including *Ernie Pyle's War* by James Tobin) may be of interest. Other books by intrepid reporters might be suggested, such as William Vollmann's *Poor People*, Jed Horne's *Breach of Faith: Hurricane Katrina and the Near Death of a Great American City*, Joan Didion's *Salvador*, or any number of books about the Iraq War (particularly the illustrated book *Unembedded: Four Independent Photojournalists on the War in Iraq*). Other books about the lives of journalists might also appeal, such as John Hockenberry's *Moving Violations*, Frank Rich's *The Greatest Story Ever Sold*, or Joe Sacco's *The Fixer*.

Chandrasekaran, Rajiv

🏵 *Imperial Life in the Emerald City: Inside Iraq's Green Zone.* Knopf. 2006. 320 pp. ISBN 9781400044870.

American journalist and the Baghdad bureau chief for the *Washington Post*, Chandrasekaran provides a straightforward but not unsympathetic look at the postwar (post-2003) administration of Iraq by Paul Bremer and others involved with the Coalition Provisional Authority. In addition to listing mistakes that most likely could have been avoided in Iraq, the author examines individual acts of bravery and common sense in the "Green Zone," the American and military enclave in the center of Baghdad.

> **Subjects:** Book Groups, Paul Bremer, Foreign Relations, Government, Iraq, Iraq War (2003), Politics, War Reporting

> **Awards:** New York Times Notable

> **Now Try:** George Packer's superlative and detailed *The Assassins' Gate: America in Iraq*, and Anthony Shadid's *Night Draws Near: Iraq's People in the Shadow of America's War*, might provide more contextual detail for the Iraq War. Other investigative works on the subject include *Fiasco: The American Military Adventure in Iraq* by Thomas Ricks; *The Greatest Story Ever Sold* by Frank Rich; *Hubris: The Inside Story of Spin, Scandal, and the Selling of the Iraq War* by Michael Isikoff; *Cobra II* by Michael Gordon; or *The Last True Story I'll Ever Tell* by John Crawford. Other titles such as

Åsne Seierstad's *The Bookseller of Kabul*, Geraldine Brooks's *Nine Parts of Desire: The Hidden Lives of Islamic Women*, or Judith Miller's *God Has Ninety-Nine Names* might also appeal to these readers.

Cockburn, Patrick

🏅 *The Occupation: War and Resistance in Iraq.* Verso. 2006. 229 pp. ISBN 9781844671007.

Cockburn, who has been visiting and reporting from Iraq since 1978, went back to Baghdad shortly before the U.S. invasion in 2003 and has been reporting from there ever since. With background knowledge gained from his previous reporting in the country, Cockburn describes the fighting on the ground, the collapse of Saddam Hussein's army, the looting of Baghdad, what he terms America's "occupation" of the city and the country, as well as the resistance to that occupation and the response to it by three main communities: Iraq's Shia, Sunni, and Kurds. Cockburn does not mince words, stating on the second page of his narrative that "the debate on why the U.S. invaded Iraq has been over-sophisticated. The main motive for going to war was that the White House thought it could win such a conflict very easily and to its own great advantage."

Subjects: George W. Bush, Foreign Relations, Government, Saddam Hussein, Iraq, Iraq War (2003), Islam, Military, Multicultural Issues, Politics, War Reporting

Awards: Martha Gellhorn Prize

Now Try: Cockburn has won the Martha Gellhorn Prize for war reporting; war reporting classics by Gellhorn or other journalists such as Ernie Pyle or John Hersey might also appeal to these readers. Also consider offering George Packer's comprehensive *The Assassins' Gate: America in Iraq*, Rajiv Chandrasekaran's *Imperial Life in the Emerald City: Inside Iraq's Green Zone*, Michael Gordon's *Cobra II*, Vincent Bugliosi's *The Prosecution of George W. Bush for Murder*, or Thomas Ricks's *Fiasco: The American Military Adventure in Iraq*. Other authors whose investigative works might appeal to Cockburn's fans include William Langewiesche, Michael Isikoff, and Frank Rich. Any number of books about the George W. Bush administration might also work as read-alikes, including Jacob Weisberg's *The Bush Tragedy*, James Risen's *State of War*, or Robert Draper's *Inside the Bush White House*.

Gellhorn, Martha

The Face of War. Simon & Schuster. 1959. 244 pp. ISBN 9780871132116.

Gellhorn was an independent, intrepid, and empathetic reporter of worldwide war and violence; in this book she reports on the effects and aftermath of World War II in such countries as Spain, Finland, and China. Unfolding over the course of eight years spent traveling in twelve countries, Gellhorn's personal and lyrical writing and character portraits based on her interviews with the individuals put a human—and particularly a civilian—face on the effects of war.

Subjects: American History, Classics, Journalism, Memoirs, Quick Reads, War Reporting, Women Travelers, World War II

Now Try: Gellhorn's work is old in years but contemporary in subject; books by or about other such well-known war reporters as Ernie Pyle, John Hersey,

Marguerite Higgins, Michael Herr, and Robert Capa might also be offered to her readers. Gellhorn also lived a fascinating life in her own right; she was married to Ernest Hemingway for a time and wrote a memoir of their travels together, titled *Travels with Myself and Another*; her fans might also consider Caroline Moorehead's biography *Gellhorn: A Twentieth Century Life* or *The Selected Letters of Martha Gellhorn* (these readers might also consider Hemingway's novels, including *For Whom the Bell Tolls* and *To Have or Have Not*).

Gourevitch, Philip, and Errol Morris

Standard Operating Procedure. Penguin. 2008. 286 pp. ISBN 9781594201325.

Although Errol Morris originally interviewed the American soldiers who appeared in and took the digital photographs proving the prisoner abuse at the Abu Ghraib prison in Iraq, Gourevitch used those interviews to tell the deeply unsettling story of the prison's history, the work of the military members in charge of the facility during the Iraq War, and the aftermath and aftershocks of the revelations of the torture. Divided into three sections—Before, During, and After—this is a story of the occupation of Iraq that explores its effects on both the prison's inmates and its guards.

> **Subjects:** Abu Ghraib, Abuse, Iraq, Iraq War (2003), Military, Oral Histories, Politics, Prisons, Torture, War

> **Now Try:** Gourevitch has long been known for his ability to explore shocking stories; his previous books, *We Wish to Inform You That Tomorrow We Will Be Killed with Our Families* (about the Rwandan genocide) and *A Cold Case* (a True Crime book) might be suggested, as might Errol Morris's documentary films, including *Standard Operating Procedure*, *The Fog of War*, and *Fast, Cheap, and Out of Control*. Other books about the subject might be suggested, such as Alfred McCoy's *A Question of Torture: CIA Interrogation from the Cold War to the War On Terror*, John Conroy's *Unspeakable Acts, Ordinary People: The Dynamics of Torture*, Mark Danner's *Torture and Truth: America, Abu Ghraib, and the War on Terror*, Joseph Margulies's *Guantánamo and the Abuse of Presidential Power*, or Lawrence Wright's *The Looming Tower: Al-Qaeda and the Road to 9/11*. Other investigative works by authors similar in style to Gourevitch might hold some appeal, including *American Ground* by William Langewiesche, *Voices from Chernobyl* by Svetlana Alexievich, or *Imperial Life in the Emerald City* by Rajiv Chandrasekaran.

Hedges, Chris

War Is a Force That Gives Us Meaning. PublicAffairs. 2002. 211 pp. ISBN 9781586480493.

In his career as a war correspondent, Hedges has traveled to such war-torn areas as Central America, the Sudan, and the Middle East; he has also survived being beaten, imprisoned, and ambushed. Over the course of his career, he has seen more violence, privation, and human cruelty than any one person should, and yet, as he tells it, he remains almost "addicted" to the exhilaration of war, speculating on how its practice is a force that gives humankind meaning. In addition to drawing on his own experience, Hedges, who is a former student of divinity, also explores the experiences of war as portrayed in such nonfiction and fiction works as those by Homer, Michael Herr (*Dispatches*) and many others. Although Hedges recognizes war's awesome power both to divide and to unite, his various chapters explore its many facets, from war myths to nationalism, the seduction of battle to the destruction of culture, and even the hijacking and revision of postwar history and memory.

> **Subjects:** Journalism, Making Sense . . ., Memoirs, Military, Politics, Psychology, Travel, War Reporting, World History

> **Now Try:** Readers who pick up Hedges's book (or his other books, *What Every Person Should Know about War*, *American Fascists*, and *Collateral Damage*) will be treated to a rich list of related readings and read-alikes in his bibliography; the authors to whom he refers include Hannah Arendt, Philip Caputo, Joseph Conrad, Niall Ferguson, Paul Fussell, Robert Graves, Michael Ignatieff, Christopher Lasch, poet Wilfred Owen, and Ernie Pyle. Authors who write in a similar style and tone to Hedges also include Christopher Hitchens, Chalmers Johnson, and William Vollmann.

Herr, Michael

Dispatches. Knopf. 1977. 260 pp. ISBN 9780394417882.

In this classic of war reportage, Herr relates his experiences covering the Vietnam War for *Esquire* magazine in the 1970s. Filled with immediate and stream-of-consciousness writing, graphic imagery of violence, and numerous instances of soldiers' almost constant and unthinking use of profanity, Herr relates the details of infamous encounters at Khe Sanh and other locations, as well as the horror and extreme anxiety and alienation felt by the soldiers who fought on the war's ever-shifting lines and landscapes.

> **Subjects:** 1960s, 1970s, American History, Book Groups, Classics, Memoirs, Military, Profanity, True Adventure, Vietnam War, War Reporting

> **Now Try:** Herr's volume is a classic of war reporting and memoir; although it now probably qualifies more as a work of history than current affairs, the style of the writing places the book firmly in the journalistic tradition. There is (sadly) no shortage of other classic works about the Vietnam War; these include Philip Caputo's *A Rumor of War*, Neil Sheehan's *A Bright Shining Lie*, David Halberstam's *The Best and the Brightest*, Seymour Hersh's *My-Lai 4*, Jeffrey Meyers's *Inherited Risk*, Tobias Wolff's *In Pharaoh's Army*, Robert Mason's *Chickenhawk*, or Tom Bissell's *The Father of All Things*; fiction by Tim O'Brien (*The Things They Carried* or *Going after Cacciato*) or Denis Johnson's *Tree of Smoke* might also be offered. Other War Reporting classics by authors including Ernie Pyle, John Hersey, or Donald Kirk might also be suggested.

Hitchens, Christopher

Love, Poverty, and War: Journeys and Essays. Nation Books. 2004. 475 pp. ISBN 9781560255802.

Hitchens, everyone's favorite contrarian, wastes little time in showing his writing style, when he states: "I did not, I wish to state, become a journalist because there was no other 'profession' that would have me. I became a journalist because I did not want to rely on newspapers for information." In this collection of opinion and personal essays highlighting his experiences traveling around the world from Iraq to Cuba to Indonesia, working as a war and foreign correspondent, and waxing eloquent on the foibles of such individuals as William Clinton, Mother Teresa, Michael Moore, and

Noam Chomsky, all of his wit and sharp writing style talents are on display. Each essay is dated and marked with its source, including magazines such as *The Nation*, *Vanity Fair*, and *The Atlantic*.

Subjects: 9/11, Character Profiles, Essays, Journalism, Literature, Sociology, Travel, War

Now Try: As noted, the essays in this collection came largely from the magazines *The Nation*, *Vanity Fair*, and *The Atlantic*; books by other correspondents and writers for those magazines might also be suggested (although it should be noted that Hitchens is no longer the "darling of the left" that he once was), such as Mark Bowden, William Langewiesche, Caitlin Flanagan, or Barbara Ehrenreich. Books by veteran reporters Chris Hedges (***War Is a Force That Gives Us Meaning***) and John Burnett (***Uncivilized Beasts and Shameless Hellions***) might also appeal. Hitchens has become more popular in recent years because of his staunch support of atheism (as shown in his own book ***God Is Not Great***), and thus books by authors Richard Dawkins, Daniel Dennett, and Sam Harris might also be suggested to his fans, as might William Vollmann, who also writes a wide variety of war and personal journalism.

Kaplan, Robert M.

Imperial Grunts: On the Ground with the American Military, from Mongolia to the Philippines to Iraq and Beyond. Random House. 2005. 421 pp. ISBN 9781400061327.

Kaplan, an author and correspondent for *The Atlantic*, presents an account of his travels to accompany and live with members of America's military from such locations as Yemen and Colombia to Iraq and the Middle East. In his interviews with them, Kaplan is able to hear their version of their work, which many see as the taming of "unruly" frontiers and performing humanitarian missions. His account is obviously a heartfelt one, although his personal acceptance and enthusiasm for American "imperialism" nearly edge this account from a firsthand immersion one into political proselytizing. What there can be no doubt of is Kaplan's admiration for all the members of the U.S. Marines, Army, Air Force, and Navy whom he meets. The book is organized geographically, with each section corresponding to different theaters of operations referred to as "coms" (e.g., CENTCOM and PACOM) and covers events during the years of 2002 to the 2004 Battle of Fallujah.

Subjects: Government, Iraq, Middle East, Military, Politics, Travel, War Reporting, World History

Now Try: Other books that provide insight into the experiences of military infantry and other personnel on the front lines include ***Black Hawk Down*** by Mark Bowden, ***The Long Road Home*** by Martha Raddatz, Bing West's ***No True Glory: A Frontline Account of the Battle for Fallujah***, Marcus Luttrell's ***Lone Survivor***, and Michael Gordon's ***Cobra II***, as well as titles by venerable war reporter Ernie Pyle, might be suggested. Also of interest might be novels by such military fiction and techno-thriller authors as Tom Clancy, James Bradley, Dale Brown, W. E. B. Griffin, or Larry Bond.

O'Donnell, Patrick

We Were One: Shoulder to Shoulder with the Marines Who Took Fallujah. Da Capo. 2006. 244 pp. ISBN 9780306814693.

In this riveting firsthand account of the brutal 2004 Battle of Fallujah in Iraq, journalist O'Donnell writes not only with battleground immediacy but also with an eye for the telling human detail. In the Marine platoon with which O'Donnell traveled, he found four pairs of best friends who lived and fought in close quarters with one another, and he tracks their reactions when each of the four lose their compatriot in battle. Nor does O'Donnell sugarcoat the realities of battle; he describes insurgents fighting to the death, as well as other such disturbing scenes as the use of civilians to lure military personnel into buildings that were rigged with explosives. In true journalistic style O'Donnell concludes his narrative with a detailed chronology of the Battle of Fallujah and an epilogue detailing the whereabouts of those individuals he described throughout his text.

Subjects: Friendships, Iraq, Iraq War (2003), Marines, Military, Oral Histories, War Reporting, Work Relationships

Now Try: Readers pulled along by the force of O'Donnell's personal reporting might consider other firsthand military accounts, such as Anthony Swofford's *Jarhead*, Robert Kaplan's *Imperial Grunts: On the Ground with the American Military, from Mongolia to the Philippines to Iraq and Beyond*, Martha Raddatz's *The Long Road Home*, Mark Bowden's *Black Hawk Down*, Marcus Luttrell's *Lone Survivor*, or War Reporting classics by Martha Gellhorn, Ernie Pyle, or Donald Kirk (not to mention historians such as Stephen Ambrose or James Bradley).

Raddatz, Martha

The Long Road Home: A Story of War and Family. Putnam. 2007. 310 pp. ISBN 9780399153822.

ABC news correspondent Raddatz relates the story of the April 4, 2004, battle between American forces and insurgents in Baghdad's Sadr City from the viewpoints of multiple commanding officers of the operation, as well as ground troops. Numerous interviews with those involved in the battle gives this account a personal and immediate feel as opposed to a political stance.

Subjects: Character Profiles, Family Relationships, Friendships, Iraq, Iraq War (2003), Military, War Reporting

Now Try: Fans of Raddatz's more human-interest style reporting might enjoy related works such as Lee Woodruff's *In An Instant: A Family's Journey of Love and Healing*, Patrick O'Donnell's *We Were One: Shoulder to Shoulder with the Marines Who Took Fallujah*, Richard Jadick's and Thomas Hayden's *On Call in Hell: A Doctor's Iraq War Story*, David Danelo's *Blood Stripes: The Grunt's View of the War in Iraq*, and Jay Kopelman's *From Baghdad, with Love: A Marine, a War, and a Dog Named Lava*. Other True Adventure nonfiction works on the subjects of battles and war might also appeal to these readers, including Mark Bowden's *Black Hawk Down*, David Howarth's *We Die Alone*, Hampton Sides's *Ghost Soldiers*, or James Hirsch's *Two Souls Indivisible: The Friendship That Saved Two POWs in Vietnam*.

Cultural Criticism

I'm not trying to put you to sleep with a heading like "Cultural Criticism"—honestly! It's just the best phrase available to describe the following collections of critical writings and essays, in which authors review and critique creative endeavors from artwork to books and literary concerns, theater to television, film to avant-garde pop culture art forms for which there is, as yet, no heading.

So what are cultural and critical essay collections doing in a chapter on "In-Depth Reporting"? Although most of the titles in this chapter have emphasized "in the field" investigations, research, travels, and interviews, the following are titles in which the authors largely stay put. But this does not really make their books any less investigative; there is simply a different focus on what is being investigated. In these books, the authors report on cultural trends, writers' and artists' bodies of work, and generally display their broad knowledge in their specific areas of expertise. These books also belong firmly in both the investigative and journalistic canon, because many of the authors in this category are well-known in their own critical spheres and their careers in writing reviews for newspapers, magazines, and other periodicals; as such, they may appeal to readers based on their name recognition alone (John Leonard or Lee Siegel, for instance). Whereas other In-Depth authors interview those individuals and stories that make up our culture, these authors simply remove themselves one step from the action, and investigate the products of those cultural producers and artists. And they do so in a highly knowledgeable way, considering not only individual artists and works of art but also how that art affects (and is affected by) the rest of our society.

The authors who write books of this type tend to be well-read and skilled stylists in their own right, and because they are often reviewing or discussing the work of others, these books can have a very thoughtful and reflective tone. Readers who enjoy these books might enjoy other reflective types of nonfiction, including Reflective Environmental Writing titles (many of which themselves contain or are collections of essays) or a wide variety of more scholarly or Making Sense . . . books (including titles by such well-regarded and knowledgeable authors as Malcolm Gladwell, Jared Diamond, Alain de Botton, David Denby, Lawrence Lessig, or Alberto Manguel. Literary fiction by more adventurous authors such as David Foster Wallace, Thomas Pynchon, Vladimir Nabokov, and, of course, by any of the authors reviewed in the following books, might also appeal to these readers.

Cultural Criticism books are written by specialized journalists and commentators who have expertise in a variety of media, from books and literature to television, movies, and entertainment (as well as cultural and societal movements and trends). These books don't typically feature interviews, but they do display their authors' research skills and subject expertise, and they are often produced in the form of essay and review collections.

Berger, John

🏵 *Selected Essays of John Berger.* Pantheon Books. 2001. 588 pp. ISBN 9780747554196.

Various reviewers have hailed Berger as "one of the greatest living writers of the English language" and a writer who can find "infinite meanings in that common but extraordinary thing, noticing." Among the things Berger notices in this collection of essays are styles of and reactions to artists (including Matisse, Goya, and Gauguin), essays inspired by Berger's life on a farm in the French Alps, his critiques of works of literature, and even personal revelations about his changing relationship with animals and their residence in zoos.

> **Subjects:** Art and Artists, Environmental Writing, Essays, France, Literary Lives
>
> **Awards:** ALA Notable
>
> **Now Try:** Readers who enjoy Berger's smart but personable essays might also enjoy his small volume *Hold Everything Dear: Dispatches on Survival and Resistance* (which is very serious in subject but displays Berger's unique style), as well as essay collections by Barbara Holland (*They Went Whistling*, *Endangered Pleasures*, and *The Joy of Drinking*), Roland Barthes (*Mythologies* or *The Rustle of Language*), or Alain de Botton (*On Travel* and *Status Anxiety*). Expatriate travel books might also appeal, such as Frances Mayes's *Under the Tuscan Sun* or Peter Mayle's *A Year in Provence*.

Capote, Truman

Portraits and Observations: The Essays of Truman Capote. Random House. 2007. 518 pp. ISBN 9781400066612.

Most well known for his True Crime and new journalism classic *In Cold Blood*, Capote was also a skilled essayist; in this collection, readers can choose from among his travel essays (describing such locations as Brooklyn and Hollywood), thoughtful essays on the nature of fame and the demands of art, and character profiles of such individuals as Isak Dinesen, Mae West, Marcel Duchamp, Willa Cather, and Marilyn Monroe.

> **Subjects:** 20th Century, Book Reviews, Character Profiles, Essays, Literary Lives, Movie Stars, Pop Culture, Writers and Writing
>
> **Now Try:** Among his literary influences, Capote listed a number of classic and literary fiction writers, including such notables as Gustave Flaubert, Marcel Proust, Charles Dickens, Sarah Orne Jewett, and Edith Warren. Fans of his character profiles might consider *The Gay Talese Reader* (Talese being widely considered an infamous practitioner of the new journalism and a skilled writer of character profiles); likewise, Capote's own nonfiction and novels (including *Breakfast at Tiffany's* and *Other Voices, Other Rooms*) might appeal, as might fiction by Willa Cather, whom he describes in this essay collection with tenderness and grace.

Dirda, Michael

Bound to Please: Essays on Great Writers and Their Books. Norton. 2005. 525 pp. ISBN 9780393057577.

Dirda, contributor and editor at the *Washington Post Book World*, offers a collection of book reviews and literary musings from the past twenty years, covering largely ancient classics (Herodotus, the Bible, Ovid) but also more recent authors (Umberto Eco and Terry Pratchett). Organized in sections such as "Romantic Dreamers," "Visionaries and Moralists," and "Lovers, Poets, and Madmen," there should truly be something here for every lover of literature.

> **Subjects:** Book Reviews, Books and Learning, Essays, Literary Lives, Writers and Writing

> **Now Try:** Other "books on books" might appeal to these readers, including Anne Fadiman's *Ex Libris*, Sven Birkerts's *Readings*, Anna Quindlen's *How Reading Changed My Life*, A. J. Jacobs's *The Know-It-All*, or David Denby's *Great Books*. Other books by Dirda might also appeal to his readers, including his *Book by Book* and his memoir *An Open Book*. Other collections of book reviews, particularly volumes by Donna Seaman, Joyce Carol Oates, and Margaret Atwood might also be suggested.

Gross, Terry

All I Did Was Ask: Conversations with Writers, Actors, Musicians, and Artists. Hyperion. 2004. 353 pp. ISBN 9781401300104.

Longtime host of National Public Radio's *Fresh Air* program Gross offers a collection of some of her most memorable and provocative interviews over the past two decades (although a surprising number date from the earlier years of the program, without ever giving this collection a dated feel). At least one reviewer noted that good interviewing requires exhaustive research and good timing, two attributes Gross has developed to the highest degree. The luminaries interviewed here include Albert Brooks, Nicolas Cage, Johnny Cash, Samuel L. Jackson, Mary Karr, Chris Rock, John Updike, and many others.

> **Subjects:** Art and Artists, Celebrities and Superstars, Entertainers, Journalism, Literary Lives, Music and Musicians, Pop Culture

> **Now Try:** Other collections of interviews might be offered to fans of this volume, including Donna Seaman's *Writers on the Air: Conversations about Books*, *I Thought My Father Was God: And Other True Tales from NPR's National Story Project*, or Studs Terkel's *Working*. A wide variety of Celebrities and Superstars biographies, or biographies of Artists, Entertainers, and Writers might also appeal to these readers.

Hardwick, Elizabeth

American Fictions. Modern Library. 1999. 352 pp. ISBN 9780375754821.

Author Hardwick was also a novelist of some repute but is most well known for her literary criticism and essays about authors and books. In this collection, she offers reviews on such authors as Sylvia Plath, Truman Capote, Norman Mailer, and Edith Wharton, among many others. Lively and erudite, many of these essays consider classic American authors and may be considered to be out-of-date in its coverage, but her skill at combining biographical, literary, and cultural details makes this a classic still very much worth reading.

> **Subjects:** Authors, Book Reviews, Books and Learning, Classics, Essays, Literary Lives

> **Now Try:** In addition to novels by Hardwick (*Sleepless Nights*, *Simple Truth*, and *The Ghostly Lover*), these readers might also consider works by the authors she writes about, including their essay and literary collections (e.g., Truman Capote's *Portraits and Observations*). Books by other classic authors might also be suggested, including those by Virginia Woolf, Joan Didion, Mary McCarthy, M. F. K. Fisher, or Gertrude Stein; Dubravka Ugresic's enjoyable critique of the current publishing business, *Thank You for Not Reading*, might also be suggested.

Hornby, Nick

🏷 *Songbook.* McSweeney's Books. 2002. 147 pp. ISBN 9781573223560.

British author and essayist Hornby offers thirty-one essays (each about five to ten pages in length) that read like love letters to his favorite songs. Always an engaging read, Hornby is no different in this collection, managing to find surprising levels of meaning and enjoyment in listening to and writing about a wide variety of songs and music, including Nelly Furtado, Rufus Wainwright, the Beatles, Paul Westerberg, Aimee Mann, Bruce Springsteen, and many others. Depending on where you find this book, also, it should be accompanied by a CD with all of the songs about which Hornby writes.

> **Subjects:** Essays, Humor, Music and Musicians, Pop Culture, Quick Reads, Small Press
>
> **Awards:** New York Times Notable
>
> **Now Try:** Music plays a big part in Hornby's fiction and other essay collections, including his novels *High Fidelity* and *About a Boy*, and his essay collections *Housekeeping vs. The Dirt* and *The Polysyllabic Spree* (okay, music not so much in that last one, in which he provides essays on his reading habits and choices). Other pop culture essay collections, particularly those written by Chuck Klosterman *(Fargo Rock City)* or Steve Almond *(Not That You Asked)* might also appeal, as might titles by David Rakoff and Jim Knipfel.

Leonard, John

Lonesome Rangers: Homeless Minds, Promised Lands, Fugitive Cultures. Norton. 1997. 318 pp. ISBN 9781565846944.

Longtime book reviewer for *The Nation* and former editor of the *New York Times Book Review* offers a collection of his literary and cultural reviews, discussing such literati and their works as Mary McCarthy, Elizabeth Hardwick, Saul Bellow, Norman Podhoretz, Bruce Chatwin, and Salman Rushdie. Although not received well by various critics, this is nonetheless a wide-ranging volume by a sharp writer who has witnessed a lot of literary and cultural history of the past several decades.

> **Subjects:** Book Reviews, Essays, Literary Lives, Pop Culture, Writers and Writing
>
> **Now Try:** Any of the authors Leonard reviews might be enjoyed by these readers; readers may consider works by other writers whose work Leonard has introduced, such as Joan Didion (in the collection *We Tell Ourselves Stories In Order to Live*) or *These United States: Original Essays by Leading American Authors on Their State within The Union*. Other art and cultural critics such as Anthony Lane (*Nobody's Perfect: Writings from the New Yorker*) and Lee Siegel might also appeal to Leonard's readers.

Oates, Joyce Carol

Uncensored: Views & (Re)views. Ecco. 2005. 370 pp. ISBN 9780060775568.

In this collection Oates, herself a prolific novelist and essayist, offers her literary reviews (most of which are positive but not fawning; Oates introduces her collection by saying it was not her intention to review books negatively) of such authors as Willa Cather, Sylvia Plath, William Trevor, Anita Brookner, Mary Karr, and many more; she also comments on such literary world discussions as the memoir crisis after allegations of James Frey's fabricating knowledge, as well as on a variety of other cultural figures including Muhammad Ali and Bela Lugosi.

> **Subjects:** Book Reviews, Essays, Literary Lives, Pop Culture, Writers and Writing
>
> **Now Try:** Those readers who most enjoy Oates's skillful writing might consider any of her many novels; her most recent include *The Gravedigger's Daughter*, *Black Girl/White Girl*, *Sexy*, and *The Falls*; her other nonfiction collections *Joyce Carol Oates: Conversations, 1970 to 2006* or *The Faith of a Writer* might also appeal. Any of the many authors she reviews, including those listed earlier, as well as Kazuo Ishiguro, Alice Sebold, and Carson McCullers might be suggested; as might other literary essay collections such as *Ex Libris* or *Rereadings* by Anne Fadiman, Sven Birkerts's *Reading Life*, Cynthia Ozick's *The Din in the Head*, or Margaret Atwood's *Writing with Intent*.

Rosenbaum, Ron

The Secret Parts of Fortune: Three Decades of Intense Investigations and Edgy Enthusiasms. Random House. 2000. 799 pp. ISBN 9780375503382.

This wide-ranging collection of journalistic pieces reflects Rosenbaum's three decades of columns, feature writing, and essays published in such magazines as *Harper's*, *The New Yorker*, *Esquire*, and the *New York Times Magazine*; they cover topics from literature to politics, thoughts on such public figures as Elvis, Bill Gates, and Oliver Stone; "secret" stories such as the rituals undertaken by Yale's Skull and Bones society, his love letter to Rosanne Cash, and the birth of hacker culture. The pieces were published in the decades of the '70s, '80s, and '90s, and although the book itself is very long, each piece ranges from ten to twenty pages in length, and most are compellingly written quick reads. If you have readers who pride themselves on being "generalists" or having a wide spectrum of interests, this is most certainly the collection for them.

> **Subjects:** 1970s, 1980s, 1990s, Character Profiles, Epic Reads, Essays, Pop Culture, Society
>
> **Now Try:** Rosenbaum is a well-known author in literary nonfiction circles; his fans might consider titles by other giants in the genre, including *Up in the Old Hotel* by Joseph Mitchell, *Fame and Obscurity* by Gay Talese, *Road Work* by Mark Bowden, *Saturday Night* by Susan Orlean, or essay collections by E. B. White, Susan Sontag, or John Updike. Rosenbaum also offers his thoughts on classic fiction works by authors such as J. D. Salinger, Thomas Pynchon, and even Charles Dickens; titles by any of those authors and other "classic" authors might also appeal to these readers.

Siegel, Lee

Falling Upwards: Essays in Defense of the Imagination. Basic Books. 2006. 337 pp. ISBN 9780465078004.

Cultural critic and essayist Siegel provides his opinions on such pop culture staples as films (*Eyes Wide Shut*), television (*Sex and the City*), literature (Saul Bellow, Dante, J. K. Rowling), and art (Soviet paintings in Soho). Siegel is a skilled and witty writer and brings a level of seemingly heartfelt engagement with his subject, even when he is being less than complimentary toward it, which makes this a quick-reading but still culturally enlightening collection. One of the themes throughout his work is a fascination with calling the creators of art he considers blatantly manufactured for only its financial (rather than aesthetic) rewards on their disservice to art and imagination.

Subjects: Book Reviews, Essays, Literary Lives, Pop Culture

Now Try: Siegel's other nonfiction titles, *Not Remotely Controlled* or *Against the Machine: Being Human in the Age of the Electronic Mob* might also appeal. Other pop culture and literary essayists might be offered to Siegel's readers, including Chuck Klosterman, Dale Peck, and David Rakoff; readers might also consider classic fiction by authors Siegel writes about, including Jane Austen and Saul Bellow. Authors who provided blurbs for Siegel's book might also be considered: Pete Hamill or David Rieff; books by such nonfiction virtuosos as Calvin Trillin and John Gregory Dunne might also appeal.

Updike, John

🎗 *Due Considerations: Essays and Criticism.* Knopf. 2007. 703 pp. ISBN 9780307266408.

Novelist Updike has also produced a healthy number of book reviews, cultural essays, and introductions to other books; they are collected together in this volume, which consists of every nonfiction piece he's published over the eight years before its publication. From discussions of art and sexual politics to reviews of contemporary novels, all of these essays highlight Updike's trademark eloquence, none more so than the essay in which he admits his love of books as objects: "Smaller than a breadbox, bigger than a TV remote, the average book fits into the human hand with a seductive nestling, a kiss of texture, whether of cover cloth, glazed jacket, or flexible paperback."

Subjects: Book Reviews, Books and Learning, Essays, Literary Lives, Writers and Writing

Awards: New York Times Notable Books

Now Try: Authors reviewed by Updike include Gabriel García Márquez, Alan Hollinghurst, Alice Munro, Margaret Atwood, Orhan Pamuk, and Michael Ondaatje; any of these literary fiction authors' works might be offered to his readers. His earlier essay collections, *Hugging the Shore* and *Odd Jobs* might also appeal, as might his novels. Other collections of literary reviews, such as Michael Dirda's *Bound to Please*, David Remnick's *Reporting: Writings from The New Yorker*, Margaret Atwood's *Writing with Intent*, or Joyce Carol Oates's *Uncensored: Views & (Re)views* might also be offered.

Fiction Read-Alikes

- **Achebe, Chinua.** Achebe's socially conscious novels *Things Fall Apart*, *A Man of the People*, or *Home and Exile* might appeal to fans of In-Depth Reporting.

- **Atkinson, Kate.** Fans of True Crime Reporting might enjoy Atkinson's tightly plotted suspense novels *Case Histories* and *One Good Turn*.

- **Banks, Russell.** Banks's realistic and nuanced novels of working-class families and communities explore how different characters arrive at the truth of events; they include *Continental Drift, Affliction,* and *The Sweet Hereafter.*

- **Brooks, Geraldine.** Brooks puts her journalistic background to use in her detailed yet lively historical fiction novels *March, People of the Book,* and *Year of Wonders: A Novel of the Plague.*

- **Crichton, Michael.** Crichton's thrillers, which range from techno-thrillers to science fiction, might appeal to readers who enjoy the focus in In-Depth Reporting on evidence and research; his titles include *The Andromeda Strain, Congo, Jurassic Park,* and *Next.*

- **Deford, Frank.** Deford is a well-known sports journalist who has also written a number of sports novels, including *The Entitled, Everybody's All-American,* and *An American Summer.*

- **Hemingway, Ernest.** Hemingway's classic novels and short stories might particularly appeal to readers who enjoy Historical Perspectives or War Reporting books; they include *The Sun Also Rises, A Farewell to Arms, For Whom the Bell Tolls,* and *The Snows of Kilimanjaro.*

- **Hiaasen, Carl.** Hiaasen is an award-winning investigative journalist who also writes humorous, incisive novels such as *Tourist Season, Double Whammy, Strip Tease,* and *Basket Case.*

- **Margolin, Phillip.** Margolin, a former attorney, also writes legal thrillers featuring young attorneys as characters; they might particularly appeal to True Crime Reporting readers, and include *The Last Innocent Man, Gone, but Not Forgotten, Wild Justice,* and *Lost Lake.*

- **Russo, Richard.** Russo's realistic novels, often offering an unflinching look at communities struggling economically and socially, might appeal to these readers: *Nobody's Fool, Straight Man, Empire of Falls,* and *Bridge of Sighs.*

Further Reading

Auletta, Ken. 2003. *Backstory: Inside the Business of News.* New York: Penguin Press.

The Best American Crime Writing (serial). 2002–2006. New York: Pantheon.

The Best American Magazine Writing (serial). 2000–. Boston: Houghton Mifflin.

The Best American Nonrequired Reading (serial). 2002–. Boston: Houghton Mifflin.

The Best American Science and Nature Writing (serial). 2000–. Boston: Houghton Mifflin.

The Best American Sports Writing (serial). 2001–. Boston: Houghton Mifflin.

Madigan, Charles, ed. *30: The Collapse of the Great American Newspaper.* 2007. Chicago: Ivan R. Dee.

Schechter, Harold, and David Everitt. 2006. *The A to Z Encyclopedia of Serial Killers.* New York: Pocket Books.

References

Fallows, James. 2006. *Blind into Baghdad: America's War in Iraq*. New York: Vintage.

Glass, Ira, ed. 2007. *The New Kings of Nonfiction*. New York: Riverhead Books.

Hennessy, Brendan. 2006. *Writing Feature Articles*. 4th edition. Burlington, MA: Focal Press.

Knightley, Phillip. 1975. *The First Casualty, From the Crimea to Vietnam: The War Correspondent as Hero, Propagandist, and Myth Maker*. New York: Harcourt Brace Jovanovich.

Stephens, Mitchell. 1988. *A History of News: From the Drum to the Satellite*. New York: Viking.

Talese, Gay. 1969. *The Kingdom and the Power*. New York: World.

Tebbel, John. 1969. *The Compact History of the American Newspaper*. New York: Hawthorn Books.

Tebbel, John. 1974. *The Media in America: How They Have Shaped Our History and Culture*. New York: Crowell.

Weintraub, Robert. 2007. "Play (Hard) Ball! Why the Sports Beat Must Evolve." *Columbia Journalism Review* (September/October): 14–16.

Chapter 2

Exposés

Definition of Exposés

There are nearly as many definitions for what exposés are as there are skilled writers of them; the latest edition of *Merriam-Webster's Collegiate Dictionary* defines them as both a "formal statement of facts" and "an exposure of something discreditable"; Lincoln Steffens, one of the first producers of this type of writing for magazines and newspapers, called it "journalistic investigations." *Chicago Tribune* columnist Bob Greene defined it as "uncovering something somebody wants to keep secret" (Shapiro 2003, xv). For many years, at the turn of the twentieth century, it was referred to simply as "muckraking," a term introduced by Teddy Roosevelt, who had grown weary of this type of journalism exposing numerous examples of government and corporate abuses of power and corruption. At Wikipedia, the definition for "journalism" includes categories of "advocacy journalism" (in which authors "intentionally and transparently adopt a non-objective viewpoint") and "watchdog journalism," which is defined as journalism in which authors want to hold "accountable public personalities and institutions whose functions impact social and political life" (Wikipedia 2008). Because I have already used the phrase "investigative writing" to explore this stylistic genre as a whole, and because the word muckraking is very much linked to the early twentieth century, I have decided to refer to the books in this chapter as Exposés. I also, quite simply, like the connection between that word and the authors' intent, in the following titles, to expose stories of corruption, greed, incompetence, evil, and wrongdoing in various forms.

As was the case in the chapter on works of In-Depth Reporting, these titles rest solidly upon a strong historical tradition. It is suggested in Ann Bausum's history *Muckrakers* that one of the first truly muckraking journalistic articles appeared in 1858 (when "The Swill Milk Trade of New York and Brooklyn" ran in *Frank Leslie's Illustrated Newspaper*, and blew wide open the story of city cows producing poor milk because they were being fed swill); later in the nineteenth century, war correspondents would file stories from their vantage points on the front lines of Civil War battles to describe the horrors of war. By 1871 reporters for the *New York Times* had told the story of Boss Tweed's stranglehold on government power and corruption, and Nellie Bly went undercover in a mental asylum for ten days in 1887 to write a damning account of her experiences (and those of her truly suffering co-residents of the institution) for the *New York World*. Book-length works supported with facts, eyewitness reports, and even photography soon followed with the publication of Jacob Riis's *How the Other Half Lives* in 1890, documenting the ghetto conditions in Manhattan's immigrant neighborhoods; Ida Tarbell's two-volume book *The History of the Standard Oil Company* was published in 1904; Upton Sinclair's novel (although it was based on fact and Sinclair's research in Chicago) *The Jungle*, published in 1906, told readers much more than they ever wanted to know about the meatpacking industry.

Although the golden age of muckraking passed after the first two decades of the twentieth century, author Bruce Shapiro traces its continued presence and development in the women's magazines of the 1920s and the radical modern journalists (many of whom were writers of realistic novels, including John Steinbeck, F. Scott Fitzgerald, and Ernest Hemingway) of the 1930s; the format exploded into popularity once more with the publication in 1962 of the classic *Silent Spring* (an environmental exposé) by Rachel Carson. Jessica Mitford's *The American Way of Death*, about unscrupulous business practices in the funeral industry, published in 1963, and Ralph Nader's *Unsafe at Any Speed*, about automobile safety standards (or the lack thereof), published in 1965, made this decade one of the richest ever for investigative books. Journalists also kept busy during the 1960s, particularly Seymour Hersh, who broke the story of the My Lai massacre in Vietnam in 1969, although at first no newspapers wanted to publish the report. It was eventually distributed to only thirty-five newspapers by the tiny Dispatch News Service (Johnson 1971, 115). In 1974 two relatively unknown reporters named Bob Woodward and Carl Bernstein published their book about burglaries at the Washington, D.C., Watergate Hotel and President Richard Nixon's connections to that crime, *All the President's Men*. More than three decades later, their names are still two of the most well known among American journalists.

More recent advances have become too numerous to list here (even with their increase in numbers, many of these books continue to be not only story-breakers but well-crafted works of prose as well), although hugely popular titles as Eric Schlosser's 2001 *Fast Food Nation* and John Perkins's 2004 *Confessions of an Economic Hit Man* continued to resonate with readers and maintained their spots on best-seller lists long after their initial publication dates. In addition to the historical tradition the authors listed in this chapter share with their muckraking counterparts from the last century, they also share a dedication to constant and common themes: "electoral corruption, slavery, Jim Crow, and the legacy of racism; workplace exploitation, the concentrated power of corporations and financiers" among them, as noted in Bruce Shapiro's *Shaking the Foundations* (Shapiro 2003, xix). Shapiro further notes that Exposé authors also have hammered out a unique literary style all their own, because these "journalists have had to be literary and intellectual innovators, constantly creating the techniques of research and storytelling and analysis for a democratic and unregulated press" and further noting that these journalists often have to shape compelling stories out of the driest court, financial, and forensic evidence (Shapiro 2003, xxii).

Veteran journalist and author Pete Hamill, writing in the foreword to Shapiro's history of the form, also offers his idea of what makes this subgenre of Exposé writing truly unique, noting that its reporters don't often need to place themselves in physical danger or be in the right spot at the right time to celebrate triumphs of human nature and will (as do many other reporters, war correspondents and sports and human interest reporters among them). Instead, he notes, these authors share "an almost obsessive tenacity" that allows them to work and investigate and question until they have the answers that they set out to find. They also, he concludes, are surprising people, with vague politics, but rather "an almost permanent skepticism about human virtue, political or otherwise" (Shapiro 2003, x). These qualities may not make them the cheeriest of human beings, but it does seemingly help them to produce books that tell the untold stories, reveal the secret histories, and find things that others have wanted to keep hidden.

> Investigative Exposés are fact-heavy stories that expose the details behind shocking stories, government cover-ups, appalling incidences of incompetence or evil design, or widespread and pervasive conspiracies. Exposé authors use their considerable narrative skills to tell compelling stories, and often offer suggestions or opinions for change.

Appeal of Exposés

Readers will often be drawn to these titles depending on their subject interests, but not always. Many readers, for instance, who heard about, read about, were disturbed by, and went on to rave about Eric Schlosser's *Fast Food Nation* probably didn't stop by the library one day and ask for a recent book on either the business models of fast-food chains or the health risks inherent in a diet high in saturated fats and sugar. Indeed, until these authors make it clear what subjects and stories have been hidden from public view, how will readers know what stories to ask for? Yes, readers with an interest in green or sustainable lifestyles might be particularly drawn to Exposés of chemical-producing companies and the mechanics of food engineering and genetically modified crops, whereas those readers with an interest in conspiracy theories might find a lot to like in a variety of titles exposing political misdeeds. But subject is not the only aspect of these books that might appeal to readers.

Perhaps more than any stylistic subgenre in this collection, the appeal of the Exposé is directly linked to its author's ability to tell the story, and not only that: these readers demand the true story, the real story, the absolute inside scoop, the story *behind* the story. This is instructive when trying to define what it is that readers really like about these books, and most often it comes down not only to the story and the back story, but also the author's telling of that story in such a way and with such pacing that the reader finds herself unable to put the book down or stop reading, just as she might have difficulty with the most story-driven of page-turners and edge-of-the-seat novels. The appeal of the stories and pacing in these titles cannot be overstated. S. S. McClure, founder of *McClure's Magazine* and one of the most important supporters of muckraking journalism, understood this fact and paid his reporters a salary rather than a fee per story, so they could perform research for years and concentrate on writing up their findings; he stated that when writers who worked for him wrote, they "must never be conscious of anything else . . . other than telling an absorbing story: the story is the thing" (Bausum 2007, 29).

These books might also be very popular now because of continuing recent trends noted by many who comment on and study journalism: the trends toward increased secrecy in government and the continuing concentration of media ownership into ever-fewer controlling corporations and individuals. (Readers interested in exactly who owns what, in terms of publishers and media sources, are advised to consult the online edition of the *Columbia Journalism Review* for their "Who Owns What" database, available at http://www.cjr.org/.) Ann Bausum is right to point out that "often it is journalists and other writers—not lawyers, government officials, or politicians—who step forward during those crucial moments when the country wobbles out of balance" (Bausum 2007, 13); readers' advisors should remember that, although these books are often discomfiting to read, their fans might still be comforted by the very fact that they're still being published.

All of the subgenres of Exposés relate closely to nonfiction History, particularly New Perspectives and Secret Histories. In this chapter perhaps more than in others, readers who enjoy titles in one subgenre will enjoy books from the other subgenres; many readers interested in learning more about business secrets will probably also be interested in government secrets, and vice versa. Essay collections might also appeal to these readers, because many essay authors are also typically opinionated and very skillful prose stylists who want to keep their readers turning the pages while simultaneously engaging their interest and thought. Fiction page-turners and thrillers, particularly those that offer conspiracy and cover-up plots, might particularly appeal to these readers, as might mainstream fiction novels with complex story lines (such as Donna Tartt's *The Secret History*). These readers might also consider a wide variety of titles from the In-Depth Reporting chapter, as well as the Business and Political Reporting chapters, depending on the subjects in which they are most interested.

Organization of the Chapter

Because two of the subgenres are so similar, it was rather a toss-up as to which should come first: *Government Exposés* or *Corporate Exposés*. Both offer titles that are story-driven, and both consider ways in which larger societal institutions (and the individuals who run them) sometimes abuse positions of power and influence. The decision to lead off with *Government Exposés* was made because the government is so often the target of conspiracy theorists and mistrust, and to mirror the larger structure of this book, in which Political Reporting precedes Business Reporting. *Social Exposés* follow immediately after, because the titles found in that category often combine a bit of malfeasance by both governments and corporations and also explore issues in a larger cultural framework. The chapter concludes with *International Exposés*, which, in addition to offering compelling stories and interesting characters, also offer a bit of variety and interest based on their settings (from Russia to countries in Africa and India to Mexico).

Government Exposés

Thanks to Woodward and Bernstein, the *Washington Post* reporters who wrote the scoop on the Watergate story and President Richard Nixon's role in it, Exposés of government corruption and misdeeds are generally the first type we think of when we picture this kind of writing. Sadly, there never seems to be any shortage of political corruption to expose, as the authors in this section prove time and time again. Although the broad subject is governmental and political corruption, incompetence, and cover-ups, the authors in this section investigate all manner of stories—from disaster and recovery stories, to narratives of poorly planned military offensives and policies, to secret histories and hidden stories of government surveillance, payoffs, abuses and misuses of power by presidents and other politicians, to human rights abuses.

As with most titles in this chapter, the majority of Government Exposés are story-driven narratives, although some also offer unsavory details and revelations about a number of less-than-sympathetic characters. Readers who enjoy these books might also find read-alikes in the Political Reporting chapter (particularly those in the Politics in Practice subgenre, in which authors provide more details about nitty-gritty details of democracy, such as how voting machines actually work and what the proliferation of blogs is doing to political campaigning). Nonfiction history books might also particularly appeal to these readers (especially those history books that provide new perspectives or are considered "secret histories"), as well as biographies of American presidents and other political leaders. Interestingly enough, governmental corruption and control has long been a theme in many novels in the Science Fiction genre (think George Orwell's *1984* or Max Barry's *Jennifer Government*), so many science fiction novels that are considered works of dystopian or bleak futures might also be suggested to these readers.

> Government Exposés are story-driven nonfiction narratives in which authors typically expose specific deeds, instances, or histories of corruption or wrongdoing in governmental and political affairs. They also feature strongly drawn and typically ambitious, if not overly sympathetic, characters, as well as the sensation of learning "secret" histories or previously untold stories that the authors go to some lengths to uncover and verify. They are often written by authors with a good deal of insider expertise in politics or political and governmental reporting.

Bernstein, Carl, and Bob Woodward

All the President's Men. Simon & Schuster. 1999 (1974). 349 pp. ISBN 9780671217815.

> The authors of this book, the nation's two most famous investigative reporters, tell the blow-by-blow history of one of the biggest news stories of the twentieth century. From the very first phone call relating that a burglary had been reported at the Watergate Hotel in Washington, D.C., on June 17, 1972, right through to the resignation of President Nixon, Bernstein and Woodward provide an action-filled narrative complete with secret sources ("Deep Throat") , threats to their safety, and a powerful president surrounded by loyal supporters.

Subjects: American History, Classics, Government, Journalism, Richard Nixon, Politics, Professions, Work Relationships

Now Try: The identity of Deep Throat has been revealed, and Bob Woodward got to write the sequel to his own classic, *The Secret Man: The Story of Watergate's Deep Throat*. A related autobiography to this story of investigative journalism is Katharine Graham's Pulitzer Prize–winning *Personal History*, in which her years spent working at the *Washington Post* and with Bernstein and Woodward occupy a large place in the narrative. Bernstein and Woodward, of course, have authored many books since this one was published; Carl Bernstein has produced a fantastic historical and literary biography of Pope John Paul II with *His Holiness: John Paul II and the Hidden History of Our Time* and *A Woman in Charge: The Life of Hillary Rodham Clinton*, and Woodward also received critical acclaim for *Plan of Attack* and *Bush at War*, both about the inner workings of George W. Bush's administration and foreign policy. A new perspective on Nixon's place in American culture and history is Rick Perlstein's *Nixonland: The Rise of a President and the Fracturing of America*.

Block, Robert C., and Christopher P. Cooper

Disaster: Hurricane Katrina and the Failure of Homeland Security. Times Books. 2006. 333 pp. ISBN 9780805081305.

Wall Street Journal reporters Block and Cooper make the case, using material from exclusive interviews with victims and local, state, and federal disaster response officials, that the emergency response systems in the United States are dangerously flawed, a theory they seek to prove by investigating the lack of coordination in the response to the devastation of the 2005 Hurricane Katrina disaster. In the course of their narrative, the authors take their readers behind the scenes in Louisiana, as well as inside the Federal Emergency Management Agency (FEMA) and the Department of Homeland Security. The narrative comprises three parts: planning before Hurricane Katrina, which included a hurricane simulation program that was underfunded and therefore cancelled; the actual events of the storm and its immediate aftermath; and finally, the response (or lack thereof) of relief agencies to evacuate citizens to safety and manage civil unrest and continuing environmental damage. Providing a list of what they feel were bad decisions, ignored facts, and poor management and communication, this is a book designed to serve as a wake-up call for Americans to demand more and better large-scale emergency response plans and procedures; otherwise, as the authors state, the most important lesson to emerge from the hurricane is that "when disaster strikes, we are all on our own" (p. 306).

Subjects: Disasters, Government, Hurricane Katrina, Hurricanes, New Orleans, Politics, Weather

Now Try: A number of other more descriptive books on Hurricane Katrina and its aftermath might be suggested, such as Jenni Bergal's *City Adrift*, Douglas Brinkley's *The Great Deluge*, Jed Horne's *Breach of Faith*, or even Andrei Codrescu's literary anthology *New Orleans, Mon Amour*. Other books about natural disasters might also be suggested, such as Mark Levine's *F5* (about tornadoes) or Erik Larson's *Isaac's Storm*. Other exposés about the government might appeal, such as Frank Rich's *The Greatest Story Ever Sold* or Jack Cafferty's *It's Getting Ugly Out There*.

Chait, Jonathan

The Big Con: The True Story of How Washington Got Hoodwinked and Hijacked by Crackpot Economics. Houghton Mifflin. 2007. 294 pp. ISBN 9780618685400.

> Senior editor at *The New Republic*, Chait offers his heavily researched evidence that the individuals most responsible for taking over the American political system are not neocons or theocons, but rather a small group of economic theorists who basically conned politicians and the media into pushing the adoption of their radical and unproved policies. With bleak humor and engaging writing, Chait offers outrageous character portraits of greedy politicians and pseudo-scientific academics alike, focusing particularly on the transformation of the Republican Party into a refuge for all comers with radical free market ideas.
>
> **Subjects:** 20th Century, Classism, Economics, Government, Politics, Society
>
> **Now Try:** Chait's well-researched book provides a ready-made bibliography for his readers, including titles from authors Thomas Frank (*What's the Matter with Kansas?*), Naomi Klein (*The Shock Doctrine*), Sidney Blumenthal (*How Bush Rules*), Ron Suskind (*The One-Percent Doctrine*), and Paul Krugman (*The Great Unraveling*). Those readers with a particular interest in economics and the theorists who were most influential in the twentieth century might also consider books by or about Milton Friedman, Alan Greenspan (*The Age of Turbulence*), Joseph Schumpeter, or Friedrich von Hayek (*The Road to Serfdom*).

Coll, Steve

🏅 *Ghost Wars: The Secret History of the CIA, Afghanistan, and Bin Laden, from the Soviet Invasion to September 10, 2001.* Penguin Press. 2004. 695 pp. ISBN 9781594200076.

> Coll, who covered Afghanistan for the *Washington Post* from 1989 to 1992, provides both an investigative tour de force and an impressive volume of history, exploring the aftermath of the Soviet invasion and occupation in Afghanistan and the subsequent rise of the Taliban, as well as the CIA's role in training and working with various factions in the region. Coll presents both the failures and successes of the agency, as well as a great amount of historical detail about politics and culture in Afghanistan and other nearby Islamic countries, and also investigates the roles of such individuals as "antiterrorism czar" Richard Clarke and George Tenet.
>
> **Subjects:** 1980s, 1990s, 9/11, Afghanistan, CIA, Epic Reads, Espionage, Government, Islam, Secret Histories, Taliban, Terrorism, World History
>
> **Awards:** Pulitzer Prize
>
> **Now Try:** Clarke and Tenet both play large roles in this narrative; their subsequent books *Against All Enemies* and *At the Center of the Storm* (respectively) might be suggested. Other books about history and politics might be offered, including Lawrence Wright's *The Looming Tower*, Tim Weiner's *Legacy of Ashes: The History of the CIA*, Robert Baer's *Sleeping with the Devil: How Washington Sold Our Soul for Saudi Crude*, or George Crile's *Charlie Wilson's War*; other secret histories such as James Risen's *State of War* or Linda Robinson's *Masters of Chaos* might also appeal. Coll's writing has been compared

favorably to Tom Clancy's; novels by that author or authors like Nelson DeMille and Frederick Forsyth might also be offered.

Gordon, Michael R., and Bernard Trainor

Cobra II: The Inside Story of the Invasion and Occupation of Iraq. Pantheon Books. 2006. 603 pp. ISBN 9780375422621.

Journalist Gordon and former Marine lieutenant general Trainor provide the insider's view of the 2003 invasion and occupation of Iraq, written in a style that aims for dispassionate, but which still asks many questions about the Bush administration's invasion planning and methods (or lack thereof). In addition to extensive research, the authors also draw on interviews with General Tommy Franks, Condoleezza Rice, and many other political officials and military personnel.

> **Subjects:** Book Groups, George W. Bush, Government, Iraq, Iraq War (2003), Middle East, Military
>
> **Now Try:** Michael R. Gordon and Bernard E. Trainor have collaborated before; fans of this title might also consider their earlier work, *The Generals' War: The Inside Story of the Conflict in the Gulf*. Other titles on the subject of the Iraq War might be offered, including *The Assassin's Gate: America in Iraq* by George Packer, *Fiasco* by Thomas Ricks, and *The One Percent Doctrine* by Ron Suskind (or even David Halberstam's reporting classic *The Best and the Brightest*, about the Vietnam War). Other books which describe ground combat, such as *Black Hawk Down*, by Mark Bowden, and *Tell It To the Dead*, by Donald Kirk, might also appeal to these readers.

Gup, Ted

Nation of Secrets: The Threat to Democracy and the American Way of Life. Doubleday. 2007. 322 pp. ISBN 9780385514750.

Gup's overall contention in this narrative is that a preoccupation with secrets and secrecy in our government, economic, and social institutions is steadily undermining the very facets of democracy—security, patriotism, and privacy—that the classification of secret information were originally intended to bolster. This confused thinking about which secrets should be made available to the public and which truly should be protected has led, in Gup's contention, to a "shadow system" of justice that is neither a workable system nor particularly just. Although the author spent years investigating this issue and his text is often complex, this is also a readable treatise and will appeal to many readers with broader interests in political science, sociology, and history.

> **Subjects:** American History, Companies, Government, Law and Lawyers, Privacy, Society
>
> **Now Try:** With their focus on surveillance methods and the new technologies behind them, books such as Katherine Albrecht's and Liz McIntyre's *Spychips: How Major Corporations and Government Plan to Track Your Every Move with RFID*, Dominic Streatfield's *Brainwash*, or Patrick Radden Keefe's *Chatter: Dispatches from the Secret World of Global Eavesdropping* might be suggested; the classic *Civil Disobedience* by Henry David Thoreau might also appeal to readers seeking to understand the philosophical underpinnings of democracy and other societal forces. The author also suggests Simon Singh's book *The Science of Secrecy* and Bob Woodward's *State of Denial*; political thrillers by authors including Jeffrey Archer, Frederick Forsyth, Joseph Finder, and David Morrell.

Hersh, Seymour M.

Cover-up: The Army's Secret Investigation of the Massacre at My Lai 4. Random House. 1972. 305 pp. ISBN 9780394474601.

This classic work details the Vietnam War incident at My Lai, where U.S. military personnel were charged with killing civilian men, women, and children in the absence of any attack or the presence of enemy soldiers. Hersh offers a story-driven narrative in which he systematically traces the cover-up from the event to the personnel in question to the commanding officers in the military and the planning of the attack and the Vietnam War in general. As explained in his preface, Hersh based the work primarily on "official transcripts and documents of an extended military investigation into the cover-up of My Lai 4."

> **Subjects:** 1960s, American History, Atrocities, Classics, Explicit Violence, Homicides, Military, My Lai, Vietnam War, War Reporting, World History

> **Now Try:** Other books about atrocities, although they are not light or easy books to read or suggest, might nonetheless be offered as read-alikes for this classic of investigative reporting, including Jean Hatzfeld's oral histories *Machete Season* or *Life Laid Bare* (about the Rwandan genocide), Iris Chang's *The Rape of Nanking* (about China in World War II), or Elie Wiesel's *Night* (or other titles about the Holocaust). Other books about the Vietnam War might be suggested, such as Neil Sheehan's classic *A Bright Shining Lie* or Tom Bissell's travel memoir *The Father of All Things*, as might more scholarly books about the effects of war and violence such as Theodore Nadelson's *Trained to Kill* or Chris Hedges's *War Is a Force That Gives Us Meaning*. Books from the time period might also be suggested, such as Dan Wakefield's *Supernation at Peace and War*. Hersh is one of America's most well-known investigative journalists; his other books include *Chain of Command: The Road from 9/11 to Abu Ghraib* and *The Dark Side of Camelot*.

Kean, Thomas H., Lee H. Hamilton, and Benjamin D. Rhodes

Without Precedent: The Inside Story of the 9/11 Commission. Knopf. 2006. 370 pp. ISBN 9780307263773.

Kean and Hamilton, chairman and vice-chair of the 9/11 Commission, respectively, offer their take on the political machinations that sometimes helped but mostly hampered their efforts to offer a coherent report of what really happened in the terrorist attacks of 9/11. The authors strive for an objective tone as they describe their interactions with politicians of both parties, Congress, family members of the victims, and the George W. Bush White House.

> **Subjects:** 9/11, George W. Bush, Government, Law and Lawyers, Politics, Terrorism

> **Now Try:** Those readers interested in this subject might also consider the official 9/11 Commission Report, Kristen Breitweiser's *Wake-Up Call: The Political Education of a 9/11 Widow*, Lawrence Wright's *The Looming Tower: Al-Qaeda and the Road to 9/11*, or William Langewiesche's *American Ground: Unbuilding the World Trade Center*.

MacArthur, John

The Selling of "Free Trade": NAFTA, Washington, and the Subversion of American Democracy. Hill and Wang. 2000. 388 pp. ISBN 9780809085316.

MacArthur, the publisher and president of *Harper's* magazine, provides a comprehensive history of the NAFTA (North American Free Trade Agreement) legislation and its passage through the political process, as well as how it really affected workers in America and across our borders, particularly in Mexico. In addition to examining the economic and social effects of the bill, the author also considers the personal and political motivations of the bill's "liberal" proponents, including President Bill Clinton, Richard Gephardt, and Bill Richardson.

> **Subjects:** 1990s, Business, Canada, Bill Clinton, Economics, Foreign Relations, Government, Mexico, NAFTA, Politics, Professions

> **Now Try:** Books on globalization and outsourcing might also appeal to these readers, including Louis Uchitelle's *The Disposable American*, John Bowe's *Nobodies*, or books on immigration and immigration policy such as Ruben Martinez's *Crossing Over: A Mexican Family on the Migrant Trail* or Miriam Davidson's *Life on the Line*. A wide variety of titles from the Political Reporting chapter (particularly those more on the left side of the political spectrum) might also appeal.

Margulies, Joseph Y.

Guantánamo and the Abuse of Presidential Power. Simon & Schuster. 2006. 322 pp. ISBN 9780743286855.

Although the author of this book is a human rights attorney and not a journalist, he still provides a valuable look at the often out-of-sight, out-of-mind world of political prisoners in detainee camps across the world. In four parts and concentrating on prison management and abuses since 2001, this book tells the story of Camp Delta in Cuba, how detainees' rights are currently being curtailed, how these abuses reflect on the administration of George W. Bush and the American rule of law, and the future of Camp Delta and similar camps. In addition to relating the history and background of such military facilities, Margulies also recounts the legal battle in which he was lead counsel: that of *Rasul v. Bush*, in which the Supreme Court eventually ruled that prisoners at Guantánamo Bay had the right to challenge the legality of their detention in a federal court of law.

> **Subjects:** Cuba, Guantánamo Bay, Human Rights, Law and Lawyers, Military, Politics, Prisons, Scholarly, Terrorism, Torture

> **Now Try:** Other books about political prisons and torture might be suggested, such as Mark Danner's *Torture and Truth*, Alfred McCoy's *A Question of Torture*, John Conroy's *Unspeakable Acts, Ordinary People: The Dynamics of Torture*, or Jon Ronson's less scholarly but still scary book *The Men Who Stare at Goats*. Other micro-histories such as Dominic Streatfeild's *Brainwash* or Phillip Zombardo's unsettling *The Lucifer Effect* might also be offered.

Marks, Stephen

Confessions of a Political Hitman: My Secret Life of Scandal, Corruption, Hypocrisy and Dirty Attacks That Decide Who Gets Elected (and Who Doesn't). Sourcebooks. 2007. 389 pp. ISBN 9781402208546.

After working for more than a decade as an "oppositional research" professional (read: one who performs research, or digs up the dirt, on political opponents) in politics, Marks heeded the call of his failing mental and physical health and left the field to write this tell-all, behind-the-scenes memoir. Relating stories from his own coming-of-age and growing political awareness, Marks relates anecdotes from his early days as "Oppo Man" and what he views as his many triumphs in finding obscure and harmful information regarding his clients' opponents, as well as how he helped create negative (and highly effective) negative campaign ads. In this quickly paced story, Marks makes it clear that his work, performed largely for members of the Republican Party, helped him see that no one is innocent in the high-stakes game of politics.

Subjects: Corruption, Elections, Government, Mass Media, Memoirs, Politics, Professions

Now Try: Fans of Marks's forthright and quickly paced tell-all might consider other "insider's looks" at a wide variety of professions, such as John Perkins's *Confessions of an Economic Hitman*, Richard Yancey's *Confessions of a Tax Collector*, or Tom Breitling's and Cal Fussman's *Double or Nothing: How Two Friends Risked It All to Buy One of Las Vegas's Legendary Casinos*; other nonfiction titles with larger-than-life characters might also be suggested, including Frank Abagnale's *Catch Me If You Can* or Ben Mezrich's *Rigged*. A wide variety of titles from the Political Reporting subgenre might also be of interest to these readers, including Jack Cafferty's *It's Getting Ugly Out There* or Eileen McGann's and Dick Morris's *Outrage*.

Mayer, Jane

The Dark Side: The Inside Story of How the War on Terror Turned into a War on American Ideals. Bantam Dell. 2008. 392 pp. ISBN 9780385526395.

New Yorker magazine correspondent Mayer exposes the details of the war on terrorism that the United States has pursued since 9/11, focusing specifically on preemptive wars, a willingness to engage in previously unused torture techniques, and a greater emphasis on monitoring the activities of private citizens. Mayer argues—forcefully—that these actions, among others, have consistently damaged America's reputation worldwide and have eroded previously untouchable Constitutional rights and practices.

Subjects: 9/11, Al Qaeda, Constitution, Foreign Relations, Government, Politics, Terrorism, Torture

Now Try: Many other exposés about the abuse of power by government might also be offered, including Steve Coll's *Ghost Wars: The Secret History of the CIA, Afghanistan, and Bin Laden* or *The Bin Ladens*, Ted Gup's *Nation of Secrets: The Threat to Democracy and the American Way of Life*, Joseph Margulies's *Guantánamo and the Abuse of Presidential Power*, or even Jon Ronson's *The Men Who Stare at Goats*. Other books about torture and the erosion of constitutional rights might also be suggested, such as Philip Gourevitch's *Standard Operating Procedure*, Dominic Streatfeild's *Brainwash: The Secret History of Mind Control*, or John Conroy's *Unspeakable Acts, Ordinary People: The Dynamics of Torture*. Political Reporting books from a more progressive viewpoint might also be suggested, such as Molly Ivins's *Bill of Wrongs* or Naomi Klein's *The Shock Doctrine: The Rise of Disaster Capitalism*.

Ronson, Jon

The Men Who Stare at Goats. Simon & Schuster. 2004. 259 pp. ISBN 9780743270601.

British journalist Ronson narrates one of the strangest investigative journalism trips ever taken: his journey to infiltrate a secret wing of the U.S. military named the First Earth Battalion, created in 1979 with the purpose of creating "Warrior Monks," or soldiers who were capable of such phenomenal abilities as walking through walls and killing goats simply by staring at them. Although the premise is fantastic, Ronson makes clear how deadly serious his investigation is, linking it to current military and psychological research on torture and mental warfare techniques. Although many of the individuals he interviews, including generals and other elite personnel from the unit, seem simply offbeat, the surreal nature of their training and techniques combines to make this an unsettling and fascinating read. Although bleakly humorous, Ronson clearly wants his reader to make a note of the import of his opening words: "This is a true story."

> **Subjects:** Animals, Character Profiles, Eccentrics, Government, Humor, Military, Parapsychology, Psychology, Quick Reads, Torture

> **Now Try:** Ronson's earlier book, *Them: Adventures with Extremists*, might also appeal to these readers, as might other books about torture, such as the essay collection *Torture* (edited by Kenneth Roth and Minky Worden), Phillip Zombardo's *The Lucifer Effect*, or Joseph Margulies's *Guantánamo and the Abuse of Presidential Power*. Dominic Streatfeild's compelling micro-history *Brainwash* might appeal, as might British ambassador Craig Murray's darkly humorous memoir *Dirty Diplomacy: The Rough-and-Tumble Adventures of a Scotch-Drinking, Skirt-Chasing, Dictator-Busting, and Thoroughly Unrepentant Ambassador Stuck on the Front Line against Terror.*

Stone, Peter Bennet

Heist: Superlobbyist Jack Abramoff, His Republican Allies, and the Buying of Washington. Farrar, Straus & Giroux. 2006. 214 pp. ISBN 9780374299316.

Stone blows the lid off at least one political lobbying scandal with this in-depth look into the connections and activities of "superlobbyist" Jack Abramoff, whose ties to Tom DeLay, Bob Ney, Ralph Reed, antitax activist Grover Norquist, and other members of the George W. Bush administration helped him and his partners become rich. Eventually his and former DeLay aid Michael Scanlon's plan to trade their influence in Congress for money (in the forms of "fees" to the amount of $82 million) from several Native American tribes seeking expanded casino rights would lead to a federal corruption probe and several criminal indictments of Abramoff and his associates.

> **Subjects:** Jack Abramoff, Companies, Corruption, Tom DeLay, Government, Politics

> **Now Try:** Other books about political corruption might be offered, including Lou Dubose's *The Hammer: Tom DeLay, God, Money and the Rise of the Republican Congress*, Matthew Continetti's *The K Street Gang*, or Frank Rich's *The Greatest Story Ever Sold*. Other books from the Political Reporting chapter might be offered, as might John Bowe's *Nobodies: Modern American Slave Labor and the Dark Side of the New Global Economy* (in which DeLay and his political activities make an appearance).

Corporate Exposés

The number and quality of titles in the Government Exposés subgenre are rivaled most closely by the number and quality of Corporate Exposés. If you have readers who want to read secret histories and inside stories, chances are you have a reader who will be open to reading about wrongdoing by either the government or by corporations and corrupt or incompetent business people. There was a reason that the Enron business scandal was so loudly reported and carefully followed by many individuals, even those who weren't employed by the company nor had any connection with it. It is as American as apple pie to believe, deep down, that everyone is out to take advantage of you, and nowhere is this belief more entrenched than in our daily dealings with companies, the free market, and, most annoyingly, those voicemail phone trees you have to call for any kind of service and that never let you talk to a real person.

But I digress. The titles in this section all report on a wide variety of corrupt or incompetent chief executives, questionable business practices, ethical dilemmas, and broadly based corporate malfeasance and malevolence in all its forms. Because they are about business—albeit some of the less savory aspects of business—many readers who are fascinated by these books might also enjoy a wide variety of books from the Business Reporting chapter, many of which offer more uplifting stories in the form of successful business's histories and business how-to books. Those readers who love getting the inside story might also of course consider the closely related titles above, from the Government Exposé section, as well as from the Social Exposés section. Also of particular interest might be Working World titles from the Immersion chapter, in which intrepid journalists actually work the jobs they're reporting; novels in which people's professions play a central part might also be of some interest, such as Stanley Bing's *You Look Lovely Today*, Douglas Coupland's Gen-X classic *Microserfs*, or Joshua Ferris's *Then We Come to the End*.

Corporate Exposés are story-driven nonfiction narratives in which authors typically expose specific deeds, instances, or histories of corruption or wrongdoing in business and particularly corporate affairs. They also feature strongly drawn and typically ambitious, if not overly sympathetic, characters, as well as the sensation of learning "secret" histories or previously untold stories that the authors go to some lengths to uncover and verify. They are often written by authors with a good deal of expertise in the business field or business reporting.

Barber, Charles

Comfortably Numb: How Psychiatry Is Medicating a Nation. Pantheon Books. 2008. 280 pp. ISBN 9780375423994.

Author Charles Barber, who spent more than a decade working with the mentally ill and homeless in New York City, provides an in-depth study on the prevalence of prescribing antidepressants in American psychiatry.

In addition to relating the latest statistics and research about the pharmaceutical industry (starting with the fact that the United States accounts for 66 percent of the global antidepressant market), Barber also traces the changing perceptions of mental health and our culture of "quick fixes," which has led to the treatment of a wide variety of mental and emotional issues solely with drugs. The second half of the book explores treatment alternatives and provides the author's findings about cognitive-behavioral therapy, more human interaction with patients, and emotional rescue.

Subjects: Business, Health Issues, Medicine, Mental Health, Pharmacology, Psychology

Now Try: Other books by and about those who have suffered from mental illness might be suggested, including Pete Earley's memoir *Crazy: A Father's Search through America's Mental Health Madness*, Kay Redfield Jamison's *The Unquiet Mind*, or Andrew Solomon's *The Noonday Demon: An Atlas of Depression*. Also of interest might be other exposés, particularly those about the medical field, such as Pete Rost's *The Whistleblower* or Stephen Klaidman's *Coronary: A True Story of Medicine Gone Awry*; other fiction and nonfiction titles about drug addictions or abuse might also be offered, such as William Cope Moyers's *Broken*, David Sheff's *Beautiful Boy*, or Augusten Burroughs's *Dry*. These readers might also consider books by authors who provided blurbs on this book, including David Healy (*Let Them Eat Prozac*) or Susan Jacoby (*The Age of American Unreason*).

Caldicott, Helen

Nuclear Power Is Not the Answer. New Press. 2006. 221 pp. ISBN 9781595580672.

Caldicott is no uninterested observer on the topic of nuclear power but is recognized worldwide for her antinuclear activism. In this manifesto, she makes her case regarding the myths of nuclear power (that it is "clean and green") and both the risks and costs of developing nuclear power plants. The author explains the timing of this book by pointing out the many controversies about the use of oil as an energy source, which is leading to a frenzied search for new and alternative sources of energy; most often that search leads to a push for more nuclear power-producing plants. Systematically answering what she refers to as the nuclear power industry's "propaganda," Caldicott lists her contentions that nuclear power contributes to global warming, the cost of producing such power is often high and relayed directly to taxpayers, uranium is scarce, and the potential for plant accidents or terrorist attacks to nuclear facilities is high. Throughout, her writing is impassioned but straightforward and concise, as is shown in this extract from her introduction: "It is also doubtful that the 8,358 individuals diagnosed between 1986 and 2001 with thyroid cancer in Belarus, downwind of Chernobyl, would choose the adjective 'safe' to describe nuclear power."

Subjects: Energy, Government, Military, Nuclear Power, Politics, Science, Sustainability

Now Try: William Langewiesche's coolly succinct look at nuclear weapons and power worldwide, *The Atomic Bazaar: The Rise of the Nuclear Poor*, might appeal to these readers, as might the more impassioned *Voices from Chernobyl* by Svetlana Alexievich. Other social critic authors including Bill McKibben or Naomi Klein might also be suggested, as might other titles about the energy industry, including Gordon Lee Weil's *Blackout: How the Electric Industry Exploits America* or Kurt Eichenwald's *Conspiracy of Fools* (about Enron).

Cohn, Jonathan

Sick: The Untold Story of America's Health Care Crisis—and the People Who Pay the Price. HarperCollins. 2007. 302 pp. ISBN 9780060580452.

Journalist Cohn exposes the crisis in health care in America—currently the only country in the developed world not to guarantee access to medical care as a basic right of citizenship—by offering primarily anecdotal and personal stories of individuals' experiences seeking health care that, in many cases, they cannot afford even when they can gain access to it. From Boston to South Central Los Angeles to the Midwest, Cohn interviews people who suffer heart attacks, blindness, and other debilitating effects of long-term illnesses such as heart disease and diabetes. In addition to relating these tragic and very personal stories, Cohn also offers a history and critique of how the health care industry has come to such a state through governance, a network of special interest influences, and lobbying by insurance companies. As a senior editor at the *New Republic*, Cohn's political tendency toward liberalism should be understood, but his in-depth reporting makes this an important and readable book.

Subjects: Character Profiles, Companies, Economics, Health Issues, Medicine, Politics, Society

Now Try: Shannon Brownlee's *Overtreated: Why Too Much Medicine Is Making Us Sicker and Poorer*, Melody Petersen's *Our Daily Meds: How the Pharmaceutical Companies Transformed Themselves into Slick Marketing Machines and Hooked the Nation on Prescription Drugs*, or Peter Rost's eye-opening memoir *The Whistleblower: Confessions of a Healthcare Hitman* might be suggested to these readers, as might Jamie Reidy's more lighthearted but still thoughtful *Hard Sell: The Evolution of a Viagra Salesman*. Andy Kessler's more personal *The End of Medicine: How Silicon Valley (and Naked Mice) Will Reboot Your Doctor* might appeal to Cohn's readers, as might books by more political authors including Barbara Ehrenreich, Thomas Frank, and David Shipler (or authors offering more insight into medicine, such as Atul Gawande or Jerome Groopman).

Curtis, Drew

It's Not News, It's Fark: How Mass Media Tries to Pass Off Crap as News. Gotham Books. 2007. 278 pp. ISBN 9781592402915.

Creator of the news Web site Fark.com, Curtis takes his readers on a sardonic tour of the current state of the news media, pointing out the non-newsworthy news that often dominates in the traditional media. He takes aim at seasonal stories ("roads will be crowded this holiday season"), fear-mongering and blatant supposition ("a tsunami could hit the Atlantic any day"), and a wide variety of other time-fillers and stock stories, including unpaid product placements masquerading as news articles and celebrity news and commentary) the media depends on to cheaply fill up newspapers, airwaves, and Internet publications.

Subjects: Business, Journalism, Mass Media, Pop Culture, Society

Now Try: There has never been any shortage of nonfiction books decrying the state of news coverage and the mass media in America; these include Bernard Goldberg's *Bias: A CBS Insider Exposes How the Media Distorts the News*, Ben Bagdikian's *The New Media Monopoly*, Eric Klinenberg's *Fighting for*

Air: The Battle to Control America's Media, Matt Drudge's *Drudge Manifesto*, Bonnie Anderson's *News Flash: Journalism, Infotainment, and the Bottom-Line Business of Broadcast News*, Barry Glassner's more scholarly *The Culture of Fear*, or titles by Robert McChesney; other books about the mass media include *The Gawker Guide to Conquering All Media*, while news satires such as Jon Stewart's *America: The Book*, Stephen Colbert's *I Am America (And So Can You!)*, and those published by the *Onion* newspaper might also make fun read-alikes.

Derber, Charles

Corporation Nation: How Corporations Are Taking Over Our Lives and What We Can Do about It. St. Martin's Press. 1998. 374 pp. ISBN 9780312192884.

Although now a decade old, Derber's investigation into what he contends is the growth in influence of the business and corporate culture on American society still offers many valid points for thought. Starting with the contentions that the United States is currently entering another Gilded Age, that thirty companies (at the time the book was written) dominate branding and market share, and that corporations display an outward disdain for federal assistance while depending on tax breaks and loopholes, Derber, a professor of sociology, strives to make the point that Americans should take a closer look at the histories and practices of the corporations whose products and services and they purchase and in whose stock they invest.

> **Subjects:** Business, Capitalism, Companies, Democracy, Foreign Relations, Politics, Professions, Society

> **Now Try:** Joel Bakan's *The Corporation: The Pathological Pursuit of Power* (and the documentary by the same title) might be suggested, as might Robert Reich's *Supercapitalism*, or Naomi Klein's *The Shock Doctrine*; other political books by authors from the left side of the political spectrum might also appeal, including those by William Greider, Thomas S. Frank, Tom Engelhardt, or Michael Moore. Other books about society and consumerism might be offered, including those by Juliet Schor or Christopher Lasch, while memoirs about individual workers' experiences in corporations might also appeal, such as *Hard Sell: The Evolution of a Viagra Salesman* by Jamie Reidy, James Marcus's *Amazonia*, or Peter Rost's *The Whistleblower*.

Fainaru-Wada, Mark and Lance Williams

Game of Shadows: Barry Bonds, BALCO, and the Steroids Scandal That Rocked Professional Sports. Gotham Books. 2006. 332 pp. ISBN 9781592401994.

Fainaru-Wada and Williams delved deep into the secret world of performance-enhancing sports drugs and offer a complete story of both those who develop and administer steroids and other drugs, as well as the athletes who are their customers and patients. Of particular interest in this volume is the Bay Area Laboratory Co-Operative (BALCO) in San Francisco and its presence in sports circles, as well as numerous big-name athletes whose careers have been rocked by this scandal, including Marion Jones, Mark McGwire, Barry Bonds, and Jason Giambi. The authors also profile Victor Conte, the director of BALCO, Barry Bonds, and even some of the fans whose ever-growing demands for the excitement of power hitters in the game led many all-round talented players to shift their focus to power hitting as well.

> **Subjects:** Baseball, Barry Bonds, Companies, Corruption, Health Issues, Sports, Steroids

Now Try: Readers who find this title will probably already be avid readers of baseball books; consider offering other books on that subject including Jose Canseco's *Juiced*, Seth Mnookin's *Feeding the Monster*, Michael Lewis's classic *Moneyball*, Gene Wojciechowski's *Cubs Nation: 162 Games. 162 Stories. 1 Addiction, Summer of '49* by David Halberstam, *The Ticket Out* by Michael Sokolove, or *The Last Best League* by Jim Collins. Sadly, books about systemic corruption might also be suggested, such as David Callahan's *The Cheating Culture*, John Perkins's *The Secret History of the American Empire: Economic Hit Men, Jackals, and the Truth about Global Corruption*, or Kurt Eichenwald's business classic *Conspiracy of Fools*.

Harney, Alexandra

The China Price: The True Cost of Chinese Competitive Advantage. Penguin. 2008. 336 pp. ISBN 9781594201578.

Harney exposes one of the causes of cheaper goods worldwide—namely, the Chinese economic model of exploiting workers and corruption in its factory economy. She also exposes the hypocrisy of such global corporations as Wal-Mart that pay lip service to human rights issues and "social responsibility codes" but whose demand (and the demand of consumers worldwide) for ever-cheaper goods leads to horrific and dangerous labor conditions throughout China and the world. The narrative also includes a closer look at growing grassroots and activist efforts for better regulation and more workers' rights for those employed in Chinese factories.

Subjects: Business, China, Consumerism, Globalization, Human Rights, Labor History

Now Try: Other books about global economics and working conditions might be suggested to these readers, such as John Bowe's *Nobodies: Modern American Slave Labor and the Dark Side of the New Global Economy* or Rachel Louise Snyder's *Fugitive Denim*. More stereotypical Business Reporting books about the rise of China's economy might also provide context for these readers; these include Ted C. Fishman's *China, Inc.*, James Kynge's *China Shakes the World*, Joe Studwell's *Asian Godfathers: Money and Power in Hong Kong and Southeast Asia*, or even Edward Luce's related *In Spite of the Gods: The Rise of Modern India*. Books about consumerism in America might also appeal, such as Sara Bongiorni's *A Year without "Made in China": One Family's True Life Adventure in the Global Economy*.

Harr, Jonathan

🏵 *A Civil Action.* Random House. 1995. 500 pp. ISBN 9780394563497.

Harr's book comes as close to novelistic writing as any work of nonfiction can be said to; using foreshadowing and building both strong characterizations and a suspenseful story, he relates the struggle of a number of residents of Woburn, Massachusetts, to prove that their children's diseases were attributable to heavy-metal pollution in their water. Part environmental history and part courtroom drama, the book focuses primarily on Anne Anderson, whose son died from leukemia, and Jan Schlichtmann, the lawyer who represented her and her neighbors and bankrupted himself in the process of proving corporate negligence in toxic waste disposal.

There is no real happy ending here, but the book, once started, is extremely hard to put down.

> **Subjects:** Book Groups, Business, Cancer, Classics, Community Life, Health Issues, Law and Lawyers, Pollution, Trials
>
> **Awards:** National Book Award
>
> **Now Try:** Other stories about underdogs and their days (or not) in court, including William Mishler's *A Measure of Endurance: The Unlikely Triumph of Steven Sharp*, Dennis Love's *My City Was Gone: One American Town's Toxic Secret, Its Angry Band of Locals, and a $700 Million Day in Court*, or Joy Horowitz's *Parts Per Million* might be good read-alikes, as might Terry Tempest Williams's environmental classic about her mother's health and the government's nuclear tests, *Refuge*. Gillian Klucas's *Leadville: The Struggle to Revive an American Town* tells the story of the battle to clean up toxic mining by-products in the town of Leadville, Colorado, and the town residents' complicated relationship with the Environmental Protection Agency and the mining companies. Legal thrillers by authors including John Grisham, Phillip Margolin, or Scott Turow might also appeal, as might Harr's other work of investigative journalism about the art world, *The Lost Painting*.

Horowitz, Joy

Parts Per Million: The Poisoning of Beverly Hills High School. Viking. 2007. 442 pp. ISBN 9780670037988.

In this in-depth description of the oil fields beneath Beverly Hills High School (the author's alma mater) and what may or may not be those fields' effects on the health of the school's students and teachers, Horowitz offers an impressively objective treatise on the difficulty of trying to attribute effects such as higher incidences of certain cancers to environmental causes. The book is organized into three parts, in which Horowitz relates the history of the oil industry in California and the specific fields under the school, the documented health crises related by the school's and community's residents, and detailed information from the lawsuit that was filed (and with which the infamous Erin Brockovich became involved) but largely dismissed by a local judge in 2006.

> **Subjects:** Beverly Hills, Erin Brockovich, Business Histories, California, Cancer, Community Life, Health Issues, Law and Lawyers, Oil
>
> **Now Try:** Other nonfiction classics featuring legal cases might be suggested, including Jonathan Harr's *A Civil Action*; William Mishler's *A Measure of Endurance*; and Terry Tempest Williams's environmental classic *Refuge*, about her mother's death from cancer (as well as Brian Fies's superlative graphic novel *Mom's Cancer*). Other books about the oil business might be offered, such as Lisa Margonelli's *Oil on the Brain* or Daniel Yergin's classic *The Prize*, as might books about other disasters and government cover-ups, such as Svetlana Alexievich's *Voices from Chernobyl* or Dennis Love's *My City Was Gone: One American Town's Toxic Secret, Its Angry Band of Locals, and a $700 Million Day in Court*, not to mention books about the culture of the state of California such as Joan Didion's *Where I Was From* or Mark Arax's *In My Father's Name*.

Hurley, Dan

Natural Causes: Death, Lies and Politics in America's Vitamin and Herbal Supplement Industry. Broadway Books. 2006. 324 pp. ISBN 9780767920421.

Hurley breaks the story of the number of deaths, disfigurements, and other injuries caused to consumers by herbal and dietary supplements, many of which are taken by individuals looking for more "safe" or "natural" alternatives than those offered them by the medical establishment. Although the media has been vocal about the risks of the weight-loss supplement Ephedra (the use of which was linked to the 2003 death of Baltimore Orioles pitcher Steve Belcher), the author suggests that not only are there risks involved with the unsupervised use of these unregulated products but that those risks are not being sufficiently investigated by consumers, health and government officials, or journalists or authors. Highlighting the passage of the Dietary Supplement Health and Education Act of 1994, he also shows how that act basically freed the industry from the more stringent FDA standards and regulations; combining horrific personal stories with case studies in which he proves the industry's knowledge regarding the truth of some of their more controversial products, Hurley provides a compelling and detailed read.

> **Subjects:** Business, Companies, Health Issues, Medicine
>
> **Now Try:** Related investigative works on health issues might be suggested, such as Randall Fitzgerald's *The Hundred-Year Lie*, Peter Rost's memoir *The Whistleblower: Confessions of a Healthcare Hitman*, or Dan Agin's *Junk Science: How Politicians, Corporations, and Other Hucksters Betray Us*. Mark Schapiro's *Exposed: The Toxic Chemistry of Everyday Products and What's At Stake for American Power* might also be of particular interest to these readers.

Kanner, Bernice, and David Verklin

Watch This, Listen Up, Click Here: Inside the 300 Billion Dollar Business Behind the Media You Constantly Consume. John Wiley. 2007. 221 pp. ISBN 9780470056431.

With the help of author and marketing expert Kanner, media-buying company CEO David Verklin gives his readers the inside scoop on how advertising dollars dictate the content of nearly all television, film, and Internet programming. Systematically providing information on how advertising spots are purchased in "medialand," the authors also explain how and why Oprah gives away cars, which magazines continue to get published, and how those individuals hoping to get a peek at how new technologies can be used for niche programming, dissemination, and billing should look at trends in the pornography industry, which is always on the cutting edge of broadcasting and publishing.

> **Subjects:** Advertising, Business, Companies, Marketing, Mass Media, Quick Reads
>
> **Now Try:** Although this is a business Exposé, the authors do not seem opposed to other books that are more favorable of business, such as Thomas Friedman's *The World Is Flat* or Stephen Dubner's and Steven Levitt's *Freakonomics* (they refer to both in their introduction). Other business books by Seth Godin or Chris Anderson (including his classic *The Long Tail*) might appeal, as might other books about the media and future technologies, such as Drew Curtis's *It's Not News, It's Fark* or Eric Klinenberg's *Fighting for Air*, or David Weinberger's *Everything Is Miscellaneous: The Power of the New Digital Disorder*.

Klaidman, Stephen

Coronary: A True Story of Medicine Gone Awry. Scribner. 2007. 303 pp. ISBN 9780743267540.

Journalist Klaidman tells the inside story of the Redding Medical Center, a for-profit hospital in California, and how two of its most prestigious surgeons performed numerous unnecessary heart bypasses and other surgical procedures simply to boost the hospital's financial earnings. In addition to examining the horrific consequences of fraud in a medical setting, Klaidman also examines the legal proceedings in these cases, which resulted in the offending doctors never being charged and unequal settlements for their many victims.

Subjects: Corruption, Doctors, Fraud, Health Issues, Hospitals, Medicine, True Crime

Now Try: Fans of Klaidman's scary exposé might enjoy similar investigative works on health care, including Thomas Edward Gass's memoir *Nobody's Home: Candid Reflections of a Nursing Home Aide,* Jonathan Cohn's *Sick: The Untold Story of America's Health Care Crisis,* Anne Fadiman's *The Spirit Catches You and You Fall Down,* Marcia Angell's *The Truth about the Drug Companies,* or Peter Rost's *The Whistleblower: Confessions of a Healthcare Hitman.* Medical thrillers by authors such as Robin Cook, Tess Gerritsen, or Michael Palmer might be suggested; as might financial thrillers by Joseph Finder or Stephen Frey.

Klinenberg, Eric

Fighting for Air: The Battle to Control America's Media. Metropolitan Books. 2007. 339 pp. ISBN 9780805078190.

Klinenberg explores how the quiet but insidious takeover of local media outlets by national and international corporations has adversely affected the dissemination of important local news and messages. The author opens his narrative with the shocking example of the 2002 train derailment accident in Minot, North Dakota, which sent a huge cloud of poisonous gas floating across the town, and which wasn't reported on the radio because all six local stations were owned by Clear Channel, and attempts to break into their programming to make a public service announcement were unsuccessful. Nor are radio stations the only ones affected; the author leads his reader on a tour of empty television news studios and newspapers filled only with content from the national wires and argues that the demise of independent and local media is directly attributable to political policies favoring deregulation and a lessening of government oversight.

Subjects: Business, Democracy, Government, Mass Media

Now Try: Drew Curtis's critique of the mass media, *It's Not News, It's Fark,* might appeal to these readers, as might Bernice Kanner's and David Verklin's *Watch This, Listen Up, Click Here: Inside the 300 Billion Dollar Business behind the Media You Constantly Consume,* Susanne Daniels's and Cynthia Littleton's memoir *Season Finale: The Unexpected Rise and Fall of the WB and UPN,* or Seth Mnookin's *Hard News: Twenty-one Brutal Months at the New York Times and How They Changed the American Media.* Other titles about corporations and their effect on American society might be offered, such as Charles Derber's *Corporation Nation: How Corporations Are Taking Over Our Lives and What We Can Do about It* or Stacy Mitchell's *Big-Box Swindle.*

Kluger, Richard

🏵 *Ashes to Ashes: America's Hundred-Year Cigarette War, the Public Health, and the Unabashed Triumph of Philip Morris.* Knopf. 1996. 807 pp. ISBN 9780394570761.

This vast history of an institution examines the public's love affair with cigarettes and smoking in the context of the tobacco industry, from cultivation to production to marketing, and all points in between. *Wall Street Journal* reporter Kluger's densely factual text is a vast and tirelessly researched work of investigative journalism that exposes all sides of the smoking debate and provides particular insight into the company histories of both R. J. Reynolds and Philip Morris, offering predictions regarding the future of the industry and possible paths that might be followed by tobacco companies, government regulators, and individual smokers.

> **Subjects:** Business, Cigarettes, Epic Reads, Health Issues, Secret Histories, Smoking
>
> **Awards:** Pulitzer Prize
>
> **Now Try:** A more culture- and business-oriented history of smoking, Allan Brandt's *The Cigarette Century*, might also be considered by these readers, as might Bryan Burrough's and John Helyar's *Barbarians at the Gate: The Fall of RJR Nabisco*, often referred to as one of the seminal works of business history and featuring the story of the leveraged buyout of RJR Nabisco (a company that also produces cigarettes) and the massive egos and amounts of money involved. Another story of business deception and egos, Kurt Eichenwald's *A Conspiracy of Fools*, about Enron, might also be suggested. Richard Kluger also recently published a massive and favorably reviewed account of civil rights and legal battles, *Simple Justice: The History of Brown v. Board of Education and Black America's Struggle for Equality*.

Mead, Rebecca

One Perfect Day: The Selling of the American Wedding. Penguin Press. 2007. 245 pp. ISBN 9781594200885.

Mead dissects the $160 billion beast that is the American wedding industry with good-natured but still insightful questions such as, why have weddings become so extravagant? Why are brides and grooms constantly told they must adhere to a wide variety of (often expensive) traditions while simultaneously finding ways to (even more expensively) personalize their weddings? What do our weddings tell us about consumption patterns and our culture at large? Mead tells her story by offering comprehensive research, complete with some very big numbers, as well as interviewing engaged couples, wedding consultants, registry workers at department stores, all the way up the ladder to the massive Walt Disney Company and their new Fairytale Weddings initiative meant to tap into the lucrative nuptial market.

> **Subjects:** Business, Consumerism, Marriage, Retail, Society, Weddings, Women's Nonfiction
>
> **Now Try:** Many business histories include questions about the environment in which they thrive; fans of this book might consider Jessica Mitford's classic *The American Way of Death Revisited* (as well as Lisa Takeuchi Cullen's *Remember Me: A Lively Tour of the New American Way of Death*), Taylor Clark's

Starbucked, Matthew Hart's *Diamond*, and even Paco Underhill's *The Call of the Mall* or *Why We Buy*. The authors who provided blurbs for Mead's book have also written a number of interesting sociological books; they include Laura Kipnis (*Against Love* and *The Female Thing: Dirt, Sex, Envy, and Vulnerability*) and Eric Schlosser (*Fast Food Nation*).

Mitford, Jessica

The American Way of Death Revisited. Knopf. 1998 (1963). 296 pp. ISBN 9780679450375.

First published in 1977 as *The American Way of Death*, Mitford's classic of investigative journalism took her readers deep into the world of the "dismal trade," highlighting numerous dodgy, corrupt, and just plain greedy methods used by individuals in the funeral trade to capitalize on their customers' grief and disturbed states of mind when selling them funereal products and services. Both serious and impassioned, as well as bleakly humorous, Mitford's lively writing makes this book as readable and pertinent now as it ever was, and in this updated edition, she offers research on new funeral trends, the power of the industry's lobbyists in political circles, and the atmosphere of corporate takeovers and huge faceless and uncaring national conglomerates that now control most of the business.

Subjects: Business, Classics, Death and Dying, Humor, Professions, Society

Now Try: Fans of Mitford's lively writing might consider her similar title *The American Way of Birth*, as well as her autobiography *Hons and Rebels*. A very similar book, Lisa Takeuchi Cullen's *Remember Me: A Lively Tour of the New American Way of Death*, provides an updated look at the funeral industry, and Mary Roach's lively *Stiff: The Curious Lives of Human Cadavers* or *Spook: Science Tackles the Afterlife* might also appeal. Nonfiction and fiction authors with rather darker senses of humor might be suggested, such as Mary McCarthy, Jim Knipfel, or novelist Magnus Mills.

Mnookin, Seth

Hard News: Twenty-one Brutal Months at the New York Times and How They Changed the American Media. Random House. 2004. 330 pp. ISBN 9781400062447.

Organized in three sections, "Before," "2003," and "After," Mnookin's narrative briefly traces the rise of the *New York Times* to prominence and its status as the newspaper of record, its editorial practices as they stood in 2002; the Jayson Blair scandal (Blair faked stories, sources, and plagiarized on a grand scale) in 2003 that rocked the paper, its staff, and its readers' trust to the very core; and concludes by looking at the current atmosphere at the paper and greater trends in the news and publishing businesses worldwide. Looming large in the narrative are the personalities of Howell Raines, the editor during whose watch the scandals exploded, and the paper's venerable publisher Arthur Sulzberger. The story will appeal most to hard-core news junkies and those interested in cultural and social histories, but Mnookin's vantage point from inside the organization makes it a fascinating behind-the-scenes narrative for any reader.

Subjects: Jayson Blair, Business, Journalism, Mass Media, New York City, Howell Raines

Now Try: Other books on the media and journalism history might be suggested to these readers, including Gay Talese's *The Kingdom and the Power* (also about the *New York Times*), Drew Curtis's *It's Not News, It's Fark*, Katharine Graham's autobiography *Personal History*, or Charles Madigan's *30: The Collapse of the Great American Newspaper*. A wide variety of notable authors provided blurbs for this title, including Jeffrey

Toobin (*The Nine: Inside the Secret World of the Supreme Court*) and Sarah Vowell (*The Partly Cloudy Patriot* and *Take the Cannoli*), and the book is dedicated to gonzo journalist Hunter S. Thompson.

Nestle, Marion

Food Politics: How the Food Industry Influences Nutrition and Health. University of California Press. 2002. 457 pp. ISBN 9780520224650.

Nestle warns her readers early on not to trust that government authorities and corporate advertisers have our best interests at heart when it comes to food and our dietary choices. In this benchmark work on food policy and agricultural production, the author fixates primarily on the particularly American "paradox of plenty," or the recognition that we have so many calories and choices available that we should all eat more to help our food producers maximize their profits. A leading researcher in nutrition at New York University, Nestle argues that increased food consumption leads to increased obesity, making the population as a whole more vulnerable to cancer, strokes, and heart and lung diseases. From inadequate food pyramid guidelines to the marketing of junk food and soda to children, especially in schools, this book covers the ongoing drama of the American dilemma of eating and living healthy in the face of a plethora of bad choices and an abundance of food marketing.

> **Subjects:** Agribusiness, Agriculture, Business, Food, Foodies, Government, Health Issues, Marketing, Science, Small Press, Society, Sustainability
>
> **Now Try:** Other illuminating books on the eating habits of Americans include Eric Schlosser's *Fast Food Nation*, Greg Critser's *Fat Land*, Michael Pollan's *In Defense of Food*, Michele Simon's *Appetite for Profit*, Eric Finkelstein's and Laurie Zuckerman's more economics-minded *The Fattening of America: How the Economy Makes Us Fat, If It Matters, and What to Do about It*, or Thomas Pawlick's *The End of Food*. Books by such well-known authors as Frances Moore Lappé and Anna Lappé might be suggested, as might a wide variety of "foodie" books such as Ruth Reichl's *Tender at the Bone*, Michael Ruhlman's *The Making of a Chef*, Elizabeth Gilbert's *Eat, Pray, Love*, or Bill Buford's *Heat*.

Off, Carol

Bitter Chocolate: The Dark Side of the World's Most Seductive Sweet. Norton. 2008. 328 pp. ISBN 9781595583307.

In addition to exploring the global history of one of the world's most decadent and beloved foods, chocolate, reporter Carol Off also relates stories of the nefarious business and labor practices, including slavery and child labor, that are often involved with the production of the commodity while traveling from West Africa and other cocoa-producing regions to the headquarters of such companies as Cadbury and Hershey.

> **Subjects:** Business, Chocolate, Food, Globalization, Micro-Histories, Slavery, World History
>
> **Now Try:** Off masterfully combines micro-history writing with investigative journalism; micro-histories that might appeal to these readers include Mark Kurlansky's classics *Cod* and *Salt*, Peter Chapman's *Bananas!*, and Jack Turner's *Spice*; investigative works about globalization and commodities include Amy Stewart's *Flower Confidential*, Matthew S. Hart's *Diamond*, Eric

Schlosser's *Fast Food Nation*, or John Bowe's *Nobodies: Modern American Slave Labor and the Dark Side of the New Global Economy*. Other books about chocolate, although they may be more lighthearted, might also prove to be interesting read-alikes, such as Steve Almond's travelogue *Candyfreak* or Tim Richardson's *Sweets: A History of Candy*. Titles cited in Off's bibliography might also be of interest, including Adam Hochschild's *King Leopold's Ghost: A Story of Greed, Terror, and Heroism in Colonial Africa* and Joel Glenn Brenner's *The Emperors of Chocolate: Inside the Secret World of Hershey and Mars*.

Ortega, Bob

In Sam We Trust: The Untold Story of Sam Walton and How Wal-Mart Is Destroying America. Times Business. 1998. 413 pp. ISBN 9780812963779.

Although fans of Wal-Mart may fault this book for its strong allegations, Ortega is an award-winning journalist with the *Wall Street Journal* and has a reputation that can withstand criticism. Wal-Mart is currently the largest private-sector employer in North America, and Ortega examines all aspects of its being, from its founding by Sam Walton as a discount store to rival the Ben Franklin chain to its current status as retail behemoth. Although the author also provides biographical details about Walton and his family, the main focus of this narrative is the company history and a consideration of its current business practices.

Subjects: Arkansas, Biographies, Business, Companies, Professions, Retail, Wal-Mart, Sam Walton

Now Try: Those readers who are particularly fascinated by Wal-Mart might also find Robert Slater's *The Wal-Mart Decade: How a New Generation of Leaders Turned Sam Walton's Legacy into the World's #1 Company* or Charles Fishman's *The Wal-Mart Effect* to be illuminating reads (they definitely offer a different viewpoint; Amazon.com reviewers point out that Slater gave up "critical journalism" for unprecedented access); Liza Featherstone's *Selling Women Short: The Landmark Battle for Worker's Rights at Wal-Mart*, Stacy Mitchell's *Big-Box Swindle* or Anthony Bianco's *The Bully of Bentonville* might appeal more to readers who are not fans of the company. Constance Hays's enlightening look at the Coca-Cola company's contentious history with its own bottlers and within its managing hierarchy, *The Real Thing: Truth and Power at the Coca-Cola Company*, is much more interesting than its dry subject heading of "business" might lead the reader to believe.

Pawlick, Thomas

The End of Food: How the Food Industry Is Destroying Our Food Supply—And What We Can Do about It. Barricade Books. 2006. 256 pp. ISBN 9781569803028.

Rather than focusing on convenience, processed, and "fast" foods, which most often take the brunt of observation in journalistic and current affairs news stories, Pawlick seeks to illuminate the methods and processes by which all foods, even produce, dairy, and meats are produced and transported to market. Central to his argument is the development of agribusiness companies and scientific advances that prolong the shelf life and "packability" of food items but that also drastically reduce vitamin content, flavor, and biodiversity and often contain harmful additives such as antibiotics and other toxic chemicals. Overall the picture that Pawlick paints is bleak, but he also provides references and interviews with experts in the field who believe there are still ways for consumers to make wiser and healthier food purchasing choices.

Subjects: Agriculture, Business, Chemicals, Environmental Writing, Food, Quick Reads, Science, Small Press, Society, Technology

Now Try: Many books have been written on the subject of agribusiness and our food supply; these include Michele Simon's *Appetite for Profit*, Barbara Kingsolver's *Animal, Vegetable, Miracle*, Michael Pollan's *The Omnivore's Dilemma* and *In Defense of Food*, Eric Schlosser's *Fast Food Nation*, and a number of books by such food scientists and activists as Frances Moore Lappé, Anne Lappé, Marion Nestle, and Nina Planck. Titles about other industries, as well as chemical use in our society, might also appeal: Mark Schapiro's *Exposed: The Toxic Chemistry of Everyday Products and What's at Stake for American Power*, Randall Fitzgerald's *The Hundred-Year Lie*, or Rachel Carson's classic *Silent Spring*.

Petersen, Melody

Our Daily Meds: How the Pharmaceutical Companies Transformed Themselves into Slick Marketing Machines and Hooked the Nation on Prescription Drugs. Farrar, Straus & Giroux. 2008. 432 pp. ISBN 9780374228279.

Journalist Petersen exposes the marketing and advertising techniques used by pharmaceutical companies to persuade consumers to buy all manner of medications. A true reporter's reporter, she not only offers examples of drug companies' blatant deceptions and deliberate half-truths in the pursuit of profits (at the expense of consumers' health) but also digs deeper and showcases instances of articles in medical journals being ghostwritten by advertising agencies, as well as the unexamined environmental dangers of excess medications being flushed into our drinking water sources. Petersen also includes policy recommendations that would hold this industry and health care professionals responsible for their advertising claims and promises.

Subjects: Business, Companies, Health Issues, Marketing, Medicine, Pharmacology

Now Try: Recent years have seen a slew of titles similar to Petersen's; they include Marcia Angell's *The Truth about the Drug Companies*, Shannon Brownlee's *Overtreated*, Charles Barber's *Comfortably Numb*, Stephen Klaidman's *Coronary*, and Peter Rost's *The Whistleblower*. Other books about the health care culture might be offered, including Anne Fadiman's *The Spirit Catches You and You Fall Down* or Jerome Groopman's *How Doctors Think*; likewise, tales of dangers to our health might be suggested, including Jonathon Harr's *A Civil Action* or Joy Horowitz's *Parts Per Million: The Poisoning of a Beverly Hills High School*. Other books about the business of health care might also appeal, such as Allan Brandt's *The Cigarette Century* or Jamie Reidy's *Hard Sell: The Evolution of a Viagra Salesman*.

Reece, Erik

Lost Mountain. Riverhead Books. 2006. 250 pp. ISBN 9781594489082.

A native of Kentucky and the son of a coal worker, Reece became fascinated by the practices of coal-mining companies operating the mountains of Appalachia; in this book, he documents specifically the process of what the companies call "radical strip mining," which Reece learns is really a euphemism for mountaintop removal. As he watches the appropriately named "Lost Mountain" disappear to release the coal that provides the energy of which Americans can't get enough, he works to provide a detailed picture of the harmful practices that are endangering not only the Appalachian ecology but a wide variety of species extinctions and other farther-reaching environmental consequences. The book is organized chronologically, each chapter comprising a month's worth of Reece's experiences (starting in September 2003), and the enormity of the issue is summed up nicely by Wendell Berry in the foreword: "American coal companies extracted over one billion tons of coal in 2004, and 40 million tons more in 2004 than in the previous year. Nearly 70 percent of that coal comes from surface mines."

> **Subjects:** Appalachian Mountains, Business, Companies, Environmental Writing, Industry, Kentucky, Mining, Quick Reads, Year in the Life

> **Now Try:** A number of big-name authors provided blurbs for Reece's book, including Wendell Berry (whose novels set in Kentucky, particularly *Jayber Crow*, might particularly appeal to these readers), Bill McKibben, and Charles Bowden. Other books about industry and environmental concerns might be suggested, such as John Vaillart's *The Golden Spruce*, Helen Caldicott's *Nuclear Power Is Not the Answer*, Barbara Freese's micro-history *Coal*, or Dennis Love's *My City Was Gone*; Michelle Slatalla's fascinating book about a Kentucky community, *The Town on Beaver Creek*, might be enjoyed by these readers, as might any number of titles by classic environmental authors including Henry David Thoreau, Aldo Leopold, Rachel Carson, or Edward Abbey.

Rost, Peter

The Whistleblower: Confessions of a Healthcare Hitman. Soft Skull Press. 2006. 224 pp. ISBN 9781933368399.

> Former pharmaceutical company Pfizer executive Rost relates the blow-by-blow story of his decision to go public about his company's corporate policies and activities, including takeovers and layoffs, physician payoffs, marketing to juvenile patients, and tax dodging. By relating details to which only an insider executive would be privy, Rost's account provides valuable details into the often secretive world of Big Pharma; his narrative takes on added significance when he relates the lengths to which Pfizer tried to go, personally and legally, to intimidate him into not telling his story. This quickly paced and shocking book provides ample evidence of Rost's assertion that the current U.S. health care system is "certainly the best system for the drug companies."

> **Subjects:** Business, Companies, Corruption, Medicine, Memoirs, Pharmacology, Quick Reads, Small Press, YA

> **Now Try:** Other books about the current health care system might be suggested, such as Jonathan Cohn's *Sick* or Andy Kessler's *The End of Medicine: How Silicon Valley (and Naked Mice) Will Reboot Your Doctor*, as well as memoirs such as Jamie Reidy's *Hard Sell: The Evolution of a Viagra Salesman*, Jerome Groopman's *How Doctors Think*, or Thomas Edward Gass's *Nobody's Home*. Other industry exposés such as Richard Kluger's *Ashes to Ashes* or William Langewiesche's *The Outlaw Sea* might also appeal.

Scahill, Jeremy

Blackwater: The Rise of the World's Most Powerful Mercenary Army. Nation Books. 2007. 452 pp. ISBN 9781560259794.

> Scahill, a longtime contributor to *The Nation* magazine, explores the history and influence of Blackwater USA, a private security firm that has been employed as a

private army in Afghanistan, Iraq, and such American domestic situations as the War on Terror and the aftermath of Hurricane Katrina. Headquartered in North Carolina and founded by Erik Prince, a former Navy Seal and, according to Scahill, "an extreme right-wing fundamentalist Christian mega-millionaire," Blackwater has been hugely successful as a corporation but is increasingly under fire for its role in human rights abuses at home and abroad. Scahill's text is dense but readable, and he provides a multitude of sources for his contentions regarding the company's mission, founding, history, and future direction.

Subjects: Afghanistan, Business Histories, Christianity, Government, Iraq, Iraq War (2003), Military, Politics, Erik Prince

Now Try: Scahill's political perspective fairly obviously leans left; his readers might consider authors espousing similar doctrine, including Naomi Klein (*No Logo* and *Shock Doctrine*), Naomi Wolf (*Letters to a Young Patriot*), Chalmers Johnson (*The Sorrows of Empire*), or Chris Hedges (*American Fascists*). Other more journalistic works on the Iraq War (as opposed to primarily political ones) might also be offered; these include Lawrence Wright's *The Looming Tower: Al-Qaeda and the Road to 9/11*, James Risen's *State of War*, or George Packer's *The Assassins' Gate: America in Iraq*. Other investigative works might appeal to these readers, particularly those by such detailed authors as William Langewiesche, Samantha Powers, and Michael Isikoff.

Schapiro, Mark

Exposed: The Toxic Chemistry of Everyday Products and What's at Stake for American Power. 2007. Chelsea Green. 216 pp. ISBN 9781933392158.

Schapiro compares and contrasts the very different attitudes toward and policies regarding chemicals and their inclusion in thousands of everyday and household products between America and Europe. Pointing out the European trend to more carefully test possible ingredients and their effects on both the environment and human health *before* including them in their products (as opposed to the more American way of using a wide array of chemicals and waiting to see if they have adverse effects), the author explains why many toxins that are currently illegal to use in Europe are still in widespread use in the United States. Although the book is densely researched, it is also compellingly told and might appeal not only to readers concerned with American production methods but also those business readers who fear America may be losing the edge in global competition and innovation.

Subjects: Business, Chemicals, Economics, Environmental Writing, Europe, Government, Quick Reads, Small Press, Toxins

Now Try: Other environmental and health titles such as Randall Fitzgerald's *The Hundred-Year Lie*, Andrew Szasz's *Shopping Our Way to Safety*, or Michael Pollan's *The Omnivore's Dilemma* might appeal to these readers, and social critic Jeremy Rifkin's title *The European Dream* or Jane Kramer's book of essays *The Europeans* might help make clearer the social and cultural differences between America and Europe. Other books about globalization, particularly its dark side, might be suggested; these include Naomi Klein's *The Shock Doctrine* or John Bowe's *Nobodies: Modern American Slave Labor and the Dark Side of the New Global Economy*; Amy Stewart's lighter *Flower Confidential* also has a chapter on the chemicals used in the worldwide floral industry.

Schlosser, Eric

🏵 *Fast Food Nation: The Dark Side of the All-American Meal.* Houghton Mifflin. 2001. 356 pp. ISBN 9780395977897.

Arguably the most immediately recognizable book in this chapter, Schlosser's investigative account of the state of fast-food preparation and consumption in America was a huge best seller and immediately sent shock waves through many consumers who had happily been devouring McDonald's hamburgers without giving their origins any thought whatsoever. Schlosser's tone, although alarmist at times, is justified by much of his comprehensive research, but the amount of information and rather dense prose in the narrative means that it, unlike the meals offered by the establishment he's questioning, cannot be devoured quickly.

Subjects: Book Groups, Business, Classics, Food, Health Issues, Retail, YA

Awards: ALA Notable

Now Try: Schlosser's groundbreaking work has spawned a host of related texts; two of the most readable are Peter Pringle's examination of genetically modified foods, *Food, Inc.: Mendel to Monsanto—The Promises and Perils of the Biotech Harvest*, and Ken Midkiff's shorter *The Meat You Eat: How Corporate Farming Has Endangered America's Food Supply*, which also offers more concrete suggestions for obtaining food that is produced in accordance with more organic and environmentally friendly methods. Michael Pollan's popular titles *The Omnivore's Dilemma* and *In Defense of Food* have also been popular titles on these subjects and might be offered. Readers seeking a more character-driven and less dense narrative on a similar subject might be better served by Peter Lovenheim's *Portrait of a Burger as a Young Calf: The Story of One Man, Two Calves, and the Feeding of a Nation*, in which the author follows his food from birth to consumption and observes current farming techniques up close while doing so. Of course, those readers who are not averse to classics may find Upton Sinclair's famous work of muckraking fiction about stockyard conditions at the beginning of the twentieth century, *The Jungle*, an appropriate if depressing companion read to Schlosser's nonfiction work.

Shah, Sonia

The Body Hunters: How the Drug Industry Tests Its Products on the World's Poorest Patients. New Press. 2006. 242 pp. ISBN 9781565849129.

In this modern-day medical horror story, Shah explores the necessity of human trials to further medical research and exposes how most of the humans being studied across the globe today are its poorest and least able to protest or complain inhabitants. She draws on historical context and precedent from such controversial studies as the Tuskegee Syphilis Study, over the course of which (from 1932 to 1972) the syphilis cases of hundreds of poor African American males were left untreated, to more recent trials in which pharmaceutical companies are quietly testing risky drugs that they hope will become their next big moneymakers in such countries as India, Zambia, and across Africa and Asia. Although Shah's case is bolstered by statistical research and firsthand observation, her interest in the subject is rooted in the belief that "turning the body into a thing rightly offends our sensibilities about what it means to be human."

Subjects: Africa, Business, Companies, Economics, Health Issues, Medicine, Pharmacology, Scholarly

Now Try: Other books about the history of medicine (and how a variety of treatments have been developed) might be suggested, including David Oshinsky's *Polio: An American History*, Arthur Allen's *Vaccine: The Controversial Story of Medicine's Greatest Lifesaver*, Denise Bookchin's and Jim Schumacher's *The Virus and the Vaccine*, and Sherwin Nuland's *The Doctor's Plague*. Medical thrillers might also be offered, particularly titles by Robin Cook, Tess Gerritsen, or Harry Lee Kraus. Other books offering insight into less-than-ethical pharmaceutical and medical practices might be suggested, including Peter Rost's *The Whistleblower* or Stephen Klaidman's *Coronary*.

Simon, Michele

Appetite for Profit: How the Food Industry Undermines Our Health and How to Fight Back. Nation Books. 2006. 392 pp. ISBN 9781560259978.

During the past decade, the American public has become increasingly interested in the food it eats, as well as where and how it is grown, produced, or processed. In this heartfelt treatise, Simon investigates not how major corporations (including McDonald's, Coca-Cola, Kraft, and General Mills) process and produce less-than-healthy products, but rather how they have both done that and increasingly gone on the marketing offensive of highlighting their new and "healthier" selections, positioning themselves as part of the solution rather than the problem. This could be seen as a positive step, but the same companies have combined those marketing efforts with much quieter lobbying and political machinations to block commonsense nutrition policies and regulation. By exposing their hypocrisy and warning consumers that they really cannot trust food companies to "do the right thing," the author, a public health attorney, makes a strong case for consumers to think critically about all of their food purchases and even offers a glossary to explain corporate rhetoric such as "better-for-you foods," among many other such stock phrases.

> **Subjects:** Advertising, Business, Companies, Food, Health Issues, Marketing, Politics, Restaurants

> **Now Try:** Well-known food writers and activists who provided blurbs for this book included Frances Moore Lappé and Marion Nestle; their books, along with Anna Lappé's *Grub*, might appeal to these readers. Recent years have seen an explosion in publication of books of this type; readers might also consider Barbara Kingsolver's *Animal, Vegetable, Miracle*, Michael Pollan's *The Omnivore's Dilemma* or *In Defense of Food*, Peter Pringle's *Food, Inc.: Mendel to Monsanto*, Eric Schlosser's *Fast Food Nation*, or Thomas Pawlick's *The End of Food*. Other "sustainability" books such as Bill McKibben's *Deep Economy*, or Environmental Writing books like Edward Abbey's *Desert Solitaire* might also be offered, as might related exposés like Randall Fitzgerald's *The Hundred Year Lie* or Stephen Klaidman's *Coronary: A True Story of Medicine Gone Awry*.

Wallis, David, editor

Killed Cartoons: Casualties from the War on Free Expression. W. W. Norton. 2007. 282 pp. ISBN 9780393329247.

This tiny book packs a big punch: it comprises entirely of one hundred political cartoons that were banned by the publications to which they were submitted (and have subsequently remained unseen, until now). Ranging from such emotionally charged issues as pedophile priests and capital punishment to President George W. Bush's "bring 'em on!" speech to terrorists and the disputed 2000 election, this collection features contributions from such big names in cartooning as Garry Trudeau, Doug Marlette, Paul Conrad, Mike Luckovich, Matt Davies, and Ted Rall (all Pulitzer Prize winners or finalists), as well as unearthed illustrations by Norman Rockwell, Edward Sorel, Anita Kunz, Marshall Arisman, and Steve Brodner. In addition to the cartoons, readers will also find short explanations of the reasoning behind the censoring and brief thoughts on the nature and practice of free speech in America.

> **Subjects:** American History, Cartoons, First Amendment, Graphic Novels, History, Illustrated Books, Politics, Quick Reads

> **Now Try:** Wallis was also the editor of *Killed: Great Journalism Too Hot to Print*, which might also appeal to these readers, as might Matthew Diffee's and Robert Mankoff's collections *The Rejection Collection* and *The Rejection Collection Volume 2*, which feature cartoons that were deemed "too risqué, silly, or weird for *The New Yorker*." These readers might also enjoy cartoon collections by artists whose work is on display here; these include Garry Trudeau and Ted Rall; likewise, graphic novels by Larry Gonick, Brian Fies, or Paul Madonna might also be suggested, as might more political works by authors such as Howard Zinn or James Loewen.

Weil, Gordon Lee

Blackout: How the Electric Industry Exploits America. Nation Books. 2006. 249 pp. ISBN 9781560258124.

Author Weil opens his narrative with a disturbingly evocative description of the huge 2003 blackout across most of northeast America, which stalled traffic, business, and all routine aspects of people's energy-dependent lives from Canada to New York City to Philadelphia. Even more distressing than the blackout itself, Weil argues, is the fact that no company or individual was ever held accountable for the disaster; he uses that point as a springboard to further explore the stranglehold the electric industry maintains over both its customers and government policy. In the first part of his narrative, the author provides a comprehensive history of the industry and its monopolistic tendencies; in the second part, he suggests new and possible avenues for reform to avoid such future failures in the competitive marketplace, as well as disasters such as debilitating blackouts.

> **Subjects:** Business, Companies, Energy, Politics, Technology

> **Now Try:** Another look at an energy company known for corruption in its accounting practices, Kurt Eichenwald's *Conspiracy of Fools* (about Enron), might also be offered. Other nonfiction titles about corruption in business or dodgy business practices might be suggested; these include Jeff Goodell's *Big Coal: The Dirty Secret behind America's Energy Future*, Lisa Margonelli's *Oil on the Brain*, or John Bowe's *Nobodies: Modern American Slave Labor and the Dark Side of the New Global Economy*. The historical fiction novel *City of Light*, by Lauren Belfer, about the city of Buffalo and the tapping of Niagara Falls for energy, might also provide an enjoyable related read.

Social Exposés

Did you ever feel like the whole world is conspiring against you? Can't decide who you trust less, the government or the marketplace (or maybe it's a little from column A, a little from column B?). Feel that something in the entire system is off? That feeling, that slight raising of the hairs on the back of your neck, is what the authors of these Social Exposés are addressing in their tell-alls. As happens a lot of time in other parts of our lives, it is hard to pin down exactly what the problem is (or even what your perception of the problem is). When examples of wrongdoing are not strictly attributable to governments, or companies, or certain individuals, at whose door do we place the blame? These titles, in which the authors more closely examine such broad issues as our criminal justice system, technology, feminism and gender equality issues, economics, health issues, and even something as amorphous as the broad ideal of happiness and well-being, can be every bit as shocking as their counterparts in the Government and Corporate subgenres. In fact, they are often a bit more unsettling, because their authors try and try, logically and conclusively, to relate causes and effects but just as often have to admit that, although many issues *may* be related, they're not exactly sure how or to what extent. These are stories in which we all have a stake; they cover pervasive cultural and societal demands and norms. If you went to a bookstore, you might find these titles sprinkled throughout a variety of categories, including Sociology, Current Affairs, Psychology, Economics, and even Nature. They are gathered here together because they explore previously unexplored aspects of many familiar institutions and constructs (e.g., grocery stores, giving birth, the very water we drink), and their authors do so by offering often copious amounts of research and interview answers from a wide variety of sources.

Although "enjoy" might really be the wrong word for how readers react to these titles, their fans might also consider a number of titles from both the Government and Corporate Exposés subgenres, as well as Historical Perspectives from the In-Depth Reporting chapter. Immersion titles about Society might also appeal, because these readers tend to be very curious and read nonfiction largely because they enjoy learning about new things (even if that knowledge doesn't always translate into increased happiness); for the same reason, essay collections in which authors carefully examine the world and people around them and reveal their own reactions and thoughts about them, might also be suggested.

Social Exposés are story-driven nonfiction narratives in which authors typically expose larger societal wrongdoings and corruptions (and specifically events that cannot be fairly attributed to specific individuals, government, or industries). Although they do not typically offer as many strongly drawn characters as do other types of nonfiction Exposés, they do offer the sensation of learning "secret" histories or previously untold stories that the authors go to some lengths to uncover and verify. They include elements of "secret histories" and the unveiling of secrets, and their authors also typically offer more sociological and psychological analysis of their subjects than they do in Government and Corporate Exposés; the emphasis is often less on purely exposing a story than it is on exploring a story and possible solutions.

Abramsky, Sasha

American Furies: Crime, Punishment, and Vengeance in the Age of Mass Imprisonment. Beacon Press. 2007. 213 pp. ISBN 9780807042229.

Abramsky details the latter-twentieth-century trend in American prisons away from rehabilitation and toward vengeance by researching such aspects of the current punitive atmosphere of life sentences for nonviolent crimes, prison overcrowding and poor living conditions, private prisons run for profit, and treating juveniles as adults. In addition to exposing conditions within prisons, the author also seeks to address how those living conditions and experiences affect the formerly incarcerated and make it harder for them to readjust to society outside the prison walls. The book is organized in two parts: "A Mindset Molded," and "Populating Bedlam," and throughout Abramsky points out consequences for the American public as well as for convicted criminals: in mid-2006 there were two million people behind bars, and more than $57 billion was spent annually on corrections.

Subjects: Economics, Law Enforcement, Prisons, Scholarly, Society, True Crime

Now Try: A number of other well-reviewed nonfiction works have been published in the last decade about the experiences of prison life and prison reform; these include Joseph Hallinan's *Going Up the River: Travels in a Prison Nation*, Jennifer Gonnerman's *Life on the Outside: The Prison Odyssey of Elaine Bartlett*, Jennifer Wynn's *Inside Rikers*, Ted Conover's *Newjack: Guarding Sing Sing*, or even Ralph Blumenthal's *Miracle at Sing Sing*. T. J. Parsell's searing memoir *Fish: A Memoir of a Boy in a Man's Prison* might serve as a related read (although its often-graphic subject matter means it may not be for all readers), as would books about other human rights issues such as Dominic Streatfeild's *Brainwash*, Anne Applebaum's history *Gulag*, or Helen Prejean's *Dead Man Walking*. Authors who provided blurbs for this book included such investigative journalists as Eric Schlosser, Barbara Ehrenreich, and Simon Winchester.

Agin, Dan

Junk Science: How Politicians, Corporations, and Other Hucksters Betray Us. Thomas Dunne Books. 2006. 323 pp. ISBN 9780312352417.

Editor of the online journal *ScienceWeek*, Agin sets out to rescue the misuse of science and scientific news from government, industry, and faith groups that seek to use discoveries and stories to bolster their own arguments. In sections titled "Buyer Beware," "Medical Follies," "Poison and Bombs in the Greenhouse," and "Genes, Behavior, and Race," the author systemically deconstructs the misinformation on such topics as genetically modified foods, health care, pollution, global warming, and cloning (among many others) to show how data can be manipulated to further public ignorance. Although his subject matter is complex, his writing is clear, and he is careful to define the difference between "bad science" (that which is flawed in methodology) and "junk science," which he defines as the "clouding of the human examination of reality by carelessness, fear, myth, and deliberate falsehood."

Subjects: Health Issues, Politics, Pollution, Religion, Science, Society

Now Try: Other investigative science titles (particularly from the Science Reporting subgenre of the In-Depth Reporting chapter) might appeal to these readers, such as Jessica Snyder Sach's *Good Germs, Bad Germs*, Elizabeth Kolbert's *Field Notes from a Catastrophe*, John Henshaw's *Does Measurement Measure Up?*, or Chris Mooney's more partisan *The Republican War on Science*. Other exposés on related subjects might be suggested, such as Peter Rost's *The Whistleblower: Confessions of a Healthcare Hitman*, Jonathan Cohn's *Sick: The Untold Story of America's Health Care Crisis—and the People Who Pay the Price*, or Dan Hurley's *Natural Causes: Death, Lies and Politics in America's Vitamin and Herbal Supplement Industry*.

Albrecht, Katherine, and Liz McIntyre

Spychips: How Major Corporations and Government Plan to Track Your Every Move with RFID. Nelson Current. 2005. 270 pp. ISBN 9781595550200.

Authors and privacy advocates Albrecht and McIntyre provide a detailed and concerning description and history of RFID, which stands for Radio Frequency Identification—a technology that uses computer chips to track all manner of items, including things we purchase to eat, wear, and use. Although the technology is being lauded as a way to streamline the processing of goods and information, the authors also suggest that the chips give everyone from government officials to business owners the capacity to track all of our daily and most mundane actions. It is the authors' contention that this ability translates to de facto spying on individuals without their knowledge and consent, and they conclude their narrative with suggestions for consumer action to limit the use of the technology and preserve our privacy and civil liberties before it is too late.

Subjects: Business, Companies, Government, Privacy, Society, Technology

Now Try: Other books about government, spying, and technological advances might be suggested, such as Ted Gup's *Nation of Secrets*, Henry David Thoreau's classic *Civil Disobedience*, or Patrick Radden Keefe's *Chatter: Dispatches from the Secret World of Global Eavesdropping*. Also of interest might be Simon Singh's book *The Science of Secrecy*, Jeremy Rifkin's *The Age of Access*, or dystopian science fiction novels such as Geoff Ryman's *Air*, William Gibson's *Neuromancer*, or Max Barry's *Jennifer Government*.

Bennetts, Leslie

The Feminine Mistake: Are We Giving Up Too Much? Hyperion. 2007. 350 pp. ISBN 9781401303068.

Bennetts explores the current state of women in the workplace, in their homes and relationships, and in the culture and concludes that the choices many women have made to temporarily leave careers to raise children or respond to other family and relationship demands often leaves them financially and personally vulnerable. The book rests mainly on Bennetts's personal interviews with numerous women in various stages of their careers, parenthood, and such special circumstances as divorce; she also includes statistical research and concludes with recommendations for all women to achieve financial independence, work fulfillment, and personal identities in which they can feel pride.

Subjects: Family Relationships, Feminism, Money, Parenting, Professions, Society, Women's Contributions, Women's Nonfiction, Work Relationships

Now Try: There has been a boom in publishing of books of this type: they include the anthologies *The Mommy Wars*, Pamela Stone's *Opting Out?*, and Ellen Bravo's *Taking On the Big Boys*. Authors who provided blurbs for this book include Linda Hirshman (*Get to Work*), and Bennetts refers to a wide variety of investigative and social policy authors including David Brooks, Barbara Ehrenreich, Ann Crittenden, Betty Friedan, and Gloria Steinem.

Block, Jennifer

Pushed: The Painful Truth about Childbirth and Modern Maternity Care. Da Capo. 2007. 316 pp. ISBN 9780738210735.

Author Block traveled across the nation and interviewed numerous women who were preparing to go through the process of childbirth. Her provocative viewpoint questions how the practice of birth has become more of a managed and pharmaceutical process of inducing birth and cesarean sections rather than a natural progression and emergence. Block also strives to make the case that not only is "managed care" the norm, but that it is often the only available choice; the use of midwives is even illegal in eleven states. After witnessing several births, interviewing medical personnel, and expectant mothers, Block is able to write a thought-provoking, if sometimes uncomfortably graphic, account of the current state of childbirth practices in America.

Subjects: Childbirth, Feminism, Health Issues, Medicine, Parenting, Women's Nonfiction, Women's Rights

Now Try: Tina Cassidy's *Birth: The Surprising History of How We Are Born*, Jessica Mitford's *The American Way of Birth*, or F. Gonzalez-Crussi's fascinating *On Being Born* might be suggested (as might Sherwin Nuland's historical *The Doctor's Plague*, about how and why so many women used to die in childbirth); other Exposés on health issues might also be good companion reads, such as Jonathan Cohn's *Sick*, Randall Fitzgerald's *The Hundred-Year Lie: How Food and Medicine Are Destroying Your Health*, Beth Kohl's *Embryo Culture*, or Robin Marantz Henig's *Pandora's Baby*.

Bowe, John

Nobodies: Modern American Slave Labor and the Dark Side of the New Global Economy. Random House. 2007. 304 pp. ISBN 9781400062096.

Investigative reporter Bowe travels to Florida, Tulsa (Oklahoma), and the Pacific island of Saipan to tell the stories of migrant and indentured workers who are lured to companies and locations with the promise of good wages and honest work; Bowe relates details of how they are often either physically restrained or their personal safety (and the safety of their families) is threatened to the point where they become, in fact if not in name, modern-day slaves. Bowe also provides historical and economic context to prove that employers are not the only ones complicit in this system, and logically makes the case that governments and the haves of the world conspire, knowingly and unknowingly, to take advantage of the have-nots.

Subjects: American History, Community Life, Economics, Florida, Globalization, Labor History, Oklahoma, Politics, Saipan

Now Try: A wide variety of other Exposés might appeal to Bowe's readers, including Douglas Farah's *Blood from Stones: The Secret Financial Network of Terror*, William Langewiesche's *Cutting for Sign* or Ruben Martinez's *Crossing Over: A Mexican Family on the Migrant Trail*, and John Perkins's *Confessions of an Economic Hit Man* or *The Secret History of the American Empire*, while the slightly lighter titles *Flower Confidential* by Amy Stewart, *Fugitive Denim* by Rachel Louise Snyder, or *A Year without "Made in China"* by Sara Bongiorni might also appeal. John Bowe is also the editor of an earlier work of oral history, titled *Gig: Americans Talk about Their Jobs*.

Bryce, Robert

Gusher of Lies: The Dangerous Delusions of "Energy Independence." Perseus Books, 2008. 371 pp. ISBN 9781586483210.

Journalist Bryce systematically dismantles the idea that "energy independence" is something that could be achieved in the United States, as well as offering a coherent argument for why it should not even be held up as an ideal. Called "high-order muckraking" by review journals, the book is organized into four succinctly written and well-researched segments focusing on how energy independence as a concept has been marketed to the American public, a history of American energy policy and oil dependence, why energy independence would be impossible to achieve, and suggestions for how a more interdependent but still workable oil supply could be achieved. The author also professes not to bring any political agenda to his book, lending it a fairly balanced tone for an Exposé.

Subjects: American History, Business, Energy, Environment, Globalization, Iraq War (2003), Middle East, Oil, Politics, Technology

Now Try: Bryce cites a good many influential books throughout his chapters, including his own earlier titles, *Pipe Dreams: Greed, Ego, and the Death of Enron* and *Cronies: Oil, the Bushes, and the Rise of Texas*, as well as Michael Klare's *Blood and Oil*, James Howard Kunstler's *The Long Emergency: Surviving the Converging Catastrophes of the Twenty-First Century*, and Paul Roberts's *The End of Oil* (two other titles which received somewhat critical mention might also be of interest; these are Al Gore's *An Inconvenient Truth* and Thomas Friedman's *The World Is Flat*). Other Investigative works about oil and energy might be suggested, such as Lisa Margonelli's *Oil on the Brain* or Daniel Yergin's *The Prize*, as well as titles about the Iraq War, such as Bob Woodward's *Plan of Attack* or Michael R. Gordon's and Bernard E. Trainor's *Cobra II: The Inside Story of the Invasion and Occupation of Iraq*. Other authors who write detailed but still readable nonfiction about technology and how things work include William Langewiesche (*American Ground* and *The Atomic Bazaar*) and John McPhee (*Uncommon Carriers* and *Annals of the Former World*).

Burbick, Joan

Gun Show Nation: Gun Culture and American Democracy. New Press. 2006. 232 pp. ISBN 9781595580870.

Burbick believed that to understand the gun culture and how gun ownership has become such a passionately held right in America, she had to jump right in and attend gun shows, National Rifle Association (NRA) conventions, shooting ranges, and also interview gun lobby strategists. By relating the history of the "rise of the gun" in our national mythos, from stories of Buffalo Bill and the wild frontier to Ronald Reagan's speeches to the NRA, Burbick also explores how the gun culture developed and how gun ownership issues became such a large part of most political discussions. A gun owner herself, the author is uniquely able to decipher the language and appeal of the weapon, wonder why 44 percent of American men own guns while only 12 percent of women do, and other issues related to this incendiary topic.

> **Subjects:** American History, Guns, Hobbies, Quick Reads, Racism, Religion, Society, Weapons, Year in the Life
>
> **Now Try:** Other books that explore the meaning and tradition of the second amendment include the pictorial collection *Armed America: Portraits of Gun Owners in Their Homes*, by Kyle Cassidy; *Ricochet: Confessions of a Gun Lobbyist*, by Richard Feldman; or *Deer Hunting with Jesus*, by Joe Bageant. Although Burbick investigates a more serious hobby than most, other books in which authors travel among and interview members of hobbyist subcultures might also be offered, such as Stefan Fatsis's *Word Freak*, Amy Stewart's *Flower Confidential*, Shari Caudron's *Who Are You People?*, or Mark Singer's *Character Studies*.

Canton, James

The Extreme Future: The Top Trends That Will Reshape the World for the Next 5, 10, and 20 Years. Dutton. 2006. 371 pp. ISBN 9780525949381.

Futurist and CEO of the Institute for Global Futures Canton lists what he believes will be the most important changes and breakthroughs of the next two decades. Referring to the future as the "Extreme Future," Canton offers predictions for climate and energy trends, population forecasts, workplace and business innovations, terrorism threats, medical advances and new global power balances; included in the fast-paced and accessible text are numerous sidebars explaining the trend predictions and other future forecast possibilities.

> **Subjects:** Demographics, Futurism, Science, Society, Technology, Trivia
>
> **Now Try:** Other books by futurists might be suggested, including Alvin Toffler's *Future Shock* and *Revolutionary Wealth*, Ray Kurzweil's *The Age of Spiritual Machines*, James Gleick's *Faster*, or David Weinberger's *Everything Is Miscellaneous*; books by Jared Diamond and Michael Frayn (*Human Touch: Our Part in the Creation of a Universe*) might also be suggested, as well as "trends" books like Malcolm Gladwell's *The Tipping Point* or Mark Penn's *Microtrends*. Fans of these books might also check out magazines like *Wired* and *The Futurist* for future reading suggestions, while science fiction novels of all types might provide good read-alikes as well.

Critser, Greg

🏆 *Fat Land: How Americans Became the Fattest People in the World.* Houghton Mifflin. 2003. 232 pp. ISBN 9780618164721.

Although it arguably covers the same ground as Eric Schlosser's best-selling favorite *Fast Food Nation*, Critser covers a broader swath and adopts a less combative tone in his seven chapters explaining some of the possible reasons for the fact that nearly 60 percent of Americans are considered overweight, where all those calories are coming from, our fascination with and dependence on a lifestyle of constant dieting, and how our weight affects our bodies, our mental health, and our overall physical well-being. The author also concludes with a chapter of suggestions for not only reducing one's own caloric intake and weight but also acting as a more responsible consumer and thinking critically about lifestyle and purchasing choices that affect this issue and the agriculture and food industries in general.

Subjects: Food, Health Issues, Obesity, Quick Reads, Society

Awards: New York Times Notable

Now Try: Eric Schlosser's more inflammable *Fast Food Nation* might be suggested to these readers, as might Morgan Spurlock's humorous (even if it is on a serious topic), *Don't Eat This Book: Fast Food and the Supersizing of America* or even books on classism and the economics that promote unhealthy eating habits, including the anthology *Class Matters* or Katherine Newman's and Victor Tan Chen's *The Missing Class*. Other books about food and food politics by such authors as Frances Moore Lappé, Anna Lappé, Nina Planck, Marion Nestle, Thomas Pawlick (*The End of Food*), and Michael Pollan (*In Defense of Food*) may be of interest, as might Vince Staten's illuminating *Can You Trust a Tomato in January?*

Davis, Devra

The Secret History of the War on Cancer. Perseus Books Group. 2007. 505 pp. ISBN 9780465015665.

As director of the Center for Environmental Oncology at the University of Pittsburgh, Davis can discuss both the medical and social history of the war on cancer, which she contends was largely waged with money from the corporations and individuals who profit primarily from things that cause cancer (including tobacco and radiation). Part history, part Exposé, this book is a compelling narrative of the disease, its causes, and the mystery of how so many resources have been allocated to combating it with so little success.

Subjects: Cancer, Corporations, Government, Health Issues, Medicine, Science, Women's Nonfiction

Now Try: Davis is also the author of *When Smoke Ran Like Water: Tales of Environmental Deception and the Battle against Pollution*. Other books about the medical and cultural aspects of cancer include Barron Lerner's *The Breast Cancer Wars*, or the more personal memoirs *Refuge* (by Terry Tempest Williams), *Welcome to Shirley: A Memoir from an Atomic Town* (Kelly McMasters), or *Mom's Cancer* (Brian Fies). Other exposés might also be suggested, including Charles Barber's *Comfortably Numb: How Psychiatry Is Medicating a Nation*, Richard Kluger's *Ashes to Ashes: America's Hundred-Year Cigarette War*, Melody Petersen's *Our Daily Meds*, or Eric Schlosser's classic *Fast Food Nation*.

DeParle, Jason

❀ *American Dream: Three Women, Ten Kids, and a Nation's Drive to End Welfare.* Viking. 2004. 422 pp. ISBN 9780670892754.

DeParle, a "social policy reporter" with the *New York Times*, set out to examine the aftereffects of the 1990s drive to "end welfare as we know it" by observing and interviewing three women and their families who were affected by welfare reform policy changes in Washington, D.C. (and the state of Wisconsin). DeParle, in offering compelling character portraits of the three women he interviewed, also examines how issues of economic security, class, and race are all intertwined in America.

> **Subjects:** Character Profiles, Economics, Family Relationships, Government, Poverty, Welfare, Wisconsin, Women's Nonfiction
>
> **Awards:** New York Times Notable
>
> **Now Try:** Other books exploring issues of poverty, class, and race might be suggested, including but not limited to Sharon Hays's *Flat Broke with Children*, David Shipler's *The Working Poor*, Katherine Newman's and Victor Tan Chen's *The Missing Class*, Jonathan Kozol's *Savage Inequalities*, or even Barbara Ehrenreich's *Nickel and Dimed*. Other books offering particularly rich character profiles, including Adrian Nicole LeBlanc's *Random Family*, Leon Dash's *Rosa Lee*, or Sudhir Venkatesh's *Gang Leader for a Day* might also be suggested.

Easterbrook, Gregg

The Progress Paradox: How Life Gets Better While People Feel Worse. Random House. 2003. 376 pp. ISBN 9780679463030.

Easterbrook seeks to prove definitively that money definitely cannot buy happiness by offering a laundry list of quality-of-life improvements made over the past century (including higher wages, larger homes, lower crime rates, and numerous personal and affordable luxuries) and illustrating that none of these factors has really made people feel any happier. Offering definitions and examples of such sociological phenomena as "choice anxiety" (wherein consumers become stressed by the sheer number of choices available to them), "abundance denial" (where people refuse to believe they have enough material goods to be comfortable), and many others, the senior editor of *The New Republic* concludes that Americans will never be considerably happier until we accept how good we truly have it. At that point, he argues, we as a society will feel compelled to share our resources worldwide to alleviate hunger and privation, which will, in turn, have a positive effect on our mental and physiological states.

> **Subjects:** Book Groups, Community Life, Economics, Happiness, Making Sense ..., Psychology, Society, Sociology
>
> **Now Try:** Other books on psychology and the idea of happiness might appeal to these readers, including Barry Schwartz's *The Paradox of Choice*, Daniel Gilbert's *Stumbling on Happiness*, Alain De Botton's *Status Anxiety*, Peter Whybrow's *American Mania: When More Is Not Enough*, Kay Redfield Jamison's *Exuberance*, or Robert H. Frank's *Falling Behind*. Other books on community and culture, including Robert Putnam's *Bowling Alone*, Daniel Goleman's *Social Intelligence*, Malcolm Gladwell's *Blink* or *The Tipping Point*, Bill Clinton's *Giving*, or Stephanie Coontz's *The Way We Never Were* might all appeal.

Eberhart, Mark

Feeding the Fire: The Lost History and Uncertain Future of Mankind's Energy Addiction. Harmony Books. 2007. 283 pp. ISBN 9780307237446.

Eberhart offers a multifaceted look at energy: how it is made, how it is consumed, how dependent on it we are, and what renewable energy sources are being developed right now. Although his writing is based on scientific research, he does an excellent job of making it readable for the general reader, and also provides a history of the industry.

Subjects: American History, Energy, Oil, Science, Society, Sustainability

Now Try: Eberhart is also the author of the science book *Why Things Break* and has a talent for explaining scientific ideas clearly. Other books about oil and energy might be suggested, such as Daniel Yergin's *The Prize*, Lisa Margonelli's *Oil on the Brain*, Gordon Lee Weil's *Blackout: How the Electric Industry Exploits America*, or James Howard Kunstler's *The Long Emergency*. Eberhart also lists other sociological and science authors in his bibliography, including Jared Diamond and Neil DeGrasse Tyson; other science books by Henry Petroski, Paul Ehrlich, and John McPhee might also be offered.

Finnegan, William

Cold New World: Growing Up in a Harder Country. Random House. 1998. 421 pp. ISBN 9780679448709.

In his work of "social journalism," Finnegan spent six years with four families across America during the late 1980s and early 1990s, seeking to learn the new challenges—personal, interpersonal, and financial—that were being faced by regular Americans. Spending time in the communities of New Haven (Connecticut), Texas, Washington state, and Los Angeles, Finnegan watched drug deals, family fights, immigrant teens struggling to leave their parents' values behind, gang activity, and a variety of other harsh realities that led him to conclude that "a new American class structure is being born—one that is harsher, in many ways, than the one it is replacing."

Subjects: Classism, Classics, Community Life, Drugs, Family Relationships, Poverty, Race Relations

Now Try: Authors who provided blurbs for Finnegan's classic work are authors of nonfiction classics themselves; they include Alex Kotlowitz, David Remnick, Tracy Kidder, and Bill McKibben. Other books about society, economics, and family and social life might also be suggested, such as Leon Dash's *Rosa Lee*, Adrian Nicole LeBlanc's *Random Family*, Jason DeParle's *American Dream*, or David Shipler's *The Working Poor*. Novels in which working-class families struggle to make a go of it might also be suggested, such as Richard Russo's *Nobody's Fool*, Richard Ford's *The Sportswriter*, John Updike's classic *Rabbit, Run*, or Russell Banks's *Continental Drift*. Another of Finnegan's books, cowritten with Philip Gourevitch, might also appeal: *Crossing the Line: A Year in the Land of Apartheid*.

Fitzgerald, Randall

The Hundred-Year Lie: How Food and Medicine Are Destroying Your Health. Dutton. 2006. 293 pp. ISBN 9780525949510.

Journalist and *Reader's Digest* contributing editor Fitzgerald tells a shocking tale of the effects to our health from the nasty cocktails of toxic chemicals in everything from our cleaning supplies and food to our medicine. Starting with the fact that the average American now carries a "body burden" of seven hundred or more synthetic chemicals in our bodies (including plastics and pesticides), the author laments the fact that we are rapidly becoming not only a source of pollution but ourselves one of the most polluted species on the planet. Any reader who does not want to be unduly shocked by the current ingredients in our drinking water and food may wish to leave this volume alone, because Fitzgerald also addresses and attempts to shatter such comfortable consumer myths as "the government will protect me." He also provides numerous suggestions throughout his text for both lessening our personal ingestion of chemicals, as well as recommendations for organizing and acting to make business and industry more responsible in their use of ingredients and production methods (a rich bibliography and appendix also offers further resources and organization to contact for more information).

Subjects: Chemicals, Environmental Writing, Food, Health Issues, Medicine, Science, Self-Help

Now Try: These readers might consider related works such as Mark Schapiro's *Exposed*, Thomas Pawlick's *The End of Food*, Frances Moore Lappé's *Diet for a Poisoned Planet*, or Rachel Carson's *Silent Spring*. Other books by food activists such as Marion Nestle, Nina Planck, and Michael Pollan might be suggested, as might a wide variety of books about health, such as Andy Kessler's more optimistic *The End of Medicine: How Silicon Valley (and Naked Mice) Will Reboot Your Doctor* or Anne Fadiman's *The Spirit Catches You and You Fall Down*.

Frank, Robert H.

Richistan: A Journey through the American Wealth Boom and the Lives of the New Rich. Crown. 2007. 277 pp. ISBN 9780307339263.

This good-natured tour through the America of the rich catalogues their possessions, including homes in excess of 30,000 square feet, 400-foot-yachts, and large personal staffs. Author Frank cunningly gains entrance to all manner of events for which he does not meet the minimum income requirements, including yacht marinas, charity balls, and top-shelf real estate agents. In addition to exploring the lifestyles of these newly rich, Frank also interviews the consultants they can't hire fast enough to train them how to display their wealth, including such staff as butlers and household managers. Their lives are not all fun and games, however; many members of the "Richistani" class are more interested in results-oriented philanthropy and display different, more Democratic than Republican, political allegiances. In a nation where the number of millionaire households more than doubled from 1995 to 2003, Frank details a segment of the population that is significant in its numbers and far-reaching in its influence.

Subjects: Book Groups, Business, Character Profiles, Economics, Society, Statistics

Now Try: The fascinating *All the Money in the World: How the Forbes 400 Make—and Spend—Their Fortunes* (by Peter Bernstein and Annalyn Swan) also provides valuable insight into the lives of the rich and famous; also consider other books about the wealthy, such as Ronald Kessler's *The Season* or Roger Lowenstein's *Buffett: The Making of an American Capitalist*. Other books about class and economics might also make good read-alikes; these include Daniel Brook's *The Trap: Selling Out to Stay Afloat in Winner-Take-All America*, Anya Kamenetz's *Generation Debt*, or Mark Buchanan's *The Social Atom*. Other titles from the Business Reporting chapter might also be suggested, by authors such as Michael Lewis (*Liar's Poker*), David Brooks (*On Paradise Drive* or *Bobos in Paradise*, or Daniel Gross (*Pop!: Why Bubbles Are Great for the Economy*).

Gardner, Daniel

The Science of Fear: Why We Fear the Things We Shouldn't—and Put Our-selves in Greater Danger. Penguin. 2008. 339 pp. ISBN 9780525950622.

Canadian journalist Gardner explores the biological underpinnings of the human experience of fear, as well as how individuals, governments, and corporations manipulate (largely) irrational fears to influence the perceptions and behaviors of others. Using examples such as the U.S. government's response to 9/11 and terrorism, Gardner proves how numbers can be used to misinform, and other "scientific" measures co-opted to increase rather than decrease the fears of the populace.

> **Subjects:** 21st Century, Biology, Brain, Emotion, Fear, Irrationality, Mass Media, Psychology, Society, Sociology, Statistics

> **Now Try:** Other books about how our brains work, as well as how we function in society, might also appeal to these readers, including Malcolm Gladwell's *The Tipping Point* or *Blink*, Nassim Nicholas Taleb's *The Black Swan*, Barry Glassner's *The Culture of Fear*, Gregg Easterbrook's *The Progress Paradox: How Life Gets Better While People Feel Worse,* or even Norman Doidge's *The Brain That Changes Itself.* Two other books that might appeal to Gardner's readers are Stephen Dubner's and Steven Levitt's *Freakonomics*, or Dan Ariely's *Predictably Irrational.*

Grossman, Elizabeth Greenwell

High Tech Trash: Digital Devices, Hidden Toxics, and Human Health. Shearwater Books. 2006. 334 pp. ISBN 9781559635547.

Grossman strips away the sleek and clean façade of technology and gadgets to reveal the complex bundles of lead, mercury, plastics, and other heavy metals and toxic building blocks beneath our computers, electronic devices, cell phones, and the other tools of our superconnected lives. In addition to explaining the less than environmentally friendly production methods used to produce these devices, Grossman also explores the current and future repercussions, to both our environment and our health, of our constant discarding of such items (Americans produce five to seven million tons of such high-tech waste annually) when we buy a new one or the technology becomes obsolete. In addition to local concerns, also highlighted are global concerns for the health of workers in China and India where workers pick through such trash by hand to recycle elements of use; later chapters offer insight into European methods of regulating the use of such materials and safer recycling.

> **Subjects:** Environmental Writing, Garbage, Health Issues, Industry, Technology, Toxins

> **Now Try:** A number of books about technology, obsolescence, and trash might be suggested, including Giles Slade's *Made to Break*, Elizabeth Royte's *Garbage Land*, and Fred Pearce's *Confessions of an Eco-Sinner: Tracking Down the Sources of My Stuff.* Other environmental and science writers might be offered, including Rachel Carson (*Silent Spring*), James Gleick, Richard Manning, Henry Petroski, or Mark Schapiro.

Hallinan, Joseph T.

🏵 *Going Up the River: Travels in a Prison Nation.* Random House. 2001. 262 pp. ISBN 9780375502637.

Hallinan investigates what he terms the "prison-industrial complex" by researching the current trends of rising incarceration rates and the boom in prison construction. Hallinan, who visited several prisons, describes their sometimes psychosis-inducing environment, considers the desire of communities to build prisons to create jobs, and describes the dangerous living conditions for both staff and inmates. The tone of the work is definitely no-nonsense journalistic reporting.

> **Subjects:** Community Life, Economics, Prisons, Professions
>
> **Awards:** ALA Notable
>
> **Now Try:** Readers more interested in personal prison narratives might try Jennifer Wynn's collection of interviews with inmates, *Inside Rikers: Stories from the World's Largest Penal Colony,* Ted Conover's undercover classic *Newjack: Guarding Sing Sing,* Jennifer Gonnerman's exploration of life after prison in *Life on the Outside: The Prison Odyssey of Elaine Bartlett,* or even Adrian Nicole LeBlanc's *Random Family: Love, Drugs, Trouble, and Coming of Age in the Bronx,* in which many of the principal characters spend much of their time going into and being released from prison.

Jaspin, Elliot

Buried in the Bitter Waters: The Hidden History of Racial Cleansing in America. Basic Books. 2007. 341 pp. ISBN 9780465036363.

Current events are not the only ones that sometimes merit close investigation; in this Exposé of American history, Pulitzer Prize–winning journalist Jaspin explores the hidden history of racial cleansing in America, describing incidents of lynching in the Deep South but also exploring other incidents of communities seeking to purge their populations of African Americans, in locations both below and above the Mason-Dixon Line, primarily in the period between Reconstruction and the 1920s. Employing methods of intimidation, violence, and subtle housing and employment discrimination, Jaspin clearly illustrates the coordinated efforts to keep their counties and cities racially "pure." The author's narrative also brings the reader up-to-date through the current day, researching the areas where such cleansing took place and finding them to be still almost exclusively white; although the tone of the book is academic and Jaspin performed research over the course of nearly a decade, he tells an important and compelling story.

> **Subjects:** 20th Century, American History, American South, Community Life, Explicit Violence, Homicides, New Perspectives, Race Relations, Racism, Scholarly, Secret Histories
>
> **Now Try:** Other books about American history, particularly those offering new perspectives, might also be suggested, including Kevin Boyle's *Arc of Justice: A Saga of Race, Civil Rights, and Murder in the Jazz Age,* Steve Oney's *And the Dead Shall Rise: The Murder of Mary Phagan and the Lynching of Leo Frank,* Jeffrey Rothfeder's business history *McIlhenny's Gold: How a Louisiana Family Built the Tabasco Empire,* Dee Brown's *Bury My Heart at Wounded Knee,* Nelson George's *Post-Soul Nation,* and Larry Tye's *Rising from the Rails: Pullman Porters and the Making of the Black Middle Class.*

Kilbourne, Jean

Can't Buy My Love: How Advertising Changes the Way We Think and Feel. Simon & Schuster. 1999. 366 pp. ISBN 9780684866000.

In this classic of sociological and investigative writing, Kilbourne examines the history and development of the advertising industry, as well as how that industry has affected Americans' consumption habits, self-images, and their very culture. The author begins her narrative with her own personal coming-of-age stories and her struggles with self-identity and objectification (she readily admits having slept with men to get jobs), offering her history as the explanation for her interest in how, in her words, we are sold to, accept an environment saturated with advertising, and how those advertisements twist and corrupt our human desires for relationships and fulfillment. Although Kilbourne's tone can be scholarly and the text contains numerous and broad references to other resources and disciplines, her writing is lively and heartfelt, and the book contains many fascinating illustrations from actual advertising campaigns and promotions; the result is a book that illustrates, beyond a doubt, the author's opening assertion that "if you're like most people, you think that advertising has no influence on you. This is what advertisers want you to believe."

Subjects: Addiction, Advertising, Business, Consumerism, Feminism, Memoirs, Pop Culture, Psychology, Society, Women's Rights

Now Try: Other books on the history of consumerism and marketing might be suggested, from Mark Tungate's business history *Adland* or James Twitchell's *Lead Us into Temptation* to Naomi Klein's more adversarial *No Logo*, Juliet Schor's *The Overspent American*, or Judith Levine's memoir *Not Buying It*. Other business Exposés such as Jessica Mitford's *The American Way of Death Revisited* or Richard Kluger's *Ashes to Ashes* might be offered, as well as books by such authors as Susan Faludi or Barbara Ehrenreich.

Kotlowitz, Alex

There Are No Children Here: The Story of Two Boys Growing Up in the Other America. Doubleday. 1991. 324 pp. ISBN 9780385265263.

Kotlowitz tells the story of two young boys, brothers LaFayette and Pharaoh Rivers, growing up in Chicago's Henry Horner Homes project in the 1980s. The brothers, drawn more vividly than most characters in novels, struggle to make their way through run-ins with violence, drugs, poverty, educational challenges, and complex family dynamics; the author spent years getting to know the pair, interviewing them, and spending time with them in their home and neighborhood. The result is an unforgettable and detailed glimpse into urban life and the many difficulties facing those minorities and other individuals living in dangerous situations and, as often as not, poverty.

Subjects: Character Profiles, Chicago, Classics, Family Relationships, Poverty, Racism, Society, Urban Life, YA

Now Try: Although Kotlowitz has particular skill with this format (another of his books, *Down by the River*, might also appeal to these readers), a number of other nonfiction classics on similar subjects are available, including Jonathan Kozol's *Savage Inequalities*, Tracy Kidder's *Among Schoolchildren*, Ron

Suskind's *A Hope in the Unseen*, James McBride's stirring memoir *The Color of Water*, Adrian Nicole LeBlanc's *Random Family*, and Edward Humes's *No Matter How Loud I Shout*. Other slightly more scholarly books about urban life might also be suggested, such as Sudhir Venkatesh's *American Project: The Rise and Fall of a Modern Ghetto* or *Off the Books* (as well as his Immersion Journalism title *Gang Leader for a Day*, set in Chicago's Robert Taylor Homes projects), or Mitchell Duneier's *Sidewalk*.

Kozol, Jonathan

The Shame of the Nation: The Restoration of Apartheid Schooling in America. Crown. 2005. 404 pp. ISBN 9781400052448.

Investigative writer and education activist Kozol explores the hard reality of segregation still present in America's educational institutions in the twenty-first century. On the basis of his observation of 60 schools and numerous interviews with students and educators, Kozol argues that nothing short of a new civil rights campaign will even begin to address the educational inequalities facing those who attend America's poorest and most racially segregated schools.

Subjects: Economics, Education, Government, Poverty, Race Relations, Racism, Schools, Society, Urban Life

Now Try: Jonathan Kozol has been writing on educational and societal issues for decades; readers might also consider his earlier books *Savage Inequalities* or *Death at an Early Age*; Alex Kotlowitz's *The Other Side of the River* is similar in tone and subject matter. Similar books about the challenges facing America's educational system might also be offered: Lee Stringer's *Sleepaway School*, Ron Suskind's *A Hope in the Unseen*, Sam Swope's *I Am a Pencil*, Melba Pattillo Beals's *Warriors Don't Cry*, and Abby Goodnough's *Ms. Moffett's First Year* are all personal and insightful memoirs on the subject. Other works focusing on poverty and urban poverty in particular might also appeal; try David Shipler's *The Working Poor*, Barbara Ehrenreich's *Nickel and Dimed*, or Adrian Nicole LeBlanc's *Random Family*.

Kunstler, James Howard

The Long Emergency: Surviving the End of Oil, Climate Change, and Other Converging Catastrophes of the Twenty-First Century. Atlantic Monthly Press. 2005. 307 pp. ISBN 9780871138880.

Kunstler, who has previously written on architectural and urban design, here turns his attention and prediction powers to the thought of an American future without oil. By drawing attention to the country's extreme dependence on fossil fuels, the author explores how life may change radically (and not for the better) when cheap and nonrenewable energy sources are depleted. In various chapters outlining the history of the last two centuries' mechanical and technological progress, explaining the finite nature of fossil fuels and geopolitics, and the natural threats such as massive climate changes and the possibilities for widespread water shortages and disease epidemics, the author offers a look at the future that is scarier than any bleak future horror or science fiction novels.

Subjects: Climate, Economics, Environmental Writing, Fossil Fuels, Oil, Politics, Science

Now Try: Kunstler is always an entertaining and thoughtful writer; his other nonfiction titles, including *The Geography of Nowhere* and *Home from Nowhere* (as well as his novels *Maggie Darling* and *World Made by Hand*) might be suggested, as well as other environmental books such as Al Gore's *An Inconvenient Truth*, Rachel Carson's

Silent Spring, or Wendell Berry's *The Long-Legged House.* Other books about oil or other scarce resources might also be suggested, such as Lisa Margonelli's *Oil on the Brain* or Vandana Shiva's *Water Wars.*

Lambrecht, Bill

Dinner at the New Gene Cafe: How Genetic Engineering Is Changing What We Eat, How We Live, and the Global Politics of Food. St. Martin's Press. 2001. 383 pp. ISBN 9780312265755.

In addition to reporting on the history, science, and ethical issues surrounding the development, planting, and consumption and use of genetically modified crops, Lambrecht takes his reporting a step further and attempts to grow genetically modified soybean seeds from Monsanto in his own backyard. A journalist with the *St. Louis Dispatch*, the author tells his story through basic reporting techniques, interspersing information gained from research and interviews with scientific, economic, and corporate sources, and also explores in depth the different cultural attitudes toward this issue between, specifically, the United States and Europe (in Europe, labeling is required on foods containing ingredients from genetically modified crops; in the United States, it is not).

> **Subjects:** Activism, Agriculture, Business Histories, Food, Genetics, Science, Technology
>
> **Now Try:** Other writers who explore the new frontiers of agribusiness and food production include Michael Pollan (*In Defense of Food*), Wendell Berry, Bill McKibben, Eric Schlosser (*Fast Food Nation*), Jeremy Rifkin (*The Biotech Century*), and Thomas Pawlick (*The End of Food*). Other provocative science books might be suggested, including Peter Pringle's *Food, Inc.,* Mark Schapiro's *Exposed: The Toxic Chemistry of Everyday Products and What's at Stake for American Power,* or Alan Weisman's *The World without Us,* as well as History of Medicine and Science books such as Robert Morris's *The Blue Death: Disease, Disaster, and the Water We Drink* or Henry Gee's *Jacob's Ladder: The History of the Human Genome.*

Love, Dennis

My City Was Gone: One American Town's Toxic Secret, Its Angry Band of Locals, and a $700 Million Day in Court. William Morrow. 2006. 344 pp. ISBN 9780060585501.

The cancer rate in Love's hometown of Anniston, Alabama, home to both a Monsanto chemical plant and a federal depot for chemical weapons (as well as the city where a Freedom Riders bus was set on fire in 1961), is 25 percent above the state norm, and Love went home to investigate why. Love unfolds a story-driven narrative centering on two of the town's most vocal and determined citizens: David Baker, the community and environmental activist leading the charge against the polluters, and Chip Howell, the mayor who defended the army's arms incineration practices at the weapon depot. Love also shares his own childhood memories and insight's into the town's racial and social tensions and paints a vivid picture of Anniston as "created from whole cloth to serve exclusively at the pleasure of commerce, a Reconstruction-era 'model city' envisioned by its profiteering yet starry-eyed founders as a Utopian centerpiece of the Industrial Age." The story culminates with the town's residents winning a financial settlement worth twice that of the one more famously won by Erin Brockovich, but as Love points out, even money may not be enough to re-build the city where he grew up.

> **Subjects:** Alabama, Business, Companies, Community Life, Environmental Writing, Health Issues, Law and Lawyers, Military, Toxins, Trials

> **Now Try:** Other books about community trials and environmental challenges, such as Joy Horowitz's *Parts Per Million: The Poisoning of Beverly Hills High School*, Gillian Klucas's *Leadville*, or Kelly McMasters's *Welcome to Shirley: A Memoir from An Atomic Town* might appeal, as might books like Jonathan Harr's *A Civil Action* or William Mishler's *A Measure of Endurance*. Other social histories like Terry Tempest Williams's *Refuge* or Melissa Fay Greene's *Praying for Sheetrock* might also be suggested; other titles from both the Corporate and Government Exposé sections might also be good related reads.

Restak, Richard M.

The Naked Brain: How the Emerging Neurosociety Is Changing How We Live, Work, and Love. Harmony. 2006. 255 pp. ISBN 9781400098088.

Restak lays bare the brave new world of neuroscience and brain scans—new tech-nologies that may soon be used by marketers to determine consumer interests, politicians to target voters, and employers to screen prospective employees for their suitability for their jobs and corporate cultures. Part science, part Exposé, Restak explains both the technological aspects of the coming "neurosociety," in which we will come to view our habits of learning, communication, and relation-ships much differently. Although the possibilities for good in such a society are many and varied, the author also warns that the possibilities for abuse of these advances are also present and must be safeguarded against.

> **Subjects:** Brain, Business, Medicine, Neuroscience, Psychology, Science, Technology

> **Now Try:** Restak himself is a prolific author; his readers might consider his other titles like *Mozart's Brain and the Fighter Pilot* or *Poe's Heart and the Mountain Climber*. Other books by Science authors might be offered, including Oliver Sacks, Carl Zimmer, William Wright, Diane Ackerman, or Louann Brizendine; other books about futurism and technology might be offered, such as David Weinberger's *Everything Is Miscella-neous* or Ray Kurzweil's *The Singularity Is Near*. Also consider offering Science Fiction novels by authors such as William Gibson, Phillip K. Dick, Isaac Asimov, or Neal Stephenson.

Robbins, Alexandra

The Overachievers: The Secret Lives of Driven Kids. Hyperion. 2006. 439 pp. ISBN 9781401302016.

Robbins dealt with her ten-year high school reunion slightly differently than do most people in their late twenties; she decided to get to know and interview cur-rent students in her former high school to get a better feel for their lives, worries, and social pressures. In the course of getting to know such teens as C. J., Julie, Frank, and many others, Robbins's eyes were opened to a world of ever-increas-ing pressure on kids to excel at academics and sports; to be popular; to wear the right clothes and look the right way and talk to the right people. In an academic environment increasingly ruled by benchmarks and test scores, Robbins also learned that kids and their parents are becoming more astute at finding ways to "game the system" than to actually learn the material. In providing these poignant character portraits, as well as offering quantitative research on college admissions and academic standards, Robbins illuminates a world most people can't wait to forget about once they graduate.

Subjects: Character Profiles, Education, Schools, Year in the Life

Now Try: Other books about challenges in education might be suggested, such as Tracy Kidder's *Among Schoolchildren*, Michael Bamberger's Immersion title *Wonderland*, Michael Weinreb's *The Kings of New York*, Jonathan Kozol's *Savage Inequalities*, Abby Goodnough's *Ms. Moffett's First Year*, or Sam Swope's *I Am a Pencil*. Robbins's Immersion Journalism title, *Pledged*, about her experiences joining a college sorority, might also be suggested. Character-driven novels featuring younger characters such as Curtis Sittenfeld's *Prep*, John Green's *Looking for Alaska* or *An Abundance of Katherines*, or Marisha Pessl's *Special Topics in Calamity Physics* might also provide good read-alikes.

Rosenbaum, Ron

Travels with Dr. Death: And Other Unusual Investigations. Penguin Books. 1991. 482 pp. ISBN 9780140138450.

Rosenbaum sets out to relate those stories he finds most interesting—that is, the stories in which the investigations themselves become the subject of investigations. Although the book is slightly dated in subject matter (one of the chapters finds Rosenbaum investigating the Watergate break-in and trying to find more information about Deep Throat, who was revealed in 2005 to be Mark Felt and is named as a possible suspect here), Rosenbaum's unique style and his fascination with the secrets often kept by those engaging in and revealing secrets is enthralling in itself. Also included here are chapters on public scandals (including spy stories and the Watergate case), private investigations such as the murder of JFK's mistress Mary Meyer, and clandestine subcultures such as the "cancer cure underground" and the Skull and Bones society. Suspenseful, intensively researched, and bolstered with numerous interviews, this is not only a fascinating narrative read but also a valuable look into the methods used by the most tenacious journalists and writers.

Subjects: American History, Character Profiles, Classics, Essays, Secret Histories, True Crime

Now Try: Rosenbaum is a respected practitioner of the "new journalism" style; his other books, including *Explaining Hitler* and *The Secret Parts of Fortune* might appeal, as might titles by other "new journalists," including Leon Dash, William Langewiesche, Richard Ben Cramer, and Lawrence Weschler.

Royte, Elizabeth

🏵 *Garbage Land: On the Secret Trail of Trash.* Little, Brown. 2005. 311 pp. ISBN 9780316738262.

Journalist Royte offers one of the stranger travelogues available, as she set out to follow the path of everything that she threw away as garbage. Her tour followed four main journeys: those of her household trash, compostable matter, recyclables, and even her sewage. The book is written with an engagingly light tone, and Royte's descriptions, although detailed, never veer into the sensationalistic; her encounters with individuals involved along the way offer delightfully matter-of-fact and prosaic interviews. Melding science and anthropology, Royte seeks to discover not only where our garbage ends up but the implications in our producing ever larger amounts of it.

Subjects: Environmental Writing, Garbage, Professions, Recycling, Sustainability

Awards: New York Times Notable

Now Try: Fans of Royte's accessible writing on a serious subject might also appreciate Michael Pollan's *The Botany of Desire* or *The Omnivore's Dilemma*, Robert Sullivan's classic *Rats*, or Amy Stewart's *The Earth Moved* or *Flower Confidential* (the former title about earthworms; the latter about the floral industry); readers more interested in Royte's worries about our (over)consumption habits might also consider Al Gore's *An Inconvenient Truth*, Bill McKibben's *Deep Economy*, Giles Slade's *Made to Break*, or Barbara Kingsolver's *Animal, Vegetable, Miracle*.

Shipler, David K.

🏶 *The Working Poor: Invisible in America.* Knopf. 2004. 319 pp. ISBN 9780375408908.
Shipler examines the lives of many members of the class he refers to as "the working poor"—those who work, and often work multiple jobs, but who cannot make enough money to raise themselves or their families above the national poverty line. He leaves no aspects of their lives unexplored, from the jobs they work to their struggles with unsafe or substandard housing, lack of access to health care, few educational opportunities, and disturbing but continuing patterns of substance and child abuse. Although some of Shipler's assertions may leave more conservative readers cold (e.g., his labeling of cable television as a necessary expense), this remains a thoroughly researched, investigated, and empathetic exploration of the experiences of the working poor (including many immigrants and minorities), and one which the author investigated in many different regions of the United States, including North Carolina, New Hampshire, and California.

Subjects: Book Groups, Business, Classics, Classism, Economics, Family Relationships, Politics, Poverty, Professions, Society

Awards: New York Times Notable

Now Try: A wide variety of books about class and economics are currently available; they include but are not limited to Louise Uchitelle's *The Disposable American*, William Finnegan's *Cold New World*, Barbara Ehrenreich's *Nickel and Dimed* or *Bait and Switch*, Anya Kamenetz's *Generation Debt*, Thomas Frank's *One Market under God*, Katherine Newman's and Victor Tan Chen's *The Missing Class*, Robert H. Frank's *Falling Behind*, or Joe Bageant's *Deer Hunting with Jesus*. Anthologies such as *Class Matters* or Daniel Rothenberg's oral history *With These Hands: The Hidden World of Migrant Farmworkers Today* might also be suggested.

Staten, Vince

Can You Trust a Tomato in January? Simon & Schuster. 1993. 239 pp. ISBN 9780671769413.

In this engaging and humorous book, Staten takes his reader on an in-depth tour of his local grocery store, examining his food and sundry purchases aisle by aisle, and offering fun facts and sometimes surprising revelations about where our food comes from, why it costs what it does, how it is marketed and distributed, and how all of these things have changed over the course of the past century. The result is a book that is both quick to read and also leaves the reader with a number of historical and cultural issues to ponder.

> **Subjects:** American History, Business, Food, Health Issues, Humor, Quick Reads, Retail, Technology, Trivia
>
> **Now Try:** Staten is the author of numerous books of this type, including *Do Bald Men Get Half-Price Haircuts?*, *Did Monkeys Invent the Monkey Wrench?*, and *Do Pharmacists Sell Farms?*; other trivia books such as *The Book of General Ignorance* (by John Lloyd) or Rick Beyer's *The Greatest Stories Never Told* might appeal, as might humor books by authors such as Dave Barry, Bill Bryson, A. J. Jacobs, or Bob Tarte. Books on food and sustainability issues might also be offered, such as Michele Simon's *Appetite for Profit*, Thomas Pawlick's *The End of Food*, or Michael Pollan's *In Defense of Food*.

Stossel, John

Myths, Lies, and Downright Stupidity: Get Out the Shovel—Why Everything You Know Is Wrong. Hyperion. 2006. 304 pp. ISBN 9781401302542.

Popular television commentator and investigative reporter John Stossel unearths contradictions, untruths, and myriad other topics that he feels are defined by their "downright stupidity" (including what he terms myths like "businesses rip us off" and "government must make rules to protect us from business") and offers suggestions for commonsense improvements and better regulation in government and other institutions. Stossel's style is sarcastic but practical, and his straight talk often strikes a libertarian tone (although many of his suggestions might be better appreciated by those readers with political sensibilities slightly to the right of center).

> **Subjects:** Government, Mass Media, Politics, Quick Reads, Society
>
> **Now Try:** Fans of this title might also want to consider John Stossel's earlier best seller *Give Me a Break*, published in 2004. Other media commentators who may appeal to these readers include Bernard Goldberg, Bill O'Reilly, Ann Coulter, Michelle Malkin, and Mona Charen.

Streatfeild, Dominic

Brainwash: The Secret History of Mind Control. St. Martin's Press. 2006. 418 pp. ISBN 9780312325725.

Streatfeild delves into all types and varieties of brainwashing and mind control in this chilling history, covering hypnosis, sensory deprivation, subliminal messages, indoctrination, and a variety of truth serums and other pharmacological tools. Parts of the narrative veer into dark humor, particularly those sections dealing with Cold War anecdotes and CIA interest in these techniques, but the author has been positively reviewed for his "meticulous research."

> **Subjects:** Brain, CIA, Cold War, Government, Hypnotism, Micro-Histories, Pharmacology, Psychology, Secret Histories, Torture, World History
>
> **Now Try:** Histories and investigation of mind control techniques are often compelling, if unnerving, reads; similar titles include Jon Ronson's nonfiction *The Men Who Stare at Goats*, as well as fiction titles such as Dean Koontz's

Night Chills or Douglas Clegg's *The Nightmare Chronicles*. Other New Perspectives history books, such as James Risen's *State of War: The Secret History of the CIA and the Bush Administration* or Tim Weiner's *Legacy of Ashes: The History of the CIA*, as well as other micro-histories (such as Stephen Murdoch's *IQ: A Smart History of a Failed Idea*) or spy and espionage novels by Robert Ludlum, Frederick Forsyth, or John Le Carré might also appeal.

Vaillant, John

The Golden Spruce: A True Story of Myth, Madness, and Greed. Norton. 2005. 255 pp. ISBN 9780393058871.

In this work of investigative journalism, true crime narrative, and true adventure environmentalism, Vaillant offers the story of logger-turned-activist Grant Hadwin, who disappeared after felling the "golden spruce," a 165-foot-tall Sitka spruce in British Columbia's Queen Charlotte Islands forest. Vaillant tells the story of this passionate act of eco-tourism, placing the tale in the greater context of the region's history, logging industry, and the tribe of Haida Indians who worshipped the tree. The violence and mystery of Hadwin's protest act, combined with the often violent history of the area between native residents and fur traders (in the past) and loggers (in the present), makes this a suspenseful, dark read.

> **Subjects:** Book Groups, British Columbia, Environmental Writing, Forestry, Grant Hadwin, Native Peoples, Nature, True Crime

> **Now Try:** Various angles of this book might appeal to different readers; those enthralled by the adventure aspect might consider books by Jon Krakauer (*Into the Wild, Into Thin Air,* or *Under the Banner of Heaven*), Richard Preston's investigative *The Wild Trees* or Erik Reece's *Lost Mountain*; other character profiles of singular and driven individuals might also be suggested, such as Elizabeth Gilbert's *The Last American Man* or Eric Blehm's *The Last Season*. Travel books by Jonathan Raban (*Passage to Juneau*) might also appeal, as might a number of environmental titles by Farley Mowat, Edward Abbey, or Robert Sullivan (*A Whale Hunt*).

Walker, Rob

Buying In: The Secret Dialogue Between What We Buy and Who We Are. Random House. 2008. 291 pp. ISBN 9781400063918.

Walker seeks to dispel the myth that Americans have become immune to advertising and marketing messages simply because they have been exposed to so many for so long. Through intensive research and detail-oriented reporting on specific (and very successful) ad campaigns such as those recently used by Red Bull and Pabst Blue Ribbon, the *New York Times* journalist makes a compelling case that new advertising techniques, word-of-mouth campaigns, and sponsorships continue to contribute to society's commercialization and consumerism in general.

> **Subjects:** Advertising, Business, Companies, Consumerism, Marketing, Psychology, Society

> **Now Try:** Other Exposés, particularly about companies and advertising, might also be suggested, such as Rebecca Mead's *One Perfect Day: The Selling of the American Wedding*, Jean Kilbourne's *Can't Buy My Love: How Advertising Changes the Way We Think and Feel*, and Melody Petersen's *Our Daily Meds: How the Pharmaceutical Companies Transformed Themselves into Slick Marketing Machines and Hooked the Nation on Prescription Drugs* might be suggested, as might more scholarly books about consumerism, spending, and materialism, such as Juliet Schor's *The Overspent*

American, James Twitchell's *Adcult USA* or *Lead Us into Temptation*, Naomi Klein's *No Logo*, or Sam Gosling's *Snoop: What Your Stuff Says about You*.

International Exposés

It is truly unfortunate that the concepts of evildoing, corruption, and ineptness know no borders in our world. The only thing more shocking than the fact that many acts of wrongdoing, systems that are rotten to the core, and individuals willing to ignore ethics and basic human rights go on in our world is in learning in how many countries and societies these acts occur around the globe. That is what the authors and titles in this subgenre, many of them journalists working outside the United States (at least one of whom lost her life in the pursuit of publishing true stories of government corruption) and writing in other languages, have in common: they all tell hidden stories and secret histories of events that took place outside of the United States. It seems odd in this era of globalization to classify a set of Exposés simply by setting or location (and further to classify those settings as "not America"), but the sad fact of the matter is that it is not often easy to find books in translation (which many of these are) or books that deal solely with tragedies, human rights violations, and events that do not immediately affect our experiences and lives as Americans. These books might particularly appeal to your most dedicated and hardcore nonfiction readers, because they often assume a great deal of historical, geographical, and general world knowledge; but what they demand is in direct proportion to what they provide. They are some of the most intense, vividly drawn, and compelling narratives in this entire book, and they deserve to sell and to circulate—if nothing else, so that their publishers are encouraged to keep finding and publishing translated and new perspectives.

That said, a very strong appeal of these books is their foreign (if not necessarily exotic) locales. Readers with interests in particular regions, especially their histories, might enjoy these books; for example, a person of Russian heritage who is interested in the politics and society of that country might be drawn to the appropriate titles here. In addition to setting, these books, like all Exposés, have much to offer in the way of story, even if they are not often pleasant stories. Because people are not really all that different the world over, many of these books, even if they are set in different countries, still focus on instances of political or business corruption; as such, their readers might also consider a wide variety of other titles from this chapter on those subjects. Business Reporting books, particularly those on the subject of globalization, might also appeal, as might Political Reporting books on the subject of foreign relations. It will not come as a surprise, perhaps, that many readers of these books might also enjoy a wide variety of nonfiction Travel narratives (including those by such sociocultural commentators as Colin Thubron, Eric Newby, or Pico Iyer), and readers of nonfiction History and Historical Fiction alike might also consider some of these titles (and vice versa).

International Exposés are story-driven nonfiction narratives in which authors typically expose specific deeds, instances, or histories of corruption or wrong-doing in international and foreign affairs (and particularly in international settings). They can feature strongly drawn characters, many of whom the readers may feel a strong sympathy for, but they also offer unique settings and locations that may themselves be of interest to readers (particularly those who enjoy multicultural stories and issues). They are often written by reporters and correspondents covering foreign affairs news stories, as well as by journalists based in other countries; this subgenre features perhaps the widest variety of "books in translation" as any nonfiction subgenre.

Alexievich, Svetlana, translated by Keith Gessen

🎗 *Voices from Chernobyl.* Dalkey Archive Press. 2005. 240 pp. ISBN 9781564784018.
Journalist Alexievich spent more than three years traveling and gathering testimonials from those who were most intimately acquainted with the Chernobyl Nuclear Power Station disaster—those who worked there in 1986, lived in the area, and many who lost family members to radiation poisoning in the aftermath of the disaster (most were exposed because they were frontline workers trying to secure and clean the area). These oral histories are immediately affecting; they are heartfelt, containing horrible descriptions of physical and medical agony, as well as an awareness that these workers and residents were not given the full story regarding the accident and its repercussions by their government.

> **Subjects:** 1980s, Belarus, Books in Translation, Chernobyl, Disasters, Family Relationships, Government, Nuclear Power, Oral Histories, Small Press, Soviet Union, Survival Stories, Ukraine

> **Awards:** ALA Notable, National Book Critics Circle

> **Now Try:** Regardless of its horrifying story, this is a beautifully written oral and investigative history; readers might consider similar titles like Melissa Fay Greene's *There Is No Me without You*, Studs Terkel's *Hard Times* or *Working*, Jean Hatzfeld's *Machete Season*, Philip Gourevitch's *We Wish to Inform You That Tomorrow We Will Be Killed with Our Families*, John Hersey's *Hiroshima*, Catherine Collins's *Death on the Black Sea,* or Adam Hochschild's *King Leopold's Ghost*. Other nonfiction titles about Russia might also appeal, including Anne Applebaum's *Gulag: A History*, Orlando Figes's *A People's Tragedy*, Robert Friedman's *Red Mafiya*, or Aleksandr Solzhenitsyn's *The Gulag Archipelago*.

Campbell, Greg

🎗 *Blood Diamonds: Tracing the Deadly Path of the World's Most Precious Stones.* Westview Press. 2002. 251 pp. ISBN 9780813339399.
Investigative journalist Campbell traces the paths taken in the illegal diamond trade. From Sierra Leone, where revolutionaries on all sides mine diamonds to fund their civil wars, to Lebanese diamond markets where all the complex politics of setting diamond prices and the trade intersect, Campbell interviewed key players at all levels in the illicit industry, from impoverished miners to De Beers company executives. The diamonds are used to fund violence, and readers should be aware that there are graphic descriptions in this book.

> **Subjects:** Business, Diamonds, Micro-Histories, Sierra Leone, True Crime

> **Awards:** ALA Notable

Now Try: Matthew Hart's *Diamond: A Journey to the Heart of an Obsession* details more of the geological origins of diamonds but also reflects on their often violent milieu. Michael Klare's *Resource Wars: The New Landscape of Global Conflict* examines a variety of scarce resources (diamonds, water, oil, etc.) and their role in global warfare. Other books set in Sierra Leone, including Graham Greene's classic *Journey without Maps* might be suggested, as might Dave Eggers's novel *What Is the What*, or other nonfiction narratives about violence in Africa, such as Jean Hatzfeld's oral histories of the Rwandan genocide, *Machete Season* and *Life Laid Bare*.

Chehab, Zaki

Inside Hamas: The Untold Story of the Militant Islamic Movement. Nation Books. 2007. 244 pp. ISBN 9781560259688.

Palestinian journalist Chehab offers coverage of the landslide election victory won by the radical Islamist movement Hamas in January 2006. In his quest to explain the popularity of Hamas in the Palestinian occupied territories, Chehab shows how they built a base for their popularity through social welfare programs but does not shy away from the reality that their strategy of terrorist acts and armed retaliation contrasts favorably with the perceived failures of the Oslo Peace Accord and general peace policies in the region. Although readers with a basic understanding of the situation in Israel and the history of the Middle East since the middle of the twentieth century will find this narrative easier to follow, Chehab's writing is clear and instructive and his fluency in both Arabic and English is used to great effect to tell the stories of civilians affected by the ongoing civil unrest in the area.

Subjects: 20th Century, Arab-Israeli Conflict, Foreign Relations, Government, Hamas, Israel, Middle East, Palestine, Terrorism, World History

Now Try: Other books by Chehab might be suggested, including *Inside the Resistance: The Iraqi Insurgency and the Future of the Middle East*, as might other books with the subjects of Hamas or Hezbollah. Other books about the region and its complex history and politics include Jimmy Carter's best seller *Palestine: Peace, Not Apartheid*, Robert Fisk's *Pity the Nation: Lebanon at War*, Richard Ben Cramer's *How Israel Lost: The Four Questions*, or George Jonas's masterpiece of reporting, *Vengeance: The True Story of an Israeli Counter-Terrorist Team*. David Shipler's *Arab and Jew: Wounded Spirits in a Promised Land*, Sandy Tolan's *The Lemon Tree*, and George Packer's *The Assassins' Gate: America In Iraq* are all fascinating histories and current affairs books on the region; Suad Amiry's more personal memoir *Sharon and My Mother-in-Law: Ramallah Diaries* might also be offered.

Drakulic, Slavenka

They Would Never Hurt a Fly: War Criminals on Trial in The Hague. Viking. 2004. 209 pp. ISBN 9780670033324.

For the most part, once war criminals are captured, their stories tend to fade from public view and media headlines. Drakulic provides the story after the story, often finding herself the only journalist (or witness, period) present at the international trials of both Croatians and Serbs who committed terrible crimes during the struggle for independence in Yugoslavia from 1991 to 1995. The author's writing is investigative, but her tone is reflective; she cynically notes that even the most hard-core of idealistic enemies imprisoned together in The Hague typically forget their differences long enough to work together to receive the best possible treatment. Quietly chilling, this book reads quickly but is hard to forget.

> **Subjects:** Europe, Government, Homicides, Human Rights, Prisons, Quick Reads, World Leaders, Yugoslavia
>
> **Now Try:** Drakulic's ALA Notable Book *The Balkan Express: Fragments from the Other Side of War* is a fascinating and evocative account of living in Yugoslavia during the ethnic violence of the early 1990s; she has also written a novel, *S: A Novel about the Balkans*. Courtney Angela Brkic's *The Stone Fields: An Epitaph for the Living* is a poignant memoir about her family's history, intertwined with her experiences interviewing victims of ethnic violence in the area. Tom Gjeltsen's ALA Notable Book *Sarajevo Daily: A City and Its Newspaper under Siege* examines the surreal nature of continuing life and professional duties under the shadow of war, while Samantha Power's classic *"A Problem from Hell": America and the Age of Genocide* might also provide a compelling read-alike experience.

Epstein, Helen

🐾 *The Invisible Cure: Africa, the West, and the Fight Against AIDS.* Farrar, Straus & Giroux. 2007. 326 pp. ISBN 9780374281526.

Public health specialist Epstein offers a lucid and thorough portrait of the different social and cultural constructs that lead to the spread of AIDS in Africa, and points out how Western countries' efforts to promote AIDS prevention often fail because of a lack of understanding about such practices as concurrency (in which individuals engage in long-term relationships with two or three other people). She also makes a case for African individuals and leaders to be more involved in education and prevention efforts, and offers specific case studies as Uganda, in which the infection rate dropped seventy percent between 1992 and 1997.

> **Subjects:** Africa, AIDS, Foreign Relations, Health Issues, Medicine, Multicultural Issues, Science, Society, Uganda
>
> **Awards:** New York Times Notable
>
> **Now Try:** Stephanie Nolan's *28: Stories of AIDS in Africa*, Melissa Fay Greene's *There Is No Me without You: One Woman's Odyssey to Rescue Her Country's Children*, or Randy Shilts's *And the Band Played On* might be good read-alikes; other books on health professionals and issues such as Sonia Shah's *The Body Hunters: Testing New Drugs on the World's Poorest Patients*, Anne Fadiman's *The Spirit Catches You and You Fall Down*, or Tracy Kidder's *Mountains beyond Mountains: The Quest of Dr. Paul Farmer* might provide good related reads. Other books featuring African stories, albeit tragic ones, might also be offered, such as Ishmael Beah's *A Long Way Gone*, or Jean Hatzfeld's enormously affecting oral histories *Machete Season* and *Life Laid Bare*, both about the Rwandan genocide.

Farah, Douglas

Blood from Stones: The Secret Financial Network of Terror. Broadway Books. 2004. 225 pp. ISBN 9780767915625.

Investigative journalist Farah traveled deep into what he terms "the interlocking web of commodities, underground transfer systems, charities, and sympathetic bankers supporting terrorist activities throughout the world." As the foreign correspondent for the *Washington Post*, Farah's grasp of world events and political ideologies, as well as his personal contacts at all levels of the terror network, provide his writing with frightening immediacy and authenticity, as well as a straightforward style that includes little in the way of partisan political commentary. Instead he provides in-depth chapters on a variety of aspects of worldwide terrorist activities and weapons purchasing, including the events of 9/11, how diamonds and money can be exchanged for weapons, the case of Viktor Bout, the "merchant of death," al-Qaeda, and many others.

> **Subjects:** 9/11, Africa, Corruption, Diamonds, Economics, Politics, Terrorism, Travel

> **Now Try:** Three other books on diamonds might also appeal to these readers; Matthew Hart's more scientific but still fascinating *Diamond: A Journey to the Heart of an Obsession*, Tom Zoellner's ALA Notable book *The Heartless Stone: A Journey through the World of Diamonds, Deceit, and Desire*, or Greg Campbell's *Blood Diamonds*; likewise, this author's other book, *Merchant of Death* (about Viktor Bout), might also be suggested. Other books set in Africa might be suggested, including Ishmael Beah's *A Long Way Gone: Memoirs of a Child Soldier* or Jean Hatzfeld's *Machete Season* (although both are tragic tales), while other political and global Exposés such as Jeremy Scahill's *Blackwater* or John Bowe's *Nobodies* might also appeal.

Hersey, John

Hiroshima. Knopf. 1946. 117 pp. ISBN 9780394548449.

This small but horrific book-length article first appeared in *The New Yorker*. It follows Hersey's experience interviewing the survivors of the atomic bomb in Hiroshima just days after it happened. As a journalist, Hersey is completely absent in his own text, which leaves him able to describe the horrific aftermath and unbelievable medical and emotional fallout of the weapon without any egotistical distractions or pat interpretations.

> **Subjects:** 1940s, Atomic Bomb, Atrocities, Classics, Health Issues, Japan, Quick Reads, Radiation, War Reporting, Weapons, World History, World War II

> **Now Try:** For those readers who can stand to learn any more about the effects of the atomic bomb on human bodies, as well as on landscapes, the illustrated *Rain of Ruin: A Photographic History of Hiroshima and Nagasaki*, by Donald Goldstein, J. Michael Wenger, and Katherine V. Dillon, might be a powerful complementary and visual read, as might Svetlana Alexievich's oral history *Voices from Chernobyl*. John Hersey was also a Pulitzer Prize–winning author of fiction; his novel *A Bell for Adano* is set in World War II Italy, and *The Wall* is a story of life inside the Jewish ghetto of Warsaw during the same time period; his classic of War Reporting, *Storming the Valley*, might also be suggested to these readers. Another atrocity of war is described in well-known journalist Seymour Hersh's Exposé *My Lai 4: A Report on the Massacre and Its Aftermath*.

Hiro, Dilip

Blood of the Earth: The Battle for the World's Vanishing Oil Resources. Nation Books. 2007. 403 pp. ISBN 9781560255444.

Numerous trends will affect the geopolitics of oil in the twenty-first century: China only narrowly trails behind America as the second largest energy consumer; India has moved rapidly into fourth place, behind Russia; and, although the demand for oil and energy is continually rising, the competition for oil will sharpen as the number of countries exporting petroleum will shrink in the future. Hiro also illustrates how most of the exporting countries in the Middle East are largely Muslim and may be hostile to Western interests (as might other countries, such as Venezuela, where the government's disagreements with American principles are more secular in nature). As a contributor to *The Nation* magazine, Hiro sometimes brings a left-of-center sensibility to his writing; but he is also a writer for the *New York Times* and the *Washington Post*, and his extensive research and interview skills show in his overall objectivity.

> **Subjects:** 19th Century, 20th Century, Business Histories, Economics, Middle East, Oil, Politics, World History

> **Now Try:** Dilip has written a number of other books which readers may want to try; including *The Iranian Labyrinth* and *Sharing the Promised Land: A Tale of the Israelis and Palestinians.* Other books on oil might be offered, such as Lisa Margonelli's *Oil on the Brain*, Daniel Yergin's *The Prize*, or Howard Kunstler's *The Long Emergency*, while books on other scarce resources might also appeal, such as Greg Campbell's *Blood Diamonds*. Dilip also lists a number of history and political books in his bibliography, including Barbara Freese's *Coal: A Human History*, Steven Emerson's *The American House of Saud*, or Robert Lacey's *The Kingdom*.

Jonas, George

Vengeance: The True Story of an Israeli Counter-Terrorist Team. Simon & Schuster. 1984. 376 pp. ISBN 9780671506117.

Canadian journalist Jonas's account of the actions of an Israeli counter-terrorist team is based largely on interviews with his source, an Israeli man named Avner who claimed to be the leader of a team of operatives sent to assassinate eleven Palestinian terrorists held responsible for the 1972 murder of eleven Israeli Olympic athletes in Munich. Although there has been some controversy regarding the truth of Avner's account, Jonas is forthright about the many reasons he believes his source's account to be true. Ranging across time and European countries, this is a chilling tale of politics and revenge, and was the basis for Steven Spielberg's 2005 film *Munich*.

> **Subjects:** 1970s, Arab-Israeli Conflict, Assassinations, Classics, Espionage, Friendships, Israel, Golda Meir, Middle East, Military, Palestine, Politics, Terrorism

> **Now Try:** Jonas's shocking true tale of terrorism, counter-terrorism, and foreign relations is more timely than ever in its subject matter; readers drawn to this account might consider other related histories such as David Shipler's *Arab and Jew: Wounded Spirits in a Promised Land*, Thomas Friedman's *From Beirut to Jerusalem*, or Suad Amiry's *Sharon and My Mother-in-Law: Ramallah Diaries*. Autobiographies or Biographies of numerous historical figures described in Jonas's book, including Golda Meir's *My Life* or Nir Hefez's *Ariel Sharon: A Life*, might also appeal. Other insiders' stories like John Perkins's *Confessions of an Economic Hit Man* might be suggested, as might Political Reporting or history books about the Middle East.

Keefe, Patrick Radden

Chatter: Dispatches from the Secret World of Global Eavesdropping. Random House. 2005. 300 pp. ISBN 9781400060344.

Keefe throws open a highly secretive world for his readers' consideration by investigating the global eavesdropping trade. Offering a nonpartisan review of the science and technology that makes much eavesdropping, spying, and listening (covert or not) possible, the author also segues into a balanced discussion of both the pros and cons of a world in which, increasingly, pretty much everything is being overheard by someone, somewhere. In the course of researching his book, the author traveled to Menwith Hill in Yorkshire (one of the largest satellite installations in the world), as well as various locations in the United States, Australia, and Eritrea. In addition to relating the hows and whys of the practice, the author also explores possible reasons for why the topic is not widely or openly discussed in the United States, either in social or political circles, although at least one of the planet-spanning surveillance networks, Echelon, is based in the United States and intercepts, on a daily basis, a huge number of private phone calls and e-mails.

Subjects: Espionage, Foreign Relations, Politics, Sociology, Technology

Now Try: Other closer looks into secretive subjects might be suggested, such as Jon Ronson's *The Men Who Stare at Goats*, Katherine Albrecht's and Liz McIntyre's *Spychips*, or Dominic Streatfeild's *Brainwash*, as might books by authors who provided blurbs for this title, such as James Carroll (*House of War: The Pentagon and the Disastrous Rise of American Power*), Seymour Hersh (*Chain of Command: The Road from 9/11 to Abu Ghraib*), or Amy Chua (*Day of Empire*). Nonfiction by authors such as Robert Baer and Chalmers Johnson might be offered, as might a wide variety of dystopia science fiction titles such as William Gibson's *Pattern Recognition*, or spy and espionage novels by Robert Ludlum or Len Deighton.

Langewiesche, William

The Atomic Bazaar: The Rise of the Nuclear Poor. Farrar, Straus & Giroux. 2007. 179 pp. ISBN 9780374106782.

It's the rare author who can sum up the global situation regarding nuclear arsenals (and developing nations' determination to develop them) in fewer than 200 pages, but Langewiesche is that author. In his simultaneously succinct and graceful prose he offers a brief history of the development and use of nuclear weapons, explains with unnerving detail how the materials necessary to build bombs could be obtained and assembled by any sufficiently motivated group or individuals, examines in close detail the case study of the driving force behind Pakistan's nuclear program, Dr. Abdul Qadeer Khan, and speculates on what future nuclear weapon proliferation will mean to world alliances and politics. He also interviews both Russian nuclear officials receiving American grants to "consolidate, secure, and to some degree destroy nuclear warheads," as well as American staff members of the National Nuclear Security Administration (NNSA) sent to Russia to provide them with support and expertise. The book first saw publication as a series of articles for The Atlantic Monthly, where Langewiesche was a national correspondent; he is now the international editor at *Vanity Fair* magazine.

> **Subjects:** 20th Century, Atomic Bomb, Cold War, Government, A. Q. Khan, Pakistan, Politics, Radiation, Russia, Weapons

> **Now Try:** Those readers looking for a much more in-depth consideration of this topic might be well served by Gordon Corera's more scholarly *Shopping for Bombs: Nuclear Proliferation, Global Insecurity, and the Rise and Fall of the A. Q. Khan Network*; other titles about atomic weapons and power might also be considered, such as Richard Rhodes's *The Making of the Atomic Bomb*, Jim Ottaviani's historical graphic novel *Fallout*, John Hersey's *Hiroshima*, or Svetlana Alexievich's *Voices from Chernobyl*. Other new historical perspectives on the twentieth century might also appeal: these include Tim Weiner's *Legacy of Ashes: The History of the CIA* or Linda Robinson's *Masters of Chaos: The Secret History of the Special Forces*; these readers might also like fast-paced thrillers by authors such as Robert Ludlum, Frederick Forsyth, Tom Clancy, or Alan Furst.

Martinez, Ruben

🟑 *Crossing Over: A Mexican Family on the Migrant Trail.* Metropolitan Books. 2001. 330 pp. ISBN 9780805049084.

In April 1996, eight illegal Mexican migrant workers were killed while being smuggled into the United States; pursued by Border Patrol officers, the driver lost control of their truck and crashed. Journalist Martinez spent two years following migrant families on their journeys back and forth between their homes in Mexico and their jobs in the United States, and in particular tells the story of María Elena Chávez, who lost three sons in the 1996 accident, and her Mexican village, Cherán. Quietly factual in tone, the book presents a comprehensive picture of the current state of border policy as well as the personal story of the migrants whose lives it most directly affects.

> **Subjects:** Culture Clash, Family Relationships, Globalization, Immigration, Law Enforcement, Mexico, Multicultural Issues

> **Awards:** ALA Notable

> **Now Try:** William Langewiesche's journalistic but still lyrical *Cutting for Sign* also describes life on both sides of the border, as well as the mechanics of crossing it, as does John Bowe's disheartening *Nobodies: Modern American Slave Labor and the Dark Side of the New Global Economy*. There are also blurbs on the back of the book from fiction authors Sandra Cisneros and Julia Alvarez; this seems fitting, as a large part of the narrative focuses less on the politics of border crossing and more on its effects on family relationships. Cisneros's *The House on Mango Street* (set in one of Chicago's Hispanic neighborhoods) or Alvarez's *In the Time of the Butterflies* (set in the Dominican Republic but still applicable) might be good places for interested readers to start. Another investigative work that explores issues of race, economics, and family is J. Anthony Lukas's Pulitzer Prize–winning *Common Ground: A Turbulent Decade in the Lives of Three American Families*.

Moorehead, Caroline

🟑 *Human Cargo: A Journey among Refugees.* Holt. 2005. 330 pp. ISBN 9780805074437.

British author Moorehead examines the experiences of those millions of the world's residents who are refugees— those people fleeing their homes and the effects of war, famine, and other disasters, as well as those making their way from location to location simply searching for a better life for themselves and their families. Moorehead is also a biographer, and she makes this narrative a powerful one hinging on its featured subjects: Liberian refugees in Cairo; immigrants from Mexico traveling across the U.S. border, and Middle Eastern and Palestinian refugees displaced by unrest in that region.

Subjects: Africa, Character Profiles, Human Rights, Refugees, Society, Travel, War Reporting

Awards: ALA Notable

Now Try: Other books about refugees and war in Africa might be suggested, such as Jean Hatzfeld's oral histories *Machete Season* and *Life Laid Bare* (about the aftermath of the Rwandan genocide), Ishmael Beah's memoir *A Long Way Gone: Memoirs of a Boy Soldier*, Dan Bortolotti's *Hope in Hell: Inside the World of Doctors Without Borders*, or John S. Burnett's *Where Soldiers Fear to Tread: A Relief Worker's Tale of Survival*. Other books about immigrants from Mexico might be suggested, such as Ted Conover's Immersion title *Coyotes*, Ruben Martinez's *Crossing Over*, William Langewiesche's *Cutting for Sign*, or John Bowe's *Nobodies*. Other books by Moorehead, particularly her biography of war correspondent and journalist Martha Gellhorn (*Gellhorn: A Twentieth Century Life*), might also be suggested.

Perkins, John

The Secret History of the American Empire: Economic Hit Men, Jackals, and the Truth about Global Corruption. Dutton. 2007. 365 pp. ISBN 9780525950158.

In Perkins's earlier book, his tell-all memoir *Secrets of an Economic Hitman*, about his work with the World Bank, he dished on his personal role as an economic "hit man" charged with lending money to countries with cultural and economic strings attached. In this follow-up volume, he travels the world interviewing other hit men, jackals, reporters, and activists who are tracking the economic and social trends of globalization. What he finds is that instability is the norm; in various countries across the world governments and markets are clinging tenuously to systems that are not sustainable over the long term and which may shortly descend into chaos in such areas as Israel and the Middle East, African nations such as the Congo, as well as South America and Asia. Perkins also concludes his volume with a number of suggestions that individuals can follow to personally affect real social and economic changes.

Subjects: Africa, Asia, Business, Companies, Economics, Latin America, Middle East, Secret Histories

Now Try: Perkins's earlier book, *Confessions of an Economic Hitman*, might particularly appeal, as might other whistleblowers' tales such as Peter Rost's *The Whistleblower*, Cynthia Cooper's *Extraordinary Circumstances: The Journey of a Corporate Whistleblower*, or Bethany McLean's and Peter Elkind's *Smartest Guys in the Room: The Amazing Rise and Scandalous Fall of Enron*. Other books about capitalism and consumerism and their effects on globalization might appeal, such as John Bowe's *Nobodies*, Naomi Klein's *The Shock Doctrine*, or Robert Reich's *Supercapitalism*, as well as titles from authors who blurbed Perkins's book, including Greg Palast (*Armed Madhouse* and *The Best Democracy Money Can Buy*) and Howard Zinn (*The People's History of the United States*).

Pilger, John

Freedom Next Time: Resisting the Empire. Nation Books. 2006. 364 pp. ISBN 9781568583266.

Documentary filmmaker and journalist Pilger exposes what he believes are some of the biggest news stories that have been treated as "slow news" (defined as the news stories that viewers and readers perceive as affecting others, not themselves, and which they view with less interest) in the past forty years: the moving of two thousand residents from an Indian Ocean archipelago to make room for an American military base, the realities of life for Palestinians living in Israel, the continuation of apartheid in South Africa, India's development as an economic force, and the bombing of Afghanistan since 2001.

> **Subjects:** Afghanistan, Essays, Government, India, Israel, Politics, South Africa, War Reporting, World History

> **Now Try:** Pilger's book is impressively researched and footnoted; he provides a ready-made bibliography of further reading for his readers. Authors mentioned in his book include Edward Said (*Orientalism*), Chalmers Johnson (*The Sorrows of Empire*), Amira Hass (*Drinking the Sea at Gaza*), Noam Chomsky (*Hegemony or Survival*), Robert Fisk (*Pity the Nation: Lebanon at War*), and Suketu Mehta (*Maximum City: Bombay Lost and Found*). Other books about the mass media such as Drew Curtis's *It's Not News, It's Fark*, Barry Glassner's *The Culture of Fear*, or Ben Bagdikian's *The New Media Monopoly* might be recommended.

Politkovskaya, Anna, Scott Simon, and Arch Tait

A Russian Diary: A Journalist's Final Account of Life, Corruption, and Death in Putin's Russia. Random House. 2007. 369 pp. ISBN 9781400066827.

Russian journalist Anna Politkovskaya was shot in a contract killing in Moscow in the fall of 2006; just before her death, Politkovskaya completed this manuscript, providing an insider's view of life in Russia from the parliamentary elections of December 2003 to the summer of 2005. Exposed here are the details of a nation struggling with extreme corruption and cynicism, as well as President Vladimir Putin's penchant for neutralizing or jailing his opponents and silencing the press. One horrific episode described at length is the terrorist attack in September 2004 when armed assailants took more than twelve hundred people hostage in the Beslan school in North Ossetia-Alania in the Russian Federation. This is a horrifying account, dense with detail and best read by those with some understanding of Russian politics and society in the twenty-first century; the author was a journalist who sought to illuminate corruptions in her country and has been described by Salman Rushdie as a person who "brought forward human truths that rewrote the official story."

> **Subjects:** Books in Translation, Chechnya, Corruption, Human Rights, Vladimir Putin, Russia, World History

> **Now Try:** Politkovskaya's book is not for the reader looking for light, escapist fare; her readers might consider her other books such as *A Small Corner of Hell: Dispatches from Chechnya* or *Putin's Russia: Life in a Failing Democracy*. Other books on Russia and Russian history might also appeal, such as Svetlana Alexievich's *Voices from Chernobyl*, Anne Applebaum's *Gulag*, Orlando Figes's *A People's Tragedy*, or David Remnick's *Lenin's Tomb*.

Power, Samantha

✱ *"A Problem from Hell": America and the Age of Genocide.* Basic Books. 2002. 610 pp. ISBN 9780465061501.

Power spent three years as a correspondent in Bosnia and Srebrenica, witnessing war and violence and expressing frustration that America in particular was not doing more to decry or counteract the genocide there. Power also provides historical context on such events as the Armenian genocide in early twentieth-century Turkey, the Holocaust, the activities of the Khmer Rouge in Cambodia, Iraqi attacks on the Kurds, and the Rwandan genocide, and although she does not speculate that America's involvement would have prevented such events, she does explore whether a more forthright response in any of the above examples would have alleviated their effects.

Subjects: Atrocities, Bosnia, Explicit Violence, Foreign Relations, Genocide, Government, World History

Awards: Pulitzer Prize

Now Try: Sadly, there is no shortage of books about human atrocities and genocide. Consider books on the Holocaust such as Art Spiegelman's *Maus*, Catherine Collins's *Death on the Black Sea*, Anne Frank's *The Diary of a Young Girl*, or Elie Wiesel's *Night*; other books like Jean Hatzfeld's superlative oral histories about Rwanda, *Machete Season* and *Life Laid Bare*, might be good suggestions, as might books about Bosnia and that region including Slavenka Drakulic's *They Would Never Hurt a Fly: War Criminals on Trial in The Hague*, Joe Sacco's *The Fixer*, or Rebecca West's historical classic *Black Lamb and Grey Falcon*.

Roberts, Adam

The Wonga Coup: Guns, Thugs and a Ruthless Determination to Create Mayhem in an Oil-Rich Corner of Africa. PublicAffairs. 2006. 303 pp. ISBN 9781586483715.

Covering roughly the same land-size area as the state of Maryland and called "Devil Island" by its residents, Equatorial Guinea is not a country that gets a lot of attention in news reports or history books—until, that is, a contingent of British, South African, and Zimbabwean mercenaries were flown into the country by American pilots on planes previously owned by the National Guard. The mercenaries were there to overthrow the government of Obiang Nguema, ostensibly for his billion-dollar corruption and rule by terror, but journalist Roberts also suggests that their mission might have had more to do with the oil fields to be found under the ocean floor surrounding the island than humanitarian motives. In this action-packed narrative, Roberts also compares the true story to the disturbingly similar coup plotline of Frederick Forsyth's adventure novel *The Dogs of War*—which was originally published in 1972.

Subjects: Africa, Corruption, Dictators, Economics, Equatorial Guinea, Foreign Relations, Government, Military, Teodoro Obiang, Oil, Politics, Poverty

Now Try: Other books about world events and foreign relations include John Perkins's *Confessions of an Economic Hit Man* or *The Secret History of the American Empire*, Mark Bowden's *Guests of the Ayatollah*, Joan Didion's *Salvador*, or Lynne Duke's *Mandela, Mobutu, and Me: A Newswoman's African Journey*. Forsyth's novel *The Dogs of War* might certainly be suggested, as might a number of authors listed in Robert's bibliography: Jeffrey Archer, Graham Greene, or Niall Ferguson.

Skinner, E. Benjamin

A Crime So Monstrous: Face-to-Face with Modern-Day Slavery. Free Press. 2008. 328 pp. ISBN 9780743290074.

Journalist Skinner makes a sobering case for his statement that there are more slaves worldwide today than at any other time in history, most particularly by visiting such human trafficking and slavery global hot spots as Haiti, Sudan, India, Eastern Europe, Dubai, and even in America. At various points in his scathing narrative, Skinner posed as an arms dealer to talk to weapons traffickers, as well as a woman so he could interview women held in sexual slavery in a brothel. The result is a horrifying glimpse inside the global criminal underworld that seeks to provide slave labor where it is needed; however, Skinner tempers the disturbing details by also examining the efforts of antislavery activists and groups worldwide.

Subjects: Economics, Globalization, Prostitution, Slavery, Travel, True Crime

Now Try: Other Investigative Writing books on the effects of globalization might also appeal to these readers, including John Bowe's *Nobodies: Modern American Slave Labor and the Dark Side of the New Global Economy*, Douglas Farah's *Blood from Stones: The Secret Financial Network of Terror*, Naomi Klein's *The Shock Doctrine: The Rise of Disaster Capitalism*, or Roberto Saviano's True Crime exposé of illicit trafficking, *Gomorrah: A Personal Journey Into the Violent International Empire of Naples' Organized Crime System*. Other books published by the progressive imprint Nation Books might also be suggested, such as Aram Roston's *The Man Who Pushed America to War*, Jeremy Scahill's *Blackwater*, or Barbara Coloroso's *Extraordinary Evil: A Short Walk to Genocide*.

Fiction Read-Alikes

- **Atwood, Margaret.** Canadian author Atwood writes convincing dystopian future speculative fiction; her novels might appeal to readers of both Government and Corporate Exposés. They include *The Handmaid's Tale*, *Cat's Eye*, and *Oryx and Crake*, as well as her historical novel *Alias Grace*.

- **Barry, Max.** Australian author Barry has been described by reviewers as an author of "smartass, punky satire for the late capitalist era"; as such, his novels *Syrup*, *Jennifer Government*, and *The Company* might all appeal to Exposé readers.

- **Cook, Robin.** Cook is a practicing doctor and includes snippets of actual news stories about horrific medical experiments and discoveries in most of his medical thrillers; readers of Corporate Exposés in particular might enjoy his novels *Coma*, *Seizure*, *Shock*, or *Critical*.

- **Gaskell, Elizabeth.** Gaskell, a nineteenth-century British author, may be considered more of a romance author for her novel *North and South*, but she was also a skilled reporter of social injustices and status in other novels including *Mary Barton* and *Ruth*.

- **Grisham, John.** Many Exposé books feature court cases and legal proceedings (or the circumventing of legal proceedings); as such, their readers might also enjoy legal thrillers from the master in the genre. His best-selling titles include *A Time To Kill*, *The Firm*, *The Client*, *The Rainmaker*, *The Summons*, *The King of Torts*, and *The Appeal*.

- **Ozeki, Ruth.** Ozeki's story-driven novels might particularly appeal to readers who enjoy the fast pace of most exposés; they include *My Year of Meats* and *All Over Creation*.

- **Palahniuk, Chuck.** Secret fight clubs, stories revealed in reverse, the fashion industry, and horror motifs appear in Palahniuk's unconventional and often violent (but never dull) novels, including *Fight Club*, *Survivor*, *Invisible Monsters*, and *Lullaby*.

- **Palmer, Michael.** Palmer, a former emergency room physician, writes suspenseful and detailed medical thrillers that often include plots about drug company practices; they include *Side Effects*, *Extreme Measures*, *Miracle Cure*, and *The Fifth Vial*.

- **Shteyngart, Gary.** Fans of international Exposés in particular might enjoy Shteyngart's satirical novels *The Russian Debutante's Handbook* and *Absurdistan*.

- **Sinclair, Upton.** His classic novel *The Jungle*, set in the stockyards of Chicago and based on investigative reporting, should definitely be offered to any reader interested in Corporate (specifically food production) exposés.

- **Trollope, Anthony.** He may be a hard sell for modern readers, but I would be remiss if I didn't mention Trollope's classic *The Way We Live Now*, set in the nineteenth century, but nonetheless a scathing fictional exposé of greedy wealth-seekers and those of whom they take advantage on their roads to riches.

Further Reading

Borjesson, Kristina, ed. 2002. *Into the Buzzsaw: Leading Journalists Expose the Myth of a Free Press*. Amherst, NY: Prometheus Books.

Columbia Journalism Review (serial). 1962–. New York: Graduate School of Journalism at Columbia University.

Jensen, Carl. 2000. *Stories That Changed America: Muckrakers of the 20th Century*. New York: Seven Stories Press.

References

Bausum, Ann. 2007. *Muckrakers: How Ida Tarbell, Upton Sinclair, and Lincoln Steffens Helped Expose Scandal, Inspire Reform, and Invent Investigative Journalism.* Washington, DC: National Geographic.

Johnson, Michael L. 1971. *The New Journalism: The Underground Press, the Artists of Nonfiction, and Changes in the Established Media.* Lawrence, KS: University of Kansas Press.

Serrin, Judith, and William Serrin, eds. 2002. *Muckraking! The Journalism that Changed America.* New York: Free Press.

Shapiro, Bruce, ed. 2003. *Shaking the Foundations: 200 Years of Investigative Journalism in America.* New York: Thunder's Mouth Press.

Wikipedia. 2008. http://en.wikipedia.org/wiki/Watchdog_journalism (accessed March 3, 2008).

Chapter 3

Immersion Journalism

Definition of Immersion Journalism

If titles in the In-Depth Reporting chapter can be most closely related to the style and historical tradition of journalistic writing, Immersion Journalism titles can be considered to be the direct descendants of the "new journalism" movement. That movement, which had its roots in the 1960s, was noted for its authors' willingness to combine reporting and nonfiction facts and events with more narrative writing techniques including the use of dialogue and relating stories from the first-person point of view. Such authors, including Tom Wolfe (*The Electric Kool-Aid Acid Test*), Norman Mailer (*The Executioner's Song*), and John Howard Griffin (*Black Like Me*), in turn owed a debt of gratitude to their literary ancestors, not only the muckrakers and investigative journalists of the early twentieth century, who wrote personal and passionately argued treatises, but also to such literary stylists as A. J. Liebling and Joseph Mitchell (both of whom wrote for *The New Yorker*) in the 1930s and 1940s.

Perhaps the best definition of the "new journalism" style, and Immersion Journalism by extension, is the one offered by Michael Johnson in his scholarly work *The New Journalism*: "the principal distinguishing mark of New Journalistic style is the writer's attempt to be personalistic, involved, and creative in relation to the events he reports and comments upon. His journalism, in general, has no pretense of being 'objective' and it bears the clear stamp of his commitment and personality" (Johnson 1971, 46). Immersion Journalism authors not only tell stories in which they are interested; they tell stories in which they have become involved. It is precisely that method of their authors' personally living the stories and surroundings they are investigating that makes these books so cohesive as a stylistic genre; for the most part, they are written almost like memoirs, with a willingness on the part of their authors to share not only their research findings and interview material but also their own personal reactions to and thoughts about those findings.

Whether these reporters inform their subjects they are writing about them or whether they go undercover, the result is the same; highly personal stories that are told from a highly personal point of view but that still rely for their telling on the authors' powers of observation and thoughtful analysis of their chosen subjects and topics. In one of the defining titles of the genre, Ted Conover's *Newjack: Guarding Sing Sing* (in which Conover relates the story of his going "undercover" and working as a prison guard himself), the author's attention to detail was so minute that Sing Sing inmates, reading the book after it was published, referred to it to learn how to pose as prison guards and escape. (Breathe easier: their plan failed.)

Many of the titles in this subgenre took a good deal of time for their authors to research and write, which is another hallmark of the new journalism form as well. Robert Boynton speaks to that truth in his collection *The New New Journalism* when he states that many of these authors "experiment more with the way one gets the story. To that end, they've developed innovative immersion strategies and extended the time they've spent reporting" (Boynton 2005, xii). These are not quick journalistic dispatches; these are stories that the authors watched unfold, may even have participated in, and about which they have taken the time to be thoughtful and reflective. They are frequently told in the first person, and they vary widely in tone and mood, from light and humorous to extremely serious. They share the same problem with the rest of the Investigative Writing stylistic genre, in that these titles go by many names. One of the labels suggested for some of its titles (most notably those by Hunter S. Thompson and Tom Wolfe) was "Gonzo Journalism," used to describe those authors' complete immersion in their stories, sometimes involving drug use that they claimed increased their clarity and insight, and often featuring a punchy style, the inclusion of vernacular, and even mention of monsters and other fantastic elements that seemed real to the authors at the time. Immersion Journalism has also been referred to as Participatory Journalism, and "Memoirist-Reportage" (Boynton 2005, 73), although author Jonathan Harr offers what I think is the most evocative term for the subgenre: "perhaps *inundated* or *drowning* journalism would be more accurate" (Boynton 2005, 114).

> Immersion Journalism is what writers engage in when they go beyond the bounds of objectively researching a story and instead step directly into it, living whatever experience they're writing about and periodically injecting their own reactions and thoughts into their narrative. They are often researched over long periods of time and are sometimes referred to as the "literature of the everyday" for the insight into ordinary lives and mundane details that they provide. They are firsthand accounts and rely heavily for their appeal on their authors' skill in storytelling and use of language.

Appeal of Immersion Journalism

Immersion Journalism titles typically offer two main features: compelling stories and interesting characters whom the writer is typically observing or interviewing (as well as the character of the authors themselves). In titles listed in the Personal Journey, Work World, and Community and Society sections, the draw is pretty clearly the authors' degree of engagement with their story and their revealing of the inside stories of their subjects as they experienced them. Because they take time to observe and write, these books are simultaneously story-driven and thoughtful, which is a rare combination in both fiction and nonfiction. They often include the stylistic conventions of the new journalism, including realistic dialogue and stories told through specific and representative scenes; because of this, they also resemble Memoirs, which are also told in the first-person voice and often feature dialogue re-creation. It might in fact be argued that several of the titles included below are closer in style to Memoirs than to Investigative Writing; however, an effort has been made to include only those books in which the authors, although they became personally involved in their narratives, retain their focus on the investigation of other peoples' stories. These titles, although they are often personally and informally told, still rely heavily on research, interviews, and journalistic observations.

Because they are slightly more personal and reflective than In-Depth Reporting titles, their readers might also consider a wide variety of essay collections and nonfiction titles that are part of the Making Sense . . . genre (defined in *The Real Story* as those books in which are characterized by their "authors' neologisms, theorizing, and subject synthesis"); examples of such titles include Malcolm Gladwell's *The Tipping Point* and Steven Johnson's *Everything Bad Is Good for You*. Those Immersion Journalism titles found in the International subgenre offer a further appeal of setting; in traveling and placing themselves in often unfamiliar surroundings, the authors of those books offer their readers an experience that is similar to reading Travel nonfiction books and fiction that relies heavily on setting for its appeal.

Organization of the Chapter

The organization of the chapter parallels the writers' experiences of immersing themselves in their own *Personal Journeys*, through immersion in a slightly larger *Work World*, then into *Community Life and Society*, and finally into the much larger world of *International Affairs*. Those titles in the *Personal Journeys* subgenre tend to be the most informal and intimate and are heavily dependent for their appeal on theirs authors' voices and style; at the other end of the spectrum, in the *International Affairs* subgenre, a bit more is demanded of the reader in terms of social, cultural, and geographical knowledge.

Personal Journeys

Immersion Journalism titles in which authors decide to engage in their own or others' personal obsessions, usually for a set period of time, and then report on their experiences can be called Personal Journeys. This heading is meant to be a play on words; in some of these books, the authors do in fact travel from place to place, meeting and talking with people and always learning more about their particular area of interest; in other titles, the journey is more a spiritual or knowledge quest, as when an author sets him- or herself a task to be completed and then sets out, figuratively, to conquer it. These can be very similar to a wide variety of In-Depth Reporting titles, in which authors so closely observe and get to know those people and events on which they are reporting that they eventually *seem* to be living the lifestyle themselves; but the difference is largely in the direction of the storytelling. The authors of Personal Journey titles are not reluctant, like many journalists and reportage authors, to step in and make themselves part of the story. Björn Türoque interviews a lot of people who take part in air guitar contests, but the driving focus of the narrative is his quest to become an air guitar champion. These authors let everyone they talk to know what they are doing (no undercover concerns here) and often enlist their assistance, at which point they become characters in the author's story.

There may be some quibbling on this classification, with many readers considering these titles to be nothing more than very specific Memoirs. They have been classified separately here for two reasons: because they contain more reporting and interviewing of others than do many Memoirs, which tend to focus more on the memoirist's interior life, and because many of them are written by journalists and authors who write essays and magazine reporting pieces for a living. Calvin Trillin, for instance, is a longtime *Nation* and *New Yorker* contributor; A. J. Jacobs writes for a number of national magazines as well. Whereas the timeframe in a Memoir is usually dictated by changes or growth in the author's personal life, the timeframe and setting in these books are more often determined by the subject or the event or the interest the readers are investigating. These titles also vary slightly from more typical Memoirs in their subject matters, many of which focus on leisure activities and hobbies (and hobbies which have blossomed into full-blown obsessions); the subjects in Memoirs often tend to be weightier and focus on broader themes such as relationships, overcoming adversities, professional developments and crises, or the process of coming of age or discovering one's self. The subjects of these Personal Journey books may indeed take their hobbies and interests very seriously, but in the end, the tone of these narratives tends to be more on the lighthearted side.

As noted, readers who enjoy this rather specialized subgenre might also be open to a wide variety of In-Depth Reporting titles, particularly Feature Stories. They might also consider a wide variety of Memoirs and even Journey Narratives or Travel Humor books that are considered nonfiction Travel (such as Paul Theroux's *The Old Patagonian Express* or Bill Bryson's *A Walk in the Woods*). Of particular importance in these titles are the writing style, humor, and personality displayed by the author. In that sense, they can be considered to appeal according to both their characters and their language and literary style. These readers might also be open to reading fiction as well, particularly novels that are humorous or cleverly written.

Personal Journeys Immersion Journalism titles find their authors not only reporting on specific stories but also actively taking part in them; in addition to interviewing other participants who share particular obsessions or interests and doing research on said obsessions, these authors insert themselves into their own narratives, mixing the Memoir and reporting formats. They are often written by reporters or journalism professionals, and are often narrated in the first person voice. Objectivity has very little part in these narratives, and strong storylines rarely make appearances as these authors amble through their subject of choice, primarily describing characters and their own reactions to them.

Burke, Monte

Sowbelly: The Obsessive Quest for the World Record Largemouth Bass. Dutton. 2005. 250 pp. ISBN 9780525948636.

A largemouth bass fisherman himself, the author of this investigative travelogue is perfectly situated to understand the obsession that drives other anglers to try and catch a bass larger than twenty-two pounds and four ounces (the largemouth bass record, set by a man named George Washington Perry all the way back in 1932). Traveling from coast to coast and abroad, even to Cuba, Burke interviews not only those chasing the record, but also historians, biologists, and fed-up spouses. In each chapter Burke explores a new location and gets to know a different fisherman, but all of the stories provide a quickly paced narrative of the labor of love that is largemouth bass fishing.

Subjects: Character Profiles, Fishing, Hobbies, Sports, Travel, True Adventure

Now Try: Other books about hobbies and obsessions might appeal to Burke's readers, including George Black's *Casting a Spell: The Bamboo Fly Rod and the American Pursuit of Perfection*, Susan Orlean's *The Orchid Thief*, Susan Warren's *Backyard Giants*, Sam Walker's *Fantasyland*, Amy Sutherland's *Cookoff: Recipe Fever in America*, or Shari Caudron's *Who Are You People?* Mike Iaconelli's *Fishing on the Edge*, about bass fishing, might also be offered; it's more of a Memoir than is Burke's narrative but is also highly informative about the sport.

Caputo, Philip

Ghosts of Tsavo: Stalking the Mystery Lions of East Africa. National Geographic. 2002. 275 pp. ISBN 9780792263623.

Caputo journeyed to Africa to unravel the legend and truth behind attacks on humans by the "man-eating lions of Tsavo." Caputo is a master of using language to set his scene, and his retelling of the attacks on humans by two man-eaters (named Ghost and Darkness), as well as the subsequent hunt for and shooting of the lions, is evocative enough to raise goose pimples on his readers' arms. In addition to the travel and true adventure aspects of his tale, Caputo also examines the history of Kenya, the environmental factors that make the area a natural habitat for the intimidating animals, and the lives of African safari tour guides.

Subjects: Africa, Animals, Kenya, Lions, Travel, True Adventure

Now Try: Several other books exist on this subject, including John Henry Patterson's classic *The Man-Eaters of Tsavo* (first published in 1907) and Robert Frump's more recent *The Man-Eaters of Eden*; other books mixing animals, adventure, and travel might also be suggested, such as *Carnivorous Nights: On the Trail of the Tasmanian Tiger* (by Margaret Mittelbach and Michael Crewdson), Peter Matthiessen's *The Snow Leopard*, Joy Adamson's *Born Free*, Tim Flannery's *Chasing Kangaroos*, or Farley Mowat's *Never Cry Wolf*. Fiction titles set in Africa, such as Dave Eggers's *What Is the What*, Michael Ondaatje's *The English Patient*, or Alexander McCall Smith's "The No. 1 Ladies Detective Agency" mystery series might also make for interesting read-alikes.

Cohen, Leah Hager

♣ *Without Apology: Girls, Women, and the Desire to Fight.* Random House. 2005. 192 pp. ISBN 9781400061570.

Boxing is no longer exclusively a male sport, and Cohen set out in the fall of 2001 to find women training to be boxers and to understand their singular desire and choice to channel their aggression through their fists. Training alongside and becoming close to four women and their coach at the Somerville Boxing Club, she learned not only about their sport but also about their home lives, the projects where they lived, and their complex and often fiercely loyal relationships with their families and friends. In addition to exploring her subjects' motivation for boxing, Cohen also finds herself working through issues of both physical strength and emotional challenges.

Subjects: Boxing, Family Relationships, Friendships, Sports, Women's Nonfiction

Awards: New York Times Notable

Now Try: Cohen is a prolific author, with both investigative nonfiction titles and novels to her credit; her readers might also try *Train Go Sorry: Inside a Deaf World*, *The Stuff of Dreams: Behind the Scenes of an American Community Theater*, her essay collection *Glass, Paper, Beans*, or her novels *Heart, You Bully, You Punk* or *House Lights*. Other books about women's friendships and lives might be offered, such as Isabel Allende's *Paula*, Elizabeth Gilbert's *Eat, Pray, Love*, Haven Kimmel's *A Girl Named Zippy*, or Anne Lamott's *Traveling Mercies*; women's fiction titles by authors including Julia Alvarez, Rebecca Wells, or Anne Tyler might also be suggested.

Covington, Dennis

🔖 *Salvation on Sand Mountain: Snake Handling and Redemption in Southern Appalachia.* Addison-Wesley. 1995. 240 pp. ISBN 9780201622928.

In the course of researching the story of snake-handling preacher Glenn Summerford, who was convicted of attempted murder for holding a gun to his wife's head and forcing her to stick her arm into a rattlesnake's cage, Covington's travels and interviews in Appalachia affected him much more personally and spiritually than he had imagined. Over the course of the narrative, he describes his own experiences attending snake-handling worship services, his own snake-handling and preaching experiments, and his discovery that the quintessentially Southern practice has a long history in his own family.

Subjects: American South, Appalachian Mountains, Family Relationships, Quick Reads, Religion, Spirituality

Awards: ALA Notable

Now Try: *Spirit and Flesh: Life in a Fundamentalist Baptist Church* by James M. Ault Jr. also provides an "inside look" at the religious experience. Kim Barnes's memoir *In the Wilderness: Coming of Age in Unknown Country* examines her family's turn to fundamentalist religiosity as a way to deal with economic and social turmoil. Barbara Kingsolver's novel *The Poisonwood Bible* features a family driven by their evangelical Baptist father to become missionaries to the Belgian Congo.

Davis, Joshua

The Underdog: How I Survived the World's Most Outlandish Competitions. Villard. 2005. 198 pp. ISBN 9780345476586.

Intrepid writer Davis, who'd already spent the majority of his life feeling like a physical and social underdog, decided to make it official and set out to face challenges and challengers he had absolutely no business facing, from arm-wrestling champions to sumo wrestlers, "extreme sauna" competitors to even a bull (when he logically took a turn as a bullfighter).

Subjects: Family Relationships, Hobbies, Humor, Memoirs, Quick Reads, Sports, Travel, Underdogs, Year in the Life

Now Try: Other writers who have undertaken strange challenges for their books include Tony Hawks (whose titles *Round Ireland with a Fridge* and *Playing the Moldovans at Tennis* say it all, really), Danny Wallace's *Join Me!* or *Yes Man*, Maria Dahvana Headley's *The Year of Yes*, or Norah Vincent's *Self-Made Man* might all appeal, as might other immersion works such as Jason Fagone's *The Horsemen of the Esophagus* and titles from the Character Profiles chapter such as Mark Singer's *Character Studies* or Hank Stuever's *Off Ramp*. Many anecdotes in Davis's memoir also concern his mother, with whom his relationship is never dull; similar books like Brett Leveridge's *Men My Mother Dated* or J. R. Moehringer's very enjoyable memoir *The Tender Bar* might also be offered.

Fatsis, Stefan

Word Freak: Heartbreak, Triumph, Genius, and Obsession in the World of Competitive Scrabble Players. Houghton Mifflin. 2001. 372 pp. ISBN 9780618015849.

Fatsis set out to explore the world of competitive Scrabble playing and found a cutthroat world of high-stakes competition, driven training sessions, and obsession. A Scrabble player himself, Fatsis hoped his skills would be sufficient to lead him to the highest levels of international competition, and along the journey he provides a history of the game and its rules, character portraits of the many players (such as "G.I." Joel Sherman, who runs the Manhattan Scrabble Club), and the challenges along the road to becoming a Scrabble player who can name multiple words that start with "q" but don't require "u" and who lays awake at night envisioning strategy and reciting memorized lists of words.

> **Subjects:** Book Groups, Character Profiles, Games, Grammar, Hobbies, Scrabble, Year in the Life

> **Now Try:** A wide and entertaining variety of other books about hobbies and journalists immersing themselves in very distinct worlds are available, including Michael Weinreb's *The Kings of New York* (about chess), Shari Caudron's *Who Are You People?*, *Sundays with Vlad* by Paul Bibeau, Mark Singer's *Character Studies: Encounters with the Curiously Obsessed*, Sam Walker's *Fantasyland*, and Charlie LeDuff's *US Guys*. Humorous Memoirs might also appeal to these readers, including those by authors David Sedaris, Anthony Bourdain, Chuck Klosterman, and Jim Knipfel.

Greenspan, Jay

Hunting Fish: A Cross-Country Search for America's Worst Poker Players. St. Martin's Press. 2006. 226 pp. ISBN 9780312347833.

Greenspan set out not only to find some of the worst poker players across America but also to take their money ("hunting fish" refers to finding suckers to fleece). Starting in New York and heading west, he sought to grow the tiny bankroll he started with across such communities as tiny bordertowns in Mississippi, Texas, and Arizona, as well as in Las Vegas and Los Angeles. As he pursued his goal of making $20,000 through poker alone (enough to enable him to play in the Commerce Casino game against true professionals), he got to know a number of cities across America, including Philadelphia, Atlantic City, and New Orleans. In addition to his travelogue, Greenspan relates many of the more technical details of the poker games he played along the way; this may be a narrative best suited to those already in the game's thrall.

Subjects: Card Games, Gambling, Hobbies, Memoirs, Poker, Travel

Now Try: Other books on poker and card games might be offered, such as James McManus's *Positively Fifth Street*, Ben Mezrich's *Bringing Down the House*, or even Edward McPherson's *The Backwash Squeeze and Other Improbable Feats: A Newcomer's Journey into the World of Bridge* (about bridge). (For those readers interested in learning how to play poker, Herbert Yardley's classic *The Education of a Poker Player*, first published in 1957, might also be a fun place to start.) Although Greenspan does not indulge in illegal activities, his readers might enjoy other quickly paced narratives about con artists, such as Marcus Richard's *American Roulette: How I Turned the Odds Upside Down—My Wild Twenty-Five-Year Ride Ripping Off the World's Casinos*, Frank Abagnale's *Catch Me If You Can*, Mitchell Zuckoff's *Ponzi's Scheme*, or Bill Mason's *Confessions of a Master Jewel Thief*.

Jacobs, A. J.

The Year of Living Biblically: One Man's Humble Quest to Follow the Bible as Literally as Possible. Simon & Schuster. 2007. 388 pp. ISBN 9780743291477.

Writer Jacobs relates the experiences of his year spent living as closely to biblical tenets as possible, including growing his beard, being fruitful and multiplying, eating crickets, as well as the Ten Commandment standards including tithing and controlling lustful thoughts. Interested in finding out more about other such religious literalists, Jacobs also travels to interview snake handlers in Appalachia, the Amish in Pennsylvania, and Samaritans in Israel.

Subjects: Book Groups, Books and Learning, Humor, Judaism, Memoirs, Pop Culture, Religion, Society, Travel

Now Try: Jacobs is a spirited and humorous writer but is always able to maintain a good-natured tone of broad acceptance of others and their lifestyles; other nonfiction authors offering the same thoughtful and surprisingly gentle humor include Alain de Botton, Robert Sullivan, and Michael Perry. Other Memoirs about religion and spirituality might also appeal, including Shalom Auslander's slightly angrier *Foreskin's Lament*, Dennis Covington's *Salvation on Sand Mountain* (about snake handling), Mary McCarthy's *Memories of a Catholic Girlhood*, or Cheryl Reed's *Unveiled: The Hidden Lives of Nuns*. Jacobs is also the author of *The Know-It-All*, in which he recounts his effort to read the entire 2002 *Encylopaedia Britannica* set; he is also an editor at *Esquire*, and other contributors to that magazine might be offered, including Chuck Klosterman, Robert Kurson, and Scott Raab.

Kohl, Beth

Embryo Culture: Making Babies in the Twenty-first Century. Farrar, Straus & Giroux. 2007. 288 pp. ISBN 9780374147570.

In a nation where there are an estimated 6.1 million clinically infertile men and women, fertility services and in vitro clinics in the business of helping people make babies are finding more clients and business than they can keep up with. Embarking on her own quest to overcome her infertility and bear a child of her own, Kohl is uniquely situated to provide an up-close examination of the science and process of in vitro fertilization and other pharmaceutical and medical procedures; she also uniquely highlights the new ethical issues raised by this field of medicine, including genetic testing of fertilized eggs, "selectively reducing" the number of embryos with which she is implanted to curb pregnancy complications, and other repercussions of the procedures.

> **Subjects:** Family Relationships, Health Issues, Medicine, Memoirs, Parenting, Science
>
> **Now Try:** Other books about the science and medical issues involved with parenting include Jennifer Block's *Pushed: The Painful Truth about Childbirth and Modern Maternity Care*, Robin Marantz Henig's *Pandora's Baby*, or Debora Spar's *The Baby Business*. The only books being published with more frequency than those about the health aspects of parenthood are those examining its social impact, such as Pamela Stone's *Opting Out* or Leslie Morgan Steiner's collection *Mommy Wars*. Books by science writers including Mary Roach and Diane Ackerman might be suggested, as might parenting Memoirs such as Ann Leary's *An Innocent, A Broad*, Lisa Belkin's *Life's Work*, Austin Murphy's *How Tough Could It Be: The Trials and Errors of a Sportswriter Turned Stay-at-Home Dad*, or Dan Savage's *The Kid: What Happened after My Boyfriend and I Decided to Get Pregnant*.

Langewiesche, William

Sahara Unveiled: A Journey across the Desert. Pantheon Books. 1996. 301 pp. ISBN 9780679429821.

> Langewiesche set out to traverse one of the harshest and most unforgiving of physical terrains on Earth: the vast and deceptive Sahara desert. Although he offers himself more as a character in this narrative than is typical in his writing, his focus, as always, is on finding the stories of others and interviewing them to provide an insight into their culture and worldview. Along the route of his 12,000-mile journey, Langewiesche explores the small towns and their inhabitants clinging to life around the desert and in its oases, learns about the ancient and more recent history of the region, and writes about all of it in a poetically descriptive, but still informative, style.

> **Subjects:** Africa, Multicultural Issues, Sahara Desert, Society, Travel, True Adventure
>
> **Now Try:** Other straightforward prose stylists might be offered to Langewiesche fans; these authors include John McPhee, Marq de Villiers, Joan Didion, or George Packer. Fiction about Africa might also appeal to these readers, such as Clive Cussler's adventure novel *Sahara*, Michael Ondaatje's *The English Patient*, Giles Foden's *The Last King of Scotland*, or Chinhua Achebe's *Things Fall Apart*; nonfiction life stories set in Africa, such as Alexandra Fuller's *Don't Let's Go to the Dogs Tonight* or Ishmael Beah's *A Long Way Gone: Memoirs of a Boy Soldier* might also be suitable read-alikes.

Lisick, Beth

Helping Me Help Myself: One Skeptic, Ten Self-Help Gurus, and a Year on the Brink of the Comfort Zone. William Morrow. 2008. 264 pp. ISBN 9780061143960.

> When Beth Lisick woke up in pain and regretting a few poor choices she'd made at her New Year's Eve party (including trying to do the splits), she made a resolution to improve twelve things in her life (one for every

month of the new year) and to seek out self-help and motivational gurus, such as Richard Simmons, Tony Robbins, and Jack Canfield, to provide inspiration and guidance during her earnest and hilarious year of self-improvement.

> **Subjects:** Humor, Mind Body Spirit, Quick Reads, Self Help, Women's Nonfiction, Year in the Life

> **Now Try:** Lisick is a light-hearted, humorous author who also knows how to work in thoughtful moments; other essayists and humorous memoirists who might appeal to her readers include Nora Ephron (*I Feel Bad about My Neck*), David Sedaris (*Me Talk Pretty One Day*), David Rakoff (*Don't Get Too Comfortable*), Jim Knipfel (*Ruining It for Everybody*), Hollis Gillespie (*Bleachy-Haired Honky Bitch*), and David Foster Wallace (*Consider the Lobster*). Other books which highlight their authors' New Years' resolutions are Judith Levine's *Not Buying It* and Sara Bongiorni's *A Year without Made in China: One Family's True Life Adventure in the Global Economy*, while other Immersion books such as Barbara Ehrenreich's *Nickel and Dimed*, A. J. Jacobs's *The Year of Living Biblically*, or Jonathan Black's *Yes You Can!: Behind the Hype and Hustle of the Motivation Biz* might also be offered.

McPherson, Edward

The Backwash Squeeze and Other Improbable Feats: A Newcomer's Journey into the World of Bridge. HarperCollins. 2007. 340 pp. ISBN 9780061127649.

McPherson sets out to explore the intricate, hugely popular card game that numbers among its devotees Warren Buffett, Hugh Hefner, and Sting—and the game isn't poker. It's bridge, and as the author argues, it's perhaps one of the most complex and psychologically absorbing card games ever to be invented. In this narrative, he describes his own adventures trying to play and master the game in such high-stakes contests as the North American Bridge Championships, while also providing a history of the game that was invented by Harold Stirling Vanderbilt in 1925 and has been a source of comfort and amusement to such notable figures as the Marx Brothers, Winston Churchill, and Dwight Eisenhower. In a story aptly described by his publisher as a "spirited homage," the author also travels from city to city (including Dallas, Kansas City, Las Vegas, and London) to try to pick up tips from amateurs and professionals alike and eventually meets his match when he partners with an octogenarian from New York named Tina.

> **Subjects:** Bridge, Card Games, Games, Hobbies, Humor, London, Year in the Life

> **Now Try:** Other books on poker and card games might be offered, such as James McManus's *Positively Fifth Street*, Ben Mezrich's *Bringing Down the House*, or Jay Greenspan's *Hunting Fish*. Other books about "sports" such as Scrabble and chess might be suggested, such as Stefan Fatsis's *Word Freak*, Michael Weinreb's *The Kings of New York*; other offbeat Travel narratives by authors such as Hank Stuever, Louis Theroux, or Mark Singer might also be suggested.

Preston, Richard

The Wild Trees: A Story of Passion and Daring. Random House. 2007. 294 pp. ISBN 9781400064892.

Best known for his nonfiction "biothrillers" (*The Hot Zone* and *The Demon In the Freezer*), the journalist and *New Yorker* contributor here turns his attention to a world high above our heads: that of the ecosystem at the heights of California redwood trees. In addition to the presence in the tops of these trees of plants and animals, Preston also illuminates a world of individuals who climb these trees in search of the beauty of their heights as well as spiritual sustenance; two of the individuals he profiles are Steve Sillett and Michael Taylor, who also show Preston the art of studying and summiting these trees (some of which reach heights in excess of 350 feet).

> **Subjects:** Character Profiles, Ecology, Environmental Writing, Nature, Redwood Trees, Science
>
> **Now Try:** This book was reviewed for *Publishers Weekly* by John Vaillant, who is the author of a similarly investigative work titled *The Golden Spruce: A True Story of Myth, Madness, and Greed*. Other books highlighting characters seeking ecosystems with which they can live in harmony might also appeal to these readers, such as Elizabeth Gilbert's *The Last American Man* or Jon Krakauer's *Into the Wild*. Also of interest might be other natural science micro-histories like William Logan's *Oak: The Frame of Civilization* or Janisse Ray's *Pinhook: Finding Wholeness in a Fragmented Land*.

St. John, Warren

Rammer, Jammer, Yellow, Hammer: A Journey into the Heart of Fan Mania. Crown Publishers. 2004. 275 pp. ISBN 9780609607084.

Author St. John not only got to know the fans of the Alabama Crimson Tide (University of Alabama) football team who own RVs and follow the team around, he even bought his own beater RV, nicknamed it "Hawg," and joined in the season's and fans' travels. In doing so, he became part of the huge Alabama tradition; as he points out, "to understand what an absolute minority nonfans are in Alabama, consider this: they are outnumbered there by atheists." Along the way St. John, who is a writer for the *New York Times*, got to know such infamous Alabama personalities as ticket scalper John Ed; Episcopalian minister Ray Pradat, who is a fan first and a minister second; and even has his photo taken with legendary coach Bear Bryant. Although the team finishes lower in the college polls than their hardcore fans would have liked, St. John paints a picture of a season of excitement and unfettered love for one's team.

> **Subjects:** Alabama, American South, Character Profiles, Fandom, Football, Hobbies, Memoirs, Sports, Travel, YA, Year in the Life
>
> **Now Try:** Other books about serious fandom might be offered to St. John's readers, including Sports Reporting titles like Gene Wojciechowski's *Cubs Nation: 162 Games. 162 Stories. 1 Addiction*, John Feinstein's books *A Season on the Brink* or *Last Dance: Behind the Scenes at the Final Four*, H. G. Bissinger's *Friday Night Lights*, Joe McGinniss's *The Miracle of Castel Di Sangro*, or Michael Lewis's *The Blind Side*. Other lighthearted travelogues might also appeal to these readers, including Tony Hawks's sports-themed *Playing the Moldovans at Tennis*, Doug Lansky's *Up the Amazon without a Paddle*, or Bill Bryson's *A Walk in the Woods*.

Sutherland, Amy

Cookoff: Recipe Fever in America. Viking. 2003. 333 pp. ISBN 9780670032518.

Author Sutherland became fascinated with the idea of modern-day cooking and recipe contests across America and pledged not only to attend and investigate them but also to get her own recipes into similar contests. After attending such contests as the 2001 National Beef Cook-Off, the Pillsbury

Cookoff, and the National Chicken recipe competitions, Sutherland gets a feel for not only the competitive cooking circuit but also for its dedicated band of competitors. In addition to telling the stories of the cook-offs, their judges and rules, and their participants, Sutherland also includes award-winning recipes throughout her chapters and relates the details of how she too became swept up in cook-off fever.

Subjects: Character Profiles, Cooking, Food, Foodies, Hobbies, Recipes, Travel, Year in the Life

Now Try: Foodie books have become hugely popular of late, and a variety of Investigative, Memoir, and Travel titles might be offered to these readers, including *Two for the Road* by Jane and Michael Stern, *Feeding a Yen* by Calvin Trillin, *Home Cooking* by Laurie Colwin, *The Making of a Chef* by Michael Ruhlman, *The Horsemen of the Esophagus* by Jason Fagone, or *Julie and Julia* by Julie Powell; books by and about M. F. K. Fisher or Julia Child might also appeal. Ruth Reichl's books, many of which include recipes (as does this book), might make for particularly enjoyable readalikes, including *Tender at the Bone, Comfort Me with Apples*, or *Garlic and Sapphires*. Likewise, "Year in the Life" books such as Shari Caudron's *Who Are You People?* or Susan Warren's *Backyard Giants* might be offered as well.

Trillin, Calvin

Alice, Let's Eat: Further Adventures of a Happy Eater. Random House. 1978. 182 pp. ISBN 9780394425009.

New Yorker and food writer Trillin set out across the nation, often with his intrepid wife Alice at his side as an eating companion, in search of "something decent to eat." From crabs in California to mutton in Kentucky (as well as some international trips to London for potato latkes and Martinique for blaff d'oursins), Trillin displays his trademark humor and travel writing, and even provides character portraits of those with whom he shares his meals, including Alice (who "has a weird predilection for limiting our family to three meals a day"), New York pizza baron Fats Goldberg, and even his six-year-old daughter Sarah, who likes to take a bagel along to most restaurants "just in case."

Subjects: Classics, Food, Foodies, Humor, Marriage, Quick Reads, Travel

Now Try: Trillin went on to write more food and travel books, including the compilation *The Tummy Trilogy* and *Feeding a Yen*, as well as the beautiful tribute to Alice after her death, *About Alice*. Other foodie books might be suggested, particularly Michael and Jane Stern's *Roadfood* and *Two for the Road*, Bill Buford's *Heat*, Michael Ruhlman's *The Making of a Chef*, or Ruth Reichl's *Tender at the Bone*. Other essay collections by authors including M. F. K. Fisher or Jeffrey Steingarten might be offered, as well as Memoirs by Laurie Colwin or Julie Powell.

Türoque, Björn

To Air Is Human: One Man's Quest to Become the World's Greatest Air Guitarist. Riverhead Books. 2006. 304 pp. ISBN 9781594482106.

Although he knew how to play a "there" guitar, mild-mannered *New York Times* reporter Dan Crane happily put it down to pick up an air guitar and reinvent himself as Björn Türoque (say it out loud). Eventually becoming America's second greatest air guitarist, Türoque traveled to a variety of air guitar contests and eventually even the 2003 world championships in Oulu, Finland. In this humorous mix of Memoir, music, and reportage, Türoque provides interviews with the founders of the art form, his competitors, and the fans who, just as they do with "there" musicians, make it all worthwhile.

Subjects: Finland, Friendships, Humor, Memoirs, Music and Musicians, Pop Culture, Travel, YA, Year in the Life

Now Try: Luckily, there's no shortage of intrepid journalists who are prepared to do all sorts of things to keep their readers amused; fans of this Immersion memoir might also consider Tony Hawks's travelogues *Round Ireland with a Fridge* or *Playing the Moldovans at Tennis*, Danny Wallace's *Yes Man* or *Join Me!*, Bill Buford's foodie memoir *Heat*, Tim Cahill's *Hold the Enlightenment*, or A. J. Jacobs's *The Know-It-All* and *The Year of Living Biblically*. Other authors who often write about music and pop culture and might appeal to these readers include Neal Pollack, Chuck Klosterman, and Nick Hornby.

Vollmann, William T.

Riding toward Everywhere. Ecco. 2008. 206 pp. ISBN 9780061256752.

Vollmann is an avant-garde fiction and nonfiction writer who very rarely covers the same subject twice, although his interest in meeting, talking with, and living alongside those people whose lives he is exploring is a constant throughout his narratives. In this personal investigation of riding the rails with individuals still living the "hobo life," Vollmann combines Memoir, interviews, stream-of-consciousness writing, and photography to paint an evocative picture of one of the remaining lifestyles still characterized by its simultaneous danger and freedom.

Subjects: American West, Memoirs, Rail Travel, Society, Trains, Travel

Now Try: Vollmann is a respected author whose nonfiction titles (including *Rising Up and Rising Down*, *Poor People*, and *The Atlas*) and fiction titles (the National Book Award–winning *Europe Central*) always feature unique viewpoints and skilled if unconventional prose. Readers particularly interested in the travel aspect of this title might consider Ted Conover's similar *Rolling Nowhere: Riding the Rails with America's Hoboes*, Paul Theroux's *The Old Patagonian Express*, or even Eric Newby's *Slowly Down the Ganges*; those readers more interested in unique individuals seeking freedom in their own ways might consider James Agee's *Let Us Now Praise Famous Men*, Jon Krakauer's classic *Into the Wild*, or Elizabeth Gilbert's *The Last American Man*. Vollmann also refers to many works of literature in his text, including Jack Kerouac's *The Dharma Bums* (*On the Road* might also appeal), and authors mentioned include John Muir, Thomas Wolfe, and Mark Twain.

Walker, Sam

Fantasyland: A Season on Baseball's Lunatic Fringe. Viking. 2006. 354 pp. ISBN 9780670034284.

A *Wall Street Journal* writer seeks to immerse himself in a season of professional baseball, but he takes a rather roundabout approach by enrolling in the "Tout Wars" Rotisserie Baseball League, one of the most competitive and hardcore fantasy baseball leagues in the country. With great humor and an appreciation for number-crunching, Walker highlights an aspect of professional baseball with which many fans are more enamored than the actual games and championships. In his own quest to hold his own in his fantasy league, he enlists the help of both a dedicated research assistant and a NASA scientist to analyze player statistics to his advantage; he also figures he's a dead lock to win the contest, because his sportswriter background grants him access to players and locker room news to which other competitors may not be privy (even though this approach makes him no fans among the baseball players with whom he shares his plans). In the end, his best-laid plans and insider information do nothing but help him spend a massive amount of his own money to win a contest with no cash prize and place far back in his league's standings.

Subjects: Baseball, Hobbies, Humor, Mathematics, Sports, Statistics, YA, Year in the Life

Now Try: Michael Lewis's classic *Moneyball*, also about statistics and baseball, might particularly appeal to these readers, as might other books about baseball such as Seth Mnookin's *Feeding the Monster*, Gene Wojciechowski's *Cubs Nation: 162 Games. 162 Stories. 1 Addiction*, or H. G. Bissinger's *Three Nights in August* (or any number of Sports Reporting books from the In-Depth Reporting chapter). Other books on hobbies and "year in the life" writers' adventures might also be suggested, such as Joe Drape's *The Race for the Triple Crown*, A. J. Jacobs's *The Year of Living Biblically*, or Stefan Fatsis's *Word Freak*.

The Work World

Although we might dream about a world in which it were otherwise, there's no denying the fact that we spend most of our adult lives working our jobs or climbing our way up through our chosen professions. It seems only fair that a great many nonfiction narratives, of all types, explore the working world and offer commentary on it. In these Immersion titles, as in others in this chapter, the authors go a step beyond observing, interviewing, researching, and reporting, and go right out there and actually work the jobs about which they are writing. Again these books are very similar in tone and style to Memoirs, particularly those in which the authors describe their professional lives (such as Anthony Bourdain's *Kitchen Confidential*), but they are different in focus and the author's point of view. These authors are not experts in their fields, and they normally do not spend a lifetime, as do most memoirists, working the jobs and careers about which they're writing.

In most of these titles, the authors are forthright with their coworkers and bosses about their desires to learn all they can about their professions, but sometimes the authors adopt more of an undercover style to get a truer flavor for the jobs in question (many of the classics of the genre, including Ted Conover's *Newjack* and Barbara Ehrenreich's *Nickel and Dimed* fall into this category). Those readers who particularly enjoy those titles might also enjoy Corporate Exposés (or Exposés in general, in which authors endeavor to bring to light previously misunderstood or obscured truths and topics). Many of these titles, although they are primarily narrative and story-driven, also offer a unique reading experience in their authors' abilities to weave their first-person stories with research and interview materials. In-depth Science, Sports, and True Crime Reporting might also appeal, as many of those books also offer inside looks at professionals doing their jobs. Above all, these are often very surprising stories, and even include moments of levity; other essay collections and fiction in which nuanced characters, stories, and writing styles are combined might be suggested (such as Joshua Ferris's second-person novel set in an office setting, *Then We Come to the End*, or

Douglas Coupland's unique *Microserfs* and *Jpod*, or even Max Barry's futuristic *The Company*). One word that particularly comes to mind with these titles is offbeat: offbeat jobs, offbeat characters, and an offbeat approach to writing that comes from authors who look at places like prisons and Wal-Mart and ask themselves, what's it really like to work there?

1

The Work World Immersion Journalism titles find their authors not only reporting on very specific stories and surroundings—those found in a variety of jobs and professions—but also, to whatever extent possible, working the jobs themselves and writing about their own experiences. They also interview other individuals and professionals with whom they work and typically perform research on their chosen industry, but again, they combine elements of personal Memoir and journalistic reporting in their narratives. The stories are not so much dictated by distinct beginnings and endings, but rather by the authors' stated time or event commitments. Setting also plays a role in the appeal of these titles, as the authors often describe their surroundings, both geographical and interior, in great detail.

2

3

Black, Jonathan

Yes You Can!: Behind the Hype and Hustle of the Motivation Biz. Bloomsbury. 2007. 228 pp. ISBN 9781596910003.

4

Although most people have indicated that they would rather be the person in the casket at a funeral than be the one charged with giving the eulogy, Black finds there is no shortage of individuals hoping to be the next great inspirational speaker and author of the business, spiritual, or self-help worlds. Delving deep into the world of professional public and motivational speaking, Black got to know such speakers as Ronan Tynan and Vince Poscente, attended numerous conferences and presentations, and sought to explore what it is to try to be the person who tells other people how to better their lives (and turn a tidy profit doing so). This informative look into the billion-dollar industry that has spawned such ubiquitous motivators as Tony Robbins and Zig Ziglar is also a well-researched and compellingly told story. In addition to relating the history of the industry, the merchandising of products to supplement speaking incomes, and the techniques necessary to network and become successful, Black also takes the phrase "participatory journalism" seriously and tries to put together his own motivational presentation and launch himself on the speaking circuit, learning along the way its many pitfalls and challenges (not the least of which is his own skepticism regarding the efficacy of any such presentations).

5

6

Subjects: Business, Character Profiles, Memoirs, Motivation, Professions, Self-Help

Now Try: Other Immersion titles such as Barbara Ehrenreich's *Nickel and Dimed*, Alex Frankel's *Punching In*, or Beth Lisick's *Helping Me Help Myself: One Skeptic, Ten Self-Help Gurus, and a Year on the Brink of the Comfort Zone*

might be suggested, as might a wide variety of titles from the Business Reporting chapter (including titles from the Biz Crit and Business Histories and Profiles subgenres). Another, more scholarly book mentioned in Black's text is Peter Whybrow's *American Mania: When More Is Not Enough*.

Bourdain, Anthony

The Nasty Bits: Collected Varietal Cuts, Usable Trim, Scraps, and Bones. Bloomsbury. 2006. 288 pp. ISBN 9781582344515.

Chef and memoirist Bourdain's always delightfully frank stories about travel, eating, and the business aspects of the restaurant business (many of them including his unique and frequent use of profanities) include tales from his travels; his work in New York and other kitchens, often side-by-side with the immigrants who basically hold up the entire American restaurant industry; and his experiences eating everything from sushi to the nasty, leftover bits of animals that most other foodies won't touch.

Subjects: Essays, Food, Foodies, Humor, Profanity, Travel, Work Relationships

Now Try: Bourdain's other nonfiction titles, *Kitchen Confidential* and *A Cook's Tour*, as well as his novels *Bone in the Throat* and *Gone Bamboo* might also be enjoyed by these readers. Other contrarian but still hilarious nonfiction authors and essayists such as Jim Knipfel, Christopher Hitchens, and David Rakoff might be offered, as might other foodie writers of straightforward narratives of the joys of eating, including Calvin Trillin (*Alice, Let's Eat* and *Feeding a Yen*), Bill Buford (*Heat*), Michael Ruhlman (*The Making of a Chef*), or Ruth Reichl (*Garlic and Sapphires*) might also be enjoyed.

Buford, Bill

🌶 *Heat: An Amateur's Adventures as Kitchen Slave, Line Cook, Pasta Maker, and Apprentice to a Dante-Quoting Butcher in Tuscany*. Knopf. 2006. 318 pp. ISBN 9781400041206.

New Yorker writer Buford set out to find what it means to become a chef by apprenticing himself to celebrity chef Mario Batali. In addition to performing the grunt work in Batali's kitchen, Buford also traveled to Italy to learn pasta making, butchering, and numerous other culinary skills from Batali's relatives.

Subjects: Mario Batali, Book Groups, Chefs, Cooking, Food, Foodies, Humor, Italy, Memoirs, New York City, Professions, Travel

Awards: New York Times Notable

Now Try: Fans of Buford's straightforward and sometimes salty language might also appreciate Anthony Bourdain's *Kitchen Confidential* or *The Nasty Bits*, or Michael Ruhlman's slightly less risqué *The Making of a Chef*. Other foodie writers such as Ruth Reichl, Calvin Trillin, Laurie Colwin, Steven Rinella (*The Scavenger's Guide to Haute Cuisine*), or M. F. K. Fisher might be offered to these readers, as might *My Life in France* by Julia Child. Buford also wrote the earlier investigative title *Among the Thugs* (about rabid soccer fans); his readers might enjoy titles by authors including Barbara Ehrenreich, Jon Ronson, and Ted Conover.

Byer, Heather

Sweet: An Eight-Ball Odyssey. Riverhead Books. 2007. 287 pp. ISBN 9781594489365.

When thirty-year-old Heather Byer found the thrill had worn off of her career at a New York City feature film company, she sought comfort and fulfillment from another source: the world of competitive pool. In this memoir, she takes the reader inside the game's history, current culture, and her own reverence for the beauty of the game.

> **Subjects:** Billiards, Coming of Age, Memoirs, Pool, Sports, Women's Nonfiction, YA, Year in the Life
>
> **Now Try:** Byer's voice is a fresh one, and her readers might enjoy other new memoirists such as Jancee Dunn (*But Enough about Me: A Jersey Girl's Unlikely Adventures among the Absurdly Famous*), Julie Powell (*Julie and Julia: My Year of Cooking Dangerously*), Toby Cecchini (*Cosmopolitan*), or Hollis Gillespie (*Bleachy Haired Honky Bitch: Tales from a Bad Neighborhood*). Another notable pool-playing Memoir, David McCumber's *Playing Off the Rail*, might be offered to these readers, as might fiction by such novelists such as Melissa Bank, Curtis Sittenfeld, or Rita Ciresi.

Conover, Ted

❦ *Newjack: Guarding Sing Sing.* Random House. 2000. 321 pp. ISBN 9780375501777.

When the New York state Department of Correctional Services wouldn't allow Ted Conover into its training academy or prisons to write a story about corrections officers, he got in the only way he could think of: as a new recruit. Conover shares the often bleak details of his life and work as a corrections officer (one of the first things he noted is that none of them liked to be called "prison guards") for a year in the maximum security Sing Sing prison in Ossining. From the training academy to his regular work detail, interacting with his colleagues and the inmates, Conover provides the reader with a clearer understanding of both prison myths and truths.

> **Subjects:** Book Groups, Classics, Prisons, Professions, True Crime, Work Relationships
>
> **Awards:** National Book Award
>
> **Now Try:** Ted Conover is an institution in the world of investigative journalism; he also wrote *Rolling Nowhere: Riding the Rails with America's Hoboes*, *Coyotes: A Journey Through the Secret World of America's Illegal Aliens*, and *Whiteout: Lost in Aspen*. Although he is alluded to only briefly, Lewis Lawes was the warden of Sing Sing for twenty years and eventually became an outspoken critic of capital punishment; readers who enjoy Conover's account of prison life might also be interested in Lawes's work, described in Ralph Blumenthal's *Miracle at Sing Sing: How One Man Transformed the Lives of America's Most Dangerous Prisoners*.

Ehrenreich, Barbara

Bait and Switch: The (Futile) Pursuit of the American Dream. Metropolitan Books. 2005. 237 pp. ISBN 9780805076066.

Best known for her book *Nickel and Dimed*, in which she tried to make a living working various service industry jobs (as a waitress, housecleaner, and Wal-Mart employee), Ehrenreich broadened her query to see how far she could get in the white-collar world of employment. In this title she relates her journey to simply try and obtain a job (which she never did, over the course of her research) by making use of networking opportunities and groups, image and employment consultants, and the same classifieds available to everyone else.

Subjects: Business, Careers, Economics, Retail, Society, Work Relationships

Now Try: Fans of Ehrenreich's willingness to live her research might also appreciate Adrian Nicole LeBlanc's *Random Family*, Alex Kotlowitz's *There Are No Children Here*, and Jonathan Kozol's *Savage Inequalities*, while those more interested in the current state of the workplace environment might consider Louis Uchitelle's *The Disposable American: Layoffs and Their Consequences*, David Shipler's *The Working Poor*, Jason DeParle's *American Dream: Three Women, Ten Kids, and a Nation's Drive to End Welfare*, Joe Bageant's *Deer Hunting with Jesus*, or *Class Matters* (by a number of *New York Times* journalists).

Ehrenreich, Barbara

Nickel and Dimed: On (Not) Getting By in America. Metropolitan Books. 2001. 221 pp. ISBN 9780805063882.

The Nation and *The Progressive* magazine contributor Ehrenreich decided that if she was going to understand the world of trying to support oneself on minimum wage, she was probably going to have to live it. She spent a year working in various jobs (including housecleaner, waitress, and Wal-Mart associate) in different locations, and found that all the jobs she held were not only physically and mentally demanding but were also so poorly compensated that making a living from them wasn't really feasible. Ehrenreich provides a lot of disturbing financial and economic statistics but also uses her strident voice and first-person storytelling to make her case that these demoralizing jobs aren't good for the employees or our society.

Subjects: Book Groups, Business, Classics, Economics, Labor History, Poverty, Retail, Society, Work Relationships, YA

Now Try: Barbara Ehrenreich has long been an outspoken and liberal writer on many sociological topics, from *Fear of Falling: The Inner Life of the Middle Class* to her more feminist texts such as *For Her Own Good: Two Centuries of the Experts' Advice to Women* (co-authored with Deirdre English); she also wrote a sequel to this book titled *Bait and Switch*. Readers interested in her "insider's look" at minimum wage jobs might also consider David Shipler's *The Working Poor: Invisible in America*, while another, more personal story of poverty is related by Michelle Kennedy in her memoir *Without a Net: Middle Class and Homeless (with Kids) in America*. Readers more intrigued by Ehrenreich's personal reactions to working service industry jobs may also enjoy Louise Rafkin's straightforward and amusing memoir of her life as a housecleaner, *Other People's Dirt: A Housecleaner's Curious Adventures*.

Esposito, Richard, and Ted Gerstein

Bomb Squad: A Year Inside the Nation's Most Exclusive Police Unit. Hyperion. 2007. 335 pp. ISBN 9781401301521.

Journalists Gerstein and Esposito spent a year alongside members of the New York City Bomb Squad, where they gained a real appreciation for the thirty-three members of the squad, as well as for their ability to focus under very real pressure.

Subjects: Character Profiles, Friendships, Law Enforcement, New York City, Public Safety, Terrorism, Work Relationships

Now Try: Fans of this book might also consider other "insider's looks" into similarly dangerous professions, such as Michael Connelly's *Homicide Special: A Year with the LAPD's Elite Detective Unit* or *Crime Beat: A Decade of Covering Cops and Killers*, Edward Conlon's *Blue Blood*, Ted Conover's *Newjack: Guarding Sing Sing*, or Terry Golway's *So Others Might Live: A History of NY's Bravest*. Other titles from the True Crime Reporting subgenre of In-depth Reporting might be offered, such as Steve Bogira's *Courtroom 302: A Year behind the Scenes in an American Criminal Courthouse* or Stacy Horn's *The Restless Sleep: Inside New York City's Cold Case Squad*.

Feiler, Bruce S.

Under The Big Top: A Season with the Circus. Scribner. 1995. 288 pp. ISBN 9780684197586.

Giving in to a lifelong interest in the circus and trading on his ability to work as a clown, Feiler joined the Clyde Beatty-Cole Bros. Circus and spent a season with them, traveling and working. In addition to providing details to which a unique few have been privy, such as the tricks and techniques of hoisting the big tent, providing veterinary care to elephants, and training tigers, he also writes sympathetic character portraits of the many fascinating individuals who have made traveling with circuses their career, as well as providing a nuanced picture of the difficult nature of remaining in the business of managing, moving, and marketing a traveling circus.

Subjects: Animals, Business, Character Profiles, Circus, Friendships, Hobbies, Travel, Work Relationships

Now Try: A wide variety of Investigative works in which journalists try their hands at other people's jobs might appeal to these readers, including Barbara Ehrenreich's *Nickel and Dimed*, Alex Frankel's *Punching In*, Bill Buford's *Heat*, or Jason Fagone's *Horsemen of the Esophagus: Competitive Eating and the Big Fat American Dream*; work memoirs such as Debra Ginsberg's *Waiting* or Reg Theriault's *How to Tell When You're Tired* might also be offered. Those readers interested in the circus life might also consider Sara Gruen's hugely popular novel *Water for Elephants*.

Frankel, Alex

Punching In: The Unauthorized Adventures of a Front-Line Employee. HarperCollins. 2007. 222 pp. ISBN 9780060849665.

Frankel spent a year immersing himself in jobs and the corporate cultures he found most interesting; his jobs included a stint as a delivery person with UPS, a barista at Starbucks, a salesperson with Enterprise Rent-A-Car, a floor salesperson at the Gap, and a sales associate at an Apple Store. Quickly paced, with as many business details as Frankel could glean from his "inside look" at the jobs themselves, as well as at the attitudes and directives of management, this is a lively exploration of business and customer service at the opening of the twenty-first century.

Subjects: Business, Companies, Quick Reads, Retail, Work Relationships, Year in the Life

Now Try: Fans of Frankel's title may enjoy Barbara Ehrenreich's immersion classics *Nickel and Dimed* and *Bait and Switch*; other slightly less business-oriented work titles and memoirs such as Iain Levison's *A Working Stiff's Manifesto*, Pete Jordan's *Dishwasher*, and Reg Theriault's *How to Tell When You're Tired* might be suggested. Likewise, books that are a bit more straightforwardly business-oriented might appeal, such as Chris Anderson's *The Long Tail*, Taylor Clark's *Starbucked*, and Rachel Louise Snyder's *Fugitive Denim*.

Holden, Anthony

Bigger Deal: A Year inside the Poker Boom. Simon & Schuster. 2007. 291 pp. ISBN 9780743294829.

Holden, author of the poker-playing memoir *Big Deal*, returns to the high-stakes world of poker, made ever more popular by the huge prizes in the World Series of Poker and other contests, as well as by the boom in Internet poker and gambling. In this investigative work, insider Holden explores how the poker world has changed since he won the 1988 World Series of Poker, often adopting a wistful tone at poker's new "respectable" image and lamenting the loss of "seedy rooms" where you could smoke at the table and play the game against characters whose background you didn't want to know too much about. Now, as Holden points out, you're just as likely to find Hollywood celebrities playing high-stakes competitive poker as ex-cons, and the business has spawned a whole net set of personalities along with its multibillion dollar revenue-making status.

Subjects: Gambling, Las Vegas, Memoirs, Poker, Sports, Technology, True Adventure, Year in the Life

Now Try: Other books on poker and card games might be offered, such as James McManus's *Positively Fifth Street*, Ben Mezrich's *Bringing Down the House*, Jay Greenspan's *Hunting Fish*, or even Edward McPherson's *The Backwash Squeeze and Other Improbable Feats: A Newcomer's Journey into the World of Bridge* (about bridge). Other books about hobbies and obsessions might be suggested, such as Stefan Fatsis's *Word Freak*, Michael Weinreb's *The Kings of New York*, or Sam Walker's *Fantasyland*. (For those readers interested in learning how to play poker, Herbert Yardley's classic *The Education of a Poker Player*, first published in 1957, might also be a fun place to start.)

McPhee, John A.

Assembling California. Farrar, Straus & Giroux. 1993. 303 pp. ISBN 9780374106454.

Journalist and creative nonfiction stalwart McPhee relates the story of his geological "field trips" across the state of California, typically in the company of Eldridge Moores, a tectonicist at the University of California—Davis. In addition to geological facts and research, McPhee also explores the history of the area, from the Donner Pass's tragic history to the development of California's wine country and industry; he also travels to Arizona, Greece, and Cyprus to better understand the concept and reality of plate tectonics worldwide. A writer with *The New Yorker* and one of the most critically acclaimed writers of the twentieth century, McPhee is known for his graceful prose, and in this book he combines scientific data with the inevitability of the state's complex fault lines and susceptibility to earthquakes; striving to make understandable to the reader his geologist companion's assertion that "You can't cope with this in an organized way, because the rocks aren't organized."

> **Subjects:** California, Classics, Environmental Writing, Geology, Eldridge Moores, Science, Travel
>
> **Now Try:** This volume completes McPhee's "Annals of the Formal World" series, the first three titles in which are *Basin and Range*, *In Suspect Terrain*, and *Rising from the Plains*; his other books such as *Uncommon Carriers* or *The Founding Fish* might also appeal; another book about earthquakes and California, David Ulin's *The Myth of Solid Ground*, might be a good related read. McPhee is an institution in the field of literary journalism; other venerable authors of both journalism and environmental writing might also appeal, including Henry David Thoreau, Rachel Carson, Edward Abbey, John Hersey, Lee Gutkind, or Joan Didion, as might setting-driven fiction by Wallace Stegner or Jim Harrison.

Plimpton, George

Paper Lion: Confessions of a Last-String Quarterback. Harper & Row. 1966. 362 pp. ISBN 9781592280155.

> Intrepid reporter and founder of the *Paris Review*, Plimpton stopped at nothing to get his insider's view of football in this classic of sports and narrative journalism. Although the majority of the story focuses on his learning the quarterback position and observing the interactions between the 1963 Detroit Lions team members and their coaching staff in both training camp and real games, Plimpton also weaves into the story the details of his persistent quest to get some football team to add him to the roster, to great effect. Thirty-six-year-old Plimpton did eventually get to take the field for five plays in an exhibition game, an experience he relates with self-deprecating honesty and humor.

> **Subjects:** Classics, Detroit, Football, Humor, Sports, Work Relationships, Year in the Life
>
> **Now Try:** This is George Plimpton's most infamous insider's sports story, but he went on to produce a number of works in the same vein, including *Out of My League: The Classic Hilarious Account of an Amateur's Ordeal in Professional Baseball* (which was actually published, without the overblown subtitle, before *Paper Lion*, in 1961), *The Bogey Man: A Month on the PGA Tour*, *Shadow Box: An Amateur in the Ring*, and *Open Net*. Readers who enjoy this mixture of sports and humor might also enjoy Tim Moore's anecdotal *French Revolutions: Cycling the Tour de France*, as well as any number of titles from the Sports Reporting subgenre of In-Depth Reporting, particularly the titles by John Feinstein.

Reavill, Gil

Aftermath, Inc.: Cleaning Up after CSI Goes Home. Gotham Books. 2007. 284 pp. ISBN 9781592402960.

Crime reporter and author Reavill wastes no time displaying his crime-writing chops; in the first chapter he recreates the murders that created one of the messier crime scenes that the "bioremediation" company Aftermath, Inc., would become responsible for remediating. Reavill was interested in the work Aftermath and other similar crime scene-cleanup companies were doing, so he joined the staff at Aftermath to describe it more accurately. One of the scenes on which he assisted is definitely not for the faint of heart: "The body fluids had drained from the deceased onto the floorboards onto the subflooring, then through the subflooring to dribble down the floor joists and drop onto a chest of drawers in the basement." The author is not specifically trying to be shocking but rather intends to provide enlightening narrations of actual cleaning procedures, as well as surprisingly nuanced interviews with the company's founders. Also explored are the work lives of the techs who do the cleanups, often working in pairs and based in specific geographic locations designed to provide coverage for multistate regions, while those who have died also merit surprisingly gentle treatment from Reavill.

> **Subjects:** Business, Explicit Violence, Homicides, Law Enforcement, Professions, Science, True Crime, Work Relationships

> **Now Try:** A wide variety of nonfiction narratives might appeal to these readers, such as True Crime titles like Stacy Horn's *The Restless Sleep: Inside New York City's Cold Case Squad*, Dominick Dunne's *Justice*, or Michael Connelly's *Crime Beat*; also consider other "inside looks" at jobs and professions like Anthony Bourdain's *Kitchen Confidential*, Edward Conlon's *Blue Blood*, or Steve Bogira's *Courtroom 302*. Fiction thrillers featuring medical examiner and other crime investigator characters, by authors including Kathy Reichs, Patricia Cornwell, or Linda Fairstein might be suggested, as might thrillers by authors such as Jonathan Kellerman or James Patterson.

Ribowsky, Shiya, and Tom Shachtman

Dead Center: Behind the Scenes at the World's Largest Medical Examiner's Office. Regan. 2006. 262 pp. ISBN 9780061116247.

Shiya Ribowsky worked as a medico-legal investigator in New York City's medical examiner's office for fifteen years, led the investigations of more than eight thousand individual deaths, and eventually took charge of the forensic investigation in the aftermath of 9/11 in which he and his staff struggled to identify the many dead from the tragedy. Although this book includes details of Ribowsky's professional career, it also contains memoir-like revelations of his childhood in an orthodox Jewish community in New York City, and his tale, told with the help of journalist Shachtman, is a compelling one of the choices he made not to practice medicine on the living, but rather to identify causes of death in locations as varied as city flophouses and posh Upper East Side apartments. Although Ribowsky provides details that could only come from his work in the Office of the Chief Medical Examiner, he does not describe them graphically, and his story is told throughout with great empathy for both the victims he examines and their families.

> **Subjects:** 9/11, Judaism, Medicine, Memoirs, New York City, Professions, Religion, True Crime

Now Try: Stacy Horn's superlative *The Restless Sleep: Inside New York City's Cold Case Squad* offers a similar reading experience, as might Mary Roach's *Stiff*, while Memoirs of medical professionals might also particularly appeal, such as Jerome Groopman's *How Doctors Think*, Sherwin Nuland's *Lost in America*, Atul Gawande's *Complications*, or Richard Selzer's *Down from Troy*. Of course, one of the most tragic tales in this book is Ribowsky's description of his work identifying 9/11 victims; books about that tragedy, such as Jim Dwyer's *102 Minutes* or Art Spiegelman's *In the Shadow of No Towers*, might also be suggested.

Rothenberg, Daniel

With These Hands: The Hidden World of Migrant Farmworkers Today. Harcourt Brace. 1998. 334 pp. ISBN 9780151002054.

Rothenberg traveled to a variety of locations across the United States in his quest to compile more than 250 interviews to provide a comprehensive oral history of the lives of migrant farmworkers at the end of the twentieth century. Organized by themes, including the nature of the work, the growers' business and financial perspective, the role of unions, illegal immigration, and children's lives as migrant workers (as well as many others), the author provides a unique and vividly detailed picture of the work and living conditions of those individuals who are, at the end of the day, responsible for picking and handling nearly all of the produce that Americans eat.

Subjects: Agriculture, Business, Character Profiles, Economics, Immigrants, Immigration, Law Enforcement, Multicultural Issues, Oral Histories, Poverty

Now Try: Three other superlative titles on this subject are available; William Langewiesche's *Cutting for Sign*, Ruben Martinez's *Crossing Over*, and John Bowe's *Nobodies*. Reg Theriault's thoughtful extended essay on the nature of physical work, *How to Tell When You're Tired*, complete with chapters on agricultural work, might also be a good read-alike. Oral histories by authors such as Studs Terkel and John Bowe might appeal to these readers, as might other investigative works about social justice issues, including Barbara Ehrenreich's *Nickel and Dimed* and Jonathan Kozol's *Savage Inequalities*.

Ruhlman, Michael

The Making of a Chef: Mastering Heat at the Culinary Institute. Holt. 1997. 305 pp. ISBN 9780805046748.

Journalist Michael Ruhlman, with a combination of determination and guile, earned a spot studying at the prestigious Culinary Institute of America and takes his readers along for the grueling but also exhilarating journey to become a professional-grade chef. His classes are both attended and taught by a variety of unique individuals, and Ruhlman's love for all things food is clearly communicated in this investigative Memoir.

Subjects: Book Groups, Cooking, Education, Food, Foodies, Friendships, Memoirs, Professions

Now Try: Michael Ruhlman has since gone on to write other cooking memoirs and cookbooks, including *The Soul of a Chef*, *The Reach of a Chef*, and *The French Laundry Cookbook*. Other Memoirs regarding the cook's and foodie's life that might appeal include Bill Buford's *Heat*, Anthony Bourdain's *Kitchen*

Confidential, Julia Child's *My Life in France*, and Ruth Reichl's *Tender at the Bone* or *Garlic and Sapphires*.

Community Life and Society

Sometimes Investigative and Immersion writers look around themselves and their natural curiosity leads them to raise questions about broader societal norms, cultural constructs, and the results of living with and near one another in our communities and society. These are the authors who then decide to investigate further, and who do so largely by experiencing the lifestyles of their subjects of interest. As in the Work World Immersion titles, the deciding factor for their collection together here is not whether these authors decide to let their subjects in on the secret (Ronald Kessler told people he was writing a book about Palm Beach high society, whereas Norah Vincent actually feared for her personal safety if the men with whom she worked and became friends, and who thought she was a fellow man, found out she was actually a female writer), but more in the nature of their participation in the events around them. These writers further combine those experiences with their opinions and thoughts on the larger issues, particularly as shaped by their supplemental research and interviews to make this another unique subset of nonfiction titles. Most of these books can be thought of as titles that provide "snapshots" of our American culture at specific times and in specific places.

Readers who enjoy these titles might also enjoy a number of Social Exposés, whose authors also explore surprising stories and come to equally surprising conclusions. Nonfiction titles that focus primarily on Relationships (as well as nonfiction titles with subjects like "community life," such as Heather Lende's *If You Lived Here, I'd Know Your Name*) might also be suggested, as might a wide variety of novels that combine setting and character details, including titles by Kent Haruf, John Steinbeck, or Jay McInerney.

> Community Life and Society Immersion Journalism titles feature stories set among communities of characters, and authors who place themselves within those communities. Although they feature strongly drawn characters and informal, typically first-person narratives, they also offer the stories of relationships between characters, as well as unique and comprehensively described settings. They also provide a bit more in the way of broader social commentary and analysis than do the other, more internal Immersion Journalism subgenres.

Agee, James and Walker Evans

Let Us Now Praise Famous Men: Three Tenant Families. Houghton Mifflin. 1936. 416 pp. ISBN 9780395489017.

> In this truly revolutionary piece of on-the-ground reportage, second only to Jacob Riis's *How the Other Half Lives* for its written and visual imagery, reporter Agee and photographer Walker went out into Depression-era America and recorded the experiences of desperately poor tenant farmers. The three families on whom the pair focused were the Ricketts, the Woods, and the Gudgers; but rather than

giving a straightforward recounting of their biographies, relationships, and struggles, Agee wrote a stream-of-consciousness narrative designed more to invoke the true worry and unceasing pressure of poverty than could be described with mere numbers or facts. Although most of the book is not graphic in its language, readers should be aware that it was written in the 1930s, when some sensibilities, particularly toward minorities and other members of the "underclasses," were different than they are now.

Subjects: Agriculture, Alabama, American History, American South, Classics, Classism, Great Depression, Illustrated Books, Poverty, Rural Life, Travel

Now Try: Fans of this classic might consider other classic works of muckraking journalism, including Jacob Riis's *How the Other Half Lives*, Ida Tarbell's *The History of the Standard Oil Company*, or Upton Sinclair's reality-based social novel *The Jungle*; novels by John Steinbeck (*The Grapes of Wrath* or *East of Eden*), who often wrote about farmers, might also be offered. More modern works of oral history, including books by Studs Terkel or William Vollmann might make for a similar reading experience, as might the more contemporary but still disheartening title *Nobodies: Modern American Slave Labor and the Dark Side of the New Global Economy* by John Bowe, or Lynn Blodgett's photography collection *Finding Grace: The Face of America's Homeless*. (Other books or collections of the photography of Walker Evans might also be offered to these readers.)

Bamberger, Michael

Wonderland: A Year in the Life of an American High School. Atlantic Monthly Press. 2004. 207 pp. ISBN 9780871139177.

Sports Illustrated journalist Bamberger spent a year mingling with a variety of high school students at Pennsbury High School, a large Pennsylvania school known for its always-elaborate spring prom. Over the course of the narrative, organized chronologically over the school year, Bamberger introduces the reader to a representative group of students: the class presidents, the couple who conceive and keep their baby but don't let it stop them from going to the prom, the star athlete, the overextended but feisty female field hockey player, and the less-popular students who dream of escorting the most beautiful girl in school to the dance. The majority of the story takes place before the prom, which makes the rather brief description of it somewhat anticlimactic, but the author provides as much closure as possible for most of the interrelated dramas he followed throughout the year.

Subjects: Community Life, Education, Friendships, Love and Dating, Pennsylvania, Year in the Life

Now Try: Education reporter Linda Perlstein also spent a year going back to school and getting to know students personally, and she used those experiences to produce a very similar book about slightly younger kids, *Not Much Just Chillin': The Hidden Lives of Middle Schoolers*. Alexandra Robbins has also written two similar books: *The Overachievers* and *Pledged: The Secret Life of Sororities*; Tracy Kidder's classic *Among Schoolchildren* might also be suggested. Curtis Sittenfeld's novel *Prep*, about a boarding school student on scholarship, may also appeal to readers enthralled by Bamberger's insider's look at the high school experience.

Conover, Ted

Coyotes: A Journey through the Secret World of America's Illegal Aliens. Vintage Books. 1987. 264 pp. ISBN 9780394755182.

Conover was one of the earliest and still best known of the "immersion journalists" who have made writing careers from living their stories. In this, one of his earlier narratives, he recounts his experiences journeying back and forth across the border separating the United States and Mexico, often in the company of other "illegals" from Mexico and Latin America and the "coyotes," or human smugglers, they often employ to help them make the journey successfully. (He refers to his experiences as a year spent "working, drinking, smoking, driving, sleeping, sweating, and shivering with Mexicans.") In addition to getting to know the coyotes themselves and the Mexican residents pursuing (most often) work opportunities in the United States, Conover also recounts his experiences trying to get past border officials, as well as getting stopped and interviewed by them. Although the book is two decades old, many of Conover's reports seem as timely as ever for a nation still struggling with how best to balance security and immigration concerns on the southern border with Mexico.

> **Subjects:** Classics, Immigrants, Immigration, Law Enforcement, Multicultural Issues, Politics, Mexico, Travel, True Adventure, Year in the Life

> **Now Try:** Many books written on this subject are classics in the field, including William Langewiesche's *Cutting for Sign*, Ruben Martinez's *With These Hands: The Hidden World of Migrant Farmworkers Today* or *Crossing Over*, Paul Cuadros's *A Home on the Field*, or John Bowe's *Nobodies*. Novels by Latino authors or with multicultural themes might also be offered, such as Sandra Cisneros's *The House on Mango Street*, Julia Alvarez's *In the Time of the Butterflies*, or Laura Esquivel's *Like Water for Chocolate*.

Conover, Ted

Whiteout: Lost in Aspen. Random House. 1991. 269 pp. ISBN 9780394574691.

As a native of the state of Colorado, Ted Conover already had a pretty good grasp on the realities of the cultural and social milieu of Aspen, the city known internationally for its skiing, number of celebrity part-time residents, expensive real estate, and John Denver's music about the Rocky Mountains. Although the book was first published in the early 1990s and feels a bit dated as an "ethnography of hedonism" (which is how Conover himself described his aim), Conover is an important and popular author in the genre, and this is an early example of his ability to immerse himself deeply into a subject and trick out observations and insights that many others miss; he can also be quite funny at times, particularly when describing such surreal events as the John Denver holiday special.

> **Subjects:** Aspen, Classics, Colorado, Community Life, Memoirs, Society, Travel

> **Now Try:** This early Conover book is getting on in years but is still an enjoyable read; his readers might also consider early works by Susan Orlean (*Saturday Night*), Tracy Kidder (*Home Town*), or Ron Rosenbaum (*Manhattan Passions*). Books in which authors explore the cohesiveness of specific communities might also appeal; these include Heather Lende's *If You Lived Here, I'd Know Your Name*, Michael Perry's *Population 485*, or Stephen Bloom's *Postville: A Clash of Cultures in Heartland America*.

Cuadros, Paul

A Home on the Field: How One Championship Team Inspires Hope for the Revival of Small Town America. Rayo. 2006. 276 pp. ISBN 9780061120275.

Paul Cuadros initially moved to Siler City in North Carolina to study the impact of the still-new and ever-growing Latino and immigrant population on the community and in the opinions of that city's earlier inhabitants. Originally he planned on investigating the culture clash between the two groups, but before long he found himself at the forefront of the battle to form a soccer team at the town's high school. When the team was formed, he became their coach, with hopes of not only teaching his team members soccer skills but also instilling them with plans of going to college and eventually finding their places in the world. After only three seasons, the Jordan-Matthews High School soccer team went to the state championship. Cuadros tells the students' story, and his own, with high emotion, and even provides a "where are they now" epilogue explaining what happened to the players after graduation.

Subjects: Character Profiles, Community Life, Government, Immigrants, Immigration, Latinos, Multicultural Issues, North Carolina, Small-Town Life, Soccer, Sports, Underdogs, Year in the Life

Now Try: Two other nonfiction titles specifically about soccer might appeal: Joe McGinniss's *The Miracle of Castel di Sangro* and Franklin Foer's *How Soccer Explains the World* are both thoughtful narratives. Other sports titles, particularly those featuring underdogs, might be offered, such as Laura Hillenbrand's *Seabiscuit* or Wayne Coffey's *The Boys of Winter*; while books about small-town and community life such as H. G. Bissinger's *Friday Night Lights* or Tracy Kidder's *Home Town* or *Among Schoolchildren* might also appeal. Sudhir Venkatesh's *Gang Leader for a Day* also provides a new perspective on a population that has not been much investigated in other nonfiction books.

Kessler, Ronald

The Season: Inside Palm Beach and America's Richest Society. HarperCollins. 1999. 326 pp. ISBN 9780060193911.

To research his book on the moneyed classes of the extreme upper class, Kessler spent time mingling with and getting to know the rich and super rich residents of Palm Beach, a community of nearly 10,000 of some of the wealthiest people in America. By getting to know them, attending their parties and social events, and interviewing them, the author got to witness firsthand their relationships, business dealings, and even their sometimes vicious ostracizing and criticism of those they feel are inferiors in their ranks. In addition to discussing such infamous people as Donald Trump, Kessler also got to know the less famous members of Palm Beach society, but ones on whom the social structure rests, including managers of the popular night club Ta-boo, the matriarchs and queens of society, and the homosexual "walkers" whose purpose is to accompany women to events during the "season" (which runs from January through March) and to provide scintillating conversation and companionship.

Subjects: Character Profiles, Classism, Community Life, Florida, Society, Year in the Life

Now Try: Kessler's writing is similar in style to Dominick Dunne's, who also often writes about high society individuals (not to mention the crimes in which they are sometimes embroiled) in such titles as *Justice: Crimes, Trials, and Punishments* and *The Way We Lived Then*. Books about the upper class, albeit from a more sociological point of view, might also be suggested, such as Robert Frank's *Richistan* or Peter Bernstein's *All the Money in the World: How the Forbes 400 Make—and Spend—Their Fortunes*; these readers might also consider Glitz and Glamour romance and fiction titles by such authors as Sidney Sheldon, Judith Krantz, or Danielle Steel.

Kingsolver, Barbara

🍎 *Animal, Vegetable, Miracle: A Year of Food Life.* HarperCollins. 2007. 370 pp. ISBN 9780060852559.

Novelist Barbara Kingsolver details her family's desire to live closer to their food sources and in more harmony with nature's seasons in this humorous Memoir. In one year Kingsolver and her family moved from Arizona to the Appalachians, where they vowed to eat only what they grew themselves or could purchase from their neighbors. Kingsolver not only relates her family's struggles with this proposition but also includes investigative details about how truly far removed many Americans have become from the source of the food they consume.

Subjects: Agriculture, Appalachian Mountains, Community Life, Environmental Writing, Family Relationships, Food, Memoirs

Awards: ALA Notable

Now Try: Investigative works and memoirs about more authentic living and learning about the food chain are becoming more popular; these readers might also consider titles like Michael Pollan's *The Omnivore's Dilemma* or *In Defense of Food*, Peter Pringle's *Food, Inc.*, Eric Schlosser's *Fast Food Nation*, Bill McKibben's *Deep Economy: The Wealth of Communities and the Durable Future*, Wendell Berry's *Sex, Economy, Freedom, and Community*, Jeanne Marie Laskas's *Fifty Acres and a Poodle*, or Jim Mullen's *It Takes a Village Idiot*. Kingsolver's many novels, including *The Poisonwood Bible* and *The Bean Trees*, might also appeal.

LeDuff, Charlie

US Guys: The True and Twisted Mind of the American Man. Penguin Press. 2006. 242 pp. ISBN 9781594201066.

Intrepid journalist LeDuff sets out to determine what really makes American men tick, lending excitement to his narrative by finding the most macho men he can. In the course of meeting with and interviewing his subjects, he also finds himself fighting guys in biker clubs, riding along on police beats, joining historical event reenactors, and participating in rodeos.

Subjects: Essays, Friendships, Gender, Gonzo Journalism, Pop Culture, Society, Travel

Now Try: Fans of LeDuff's distinctive writing might also consider classics by Hunter S. Thompson (master of the Gonzo journalism form), including *Fear and Loathing in Las Vegas* and *Hell's Angels*. Other writers who might appeal include Chuck Klosterman (*Fargo Rock City*), Hank Stuever (*Off Ramp: Adventures and Heartache in the American Elsewhere*), Mark Singer (*Somewhere in America*), Jon Ronson (*Them: Adventures* *with Extremists*), and Louis Theroux (*The Call of the Weird*); nonfiction character profiles such as Ty Phillips's **Blacktop Cowboys** and Elizabeth Gilbert's *The Last American Man* might also be suggested. Novels by such authors as Charles Bukowski, Jack Kerouac, or Robert Stone might also strike a chord with these readers.

Mailer, Norman

🏵 *The Armies of the Night: History as a Novel, The Novel as History.* New American Library. 1968. 288 pp. ISBN 9780451140708.

Referring to himself in the third person as "Mailer," the author relates the story of his protests against the Vietnam War, in the company of other members of the literati including Noam Chomsky and Robert Lowell. In two mains parts ("History as a Novel" and "The Novel as History") and centering on the four days in 1967 when antiwar protests were at their height in Washington, D.C., the story includes just as much Mailer as it does history, outlining not only the events of his and others' march on the Pentagon but also his inner monologue regarding the event, his arrest, and the effects of protest on American society and foreign policy.

Subjects: 1960s, Classics, Literary Lives, Society, Vietnam War, Washington D.C.

Awards: Pulitzer Prize

Now Try: Norman Mailer had a completely unique literary style and liked to play with the boundaries between fiction and nonfiction; his readers might also consider his fiction classic *The Naked and the Dead* or his true crime novel *The Executioner's Song*; other practitioners of this style of writing include Tom Wolfe and Hunter S. Thompson; authors writing more recently in this style include Hank Stuever and Charlie LeDuff. Other books on the Vietnam War, both fiction and nonfiction, might appeal to these readers (including Dan Wakefield's 1968 classic *Supernation at Peace and War*); and, because Noam Chomsky and Robert Lowell both appear in this narrative, readers may want to try tracking down some of their titles too.

Mitchell, Joseph

Up in the Old Hotel: and Other Stories. Pantheon Books. 1992. 718 pp. ISBN 9780679412632.

Mitchell, a long-time and influential writer for *The New Yorker*, and best known for his book *Joe Gould's Secret*, had a knack for going among ordinary people, in ordinary places (including New York City's port and waterfront bars, neighborhoods, and fish markets) and hearing and then relating fascinating stories from them about their lives, relationships, work, and experiences. In this collection, he relates true stories that were first published in the pages of *The New Yorker* in the 1930s and 1940s (meaning that some of the language is outdated and less politically correct than modern readers may be used to, although Mitchell's prose and character portraits are always strangely gentle and respectful of those individuals he portrayed).

Subjects: 1930s, 1940s, American History, Character Profiles, Classics, Epic Reads, Essays, Humor, New York City

Now Try: Fans of Mitchell's writing might consider a wide variety of Investigative Writing works, particularly titles from the Character Profiles chapter. Titles which might particularly appeal include E. B. White's classic *This Is New York* and *One Man's Meat*, A. J. Liebling's *The Most of A. J. Liebling*, or David Remnick's more recent *Life Stories* or *Reporting: Writings from the New Yorker*. Fiction and nonfiction titles set in New York City might also particularly appeal to Mitchell's fans, such as Colson Whitehead's *The Colossus of New York*, Pete Hamill's *Downtown: My Manhattan*, or Melissa Bank's novel *The Wonder Spot*.

Rakoff, David

Don't Get Too Comfortable: The Indignities of Coach Class, The Torments of Low Thread Count, The Never-Ending Quest for Artisanal Olive Oil, and Other First World Problems. Doubleday. 2005. 222 pp. ISBN 9780385510363.

Rakoff has a talent for self-deprecation and for making the ridiculous funny, and he does both of those things in this collection of essays about flying on the Concorde, spending time at a luxury resort, and attending couture shows, as well as a number of other "luxury" subjects and industries. Rakoff is not afraid to describe things as he sees them, and although some readers might describe his quips as "catty," an equal number might simply find them sharp and hilarious.

Subjects: Consumerism, Essays, GLBTQ, Humor, Luxury, Society, Travel

Now Try: Rakoff's earlier essay collection, *Fraud*, might also be offered to these readers. Other essayists who can make the sarcastic hilarious include David Sedaris (*Me Talk Pretty One Day* and *Dress Your Family in Corduroy and Denim*), Sarah Vowell (*Take the Cannoli* and *The Partly Cloudy Patriot*), Jim Knipfel (*Ruining It for Everybody*), David Foster Wallace (*A Supposedly Fun Thing I'll Never Do Again* and *Consider the Lobster*), and John Hodgman (*The Areas of My Expertise*). Other books about luxury and lifestyle might also appeal to these readers, such as Robert Frank's *Richistan*, Dana Thomas's *Deluxe: How Luxury Lost Its Luster*, or even other Investigative books like Rebecca Mead's *One Perfect Day: The Selling of the American Wedding*.

Robbins, Alexandra

Pledged: The Secret Life of Sororities. Hyperion. 2004. 372 pp. ISBN 9781401300463.

Journalist Robbins went undercover to see what life in a sorority house is really like and found a rather disturbing propensity toward hazing rituals, psychological abuse among sorority members, and a wide variety of body-image and esteem disorders. She also, mercifully, found many intelligent, empathetic, and successful women who viewed their sorority experience as one that made them feel more part of a "sisterhood" and connected with their campus and their community. By spending the entire school year of 2002–2003 as a part of the sorority house, Robbins is able to present a comprehensive and detailed look at not only the sorority of which she was a part but sororities in general, and she concludes with a number of thoughts on how to improve the experience for all young women, suggesting more of a focus on community service, improved adult supervision, and an end to pledging and hazing traditions.

Subjects: College, Education, Friendships, Sororities, Women's Contributions, YA, Year in the Life

Now Try: Other classic works of "undercover" journalistic reporting might be suggested, including Robbins's own *The Overachievers*, Norah Vincent's *Self-Made Man*, Barbara Ehrenreich's *Nickel and Dimed*, or Ted Conover's *Newjack: Guarding Sing*

Sing. Other books about education might also appeal, such as Michael Bamberger's *Wonderland*, Abby Goodnough's *Ms. Moffett's First Year*, Frank McCourt's *Teacher Man*, or Sam Swope's *I Am a Pencil*. Consider also offering novels about young and twentysomething characters, such as John Green's *Looking for Alaska*, Curtis Sittenfeld's *Prep*, Mary Gaitskill's *Veronica*, or Melissa Bank's *The Wonder Spot* (as well as books by Jane Green, Helen Fielding, Sophie Kinsella, or Jane Stanton Hitchcock).

Ronson, Jon

Them: Adventures with Extremists. Simon & Schuster. 2001. 327 pp. ISBN 9780743227070.

British journalist Ronson decided the only way to truly get to know a wide variety of extremists was to join them. This meant that in the course of researching his book, Ronson effectively joined and interacted with Islamists in London, gun enthusiasts in Montana, Irish Protestant firebrands, and even the Ku Klux Klan. Ever fascinated by the idea that throughout history individuals who believed there are groups who rule the entire world from their tiny enclaves of power, Ronson's reporting provides the true inside look into organizations whose members passionately believe in the rightness of their varied causes. By discussing them all together in one narrative, he also paints a picture of stasis and of forces mainly kept in check largely because of their staunch opposition to one another and their sometimes vast inefficiencies.

Subjects: Character Profiles, Extremists, Fundamentalism, Politics, Racism, Radicalism, World Travel

Now Try: Ronson is also the author of the fascinating exposé *The Men Who Stare at Goats*, and his fans might enjoy other character profiles such as Jane Kramer's *Lone Patriot: The Short Career of an American Militiaman* or Elizabeth Gilbert's *The Last American Man*. Essay and current affairs collections by such authors as Chuck Klosterman, Sarah Vowell, David Sedaris, or Mark Singer might also be offered to Ronson fans.

Savage, Dan

Skipping towards Gomorrah: The Seven Deadly Sins and the Pursuit of Happiness in America. Dutton. 2002. 302 pp. ISBN 9780525946755.

Sex columnist and writer Savage sets out to explore America's moral fiber by researching the seven "deadly sins." His methodology? He sets out to commit all of the sins, of course, with the exception of coveting his neighbor's wife, which is not really in his area of expertise as a gay man (although lust can and does make an appearance in the narrative). Savage is never shy or reticent to say what he means, but he is always hilarious. In addition to his own personal experiences, Savage reveals a lot about the history of sin and some of its most famous detractors; he includes numerous quotes from such (conservative) authors as Robert Bork, William J. Bennett, and Pat Buchanan. Savage sees quite a bit of America and even more in terms of truly special events, from attending swinger conventions, meeting representatives of the NAAFA (National Association for the Advancement of Fat Acceptance), and indulging his anger by firing a gun.

Subjects: Explicit Sexuality, GLBTQ, Humor, Politics, Pop Culture, Religion, Society

Now Try: There's a great little series of books about each of the seven deadly sins available from the Oxford University Press, each authored by a different literary notable: *Gluttony* by Francine Prose, *Envy* by Joseph Epstein, *Sloth* by Wendy Wasserstein, and *Lust* by Simon Blackburn; these may offer fun related reading for this title. Readers who enjoy Savage's, well, savage humor, might also consider such nonfiction authors as Augusten Burroughs, Jim Knipfel, Lewis Black, Hollis Gillespie, or Susie Bright. Fiction authors who might appeal include John Irving, Carl Hiaasen, Terry Pratchett, or Magnus Mills (all of whom also display slightly offbeat, if not bleak, senses of humor in their novels).

Talese, Gay

Thy Neighbor's Wife. Doubleday. 1980. 568 pp. ISBN 9780385006323.

Talese set out to document the sexual practices and love and family relationships throughout America not only by interviewing those subjects who would speak honestly with him but also by offering character profiles of such well-known popular culture figures as Hugh Hefner and Alex Comfort, as well as engaging in extramarital affairs and masseuse parlor services himself. The book took him nine years to complete, and the result is exactly what is heralded on its front cover: a straightforward "chronicle of American permissiveness before the age of AIDS."

Subjects: Character Profiles, Classics, Explicit Sexuality, Hugh Hefner, Love Affairs, Marriage

Now Try: Talese's other classic works might appeal to these readers, such as *The Gay Talese Reader* and *Unto the Sons* (as well as his autobiography *A Writer's Life*), as might other classics of Gonzo journalism such as Hunter S. Thompson's *Hell's Angels* or *Fear and Loathing in Las Vegas*, or Tom Wolfe's nonfiction and fiction (including the novels *The Bonfire of the Vanities* and *I Am Charlotte Simmons*). Other books in which the authors are very forthright about their own sexuality include Reinaldo Arenas's *Before Night Falls*, Zane's self-help manual *Dear G-Spot*, or even Joan Sewell's fun and honest (although slightly opposite in subject matter) *I'd Rather Eat Chocolate: Learning to Love My Low Libido*.

Thompson, Hunter S.

Fear and Loathing in Las Vegas: A Savage Journey to the Heart of the American Dream. Vintage. 1971. 204 pp. ISBN 9780679785897.

"Gonzo" journalist Thompson (often referred to as the "creator of the aggressively subjective approach to reporting") pulled out all the stops to immerse himself in the story of his reporter's lifestyle and coverage of a Las Vegas sporting event and a law enforcement conference on drug use, complete with ingesting (and describing the effects of) massive amounts of drugs. With his road-trip companion, described throughout as his attorney, Thompson tells a breathless story of drug use, random encounters with other travelers, and, only incidentally, the Mint 400 motorcycle race and the National District Attorney's Convention.

Subjects: Alcoholics and Alcoholism, Classics, Drug Addiction, Gonzo Journalism, Las Vegas, Nevada, Law Enforcement, Quick Reads, Sports, Travel

Now Try: *Fear and Loathing* was chosen for annotation because many readers recognize its title if not its subject matter, but Hunter Thompson's earlier work, *Hell's Angels: A Strange and Terrible Saga*, originally written for *The Nation* magazine, is a more powerful and less drug-heavy work of reportage. Although not often referred to as Gonzo journalists, writers who share Thompson's Immersion and new journalism style include Tom Wolfe, Gay Talese, Norman Mailer, and rock reporter Lester Bangs.

Thompson, Hunter S.

Hell's Angels: A Strange and Terrible Saga. Random House. 1967. 278 pp. ISBN 9780345410085.

"Gonzo" journalist Thompson produced one of the all-time classics in the field of immersion reporting when he decided to infiltrate and become a member of the motorcycle gang Hell's Angels. In his time of living with them, learning their unique modes of communication and their love for their motorcycles, Thompson was able to learn enough about them to write one of the most comprehensive and disturbing accounts of their activities, illegal and otherwise. His participation came with a price when members of the group turned on him and gave him a serious beating; the last chapter of this account is a stream-of-consciousness retelling of a "stomping" given by the gang to another offender; although there is a relatively low level of profanity throughout, readers should be aware that the Hell's Angels at the time Thompson knew them were a violent group, and such topics as theft, rapes, and physical violence (in the form of "stompings") do come up in the narrative. Also included are excerpts from interviews Thompson performed with gang members and other press pieces on their activities.

Subjects: Classics, Explicit Violence, Gangs, Gonzo Journalism, Journalism, Motorcycles, Sociology, Travel

Now Try: Thompson's other classic travelogue, *Fear and Loathing in Las Vegas*, features more drug use than does this title, but readers might want to try it all the same. Other authors who write in the style of Thompson include Tom Wolfe, Gay Talese, Norman Mailer, and Charlie LeDuff. Other journalists who have gone "undercover" for their story include Barbara Ehrenreich (*Nickel and Dimed: On Not Getting By in America*), Ted Conover (*Newjack* and *Coyotes*), and Norah Vincent (*Self-Made Man*).

Twitchell, James B.

Shopping for God: How Christianity Went from in Your Heart to in Your Face. Simon & Schuster. 2007. 324 pp. ISBN 9780743292870.

Twitchell, a professor of English and advertising, decides to explore the newest religious development in America; the tendency of individuals to "shop" for their church the same way they shop for other services and products. Interested in how and why Americans now switch religious denominations, sometimes several times in a lifetime, Twitchell set out to visit as many "megachurches" and other mainline Protestant churches as he could, as well as to interview their leaders, often referred to as "pastorpreneurs," and their parishioners. Although he did not visit African American churches or more staid establishments (including those in the Catholic or Jewish faiths) for fear of sticking out among the congregation or because, in his theory, the older churches aren't seeking to market their services the same way, this remains a historically grounded and personal look at contemporary American religious beliefs and experiences.

Subjects: Advertising, Business, Consumerism, Making Sense ..., Marketing, Religion, Scholarly

Now Try: Although Twitchell is a scholarly writer, his books are always extremely accessible; however, his readers might enjoy other more intense nonfiction writers and commentators, including Naomi Klein (*No Logo* and *The Shock Doctrine*), Jean Kilbourne (*Can't Buy My Love: How Advertising Changes the Way We Think and Feel*), Juliet Schor (*The Overspent American*), or even Wendell Berry (*The Long-Legged House*). A wide variety of Investigative Exposé titles might also be suggested to these readers, such as Eric Schlosser's *Fast Food Nation*, Jeremy Scahill's *Blackwater*, Charles Derber's *Corporation Nation*, or Joan Burbick's *Gun Show Nation* (not to mention other consumerism titles like Judith Levine's *Not Buying It* or Dana Thomas's *Deluxe: How Luxury Lost Its Luster*).

Vincent, Norah

🏵 *Self-Made Man: One Woman's Journey into Manhood and Back Again.* Viking. 2006. 290 pp. ISBN 9780670034666.

Vincent gave new meaning to the term "undercover" when she chose to venture into the world for more than a year disguised as her male alter-ego, Ned. Employing a crew cut and seeking the help of cosmetics experts to help her apply a believable five o'clock shadow, she joined a bowling team, a testosterone-rich sales job environment, and even dated women, visited sex clubs, and got inside a male monastery. Continually surprised by things she learned through her status as a "male," Vincent was also able to explore not only gender but also sex and relationship roles in a completely new way (Vincent herself is gay, giving her a different viewpoint on heterosexual relationships and interactions). Although she was reporting on them, Vincent also offers surprisingly sympathetic character portraits of the many men she meets and even befriends, and learns that the expectations and rituals comprising stereotypical male attitudes can be exhausting to maintain.

Subjects: Book Groups, Business, Feminism, Friendships, Gender, GLBTQ, Memoirs, Psychology, Society, Sociology, Work Relationships

Awards: New York Times Notable

Now Try: Other books of undercover reporting, particularly those by Barbara Ehrenreich, Ted Conover, and Alexandra Robbins, might be suggested to these readers; other books in which authors undertook to live a different life for a year might also be offered, such as John Howard Griffin's classic *Black Like Me* (in which Griffin, a white man, sought to live as a black man), Sudhir Venkatesh's *Gang Leader for a Day* (although he did not infiltrate the Chicago gang world as an undercover author, Venkatesh nonetheless spent many years living among the people he was studying), Barbara Kingsolver's *Animal, Vegetable, Miracle*, Judith Levine's *Not Buying It*, or *The Year of Yes* (in which the author agreed to date whoever asked her) by Maria Dahvana Headley. Books in which authors write about gender issues might be considered, such as Pagan Kennedy's *The First Man-Made Man*, Edward Ball's *Peninsula of Lies*, or books by social critics like Betty Friedan, Susan Faludi, Naomi Wolf, Camille Paglia, Andrea Dworkin, or Laura Kipnis.

International Affairs

It could be argued that many of the titles found in this Immersion subgenre might fit creditably into other Immersion categories, particularly Personal Journeys, or even into the broader nonfiction genre of Travel Writing. It may seem overly fastidious to group these Immersion titles together according to their international settings, but the current popularity of both fiction and nonfiction titles with multicultural and international themes (e.g., Khaled Hosseini's *The Kite Runner* or Elizabeth Gilbert's travel Memoir *Eat, Pray, Love*) indicates that these far-flung settings and cultures might themselves provide much more of the appeal of many books than even their characters or their authors' unique writing styles. The locations offered in these titles vary widely, from Africa to Afghanistan to Italy, but in all of them the authors sympathetically and evocatively describe the environments in which they are immersed, although those landscapes tend not to be as picturesque as those often featured in Travel Writing.

Readers who enjoy these books might also particularly enjoy International Exposés, given the same focus on new locations and settings, as well as a wide variety of Travel titles. These readers might also consider nonfiction History titles in which the authors also try to immerse themselves in historical contexts (e.g., Tony Horwitz's *Confederates in the Attic* or Mark Honigsbaum's *Fever Trail: In Search of the Cure for Malaria*); even True Adventure titles, particularly those set on continents other than North America, might also particularly appeal.

International Affairs Immersion Journalism titles find their authors not only reporting on very specific stories and surroundings in international locations but also immersing themselves in the stories on which they are reporting. Many of these books are written by authors on personal journeys or in the course of their work (rather than by professional journalists), but their authors' attention to detail and research make them more investigative than more straightforward memoirs. A large part of the appeal of these titles, in addition to the immediacy of the first-person narration, is their foreign locales and situations, many of which can be quite bleak, but in which the authors also find numerous stories of human redemption. Often these titles also offer their readers political and cultural details, acquired firsthand by their authors, and a good number of these books are also "books in translation," written by authors for whom English is not their first language.

Burnett, John S.

Where Soldiers Fear to Tread: A Relief Worker's Tale of Survival. Bantam Books. 2005. 350 pp. ISBN 9780553803747.

As a relief worker in Somalia from 1997 to 1998, Burnett describes how he faced his own death more than once: "there is going to be a shooting here and it is a toss-up who is going to get the boy's first round. The soldier, about ten years old, is jamming the barrel of his gun hard against my driver's face, and unless the kid decides to go for me, the relief worker, my driver is going to get his head blown off." In this firsthand account, he relates the dangers faced by humanitarian workers across the globe, who often find themselves caught between warring factions and facing great challenges from the opposing sides. In addition to relating his own story, Burnett reports on the use of children as soldiers, the logistics of starvation and flood relief operations, and the politics of providing both human and monetary aid and support.

Subjects: Africa, Explicit Violence, Memoirs, Somalia, Travel, True Adventure, War Reporting

Now Try: This John Burnett (John S. Burnett) is not to be confused with John F. Burnett, although John F.'s book about his experiences as an NPR journalist, *Uncivilized Beasts and Shameless Hellions*, might also appeal to these readers. Other Memoirs by well-meaning humanitarians, including Tom Bissell's *Chasing the Sea* or Tracy Kidder's biography of Dr. Paul Farmer, *Mountains beyond Mountains*, might be good read-alikes, as might Ishmael Beah's *A Long Way Gone: Memoirs of a Boy Soldier*. Other books set in Somalia or other war-torn areas of Africa, such as Scott Peterson's *Me against My Brother: At War in Somalia, Sudan, and Rwanda*, Mark Bowden's *Black Hawk Down*, Philip Gourevitch's *We Wish to Inform You That Tomorrow We Will Be Killed with Our Families*, or even Dave Eggers's novel *What Is the What*, might also appeal to these readers.

Crewdson, Michael, Margaret Mittelbach, and Alexis Rockman

Carnivorous Nights: On the Trail of the Tasmanian Tiger. Villard Books. 2005. 320 pp. ISBN 9781400060023.

Packing both their senses of humor and a pair of keen scientific minds (as well as a renowned artist, Alexis Rockman), Crewdson and Mittelbach set off on a modern safari to track down the elusive Tasmanian tiger. With its powerful jaw and terrible teeth, this carnivorous marsupial once threatened residents of Australia and Tasmania alike. Although it is speculated that the tiger was hunted into extinction in the twentieth century, the intrepid trio journey first to Australia and then to the wilds of Tasmania to search for any remaining members of the species; along the way they also come across many other terrifying examples of wildlife, including blood-sucking land leeches, venomous bull ants, and Tasmanian devils, not to mention trappers, bushwhackers, and other driven wildlife experts who refuse to give up their own personal searches for the tiger. The book entertainingly combines adventure, animal stories, travel, and humorous writing with Rockman's beautiful pencil drawings of exotic flora and fauna that they do come across on their odyssey.

Subjects: Animals, Australia, Environmental Writing, Humor, Illustrated Books, Memoirs, Science, Tasmania, Travel, True Adventure, Work Relationships

Now Try: Similar books on the interactions of humans and animals, such as Phillip Caputo's *Ghosts of Tsavo*, David Quammen's *Monster of God*, or Peter Matthiessen's *The Snow Leopard*, might also be suggested; books by natural history and science authors such as Farley Mowat, Tim Flannery, Richard Preston, Jane Goodall, Dian Fossey, or Jeffrey Moussaieff Masson might also appeal.

Ferguson, Rob

The Devil and the Disappearing Sea: Or, How I Tried to Stop the World's Worst Ecological Catastrophe. Raincoast Books. 2003. 267 pp. ISBN 9781551925998.

Ferguson went to Central Asia in 2000 with the best of all possible intentions: to play a part in the huge environmental project to help save the rapidly shrinking and disappearing Aral Sea. When he left one year later, he did so under suspicion for murder and without having achieved much in his quest to slow the progress of one of the world's worst ecological disasters. This thrilling travelogue, memoir, environmental treatise, and behind-the-scenes provides a look at the cultural, historical, and political backdrop of such Central Asian states as Kazakhstan, Kyrgyzstan, Tajikistan, Turkmenistan, and Uzbekistan. Other reviewers have referred to the Aral Sea crisis as a "slow-moving Chernobyl," and Ferguson paints a vivid and disturbing picture of corruption, bureaucratic inefficiencies, bribery, the influence of the Russian mafiya, and the deadly serious stakes of personal and political dissent in the region.

> **Subjects:** Aral Sea, Central Asia, Corruption, Government, Environmental Writing, Memoirs, Multicultural Issues, Travel, Uzbekistan, Work Relationships, World History

> **Now Try:** This title offers so many different aspects for read-alikes that it's hard to pick just a few; readers interested in idealistic memoirs might consider Tom Bissell's *Chasing the Sea: Lost Among the Ghosts of Empire in Central Asia* or Craig Murray's memoir of his time as an ambassador to Uzbekistan, *Dirty Diplomacy*; books by relief workers such as John S. Burnett's *Where Soldiers Fear to Tread: A Relief Worker's Tale of Survival, Emergency Sex and Other Desperate Measures* by Kenneth Cain or Melissa Faye Green's *There Is No Me without You* might also appeal. Ferguson also provides a handy list of related reads in his bibliography; these include books by Marq de Villiers, Robert Kaplan, and Colin Thubron.

Hafvenstein, Joel

Opium Season: A Year on the Afghan Frontier. Lyons Press. 2007. 337 pp. ISBN 9781599211312.

Hafvenstein spent a year working in the Helmand Province of Afghanistan, where he managed an American aid program with two charges: to help farmers in the region make profits from crops other than opium poppies, and to encourage good opinions about America (and lessen support for the former Taliban government). Although he set out with the best of intentions and found much to love in the landscape of the country and its people, the author still struggled with the danger and violence of the region, the tenacity of the drug trade and the remaining Taliban, and the difficulty of affecting change in cultures and peoples' hearts and minds.

> **Subjects:** Afghanistan, Drugs, Foreign Relations, Human Rights, Opium, Taliban, Travel, True Adventure, War Reporting, Year in the Life

> **Now Try:** Many individuals have sought to travel and work for positive change in international settings and told their tales; these titles include Tom Bissell's *Chasing the Sea,* Rob Ferguson's *The Devil and the Disappearing Sea,*

John Burnett's *Where Soldiers Fear to Tread*, Craig Murray's *Dirty Diplomacy*, and Heidi Postlewait's *Emergency Sex and Other Desperate Measures: A True Story from Hell on Earth*. Fiction and nonfiction titles about Afghanistan (including Jason Elliot's *An Unexpected Light: Travels in Afghanistan* and Khaled Hosseini's novel *The Kite Runner*) might appeal, as might Travel Adventures such as Tom Dyke's *The Cloud Garden: A True Story of Adventure, Survival, and Extreme Horticulture*.

Hass, Amira, Maxine Kaufman-Lacusta, and Elana Wesley

Drinking the Sea at Gaza: Days and Nights in a Land under Siege. Metropolitan Books. 1999. 379 pp. ISBN 9780805057393.

Hass, an Israeli journalist living in the Palestinian enclave of Gaza, relates her stories of living there with both a great awareness of the culture and history of the area and real empathy for the area's residents who are forced to live nearly like prisoners, facing daily difficulties merely in moving around both within Gaza and outside of its borders (as shown by her example of and interviews with college students simply trying to get to their classes being held in the West Bank). In each chapter, Hass tells a different and very personal story, using her shared residence in the area to encourage residents to really open up about their experiences and political events in the area.

> **Subjects:** Arab-Israeli Conflict, Books in Translation, Character Profiles, Gaza Strip, Israel, Middle East, Multicultural Issues, Palestine, Politics, Travel

> **Now Try:** Other books on the Arab-Israeli conflict might be suggested, such as Jimmy Carter's *Palestine Peace Not Apartheid*, Suad Amiry's *Sharon and My Mother-in-Law: Ramallah Diaries*, or Noam Chomsky's *The Fateful Triangle*; George Jonas's classic *Vengeance: The True Story of an Israeli Counter-Terrorist Team* might also appeal. Åsne Seierstad's book *With Their Backs to the Wall* (about Serbia) or Svetlana Alexievich's *Voices from Chernobyl* might also work as oral history read-alikes.

Hersey, John

Into the Valley: A Skirmish of the Marines. Knopf. 1943. 138 pp. ISBN 9780805240788.

Embedding himself with a company of Marines decades before the term "embedded reporter" would come into popular use during the Iraq War (2003), Hersey provided this concise account of a battle fought on Guadalcanal (an island in the South Pacific) during World War II from the soldier's point of view. In addition to providing details of battle experienced and reported firsthand, Hersey also spent time getting to know the company's captain, Charles Alfred Rigaud, and learning about the pressures of command such men were subject to. Although this is a classic in the genre, readers should be aware that it is very much of its time and contains some questionable references to Japanese individuals; likewise, Hersey himself admits in his introduction that he was unable to record as accurately as he might have liked many of the conversations to which he was privy, and he therefore took the liberty of recreating some of the soldiers' dialogue.

> **Subjects:** American History, Character Profiles, Military, Quick Reads, South Pacific, True Adventure, War Reporting, World War II

> **Now Try:** Hersey is also the author of the journalism classic *Hiroshima*, in which he described the aftermath of the dropping of the atomic bomb on Japan during World War II. Books by other classic war reporters, although many of their books are now more works of history than of current affairs, might also be suggested, these include Martha

Gellhorn, Michael Herr, Donald Kirk, and Ernie Pyle. History books by such authors as Stephen Ambrose, Studs Terkel, and James Bradley might also appeal to these readers.

Jones, Ann Rosalind

Kabul in Winter: Life without Peace in Afghanistan. Metropolitan Books. 2006. 321 pp. ISBN 9780805078848.

Many political and journalistic books have been written on the influence and political domination of the Taliban in Afghanistan at the end of the twentieth century; in this book, Jones explores the country and specifically Kabul after the fall of the Taliban. Although Jones originally went to the city with the hope of volunteering and providing humanitarian aid, she eventually decided instead to use her skills as an award-winning journalist who could highlight the plight of impoverished war widows, English teachers, and various women who were considered outcast because they were runaway brides, prostitutes, or victims of rape in a city and a culture where "regarding women as less than human is the norm." In addition to speaking with such women, Jones also provides insight into how Afghan history, culture, and politics have been affected by the Taliban, before them the Communists, and after them the Western contractors seeking to further a free market. The book is organized into three sections according to where Jones met and befriended her subjects; they are titled "In the Streets," "In the Prisons," and "In the Schools."

> **Subjects:** Afghanistan, Discrimination, Family Relationships, Feminism, Fundamentalism, Gender, Islam, Religion, Society, Taliban, War Reporting, Women's Contributions
>
> **Now Try:** Other books about Afghanistan might particularly appeal, such as Åsne Seierstad's *The Bookseller of Kabul* or Chris Johnson's *Afghanistan: The Mirage of Peace*; Khaled Hosseini's *The Kite Runner* or *A Thousand Splendid Suns* or Yasmina Khadra's *The Swallows of Kabul* might also be suggested. Other books with strong women characters might prove to be good read-alikes, such as Sue Monk Kidd's *The Secret Life of Bees*, Alice Walker's *The Color Purple*, or Kaye Gibbons's *Divining Women*; Memoirs about the Middle East might also be suggested, such as Azar Nafisi's *Reading Lolita in Tehran*, Greg Mortenson's *Three Cups of Tea*, or Jason Elliot's travelogue *An Unexpected Light: Travels in Afghanistan*.

McGinniss, Joe

The Miracle of Castel di Sangro. Little, Brown. 1999. 407 pp. ISBN 9780316557368.

McGinniss has always been known for immersing himself completely in the stories on which he reports (which can be controversial, as was the case when he actually lived with the husband accused of murder in his true crime account *Fatal Vision*). This narrative finds him investigating a story that would seem, on the surface, to be less serious, but that turns out to be one of major import to rabid soccer fans the world over; McGinniss traveled to Italy to stay with the soccer team of the Castel di Sangro region, which is regarded as one of the poorest and most agriculturally challenging and poor regions of the country. The author got swept up in the unique personalities of the team members and their Cinderella story of taking on and beating teams from much more affluent areas but was eventually disappointed to find that corruption even finds its way into regional soccer leagues and players who are accustomed to going along with the system just to get along.

> **Subjects:** Community Life, Corruption, Friendships, Italy, Soccer, Sports, Travel, Underdogs, Work Relationships, Year in the Life
>
> **Now Try:** Two other very good books on soccer, including Paul Cuadros's *A Home on the Field* and Franklin Foer's *How Soccer Explains the World* might be suggested to these readers, as might other books by McGinniss, who has a very unique reportorial presence (especially in his true crime classic *Fatal Vision*), or Travel books about Italy such as Bill Buford's *Heat* or John Berendt's *The City of Falling Angels*.

Sack, John

M. New American Library. 1966. 199 pp. ISBN 9780380698660.

Sack was known for his old-school dedication to facts and accuracy in reporting, but he also had a gift for placing himself in his subjects' shoes and illuminating their stories and experiences. This classic is no exception; Sack followed a company of the U.S. Army infantry ("M" Company of the 1st Advanced Infantry) from their training at Fort Dix all the way through their horrific experiences and the violence they both experienced and perpetrated during the Vietnam War.

> **Subjects:** 1960s, American History, Classics, Vietnam War, Violence, War Reporting
>
> **Now Try:** Sack's later books, *Company C: The Real War in Iraq* (about the Persian Gulf War) and *The Dragonhead: A True Story of the Godfather of Chinese Crime*, might also appeal to these readers. This classic work has often been referred to as a "nonfiction Catch-22"; Joseph Heller's novel *Catch-22* might therefore be offered, as might a number of other works on Vietnam including Seymour Hersh's *My Lai 4*, Michael Herr's *Dispatches*, Neil Sheehan's *A Bright Shining Lie*, or even Tom Bissell's Memoir of his experiences growing up with a Vietnam veteran father, *The Father of All Things*. Other classics of War Reporting might be offered, including John Hersey's *Into the Valley*, Ernie Pyle's *This Is Your War*, or even Chris Hedges's *War Is a Force That Gives Us Meaning*.

Seierstad, Åsne, and Ingrid Christopherson

The Bookseller of Kabul. Little, Brown. 2003. 287 pp. ISBN 9780316734509.

Journalist Seierstad relates the day-to-day details of the year she spent living with the Khan family in Kabul in the spring after the fall of the Taliban, providing an intimate look at Afghan culture and family life through her interactions with Sultan Khan, the family patriarch and bookseller, and the rest of his family members. Although most of the family relationships are observed and described firsthand, Seierstad does make use of some more creative nonfiction techniques in ascribing inner thoughts and feelings to several of the family members.

> **Subjects:** Afghanistan, Book Groups, Books and Learning, Books in Translation, Culture Clash, Family Relationships, Islam, Multicultural Issues
>
> **Now Try:** Geraldine Brooks's ALA Notable Book *Nine Parts of Desire: The Hidden World of Islamic Women* also closely examines the daily lives of women living in Islamic countries and contrasts them with the rule of law as described in the Koran and as lived historically by other Islamic women, including the prophet Muhammad's wives

and daughters. Judith Miller's ALA Notable Book *God Has Ninety-Nine Names: Reporting from a Militant Middle East* may also appeal to readers hoping to learn more about Middle Eastern culture and society. The love of books and learning exhibited throughout this title are also reflected in Azar Nafisi's extremely popular Memoir *Reading Lolita in Tehran: A Memoir in Books.* Jason Elliot's Travel title *An Unexpected Light: Travels in Afghanistan* might also appeal to these readers, as might multicultural novels such as Khaled Hosseini's *The Kite Runner* and *A Thousand Splendid Suns,* as well as Zadie Smith's *White Teeth* or Monica Ali's *Brick Lane.*

Shadid, Anthony

🏵 *Night Draws Near: Iraq's People in the Shadow of America's War.* Henry Holt. 2005. 424 pp. ISBN 9780805076028.

The great majority of accounts of the Iraq War have been written either by reporters embedded with American forces or by writers who rarely venture out of the closely guarded grounds of Baghdad's Green Zone, where the American Embassy and the Provisional Authority are headquartered. *Washington Post* reporter Shadid, however, writes candidly about the political situation and the war in Iraq from the point of view of Iraqi citizens, recounting stories of violence and explosions in the city's streets, blackouts, and the continuation of the privations of war with which most of them have been living for the past three decades (stretching back to the Iran-Iraq War of the 1980s). Because his take on the subject is less politically and ideologically driven than it is focused on presenting an underexplored point of view, and because of his Lebanese American heritage and his fluency in Arabic, Shadid was able to interview a wide cross-section of the Baghdad populace, from educated professionals who wax nostalgic for the country's pre-1970s golden days to Iraqi policemen, among many others. His account begins in the days leading up to the 2003 American invasion and concludes with the January 2005 elections.

Subjects: Baghdad, Death and Dying, Saddam Hussein, Iraq, Iraq War (2003), Politics, Violence, War Reporting, World History

Awards: New York Times Notable

Now Try: The number of books published on the Iraq War has been astounding; Shadid's readers might consider other investigative titles such as George Packer's *The Assassins' Gate,* Rajiv Chandrasekaran's *Imperial Life in the Emerald City,* Thomas Ricks's *Fiasco: The American Military Adventure in Iraq,* or Patrick Cockburn's *The Occupation: War and Resistance in Iraq.* Other books about the impact of war on civilians might also be offered, such as *Unembedded: Four Independent Photojournalists on the War in Iraq, Emergency Sex and Other Desperate Measures* by Kenneth Cain, David Howarth's *We Die Alone,* John Burnett's *Uncivilized Beasts and Shameless Hellions,* or Dahr Jamail's *Beyond the Green Zone: Dispatches from an Unembedded Journalist in Occupied Iraq.*

Spurlock, Morgan

Where in the World Is Osama Bin Laden? Random House. 2008. 304 pp. ISBN 9781400066520.

Spurlock has made a career out of putting himself in over-the-top situations in the pursuit of a story; in this book, the intrepid investigator and traveler decided that, if all it would take to make the world safe would be finding Osama bin Laden, he would set out and do so. Spurlock first set out to learn about Islam, Arabic culture, terrorism, and the state of world politics and religions by interviewing any experts on the subjects he could find (from imams to soldiers, scholars to terrorists) and then traveled to many locations in the Middle East (Egypt, Israel, Palestine, Morocco, Saudi Arabia, Jordan, and Afghanistan) himself to see if he could succeed where the world's governments had failed.

> **Subjects:** 9/11, Humor, Islam, Osama bin Laden, Middle East, Military, Politics, al-Qaeda, Terrorism, Travel
>
> **Now Try:** Fans of Spurlock's lively, irreverent prose might also consider his earlier book, *Don't Eat This Book: Fast Food and the Supersizing of America*, as well as his documentary (*Super Size Me*) and television series (*30 Days*). Other Immersion journalists who live their stories include A. J. Jacobs (*The Year of Living Biblically*), Matt Taibbi (*The Great Derangement*), Jon Ronson (*Them* and *The Men Who Stare at Goats*), Ted Conover (*Newjack: Guarding Sing Sing*), and Barbara Ehrenreich (*Nickel and Dimed*). Those readers with a particular interest in the subject matter might also consider Steve Coll's comprehensive family history *The Bin Ladens*, Reza Aslan's *No God but God*, or Lawrence Wright's *The Looming Tower*.

Fiction Read-Alikes

- **Chabon, Michael.** Chabon's novels offer perfectly realized, if complex, fictional worlds; readers who enjoy the experience of immersing themselves in someone else's world might particularly enjoy his titles *Wonder Boys*, *The Amazing Adventures of Kavalier and Clay*, and *The Yiddish Policeman's Union*.

- **Egan, Jennifer.** Egan's novels *Look at Me* and *The Keep* are layered and complex, yet quickly paced, stories about characters and questions of identity.

- **Eggers, Dave.** The personal journey and travel aspect of Eggers's novels might particularly appeal to Immersion readers; these include *You Shall Know Our Velocity* and *What Is the What* (as well as the short story collection *How We Are Hungry*).

- **Ishiguro, Kazuo.** Ishiguro is very concerned with the inner lives of his characters and is a master at throwing his reader directly into their worlds; he has done this in both historical fiction (*The Remains of the Day* and *When We Were Orphans*) and speculative fiction (*Never Let Me Go*).

- **Mosley, Walter.** Mosley is most well known for his series of mysteries set in 1940s Los Angeles (they eventually move through the 1960s) and featuring his character Easy Rawlins; they are richly drawn novels and Rawlins's connections to and relationships with individuals in his community make these books a good read-alike for fans of Immersion Journalism. The series starts with *Devil in a Blue Dress* and continues with *A Red Death*, *White Butterfly*, *Black Betty*, *Little Yellow Dog*, *Bad Boy Brawley Brown*, *Little Scarlet*, and *Cinnamon Kiss*.

- **O'Brien, Tim.** Although he is often considered a novelist who is drawn to psychological themes, or one who tells primarily stories based on the Vietnam War (O'Brien himself is a veteran), O'Brien is also a master at making his readers feel like they are in the (often nightmarish) world of his creation. His novels include the semi-autobiographical *If I Die in a Combat Zone*, as well as the classics *The*

Things They Carried and *In the Lake of the Woods* and his more recent titles *Tomcat in Love* and *July, July*.

- **Robbins, Tom.** Robbins began his career as a journalist and originally moved to the West Coast in the 1960s to experience and write about the culture there; eventually he would produce the cult favorite novels *Even Cowgirls Get the Blues*, *Jitterbug Perfume*, and *Half Asleep in Frog Pajamas*.

- **Steinbeck, John.** Steinbeck's classic novels provide valuable inside looks at the regions and individuals he describes, including migrant workers in *The Grapes of Wrath* or ranchers in the Salinas Valley of California in *East of Eden*; his novels *Cannery Row* and *Tortilla Flat* might also be suggested.

Further Reading

Creative Nonfiction (serial). 1993–. Pittsburgh, PA: University of Pittsburgh Press.

Fourth Genre: Explorations in Nonfiction (serial). 1999–. East Lansing, MI: Michigan State University Press.

Gutkind, Lee, ed. 2005. *In Fact: The Best of Creative Nonfiction*. New York: Norton.

Hartsock, John C. 2000. *A History of American Literary Journalism: The Emergence of a Modern Literary Form*. Amherst, MA: University of Massachusetts Press.

Weingarten, Marc. 2006. *The Gang That Wouldn't Write Straight: Wolfe, Thompson, Didion, and the New Journalism Revolution*. New York: Crown.

Wolfe, Tom, and Michael L. Johnson. 1973. *The New Journalism*. New York: Harper & Row.

References

Boynton, Robert, ed. 2005. *The New New Journalism: Conversations with America's Best Nonfiction Writers on Their Craft*. New York: Vintage Books.

Johnson, Michael L. 1971. *The New Journalism: The Underground Press, the Artists of Nonfiction, and Changes in the Established Media*. Lawrence, KS: University Press of Kansas.

Chapter 4

Character Profiles

Definition of Character Profiles

At last, a genre of Investigative Writing that sounds exactly like what it is. People are the story in these books. Authors set out to tell their stories of the characters they are profiling in these narratives, but that story always somehow ends up being secondary to the fascinating revelations of the characters' thoughts and actions, as well as their dialogues with the author. The titles included in this chapter also remain true to the underlying goal of Investigative Writing, which is always to arrive at some sort of truth and provide either the inside or the behind-the-scenes insight into the narrative. Leon Dash, one of the most skilled journalists and character profilers of his generation (which is no mean feat, considering his generation includes Gay Talese and Truman Capote) explains his style of researching and interviewing his subjects for such profiles: "I operate on the theory that everyone has a public mask. . . . The stories most reporters get—because of time constraints and deadline pressures—rarely penetrate beneath that mask. Unless you're able to get someone to remove his public mask, your story won't reflect his genuine motivation or behavior" (Boynton 2005, 57).

Although some of the individuals profiled in these works are famous or celebrities, the majority of them are not. In keeping with the hallmarks of creative nonfiction, the new journalism, and Investigative Writing, most of the characters described in these titles are very everyday sorts of people, most of whom are quietly leading whatever kinds of lives they have tricked out for themselves, and most of whom must first overcome their disbelief that an author really wants to spend years observing and interviewing them. Author Jane Kramer has described her focus on ordinary people by saying, "I like writing about people who, by most 'news' standards, would be considered marginal. I find that the perspective from the margins is usually much more telling—if you're interested in how power works—than any number of conversations with politicians and especially with important ones like presidents and prime ministers" (Boynton 2005, 188). That is the writerly attitude that leads to Melissa Fay Greene's profile of a unique but unknown African woman trying to care for her neighborhood's children orphaned by AIDS, and Susan Orlean's treks across the United States simply to observe how people from all walks of society spend their Saturday nights. These are not the stories you will see making the nightly news headlines. They are the stories of people just like you and me.

As simple as they are to describe, they are even simpler to subdivide into categories. Character Profiles come primarily in two flavors: profiles of individuals and profiles of groups. Although these titles vary within those categories from slightly fawning (a reader gets the feeling that Elizabeth Gilbert has a little crush on her subject Eustace Conway in *The Last American Man*, for instance) to the outright conflicted (Mark Bowden doesn't quite know what to make of his Philadelphian protagonist in *Money for Nothing*), those distinctions are secondary to readers who love character-driven books. The only requirement is that the characters be interesting.

> Character Profiles provide researched and comprehensive investigative stories but add the dimension of detailed (and often empathetic) character development. Although not all of the stories in this subgenre end happily or successfully, they all feature complex and nuanced character portraits of individuals or groups who are living life according to their own precepts or who are heroic in their struggle to overcome hardship or struggle.

Appeal of Character Profiles

The appeal of Character Profiles is revealed in its heading; these are character-driven nonfiction narratives. Stories emerge, as do the settings in which people live and the language and writing styles of these authors, over the unfolding of these in-depth character portraits, but readers enjoy these books because they provide intimate details of other peoples' lives. Readers (and the authors themselves) may not always love these characters, all of whom display very human weaknesses and foibles. But Richard Ben Cramer perfectly describes the heart of the matter when he says, "I think writing about a human is the hardest thing to do. But it is the most satisfying for the reader because most people learn most easily through personal acquaintance" (Boynton 2005, 51).

Readers who enjoy these titles may well enjoy many other character-driven nonfiction genres, including Memoirs, popular Biographies, and Relationships nonfiction (readers who enjoy Group Character Profiles may be particularly drawn to Relationships nonfiction in which authors describe Community Life, such as Michael Perry's *Population 485* or Heather Lende's *If You Lived Here, I'd Know Your Name*). Other nonfiction genres focusing on people (or even animals in their own right as characters, as are often found in the Animal Stories subgenre of Environmental Writing) might be suggested, even if their subject matters are more disparate; Science books such as Ken Silverstein's *The Radioactive Boy Scout* or Travel books by expatriates including Frances Mayes or Peter Mayle may also be offered. These readers might also be open to fiction suggestions, particularly character-driven works of mainstream fiction or other fiction genres in which recurring or particularly well-drawn characters appear. These are readers who might also be particular fans of interview-format television programs and public radio profiles; Kiera Butler noted listeners' hunger for personal narratives in the July/August 2006 issue of the *Columbia Journalism Review* by citing the fact that nearly 1.7 million listeners tune in to the weekly NPR program *This American Life* (Butler 2006, 29).

Organization of the Chapter

Character Profiles fall into four primary categories. The first two, *Character Portraits* and *Ordinary People, Extraordinary Stories*, primarily feature the stories of individual characters, while the *Shared Experiences* and *Group Portraits* titles offer multiple characters or groups of characters who are related by their stories or through the choice and organization of their authors. Although all of these titles feature fascinating individuals and the appeal factor of characters, the category of *Character Portraits* leads off the chapter because their characters are so unique that they completely overpower their own stories. In *Ordinary People, Extraordinary Stories*, the characters are also unique and can be described by such labels as "hero," "martyr," "eccentric," and many others, but those titles offer more in the way of complete stories, with very identifiable beginnings and conclusions. The last two categories, *Shared Experiences* and *Group Portraits*, offer a return to character-driven (rather than story-driven) collections, with the former focusing on the relationships between the characters being profiled and their reactions to their shared circumstances, whereas the latter offer more orchestration and analysis by the authors, who select their interview subjects according to their own interests.

Character Portraits

This heading may seem redundant within a genre called "Character Profiles." However, it gives the truest flavor of what these titles are all about: the people—the characters—in question. The people in question can be referred to by a wide variety of descriptive labels: true individuals, real characters, eccentrics, heroes, recluses, larger-than-life personalities, martyrs, dreamers. The list is endless, so it is hard to group together like titles under any of a sufficient number of those characteristics. When Character Portraits appear in magazines and other media, they largely tend to be of famous individuals, but that is not the case in these books. The characters profiled here are rarely widely known individuals, but they do have to fascinate their chroniclers, who in turn take it upon themselves to make their chosen subjects interesting and the book appealing to their readers (even when the individual is not really all that appealing, which can happen).

From a stylistic point of view, these titles feature character as their main appeal, with story, setting, and language tied for a distant second. These books are not driven by narrative; they do not really offer a story that has a finite beginning, middle, and end. What timelines they follow are dictated largely by their authors, the profilers; Elizabeth Gilbert followed Eustace Conway, in her opinion, "the last American man," until she thought she had learned all she could about him. It took Susan Orlean two years to sufficiently observe John Laroche, the "orchid thief," to her satisfaction. These are books in which the authors do extensive research on the history and background of the person they're writing about; they also tend to construct much of their narratives out of quotes and dialogue they gain during interviews with the person in question and others who know the person.

These titles tend to have a delightful air of uncertainty about them; whereas novelists who write character-driven stories often know who their characters are and what motivates them (even if they don't share that information with their readers, in the text or otherwise), these authors are restricted to a very limited third-person point of view. We all know how difficult it is to really know another person; even those we live or work with can often be complete mysteries to us. These authors often do ask very personal questions of their subjects; they try and get at an individual's deeper thoughts, motivations, beliefs, and feelings. But in the end, they simply have to write the story from their own point of view, trying to understand another person. They don't typically offer much in the way of story or plot resolution; the conclusions of these books are less the ending of the stories than the authors' speculation on what their characters will do in the future.

These books match up nicely with a wide variety of Memoirs and essay collections, in which authors explore either the unique lives or their unique takes on ordinary lives and typically offer slices of life rather than complete life stories or autobiographies. Personal Journeys Immersion titles, many of which also feature stories about truly unique and driven individuals, might also be offered, particularly because those titles are also typically organized along a timeline dictated by their authors rather than the stories. Fans of these titles might also enjoy character-driven mainstream fiction; novels with strong setting and language appeals might also appeal, particularly if they also offer unique characters.

Character Portraits are distinguished by their main characters, individuals who are described in great (and not always flattering) detail. They do not often feature celebrities, but rather "everyday people" or unique individuals in whom the author has become interested for a specific reason. They do not typically offer strong storylines or narratives that have a beginning, middle, and an end but instead cover time periods and events as chosen by their authors. They do often offer very personal details of the character being profiled, as gleaned through the authors' questions and observations; they can be quite surprising in terms of both character revelation and development. Although these titles can feature research anecdotes and information from outside interviews, their authors tend to focus most of their attention on the person being profiled.

Fuller, Alexandra

The Legend of Colton H. Bryant. Penguin. 2008. 202 pp. ISBN 9781594201837.
   Fuller, a memoirist and nonfiction author, offers a lyrically written and poetic "legend" of a young Wyoming man named Colton H. Bryant, who charmed everyone who met him with cornflower blue eyes, a ready smile, and an unstoppable attitude that he described as "mind over matter"—"I don't mind so it don't matter." In short chapters, Fuller describes Bryant's upbringing in Wyoming, his strong friendship with kindred spirit Jake, his family members, his marriage, and his eventual death in an oil rig accident.
   Subjects: Accidents, American West, Book Groups, Colton H. Bryant, Cowboys, Death and Dying, Family Relationships, Friendships, Quick Reads, Wyoming, YA

Now Try: Readers who enjoy this slim but uniquely styled character portrait might also consider Fuller's popular memoir *Don't Let's Go to the Dogs Tonight*, about her own childhood in Rhodesia, or her character portrait of a man known only as "K," titled *Scribbling the Cat: Travels with an African Soldier*. Other Character Portraits, particularly of strong-minded male characters, might also be suggested; these include Jane Kramer's *The Last Cowboy* or *Lone Patriot*, Elizabeth Gilbert's *The Last American Man*, or William Mishler's *A Measure of Endurance: The Unlikely Triumph of Steven Sharp*. Modern Western novels might also hold some appeal for readers who enjoy the unique Western setting; fiction titles by authors such as Elmer Kelton, Kent Haruf (*The Ties that Bind*), or Larry Watson (*Montana 1948*) might be offered.

Gilbert, Elizabeth

The Last American Man. Viking. 2002. 271 pp. ISBN 9780670030866.

Journalist and novelist Gilbert, best known for her best-selling Oprah book, the memoir *Eat Pray Love*, has a talent for getting to know people and sharing their stories in print. In this book-length character portrait, her subject is Eustace Conway, whom she (and others) considers the last true "American man." Through in-depth interviews with both Conway and those who have tried to know him best over the years, Gilbert relates the story of the man who, at the age of seventeen, left his family's suburban home to move alone into the Appalachian Mountains. In addition to speaking and teaching nature skills classes to schoolchildren, Conway has also sought to convince others to live a simpler lifestyle, similar to his. He has also sought friendships and love relationships with like-minded individuals; Gilbert shows that he has had varying levels of success with those goals, although she is also astute in portraying not only his vast store of nature knowledge and woodland skills but also his prowess in accumulating land and striking financial and other deals with his nearest neighbors. She also explores his early relationships with his family, as well as her own reactions to him and his strong personality and beliefs.

> **Subjects:** Appalachian Mountains, Biographies, Eustace Conway, Eccentrics, Environmental Writing, Family Relationships, Friendships, Nature

> **Now Try:** Other books about strong-minded individuals determined to carve out a unique life path might be offered, including Jon Krakauer's *Into the Wild* or Jane Kramer's *The Last Cowboy*; other books about strong-willed individuals who also interact with nature might also appeal, such as Eric Blehm's *The Last Season*, Richard Proenneke's *One Man's Wilderness*, Edward Abbey's *Desert Solitaire*, and Anne LaBastille's *Woodswoman* series. Gilbert's novels, *Stern Men* and *Pilgrims*, might appeal to these readers, as might other novels featuring nonconformist male characters by authors such as John Updike, Richard Ford, David Gates, and Walker Percy.

Gonnerman, Jennifer

🌹 *Life on the Outside: The Prison Odyssey of Elaine Bartlett.* Farrar, Straus & Giroux. 2004. 356 pp. ISBN 9780374186876.

Gonnerman shadowed Elaine Bartlett, a woman sentenced to prison for sixteen years following her first conviction (for selling cocaine), for several years after she had been released from prison, documenting her hardships trying to connect with the four children she'd had to leave behind when she was incarcerated, find a job, and renegotiate her way back into society after the rigid rules of the prison environment. Bartlett is a strong but sympathetic character for Gonnerman to profile, and the author also addresses the ways in which she feels "tough on crime" measures, often enacted to help society, may increase its inequalities and criminal activities.

>**Subjects:** Drugs, Family Relationships, Poverty, Prisons, Society, Sociology, Underdogs, Urban Life, Women's Nonfiction
>
>**Awards:** New York Times Notable
>
>**Now Try:** Other character profiles of individuals struggling to make it in American society might also be offered; these include Adrian Nicole LeBlanc's *Random Family*, Ron Suskind's *A Hope in the Unseen*, Jonathan Kozol's *Savage Inequalities*, Alex Kotlowitz's *The Other Side of the River*, and Michael Lewis's *The Blind Side*; books about prison life might also make valid suggestions: Joseph Hallinan's *Going Up the River*, Jennifer Wynn's *Inside Rikers*, and Ted Conover's *Newjack: Guarding Sing Sing*. Other related reads on poverty might be offered, such as David Shipler's *The Working Poor*, *Class Matters* by journalists on the staff of the *New York Times*, Barbara Ehrenreich's *Nickel and Dimed*, and Michael Sokolove's *The Ticket Out: Darryl Strawberry and the Boys of Crenshaw*.

Greene, Melissa Fay

🌸 *There Is No Me without You: One Woman's Odyssey to Rescue Africa's Children.* Bloomsbury. 2006. 472 pp. ISBN 9781596911161.

Melissa Faye Greene offers an extended character portrait of Haregewoin Teferra, an Ethiopian widow whose home has become a refuge and home for numerous children orphaned by parents suffering from AIDS (or who are suffering from AIDS themselves); Greene also interviews and offers sympathetic character portraits of Teferra's friends, family, and colleagues who assist her, as well as of the children in her care (and in some cases, their adoptive parents in other countries like the United States). Greene's writing is immediately affecting and personally written, and heavy on the descriptive details of Ethiopian society and poverty.

>**Subjects:** Africa, AIDS, Book Groups, Ethiopia, Family Relationships, Health Issues, Multicultural Issues, Orphans, Poverty, Haregewoin Teferra, Women's Contributions, Women's Nonfiction
>
>**Awards:** ALA Notable
>
>**Now Try:** Another stunning character profile of a man fighting the effects of poverty is Tracy Kidder's *Mountains Beyond Mountains: The Quest of Dr. Paul Farmer*. Those readers interested in Memoirs and narratives set in Africa might also consider Ishmael Beah's powerful child-soldier memoir *A Long Way Gone*, Neely Tucker's *Love in the Driest Season*, Adam Hochschild's historical *King Leopold's Ghost*, or Philip Gourevitch's *We Wish to Inform You That Tomorrow We Will Be Killed with Our Families*; fiction titles with similar themes include Hanna Jansen's *Over a Thousand Hills I Walk with You*, Lucinda Roy's *The Hotel Alleluia*, Barbara Kingsolver's *The Poisonwood Bible*, or Giles Foden's *The Last King of Scotland*. Related nonfiction discussing health issues and AIDS, including Randy Shilts's *And the Band Played On* or Mark Doty's memoir *Dog Years*, might also be suggested.

Halberstam, David

The Education of a Coach. Hyperion. 2005. 277 pp. ISBN 9781401301545.

The subject of Halberstam's Character Profile is a man who has had an uncannily successful career in the NFL: Coach Bill Belichick, who has spent thirty-one years in the league, first with the New York Giants, then with the Cleveland Browns, and finally, and most spectacularly, with the dominant New England Patriots team of the late 1990s and early 2000s. The author leaves no aspect of Belichick's life unexplored, offering details about his personal and family life as well as about his professional life and about the nuances of the game of football in general. Admitting that he was fascinated by his subject for a full twenty years before writing the book, Halberstam particularly focuses on the coach's signature ability to prevail with great drama and often in the second halves of games, while simultaneously maintaining a low profile. The book is organized chronologically like a work of typical biography but also combines sports writing and an investigation into Belichick's coaching style and understanding of the game (which is bolstered by Halberstam's many interviews with the coach's colleagues and players).

> **Subjects:** Bill Belichick, Biographies, Football, New England, Professions, Sports, Work Relationships
>
> **Now Try:** Halberstam was a highly regarded journalist and historian; other books of his, such as *The Best and the Brightest*, *Summer of '49*, and *The Teammates* might be offered. Other sports books, particularly those about football, might be considered: Buzz Bissinger's *Friday Night Lights*, Tony Dungy's *Quiet Strength*, Vic Carucci's and Charlie Weis's *No Excuses*, Michael Lewis's *The Blind Side*, and Lou Holtz's *Wins, Losses, and Lessons*. Other books featuring ambitious and sporting men might also appeal, such as Lance Armstrong's *It's Not about the Bike*, Mark Kriegel's *Namath: A Biography* or *Pistol: The Life of Pete Maravich*, Jonathan Eig's *Opening Day*, David Maraniss's *Clemente*, and Geoffrey C. Ward's *Unforgivable Blackness: The Rise and Fall of Jack Johnson*.

Kramer, Jane

Lone Patriot: The Short Career of an American Militiaman. Pantheon Books. 2002. 259 pp. ISBN 9781400032327.

In examining the career and followers of self-styled right-wing militiaman John Pitner (leader of the Washington State Militia), Kramer provides insight not only into his personal life and political beliefs but also into the relationships he has with those around him, including his followers, his wife, and his sister, all of whom interact with him in different and often conflicting ways. Kramer also paints a broader picture of the experiences of such individuals that leads them to view themselves as separate from and against the government; in Pitner's story, she finds parallels to other extremists, including Timothy McVeigh, and their development.

> **Subjects:** Eccentrics, Family Relationships, Government, John Pitner, Politics, Radicalism, Sociology
>
> **Now Try:** Books about other people who feel separate from or who separate themselves from society might be offered, such as Jon Ronson's *Them: Adventures with Extremists* or *The Men Who Stare at Goats*, or Elizabeth Gilbert's

The Last American Man, biographies of other extremists such as Lou Michel's *American Terrorists: Timothy McVeigh and the Oklahoma City Bombing*, or Alston Chase's *Harvard and the Unabomber* (about Ted Kaczynski). Kramer's colleague in the "new journalism" style, Lawrence Weschler, provided an author blurb for this title, as did novelist Ward Just; their titles might appeal to these readers as well.

Lieve, Joris, and Liz Waters (translator)

The Rebels' Hour. Grove Press. 2008. 272 pp. ISBN 9780802118684.

Belgian journalist Joris offers an in-depth character portrait of a high-ranking general in the Congolese army whom she calls "Assani." In chapters that move back and forward through time, from Assani's youth in the 1960s and 1970s to the present day, Joris tells the life story of a man who endured such contradictions as being taught that the "only good Tutsi is a dead Tutsi" and then learning that he himself was ethnically a Tutsi; it is also the story of a person who craved education but was instead taught to engage in war. There has been controversy over the format of this title; it is a book in translation and was originally published in France as a novel; in other countries, it has been classified as "literary reportage" nonfiction, and the author offers this note as a preface: "This book is based on real characters, situations, and places, without ever coinciding with them completely."

Subjects: Africa, Atrocities, Book Groups, Books in Translation, Democratic Republic of the Congo, Ethnicity, Explicit Violence, Military, Multicultural Issues, Rwanda, War

Now Try: Readers of this literary title might also consider books related by subject and tone, including Ishmael Beah's Memoir of his experiences as a child soldier, *A Long Way Gone*; Jean Hatzfeld's oral histories *Machete Season* and *Life Laid Bare*; or Philip Gourevitch's classic and more traditional work of history about the Rwandan genocide, *We Wish to Inform You That Tomorrow We Will Be Killed with Our Families*. Other haunting works about atrocities worldwide might provide a read-alike experience, including Svetlana Alexievich's *Voices from Chernobyl* or Eilet Negev's *In Our Hearts We Were Giants: The Remarkable Story of the Lilliput Troupe—A Dwarf Family's Survival of the Holocaust*. Novels with multicultural themes might also be suggested, such as Dave Eggers's *What Is the What* (set in the Sudan) or Chimamanda Ngozi Adichie's *Half of a Yellow Sun*. Joris has also been compared favorably to international authors V. S. Naipaul and Ryszard Kapuscinski.

Malcolm, Janet

The Crime of Sheila McGough. Knopf. 1999. 161 pp. ISBN 9780375405082.

After serving three years in prison, newly released former attorney Sheila McGough contacted investigative journalist Malcolm to tell her side of a complex story based in the labyrinthine legal and court system. McGough, a tenacious defense attorney, defended one of her clients (Bob Bailes) against charges of multiple crimes and proclaimed his innocence with so much zeal and so little success that eventually she would draw suspicion for being his accomplice. Eventually charged with and convicted of fourteen charges of complicity with Bailes's crimes, McGough was sentenced to three years in prison, which she served. Malcolm investigates the case with her own unique brand of tenacity, interviewing numerous players in the legal system, as well as reading untold numbers of legal documents; in the midst of exploring how truth, facts, and different peoples' narratives differ, she makes and offers her own judgment regarding McGough's guilt.

Subjects: Con Artists, Law and Lawyers, Sheila McGough, Quick Reads, Trials, True Crime, Women's Nonfiction

Now Try: Malcolm isn't a flashy writer but is well known for her journalistic tenacity; readers might also consider her book *The Journalist and the Murderer*, in which she examined the relationship between true crime writer Joe McGinniss and his subject in *Fatal Vision*. Other books which involve compelling trial stories might also be offered, such as Jonathan Harr's *A Civil Action*, John Berendt's *Midnight in the Garden of Good and Evil*, Steve Bogira's *Courtroom 302*, or Edward Humes's *No Matter How Loud I Shout*; legal thrillers by John Grisham or David Baldacci; or nonfiction featuring real-life con artists, such as Frank Abagnale's *Catch Me If You Can*, Mitchell Zuckoff's *Ponzi's Scheme*, or Ben Mezrich's *Bringing Down the House*.

Orlean, Susan

🏵 *The Orchid Thief: A True Story of Beauty and Obsession.* Random House. 1998. 284 pp. ISBN 9780679447399.

Part extended Character Profile of eccentric orchid hunter and all-around collecting enthusiast John Laroche, part True Adventure story of orchid hunting and traversing the competitive world of orchid conferences and shows, and part travelogue of Florida, Orlean's story of her two-year odyssey following the exploits of Laroche truly adds up to even more than the sum of all those parts. The narrative is told in the first person, and Orlean offers both commendable scientific orchid details and a highly personable account of her journalistic relationship with Laroche.

Subjects: Book Groups, Classics, Florida, Flowers, Friendships, Horticulture, Travel

Awards: ALA Notable

Now Try: Susan Orlean is a highly respected travel writer and her titles *The Bullfighter Checks Her Makeup: My Encounters with Ordinary People* and *My Kind of Place: Travel Stories from a Woman Who's Been Everywhere* may also appeal to readers who enjoy her mix of character development and descriptive journalism. Readers who enjoy a bit more adventure with their horticultural stories might also try Tom Hart Dyke's and Paul Winder's *The Cloud Garden: A True Story of Adventure, Survival, and Extreme Horticulture*, in which an orchid hunter and his friend are captured and held for ransom while backpacking through Central America; Amy Stewart's look at the floral industry, *Flower Confidential*, might also be offered.

Sacco, Joe

The Fixer: A Story from Sarajevo. Drawn & Quarterly. 2003. 105 pp. ISBN 9781896597607.

Joe Sacco tells the story of his reporting experiences in post-Balkan conflict Sarajevo by telling the story of Neven, a former soldier in the Yugoslav People's Army and current "fixer," who finds stories and prostitutes for Western journalists with equal ease and comparable expense. Stark in black-and-white and subtly horrifying, Sacco relates his first meeting with Neven, Neven's war experiences, and his current life in a city still suffering the aftermath of war.

Subjects: Friendships, Graphic Novels, Journalism, Multicultural Issues, Quick Reads, Small Press, War Reporting, Yugoslavia

Now Try: Often referred to as the first "comic book journalist," Sacco is also the author of the graphic novels *Palestine* (based on his travels to the West Bank and the Gaza Strip during the 1990s) and *Safe Area Gorazde: The War in Eastern Bosnia, 1992–1995*. Readers who enjoy this brand of history through visuals might also enjoy Memoirs such as Marjane Satrapi's *Persepolis: The Story of a Childhood* and Art Spiegelman's decidedly surreal *In the Shadow of No Towers* (about the events of 9/11 as he and his family experienced them). Character Profiles from other war-torn areas might also be suggested, such as Åsne Seierstad's *With Their Backs To the Wall* or David Howarth's *We Die Alone: A World War II Epic of Escape and Endurance*.

Thurman, Judith

🎖 *Cleopatra's Nose: 39 Varieties of Desire*. Farrar, Straus & Giroux. 2007. 427 pp. ISBN 9780374126513.

In this erudite collection of essays, most of which have been published over the last ten years in *The New Yorker*, Thurman earns her title as a cultural essayist by ruminating on celebrities (although perhaps not widely known pop culture figures) such as Italian performance artist Vanessa Beecroft, photographer Diane Arbus, fashion designer Elsa Schiaparelli, and Jackie Onassis.

Subjects: Celebrities and Superstars, Character Profiles, Essays, New York City, Pop Culture

Awards: New York Times Notable

Now Try: Thurman takes as her subjects somewhat more specialized individuals on the cultural scene, but her writing is still accessible; she is also a biographer and her readers might consider her other titles *Isak Dinesen: The Life of a Storyteller* or *The Vagabond* (about Colette). These readers might consider collections by other *New Yorker* contributors, including John Updike (*Due Considerations: Essays and Criticism*), David Remnick (*Reporting: Writings from the New Yorker*), Donald Barthelme (*Not-Knowing*), Truman Capote (*Portraits and Observations*), Jonathan Franzen (*How to Be Alone*), Louis Menand (*American Studies*), and Susan Sontag (*On Photography* and *Against Interpretation*).

Wilkinson, Alec

The Happiest Man in the World: An Account of the Life of Poppa Neutrino. Random House. 2007. 301 pp. ISBN 9781400065431.

New Yorker writer Wilkinson offers an extended Character Profile/Biography of David Pearlman, more popularly known as "Poppa Neutrino," who has spent a lifetime exploring the roads not popularly taken. Instead, he has spent his life traveling from one location, job, and life to another; keeping busy forming bands, building a raft in Mexico, and spending time on a Navajo reservation. Like many other journalists who have profiled fascinating subjects, Wilkinson spends time with Neutrino and in the end tells a compelling story of a life much less ordinary than it appears.

Subjects: American Indians, Biographies, Eccentrics, Homeless, David Pearlman, Travel

Now Try: Fans of Wilkinson's fascinating but not sycophantic profile might enjoy other such classic profiles as Joseph Mitchell's *Joe Gould's Secret*, Elizabeth Gilbert's *The*

Last American Man, William Mishler's *A Measure of Endurance: The Unlikely Triumph of Steven Sharp*, Michael Sokolove's *The Ticket Out: Darryl Strawberry and the Boys of Crenshaw*, Adrian Nicole LeBlanc's *Random Family*, or Jon Krakauer's *Into the Wild*. Character-driven works of fiction might also appeal to these readers, such as Joe Coomer's *Apologizing to Dogs* or Michael Malone's *Handling Sin* (not to mention classics like Jack Kerouac's *On the Road*), as might a variety of Travel nonfiction titles (particularly Journey Narratives).

Ordinary People, Extraordinary Stories

Many of the characters profiled in these stories are as interesting, unique, and individualistic as the characters described in Character Portraits. Like authors of Character Portraits, these authors also use extensive research and lengthy periods of personal observation to learn about the people whose stories they're telling and rely on description and dialogue to describe their characters. However, these authors often choose to profile ordinary people who have extraordinary stories, and the emphasis is often truly on the story. Character is still the key appeal of these books, but they also often offer a story with a true narrative arc, and a sometimes shocking or unbelievable one at that. Steven Sharp, profiled by William Mishler in *A Measure of Endurance*, is an interesting young man, and Mishler describes him and his family at length, but the story of how he lost his arms and made the decision to sue a large corporation for the faulty manufacturing in the machine he was using takes precedence over personal description.

Fans of these titles might also enjoy character-driven nonfiction titles, particularly Life Stories such as Autobiographies and Biographies that offer some narrative closure on individuals' life stories. True Adventure nonfiction, in which characters often find themselves drawing on inner reserves of courage and resourcefulness in response to bad situations, might also hold some appeal for these readers, as might History nonfiction, particularly New Perspectives and Historical Biography titles. Mainstream fiction titles that offer both strong character and story appeal factors might also be suggested to these readers.

Although Ordinary People, Extraordinary Stories titles also feature unique individuals, their authors often place their characters more in the context of a story-driven narrative. Character details are important here, but the story is often equally or more so, as the extraordinary stories are at least partially responsible for the characters' development. Often these titles include more anecdotes from research and outside interviews than are typically found in Character Portraits (where the main character is the one with whom the author spends the majority of their time).

Ball, Edward

Peninsula Of Lies: A True Story of a Mysterious Birth and Taboo Love. Simon & Schuster. 2004. 271 pp. ISBN 9780743235600.

Labeled by the author as a "nonfiction mystery," this book relates the story of Gordon Langley Hall. Born in England and raised by his parents on the estate of Vita Sackville-West (where they worked and lived), Hall, who maintained throughout his life that he was mislabeled a boy at birth, would eventually make his way to New York City, where he would become a close friend of the heiress Isabel Whitney, who left him a small fortune when she died. At that point, Hall moved to Charleston, South Carolina, underwent a sex reassignment, and reemerged into Charleston society as Dawn Langley Hall. Her amazing powers of transformation and her unique experiences would not end there; eventually she married John Paul Simmons, an African American laborer on her estate, and claimed to have a baby, Natasha, by him. Readers fascinated by the twists and turns in Hall's life will need to read to the end to find out what really happened, but one thing is clear throughout; Dawn is one of the most unique (and at times, sympathetic) main characters in all of American nonfiction and fiction.

> **Subjects:** 20th Century, American South, Gender, Gordon Langley Hall, Interracial Relationships, Marriage, Race Relations, Transsexuals

> **Now Try:** Readers might try Edward Ball's earlier book, *Slaves in the Family*, in which he also explored issues of race, as well as James McBride's *The Color of Water* about his interracial family and Bliss Broyard's *One Drop: My Father's Hidden Life—A Story of Race and Family Secrets*. Books dealing with sexuality and gender issues might also work as read-alikes to this title, including John Berendt's *Midnight in the Garden of Good and Evil*, Pagan Kennedy's *The First Man-Made Man*, John Colapinto's *As Nature Made Him*, and Jennifer Finney Boylan's memoirs *She's Not There* or *I'm Looking Through You: Growing Up Haunted*.

Blehm, Eric

The Last Season. HarperCollins. 2006. 335 pp. ISBN 9780060583002.

California's imposing Sierra Nevada mountain range has long been the refuge of the brave and the original; photographer Ansel Adams and naturalist John Muir are listed among their more well-known explorers. In this story, equal parts True Adventure and Character Profile, author Blehm examines the life and as yet unsolved disappearance of National Park Service backcountry ranger Randy Morgenson, who worked for twenty-eight years in the wilderness of the mountains, offering his expertise and experience to hikers and climbers. Although the solitude that is part of the job was originally a large part of its appeal, later years found Morgenson struggling in his relationships with his wife and his friends, and when he disappeared on a trip into Kings Canyon National Park, many suspected foul play or suicide, and one of the most intensive manhunts ever was initiated by the Park Service.

> **Subjects:** Accidents, California, Environmental Writing, Family Relationships, Randy Morgenson, Mountains, Sierra Nevada Mountains, True Adventure, True Crime

> **Now Try:** Other True Adventure titles might be offered, particularly Jon Krakauer's *Into the Wild* and *Into Thin Air*, Sebastian Junger's *The Perfect Storm*, or Lynn Schooler's *The Blue Bear: A True Story of Friendship, Tragedy, and Survival in the Alaskan Wilderness*. Authors who provided blurbs on this book include Bill McKibben and Aron Ralston (*Between a Rock and a Hard Place*); other authors who have profiled

enigmatic lovers of nature and solitude include Edward Abbey (who wrote about himself in *Desert Solitaire*), Elizabeth Gilbert (*The Last American Man*) and Jane Kramer (*The Last Cowboy*). In the text of this title it is also noted that Morgenson was a fan of Robert Bly's book *Iron John*; books by authors such as John Steinbeck, Wallace Stegner, and Kent Haruf might also appeal to these readers.

Bowden, Mark

Finders Keepers: The Story of a Man Who Found $1 Million. Atlantic Monthly Press. 2002. 209 pp. ISBN 9780871138590.

What would you do if you found a million dollars? Journalist Bowden attempts to tell the story of Joey Coyle, a resident of South Philly, who did stumble across two bags of unmarked casino money (for a total of 1.2 million dollars, to be more accurate). As a twenty-eight-year-old man who lived with his mother, was addicted to crystal meth, and would have worked on the docks if there'd been any work to get, the money was just too good to pass up, although Coyle's poor choices with the money and of associates eventually led to his arrest and trial; the story does not end happily. This book began as a series of articles in the newspaper the *Philadelphia Inquirer* and was made into a movie starring John Cusack.

Subjects: Biographies, Joey Coyle, Drug Addiction, Drugs, Pennsylvania, Philadelphia, Quick Reads, True Crime, YA

Now Try: Other nonfiction and fiction books about individuals not cut out to be criminals might particularly appeal, such as Jeff Diamant's *Heist!*, or Scott Smith's novel *A Simple Plan* (or even Frank Abagnale's *Catch Me If You Can*, although Abagnale was a much smoother character). Other books by Bowden might be offered, particularly *Black Hawk Down* or his collection of journalistic pieces, *Road Work*; another *Philadelphia Inquirer* colleague, Pete Dexter, might also be offered to these readers (particularly his novels *Paris Trout* and *The Paperboy*) or his nonfiction collection *Paper Trails*. Another behind-the-scenes look at the lottery business, Edward Ugel's *Money for Nothing*, might also appeal to these readers.

Colapinto, John

As Nature Made Him: The Boy Who Was Raised as a Girl. HarperCollins. 2000. 279 pp. ISBN 9780060192112.

Colapinto reveals the story of David Reimer, born in Winnipeg, Canada, in 1966, who was badly injured during his circumcision. On the advice of psychologist and famous sex researcher John Money, his parents opted to raise him as a girl (a situation that was made even more difficult by the fact that David, born Bruce, also had an identical twin brother named Brian). In this compelling and heartbreaking story, Colapinto reveals the unhappiness and confusion of Reimer's childhood, the not inconsiderable physical procedures and discomfort he had to experience, the challenges faced by his parents and his brother, Dr. John Money's controversial career and the attitude of the medical establishment toward the "intersexed" and those with genital injuries, as well as the cultural significance of this case (feminists, in particular, relied on it to illustrate the importance of nurture and the imposition of gender roles).

Subjects: Biographies, Depression, Family Relationships, Gender, Medicine, John Money, Psychology, David Reimer, Sexuality, Society, Transsexuals

Now Try: In addition to being a stunning character profile, the magnitude of tragedy in this book elevates it to a type of disaster and survival story; other books which might appeal include William Mishler's *A Measure of Endurance: The Unlikely Triumph of Steven Sharp*, Aron Ralston's *Between a Rock and a Hard Place*, and Sebastian Junger's *A Perfect Storm*. Other books dealing with gender issues might also be offered, such as Edward Ball's *Peninsula of Lies*, Pagan Kennedy's *The First Man-Made Man*, and Amy Bloom's *Normal*. Books about missteps in medicine might also be offered, such as Anne Fadiman's *The Spirit Catches You and You Fall Down*, Debbie Bookchin's and Jim Schumacher's *The Virus and the Vaccine*, or Stephen Klaidman's *Coronary*.

Hersey, John

Here to Stay: Studies in Human Tenacity. Knopf. 1962. 335 pp. ISBN 9781557781000.

In this series of essays about decidedly not famous individuals, Hersey tells the incredible stories of two women who survive a hurricane in their Connecticut apartment building (an event that took place in 1955), a family who left Hungary after the political unrest there in 1956, and a man dealing with the loss of one of his limbs and his struggle to get his life back to normal. Hersey is also not immune to the stories of more famous people and relates the series of events in August 1943 when John F. Kennedy's patrol torpedo boat crashed.

Subjects: Character Profiles, Classics, Essays, Hiroshima, Holocaust, John F. Kennedy, Nuclear Weapons, Survival Stories, War, World War II

Now Try: Although this book is old, there is no statute of limitations on character-driven essays or skilled prose writing. Other classic authors who might be offered to Hersey's readers include Joseph Mitchell, E. B. White, or Martha Gellhorn; classic fiction titles by Ernest Hemingway, John Steinbeck, John Dos Passos, Flannery O'Connor, William Faulkner, or Graham Greene might also appeal.

Kennedy, Pagan

The First Man-Made Man: The Story of Two Sex Changes, One Love Affair, and a Twentieth-Century Medical Revolution. Bloomsbury. 2007. 214 pp. ISBN 9781596910157.

Laura Dillon knew from a very early age that she should have born a boy; when she underwent one of the first sex-change operations ever performed in Great Britain to become Michael Dillon, she simply felt like she was correcting an error that had been made at birth. Growing up as a girl in Great Britain in the 1920s, Dillon struggled with her gender identity, and it was not until she met doctor Harold Gillies, who specialized in performing reconstructive surgeries on injured World War I and II veterans, that she saw a way to resolve her dilemma. After writing a book on sexual identity and endocrinology (titled *Self*) Dillon attracted the attention of Robert Cowell, who was seeking an operation of his own to become a woman. Although Michael Dillon then fell in love with Roberta Cowell, she eventually rejected his love, and he traveled to India to seek the spiritual peace and tranquility he had sought so long. He would eventually transform himself again, into the Buddhist monk known as "Jivaka," but then met his untimely death on a subsequent pilgrimage to Tibet in 1962.

Subjects: 1940s, 1950s, Biographies, Michael Dillon, Gender, Great Britain, Love Affairs, Medicine, Psychology, Quick Reads, Tibet, Transsexuals

Now Try: A wide range of nonfiction narratives on gender issues and transsexuality might be offered to fans of Kennedy's sympathetic portrait, including Jennifer Finney Boylan's memoirs *She's Not There* and *I'm Looking through You*, Amy Bloom's *Normal*, Edward Ball's *Peninsula of Lies*, and Christine Jorgensen's classic *Christine Jorgensen: Personal Autobiography*. Norah Vincent's Immersion Journalism title *Self-Made Man*, in which she dresses and lives as a man as a sociological experiment might also be offered, as might Pagan Kennedy's novels, *Spinsters* and *Confessions of a Memory Eater*.

Kurson, Robert

Crashing Through: A True Story of Risk, Adventure, and the Man Who Dared to See. Random House. 2007. 306 pp. ISBN 9781400063352.

Mike May broke world records in downhill speed skiing, worked for the CIA, and became an inventor—all after losing his eyesight when he was three years old. In this thrilling account of medical advances, Kurson tells May's story with great empathy for the challenges faced by a man who never let his blindness slow him down but was almost stopped in his tracks by fear of the consequences of the procedure to restore his sight. Although the procedure brought him the ability to see his wife and children for the first time in his life along with other miraculous firsts, it also found him questioning the very core of his own identity and self-confidence.

> **Subjects:** Biographies, Book Groups, Brain, Family Relationships, Health Issues, Michael May, Medicine, Science
>
> **Now Try:** Other nonfiction narratives of daring medical procedures and issues include Jonathan Weiner's *His Brother's Keeper: One Family's Journey to the Edge of Medicine*, Jenifer Estess's *Tales from the Bed* (about her struggles with ALS), Michael McCarthy's *The Sun Farmer*, and Pagan Kennedy's *The First Man-Made Man*; other investigative works offering strong characters who overcome long odds include William Mishler's *A Measure of Endurance: The Unlikely Triumph of Steven Sharp*, John Hockenberry's ALA Notable Book *Moving Violations: War Zones, Wheelchairs, and Declarations of Independence*, and Jim Knipfel's memoir *Slackjaw*. Other titles that are considered works of science writing might also be offered, such as Robin Henig's *Pandora's Baby*, Chris Jones's *Too Far from Home*, or Richard Preston's *The Hot Zone*.

Lewis, Michael D.

❀ *The Blind Side: Evolution of a Game.* W. W. Norton. 2006. 299 pp. ISBN 9780393061239.

Journalist Lewis, best known for his titles *Moneyball* and *Liar's Poker*, this time examines the mechanics and intangibles present in both the physical game of football and within and among some of its most valuable but underappreciated players. He provides a character portrait in the form of left tackle Michael Oher, who grew up in poverty, moved in with an affluent Memphis family to attend a private high school, and eventually became one of the best tackles at exploiting quarterbacks' biggest weakness: their blind side.

Subjects: Book Groups, Family Relationships, Football, Michael Oher, Poverty, Sports, Underdogs, YA, Year in the Life

Awards: New York Times Notable

Now Try: Fans of this book might thoroughly enjoy *Moneyball* (in the In-Depth Reporting chapter), in which Lewis examined the winning record of a baseball team that didn't boast the sport's biggest payroll. Other sports stories that might appeal to these readers include *The Ticket Out* by Michael Sokolove, *The Last Shot* by Darcy Frey, *One Great Game* by Don Wallace, *Friday Night Lights* by H. G. Bissinger, *Namath: A Biography* or *Pistol: The Life of Pete Maravich* by Mark Kriegel, or *The Boys of Winter* by Wayne Coffey.

Mishler, William

A Measure of Endurance: The Unlikely Triumph of Steven Sharp. Knopf. 2003. 306 pp. ISBN 9780375411335.

In this quiet and compelling book Mishler tells the story of Steven Sharp, who lost both his arms in a farm accident in the summer of 1992. Narrative detailing describes Steven's remarkable force of personality and drive to rehabilitate himself. The author details the story of the lengthy trial at which Sharp and his attorney, Bill Manning (a fascinating character in his own right), alleged that the Case Corporation, which manufactured a mechanism on the farm equipment that injured Sharp, was responsible for his injuries. The story makes personal the often dry details of personal injury litigation and corporate responsibility. Although labeled "current events" on its jacket, this narrative is appealing both for the momentum of its story as well as the indomitable spirit of the individuals involved.

Subjects: Accidents, Agriculture, Business, Family Relationships, Law and Lawyers, Organizations, Rural Life, Underdogs, YA

Now Try: William Mishler died in 2002, which is a tremendous loss to readers. Stories of physical accidents and hardships such as Michael McCarthy's *The Sun Farmer* or John Colapinto's *As Nature Made Him* might be offered, as might community and legal stories like Paul VanDevelder's *Coyote Warrior: One Man, Three Tribes, and the Trial That Forged a Nation*, which illuminates the legal process by telling the compelling story of three Native American tribes' battles to win compensation for the 1953 Garrison Dam flooding of their homelands, or Joy Horowitz's *Parts Per Million: The Poisoning of Beverly Hills High School*. The much older (publication date 1976) but still compelling page-turner *The Buffalo Creek Disaster: The Story of the Survivors' Unprecedented Lawsuit*, might also appeal to readers of character-driven, legal underdog stories.

Suskind, Ron

🏶 *A Hope in the Unseen: An American Odyssey from the Inner City to the Ivy League.* Broadway Books. 1998. 372 pp. ISBN 9780767901253.

Suskind details the struggle of inner-city student Cedric Jennings, whom he first encounters as a junior in crime-ridden Ballou Senior High in Washington, D.C., and his quest to gain both admittance to an Ivy League college and comfort in surroundings that are decidedly not familiar to minorities or members of lower economic classes. Driven only by his hard work and dreams, Jennings is a complex subject for Suskind's journalistic study, and the story of his eventual triumph and experiences at Brown University is a compelling and page-turning account.

Subjects: Education, Cedric Jennings, Poverty, Race Relations, Racism, Underdogs, Urban Life

Awards: ALA Notable

Now Try: Jonathan Kozol's *Savage Inequalities: Children in America's Schools* and Alex Kotlowitz's *There Are No Children Here: The Story of Two Boys Growing Up in the Other America* might provide complementary reading to fans of Suskind's character-driven narrative, as might Tracy Kidder's superlative story of a fifth-grade classroom, *Among Schoolchildren*. Character-driven works of investigative writing might also be offered, such as Michael Lewis's *The Blind Side* or Michael Sokolove's *The Ticket Out*.

Shared Experiences

In these titles, authors profile groups of individuals who know each other or who participate in a shared experience or location (in Adrian Nicole LeBlanc's classic *Random Family*, her subjects are relatives, friends, or neighbors; in Michael Weinreb's *The Kings of New York*, the shared link is the competitive chess team at the Edward R. Murrow high school in Brooklyn). They can be very personal stories, many of which take the authors years to observe, research, and write (both LeBlanc and Leon Dash, for example, spent years getting to know the communities of people they describe); however, for all their time spent getting to know the groups they're profiling, these authors keep a very low profile in their own stories. Although they are similar in tone to many Immersion Journalism titles, authors in this subgenre tend to keep themselves completely out of their stories.

These are often stories of relationships as much as they are about individual characters; readers who particularly enjoy those (e.g., Leon Dash's *Rosa Lee* or Michael Sokolove's *The Ticket Out*) might also enjoy nonfiction Life Stories that focus on Relationships, such as Augusten Burroughs's *Running with Scissors* or Michael Perry's *Population 485*. Any nonfiction title with the subject of community life might also appeal to these readers, as might a wide variety of fiction titles exploring relationships between characters, such as Anne Tyler's classic *Dinner at the Homesick Restaurant* or Rebecca Well's *Divine Secrets of the Ya-Ya Sisterhood*. Biographies featuring groups of characters, also known as "Buddy Bios" might also appeal to these readers; examples from that subgenre include Jon Meacham's *Franklin and Winston* and Doris Kearns Goodwin's *Team of Rivals*. Because these authors largely strive to keep their presence understated, fans of these titles might also consider a wide variety of titles from the In-Depth Reporting subgenre, particularly by authors such as Tracy Kidder, William Langewiesche, or Mark Bowden.

Shared Experiences titles feature profiles of not only one character, but instead a group or multiple individuals. They are also people or groups who share experiences in some way, either by living the same experience in close physical proximity (without really knowing or being aware of one another) or by knowing each other (as is the case with family members, friends, or other acquaintances). The major appeal of these titles is still their authors' attention to character details, but the relationships between and among the related characters is also an important part of these stories.

Alvarez, Julia

Once Upon a Quinceañara: Coming of Age in the USA. Viking. 2007. 278 pp. ISBN 9780670038732.

Novelist Alvarez takes as her subject the Hispanic tradition of throwing a quinceañara, or coming-of-age party, for girls turning fifteen years old. In her yearlong investigation of the event, she became particularly close to one of the girls (Monica Ramos) and her family as they prepared for the party, on which many Hispanic American families spend thousands of dollars and plan for extensively. With good humor and a wealth of understanding based on her own multicultural background, Alvarez not only explains the tradition but also provides nuanced character portraits of the girls involved.

> **Subjects:** Celebrations, Coming of Age, Family Relationships, Friendships, Multicultural Issues, Pop Culture, Society, Women's Nonfiction, YA, Year in the Life

> **Now Try:** Fans of Alvarez's thoughtful narrative might also enjoy her novels, including *How the García Girls Lost Their Accents* and *In the Time of the Butterflies*, as well as her poetry collections *The Housekeeping Book, Homecoming*, or *The Woman I Kept to Myself*. Other authors who might appeal to these readers include Isabel Allende (Allende writes both novels, such as *The House of the Spirits*, and memoirs, such as *The Sum of Our Days*), Cristina García (*Dreaming in Cuban*), or Laura Esquivel (*Like Water for Chocolate*). Also of interest might be more scholarly books about girls and how they come of age, two of which are cited in this volume: Mary Pipher's *Reviving Ophelia* and Joan Jacobs Brumberg's *The Body Project: An Intimate History of American Girls*); other In-Depth investigative works with a "year in the life" flavor might also be suggested, such as Tracy Kidder's *Among Schoolchildren* or Anne Fadiman's *The Spirit Catches You and You Fall Down.*

Belkin, Lisa

❦ *Show Me a Hero: A Tale of Murder, Suicide, Race, and Redemption.* Little, Brown. 1999. 331 pp. ISBN 9780316088053.

Journalist Belkin investigates the ten-year period from 1988 to 1998 when, by court order, public housing units were built among a majority white neighborhood in Yonkers, New York. In interviewing and telling the stories of the key players in the controversy, Belkin narrates a compelling and character-driven story. From Judge Leonard Sand, who first handed down the 1985 decision that segregation in Yonkers was deliberately planned by city leaders, to Nicholas Wasicsko, the twenty-eight-year-old mayor who would be in office when the order was enacted, to neighborhood individuals Mary Dorman and Alma Febles who found themselves on opposite sides of the debate, Belkin illustrates through personalities the challenges of economic and racial divides in urban communities.

> **Subjects:** Community Life, Government, New York City, Politics, Race Relations, True Crime, Urban Life

> **Awards:** ALA Notable

Now Try: Jonathan Harr's legal classic *A Civil Action* is similar to Belkin's title in its character-driven narrative and tale of community-wide activism; Buzz Bissinger's *A Prayer for the City* (about Philadelphia's mayor, his staff, and their struggle to revitalize the city) might also appeal. Michael Winerip's *9 Highland Road* is similar in subject and tone to Belkin's narrative; nonfiction titles which explore the relationships of communities and individuals such as *Blood Done Sign My Name* by Timothy Tyson, *The Other Side of the River* by Alex Kotlowitz, and *Midnight in the Garden of Good and Evil* by John Berendt might all be suggested. Belkin is also the author of *First, Do No Harm*, which follows the medical cases of several patients in a Houston hospital.

Bissinger, H. G.

A Prayer for the City. Random House. 1997. 408 pp. ISBN 9780679421986.

Pulitzer Prize winner and journalist Bissinger, best known for his sports classic *Friday Night Lights*, offers an in-depth, sympathetic, but never naïve character portrait of Philadelphia mayor Edward Rendell, who served in that office from 1992 to 1996. Bissinger had completely unfettered access to the mayor and his aide David Cohen but also offers the viewpoints of four of the city's residents: Jim Mangan, a Naval Shipyard employee; policy analyst Linda Morrison; city prosecutor Mike McGovern; and the elderly Fifi Mazzccua trying to raise her four grandchildren. The city of Philadelphia itself very nearly emerges as a character in its own right in this detailed, chronologically ordered narrative. The author is a contributor to *Vanity Fair*.

Subjects: Community Life, Government, Pennsylvania, Philadelphia, Politics, Edward Rendell, Society, True Crime, Urban Life, Year in the Life

Now Try: Other books about life in American cities might be offered: Adrian Nicole LeBlanc's classic *Random Family*, Tracy Kidder's *Among Schoolchildren*, Jonathan Kozol's *Savage Inequalities*, and Sudhir Venkatesh's *American Project: The Rise and Fall of a Modern Ghetto*. Another great book specifically about Philadelphia and its residents is Tom Gralish's and Michael Vitez's *Rocky Stories*; Bissinger's bibliography makes reference to city-planning books by Lewis Mumford; and books about hardships faced by American residents in poverty might also apply (such as David Shipler's *The Working Poor*, William Finnegan's *Cold New World*, or even Barbara Ehrenreich's *Nickel and Dimed*). Bissinger, of course, is also famous for his sports journalism titles such as *Friday Night Lights* and *Three Nights in August*.

Dash, Leon

Rosa Lee: A Mother and Her Family in Urban America. BasicBooks. 1996. 279 pp. ISBN 9780465070923.

Investigative reporter Dash spent four years with Washington, D.C., resident Rosa Lee Cunningham, getting to know her, her eight children, and five of her grandchildren in an effort to better understand her life, much of which had been spent in trouble with the law, either under arrest or in jail, doing and dealing drugs, and living through bouts of homelessness and extreme poverty as members of America's black urban "underclass." Dash's writing is immediate; he opens his book with a description of Rosa Lee being treated in the hospital and nearly receiving a visit there from her daughter's drug dealer to demand his money. Although many of Cunningham's children also struggled with teen pregnancy and drug abuse issues, two of her sons were living in more mainstream American society, working government service jobs. The result is a nuanced, sympathetic, but still distanced report on poverty and urban life and one that never loses sight of the very human characters (particularly Rosa Lee) at its core: "She could barely walk when she reached the emergency room four days earlier and wants to take full advantage of her hospital stay. A full night's sleep and daylong quiet are rare luxuries in her life. This is the closest she ever comes to having a vacation," (p. 3).

> **Subjects:** African American Authors, Classics, Drug Addiction, Drugs, Family Relationships, Poverty, Race Relations, Urban Life, Washington D.C., Women's Nonfiction

> **Now Try:** Other books about families, crime, and poverty might be offered these readers, including Adrian Nicole LeBlanc's *Random Family*, Alex Kotlowitz's *There Are No Children Here*, Jennifer Gonnerman's *Life on the Outside*, or David Shipler's *The Working Poor*. Other books by Leon Dash might appeal, as well as nonfiction by social issue journalists including John Bowe, Jonathan Kozol, Barbara Ehrenreich, or Tracy Kidder.

LeBlanc, Adrian Nicole

🗲 *Random Family: Love, Drugs, Trouble, and Coming of Age in the Bronx.* Scribner. 2003. 408 pp. ISBN 9780684863870.

Journalist LeBlanc spent ten years getting to know several families in the Bronx, and her subtitle admirably sums up the many challenges facing the borough's children and families. Although character-driven and as forcefully written as a physical jab to the stomach, this is a dense and nuanced narrative, and it does take some time to read (which is only fitting; it took a decade to write). Although many of the stories, particularly those involving drug use, prison life, and the many hardships faced by most of the book's extremely young mothers, have an almost unreal quality and unrelenting frequency, the author manages to present an incredibly well-written account that is gritty without being bleak.

> **Subjects:** Book Groups, Classics, Drug Addiction, Explicit Sexuality, Explicit Violence, Family Relationships, Love and Dating, Poverty, Prisons, Urban Life, Women's Nonfiction

> **Awards:** ALA Notable

> **Now Try:** Leon Dash's *Rosa Lee: A Mother and Her Family in Urban America* also focuses on family relationships; Ron Suskind's similarly journalistic but empathetic *A Hope in the Unseen: An American Odyssey from the Inner City to the Ivy League*, also details the remarkable strength of character and family relationships of its subject, Cedric Jennings. Although written by a professor of anthropology, *Sugar's Life in the Hood: The Story of a Former Welfare Mother* (written by Tracy Bachrach Ehlers through interviews with Sugar Turner) is also a personal and evocative inside look at Turner's experiences within her neighborhood and relationships. Jason DeParle's *American Dream: Three Women, Ten Kids, and a Nation's Drive to End Welfare*, focuses more on the history and efficacy of welfare programs, but does so by telling the extremely personal stories of his main characters; Jennifer Gonnerman's *Life on the Outside*, about a woman's struggle to rebuild her life after incarceration, might also appeal.

Lipper, Joanna

Growing Up Fast. Picador. 2003. 421 pp. ISBN 9780312422226.

Documentary filmmaker Lipper followed the lives of and interviewed six teenage mothers in Pittsfield, Massachusetts, a region of that state suffering from financial hardships (initiated when General Electric, the town's largest employer, closed their division there in the 1980s). The cycle of poverty, complete with family and drug abuse, that resulted from widespread unemployment, Lipper argues, also led to an increase in teen pregnancies as teenagers sought an outlet to their stressful home lives. Lipper was a sympathetic listener, and the girls she interviewed were forthcoming with their stories of their childhoods, abuse, their relationships with their families, and the challenges they face as teen parents.

> **Subjects:** Classics, Drug Addiction, Dysfunctional Families, Family Relationships, Love Affairs, Massachusetts, Parenting, Poverty, Teens, Women's Nonfiction, Year in the Life

> **Now Try:** Adrian Nicole LeBlanc's classic *Random Family* also explores the issue of young girls becoming pregnant; Leon Dash also touches on the subject in his book *Rosa Lee*. A more violent aspect of teen rebellion is seen in Rene Denfeld's *All God's Children: Inside the Dark and Violent World of Street Families*, while books about economics and the challenges of the current work environment, such as David Shipler's *The Working Poor*, Jason DeParle's *American Dream: Three Women, Ten Kids, and a Nation's Drive to End Welfare*, and Alex Kotlowitz's *There Are No Children Here*, might work as related reads.

Lipsky, David

🕯 *Absolutely American: Four Years at West Point.* Houghton Mifflin. 2003. 317 pp. ISBN 9780618095421.

Reporter Lipsky was offered full access to the West Point military academy, and spent four years following the educations and lives of the graduating class of 2002. At that time the school was undergoing a cultural change, because the practice of hazing had been largely suspended, and the events of 9/11 were lending a more charged tension than ever to the atmosphere. By telling the stories of numerous students, from those who never expected to make the military a career to those seeking to align their femininity with their training to become soldiers (women also attend West Point), Lipsky provides a valuable inside look into one of America's most venerable institutions, as well as insight into the personalities of college students who also happen to be military personnel.

> **Subjects:** Education, Friendships, Military, Year in the Life

> **Awards:** New York Times Notable

> **Now Try:** Other books in which authors immerse themselves in different educational experiences include *The Overachievers* and *Pledged* by Alexandra Robbins, *Wonderland* by Michael Bamberger, Tracy Kidder's *Among Schoolchildren*, and Sam Swope's *I am a Pencil*. Stephen Ambrose's related read *Duty, Honor, Country: A History of West Point* might also appeal to these readers, as might other books about the military such as Mark Bowden's *Black Hawk Down*, Marcus Luttrell's bestseller *Lone Survivor*, or Linda Robinson's

Masters of Chaos: The Secret History of the Special Forces, not to mention techno-thrillers by Tom Clancy, Nelson DeMille, Dale Brown, or W. E. B. Griffin.

Phillips, Ty

Blacktop Cowboys: Riders on the Run for Rodeo Gold. Thomas Dunne Books. 2006. 263 pp. ISBN 9780312330361.

Writing in part travelogue, part character-profile style, author Phillips describes life on the rodeo circuit with two modern-day cowboys, Luke Branquinho and Travis Cadwell. Chapters open with a specific location and date; each new location represents a steer wrestling competition in which Branquinho (in the beginning of his career) and Cadwell (near the end of his) both make a bid to make it to the sport's version of the Super Bowl: the National Finals Rodeo (NFR) in Las Vegas. Phillips catches much of the tone and content of the sometimes racy dialogue between many riders on the circuit, making this a quickly paced and immediate read.

Subjects: American West, Cowboys, Friendships, Profanity, Professions, Rodeos, Travel, Work Relationships, YA, Year in the Life

Now Try: The authors who provided blurbs on the back of Phillips's book aren't well known, but their books seem very appropriate as related reads: they are Ty Murray's autobiography *King of the Cowboys* and Casey Tefertiller's biography *Wyatt Earp: The Life behind the Legend*. Other books about cowboys and ambitious and unique men might be offered; these include Jane Kramer's classic *The Last Cowboy*, Elizabeth Gilbert's *The Last American Man*, Eric Blehm's *The Last Season*, or Jon Krakauer's *Into the Wild*. Westerns by such authors as Elmer Kelton, Larry McMurtry, or Cormac McCarthy might appeal, as might authors who depend heavily on setting, including Kent Haruf, Wallace Stegner, and Jim Harrison.

Slatalla, Michelle

The Town on Beaver Creek: The Story of a Lost Kentucky Community. Random House. 2006. 242 pp. ISBN 9780375509056.

In 2004 the small town of Martin, Kentucky, was bulldozed to make way for a federal flood-relief program (the low-lying town was subject to regular and destructive floods). Before the bulldozers arrived, author Slatalla returned to Martin, which was also her family's hometown, in the hopes of learning the area's stories before its residents were relocated. The book, which is told in the form of a nonfiction novel (reminiscent in style of Truman Capote's *In Cold Blood*), opens with the story of her great-grandfather Fred Mynhier and her great-grandmother Hesta, and their life in the area in the 1930s; in later chapters, she explores the complicated marriage(s) of her grandparents, Mary and Elmer, and the many struggles of small-town life in Depression and post–World War II rural America.

Subjects: 1930s, American History, Appalachian Mountains, Family Relationships, Floods, Great Depression, Kentucky, World War II

Now Try: The most singular character in Slatalla's history is her great-grandmother Hesta; other nonfiction and fiction featuring strong women characters might be good read-alikes, such as Carol Shields's novels *The Stone Diaries* and *Unless*, Khaled Hosseini's *A Thousand Splendid Suns*, Rick Bragg's memoir *All Over but the Shoutin'*, James McBride's memoir *The Color of Water*, or even Carolly Erickson's history *The Girl from Botany Bay* (also check the index to this volume for books with the subject "Women's Contributions" or "Women Travelers"). Wendell Berry's fiction titles, set in

Kentucky, including *Jayber Crow* should be suggested, as should Edgar Lee Masters's classic *Spoon River Anthology*; books about natural disasters, such as Jed Horne's *Breach of Faith* (about Hurricane Katrina) or Ashley Shelby's *Red River Rising*, may also be good fits.

Sokolove, Michael

🏵 *The Ticket Out: Darryl Strawberry and the Boys of Crenshaw.* Simon & Schuster. 2004. 291 pp. ISBN 9780743226738.

A character portrait of an entire high school baseball team, Sokolove's narrative following the school and playing careers of the 1979 Crenshaw High team begins with their heartbreaking loss of the LA City Championship to a team from a more affluent area. Heartbreaking is the operative word for this story, as Sokolove interviewed many of the players and was thus granted full access to their world of childhood poverty and hardships, personality conflicts among team members, their struggles with drugs and other temptations (a full chapter is devoted to Darryl Strawberry and his volatile career), and, above all, the failure to fulfill the hopes spawned by their aggregate amount of raw talent.

> **Subjects:** Athletes, Baseball, Biographies, California, Friendships, Los Angeles, Poverty, Sports, Underdogs, Urban Life, YA
>
> **Awards:** ALA Notable
>
> **Now Try:** Darcy Frey's ALA Notable Book *The Last Shot: City Streets, Basketball Dreams*, is set on a different coast and focuses on a different sport but provides a similarly simultaneously heartbreaking and hopeful story of the dreams of young athletes; Don Wallace's *One Great Game: Two Teams, Two Dreams, in the First Ever National Championship High School Football Game* does the same. Set even further afield, sportswriter S. L. Price's travel/sports title *Pitching around Fidel: A Journey into the Heart of Cuban Sports* portrays the slow demise of the island's fabled athletics program. H. G. Bissinger's *Friday Night Lights: A Town, a Team, and a Dream* or Michael Lewis's *The Blind Side* might also appeal to readers who enjoy character-rich sports stories.

Weinreb, Michael

The Kings of New York: A Year among the Geeks, Oddballs, and Geniuses Who Make Up America's Top High School Chess Team. Gotham Books. 2007. 288 pp. ISBN 9781592402618.

Journalist Weinreb spent a year with the chess team of Edward R. Murrow High School in Brooklyn, getting to know its coach (Eliot Weiss) as well as its highly individual members, each with his or her own distinct personality, and, more important, chess-playing styles and tactics. The players the reader is introduced to include Oscar Santana and Ilya Kotlyanskiy; while the bulk of the narrative follows the exploits of the chess players, Weinreb also provides the stories of coach Weiss and the principal of Murrow High School, Saul Bruckner. In addition to exploring the game of chess and the power of friendship, the author also does a creditable job of describing a successful alternative high school and the educational trials of the students he gets to know.

> **Subjects:** Chess, Education, Friendships, Hobbies, Immersion Journalism, New York City, Poverty, Society, Teachers, Underdogs, YA, Year in the Life

Now Try: This book offers many subjects and aspects for possible read-alikes: books about chess (*Searching for Bobby Fischer*), hobbies and obsessions (Shari Caudron's *Who Are You People?* or Stefan Fatsis's *Word Freaks*), sports and underdogs (Mark Kriegel's *Namath* or *Pistol: The Life of Pete Maravich*), education (Jonathan Kozol's *Shame of the Nation* or *Savage Inequalities*, Sam Swopes's *I Am a Pencil*, Tracy Kidder's *Among Schoolchildren*), and Immersion Journalism titles (Michael Bamberger's *Wonderland* or Alexandra Robbins's *The Overachievers: The Secret Lives of Driven Kids*).

Wolfe, Tom

🎋 *The Right Stuff.* Farrar, Straus & Giroux. 1979. 436 pp. ISBN 9780374250324.
One of the most vocal practitioners of the "new journalism," Wolfe took the charge to use dialogue and fiction-like scene construction in his nonfiction works seriously. In this classic title, he relates the stories of the seven initial astronauts in the U.S. space program, including John Glenn, Gus Grissom, and Alan Shepard. He also relates the history of the program and a variety of aerospace anecdotes, including Chuck Yeager's determination to break the sound barrier, and ponders the future of the program. When the book was first published in 1979, the patriotic enthusiasm and self-determination of the driven men Wolfe profiled seemed out of date; in 2008, however, the book still feels like it was just published.

> **Subjects:** Astronauts, Classics, Science, Space

> **Awards:** National Book Award

> **Now Try:** Other classics regarding space and flight might be suggested, including Andrew Chaikin's *A Man on the Moon*, Chris Jones's *Too Far from Home*, or even William Langewiesche's *Inside the Sky: Meditations on Flight*, as might a variety of adventurous Science and Math titles (such as Jeffrey Kluger's *Journey Beyond Selene* or Mark Wolverton's *The Depths of Space*). Books by other "new journalists" such as Gay Talese, Truman Capote, Hunter S. Thompson, or Norman Mailer might also be good read-alikes.

Group Portraits

Sometimes groups of characters present themselves to authors, being related by blood or by location or by a common purpose; those titles are to be found in the Shared Experiences subgenre. Other times, authors must decide upon their own organizing principle, then seek out characters who fulfill their requirements and can be interviewed and profiled to assuage their curiosity. What results from that style of investigation and interviewing is what I've termed Group Portraits—collections of individual stories, gathered carefully and reported nearly verbatim, and given structure by the authors, who often have a larger presence in their stories than do the authors who write Shared Experiences titles. There is no limit to the imagination found in these titles; Susan Orlean simply decided she was curious how people across the nation spent their Saturday nights (the result, *Saturday Night*, is a lively cross-country report on leisure activities and the individuals indulging in them), while Joan Cheever, curious about the lives of convicted criminals who had received reprieves from the death penalty, set out to meet and interview them.

These titles are typically not driven by their narrative; there are few cohesive stories here, but rather collections of individual impressions and beliefs. As in the Character Portraits subgenre, the authors of these titles generally decide how to organize their subjects' stories, and they do not follow a standard start-to-finish narrative arc. Readers who enjoy them might also enjoy more thoughtful, analytical nonfiction genres and subgenres, including Making Sense ... titles such as Malcolm Gladwell's *The Tipping Point*, Reflective Environmental Writing titles by authors such as Annie Dillard or Michael Pollan, New Perspectives History titles, or Oral Histories from the In-Depth Reporting chapter.

As in Shared Experiences character profiles, Group Portraits titles feature multiple characters, but they are usually individuals who have been selected by their authors because of shared characteristics, rather than for their connection to the other individuals in the narrative. Very rarely do these titles offer a start-to-finish story but rather are more reflective and ruminative books, with the opinions and characters of the individuals profiled typically being gleaned from the authors' interviews of their subjects. In addition to character, Group Portraits sometimes offer setting as an appeal factor, because sometimes the common factor among a group of people is their environment or where they live. Although the authors of Group Portraits rarely insert themselves into their own stories, their organizing and synthesizing voice is important in these books, as they decide how to group their subjects and how to present their stories.

Barkley, Charles

Who's Afraid of a Large Black Man? Speaking My Mind on Race, Celebrity, Sports, and American Life. Penguin Press. 2005. 236 pp. ISBN 9781594200427.

This fascinating collection of interviews reads more like conversations between old friends on the complex subjects of race and society than they do traditional "question-and-answer" interviews. Among those with whom Barkley spoke are Tiger Woods, Morgan Freeman, George Lopez, Bill Clinton, and Jesse Jackson.

Subjects: African American Authors, Charles Barkley, Basketball, Making Sense ..., Politics, Quick Reads, Race Relations, Racism, Society, Sports, YA

Now Try: Fans of this straightforward work of oral history on race relations might consider other works on the same topic, including Nelson George's *Post-Soul Nation*, Studs Terkel's *Race*, Ron Suskind's *A Hope in the Unseen*, and Melba Pattillo Beals's *Warriors Don't Cry*. Memoirs and Relationships nonfiction with an African American reading interest might also be offered, as might biographies of African Americans and sports figures, including Jonathan Eig's *Opening Day: The Story of Jackie Robinson's First Season*, Arthur Ashe's *Days of Grace*, and Sidney Poitier's *The Measure of a Man*. Fiction titles featuring African American protagonists, including Walter Mosley's *The Easy*

Rawlins Series, or books by authors such as Terry McMillan, Bebe Moore Campbell, or Colson Whitehead might also appeal.

Cheever, Joan

Back from the Dead: One Woman's Search for the Men Who Walked off America's Death Row. John Wiley. 2006. 308 pp. ISBN 9780470017500.

When the death penalty was abolished in 1972 (it was reinstated four years later), 589 death-row inmates then awaiting their execution had their sentences commuted. Cheever, fascinated by the question of what these convicted felons would do with their second chances, traveled across the country to interview them. In addition to profiling these individuals, Cheever also explores her own feelings and fears when meeting these (primarily) men, often armed with only a notebook and facing individuals who had committed horrific crimes. In addition to relating in detail the case of Walter Williams, who was executed in 1994, the author offers stories that end in triumph and normal lives, but also many that end in repeat violence and failure (at the time of her investigations, 226 of the 589 were back in jail serving sentences for new crimes).

Subjects: Capital Punishment, Law Enforcement, Prisons, True Crime

Now Try: The author's bibliography includes Norman Mailer's true crime classic *The Executioner's Song*; other books about capital punishment and prison life might also be suggested, such as Helen Prejean's *Dead Man Walking*, Ralph Blumenthal's *Miracle at Sing Sing*, Joseph Hallinan's *Going Up the River: Travels in a Prison Nation*, or Jennifer Wynn's *Inside Rikers: Stories from the World's Largest Penal Colony*.

Danziger, Danny

Museum: Behind the Scenes at the Metropolitan Museum of Art. Viking. 2007. 277 pp. ISBN 9780670038619.

Danziger paints a portrait of a day in the life in the Metropolitan Museum of Art in New York City by offering this compendium of interviews with fifty-two people who are involved with the Met, from waitresses and custodial staff who work there to curators and librarians and trustees. Each person's recollection or story constitutes a chapter, and all of the chapters range in length from four to ten pages, making this an enlightening but quick and light read.

Subjects: Art and Artists, New York City, Oral Histories, Professions, Work Relationships

Now Try: Books about the many fascinating aspects of the art and museum world might make good read-alikes; these include Matthew Hart's *The Irish Game*, Robin Brooks's *The Portland Vase*, Lynn H. Nicholas's *The Rape of Europa*, Herbert Krosney's *The Lost Gospel*, Reviel Netz's and William Noel's *The Archimedes Codex*. Fiction titles like Arturo Perez-Reverte's *The Flanders Panel* or Tracy Chevalier's *Girl with a Pearl Earring* might also appeal. Oral histories collected by such authors as Studs Terkel (*Working*) and John Bowe (*Gig*) might appeal, as might Memoirs about professions such as Anthony Bourdain's *Kitchen Confidential* or Edward Conlon's *Blue Blood*.

Ferner, Mike

Inside the Red Zone: A Veteran for Peace Reports from Iraq. Praeger. 2006. 164 pp. ISBN 9780275992439.

Numerous books have been written on various aspects of the Iraq War (2003) and more will continue to be written, but peace activist and journalist Ferner focuses primarily on the characters of peace activists and other individuals engaged in the conflict. Ferner himself was in Iraq both before and after the 2003 invasion; the first and second parts of the book reflect the changes in the country that he witnessed, while a third part includes his profiles of peace activists Cliff Kindy and Kathy Kelly, as well as a wide variety of other activists, military personnel, and Iraqi citizens. Although the chapters are short and the prose accessible, readers with some knowledge of the invasion and the political context of the Middle East may find it easier to read; also, with a foreword by Cindy Sheehan, it displays a more questioning stance toward the war.

> **Subjects:** Activists, Government, Iraq, Iraq War (2003), Journalism, Military, Politics, War Reporting

> **Now Try:** Books from any number of other investigative writing subgenres might be offered: War Reporting (Patrick Cockburn's *The Occupation: War and Resistance in Iraq*), Immersion Journalism (Anthony Shadid's *Night Draws Near*), Political Reporting (Michael Isikoff's *Hubris: The Inside Story of Spin, Scandal, and the Selling of the Iraq War*, Craig Unger's *The Fall of the House of Bush*), or Exposés (Jeremy Scahill's *Blackwater*, Joseph Margulies's *Guantánamo and the Abuse of Presidential Power*). Essays by such authors as Wendell Berry, Naomi Wolf, or Susan Sontag might also be offered.

Gralish, Tom, and Michael Vitez

Rocky Stories: Tales of Love, Hope, and Happiness at America's Most Famous Steps. Paul Dry Books. 2006. 129 pp. ISBN 9781589880290.

One of the most iconic moments in American film history is the sequence in which Rocky Balboa, played by Sylvester Stallone, whips himself into boxing shape and runs up the massive steps in front of the Philadelphia Museum of Art in the 1976 film *Rocky*. In this ode to the movie, the stairs and the city of Philadelphia, and the human spirit, *Philadelphia Inquirer* journalists and photographers Gralish and Vitez share the personal stories of the people who still come from all over the world to run the steps and jog in place in triumph at the top of the stairs themselves. Over the course of a year, starting on a frigid New Year's Eve, the two hung around the steps and asked people what the steps meant to them and what events and needs in their lives had influenced their decision to imitate the run; the result is an often heartwarming and inspiring look into the lives of people who have overcome health issues, tragedies, and challenges, as well as those people who just come to celebrate milestones or because they promised friends they would. Organized by season and opened with a foreword by Stallone, the book includes fifty-two character profiles and a wealth of beautiful photographs.

> **Subjects:** Illustrated Books, Movie Stars, Movies, Pennsylvania, Philadelphia, Quick Reads, Small Press, Travel, Underdogs, YA

Now Try: The movie *Rocky* presented the ultimate underdog story; other books about underdogs that readers love to love might be offered to these readers, including Laura Hillenbrand's *Seabiscuit*, Michael Sokolove's *The Ticket Out*, Wayne Coffey's *The Boys of Winter*, or William Mishler's *A Measure of Endurance*. Other nonfiction books by authors who spent at least part of their careers in Philadelphia might also be offered; these include Buzz Bissinger, Mark Bowden, and Pete Dexter. As many of the stories included in this book reveal triumphs over adversity, a variety of Overcoming Adversity Memoirs might also be offered, such as Ishmael Beah's *A Long Way Gone*, Rick Bragg's *All Over but the Shoutin'*, or Nick Flynn's *Another Bullshit Night in Suck City*.

Horne, Jed

🔥 *Breach of Faith: Hurricane Katrina and the Near Death of a Great American City*. Random House. 2006. 412 pp. ISBN 9781400065523.

By telling the stories of individuals caught up in Hurricane Katrina and its aftermath, New Orleans journalist Horne provides multiple perspectives from which to view the disaster (as well as the human spirit necessary to survive it). He profiles a Lower Ninth War resident (Patrina Peters) who is also a mother of two and disabled by epilepsy; Kiersta Kurtz-Burke, a doctor who worked throughout at the downtown New Orleans Charity Hospital; and Ivor van Heerden, deputy director of the Hurricane Center at Louisiana State University.

Subjects: Disasters, Government, Hurricane Katrina, Hurricanes, Louisiana, New Orleans, Survival Stories, Weather

Awards: ALA Notable

Now Try: Other books about Hurricane Katrina might be suggested, including Douglas Brinkley's *The Great Deluge* or Christopher Cooper's Exposé *Disaster: Hurricane Katrina and the Failure of Homeland Security*; other survival and disaster nonfiction might also appeal to these readers, including Sebastian Junger's *The Perfect Storm*, Erik Larson's *Isaac's Storm*, John Barry's *Rising Tide*, Mark Levine's *F5*, or Ashley Shelby's *Red River Rising*. Andrei Codrescu's collection *New Orleans, Mon Amour* might also appeal to these readers.

Jager-Hyman, Joie

Fat Envelope Frenzy: One Year, Five Promising Students, and the Pursuit of the Ivy League Prize. HarperCollins. 2008. 231 pp. ISBN 9780061257162.

Jager-Hyman, herself a former admissions officer at Dartmouth, decided to explore the other side of the college admissions story and offers character profiles of five very different students hoping to gain admission to Harvard University. In addition to detailing the lives of Felix, Andrew, Marlene, Nabil, and Lisa (who hail from such different locations as New Orleans and Memphis, and from a range of socioeconomic backgrounds), Jager-Hyman also provides information on higher education, the admissions process, the factors that affect acceptance, and the students' feelings about the process.

Subjects: Education, Harvard University, High School, Year in the Life

Now Try: Other "year in the life" books, particularly those about education, might be suggested to these readers, including Ron Suskind's *A Hope in the Unseen: An American Odyssey from the Inner City to the Ivy League*, Tracy Kidder's *Among Schoolchildren*, Michael Bamberger's *Wonderland: A Year in the Life of an American High School*, Abby Goodnough's *Ms. Moffett's First Year*, or David Lipsky's *Absolutely American: Four Years at West Point*. Fiction featuring high school characters or college life might also be suggested to these readers, including Marisha Pessl's *Special Topics in Calamity Physics*, Michael Chabon's *Wonder Boys*, or Tom Perrotta's *Joe College*.

Kennedy, Pagan

The Dangerous Joy of Dr. Sex and Other True Stories. Independent Publishing Group. 2008. 250 pp. ISBN 9780977679935.

Novelist and nonfiction writer Kennedy offers a variety of portraits about characters who are both squarely involved with but still outside the mainstream, including Alex Comfort, the author of the best-selling manual *The Joy of Sex* (in the title essay), inventor and MIT professor Amy Smith, female weightlifter Cheryl Haworth, and many others (including concluding chapters exploring the oddities in her own life). The result is an unpredictable and thoroughly whimsical collection of very human stories about sexuality, innovation, persistence, and personality.

> **Subjects:** Biology, Brain, Alex Comfort, Eccentrics, Essays, Humor, Inventions, Personality, Psychology, Quick Reads, Sexuality

> **Now Try:** Kennedy is also the author of several novels, including *Spinsters* and *Confessions of a Memory Eater*, as well as the biography/character portrait *The First Man-Made Man: The Story of Two Sex Changes, One Love Affair, and a Twentieth-Century Medical Revolution*. Other character profile collections might also be suggested, including Shari Caudron's *Who Are You People? A Personal Journey into the Heart of Fanatical Passion in America*, Melissa Fay Greene's *There Is No Me without You: One Woman's Odyssey to Rescue Africa's Children*, Tracy Kidder's *Mountains beyond Mountains* or *Among Schoolchildren*, or Alec Wilkinson's *The Happiest Man in the World: An Account of the Life of Poppa Neutrino*. Novels featuring decidedly eccentric characters might also be suggested, including Douglas Coupland's *All Families Are Psychotic*, Kate Atkinson's *Emotionally Weird*, or Richard Russo's *Nobody's Fool*.

Lukas, J. Anthony

🏵 *Common Ground: A Turbulent Decade in the Lives of Three American Families.* Knopf. 1985. 659 pp. ISBN 9780394411507.

Lukas's classic volume tells the story of three families in Boston, spanning a decade in time from the mid-1970s to the mid-1980s: two working-class families, one headed by an African American mother and the other by an Irish American widow, and an upper-middle-class family. In addition to relating the details of their family lives and other community and interpersonal relationships, Lukas also puts their existences in context by examining the histories of their families; also discussed are a number of public officials and government figures prominent during the time.

> **Subjects:** 1970s, 1980s, Boston, Classics, Classism, Family Relationships, Massachusetts, Poverty, Race Relations

> **Awards:** National Book Award, Pulitzer Prize

> **Now Try:** William Finnegan's classic book *Cold New World* also showcased the hardships and lives of "typical" American families, as did Adrian Nicole LeBlanc's (more urban) *Random Family*. James McBrides's affecting Memoir *The Color of Water* might also be a good read-alike. Other books on classism

and society might be offered to these readers, including Barbara Ehrenreich's *Nickel and Dimed*, Joe Bageant's *Deer Hunting with Jesus*, the *New York Times* editorial collection *Class Matters*, or David Shipler's *The Working Poor*. Also of interest might be books about integration and other education issues, including Jonathan Kozol's *Savage Inequalities* or *Shame of the Nation*, Melba Pattillo Beals's *Warriors Don't Cry*, Tracy Kidder's *Among Schoolchildren*, or Alex Kotlowitz's *There Are No Children Here*.

Orlean, Susan

Saturday Night. Knopf. 1990. 258 pp. ISBN 9780394573366.

In this thoroughly amusing, if no longer strictly current (the book was first published in 1990) story, travel writer and intrepid journalist Orlean set out on a cross-country journey to answer one question: how do Americans spend their Saturday nights? The one night of the week not preceded or followed by work, Orlean argues, has always been a special proposition, and she treats it as such as she joins individuals for their coming-out parties, cruising the streets, watching television, babysitting, hosting society parties, going to church, dancing, and even committing crimes. Each chapter offers new characters, whom Orlean describes with a true eye for detail but with a surprising gentleness and attention to their preferred pastimes. In the process, she travels from Arizona to Indiana to Los Angeles to New York and also relates important aspects of her surroundings and these settings as well. Throughout the narrative, although she offers honest and thorough descriptions of those individuals she is profiling, she does not really divulge how she spends her own Saturday nights or how she feels personally about peoples' chosen leisure activities.

> **Subjects:** Hobbies, Humor, Recreation, Travel

> **Now Try:** Other offbeat Character Profile and Travel books might be offered to Orlean's readers; these include her later books *The Orchid Thief* and *The Bullfighter Checks Her Makeup*, Shari Caudron's *Who Are You People?*, and Jason Fagone's *Horsemen of the Esophagus*; Community Life nonfiction titles such as Michael Perry's *Population 485*, David Benjamin's *The Life and Times of the Last Kid Picked*, Bill Bryson's *The Life and Times of the Thunderbolt Kid*, or Michael Bamberger's *Wonderland: A Year in the Life of an American High School* might also make good read-alikes. An interesting twist on the "day" concept might be Craig Harline's micro-history *Sunday: A History of the First Day from Babylonia to the Super Bowl*, and a more scholarly take on community recreation opportunities, Robert Putnam's classic *Bowling Alone*, might also be offered.

Rosenbaum, Ron

Manhattan Passions: True Tales of Power, Wealth, and Excess. Beech Tree Books. 1987. 285 pp. ISBN 9780688066123.

Although dated in its selection of movers and shakers in the world of 1980s Manhattan, this is still a well-written collection of character profiles, and two decades later, many of the individuals and concepts discussed by Rosenbaum in his humorous and straightforward way continue to be as influential and valid as ever. Donald Trump, who is profiled here, is still a force in both the business world and popular culture, and Jerry Bruckheimer (another profilee) continues to be a force in moviemaking. Although it no longer qualifies as a work of current affairs, it nonetheless provides an entertaining read and, interestingly, valuable historical context for issues in our current society. The majority of these essays are written in an immediate, first-person style, with Rosenbaum interjecting many of his personal and very opinionated reactions to those notables with whom he is conversing (and typically sharing lunch). Rosenbaum's book is getting on in years, but now it's just as fun to read for social history as it is for the human interest stories.

> **Subjects:** Business, Celebrities and Superstars, Essays, New York City, Pop Culture, Society

> **Now Try:** Rosenbaum has written a number of other books, including *The Secret Parts of Fortune* (essays and short pieces), *The Shakespeare Wars*, and *Explaining Hitler*. A wide variety of Biographies might appeal to Rosenbaum's fans, particularly life stories about celebrities and superstars, such as Elizabeth Kolbert's *The Prophet of Love and Other Tales of Power and Deceit*, Bill Zehme's *The Way You Wear Your Hat: Frank Sinatra and the Lost Art of Livin'*, and *The Gay Talese Reader* by Gay Talese (which includes many character portraits). Writers who capture the feel of New York City might also appeal, such as Joseph Mitchell, Pete Hamill, Don DeLillo, Robert Sullivan, and Adam Gopnik; the essay collections of the very urbane Truman Capote, Phillip Lopate, and John Updike might also be considered.

Rufus, Anneli S.

Magnificent Corpses: Searching through Europe for St. Peter's Head, St. Claire's Heart, St. Stephen's Hand, and Other Saintly Relics. Marlowe. 1999. 245 pp. ISBN 9781569246870.

Part travelogue, part history, and all strange, the characters in Rufus's book stand out not only because they are dead but also because parts of their mortal remains are displayed in cathedrals and other shrines through Europe: the author's journey centered on investigating relics of saints in the Roman Catholic churches at sites from Germany and Italy to Denmark and Great Britain. Although not a Catholic herself, Rufus relates her early fascination with the often graphic stories and legends of Roman Catholic saints, and her tour includes many quiet moments of wondering not only about the people whose remains she is visiting but also about the many pilgrims and other religiously motivated tourists she meets along the way. Although the book also features many unusual and exotic locations, Rufus does not dwell so much on the geography or her travels as she does on the saints, their lives, and the lives of those who have collected, displayed, and believed in the power of the relics.

> **Subjects:** Catholicism, Christianity, Europe, Humor, Religion, Saints, Travel, World History

> **Now Try:** Rufus is also the author of *Party of One: A Loner's Manifesto*, in which she explains her own character (and her desire not to be around others) quite clearly and with great prose style. Other slightly offbeat Investigative and Travel books might also be offered to these readers, including Mary Roach's *Stiff: The Curious Lives of Human Cadavers* and *Spook*; Jessica Mitford's *The American Way of Death Revisited* or Lisa Takeuchi Cullen's *Remember Me*, Paul Bibeau's *Sundays with Vlad*, Dea Birkett's *Serpent In Paradise*, Bruce Chatwin's *The Songlines*, or Gretel Ehrlich's *This Cold Heaven*. Offbeat fiction titles by such authors as Magnus Mills, Craig Ferguson, and Matt Ruff might also be suggested.

Seierstad, Åsne

With Their Backs to the World: Portraits from Serbia. Basic Books. 2005. 340 pp. ISBN 9780465076024.

From 1999 through 2004, journalist Seierstad traveled extensively through Serbia to record the reactions of the country's residents to Slobodan Milosevic's regime and eventual downfall. In this narrative, she tells the stories of thirteen "ordinary" Serbian people, including a television personality, a currency buyer and seller, an Orthodox church deacon, a magazine journalist, a war criminal's wife, Serbian refugees from Kosovo, and the mayor of the city of Nis. In telling these very personal stories, Seierstad paints a cohesive picture of the different individuals trying to forge a new path for a region with a troubled and divisive path. Its tone is perhaps best shown in the words of a song included by the author: "Who says, who lies Serbia is small? Who says, who lies that the planet is small?"

Subjects: Books in Translation, Croatia, European History, Government, Kosovo, Multicultural Issues, Oral Histories, Politics, Serbia, Society, War Reporting

Now Try: Seierstad is a dedicated recorder of people's personal stories; her earlier book *The Bookseller of Kabul* is also a compelling read. Other books in translation, documenting the world's tragedies, might also appeal to these readers, including Svetlana Alexievich's *Voices from Chernobyl*, Jean Hatzfeld's *Machete Season* and *Life Laid Bare*, and Anna Politkovskaya's *A Russian Diary: A Journalist's Final Account of Life, Corruption, and Death in Putin's Russia*. Other books about individuals struggling to live their lives in war-torn and troubled regions, including Greg Mortensen's *Three Cups of Tea*, Azar Nafisi's *Reading Lolita in Tehran*, and Melissa Fay Greene's *There Is No Me without You*, might be offered, as might books about Serbia and Croatia and the history of the region, including Samantha Power's *A Problem from Hell: America and the Age of Genocide* or even Rebecca West's classic travelogue *Black Lamb and Grey Falcon*.

Singer, Mark

Character Studies: Encounters with the Curiously Obsessed. Houghton Mifflin. 2005. 256 pp. ISBN 9780618197255.

Singer, a staff writer with *The New Yorker*, offers a variety of character profiles in the best tradition of offering the personal and telling details that make celebrities and personalities true individuals (Singer believes that journalists primarily engage in "sublimated voyeurism"). Among the individuals described here are Ricky Jay, a sleight-of-hand artist; Donald Trump; author Joseph Mitchell; Michael Zinman, a rare book dealer; and Martin Scorsese.

Subjects: Celebrities and Superstars, Eccentrics, Essays, Humor, Travel

Now Try: Singer's earlier books *Somewhere in America: Under the Radar with Chicken Warriors, Left-Wing Patriots, Angry Nudists, and Others* and *Mr. Personality* might also be enjoyed by these readers. One of the individuals profiled here, Joseph Mitchell, was a *New Yorker* writer and institution in his own right; his collection *Up in the Old Hotel* might appeal to these readers. Books by other authors who excel at character profiling, including Gay Talese, Charlie LeDuff, Susan Orlean, Chuck Klosterman, and Bill Zehme, might also be suggested. Also of interest might be Travel books, including those by Calvin Trillin, Hank Stuever, Geoff Dyer, and Jon Ronson, and essay collections by writers such as Joseph Epstein, Hampton Sides, or Phillip Lopate.

Weschler, Lawrence

Calamities of Exile: Three Nonfiction Novellas. University of Chicago Press. 1998. 199 pp. ISBN 9780226893938.

Weschler tells the stories of three very different expatriates: Kanan Makiya, an exile from Iraq who would publish the book *Republic of Fear* about the dictatorial reign of Saddam Hussein; Jan Kavan, a student activist in the Prague Spring of 1968, who would operate the Czech underground for decades, only to be accused of colluding with Communists when he returned to the country in the 1990s; and Breyten Breytenbach, whose art and poetry raised worldwide awareness of the evils of apartheid but which he came to feel were an inadequate response to the politics of South Africa. Although accessibly written, this is a complex work centering on many detailed and less widely studied aspects of global history; however, those readers interested in foreign affairs and history might find much to enjoy in these three very personal reactions to totalitarian regimes, as well as insight into the experience of the expatriate's life and struggles.

> **Subjects:** Apartheid, Czechoslovakia, Government, Saddam Hussein, Iraq, Small Press, South Africa, World History
>
> **Now Try:** Fans of Weschler's writing might consider his other books, *A Wanderer in the Perfect City*, *Mr. Wilson's Cabinet of Wonders*, or *Everything That Rises: A Book of Convergences*. He also has a dedicated following of readers; they may be more eclectic in their tastes and might consider other authors such as William Vollmann, Pico Iyer, William Finnegan, or even fiction by literary stylists Don DeLillo or Thomas Pynchon.

Fiction Read-Alikes

- **Bank, Melissa.** Bank has not been a prolific novelist, but her books, in which she tells the stories of characters she seems to know so well they're almost real, might particularly appeal to readers of character profiles; they include the classic (some argue it is among the first of the "chick lit" titles, but Bank disagrees with that assessment) *The Girl's Guide to Hunting and Fishing* and *The Wonder Spot*.

- **Byatt, A. S.** Byatt's novels are definitely character-driven, and in addition to telling their stories, she also carefully illustrates their inner lives and thoughts. In her most well-known books, including *Possession*, *The Biographer's Tale*, and *The Matisse Stories*, she particularly displays an insider's eye for detail in her stories about scholarly and artistic studies and pursuits.

- **Ciresi, Rita.** Ciresi's enjoyable and surprisingly nuanced novels particularly feature the thoughts and actions of characters as they relate to others and their relationships; her titles include *Blue Italian*, *Pink Slip*, and *Sometimes I Dream in Italian*.

- **Doyle, Roddy.** Doyle also tells character-driven stories, particularly ones featuring eccentric and personable characters, many of whom are connected by family, work, or larger community ties. Readers may particularly want to start with his Barrytown Trilogy, set in Dublin: *The*

Commitments, *The Snapper*, and *The Van* (all of which have also been made into spectacular feature films). Also of interest might be *Paddy Clarke, Ha-Ha-Ha* and *The Woman Who Walked into Doors* (as well as its sequel, *Paula Spencer: A Novel*).

- **Ford, Richard.** Many descriptions of Ford's Frank Bascombe novels include phrases that should appeal to readers of character-driven nonfiction and fiction; Bascombe has been described as an "everyman," while other reviewers have spoken favorably of Ford's ability to credibly display the interior world of his main character, as well as to explore all his relationships, in the titles *The Sportswriter*, *Independence Day*, and *The Lay of the Land*.

- **Haddon, Mark.** Haddon's main characters are eccentric but very sympathetically drawn; his protagonist in *The Curious Incident of the Dog in the Night-Time* is an autistic teenager; in *A Spot of Bother*, he tells the story of sixty-one-year-old George Hall and his interactions with his other family members.

- **Hornby, Nick.** Even when they're not all that likable, British author Hornby's novels all offer memorable characters, including music fanatic Rob in *High Fidelity*; Will Freeman, who pretends to be a single father to hook up with single mothers in *About a Boy*; and married couple Katie and David Carr in *How to Be Good*.

- **Kingsolver, Barbara.** Kingsolver has a talent for developing characters who reveal more by what they don't say than what they do; such as the Cherokee child Turtle who rarely speaks in her novels *The Bean Trees* and its sequel *Pigs in Heaven*; also of interest might be her popular titles *The Poisonwood Bible* and *Prodigal Summer*.

- **Lawson, Mary.** Canadian author Lawson has won numerous literary prizes, and reviewers have often commented on her skill at characterization in her novels *Crow Lake* and *The Other Side of the Bridge*.

- **Miller, Sue.** Miller not only offers strong (often female) characters in her novels but also addresses the larger questions of how identities are formed and questions of self are answered; her novels that might appeal to these readers include *The Good Mother*, *Family Pictures*, *While I Was Gone*, and *The Senator's Wife*.

- **Salinger, J. D.** Salinger has taken exploring the lives of his characters to extremes; many of his novels and stories feature tales of the brilliant, thoughtful, and eccentric members of the Glass family: they pop up in *Nine Stories*, and are the main characters in *Franny and Zooey*, *Raise High the Roof Beam, Carpenters*, and *Seymour: An Introduction*. *The Catcher in the Rye*, featuring one of the most well-known characters in American literature, Holden Caulfield, might also appeal.

- **Tyler, Anne.** The pace of storytelling in Tyler's novels is leisurely, but her skill at developing realistically flawed but still sympathetic characters is unparalleled. Readers who enjoy Character Profiles might enjoy her novels *Dinner at the Homesick Restaurant*, *The Accidental Tourist*, *Breathing Lessons*, *Saint Maybe*, or *Digging to America*.

- **Whitehead, Colson.** Whitehead's quirky literary fiction might primarily appeal for his stylistic skill, but he also portrays unique characters; his books include *John Henry Days* (in which one of the characters is a freelance journalist), *The Intuitionist*, and *Apex Hides the Hurt*.

Further Reading

Glass, Ira. 2007. *The New Kings of Nonfiction*. New York: Riverhead Books.

Walls, Jeannette. 2000. *Dish: The Inside Story on the World of Gossip*. New York: Spike.

References

Boynton, Robert, ed. 2005. *The New New Journalism: Conversations with America's Best Nonfiction Writers on Their Craft*. New York: Vintage Books.

Butler, Kiera. 2006. "Other Voices." *Columbia Journalism Review* (July/August): 28–32.

1

2

3

4

5

6

Chapter **5**

Political Reporting

Definition of Political Reporting

It is true, just as it is with Business Reporting, that the genre of Political Reporting can be viewed as cohesive primarily because of the subject matter of politics. But to assume that all works of Political Reporting are the same, ideologically or stylistically, would be to badly fail many dedicated readers of these titles. If you don't believe me, just try offering a book by Ann Coulter to a Michael Moore fan, or a work of straight-up and opinionated Political Commentary to a reader who is more interested in broader Politics in Practice titles.

Political Reporting, like the In-Depth Reporting, Exposés, and Business Reporting subgenres, also has a strong historical tradition. As noted in previous chapters, the American press grew up reporting news of politics and the government, and often did so without any kind of "objectivity." Particularly during what journalism historians refer to as the "dark ages" of the American newspaper, 1789 to 1808, the debates between Federalists and Republicans about the power a central government should have in a democracy were largely reported in openly partisan papers and news reporting. Centuries have passed and the tradition has changed, with modern journalists often striving not to reveal their own inclinations in their writing, but the fact remains that people are interested in all aspects of politics: ideological debates, the process of elections and lawmaking, and the personalities and politicians making the news. This is where Political Reporting comes in.

Political Reporting can be written by media and political pundits, in which case it tends to fall into the category of what I call Political Commentary (either on the right or on the left). These titles, like their eighteenth-century counterparts, clearly align with a party or an ideology; although they are often researched and include aspects of other investigative works, including interviews and firsthand observations, they also tend to be the most bombastic and inflammatory in tone. Other Political Reporting books, written by authors with less name recognition but more journalistic dedication (and whom often consider one particular issue or related group of issues in their titles), can be considered to be Hot-Button Issues titles; another field of titles, more focused on the processes of politics and edging more toward political science or government as a subject (as opposed to "politics") can be thought of as Politics in Practice titles and are the most understated in tone (as well as, typically, the least story-driven). A great many politicians also tend to write their own memoirs and books (although many employ cowriters or ghostwriters), and they also attract other authors to write about them; these books can be found in the Politicos subgenre. Another category of such books can be thought of as the "campaign books," which are proclaimed to be written by candidates for office (again, they usually employ help) and are rushed through publication in time to support election cycles, are always available but have not been included here because they tend to age the most quickly and can be easily found under their authors' names.

Political reporting titles are often referred to as "current affairs" books and revolve around politics and those individuals with political power. They can be written either by media pundits and commentators, in which case they are typically produced in response to current political events; they may also be written by political scientists and journalists, who produce solid works of reporting and history. Although the works of reportage tend to stand the test of time better than do the commentary titles, all of them have more backlist appeal than the flattering (or scathing) political autobiographies and vanity books that are typically published every election cycle.

Appeal of Political Reporting

There can be no escaping the fact that readers who enjoy Political Reporting are most likely driven by their desires to engage with the world and to learn more about political subjects, debates, and people. The ubiquitous nature of news programs, political commentary online and in the media, and cable news and political opinion programs (especially during 2008 and other election years) indicates that many people are interested in these subjects and may consider a wide variety of these titles for their informational and recreational reading.

Outside of the informational and subject-driven component, the subgenres of Political Reporting offer a variety of different experiences for readers to enjoy. Those readers most invested in their political opinions and who are looking for a bit of bolstering or confirming of their opinions might particularly enjoy works of Political Commentary (on the right or left, depending on their political orientation, although it should be noted that not everyone with deeply held political beliefs falls easily into one of those two camps); I tend to think of these as the "comfort reading" of a political sort. It is no jibe at Ann Coulter or Michael Moore that they each have dedicated fan bases and that they write with those fans very clearly in mind. Readers' advisors may not have a lot of success suggesting other works of political science to these readers, but they might be able to interest a Coulter fan in similar books by authors such as Laura Ingraham or Glenn Beck. In that respect, advisors may want to become knowledgeable in the biggest "names" on both the right and the left so that they are prepared to offer alternatives when the latest bestseller by the biggest name is checked out or has a waiting list.

I once heard it suggested in a readers' advisory seminar that some advisors tried to present books from both sides of the political spectrum to their patrons, in the belief that maybe they could get them to try something new or read a differing viewpoint. I'm not really one to critique whatever individual advisors use as their own personal techniques, but I must say that I can't imagine that being a popular strategy with readers of Political Commentary on either the right or the left (or even, to some extent, by more "libertarian" authors, such as Lou Dobbs or Jack McCafferty). A large part of the appeal of these titles is the assurance their readers will find that their worldview is the correct one. Again, that is not to say these are poorly written books; many of them cover topics of sufficient complexity that their readers must be well versed in politics and cultural knowledge to enjoy them. It simply means that these readers may be more drawn to complete one author's entire catalog, or to other similar authors in the same category, for recreational reading, the way some readers enjoy romance novels or have hardcore genre and subgenre loyalties (some Urban Fantasy readers, for example, might never consider Sword and Sorcery titles, although both subgenres are part of the larger Fantasy and Speculative fiction camps). For those Political Commentary readers who are interested in exploring the opposite viewpoint (to better understand the "enemy camp," so to speak), I have listed four or five of the most representative Commentary titles at the ends of both the Right and Left subgenres. These suggestions are provided as a starting point for readers' advisors who may not read widely in the genre but who are working with readers who want to see the most influential titles from the other side of the political divide.

Hot-Button Issues books, while still subjective, are less easy to categorize according to broad ideological or political party lines and may appeal to readers with less partisan reading interests, whereas Politics in Practice books might appeal particularly to nonfiction readers who are more interested in the actual workings of democratic government, as well as culture and history. Politics in Practice books in particular tend to be the least narrative or story-driven of all these titles, but they make up for the less obvious story line with more rigorous reporting and source documentation, which can be of comfort to many nonfiction readers who enjoy pursuing their reading interests by perusing source notes and bibliographies and seeking out titles they find there (and these readers do exist; just because they tend to be self-sufficient at locating their own books doesn't mean they won't eventually ask for your assistance or suggestions regarding other titles). Politicos titles, finally, bring us back into the realm of more stereotypical appeal factors, with their focus on character and on the life and career stories of figures in the political news, as well as their very personal viewpoints, immediate writing style, and often compelling story lines.

Organization of the Chapter

The Political Reporting books most recognizable to readers and readers' advisors, *Political Commentary*, open the chapter because they tend to be the most popular with readers and learning their authors' names might be of real use to anyone working a public library reference desk. Although I have labeled and organized them as "Right" or "Left" (or conservative and liberal, red or blue, or Republican and Democrat, however you'd like to think of these categories), it should be noted that not all readers align perfectly along those party lines. For those readers whose politics or inclinations might be described as "less obviously aligned," the third subgenre, **Hot-Button Issues**, might be a worthy category to explore because their authors tend to be similar in career choice (many of them well-known political journalists or other media pundits), and their books share a brisk, opinionated writing style similar to that of their counterparts in the **Political Commentary** categories. Books written by more independent journalists or authors with specific research interest follow those categories, in the **Politics in Practice** subgenre; these are the titles you may wish to look into for your self-avowed "political junky" readers, who tend to be more enthralled with the nitty-gritty workings of politics, and democracy in particular, than they are with particular parties or pundits. The final subgenre, **Politicos**, offers books written primarily by politicians and political insiders, combining the nonfiction appeal factor of subject and the broader appeal factor of character.

Political Commentary

Right

It is not as easy to define political writing from the right, or conservative, side of the political spectrum as the uninitiated might think. As with any other belief system or ideological position, the American conservative tradition encompasses many sub-classes of "isms." The complexity of the matter is admirably summed up in the introduction to Chilton Williamson Jr.'s anthology *The Conservative Bookshelf: Essential Works That Impact Today's Conservative Thinkers*: "among those who call themselves conservatives, there is substantial agreement as to what, exactly, the conservative tradition amounts to and what 'conservatism' actually *is* … a 'conservative' seeks to conserve what exists in the present, while a 'Rightist' is prepared to dismantle contemporary institutions in order to replace them with ancient ones resurrected from the past" (Williamson 2004, xiv). From there he goes on to discuss the many and minute differences between monarchists, the Catholic Rightists, paleoconservatives, nationalists, and neoconservatives; but for the most part, such distinctions are beyond the scope of this merest of introductions. Suffice it to say that there is more to the literature of the right (or the conservative) than simply announcing that these authors and all of their readers reside only in red states, although Williamson does also admit that the Republican Party is the present embodiment of this politics in the United States.

It is also probably safe to define these books as the polar opposite, in subject and belief system, of their counterparts in the Political Commentary—Left section that follows (and vice versa). These titles fall under the Investigative Writing stylistic umbrella primarily because their authors are typically journalists or media commentators of some kind, although they are not often "reporters" in the sense of the word as it used in other chapters in this book. For the most part, these authors have a worldview, and they write books to prove, support, and evangelize it, as opposed to other reporters and authors who, if not completely objective, at least reserve their judgments in writing until after they have researched and observed the subjects on which they are writing. This is not to say that these titles are shoddily researched or poorly written; many of them are best sellers because they do provide compelling statistics, examples, and interviews, as well as skillful (some might say "slick") and persuasive writing.

When providing advisory assistance to readers who enjoy these authors, it is always important to keep in mind the appeal of the authors and to make sure their catalog is exhausted, in addition to finding new authors (a reader who has found and enjoyed Ann Coulter's latest, for instance, may not be aware of her many previous titles); it may also be instructive to become familiar with magazines and publishers who publish authors with similar opinions (valuable sources include the magazine William F. Buckley, Jr.'s *National Review* and *The Weekly Standard*, edited by Bill Kristol, as well as the Regnery Publishing Web site). These readers may also enjoy books from the Politics in Practice and Politicos subgenres, although that will very much depend on who the political personality in question is (err on the side of Ronald Reagan, less so Madeleine Albright). Books from the Exposés chapter, particularly those highlighting government wrongdoing or mistakes (because the tradition in conservatism is to promote smaller, not larger, government) might also be suggested. These readers might also consider a wide variety of History nonfiction titles, particularly those focusing on American history subjects or offering stirring historical Biographies of the founding fathers (of which there are many; that has always been a popular biographical category). Above all (and this goes for the Political Commentary—Left titles as well), when working with readers who enjoy these books it may be helpful to remember Joyce Saricks's guiding principle to think nonjudgmentally about titles these readers enjoy.

Often written by popular political commentators and media hosts, Political Commentary—Right books feature strong opinions, even stronger language, and a focus on the conservative belief system of their authors. They do not typically feature as much research as most Investigative Writing books (they rarely include references, notes, or indexes) and are also light on interview material. They are quick reads, written in a punchy and clever style to be consumed as quickly as possible, largely by readers who agree wholeheartedly with the authors' political stances on the right side of the American political spectrum.

Beck, Glenn, and Kevin Balfe

An Inconvenient Book: Real Solutions to the World's Biggest Problems. Threshold Books. 2007. 295 pp. ISBN 9781416552192.

CNN Headline News television show host and conservative radio commentator Beck offers his take on the biggest problems in America today, including a surplus of political correctness, economic troubles, illegal immigration, and a variety of other current affairs issues. Beck also takes issue with such treatises as those by Al Gore (whose title *An Inconvenient Truth* provided the satirical title for this volume) and other political liberals.

Subjects: Government, Humor, Mass Media, Politics, Society

Now Try: Fans of Beck's conservative viewpoint might also consider other blockbuster best sellers from his conservative commentary colleagues, including Laura Ingraham's *Power to the People*, Ann Coulter's *Godless: The Church of Liberalism*, Mark Steyn's *America Alone: The End of the World As We Know It*, Bill O'Reilly's *Culture Warrior*, or John Stossel's *Myths, Lies, and Downright Stupidity: Get Out the Shovel—Why Everything You Know Is Wrong*.

Brooks, David R.

On Paradise Drive: How We Live Now (and Always Have) in the Future Tense. Simon & Schuster. 2004. 304 pp. ISBN 9780743227384.

Cultural and social historian Brooks sets out to investigate three related tenets of life in America in the early twenty-first century: what life is really like in middle- and upper-middle-class neighborhoods, why Americans continue to strive and move so restlessly in the pursuit of a bit more wealth and security, and whether Americans are truly as shallow as is sometimes charged in other countries and cultures. Creating such definitions as Cosmic Blondes and Brunettes, Brooks eventually concludes that Americans are an imaginative people ideally suited to lifestyles that are changing more rapidly than ever before in human history.

Subjects: Classism, Economics, Family Relationships, Making Sense . . ., Politics, Society

Now Try: Brooks's earlier classic, *Bobos in Paradise* (annotated in the Business Reporting chapter) might also be suggested, as might other titles he himself suggests in this book: Gregg Easterbrook's *The Progress Paradox*, Robert Putnam's *Bowling Alone*, or Graham Greene's novel *The Quiet American*. Robert Frank's investigative *Richistan* or his more economically motivated *Falling Behind* might be suggested, as might Peter Bernstein's and Annalyn Swan's *All the Money in the World: How the Forbes 400 Make—and Spend—Their Fortunes*.

Buckley, William F., Jr.

God and Man at Yale. Regnery. 1951. 240 pp. ISBN 9780895266972.

Founder of the conservative magazine *National Review*, Buckley's influence on American conservative thought in the twentieth century is such that any of his many nonfiction titles might well be offered to readers who enjoy political works on the right side of the spectrum. In this title, his first published nonfiction book, Buckley railed against the liberal academics at Yale, his own alma mater; among his charges, he asserted that the school's acceptance of atheism, collectivism, and the stifling political atmosphere that would brook no dissent had made his experiences there unpleasant and detrimental to his education.

Subjects: Classics, Conservatism, Education, Memoirs, Politics, Yale University

Now Try: Buckley is nothing if not prolific; in addition to political volumes such as this one and *Rumbles Left and Right* and *Happy Days Were Here Again*, he has also written autobiographies (*Cruising Speed, Overdrive, Nearer, My God to Thee: An Autobiography of Faith* and *Miles Gone By: A Literary Autobiography*), collections from the pages of *National Review* (*In Search of Anti-Semitism* and the letters collection *Cancel Your Own Goddamn Subscription: Notes and Asides from National Review*) and novels (including the Blackford Oakes, CIA agent series, starting with *Saving the Queen* in 1976). His son Christopher Buckley also writes satirical novels which may appeal to his father's readers.

Coulter, Ann

Godless: The Church of Liberalism. Crown Forum. 2006. 310 pp. ISBN 9781400054206.

1

> Political commentator Coulter offers another no-holds-barred narrative on what she terms the "Church of Liberalism," the many beliefs of which include abortion, evolution, such prophets as Alger Hiss and Cindy Sheehan, and its disdain for a Judeo-Christian ethic.

> > **Subjects:** Conservatism, Government, Liberalism, Mass Media, Politics, Religion, Society

> > **Now Try:** Coulter's writing is fast-paced and opinionated; fans of her many works might enjoy treatises from other conservative political pundits including Bill O'Reilly (*Culture Warrior*), John Stossel (*Myths, Lies, and Downright Stupidity*), Michael Savage (*The Political Zoo*), Michael Smerconish (*Muzzled*), and Rush Limbaugh (*The Way Things Ought to Be*). They might also enjoy books that explore topics of media and politics, including *100 People Who Are Screwing Up America* by Bernard Goldberg, as well as conservative presidential biographies including Doro Bush Koch's *My Father, My President*, and *President Reagan: The Triumph of Imagination* by Richard Reeves.

2

3

Coulter, Ann

If Democrats Had Any Brains, They'd Be Republicans: Ann Coulter at Her Best, Funniest, and Most Outrageous. Crown Forum. 2007. 274 pp. ISBN 9780307353450.

> Conservative media commentator Ann Coulter is known for saying exactly what is on her mind, and this volume comprises her most outrageous and pointedly inflammatory quotations and opinions on political and cultural subjects, including Democrats, Republicans, Ronald Reagan, liberal social policies, evolution, religion, terrorism, the media, dating and personal life, abortion, economics, Islam, gun control, Bill and Hillary Clinton, and the environment (among many others).

4

> > **Subjects:** Government, Mass Media, Politics, Quick Reads, Society

> > **Now Try:** Coulter's readers might enjoy nonfiction titles from a wide variety of other well-known conservative political commentators, including Laura Ingraham's *Power to the People* or *Shut Up & Sing: How Elites from Hollywood, Politics, and the UN Are Subverting America*, Dick Morris's *Outrage!* or *Rewriting History* (about the political career of Hillary Clinton), and Mark Steyn's *America Alone: The End of the World As We Know It*.

5

D'Souza, Dinesh

6

The Enemy at Home: The Cultural Left and Its Responsibility for 9/11. Doubleday. 2007. 333 pp. ISBN 9780385510127.

> D'Souza passionately argues in this manifesto that the blame for the terrorist attacks of 9/11 rests squarely on the shoulders of American liberals, who, in their quest to undermine the rights of the patriarchal family, agitate for gay marriage rights, and pursue a feminist agenda, directly attacked many traditional Islamic values and tacitly encouraged the attacks. He particularly singles out figures in both the liberal intelligentsia and

pop culture for criticism, including Noam Chomsky, Hillary Clinton, Eve Ensler, and Britney Spears.

Subjects: 9/11, Islam, Politics, Religion, Society, Terrorism

Now Try: D'Souza, a fellow at the Hoover Institution and prominent conservative author, has written prolifically on political topics, and his other books might be offered, including *The End of Racism*, *What's So Great about America*, and *Ronald Reagan: How an Ordinary Man Became an Extraordinary Leader*. His readers might also consider books by other outspoken political commentators such as Mark Steyn (*America Alone*), or by other fellows of the Hoover Institution, like Thomas Sowell (*Economic Facts and Fallacies*) or Niall Ferguson (*Colossus: The Rise and Fall of the American Empire*).

Frum, David

Comeback: Conservatism That Can Win Again. Doubleday. 2008. 213 pp. ISBN 9780385515337.

From the author of the 1995 conservative manifesto *Dead Right*, this book offers Frum's take on the controversial presidency of George W. Bush and suggests ways that the conservative faction of the Republican Party can forge its status as a truly compassionate force by promoting nuclear energy over oil dependence, addressing prison reform, enforcing stricter ethical standards, creating a comprehensive immigration policy, and restoring traditional family and social values.

Subjects: George W. Bush, Conservatism, Government, Political Science, Politics, Society

Now Try: Other books by very dedicated conservative writers and theorists might also be offered, including those by William F. Buckley, Jr., Mark Steyn, Robert Spencer, and Dinesh D'Souza. Autobiographies and biographies of conservative thinkers might also be suggested, including Clarence Thomas's *My Grandfather's Son*, Dinesh D'Souza's *Ronald Reagan: How an Ordinary Man Became an Extraordinary Leader*, Karen DeYoung's *Soldier: The Life of Colin Powell*, Patrick Buchanan's *Right from the Beginning*, or Bill Sammon's *Misunderestimated: The President Battles Terrorism, Media Bias, and the Bush Haters*.

Gingrich, Newt, Vince Haley, and Rick Tyler

Real Change: From the World That Fails to the World That Works. Regnery. 2008. 310 pp. ISBN 9781596980532.

Former Speaker of the House of Representatives (during the latter half of the 1990s) Gingrich holds forth on what he feels is the artificial division of America into red and blue states, based solely on their voting patterns. Taking the stance that Democrats can't change and Republicans won't, based on his experiences as both a political power player and one of the Republican Party's most infamous members, Gingrich instead suggests that all Americans should focus instead on affecting change on issues that the populace has indicated in surveys that it cares about: immigration, taxes, and the freedom of religion.

Subjects: Government, Politics, Religion, Society

Now Try: Gingrich is advocating a change in readers' attitudes toward governance and politics, but he still offers a conservative and Republican viewpoint; other authors who may appeal to his readers include Ann Coulter (*Godless*), Laura Ingraham (*Power to the People*), Eileen McGann (*Outrage*), and Bill O'Reilly (*Culture Warrior*). He also devotes part of his manifesto to the importance of religion and freedom of religion; other self-help books on the subject might appeal, such as Joel Osteen's *Become a Better You* or fiction by such authors as Bodie and Brock Thoene, Frank E. Peretti, or Tim LaHaye and Jerry Jenkins.

Goldberg, Bernard

100 People Who Are Screwing Up America: And Al Franken Is #37. HarperCollins. 2005. 305 pp. ISBN 9780060761288.

Media pundit Goldberg provides his list of 100 people who are "screwing up America," with various offenses against morality and integrity. Written in short chapters, each headed up with the name of an offender (included are Michael Jackson, Michael Moore, Al Franken, Howard Dean, and David Duke), Goldberg offers short and witty opinion pieces on the wrongdoing of each person on his list.

> **Subjects:** Character Profiles, Mass Media, Politics, Society

> **Now Try:** Bernard Goldberg has long been opposed to what he considers the liberal bias in America's mass media; fans of this title might consider his earlier books, *Arrogance: Rescuing America from the Media Elite* and *Bias: A CBS Insider Exposes How the Media Distort the News*. Other partisan titles such as *Do as I Say (Not as I Do)* by Peter Schweizer might appeal, as might titles by other popular media figures, such as Ann Coulter's *Godless: The Church of Liberalism*, Michelle Malkin's *Unhinged: Exposing Liberals Gone Wild*, John Stossel's *Give Me a Break!*, or even Jack Cafferty's slightly more centrist *It's Getting Ugly Out There: The Frauds, Bunglers, Liars, and Losers Who Are Hurting America*.

Goldberg, Jonah

Liberal Fascism: The Secret History of the American Left, from Mussolini to the Politics of Meaning. Doubleday. 2007. 487 pp. ISBN 9780385511841.

Goldberg, a columnist for the conservative magazine *National Review*, provides a history of the liberal and progressive movements in the United States and draws parallels between politicians on the left (including Hillary Clinton, FDR, and Woodrow Wilson) and the National Socialism of Nazi Germany and the fascism of Mussolini's Italy. With sharp and persuasive writing, this book is designed to raise controversy, particularly on what constitutes a "fascist" point of view (Goldberg points out that the Nazis believed in free health care) and in Goldberg's comparisons of such "progressives" as W. E. B. Du Bois, John Dewey, and the many liberals in modern-day Hollywood with historical figures as Hitler, Mussolini, Himmler, and many others.

> **Subjects:** Fascism, Government, Politics, Socialism, Society, World History

> **Now Try:** Goldberg's book (particularly the eye-catching cover, featuring a smiley face wearing a mustache similar to Hitler's) is clearly meant to incite interest, discussion, and argument. Other plain-speaking conservative writers including David Frum, the more intellectual Theodore Dalrymple, Ann Coulter, Bill Sammon, Michael Savage, George Weigel, Kenneth Timmerman, or Peggy Noonan might all appeal to these readers. New perspective history books, particularly by historians with more conservative angles, might also be suggested, including Amity Shlaes's *The Forgotten Man: A New History of the Great Depression*, M. Stanton Evans's *Blacklisted by History: The Untold*

Story of Senator Joe McCarthy and His Fight against America's Enemies, or John Earl Haynes's *In Denial: Historians, Communism, and Espionage.*

Ingraham, Laura

Power to the People. Regnery. 2007. 372 pp. ISBN 9781596985162.

Conservative talk radio host Ingraham offers anecdotes explaining how ordinary people are becoming fed up with government, educational, and cultural forces over which they feel they have no control and suggests a variety of actions and solutions being undertaken by people throughout the nation to embrace and further more traditional and conservative agendas. She also tells the story of her own battle with breast cancer, and how it strengthened her own faith and resolve.

Subjects: Government, Health Issues, Mass Media, Politics, Religion

Now Try: Ingraham's readers might consider other (largely) conservative authors, including Ann Coulter (*If Democrats Had Any Brains, They'd Be Republicans*), Dick Morris (*Outrage!*), Pat Buchanan (*State of Emergency*), Bernard Goldberg (*100 People Who Are Screwing Up America*), John Stossel (*Myths, Lies, and Downright Stupidity*), or Mark Steyn (*America Alone: The End of the World as We Know It*).

Kupelian, David

The Marketing of Evil: How Radicals, Elitists, and Pseudo-Experts Sell Us Corruption Disguised as Freedom. WND Books. 2005. 256 pp. ISBN 9781581824599.

Kupelian argues that in our current society, the idea of "consensuality" has supplanted previously held cultural and interpersonal ideas of right and wrong; in this book, he names numerous issues including easy access to divorce, legalized abortion, and gay rights as being marketed to the nation by corrupt individuals, corporations, the liberal media, the government, and the public school system (among others). Although Kupelian does cite research studies and statistics, the writing is accessible, and the author stridently makes his case for a return to and respect for Judeo-Christian ethics.

Subjects: Christianity, Marketing, Politics, Religion, Society

Now Try: Authors who blurbed this title include Michelle Malkin and Laura Schlessinger; their books *Unhinged: Exposing Liberals Gone Wild* and *The Proper Care and Feeding of Husbands* (respectively) might appeal to these readers. Other authors who write about conservative values and society include Patrick Buchanan (*State of Emergency: The Third World Invasion and Conquest of America*), Laura Ingraham (*Power to the People*), or Joseph Farah (*Taking America Back: A Radical Plan to Revive Freedom, Morality, and Justice*).

Lott, John R.

Freedomnomics: Why the Free Market Works and Other Half-Baked Theories Don't. Regnery. 2007. 275 pp. ISBN 9781596985063.

Author Lott seeks to provide a more conservative response to the popular economics best-seller *Freakonomics*; although his book is different in style than that book, he also seeks to explain cause-and-effect relationships through case studies, examples, and statistics and numbers, suggesting such relationships as lower crime rates being caused in part by the continuing use of the death penalty. This is more a work of economic than political theory, as Lott refers often to Adam Smith's historical ideas that individuals could enrich society by pursuing their own self-interest; however, he does often relate his arguments to political subjects and topics.

> **Subjects:** Business, Economics, Government, Politics

> **Now Try:** A wide variety of conservative political books by authors such as Michael Savage and Laura Ingraham might be offered (as might Lott's previous title, *More Guns, Less Crime*); other options are business and economics books touting the advances of the free market system, such as P. J. O'Rourke's *On the Wealth of Nations* (about Adam Smith's economics classic *The Wealth of Nations*), Thomas Friedman's *The Lexus and the Olive Tree*, Friedrich von Hayek's classic *The Road to Serfdom*, Thomas Sowell's *Economic Facts and Fallacies*, or Daniel Gross's *Pop! Why Bubbles Are Great for the Economy*. Other economics titles from Regnery might also be suggested, such as Robert Murphy's *The Politically Incorrect Guide to Capitalism*.

Podhoretz, Norman

World War IV: The Long Struggle against Islamofascism. Doubleday. 2007. 230 pp. ISBN 9780385522212.

> Podhoretz, who was editor-in-chief of the political and cultural magazine *Commentary* for thirty-five years, offers his thoughts on why what he terms "Islamofascism" must be suppressed across the globe. Positing that leaders such as the Ayatollah Khomeini and Saddam Hussein and terrorists such as Osama bin Laden are dedicated to the destruction of freedoms taken for granted in America, Podhoretz makes the claim that the current wars in Iraq and Afghanistan are every bit as important as the twentieth century's world wars and the Cold War and that the "Bush Doctrine" of preemptive war is necessary to win the current war of ideas and ideals.

> **Subjects:** 9/11, Afghanistan, George W. Bush, Conservatism, Government, Iraq, Iraq War (2003), Politics

> **Now Try:** Podhoretz has long been a leading voice on the political right; his fans might consider his earlier books, *The Prophets*, *Ex-Friends*, or *My Love Affair with America*; books by other conservative commentators including Bill Kristol, Bernard Lewis, George Will, and William F. Buckley, Jr. might also appeal to these readers.

Sammon, Bill

The Evangelical President: George Bush's Struggle to Spread a Moral Democracy throughout the World. Regnery. 2007. 232 pp. ISBN 9781596985186.

> Sammon, senior White House correspondent for the *Washington Examiner*, offers his take on the presidency of George W. Bush, which he sees as one that deserves more respect than it has thus far been given by the media and other commentators. Citing Bush's decisive actions after the 9/11 attacks, his administration's success in finding and neutralizing many powerful members of Al Qaeda worldwide, and his refusal to bow to the pressures of a national media that focused on his vice president's hunting accidents rather than the more tangible results of his presidency, Sammon makes his case that President Bush continues to be underestimated by his opponents.

Subjects: 9/11, George W. Bush, Government, Mass Media, Politics, Presidents, Quick Reads, Religion

Now Try: Sammon has proved to be one of President Bush's most reliably stalwart defenders, and his other titles might be offered to his readers, including *At Any Cost: How Al Gore Tried to Steal the Election*, *Fighting Back: The War on Terrorism from Inside the Bush White House*, *Strategery: How George W. Bush Is Defeating Terrorists, Outwitting Democrats, and Confounding the Mainstream Media*, and *Misunderestimated: The President Battles Terrorism, Media Bias, and the Bush Haters*. Books by and about other prominent conservatives might appeal to these readers, including Clarence Thomas's autobiography *My Grandfather's Son*, Stephen Hayes's *Cheney*, and Sean Wilentz's *The Age of Reagan: A History, 1974 to 2008*, as well as Bernard Goldberg's books about the liberal bias in the American media, including *Bias*, *Crazies to the Left of Me, Wimps to the Right*, and *100 People Who Are Screwing Up America (and Al Franken Is #37)*.

Savage, Michael

The Political Zoo. Nelson Current. 2006. 374 pp. ISBN 9781595550422.

Conservative radio commentator Savage describes the current political atmosphere in America as a zoo and spends most of this narrative satirically comparing numerous political movers and shakers (on both the right and the left) to wild animals.

Subjects: Government, Humor, Mass Media, Politics, Satire

Now Try: Savage's earlier titles might also appeal, such as *Liberalism Is a Mental Disorder*, *The Enemy Within*, or *The Savage Nation*. Fans of Savage's writing might enjoy other titles by conservative commentators, including Sean Hannity (*Let Freedom Ring* and *Deliver Us from Evil*), Ann Coulter (*Godless*), Glenn Beck (*An Inconvenient Book*), Michelle Malkin, Michael Smerconish (*Muzzled*), Jesse Larner, Bill O'Reilly (*Culture Warrior*), and William Bennett (*America: The Last Best Hope*).

Schweizer, Peter

Makers and Takers: How Conservatives Do All the Work while Liberals Whine and Complain. Doubleday. 2008. 258 pp. ISBN 9780385513500.

Schweizer relies heavily on recent surveys and studies to support his contention that politically conservative individuals work harder, feel happier, are less materialistic, and possess a host of other characteristics and behaviors that indicate they live fuller lives than political liberals. Among the results cited by Schweizer include such findings as Republicans calling in sick to work fewer days than liberals and Ronald Reagan giving more money to charities than Edward Kennedy.

Subjects: Happiness, Politics, Psychology, Society

Now Try: Schweizer is also the author of the provocatively titled *Do as I Do (Not as I Say): Profiles in Liberal Hypocrisy*, which might be suggested to these readers. Other books by popular conservative commentators such as Jonah Goldberg (*Liberal Fascism*), Glenn Beck (*An Inconvenient Book*), and Ann Coulter (*If Democrats Had Any Brains, They'd Be Republicans*) might also be offered.

Smerconish, Michael A.

Muzzled: From T-Ball to Terrorism—True Stories That Should Be Fiction. Nelson Current. 2006. 292 pp. ISBN 9781595550507.

Radio host and attorney Smerconish launches an all-out offensive on "the total BS of rampant PC." Caustically written and aiming to take on all that is politically correct, this title offers a variety of examples that draw the author's wrath, from handing out trophies to the losers in sports contests to overscreening the elderly and infants at airport security.

Subjects: Mass Media, Politics, Pop Culture, Society

Now Try: The cover of Smerconish's book features a wide range of author blurbs, from Bill O'Reilly and Bernard Goldberg to Arianna Huffington and Alan Dershowitz; books by any of these outspoken authors on both sides of the political spectrum might also appeal to these readers. Books by other cultural and political commentators like Ann Coulter (*If Democrats Had Any Brains, They'd Be Republicans*), Glenn Beck (*An Inconvenient Book*), or John Stossel (*Myths, Lies, and Downright Stupidity*) might also be offered.

Sowell, Thomas

Economic Facts and Fallacies. Basic Books. 2008. 262 pp. ISBN 9780465003495.

Sowell has taught economics at institutions including Cornell and UCLA, and in this he exposes how economics theories that are offered as "givens" by the popular media are more fallacy than fact. Although Sowell is an economic theorist, this book is written for the general reader, and the author explores ideas that he believes are mistaken, including the gender gap in wages, economics as a cause in a host of urban problems, and the economics of Third World countries.

Subjects: African American Authors, Economics, Politics, Race Relations, Scholarly, Society

Now Try: Although Sowell is more well known for his economics writing and theorizing than he is for his political commentary, there can be no doubt that his titles have proved popular among his conservative readership. His readers might consider his other titles, including *Knowledge and Decisions* and *Black Rednecks and White Liberals*. Other authors who might appeal to these readers include Larry Elder (*Stupid Black Men: How to Play the Race Card—And Lose* and *The Ten Things You Can't Say in America*), Shelby Steele (*White Guilt: How Blacks and Whites Together Destroyed the Promise of the Civil Rights Era*), and influential economics writer Friedrich von Hayek (*The Road to Serfdom*).

Will, George

One Man's America: The Pleasures and Provocations of Our Singular Nation. Crown Forum. 2008. 384 pp. ISBN 9780307407863.

In this collection of his opinion columns and essays from the previous five years, Will earns his reputation as what one reviewer labels the "consummate conservative high-priest." His columns focus less on current politics, specific administrations, and partisan debate than they do on what he feels makes America great: the country's history and its endless variety of unique individuals. The tone of the book features Will's trademark erudition and his staunch belief that America only falls short in view of the "uniquely high standards it has set for itself."

Subjects: American History, Character Profiles, Essays, Family Relationships, Journalism, Politics, Travel

Now Try: Will is a prolific and Pulitzer Prize–winning author who is perhaps best known for his writings about another uniquely American pastime: baseball. His readers might consider his baseball book *Men at Work*, as well as his political books *Statecraft as Soulcraft* and *The Woven Figure*. Other authors and their titles that might appeal to Will's conservative readers include Newt Gingrich (*Real Change*), William F. Buckley, Jr. (*God and Man at Yale*), Barry Goldwater (*The Conscience of a Conservative*), and William Bennett (*America: The Last Best Hope*).

York, Byron

The Vast Left Wing Conspiracy: The Untold Story of the Democrats' Desperate Fight to Reclaim Power. Crown Forum. 2005. 277 pp. ISBN 9781400082384.

White House correspondent and journalist for *The National Review*, York provides examples of how Democrats and other politicians on the left are poised to dominate in America's political and cultural environment. Offering such examples as Michael Moore, George Soros, and many others, the author lists what he feels are these individuals' willingness to use tools ranging from political interest groups like MoveOn.org and propaganda like Moore's film *Fahrenheit 9/11* to further their own agenda at any cost.

Subjects: Conservatism, Government, Politics, Society

Now Try: Popular conservative authors such as David Frum (*Comeback: Conservatism That Can Win Again*) and Laura Ingraham (*Shut Up & Sing* and *Power to the People*) might particularly appeal to York's readers. He is also a staff writer with the conservative journal *National Review* (founded by William F. Buckley, Jr., whose many books might also appeal to these readers); other authors on staff at that magazine whose books might be suggested to York's readers include Richard Brookhiser (*What Would the Founders Do?*), Rich Lowry (*Legacy: Paying the Price for the Clinton Years*), and Jonah Goldberg (*Liberal Fascism*).

Although many readers of Political Commentary on both the right and the left are often quite invested in the ideology of their choice and will not read outside of it, periodically readers will ask for either "representative" political works (if they hold the opposite viewpoint) to help them better understand or be apprised of the literature from the other side of the political spectrum. In such a case, I would suggest starting with the biggest "names" and titles in the subgenre, including Ann Coulter's **Godless: The Church of Liberalism**, Bernard Goldberg's **100 People Who Are Screwing Up America: And Al Franken Is #37**, Laura Ingraham's **Power to the People**, or Michael Savage's **The Political Zoo**.

Political Commentary

Left

Trying to describe the political history and thought of the American left is as challenging as trying to distill all of the viewpoints on the American right into one cohesive tradition. Much as American conservatism has many facets, so too does liberal thought and writing, or progressivism, and the Democratic party platform. A further discussion of political parties, traditions, and definitions might be found in one of the titles listed in this chapter—Brian J. Mitchell's *Eight Ways to Run the Country: A New and Revealing Look at Left and Right*—and a brief perusal of that title might be informative for advisors seeking to learn more about political divides.

Luckily, readers in both of these categories (left and right) will most likely have tried and trusted authors to whom they turn for an interpretation of national and world events that closely aligns with their own, and a readers' advisor may find that the most appropriate action is to locate multiple titles by favorite writers or be aware of the names of best-selling pundits on the left side. This awareness can certainly be fostered by looking through political and news magazines (including *The Nation* and *The New Republic*) as well as keeping an eye on the books produced by publishers such as The New Press, Nation Books, or the Metropolitan Press. Likewise, keep an eye on authors interviewed and books showcased on the mock news programs (coverage on which leans left, for all practical purposes, although Jon Stewart and Stephen Colbert are not above mocking Democratic politicians and actions) *The Daily Show* and *The Colbert Report*. Be warned, however; as often as not, those hosts invite guests whose books they do not particularly agree with (Stewart's interview with Jonah Goldberg, author of *Liberal Fascism*, is a case in point).

Books from the Politics in Practice or Politicos subgenres, on the other hand, might successfully be suggested to these readers (although again, it will largely depend on who the personality is—this is most likely the best place to offer books by Bill Clinton and Jimmy Carter), as might a variety of Exposés, particularly those about corporate wrongdoing and international affairs. Biz Crit books from the Business Reporting chapter might also hold some appeal.

Often written by popular political commentators and media hosts, Political Commentary—Left books feature strong opinions, even stronger language, and a focus on the liberal or progressive belief system of their authors. They do not typically feature as much research as most Investigative Writing books (they rarely include references, notes, or indexes) and are also light on interview material. They are quick reads, written in a punchy and clever style to be consumed as quickly as possible, largely by readers who agree wholeheartedly with the authors' political stances on the left side of the American political spectrum.

Alterman, Eric

Why We're Liberals: A Political Handbook for Post-Bush America. Viking. 2008. 401 pp. ISBN 9780670018604.

A professor and columnist for *The Nation* magazine, Alterman reveals how many Americans, even if they don't think they do, hold "liberal" opinions on such issues as education and health care. In this feisty manifesto, he sets out to rescue the term "liberal" from the cultural trashing it's received over the past few decades and sets an agenda for true liberals to make their mark in government and politics in "post-Bush" America.

> **Subjects:** Government, Political Science, Politics, Pop Culture, Society
>
> **Now Try:** Fans of this book might also consider the similarly themed *Conscience of a Liberal* by Paul Krugman, *Homegrown Democrat* by Garrison Keillor, or *Giving* by Bill Clinton. Other works of Political Reporting might appeal, as might a wide variety of books about American society, such as Robert Putnam's classic *Bowling Alone* or Jack Cafferty's *It's Getting Ugly Out There*.

Bageant, Joe

Deer Hunting with Jesus: Dispatches from America's Class War. Crown. 2007. 273 pp. ISBN 9780307339362.

Bageant returns to his hometown of Winchester, Virginia, after what he refers to as "thirty years spent scratching together a middle-class life out of a 'dirt-poor' childhood," only to find that residents there seem to be voting for and aligning themselves with political candidates who are not addressing the economic, social, and health problems of the town's "underclass." With no-nonsense but person-able reporting, he interviewed old friends and neighbors, many of whom still work industrial jobs they fear they could lose to outsourcing at any moment, and the majority of whom struggle under the combined weight of health, financial, and interpersonal woes. Many of Bageant's ideals and questions will appeal to readers of a liberal political persuasion, but there are no simple classifications here; the author also lambasts the left for "not getting it" and shares his decidedly conservative views on such issues as gun ownership.

> **Subjects:** Book Groups, Classism, Community Life, Economics, Humor, Politics, Profanity, Society, Virginia
>
> **Now Try:** Other books about classism and economics, particularly about the working classes, might also be suggested, such as Barbara Ehrenreich's immersion journalism classics *Nickel and Dimed* and *Bait and Switch*, Louis Uchitelle's *The Disposable American*, the collection of *New York Times* pieces *Class Matters*, and Katherine Newman's and Victor Tan Chen's more scholarly but still very readable *The Missing Class*. Other books set in Virginia or featuring working-class characters, including novels by Richard Russo, Lee Smith (*Family Linen*), Kent Haruf (*Plainsong*), and Wendell Berry (*Jayber Crow*), might be offered, as might Exposés about community life such as William Finnegan's classic *Cold New World* or Tracy Kidder's *Home Town*.

Blumenthal, Sidney

How Bush Rules: Chronicles of a Radical Regime. Princeton University Press. 2006. 420 pp. ISBN 9780691128887.

This book is a collection of previously published investigative pieces and essays, written by Blumenthal for the online magazine *Salon* and the *Guardian* newspaper of the United Kingdom. It is organized thematically and split into three sections; the first is titled "Hubris" and covers topics such as Bush's policy in Iraq and his defeat of John Kerry; and "Nemesis II: Heckuva Job," from the administration's mishandling of Hurricane Katrina and its disastrous aftermath to the resignations of many commanding military officers from the Iraq War. Although the topics on which he is writing vary, Blumenthal's overriding theme is what he refers to as the radicalism and the "fanciful conservatism" of President George W. Bush.

> **Subjects:** George W. Bush, Essays, Foreign Relations, Government, Journalism, Politics, Small Press
>
> **Now Try:** Other books that consist of journalistic and opinion pieces might be offered to these readers, including Maureen Dowd's *Bushworld* and Molly Ivins's *Bushwhacked*; other books critical of President Bush and his administration might also be suggested, such as Thomas Ricks's *Fiasco: The American Military Adventure in Iraq*, Frank Rich's *The Greatest Story Ever Sold*, Michael Isikoff's *Hubris: The Inside Story of Spin, Scandal, and the Selling of the Iraq War*, Ron Suskind's *The One-Percent Doctrine*, or Richard Clarke's *Against All Enemies: Inside America's War on Terror*.

Carville, James, and Paul Begala

Take It Back: Our Party, Our Country, Our Future. Simon & Schuster. 2006. 349 pp. ISBN 9780743277525.

Longtime Democratic strategists Carville and Begala offer a blueprint for wresting control of the United States politics and voters' hearts away from the Republican Party (and moderate, "mealy-mouthed wimps" of the Democratic Party), particularly advocating grassroots activism and community action.

> **Subjects:** Government, Liberalism, Politics
>
> **Now Try:** Fans of Carville and Begala might consider other popular Democratic autobiographies and treatises such as Bill Clinton's *My Life* or *Giving*, Hillary Clinton's *Living History*, Barack Obama's *The Audacity of Hope*, Edward Kennedy's *America Back on Track*, Paul Waldman's *Being Right Is Not Enough*, or Jerome Armstrong's *Crashing the Gate: Netroots, Grassroots, and the Rise of People-Powered Politics*. Although not really part of the Democratic Party establishment, political books by George Lakoff and Jim Wallis might also prove to be good read-alikes; these include *Don't Think of an Elephant: Know Your Values and Frame the Debate* from the former and *God's Politics: Why the Right Gets It Wrong and the Left Doesn't Get It* and *The Great Awakening* from the latter.

Chomsky, Noam

Hegemony or Survival: America's Quest for Global Dominance. Metropolitan Books. 2003. 278 pp. ISBN 9780805074000.

In this American Empire Project series title, infamous political commentator, author, and famed linguist Chomsky sets out to redefine all of the accepted tenets and definitions as they are currently applied to American foreign relations and policies, and posits that America's current military strikes in Afghanistan and Iraq are simply a continuation of the policy of "imperial grand strategy." Chomsky does not mince words here and concludes, among other things, that America is, by definition, a rogue state, and one that applies the definition of "terrorism" and "terrorist acts" so inconsistently that most of its own activities and policies fall under that umbrella themselves.

Subjects: Classics, Foreign Relations, Globalization, Government, Liberalism, Politics, Terrorism

Now Try: Chomsky is one of the most prolific and well-known writers of the American political left, even though his political affiliation is given in the Contemporary Authors Online database as "Libertarian Socialist." His other books, including *The Fateful Triangle: The United States, Israel, and the Palestinians, Rogue States, Profit Over People, On Neoliberalism, On Power and Prospects*, and *Manufacturing Consent* might be suggested, as might any title from his series of "interview" books with David Barsamian (in which Barsamian and Chomsky have question-and-answer conversations on a variety of subjects, including *What We Say Goes, The Common Good, Class Warfare*, and *Secrets, Lies, and Democracy*). Books by other influential authors including Howard Zinn, Tom Engelhardt, Chalmers Johnson, Cornel West, and Naomi Klein might also appeal, as might other works in the American Empire Project such as Robert Dreyfuss's *Devil's Game: How the United States Helped Unleash Fundamentalist Islam*, James Carroll's *Crusade: Chronicles of an Unjust War*, and Alfred McCoy's *A Question of Torture*.

Colbert, Stephen

I Am America (and So Can You!). Grand Central Publishing. 2007. 230 pp. ISBN 9780446580502.

Host of Comedy Central's political satire show *The Colbert Report*, Stephen Colbert offers the opinions of his ultraconservative commentator persona on American society, culture, politics, faith, education, morality, and sex.

Subjects: Humor, Mass Media, Politics, Pop Culture, Quick Reads, Satire, Society

Now Try: Fans of Stephen Colbert's brand of political satire might enjoy Jon Stewart and *The Daily Show*'s book *America*; as well as an earlier humor book to which Colbert contributed, *Wigfield: The Can-Do Town That Just May Not*. Jon Stewart's earlier book, *Naked Pictures of Famous People*, Lewis Black's *Nothing's Sacred*, or John Hodgman's *The Areas of My Expertise* might also appeal to these readers. Colbert has also collaborated with writer and actress Amy Sedaris on a variety of projects; Sedaris's offbeat humor book and hospitality guidebook *I Like You* might also be offered. Although Colbert's alter-ego is an ultraconservative commentator, his and Stewart's core audience skews to the left on the political spectrum and might enjoy other more liberal authors like Michael Moore, Maureen Dowd, Molly Ivins, or Thomas Frank. Colbert has also interviewed numerous other nonfiction authors on his show; these include (but are not limited to) Jeffrey Toobin, Naomi Wolf, Thomas Ricks, and Michael Shermer (among many others).

Dean, John

Worse than Watergate: The Secret Presidency of George W. Bush. Little, Brown. 2004. 253 pp. ISBN 9780316000239.

Former Nixon White House legal counsel Dean draws a number of illustrative parallels between the presidencies of Richard Nixon and George W. Bush, citing the two leaders' similarities in terms of preferring to operate in an atmosphere of extreme secrecy and the broad interpretation of the powers of the executive branch of government. President Bush is not the only politico who comes in for Dean's criticism; he also cites as disruptive the extreme influence of Vice President Dick Cheney, frequently referring to the administration as the Bush-Cheney presidency. Those subjects covered in this volume include the outing of CIA agent Valerie Plame, Cheney's corporate involvements with energy companies and Halliburton, and many others. Dean has an astute understanding of both legal and business issues, and is also able to write a compelling history of the questionable business activities and management styles of both Bush and Cheney in their careers before they entered the White House.

Subjects: George W. Bush, Richard Cheney, Government, Richard Nixon, Politics, Secret Histories

Now Try: This book is the first in Dean's trilogy, which continued with *Conservatives without Conscience* and *Broken Government* (in this last title, Dean recounts what he perceives to be the "narrowness" of the previous ten years' worth of the "Republican way of thinking"). People mentioned in this book include J. Edgar Hoover, Spiro Agnew, Phyllis Schlafly, Dick Cheney, and Tom DeLay; books with any of those individuals as their subjects might also appeal. Other historical and political hybrids by authors such as Bob Woodward, Jacob Weisberg (*The Bush Tragedy*), and Molly Ivins (*Bill of Wrongs*) might also appeal, as might books about Nixon, such as Stanley Kutler's *Abuse of Power* or *Wars of Watergate*, or even John Dean's own *Blind Ambition*.

Dershowitz, Alan

Blasphemy: How the Religious Right Is Hijacking Our Declaration of Independence. Wiley. 2007. 195 pp. ISBN 9780470084557.

In this short, punchy volume, famous attorney Dershowitz makes a succinct case for his belief that the political and religious right in America is seeking to co-opt the Declaration of Independence as a "religious baptismal certificate" for the nation and a manifesto promoting their causes.

Subjects: American History, Declaration of Independence, Government, Thomas Jefferson, Making Sense . . ., Politics, Quick Reads, Religion

Now Try: Dershowitz is well known as a lawyer and an author; his other books might also be suggested: *Finding Jefferson*, *The Case for Israel*, and *Rights from Wrongs: A Secular Theory of the Origins of Rights*. Other books about Thomas Jefferson might appeal, such as Joseph Ellis's *American Sphinx* or Stephen Ambrose's *Undaunted Courage*, as might books about the clash of politics and religion, such as Chris Hedges's *American Fascists*, Sam Harris's *The End of Faith* and *Letters to a Christian Nation*, or Christopher Hitchens's *God Is Not Great*.

Dowd, Maureen

Bushworld: Enter at Your Own Risk. Putnam. 2004. 523 pp. ISBN 9780399152580.

In this collection of columns and essays largely exploring the failures and inadequacies of President George W. Bush and various members of his administration, *New York Times* columnist Dowd doesn't hold anything back in her sharply acerbic, wittily argued, and short (most range from four to ten pages in length) pieces. Arranged by theme rather than chronologically, and exploring Bush's political career starting in the 1990s, this book will provide a quick and enjoyable read for those on the left side of the political spectrum.

> **Subjects:** George W. Bush, Essays, Foreign Relations, Government, Humor, Journalism, Politics, Terrorism

> **Now Try:** Other collections of journalistic and political essays might be suggested to these readers, including Sidney Blumenthal's *How Bush Rules*, Molly Ivins's *Molly Ivins Can't Say That, Can She?* and *Bushwhacked*, Jim Hightower's *Let's Stop Beating around the Bush*, or Tom Engelhardt's *Mission Unaccomplished*. Other witty cultural essayists might also appeal, including Nora Ephron (*I Feel Bad about My Neck*), Caitlin Flanagan (*To Hell with All That*), or Garrison Keillor (*Homegrown Democrat*).

Engelhardt, Tom

Mission Unaccomplished: TomDispatch Interviews with American Iconoclasts and Dissenters. Nation Books. 2006. 270 pp. ISBN 9781560259381.

Author and creator of the Web site TomDispatch.com, Engelhardt here functions as an editor of this collection of essays and interviews with some of the most well-known names of the American progressive and liberal tradition, including Howard Zinn, Chalmers Johnson, Barbara Ehrenreich, and *Boston Globe* columnist James Carroll, as well as activists and dissenters such as Cindy Sheehan, Mike Davis, and Ann Wright. What most of the interviewees agree on is the imperial nature of the George W. Bush administration and the need for new ways to address and formulate American global policies and actions.

> **Subjects:** American History, Economics, Government, Military, Politics, Society, War

> **Now Try:** The roster of those interviewed for this book is, in itself, a reading list for those of the liberal political persuasion. Such authors and titles as might appeal include *Nickel and Dimed* and *Bait and Switch* by Barbara Ehrenreich, *A People's History of the United States* by Howard Zinn, *House of War* by James Carroll, *The Sorrows of Empire* by Chalmers Johnson, *The New American Militarism* by Andrew Bacevich, or *Ideas Matter* by Katrina vanden Heuvel. Engelhardt is also an editor for Metropolitan Books, and other titles from their list might appeal, such as those by Noam Chomsky, Susan Faludi, Orlando Figes, or Thomas Frank.

Faludi, Susan

The Terror Dream: Fear and Fantasy in Post-9/11 America. Metropolitan Books. 2007. 351 pp. ISBN 9780805086928.

Journalist and author Faludi, best known for her feminist classic *Backlash*, provides her take on American politics, culture, and gender roles in our post-9/11 world. Identifying trends few other writers have focused on, Faludi cites examples of how she believes the response to the terrorist attacks seemed to focus on restoring traditional ideals of masculinity, gender roles, and conservative values; she also makes the controversial contention that Americans were humiliated by the terrorist attack on their own shores particularly because it was perpetrated by "nonwhite Barbarians." Strongly opinionated throughout, Faludi concludes that the wars in Afghanistan and Iraq were the disastrous results of our knee-jerk reaction to terror and laments the fact that we seem to have lost our opportunity to ask questions about the 9/11 attacks and use the answers to influence our domestic and foreign policies.

Subjects: 9/11, Feminism, Foreign Relations, Gender, Government, Mass Media, Politics, Society, Terrorism, Women's Contributions, Women's Nonfiction

Now Try: Faludi's focus on cultural shifts and gender roles in the wake of the terrorist attacks of 9/11 is unique; other books of feminist thought and politics might be suggested, including Maureen Dowd's *Are Men Necessary?*, Sara Paretsky's *Writing in an Age of Silence*, Laura Kipnis's *The Female Thing*, Naomi Wolf's *The Beauty Myth*, or Alice Walker's *In Search of Our Mother's Gardens*. Political treatises by erudite skillful female authors might be of particular interest, such as Naomi Klein's *The Shock Doctrine*, Joan Didion's *Fixed Ideas: America Since 9/11*, Arundhati Roy's *An Ordinary Person's Guide to Empire*, or Susan Sontag's *At the Same Time: Essays and Speeches*.

Franken, Al

The Truth: With Jokes. Dutton. 2005. 336 pp. ISBN 9780525949060.

Political commentator and Air America radio host Franken takes an in-depth look at the election of 2004, uncovering what he believes to be the more unsavory aspects of what he terms George W. Bush's "fear, smear, and queers" campaign. In addition to closely examining the election, Franken also comments on other political news stories, including the Terri Schiavo case, incidences of modern-day slavery on the Pacific island of Saipan, and offers some sharp comments of his own regarding political operatives like Karl Rove and Jack Abramoff, as well as media personalities like Tim Russert and Sean Hannity.

Subjects: Government, Corruption, Humor, Mass Media, Politics, Satire

Now Try: Franken's fans may consider his other titles, including *Lies and the Lying Liars Who Tell Them* and *Rush Limbaugh Is a Big Fat Idiot*. Books by other political commentators on the left, including Michael Moore, might be suggested, as might other books related by subject, such as Sam Seder's and Stephen Sherrill's *FUBAR: America's Right-Wing Nightmare* or Peter Stone's *Heist: Superlobbyist Jack Abramoff, His Republican Allies, and the Buying of Washington*.

Hartmann, Thom

Screwed: The Undeclared War against the Middle Class—and What We Can Do about It. Berrett-Koehler. 2006. 239 pp. ISBN 9781576754146.

Air America radio host and popular progressive commentator Hartmann describes how the past thirty years in American society and politics (starting with the Reagan administration) have seen a steady decline in safety nets, social programs, and other economic policies designed to help the middle class, while it has simultaneously been a time of increased deregulation for corporations and entire industries (as well as a time of rampant tax breaks and loopholes that heavily favor corporations over individuals). In addition to outlining his beliefs on these subjects, the author also provides suggestions for "leveling the playing field" in American society.

Subjects: American History, Business, Classism, Economics, Government, Politics, Poverty, Progressive, Society

Now Try: Hartmann is also the author of *Unequal Protection: The Rise of Corporate Dominance and the Theft of Human Rights* and *Cracking the Code: How to Win Hearts, Change Minds, and Restore America's Original Vision*.

Although they are slightly more bombastic in tone, other progressive and Left authors including Greg Palast (*The Best Democracy Money Can Buy* and *Armed Madhouse*), Jim Hightower (*Swim against the Current*), Naomi Klein (*Shock Doctrine: The Rise of Disaster Capitalism*), and Thomas Frank (*What's the Matter with Kansas?* and *One Market under God*) might also appeal. Other authors who focus on the plight of the middle class but who are not really considered "progressive" are Lou Dobbs (*War on the Middle Class* and *Independents Day*) and Jack Cafferty (*It's Getting Ugly Out There: The Frauds, Bunglers, Liars, and Losers Who Are Hurting America*); likewise, books from the Business Reporting chapter about the current state of American economics and the class system might be suggested, including David Shipler's *The Working Poor* and Louis Uchitelle's *The Disposable American*.

Hedges, Chris

American Fascists: The Christian Right and the War on America. Free Press. 2007. 254 pp. ISBN 9780743284431.

Journalist and war reporter Hedges doesn't mince words when he examines the empire that has been built over the course of the past twenty-five years by Christian and media evangelists, arguing that at its core the movement is fueled by unbridled nationalism and resembles the early days of fascist movements in 1920s and '30s Germany and France. Hedges, who himself grew up in rural upstate New York and is the son of a Presbyterian pastor, uses his knowledge of and citations from the Christian Bible to register his opposition to the religious right movement. Citing high approval ratings from Christian right advocacy groups for a large number of senators and members of Congress as evidence that the conservative movement now wields great power in the political process, the author also interviewed many such right-wing individuals and reports on events such as pro-life rallies and seminars on converting nonbelievers, and concludes that "debate with the radical Christian right is useless. We cannot reach this movement. It does not want a dialogue. It is a movement based on emotion and cares nothing for rational thought and discussion."

> **Subjects:** Christianity, Fascism, Memoirs, Politics, Religion, World History

> **Now Try:** Hedges's other books, *War Is a Force That Gives Us Meaning*, *Losing Moses on the Freeway*, and *I Don't Believe in Atheists*, might also appeal to these readers; any number of books listed in his bibliography might also be suggested, such as James Agee's and Walker Evans's classic *Let Us Now Praise Famous Men*, Karen Armstrong's *The Battle for God* and *The Great Transformation*, Sam Harris's *The End of Faith*, Stephen Prothero's *American Jesus: How the Son of God Became a National Icon*, or Bart Ehrman's *Misquoting Genius*. Christopher Hitchens's feisty anti-religion manifesto *God Is Not Great* might also appeal.

Hightower, Jim, and Susan DeMarco

Swim Against the Current: Even a Dead Fish Can Go with the Flow. Wiley & Sons. 2008. 212 pp. ISBN 9780470121511.

Popular progressive author and political commentator Hightower answers his critics' charges that he never stops complaining about greed and corruption (particularly in the business and political worlds) by offering an arguably more positive collection of character profiles and examples of people and organizations who are choosing to live different lives than the ones many Americans think they "have to." Along the way he provides anecdotes of cooperative businesses, political activists, and other individuals who have simply decided to follow maxims which include questioning authority, trusting your own values, and standing up for your beliefs. It also concludes with a section of resources and contact information.

Subjects: Activism, Business, Corruption, Government, Politics, Progressive, Quick Reads, Society, Sustainability

Now Try: Although they may already have read them, other books by Jim Hightower might be offered to these readers, including *Thieves in High Places* and *If the Gods Had Meant Us to Vote, They'd Have Given Us Candidates*. This book is dedicated to Molly Ivins, another popular progressive commentator who was also a Texan; her books *Bill of Wrongs: The Executive Branch's Assault on America's Fundamental Rights* and *Molly Ivins Can't Say That, Can She?* might appeal, as might books such as Naomi Wolf's *The End of America: Letter of Warning to a Young Patriot* and Paul Krugman's *The Conscience of a Liberal*. At the end of this book, Hightower's colleague and co-author Susan DeMarco also offers her own suggestions for a reading list, which include Howard Zinn's *People's History of the United States, 1492–Present*, William Greider's *The Soul of Capitalism*, Louis Uchitelle's *The Disposable American*, and John Perkins's *Confessions of an Economic Hit Man*.

Huffington, Arianna

Right Is Wrong: How the Lunatic Fringe Hijacked America, Shredded the Constitution, and Made Us All Less Safe. Knopf. 2008. 388 pp. ISBN 9780307269669.

Former member of the GOP turned progressive agitator and editor-in-chief of the popular political Web site *The Huffington Post* reveals how the conservative Republican Party gets it wrong on so many key issues: national defense, foreign relations, the economy, social issues, including health care and gay rights, abortion, and torture. She also concludes with a chapter detailing the Conservative Right's "hijacking" of presidential candidate John McCain. The result is a passionately argued and intense book about politics and American society in the early twenty-first century.

Subjects: Foreign Relations, Government, Iraq War (2003), Mass Media, Politics, Women Writers

Now Try: Huffington is also the author of the book *Pigs at the Trough: How Corporate Greed and Political Corruption Are Undermining America*; that book and others similar to it, such as Greg Palast's *The Best Democracy Money Can Buy* and Kevin Phillips's *American Theocracy* might also be suggested. Other similarly feisty books by media commentators might be suggested, such as Keith Olbermann's *Truth and Consequences* or Jack Cafferty's *It's Getting Ugly Out There: The Frauds, Bunglers, Liars, and Losers Who Are Hurting America*, as might books by other outspoken women authors such as Barbara Ehrenreich (*This Land Is Their Land*) and Molly Ivins (*Bill of Wrongs* and *Bushwhacked*).

Isikoff, Michael, and David Corn

Hubris: The Inside Story of Spin, Scandal, and the Selling of the Iraq War. Crown. 2006. 463 pp. ISBN 9780307346810.

Journalists and television news commentators Isikoff and Corn present a succinct history of George W. Bush's administration's decision and plan to invade Iraq and topple Iraqi dictator Saddam Hussein in 2003. They describe many incidents and political machinations that had previously gone unreported, including power struggles among the administration's key players, such as Richard Cheney, Donald Rumsfeld, Condoleezza Rice, Richard Perle, and Paul Wolfowitz; the blowing of CIA operative Valerie Plame Wilson's cover as political retaliation against her husband Joseph Wilson; and how false information and faulty intelligence was used to take the country to war. The book is complex and includes numerous political, intelligence, and media key players, but the order is strictly chronological, and the authors are methodical in their exposé of the Bush administration's arrogance.

> **Subjects:** George W. Bush, Richard Cheney, Government, Saddam Hussein, Iraq, Iraq War (2003), Mass Media, Political Science, Politics, Valerie Plame Wilson
>
> **Now Try:** There is no shortage of comprehensive historical and investigative works on the Iraq War. These include Thomas Ricks's *Fiasco: The American Military Adventure in Iraq*, Michael R. Gordon's *Cobra II: The Inside Story of the Invasion and Occupation of Iraq*, George Packer's *The Assassin's Gate: America in Iraq*, Ron Suskind's *The One Percent Doctrine*, James Risen's *State of War*, Frank Rich's *The Greatest Story Ever Sold*, Bob Woodward's *State of Denial*, and Rajiv Chandrasekaran's *Imperial Life in the Emerald City: Inside Iraq's Green Zone*. Related biographies, including Robert Draper's *Dead Certain* (about Bush), Stephen Hayes's *Cheney* (Hayes is a reporter with *The National Review*, and this biography is, if not fawning, at least positive), Joseph Wilson's *The Politics of Truth*, and Valerie Plame Wilson's *Fair Game* might also be offered, as might books which share the subject of the mass media, such as Robert Novak's *The Prince of Darkness*.

Johnson, Chalmers A.

Nemesis: The Last Days of the American Republic. Metropolitan Books. 2006. 354 pp. ISBN 9780805079111.

Johnson concludes his trilogy of current affairs books looking at America's world dominance in the twentieth and continuing into the twenty-first centuries (part of the American Empire Project, the first two volumes were titled *Blowback* and *The Sorrows of Empire*). In extensively endnoted chapters, Chalmers explores the militarization of American society and the impact of our military bases worldwide, the uses and more frequent misuses of the Central Intelligence Agency by presidents, and the plans in place to expand America's "hyperpower" influence not only globally but into space as well.

> **Subjects:** Foreign Relations, Government, Military, Politics, Society
>
> **Now Try:** Johnson is a prolific and well-known author; his other books might be suggested, including *The Sorrows of Empire* and *Blowback*, as might related books on American foreign and military policies, including Amy Chua's *Day of Empire: How Hyperpowers Rise to Global Dominance—And Why They Fall*, Naomi Klein's *The Shock Doctrine*, John Perkins's *The Secret History of the American Empire*, Andrew Bacevich's *The New American Militarism*, or Jeremy Scahill's Exposé *Blackwater: The*

Rise of the World's Most Powerful Mercenary Army. This book is an entry in the American Empire Project, a series of books published by the Metropolitan Books imprint that explore the "fateful exercise of empire-building and to explore every facet of the developing American imperium"; other titles include Alfred McCoy's *A Question of Torture*, Michael Klare's *Blood and Oil*, James Carroll's *Crusade: Chronicles of an Unjust War*, or Noam Chomsky's *Imperial Ambitions*.

Joshi, S. T.

The Angry Right: Why Conservatives Keep Getting It Wrong. Prometheus Books. 2006. 311 pp. ISBN 9781591024637.

In this collection of profiles of twelve leading political conservatives, Joshi considers how and why they continue to portray themselves as political and cultural "underdogs," even though Republicans have spent more years in the presidential office since 1968 than have Democrats (and have largely controlled both houses of Congress as well). Joshi posits that thinkers and leaders on the political right trade on that sense of endangerment and anger to further intimidate their adherents into becoming ever more conservative in their viewpoints. Providing quotes from historical political stances that would seem controversial today (William F. Buckley, Jr. argued in the 1950s that school desegregation violated states' rights), the author demonstrates how all of American culture has become steadily more conservative since the Great Depression and the New Deal.

> **Subjects:** American History, Essays, Government, Mass Media, Political Science, Politics, Scholarly

> **Now Try:** Other books about conservatives and their effect on American politics and society might be offered; these include Chris Hedges's *American Fascists: The Christian Right and the War on America*, Naomi Wolf's *The End of America*, Jim Wallis's *The Great Awakening* and *God's Politics: Why The Right Gets It Wrong and the Left Doesn't Get It*, or other broader books on American political science, such as Todd Gitlin's *The Bulldozer and the Big Tent: Blind Republicans, Lame Democrats, and the Recovery of American Ideals* or Jonathan Clarke's and Stefan Halper's *Silence of the Rational Center: Why American Foreign Policy Is Failing*.

Krugman, Paul R.

The Conscience of a Liberal. Norton. 2007. 296 pp. ISBN 9781591024637.

Economist Krugman, often hailed as the economic and political heir to progressive John Kenneth Galbraith, offers his take on the past eighty years of American history, outlining the reforms that evened out the excesses of the late nineteenth century's Gilded Age, as well as the unraveling of many of those reforms in the latter half of that same century. In addition to explaining many facets of America's complex economy and place on the new global stage, Krugman also reiterates his belief that a "new New Deal," specifically one that addresses military-industrial spending and the availability of health care, is necessary now to provide a social safety net and reduce inequalities present in our society.

> **Subjects:** 20th Century, Book Groups, Classism, Economics, Liberalism, Memoirs, Politics, Society

Now Try: Krugman's earlier book, the New York Times Notable *The Great Unraveling: Losing Our Way in the New Century* might also appeal to his readers. Other books about closely held personal beliefs that merge with the political, such as Garrison Keillor's *Homegrown Democrat*, Robert Reich's *Supercapitalism* or *Reasons: Why Liberals Will Win the Battle for America*, Thomas Frank's *One Market Under God* and *What's the Matter with Kansas?*, Jonathan Chait's *The Big Con*, Robert Kuttner's *The Squandering of America*, Naomi Wolf's *The End of America*, or John Kenneth Galbraith's *The Affluent Society* or *The Economics of Innocent Fraud* might all appeal. Other political and economic books by William Greider, Robert F. Frank, and Lewis Lapham might also be suggested.

Lapham, Lewis H.

Pretensions to Empire: Notes on the Criminal Folly of the Bush Administration. Norton. 2006. 288 pp. ISBN 9781595581129.

This collection of essays from Lapham's political commentaries, published as his "Notebook" column in *Harper's* magazine between August 2002 and March 2006, functions largely to create a picture of the George W. Bush administration as one rife with both incompetence and abuse of power. Lapham calls stridently throughout for Bush's impeachment, which makes it abundantly clear to the reader which side of the political divide he is on. Topics covered by Lapham include the Iraq War, Hurricane Katrina, the military-industrial complex, domestic spying programs, and concessions made by Bush's government to extreme right-wing business and religious interests.

Subjects: George W. Bush, Essays, Government, Iraq War (2003), Politics

Now Try: Other collections of journalism and magazine pieces might be suggested to these readers, including Maureen Dowd's *Bushworld*, Sidney Blumenthal's *How Bush Rules*, or even books by William Langewiesche (which, if not essay collections per se, often first see life as magazine articles). Other books by Lapham might appeal, such as *Gag Rule* and *Waiting for the Barbarians*, as might books by *Harper's* magazine contributors, including Thomas Frank's *What's the Matter with Kansas?*, Jonathan Schell's *The Seventh Decade: The New Shape of Nuclear Danger*, or even John Edgar Wideman's novel *Fanon*.

Moore, Michael

Stupid White Men—And Other Sorry Excuses for the State of the Nation! ReganBooks. 2001. 277 pp. ISBN 9780060392451.

Liberal filmmaker and author Moore has never been one to hold back on his opinions, and his writing in this book is no exception. In it he derides the results of the 2000 political election, the presidency of George W. Bush, and a wide variety of what he views to be other political and societal ills in bombastic language meant to make the blood of all readers, conservative or liberal, boil.

Subjects: George W. Bush, Government, Humor, Politics

Now Try: Moore's other titles, including *Dude, Where's My Country?* and *Will They Ever Trust Us Again?* might be suggested, as might his documentary films *Roger & Me* or *Fahrenheit 9/11*. Books by other media commentators on the left, including Al Franken, Keith Olbermann, and Jon Stewart might all appeal, as might the straightforward title *FUBAR: America's Right-Wing Nightmare* by Sam Seder and Stephen Sherrill.

Olbermann, Keith

The Worst Person in the World: And 202 Strong Contenders. Wiley. 2006. 267 pp. ISBN 9780470044957.

Olbermann is the politically liberal host of the popular MSNBC show *Countdown with Keith Olbermann,* and on each show he features a segment in which he shares his opinion on who he currently thinks is the "Worst Person in the World." In this book he has collected hundreds of these segments, which aired between July 2005 and May 2006; each chapter is one or two pages long and highlights the "idiotic moves" of such notables as Ann Coulter, Bill O'Reilly, George W. Bush, NASA, Roger Clemens, and lots of other knowns and unknowns. Witty and acerbic, this humorous collection might well prove a quick and entertaining read for progressives who enjoy Olbermann's erudite sarcasm.

> **Subjects:** Celebrities and Superstars, Character Profiles, Humor, Mass Media, Politics

> **Now Try:** Other books by popular media commentators might be suggested, including Jack Cafferty's *It's Getting Ugly Out There,* the works of satire by Jon Stewart and Stephen Colbert (*America: The Book* and *I Am America,* respectively), or Jack Huberman's satire *101 People Who Are Really Screwing Up America* (a response to Bernard Goldberg's title *100 People Who Are Screwing Up America—and Al Franken Is #37*).

Palast, Greg

Armed Madhouse: Who's Afraid of Osama Wolf?, China Floats, Bush Sinks, The Scheme to Steal '08, No Child's Behind Left, and Other Dispatches from the Front Lines of the Class War. Dutton. 2006. 360 pp. ISBN 9780525949688.

BBC television reporter Palast wastes no time in taking aim at George W. Bush and all other aspects of American government and social policies that he finds absurd, providing information and his trademark angry style in short chapters and even shorter segments within his chapters. Succinctly detailing such topics as Bush's penchant for invading oil-rich countries, economics policies that favor the haves at the expense of the have-nots, and numerous others, Palast offers a book that is dark, bitter, hilarious, serious, is easily readable in small chunks, and even challenges its readers to take a stand on the issues themselves.

> **Subjects:** George W. Bush, Classism, Exposés, Government, Humor, Politics

> **Now Try:** Other authors who mix humor with political commentary might be offered, including Molly Ivins (*Bushwhacked* and *Molly Ivins Can't Say That, Can She?*), Jim Hightower (*Thieves in High Places* and *Swim against the Current*), Joe Bageant's *Deer Hunting with Jesus,* and Keith Olbermann (*The Worst Person in the World*). Other Exposés, particularly about government and politics, might also be suggested, including Jonathan Chait's *The Big Con: The True Story of How Washington Got Hoodwinked and Hijacked by Crackpot Economics* or Peter Bennet Stone's *Heist: Superlobbyist Jack Abramoff, His Republican Allies, and the Buying of Washington.*

Rich, Frank

🌷 *The Greatest Story Ever Sold: The Decline and Fall of Truth from 9/11 to Katrina.* Penguin Press. 2006. 341 pp. ISBN 9781594200984.

New York Times op-ed columnist Rich sets out to illustrate that George W. Bush's administration is interested in one thing and one thing only: the consolidation and preservation of their own power. His main charge is that the White House created a twin-barreled propaganda spin-machine focused on the selling of the war on terror and moral values. The book is intensively researched, extensively footnoted, and provides a 70-page time line exploring political maneuvers and statements from 2001 through April 2006.

Subjects: 9/11, George W. Bush, Exposés, Government, Hurricane Katrina, Iraq War (2003), Journalism, Mass Media, Politics, Terrorism

Awards: New York Times Notable

Now Try: Fans of Rich's opinionated writing might consider other less stereotypically "objective" investigative works including *State of Denial* by Bob Woodward, *The Worst Person in the World* by Keith Olbermann, or *Hubris: The Inside Story of Spin, Scandal, and the Selling of the Iraq War* by Michael Isikoff. These readers might also consider more traditional works of history on related subjects, such as Douglas Brinkley's *The Great Deluge: Hurricane Katrina, New Orleans, and the Mississippi Gulf Coast* or George Packer's *The Assassins' Gate: America in Iraq*.

Spence, Gerry

Bloodthirsty Bitches and Pious Pimps of Power: The Rise and Risks of the New Conservative Hate Culture. St. Martin's Press. 2006. 284 pp. ISBN 9780312361532.

As you might be able to tell from the title, author and former defense attorney Spence, while seeking to expose such conservative, right-wing commentators and authors as Ann Coulter, Laura Ingraham, Nancy Grace, Bill O'Reilly, Sean Hannity, and Pat Robertson, engages in some angry language of his own. Charging that the individuals listed (among others) "occupy the bully pulpit of the new American hate culture," the author strives to expose the unnatural power wielded by these luminaries, whose programs go into millions of homes and reach millions of voting listeners every day.

Subjects: Journalism, Mass Media, Politics, Society

Now Try: It only stands to reason that a book lambasting the commentators of the right might appeal to fans of commentators on the left; authors who might appeal include Al Franken, Keith Olbermann, and Thom Hartmann (*Screwed: The Undeclared War against the Middle Class*). Spence is also a lawyer with other law and true crime books to his credit; these include *Give Me Liberty, The Making of a Country Lawyer*, and *The Smoking Gun*. Other "left" books by other authors/lawyers include Alan Dershowitz's *Blasphemy: How the Religious Right Is Hijacking Our Declaration of Independence* and Joseph Margulies's *Guantánamo and the Abuse of Presidential Power*.

Starkey, David, ed.

Living Blue in the Red States. University of Nebraska Press. 2007. 344 pp. ISBN 9780803260085.

This collection of essays is all written by individuals who consider themselves "blue staters" (read: politically and socially liberal) who reside in red states (where most voters adhere to politically and socially conservative policies). Such writers as Jonis Agee, Stephen Corey, Lee Martin, and Wyoming poet laureate David Romtvedt all explore the dissonance felt when an individual lives in a community with which he or she does not share the same political orientation. Although such timely topics as the war in Iraq and the 2004 election are discussed, the authors in this volume also sought to look beyond their current circumstances and imagine how these issues affected neighborhoods, relationships among neighbors, and communities before the red state/blue state polarization became such a divisive issue, as well as look toward the future and consider how this dichotomy will continue to affect government action and policy. The essays are organized geographically, with essays from the West, Midwest, and the South.

Subjects: Community Life, Essays, Government, Politics, Small Press, Society

Now Try: Most, if not all, of the contributors to this book have published books of their own which might be suggested, including Jonis Agee's novels *The River Wife* and *The Weight of Dreams*, Lee Martin's memoir *From Our House*, Donald Morrill's memoir *The Untouched Minutes*, or Frank Soos's story collection *Unified Field Theory*. Of course, any number of other "Political—Left" books from this subgenre might also appeal to these readers (particularly Thomas Frank's classic *What's the Matter with Kansas?*).

Tirman, John

100 Ways America Is Screwing Up the World. Harper Perennial. 2006. 258 pp. ISBN 9780061133015.

Following the popular political treatise format of lists of things "screwing up" America and the world (e.g., *100 People Who Are Screwing Up America*), Tirman offers his take on ways in which this country represents itself poorly across the world, including broadcasting our love for Wal-Mart and SUVs, and also ways in which we fail ourselves and our children, particularly through our consumption habits, of both cultural goods and, at a basic level, of unhealthy foods. Contrarian in nature and tone throughout, Tirman nonetheless concludes his volume with numerous examples of what America still does right, including our history of more open immigration policies, human rights and the rule of law, honoring diversity and creativity, and secularism.

Subjects: American History, Culture, Politics, Pop Culture, Quick Reads, Society

Now Try: Howard Zinn, author of *A People's History of the United States*, wrote the foreword for this volume; likewise, quotes from Kurt Vonnegut (*Man without a Country*) can be found within it. Other works by left political thinkers and writers will also appeal, including books by Noam Chomsky, Mark Crispin Miller, Lewis Lapham, and Greg Palast.

Unger, Craig

The Fall of the House of Bush: The Untold Story of How a Band of True Believers Seized the Executive Branch, Started the Iraq War, and Still Imperils America's Future. Scribner. 2007. 437 pp. ISBN 9780743280754.

Unger leaves very little doubt as to the nature of his own conclusions in this story in which he weaves together interview material from religious leaders, politicians, and individuals close to President George W. Bush and his family. What he concludes is that a group of powerful neoconservatives, including Dick Cheney, Richard Perle, Paul Wolfowitz, and Donald Rumsfeld, confident in their own beliefs and rights, influenced the president to start the Iraq War in the absence of verifiable intelligence information. Unger also explores the president's experience of becoming a born-again Christian and how that status makes him vulnerable to the influence of extreme right-wing religious conservatives, including Timothy LaHaye, Arthur Blessitt, and Pat Robertson.

> **Subjects:** George W. Bush, Government, Iraq War (2003), Neoconservatives, Politics

> **Now Try:** Books about the Iraq War and its genesis might be suggested to these readers, including Lawrence Wright's *The Looming Tower*, Michael Isikoff's *Hubris*, Frank Rich's *The Greatest Story Ever Sold*, Joshua Key's more personal *The Deserter's Tale*, Thomas Ricks's *Fiasco*, Bob Woodward's *State of Denial*, or Jeremy Scahill's Exposé *Blackwater*. Kevin Phillips's *American Theocracy*, about politics and religion and oil, might appeal, as might biographies of George W. Bush (by Robert Draper or Jacob Weisberg), Colin Powell, Richard Perle, and Paul Wolfowitz, as well as books by other "left" political writers including Sidney Blumenthal and Thomas Frank.

Wolf, Naomi

The End of America: A Letter of Warning to a Young Patriot. Chelsea Green. 2007. 176 pp. ISBN 9781933392790.

Wolf draws parallels between historical dictatorships in Germany, Russia, China, and Chile during the twentieth century and the state of American administration and policies in 2007, both domestically and abroad. Written in the format of a personal, impassioned letter to a "young patriot" (the style is reminiscent of that used in political pamphlets authored by Thomas Paine and others during the Revolution and founding of the American republic), Wolf argues that the increasingly pervasive curtailments of personal rights and civil liberties will lead to further totalitarianism in government. Among the points she has listed are the government's willingness to promote fear in the populace, establish secret prisons, surveil ordinary citizens, cast dissent as treason, and several others. Wolf has written this book intending to shock readers, and her language is appropriately combative for that purpose; she is also part of the American Freedom Campaign, a "grassroots effort to ensure that presidential candidates pledge to uphold the constitution and protect our liberties from further erosion."

> **Subjects:** 9/11, Book Groups, Government, Law and Lawyers, Making Sense . . ., Politics, Quick Reads, Small Press

> **Now Try:** Wolf is, of course, a well-known writer and cultural critic; her books *The Beauty Myth* and *Misconceptions* might also be offered to these readers. Other books about America's current path and its reactions to the events of 9/11 might also be suggested, including Naomi Klein's *The Shock Doctrine* and Susan Faludi's *The Terror Dream*, as well as Lawrence Wright's *The Looming Tower: Al-Qaeda and the Road to 9/11* or Susan Sontag's *At the Same Time*. Other books from the independent publisher Chelsea Green might appeal, including George Lakoff's *Don't Think of an Elephant!* or Thorne Anderson's *Unembedded: Four Independent Photojournalists on the War in Iraq*, or even Christopher Hitchens's *Letters to a Young Contrarian*.

Zinn, Howard

A People's History of American Empire. Metropolitan Books. 2008. 288 pp.
ISBN 9780805077797.

> Well-known peace and social activist and leftist historian Zinn provides a
> "people's history" (very similar to his earlier title *A People's History of the*
> *United States*) of the development of the American empire, in graphic
> novel form and by highlighting such events as the massacre of American
> Indians at Wounded Knee through the 2003 Iraq War. In addition to de-
> tailing historical events including World Wars I and II, the Vietnam War,
> and 9/11, the book also relates Zinn's personal history as the child of im-
> migrants who became one of America's most infamous historians.

> **Subjects:** American History, Government, Graphic Novels, Politics, YA

> **Now Try:** Zinn's *A People's History of the United States* has sold nearly two
> million copies since its initial publication; it and Zinn's other titles, including
> his memoir *You Can't Be Neutral on a Moving Train* and his political works
> published by smaller independent houses, *A Power Governments Cannot*
> *Suppress*, *The Unraveling of the Bush Presidency*, and *Disobedience and De-*
> *mocracy* might also appeal to these readers. Books by similar political thinkers
> including Noam Chomsky might be suggested, as might graphic novels by au-
> thors such as Joe Sacco or Jason Lutes.

> Readers who typically read titles from the right side of the Political
> Commentary divide might also sometimes seek, as noted earlier, rep-
> resentative titles from the other side of the political spectrum. In that
> case, I would suggest the more well known of these Political Commen-
> tary—Left titles, including James Carville's and Paul Begala's **Take It**
> **Back: Our Party, Our Country, Our Future**, Noam Chomsky's **He-**
> **gemony or Survival: America's Quest for Global Dominance**, Mi-
> chael Moore's **Stupid White Men—And Other Sorry Excuses for**
> **the State of the Nation!**, or Keith Olbermann's **The Worst Person**
> **in the World: And 202 Strong Contenders**.

Hot-Button Issues

The heading I have for these political reporting books in my mind is actually "less obviously aligned, ideologically" but that doesn't sound nearly as
punchy as "Hot-Button Issues." These are the authors and the books that remain opinionated, often offer feisty personal reactions and writing, but are not
typically (or as obviously) partisan in their approaches. It would also be inac-
curate to describe them as Libertarian, although undoubtedly that is the political camp in which some of their authors consider themselves. For one thing,
not all of these titles are Libertarian in their outlook, and for another, the very
nature of that political tradition does not lend itself easily to its own subgenre.
Above all, these are typically extremely thoughtful titles and are not usually
quick reads, although they often feature lively storytelling and accessible lan-

guage. They are books in which the authors definitely have an opinion on which they are editorializing; but because they are works of reporting, they also feature details gleaned from their reporters' work and observation, as well as often well-researched historical context, evidence and statistics, and interviews. They also generally focus on one specific issue or subject of interest, such as globalization, immigration, or energy policy (to name just a few).

Although they may be written by pundits (Lou Dobbs and Jack McCafferty among them) or political theorists and academics (including Francis Fukuyama), they tend more to be written by career journalists and reporters. They are books that depend heavily on ideas for their appeal and cannot be considered escapist reading, in that they often encourage their readers to become engaged, in the way their authors would like them to, with political, national, social, and world issues. Readers who enjoy these books might consider the decidedly cooler-in-tone Politics in Practice books, as well as certain titles from either of the Political Commentary subgenres, but more likely these readers might enjoy blunt and shocking titles from the Exposés chapter, as well as the more passionately written Immersion Journalism or a few In-Depth Reporting titles.

Hot-Button Issues political titles are often written in feisty, opinionated language, and typically feature a focus on specific political and cultural issues, including national security, energy policy, and immigration (among many others). Although their subject matters and their lively writing styles are two of their largest appeals, they also feature skillful writing and food for thought, as they tend to be written primarily by career journalists and authors who have honed their craft but refuse to be constrained by the precept of objectivity.

Allison, Graham

🏶 *Nuclear Terrorism: The Ultimate Preventable Catastrophe.* Times Books. 2004. 263 pp. ISBN 9780805076516.

Based on his experience and studies in politics and history, Allison, the former dean of the John F. Kennedy School of Government at Harvard, believes that the United States is vulnerable to the possibility of a terrorist attack with nuclear weapons. He asserts that preventing such a possibility is very possible but that a cohesive policy (as well as one that is "humble" and reaches out to other nations to build a world coalition against nuclear attacks) must be undertaken by the American government to safeguard against the possibility.

Subjects: Foreign Relations, Government, Politics, Terrorism, Weapons

Awards: New York Times Notable

Now Try: William Langewiesche's illuminating *The Atomic Bazaar,* in which he describes the state of nuclear weapon-building and components worldwide, might be suggested to these readers, as might other works about foreign relations and terrorism, including Richard Clarke's *Against All Enemies: Inside America's War on Terror* or Stefan Halper's *Silence of the Rational Center: Why American Foreign Policy Is Failing.* Judith Miller's *Germs: Biological Weapons and America's Secret War* might also be of interest, as might a variety of titles from the Exposés chapter.

Babbin, Jed, and Edward Timperlake

Showdown: Why China Wants War with the United States. Regnery. 2006. 226 pp. ISBN 9781596980051.

Authors Babbin and Timperlake list reasons why they believe China will eventually challenge the United States, militarily or otherwise, over the availability and use of oil. The authors argue that a showdown between the United States and China is virtually inevitable, and at the very least we are in the beginning stages of a "Pacific Cold War." Written in the style of a diary from the future in which America is engaged in war with China, this is a quickly paced policy read with rather more elements of adventure writing than can usually be found in political treatises.

> **Subjects:** American History, China, Communism, Foreign Relations, Government, Military, Politics

> **Now Try:** Other books published by Regnery publishing (a conservative publisher) might also be suggested, including Laura Ingraham's *Power to the People*, Robert Spencer's *Religion of Peace?*, Jed Babbin's *In the Words of Our Enemies*, and Rowan Scarborough's *Sabotage: America's Enemies within the CIA*; Business Reporting books about the rise of China as an economic power might also be suggested, such as Ted Fishman's *China, Inc.* or Robyn Meredith's *The Elephant and the Dragon.*

Berry, Wendell

The Way of Ignorance: and Other Essays. Shoemaker & Hoard. 2005. 180 pp. ISBN 9781593760779.

Many of the political, cultural, and agrarian essays in this collection were first delivered as speeches, lending them a conversational tone (even though Berry's prose, as always, is skillfully written). Although critics noted that many of these essays, ranging in subject from advice to John Kerry on his presidential campaign to ringing indictments of the current processes of globalization, had something of the air of "preaching to the converted," Berry as always is eloquent, impassioned, and persuasive in his arguments for a more natural and sensible society.

> **Subjects:** Community Life, Environmental Writing, Essays, Government, Politics, Small Press, Society

> **Now Try:** Berry's output has been prodigious; fans of his essays might also consider his novels *Jayber Crow* or his story collections *That Distant Land* and *Fidelity*, as well as his poetry and his other essay collections *The Unsettling of America*, *Sex, Economy, Freedom, and Community*, and *What Are People For*? Other agrarian and environmental titles by authors such as Wes Jackson, Bill McKibben (*The End of Nature* and *Deep Economy*), Annie Dillard (*Pilgrim at Tinker Creek*), Jane Brox, John Hays, and Aldo Leopold.

Buchanan, Pat

State of Emergency: The Third World Invasion and Conquest of America. St. Martin's Press. 2006. 308 pp. ISBN 9780312360030.

Political conservative author Buchanan offers a warning that the lack of a cohesive immigration policy in America is opening the future to a reclaiming of the American Southwest by Mexico and the "death of the West." Comparing the current situation to the fall of the Roman Empire and recent events in Russia and other European countries, Buchanan concludes his book with recommendations for immigration reform and border security.

> **Subjects:** Government, Immigration, Mexico, Politics, Race Relations, Society

> **Now Try:** Although Buchanan has become increasingly difficult to categorize, he previously wrote in the conservative tradition, and his other books espousing more traditionally "right" viewpoints might also be suggested, including *Day of Reckoning* and *The Death of the West*. Fans of his writings might consider works by other commentators such as Bill O'Reilly, Ann Coulter, or Sean Hannity. He is, however, emphatically not a "neo-con" and has at times been critical of the George W. Bush administration; as such, some of his readers might also consider books by Lou Dubose, as well as less blatantly partisan works such as Lawrence Wright's *The Looming Tower: Al-Qaeda and the Road to 9/11*, George Packer's *The Assassins' Gate: America in Iraq*, and Michael Gordon's *Cobra II*.

Cafferty, Jack

It's Getting Ugly Out There: The Frauds, Bunglers, Liars, and Losers Who Are Hurting America. Wiley. 2007. 269 pp. ISBN 9780470144794.

CNN commentator and longtime broadcast journalist Cafferty is known for speaking his mind, and he doesn't hold back in this, his first book, exploring George W. Bush's presidential tenure and a number of other cultural and political targets that draw his ire (including Anna Nicole Smith and numerous other politicians). Covering subjects such as immigration, corporate and political scandals, campaign finance reform, and the Iraq War, Cafferty more than earns his reputation as a curmudgeon, albeit a forthright one. Along the way he also provides details of his own media career and personal life, but the focus is definitely on society and the American cultural milieu at the beginning of the 21st century.

> **Subjects:** Government, Humor, Journalism, Mass Media, Memoirs, Politics, Society

> **Now Try:** Readers who enjoy Cafferty's curmudgeonly manner might consider other forthright political authors from all sides of the partisan divide, including Christopher Hitchens, Mark Steyn, Bernard Goldberg, Robert Novak, or John Stossel. Other political books might also appeal, including James Risen's *State of War*, Alan Greenspan's *The Age of Turbulence*, Keith Olbermann's *The Worst Person in the World*, John Dean's *Broken Government*, or Lou Dobbs's *War on the Middle Class* or *Independents Day*.

Chafets, Zev

A Match Made in Heaven: American Jews, Christian Zionists, and One Man's Exploration of the Weird and Wonderful Judeo-Evangelical Alliance. HarperCollins. 2007. 231 pp. ISBN 9780060890582.

Former director of the Israeli government press office and *New York Daily News* columnist, Chafets spent a year investigating the close ties between Christian evangelicals seeking alliances with the American Jewish establishment. Because, as Chafets points out, evangelicals view an independent and democratic Israel as imperative to their rapture timeline, many members of the liberal and secular Democratic Jewish establishment remain wary of their overtures. In this volume, the author meets Jerry Falwell, gets to know Jewish cadets at West Point, tours Pat Robertson's university, tours the Holy Land with Christian pilgrims, and even attends an event for George W. Bush with five hundred other Jewish Republicans

(Chafets himself voted for Bush). Although Chafets's writing is witty and his tone and banter light, he nonetheless explores important issues: Why do evangelicals really support Israel? How is the relationship between the two groups changing, and how will it continue to change? And what does that mean for those of the Jewish faith living in both America and in Israel?

> **Subjects:** Arab-Israeli Conflict, Christianity, Government, Judaism, Politics, Religion, Society

> **Now Try:** Other books about Israel and American politics might appeal to these readers, including Richard Ben Cramer's *Why Israel Lost*, Alan Dershowitz's *The Case for Israel* and *The Case for Peace*, and Thomas Friedman's *From Beirut to Jerusalem*, as well as more personal books like Sandy Tolan's *The Lemon Tree: An Arab, a Jew, and the Heart of the Middle East*.

Clarke, Jonathan, and Stefan A. Halper

Silence of the Rational Center: Why American Foreign Policy Is Failing. Basic Books. 2007. 312 pp. ISBN 9780465011414.

> Figures from both the political right and the left come in for criticism from conservative scholars Clarke and Halper, who argue that America's current fascination with political commentators and policy makers who are marketing their own brands of glib, simplistic thinking about foreign affairs and relations is leading to disastrous foreign policies in practice. Offering specific examples from the works of such figures as Noam Chomsky and Jeffrey Sachs, the authors maintain that Americans have become fascinated with far-fetched doomsday scenarios because that is all they have been presented with. Calling for more rational and centrist thought on this topic, this is a well-argued and scholarly but accessible treatise on politics and how it affects our nation's relations with other world nations.

> **Subjects:** Foreign Relations, Government, Politics, Scholarly

> **Now Try:** Other books on America's foreign relations might be offered, including Francis Fukuyama's *America at the Crossroads: Democracy, Power, and the Neoconservative Legacy*, John Robb's *Brave New War: The Next State of Terrorism and the End of Globalization*, or Madeleine Albright's *Mighty and the Almighty*, as well as History titles like Margaret Macmillan's *Nixon and Mao*, Robert Dallek's *Nixon and Kissinger*, or Stacy Schiff's *The Great Improvisation: Franklin, France, and the Birth of America*.

Correspondents of the *New York Times*; Introduction by Bill Keller

Class Matters. Times Books. 2005. 268 pp. ISBN 9780805080551.

> Traditionally Americans have believed themselves and their society to be largely free from class distinctions and discrimination, but as illustrated in this collection of journalistic pieces and exposes from the *New York Times* series on social class (and written by a variety of *New York Times* correspondents), individuals' classifications by income, education, wealth, and occupation do indeed have an impact on their lives and their socioeconomic status. Using individuals and families as their case studies, the reporters in this series paint a vivid picture of those who believe they have achieved prosperity through education and members of the upper middle class, as well as

the urban poor with little or no access to basic health care and others struggling to make ends meet even though they work multiple jobs. Also included are survey results that provide information on how Americans view their own class standings, as well as interviews with authors and politicians such as Diane McWhorter and Linda Chavez about their experiences with class discrimination.

Subjects: Character Profiles, Classism, Community Life, Economics, Essays, Family Relationships, Health Care, Politics, Society

Now Try: A wide variety of books from the Business Reporting and this political chapter might be offered to these readers, including David Shipler's *The Working Poor*, Barbara Ehrenreich's *Nickel and Dimed*, or Thomas Frank's *One Market Under God*; as well as books about those on the other side of the class divide, including Robert Frank's *Richistan*, David Brooks's *On Paradise Drive*, and *All the Money in the World: How the Forbes 400 Make—and Spend—Their Fortunes* by Peter Bernstein and Annalyn Swan. Books marking a middle path of the current economic situation, including Anya Kamenetz's *Generation Debt* and Daniel Brook's *The Trap: Selling Out to Stay Afloat in Winner-Take-All America* might appeal, as might more personal character studies about family relationships and socioeconomic status, including William Finnegan's *Cold New World*, Jason DeParle's *American Dream: Three Women, Ten Kids, and a Nation's Drive to End Welfare*, or Sudhir Venkatesh's *Gang Leader for a Day*.

Cramer, Richard Ben

How Israel Lost: The Four Questions. Simon & Schuster. 2004. 307 pp. ISBN 9780743250283.

Investigative reporter Cramer sets out to answer four questions that he thinks address all the issues of violence centered in Israel and between Arabs and Israelis: Why do we care about Israel? Why don't the Palestinians have a state? What is a Jewish state? Why is there no peace? Until these questions are sufficiently explored and answered, the author believes (himself the winner of a Pulitzer Prize for his reporting on the Middle East), there will be no peace in the Middle East. In refreshingly forthright and accessible language, the author makes suggestions directly to both the Israeli and the Palestinian sides and is also not afraid to admit that it is impossible to predict affairs in the region: "I know it's a fine time to tell you, now—but I'm always wrong about the Middle East. Of course, the Middle East will *make* you wrong. That's why it's a plum assignment for reporters—it preserves its capacity to shock."

Subjects: Arab-Israeli Conflict, Foreign Relations, Government, Israel, Middle East, Palestine, Quick Reads, War Reporting

Now Try: Richard Ben Cramer's other classic political work, *What It Takes: The Way to the White House*, might also appeal to these readers, as might other topical books such as Jimmy Carter's *Palestine: Peace Not Apartheid*, Noam Chomsky's *Fateful Triangle*, or Zev Chafets's *A Match Made in Heaven*. Other investigative journalists and Middle East scholars mentioned in Cramer's bibliography include Dilip Hiro, Joe Sacco, Amos Elon, and Edward Said.

Dobbs, Lou

Independents Day: Awakening the American Spirit. Viking. 2007. 237 pp. ISBN 9780670018369.

Anchor and managing editor of the CNN news program *Lou Dobbs Tonight*, Dobbs is no stranger to the concept of sharing his political opinions and prescriptions for an improved and "New America." In this volume, a sequel of sorts to his best-selling *War on the Middle Class*, Dobbs reviews American history from the past thirty years and illustrates, with clear examples and straightforward prose, how Americans' civil liberties are slowly being curtailed and the middle class disenfranchised, while workers' rights and pay are declining. Calling particularly for new leadership and policies, this is less a Republican or Democratic treatise than it is the contrarian cry of an "independent populist."

Subjects: Government, Mass Media, Politics

Now Try: Other mass media pundits who enjoy lambasting both sides of the political spectrum might be considered; these include Jack Cafferty (*It's Getting Ugly Out There*) and John Stossel (*Give Me a Break* and *Myths, Lies, and Downright Stupidity*). Lee Iacocca's feisty business and political manifesto *Where Have All the Leaders Gone?* might be suggested, as might Patrick Buchanan's *Day of Reckoning* or even Joe Bageant's (decidedly more left but still forthright) *Deer Hunting with Jesus: Dispatches from America's Class War*.

Fukuyama, Francis

America at the Crossroads: Democracy, Power, and the Neoconservative Legacy. Yale University Press. 2006. 226 pp. ISBN 9780300113990.

Fukuyama was critical of the Bush administration's decision to invade Iraq, an opinion that did not increase his popularity among his neoconservative friends inside or outside of that administration. In this scholarly but clearly argued and accessible text, he argues that the government of George W. Bush erred when it accepted the doctrine of "preventive war" as the central feature of its foreign policy, badly misjudged the reaction other countries would have to the invasion of Iraq, and underestimated the difficulty, not of deposing Saddam Hussein, but of establishing a democratic government in Iraq. By exploring the history and theory of neoconservative thought, the author provides context for the decisions made by the American government in the early twenty-first century; also included are theoretical suggestions for joining more positive aspects of the neoconservative legacy with more effective foreign policy.

Subjects: Foreign Relations, Government, Iraq War (2003), Politics, Scholarly, Small Press, War

Awards: New York Times Notable

Now Try: Fukuyama is a prolific author; his other books, including *The End of History and the Last Man*, which is a more stereotypically "neoconservative" treatise, might also be suggested, as might *The Right Nation: Conservative Power in America* by John Micklethwait and Adrian Wooldridge. Other scholarly books about America's foreign relations policies might be offered to these readers, including Jonathan Clarke's and Stefan Halper's *Silence of the Rational Center: Why American Foreign Policy Is Failing*, as might other takes on the neoconservative movement, such as John Dean's *Conservatives without Conscience* or Ryan Sager's *The Elephant in the Room*.

Hersh, Seymour M.

🎗 *Chain of Command: The Road from 9/11 to Abu Ghraib*. HarperCollins. 2004. 394 pp. ISBN 9780060195915.

Investigative journalist Hersh, best known for his writing on the My Lai massacre during the Vietnam War (*My Lai 4: A Report on the Massacre and Its Aftermath*) and for delving deep into political stories, aided by his copious insider contacts in the government and the military, here charts the lead-up to the Iraq War (2003), the personalities of various "hawks" and neoconservatives in George W. Bush's administration, the human rights violations and abuse at Abu Ghraib. Hersh also uses his well-placed contacts to address other issues such as influence peddling in our government, intelligence failures both before and after 9/11, and the development of Pakistan's nuclear arsenal. Originally these twenty-six pieces were published in *The New Yorker* magazine, so this is not so much a cohesive narrative as it is an arranged snapshot of American political influence here and abroad at the beginning of the twenty-first century.

> **Subjects:** 9/11, Abu Ghraib, Atrocities, Book Groups, Exposés, Iraq War (2003), Law and Lawyers, Prisons, Terrorism

> **Awards:** ALA Notable, New York Times Notable

> **Now Try:** Other books about the aftermath of 9/11 and the Iraq War might appeal to these readers, including Lawrence Wright's *The Looming Tower*, Mark Danner's *Torture and Truth*, or Rajiv Chandrasekaran's *Imperial Life in the Emerald City*. Other investigative classics by authors such as George Packer (*The Assassins' Gate: America in Iraq*), Bob Woodward and Carl Bernstein (*All the President's Men*), or Anthony Shadid (*Night Draws Near*); as well as books by David Remnick, who wrote the foreword for this volume, might also be suggested, including *Reporting: Writings from the New Yorker* or *Lenin's Tomb: The Last Days of the Soviet Empire*.

Hitchens, Christopher

God Is Not Great: How Religion Poisons Everything. Twelve. 2007. 307 pp. ISBN 9780446579803.

British journalist and political commentator Christopher Hitchens is never shy about speaking his mind, and never less so than when discussing religion. In this atheist manifesto, he lays the blame for most of history's tragedies squarely at the door of the world religions and their followers and makes his case for why he believes that false hope in a greater power is worse than no hope at all.

> **Subjects:** Atheism, Book Groups, God, Making Sense . . ., Religion, Spirituality

> **Now Try:** Readers who agree with Hitchens might further consider Sam Harris's *The End of Faith* or *Letter to a Christian Nation*, Richard Dawkins's *The God Delusion*, Victor Stenger's *God: The Failed Hypothesis*, Julian Barnes's more personal *Nothing to Be Frightened Of*, or Daniel Dennett's *Breaking the Spell*. More politicized books such as Kevin Phillips's *American Theocracy* or *Conservatives without Conscience* by John Dean might also be offered to these readers.

Humes, Edward

Monkey Girl: Evolution, Education, Religion, and the Battle for America's Soul. Ecco. 2007. 380 pp. ISBN 9780060885489.

Pulitzer Prize–winning journalist Humes provides a character portrait of both a town and a trial in this in-depth story of the 2005 *Kitzmiller v. Dover* case (in which parents sued the Dover, Pennsylvania, school district for voting to use a science textbook that focused on the theory of intelligent design rather than evolution). Through interviews and a compelling account of the trial itself, Humes illuminates the greater picture of the cultural divide between proponents of evolution and those who ascribe to intelligent design.

> **Subjects:** Community Life, Creationism, Education, Evolution, Intelligent Design, Law and Lawyers, Pennsylvania, Religion, Science, Trials
>
> **Now Try:** Those readers interested in the intersects between science and religion (particularly those which deal with evolution) might also consider such titles as Michael Ruse's *Darwin and Design*, or Edward Larson's *Summer for the Gods: The Scopes Trial and America's Continuing Debate Over Science and Religion*, as well as his *Evolution: The Remarkable History of a Scientific Theory*. Other investigative works which focus on smaller towns and community life include Jonathan Harr's *A Civil Action*, Gillian Klucas's *Leadville*, and Lisa Belkin's *Show Me a Hero*.

Imhoff, Daniel, and Michael Pollan

Food Fight: The Citizen's Guide to a Food and Farm Bill. University of California Press. 2007. 167 pp. ISBN 9780970950024.

Authors Imhoff and Pollan provide an in-depth and illustrated guide to the United States Farm Bill, arguably one of the most influential and least understood pieces of legislation regularly passed by the government. The Farm Bill dictates what is grown where, determines farm subsidy amounts (to the tune of $25 billion dollars annually), and affects a number of far-ranging environmental and political issues from rural economics to national security and biodiversity. This is not a narrative-driven piece of writing but is written in an engaging style with numerous pictures, illustrations, and practical suggestions for better food production and consumption methods.

> **Subjects:** Agriculture, Economics, Food, Political Science, Politics, Small Press
>
> **Now Try:** Other books by Michael Pollan, particularly *An Omnivore's Dilemma* and *In Defense of Food* might be offered to these readers, as might a number of food and Environmental Writing books by authors such as Marion Nestle, Nina Planck, and James Howard Kunstler. The authors also make references to the author Jared Diamond, whose books might appeal, as might a number of titles from the Exposés chapter, including Thomas Pawlick's *The End of Food* and Randall Fitzgerald's *The Hundred-Year Lie*.

Kuttner, Robert

The Squandering of America: How the Failure of Our Politics Undermines Our Prosperity. Knopf. 2007. 337 pp. ISBN 9781400040803.

Linking economics and politics, Kuttner argues that the increasing difficulties faced by the American middle class (more layoffs, static wages, rising prices, the high cost of health insurance) are directly linked to the consolidation of power and wealth in only the very highest ranks of American society. Among the crises that Kuttner explores are increasingly complex and unstable financial markets and speculations, subprime lending, and America's dependence on the low prices created by a system of globalization which rewards companies for flocking to global areas with the fewest regulations. Although this is a serious and nuanced work, it is written in an accessible manner and might appeal to a wide variety of both business and political readers.

> **Subjects:** Business, Economics, Finance, Globalization, Government, Politics, Scholarly

> **Now Try:** Authors who provided blurbs for this book are well-known political writers and their books might be offered as well, including Bill Moyers's *Welcome to Doomsday*, William Greider's *One World, Ready or Not* and *Who Will Tell the People: The Betrayal of American Democracy*, Barbara Ehrenreich's *Nickel and Dimed*, or James Fallows's *Blind into Baghdad* and *Breaking the News*. Other books about economics and politics together might be offered, such as the anthology *Class Matters*, Robert Putnam's *Bowling Alone*, and Joe Bageant's *Deer Hunting with Jesus*.

Mann, Brian

Welcome to the Homeland: A Journey to the Rural Heart of America's Conservative Revolution. Steerforth Press. 2006. 288 pp. ISBN 9781586421113.

Mann makes the argument that the true political divide in America is not between entire red states and blue states but rather between rural and urban populations within each state and in the country as a whole (referring to the rural schism, he says it "is the new frontier in America's culture war"). He further posits that America's fifty million rural whites, whom he terms "Homelanders," have come to dominate, in theory and in policy, the Republican Party, the Senate, and the Supreme Court. By traveling through the nation's geographical heartland and being guided by his brother, himself a true "homelander" in cultural and fundamental religious beliefs, Mann seeks to reveal the segment of the population that is having a much greater effect on its politics than its mere numbers would lead you to believe.

> **Subjects:** Conservatism, Government, Politics, Rural Life, Society, Urban Life

> **Now Try:** Although Mann steers away from the red state/blue state divide, books on that subject might be suggested, such as Thomas Frank's *What's the Matter with Kansas?*, Thomas Edsall's *Building Red America*, the essay collection *Living Blue in the Red States*, and Jim Wallis's *God's Politics*. Books on American society and culture might also appeal, including Richard C. Longworth's *Caught in the Middle: America's Heartland in the Age of Globalism*, David Brooks's *On Paradise Drive* and *Bobos in Paradise*, Joe Bageant's *Deer Hunting with Jesus*, Roger Putnam's *Bowling Alone*, or George Packer's memoir *Blood of the Liberals*. Other authors mentioned in Mann's bibliography, including Mark Kurlansky, George Lakoff, Alvin Toffler, Howard Zinn, and Wendell Berry might appeal, as might Travel and Character Profile titles such as Mark Singer's *Character Studies*, Hampton Sides's *Americana*, Calvin Trillin's *Feeding a Yen*, or Hank Stuever's *Off Ramp*.

Morris, Dick, and Eileen McGann

Outrage: How Illegal Immigration, the United Nations, Congressional Ripoffs, Student Loan Overcharges, Tobacco Companies, Trade Protection and Drug Companies Are Ripping Us Off—and What to Do about It. HarperCollins. 2007. 351 pp. ISBN 9780061195402.

Political consultant Morris and CEO (of Vote.com) McGann provide an impassioned plea to readers to take notice of the many ways lobbyists, organizations, and other groups influence governmental and business decisions, from illegal immigration to insurance payoffs (or the lack thereof) after disasters like Hurricane Katrina. The authors have also stated that they hope their book serves as a source of information and facts about "the special interests of both the left and the right."

Subjects: Business, Economics, Government, Immigration, Politics, United Nations

Now Try: Morris was a consultant to Bill Clinton for many years and now works for Fox News; McGann's Vote.com advertises itself as "neither Democrat nor Republican." Readers interested in this book might also consider related political titles such as Patrick Buchanan's *State of Emergency: The Third World Invasion and Conquest of America*, Douglas Brinkley's *The Great Deluge: Katrina, New Orleans, and the Mississippi Gulf Coast*, or Dick Morris's own *Rewriting History* (about Hillary Clinton). These readers might also consider other "presidential" works such as *The Reagan Diaries* or Michael Beschloss's *Presidential Courage*, as well as books by similarly straight-talking media pundits, including Bernard Goldberg's *Bias* or *Crazies to the Left of Me, Wimps to the Right*, or John Stossel's *Give Me a Break*.

Phillips, Kevin

American Theocracy: The Peril and Politics of Radical Religion, Oil, and Borrowed Money in the 21st Century. Viking. 2006. 462 pp. ISBN 9780670034864.

Political analyst and former Republican strategist Phillips offers three interrelated theories in this title: that America's overdependence on oil, approval of radical religious beliefs, and abundance of borrowed money, will all contribute to future problems both domestically and internationally. Phillips is currently a journalist with the *Los Angeles Times* and *Harper's Magazine*, and this work includes extensive endnotes and a comprehensive index.

Subjects: Economics, Government, Oil, Politics, Religion

Now Try: Fans of Phillips's heavily researched works might also consider his subsequent title, *Bad Money: Reckless Finance, Failed Politics, and the Global Crisis of American Capitalism,* as well as nonfiction by such economic and political authors as Paul Krugman (*The Great Unraveling* and *The Conscience of a Liberal*), John Perkins (*Confessions of an Economic Hit Man* and *The Secret History of the American Empire*), Douglas Brinkley (*The Great Deluge*), James Risen (*State of War*), and Ron Suskind (*The One Percent Doctrine*).

Ricks, Thomas

🎖 *Fiasco: The American Military Adventure in Iraq.* Penguin Press. 2006. 482 pp. ISBN 9781594201035.

Journalist Ricks (he is the Pentagon correspondent for the *Washington Post*) researched this title while living and moving with military units fighting in Iraq following the 2003 invasion. The first half of the book explores the run-up to the conflict, while the second half explores the underlying reasons for the continuing insurgencies in that country.

Subjects: George W. Bush, Exposés, Foreign Relations, Government, Iraq, Iraq War (2003), Military, Politics

Awards: New York Times Notable

Now Try: There has been no shortage of works published about the 2003 invasion of Iraq; readers of this title might also consider George Packer's comprehensive *The Assassins' Gate: America in Iraq*, Bob Woodward's *State of Denial*, or Michael Isikoff's *Hubris: The Inside Story of Spin, Scandal, and the Selling of the Iraq War*. Other more broadly political books such as Frank Rich's *The Greatest Story Ever Sold* or Ron Suskind's *The One Percent Doctrine* might also appeal, as might books about the war's effect on Iraqi civilians, including Anthony Shadid's *Night Draws Near* and Rajiv Chandrasekaran's *Imperial Life in the Emerald City*. Author Ricks has also provided a number of books that he feels are instrumental to understanding the situation in Iraq; they include Alistair Horne's *A Savage War of Peace: Algeria, 1954–1962* and *Learning to Eat Soup with a Knife* by Lt. Col. John Nagl.

Ritter, Scott

Target Iran: The Truth about the White House's Plans for Regime Change. Perseus Books Group. 2006. 228 pp. ISBN 9781560259367.

Former UN weapons inspector Ritter explores the history of America's foreign relations with the country of Iran and outlines what he feels is the current emphasis on casting Iran as a faceless evil power that is developing its nuclear capabilities. Ritter also provides a succinct summation of global views toward Iran and compares the case being made to wage war against the country to the case previously made by the George W. Bush administration to invade Iraq in 2003.

Subjects: Foreign Relations, Iran, Middle East, Nuclear Weapons, Politics

Now Try: Ritter was also the author of the book *Iraq Confidential*, in which he questioned the necessity of the invasion of that country in 2003. Other books about Iran might be suggested to these readers, including Barbara Slavin's thoughtful *Bitter Friends, Bosom Enemies: Iran, the U.S., and the Twisted Path to Confrontation* or Reese Erlich's *The Iran Agenda*. Other books about foreign relations, such as Steve Levine's *The Oil and the Glory*, Fareed Zakaria's *The Post-American World*, or Aaron David Miller's *The Much Too Promised Land: America's Elusive Search for Arab-Israeli Peace*, might also be of interest.

Slavin, Barbara

Bitter Friends, Bosom Enemies: Iran, the U.S., and the Twisted Path to Confrontation. St. Martin's Press. 2007. 258 pp. ISBN 9780312368258.

USA Today senior correspondent Slavin illustrates, with lucid prose and vivid examples, the love-hate relationship between the United States and Iran, as well as the two countries' complex history of foreign relations. As one of the few American reporters ever to interview Iranian president Mahmoud Ahmadinejad, and with an impressive understanding of the region and its culture based on her many travels there, Slavin is able to provide her reader with valuable insights and nonpartisan considerations. In addition to providing a valuable overview of Iranian history, including information about such important figures as Mohammad Mossadeq, Reza Shah, Mohammad Reza Pahlavi, and the Ayatollah Khomeini, Slavin also explores the lives and beliefs of current residents of Iran and their attitudes towards Americans and the West.

Subjects: Foreign Relations, Government, Iran, Iraq, Middle East, Nuclear Weapons, Travel, War, World History

Now Try: Other books about Iran and its culture might be suggested to these readers, including Marjane Satrapi's graphic novel memoirs *Persepolis* and *Persepolis II*, Azar Nafisi's *Reading Lolita in Tehran*, Mark Bowden's *Guests of the Ayatollah*, or Roya Hakakian's *Journey from the Land of No*; Slavin also lists a number of related books in her bibliography, including Elaine Sciolino's *Persian Mirrors*, Shaul Bakhash's *The Reign of the Ayatollahs*, or Baqer Moin's *Khomeini: Life of the Ayatolla*.

Suskind, Ron

The One Percent Doctrine. Simon & Schuster. 2006. 367 pp. ISBN 9780743271097.

Journalist Suskind investigates Vice President Dick Cheney's "one percent doctrine," first espoused in November 2001, that any threat to national security which had a one percent chance of happening should be treated as a certainty. Suskind makes no secret of the fact that he believes this doctrine is indicative of this administration's ignoring of certain facts and bases much of his exposé on information he learned from former CIA director George Tenet.

Subjects: George W. Bush, Richard Cheney, Government, Iraq, Politics, Terrorism

Now Try: Suskind's readers might also consider George Tenet's *At the Center of the Storm*, George Packer's detailed look at pre- and post-war Iraq, *The Assassins' Gate: America in Iraq*, as well as books similar in subject and ideology, such as *Fiasco: The American Military Adventure in Iraq* (Thomas Ricks), *COBRA II: The Inside Story of the Invasion and Occupation of Iraq* (Michael Gordon), *State of War: The Secret History of the CIA and the Bush Administration* (James Risen), and *American Theocracy: The Peril and Politics of Radical Religion, Oil, and Borrowed Money in the 21st Century* (Kevin Phillips).

Wright, Lawrence

🏅 *The Looming Tower: Al-Qaeda and the Road to 9/11.* Knopf. 2006. 469 pp. ISBN 9780375414862.

New Yorker reporter Wright conducted more than five hundred interviews in the course of writing this history of al-Qaeda (which doubles as an extended character portrait of Osama bin Laden). This book truly offers an "inside look" at the historical course of terrorism and the development of the 9/11 terrorism attack in particular. Based on five years of research and hundreds of interviews, Wright explores the roles of such individuals as Osama bin Laden, Ayman al-Zawahiri, John O'Neill (the FBI's counterterrorism chief), and Prince Turki al-Faisal (the former head of Saudi intelligence).

Subjects: 9/11, Al-Qaeda, Book Groups, Government, Islam, New York City, Politics, Terrorism

Awards: New York Times Notable, Pulitzer Prize

Now Try: Those readers interested in this subject might also consider the official 9/11 Commission Report, Thomas Kean's and Lee Hamilton's *Without*

Precedent: The Inside Story of the 9/11 Commission, Kristen Breitweiser's *Wake-Up Call: The Political Education of a 9/11 Widow*, William Keegan's *Closure: The Untold Story of the Ground Zero Recovery Mission*, and William Langewiesche's *American Ground: Unbuilding the World Trade Center*. Other political "inside looks" might also appeal to these readers, including *Cobra II* by Michael Gordon, *The One Percent Doctrine* by Ron Suskind, Richard Clarke's *Against All Enemies: Inside America's War on Terror*, and James Risen's *State of War: The Secret History of the CIA and the Bush Administration*.

Zakaria, Fareed

🐾 *The Post-American World.* Norton. 2008. 292 pp. ISBN 9780393062359.

Editor of *Newsweek International* Zakaria argues that the next few decades will signal a "great power shift" from America to the rest of the world, including such growing (in population and influence) countries as China, India, and Brazil. Although Zakaria points out multiple challenges facing the United States, from terrorism to poverty, religious fanaticism to energy consumption, he also concludes his treatise on a positive note, pointing out that Americans should rely more than ever on its strengths of openness and tolerance and resist the urge to fear a new world order.

Subjects: Book Groups, Economics, Foreign Relations, Globalization, Government, Politics, Society

Awards: New York Times Notable

Now Try: Fareed Zakaria is also the author of *The Future of Freedom*; numerous titles from his notes might also appeal to these readers, including such political titles as Thomas Friedman's *The World is Flat: A Brief History of the Twenty-First Century*, Niall Ferguson's *Empire: The Rise and Demise of the British World Order*, or Robert Kagan's *Of Paradise and Power*. Other Political Reporting books might appeal to these readers, including Jonathan Clarke's and Stefan Halper's *Silence of the Rational Center: Why American Foreign Policy is Failing* or Robert Kuttner's *The Squandering of America: How the Failure of Our Politics Undermines Our Prosperity*; Business Reporting books, particularly those about globalization, might also be suggested, including Jeffrey Sachs's *Common Wealth: Economics for a Crowded Planet* or David Rothkopf's *Superclass: The Global Power Elite and the World They Are Making*.

Politics in Practice

There are readers who consider themselves more "political junkies" than partisans of either side or interested in any one political party to the exclusion of all others. For these readers, books about the practical side of politics—what might be thought of as the more scholarly and detailed political science books, although political science is not always their sole or even most important subject—might be just the ticket. These books often discuss the processes of the democratic political system and place those processes squarely within their cultural and historical context. Although they, too, can be showcases for their authors' opinions and beliefs, they tend to be a bit cooler in tone and writing style and most often include much longer and more comprehensive notes and references lists, bibliographies, and indexes. As such they are often their own best source of future reading recommendations; often a perusal of the books and authors listed among their authors' references will provide many helpful avenues for suggested reading.

Readers who enjoy these books, which are often written in a slightly more sedate style than books from the Political Commentary or Hot-Button issues subgenres, might also consider a number of In-Depth Reporting titles, in which the authors typically reserve their judgments until they have fully investigated their stories, and then tend to write them in a straightforward manner; Historical Perspectives reporting in particular might be suggested. Other nonfiction books in which authors strive to present as full and as accurate a big picture as possible might also be offered, including titles from the Biz Crit subgenre of Business Reporting, International Exposés, and a wide variety of titles whose subject is History, either American or world.

> Written by and for the pure "political junkies" who are less interested in differing ideologies than they are in the actual processes of governance, administration, and elections, Politics in Practice books feature a cooler tone than most Political Reporting titles, with a heavier emphasis on research, interviews, and objective presentation. They are not typically story-driven but rather more informational and persuasive in style and are designed to appeal to readers' logic more than to their emotions.

Bai, Matt

🎗 *The Argument: Billionaires, Bloggers, and the Battle to Remake Democratic Politics.* Penguin Press. 2007. 316 pp. ISBN 9781594201332.

Bai goes deep inside the operations and machinations of the Democratic Party in America, trying to make cohesive sense of a party whose leaders are most well known for not having a cohesive message. Exploring how grassroots organizing and blogs have changed the political playing field, Bai also profiles many prominent members of the party, including Howard Dean, George Soros, union leader Andy Stern, blogger Markos Moulitsas Zuniga, and many others as they struggle to work together to inspire voters and citizens.

Subjects: Blogs, Journalism, Mass Media, Political Science, Politics

Awards: New York Times Notable

Now Try: Books by author bloggers and media critics (including Zuniga) might be suggested, including *Crashing the Gate*, books by MoveOn.org's founder George Soros (including *The Age of Fallibility*), A. J. Rossmiller's *Still Broken: A Recruit's Inside Account of Intelligence Failures, from Baghdad to the Pentagon*, Arianna Huffington's *Right Is Wrong*, Sam Seder's *F.U.B.A.R.: America's Right-Wing Nightmare*, or Eric Boehlert's *Lapdogs: How the Press Rolled Over for Bush*.

Cramer, Richard Ben

What It Takes: The Way to the White House. Random House. 1992. 1047 pp. ISBN 9780394562605.

In this massive and extensively researched volume, Pulitzer Prize–winning journalist Cramer undertook to follow the lives and political and interpersonal machinations of the 1988 candidates for American president, including George H. W. Bush, Bob Dole, Gary Hart, and Michael Dukakis. Written in an immediate and informal style ("When he stepped up to the podium for a speech to four thousand noisy muldoons of the Philadelphia Democratic City Committee, he got that crowd quiet in a hurry: 'I've been in thirty-two states, and you're the worst damn audience anywhere,' [Joe] Biden said. He started to laugh. 'I hope you can get out the vote like you talk, because you sure talk like hell . . . you're all a bunch of bums,' " p. 650). This unprecedented and never duplicated work of Political Reporting shows all sides of the candidates and the political process in unwavering and sometimes harsh detail.

> **Subjects:** Classics, Epic Reads, Government, Politics, Presidents, Profanity
>
> **Now Try:** Other books on presidents and the political process might appeal to these readers, including Bob Woodward's *The Choice*, David Halberstam's *The Powers That Be*, Sidney Blumenthal's *The Clinton Wars*, Theodore White's 1960 classic *The Making of the President*, or Joe McGinniss's *The Selling of the President* (not to mention presidential Biographies, from Robert Draper's *Dead Certain*, about President George W. Bush, to recent books about Dwight Eisenhower, Theodore Roosevelt, and John F. Kennedy, among others). Cramer is a well-known journalist, and his earlier books, *How Israel Lost* and *What Do You Think of Ted Williams Now?*, might also appeal.

Didion, Joan

Political Fictions. Knopf. 2001. 338 pp. ISBN 9780375413384.

This is a collection of political pieces originally published in the *New York Review of Books*, introduced in typical Didion fashion. The first essay is from 1988 and concerns the Republican and Democratic national conventions; from there Didion moves on to consider El Salvador and American politics at the end of the 1980s, Clinton and change in 1992, Newt Gingrich, Bob Woodward's book *The Choice* about the Clinton and Dole campaigns, Clinton and the Starr Report, and compassionate conservatives.

> **Subjects:** 20th Century, American History, Elections, Essays, History, Political Science, Politics
>
> **Now Try:** Didion's other books of political and cultural essays might also appeal to these readers, including *Fixed Ideas: America Since 9/11* and *Slouching Towards Bethlehem*, as might her memoir *The Year of Magical Thinking*; her husband's collection of nonfiction, titled *Regards: The Collected Nonfiction of John Gregory Dunne*, in which many essays consider politics, class, and culture, might also be enjoyed. Other books in the *New York Review of Books* essay collection series, including Bill Moyers's *Welcome to Doomsday*, Elizabeth Drew's *Fear and Loathing in George W. Bush's Washington*, and Mark Danner's *The Secret Way to War* might be suggested, as might John Berger's more global *Hold Everything Dear: Dispatches on Survival and Resistance*, or any number of books from the Political Reporting chapter.

Gitlin, Todd

The Bulldozer and the Big Tent: Blind Republicans, Lame Democrats, and the Recovery of American Ideals. Wiley. 2007. 327 pp. ISBN 9780471748533.

In this book, Gitlin discusses the political movements and history of the past fifty years, highlighting the rise in popularity and influence of the Republican Party (particularly its most conservative members), and argues that the disparate nature of the many groups that comprise the Democratic Party make it harder to organize into one successful and cohesive whole. The core of Gitlin's argument can be easily seen in his early contention that "it goes without saying that it is far easier to blend two constituencies than the Democrats' roughly eight: labor, African Americans, Hispanics, feminists, gays, environmentalists, members of the helping professions, and the militantly liberal."

Subjects: Government, Political Science, Politics, Scholarly

Now Try: Other books about the currently very partisan nature of American politics might also be suggested to these readers, including Thomas Frank's *What's the Matter with Kansas?*, Joan Didion's essay collection *Political Fictions*, the equally scholarly *Eight Ways to Run the Country* by Brian Patrick Mitchell, George Lakoff's *Don't Think of an Elephant!*, or Jim Wallis's *God's Politics*. Authors who blurbed this title include George Packer (*The Assassins' Gate: America in Iraq*) and Thomas Edsall (*Building Red America*).

Halberstam, David

The Best and the Brightest. Random House. 1972. 688 pp. ISBN 9780394461632.

Arguably now more of a history book than one about current affairs, this book on the "best and brightest" individuals with whom President John Kennedy sought to surround himself remains a classic of journalistic research and political reporting. Over the course of years and numerous interviews, Halberstam put together a comprehensive picture of the bad things that can happen in governance and wars, even when the very smartest people put their heads together and attempt to dictate human actions and history. Halberstam's writing style is immediate, and even though he describes events that took place nearly half a century ago, his language and character profiles feel as fresh as though they had been written yesterday.

Subjects: 1960s, American History, Classics, Epic Reads, Foreign Relations, Government, Lyndon Johnson, John F. Kennedy, Politics, Vietnam War

Now Try: Other classics of political reporting might particularly appeal to these readers, such as Joe McGinniss's *The Selling of the President* or Bob Woodward's and Carl Bernstein's *All the President's Men*; other books from and about the time might also be suggested, such as Daniel Ellsberg's *Secrets: A Memoir of Vietnam and the Pentagon Papers*, Paul Hendrickson's *The Living and the Dead: Robert McNamara and Five Lives of a Lost War*, Robert McNamara's *In Retrospect*, or even Robert Caro's three-volume biography of Lyndon Johnson. Other fiction and nonfiction about the Vietnam War, by authors such as Tim O'Brien and Stanley Karnow might be suggested, as might other books by David Halberstam, including *The Coldest Winter* (about the Korean War) or *The Powers That Be*.

Irons, Peter H.

God on Trial: Dispatches from America's Religious Battlefields. Viking. 2007. 362 pp. ISBN 9780670038510.

Author and constitutional scholar Irons provides the legal play-by-play for five landmark Supreme Court battles on the issue of separation of church and state in this heavily researched but readable story, which includes not only the legalese and details of the cases, but personal responses and interviews with people on both sides of each issue. The cases include a 1989 case in which residents of San Diego challenged a forty-three-foot-high cross in the center of a public park; a 1995 dispute in Texas over prayer at football games; a 1999 lawsuit in Kentucky against displaying the ten commandments in county courthouses; a 2000 challenge in California about the words "under God" in the pledge used at school; and a case in Pennsylvania in 2004 regarding the teaching of "intelligent design."

Subjects: American History, Christianity, Law and Lawyers,, Religion, Supreme Court, Trials

Now Try: Jeffrey Toobin's inside look, *The Nine: Inside the Secret World of the Supreme Court* or Clarence Thomas's *My Grandfather's Son* might particularly appeal to these readers, as might other books about legal proceedings such as Jonathan Harr's *A Civil Action*, Edward Humes's *Monkey Girl: Evolution, Education, Religion, and the Battle for America's Soul*, Edward Larson's *Summer for the Gods*, or Steve Bogira's *Courtroom 302* or even fiction titles by John Grisham, Phillip Margolin, or David Baldacci.

Lindsey, Brink

The Age of Abundance: How Prosperity Transformed America's Politics and Culture. Collins. 2007. 394 pp. ISBN 9780060747664.

Linking economic prosperity to citizens' participation in political issues and debates, Lindsey argues that a bold new type of libertarianism might be necessary to resolve differences between Republicans, who "want to go home to the United States of the 1950s," and the Democrats, "who want to work there." The author combines issues of history, economics, politics, and sociology in this accessible assessment of the current state of partisan American politics.

Subjects: 20th Century, American History, Economics, Making Sense . . ., Politics, Society

Now Try: Lindsey's bibliography is in itself a wonderful read-alike list; he provides such author names as Allan Bloom (*The Closing of the American Mind*), David Brooks (*On Paradise Drive*), Thomas Frank (*One Market under God*), Robert Kanigel (*The One Best Way*), Stephanie Coontz (*The Way We Never Were*), James Twitchell (*Living It Up: America's Love Affair with Luxury*), and Tom Wolfe. Broader works on culture and society written by authors such as Jared Diamond and Jacques Barzun might also appeal.

Mitchell, Brian Patrick

Eight Ways to Run the Country: A New and Revealing Look at Left and Right. Praeger. 2007. 161 pp. ISBN 9780275993580.

Recent years have seen politicians and the media depicting the United States as a polarized red-and-blue land in which only two ruling parties offer the possibility of governance. In this academic but lively and short book, author Mitchell defines and explores four traditional political traditions: republican constitutionalism, libertarian individualism, progressive democracy, and plutocratic nationalism.

Further segmenting those four traditions into eight contemporary perspectives leads to eight very different ideologies that Mitchell argues American citizens should embrace and enact in order to bring more diversity to our system of governance and our elections.

> **Subjects:** Economics, Government, Making Sense . . ., Politics, Religion, Scholarly, Society

> **Now Try:** Mitchell provides references to a wide variety of cultural and political writers, including Robert Putnam (*Bowling Alone*), William F. Buckley, Jr. (*God and Man at Yale*), Thomas Frank (*What's the Matter with Kansas?*), Robert Kagan (*Of Paradise and Power* and *The Return of History and the End of Dreams*), and Jedediah Purdy (*For Common Things*).

Rubin, Aviel D.

Brave New Ballot: The Battle to Safeguard Democracy in the Age of Electronic Voting. Morgan Road Books. 2006. 280 pp. ISBN 9780767922104.

Rubin, a computer scientist at Johns Hopkins University, studied the electronic voting machines currently in use in thirty-seven states, and he and his team unearthed a variety of disturbing facts: very rarely are programmers or computer security analysts employed by states to monitor the machines; votes are registered only on removable data cards on which it's impossible to track any tampering; and there were enough irregularities associated with the use of these machines during the 2004 machines that their use and validity should be seriously questioned going into the next election. Although much of the narrative functions more as an exposé than a political treatise, Rubin also relates his experiences being defamed by voting-machine manufacturers, as well as working with politicians who aren't interested in hearing about or fixing the problems in the system.

> **Subjects:** Computers, Democracy, Government, Politics, Society, Technology

> **Now Try:** Other books about the political process might particularly appeal to these readers, including Brian J. Mitchell's *Eight Ways to Run the Country: A New and Revealing Look at Left and Right*, William Poundstone's *Gaming the Vote: Why Elections Aren't Fair (and What We Can Do about It)*, Allen Raymond's *How to Rig an Election: Confessions of a Republican Operative*, Drew Westen's *The Political Brain: The Role of Emotion in Deciding the Fate of the Nation*, and Tracy Campbell's comprehensive history *Deliver the Vote: A History of Election Fraud, an American Political Tradition, 1742 to 2004*.

Toobin, Jeffrey

🏳 *The Nine: Inside the Secret World of the Supreme Court.* Doubleday. 2007. 369 pp. ISBN 9780385516402.

Toobin, a staff writer with *The New Yorker*, provides an inside look into the workings of the Supreme Court from the Reagan political era through the appointment of John Roberts as Chief Justice and the court in the early twenty-first century. Through interviews and analysis (the author is also a commentator on legal issues for CNN), Toobin examines the workings of the court, the political nature of its appointments and findings, the personalities and legacies of some of its most infamous members, including

Antonin Scalia, William Rehnquist, and Sandra Day O'Connor, and the influence of its decisions on American politics, culture, and society.

Subjects: Character Profiles, Government, Law and Lawyers, Politics, Supreme Court

Awards: New York Times Notable

Now Try: Titles promising the "inside story" on legal and political institutions might appeal to these readers, including James Risen's *State of War: The Secret History of the CIA and the Bush Administration*, Tim Weiner's *Legacy of Ashes: The History of the CIA*, Richard Yancey's *Confessions of a Tax Collector*, John Perkins's *Confessions of an Economic Hit Man* or *The Secret History of the American Empire*, Steve Bogira's *Courtroom 302*, or Marissa Batt's *Ready for the People: My Most Chilling Cases as a Prosecutor*. Legal thrillers, particularly those by authors such as John Grisham, Phillip Margolin, and Scott Turow, might also be offered.

Westen, Drew

The Political Brain: The Role of Emotion in Deciding the Fate of the Nation. PublicAffairs. 2007. 457 pp. ISBN 9781586484255.

Ever wondered how politicians are truly elected? Professor of psychology Westen seeks to prove that we do indeed vote with our hearts and not our heads; in this investigative and scientific treatise, he shares his theories on how, historically, the American electorates' votes have been emotionally influenced by campaign ads, debates, and personal "liking" of the available candidates. Citing new physiological research obtained through brain scanning and other similar tests, Westen illustrates that campaigns must present even their most rational platforms with irrationality to appeal to the overemotional voter.

Subjects: Brain, Marketing, Neuroscience, Politics, Science

Now Try: Other books about the political process, including Aviel Rubin's *Brave New Ballot: The Battle to Safeguard Democracy in the Age of Electronic Voting*, William Poundstone's *Gaming the Vote: Why Elections Aren't Fair (and What We Can Do about It)*, Matt Bai's *The Argument*, or Allen Raymond's *How to Rig an Election: Confessions of a Republican Operative* might all appeal to these readers, as might books about marketing such as Frank Luntz's *Words That Work* or *Applebee's America: How Successful Political, Business, and Religious Leaders Connect with the New American Community* by Ron Fournier, Douglas Sosnik, and Matthew Dowd. Authors mentioned in Westen's references, including George Lakoff and James Twitchell, might also be suggested.

Politicos

Yes, in all fairness, many of the books in this subgenre of Political Reporting might also be considered to be Commentary, on either the right or left sides of the American political spectrum. But these books, written by some of the most recognizable political names and personalities in the country, offer a little something more than commentary. They offer the personal touch; the details, the stories, the viewpoints that can only be formed by those who have spent entire lifetimes working in and near politics—true "politicos." They occupy a small but important middle ground between more traditional Biographies and Memoirs of American Presidents and other political leaders, and the Political Commentary books, which are more often written by those who observe history but don't necessarily step out there and make it. These books also differ in another important way from the other books of Political Reporting in that their appeal is primarily character-driven. Not a lot of readers would probably be drawn to a book on the subject of charitable giving, but a fan of Bill Clinton and a person who is fascinated by him as a character might certainly enjoy his book *Giving*. So if they are so character-driven, why not just consider these Life Stories? Because, more often than not, although they focus on particular and notable characters, the authors of these books tend to offer the stories of how their subjects have carved out political lives or responded to their political duties or jobs. Jimmy Carter's *Our Endangered Values* is not so much a book about Carter's life as it is about how his political experiences have shaped his worldview.

The appeal of these books resides squarely with their characters and either their recounting of political events or their insight into the personalities of the other politicos they knew or with whom they worked. As such, readers who enjoy them might enjoy other character-driven nonfiction narratives, particularly those Life Stories—biographies, memoirs, and autobiographies alike—of political and presidential figures. Nonfiction History titles might also be suggested to these readers, particularly those focusing on well-known characters in American history. Within Investigative Writing, the subgenre that may have the most to offer fans of these titles might be Character Profiles, either individual or in groups.

> Politicos titles are more noteworthy for whom they are written by (political leaders, figures, and insiders) than what they are written about (various subjects from foreign relations to corruption and scandals). Authored by political figures and insiders, these books offer a more straightforward narrative (historical stories, life stories, event stories, etc.) as well as the thrill of hearing the "insider's" account of historical and political events.

Albright, Madeleine, and William Woodward

The Mighty and the Almighty: Reflections on America, God, and World Affairs. HarperCollins. 2006. 339 pp. ISBN 9780060892579.

Former secretary of state under President Clinton, Albright draws on both that experience and on her life experience as a Catholic with Jewish roots to urge both caution and nuance in America's foreign affairs, particularly where issues of religion intersect with those of governance. In addition to offering thoughts on the future, Albright provides a firsthand look at the recent history of America's dealings with other countries, particularly those which took place under her watch throughout the 1990s.

Subjects: 1990s, Madeleine Albright, Christianity, Foreign Relations, Government, Politics, Religion, Women's Contributions, Women's Nonfiction

Now Try: Albright served under President Clinton; readers interested in that president and his eight-year tenure might also consider his autobiography, *My Life* (as well as Hillary Clinton's autobiography *Living History*, or Carl

Bernstein's biography *A Woman in Charge*). Other political books examining the role of religion in governance include Kevin Phillips's *American Theocracy* and Jim Wallis's *God's Politics*. Those readers who enjoy Albright's forthright style might also consider her memoir, **Madam Secretary** or autobiographies or biographies of other singular women in American history, including Katharine Graham's *Personal History*, Betty Friedan's *Life So Far*, or Kay Mills's *This Little Light of Mine: The Life of Fannie Lou Hamer*.

Bhutto, Benazir

Reconciliation: Islam, Democracy, and the West. Harper. 2008. 328 pp. ISBN 9780061567582.

Bhutto, former prime minister of Pakistan, offers her take on the current political situation in that country, as well as the larger world picture of relations between Islamic nations and Christian nations in the West. Written before her tragic death in 2007, the book provides not only a sense of Bhutto's optimism regarding Islam's place in the world and the possibilities for better relations between all nations, but also offers a thorough history on Pakistan, international terrorism trends, and an account of the history between America and Pakistan.

> **Subjects:** Benazir Bhutto, Foreign Relations, Government, Islam, Memoirs, Pakistan, Politics, Religion, Terrorism, Women's Contributions, Women's Nonfiction

> **Now Try:** Readers interested in similar world history and political memoir titles might also consider Barbara Slavin's *Bitter Friends, Bosom Enemies: Iran, the U.S., and the Twisted Path to Confrontation*. Jimmy Carter's *Palestine: Peace Not Apartheid*, Mark Bowden's *Guests of the Ayatollah*, Greg Mortenson's *Three Cups of Tea*, or Imam Hassan Qazwini's *American Crescent*; William Langewiesche's succinct *The Atomic Bazaar* also includes a chapter on Pakistan and the development of nuclear weapons and may be of some interest to these readers. Other Political Reporting titles might appeal, as might Biographies of American Presidents and Other World Leaders. Books written by or featuring powerful women might also be suggested, such as Madeleine Albright's *The Mighty and the Almighty* or Katharine Graham's *Personal History*.

Blumenthal, Sidney

The Clinton Wars. Farrar, Straus & Giroux. 2003. 822 pp. ISBN 9780374125028.

Love them or hate them, there can be no doubt that few politicians have garnered such public attention (both support and derision) as former president Bill Clinton and his wife, senator and strong contender for the 2008 Democratic presidential nomination Hillary Rodham Clinton. This book is billed as part history, part memoir, and part current affairs; Blumenthal worked for Clinton as a "senior advisor" starting in 1997 and would eventually have to testify at Clinton's impeachment trial. In this dense, detail-laden, but still personal, work Blumenthal provides insight into the Clintons' political methods, their marriage, and their stances on issues from health care to unrest in Kosovo.

> **Subjects:** 1990s, American History, Biographies, Bill Clinton, Hillary Clinton, Government, Politics, Presidents, Washington, D.C.

> **Now Try:** There is no shortage of autobiographical and biographical materials about both of the Clintons; these include their autobiographies *My Life* (by Bill) and *Living History* (by Hillary), and the biographies *First in His Class* by David Maraniss and *A Woman in Charge* by Carl Bernstein. Blumenthal has written a number of other titles,

including *How Bush Rules* and *The Rise of the Counter-Establishment: The Conservative Ascent to Political Power*.

Carter, Jimmy

Palestine: Peace Not Apartheid. Simon & Schuster. 2006. 264 pp. ISBN 9780743285025.

Former president Jimmy Carter draws on his experience both in office and outside it, as founder of the charitable Carter Foundation, to examine the discord-filled recent history of the Middle East, and most particularly the Arab-Israeli conflicts of the last century. Suggesting that continued strife in the region will continue to be a roadblock to any real world peace programs, Carter makes his case for mutually agreeable and negotiated solutions to the standoff between Israel and Palestine.

Subjects: 20th Century, Arab-Israeli Conflict, Jimmy Carter, Government, Israel, Middle East, Palestine, Politics, World History

Now Try: Readers interested in the history of the Middle East region might consider other titles such as Richard Ben Cramer's *How Israel Lost: The Four Questions*, Christopher Tyerman's *God's War: A New History of the Crusades*, David Fromkin's *A Peace to End All Peace: The Fall of the Ottoman Empire and the Creation of the Modern Middle East*, Sandy Tolan's *The Lemon Tree: An Arab, a Jew, and the Heart of the Middle East*, and Noam Chomsky's *The Fateful Triangle: The United States, Israel, and the Palestinians*. Those most interested in Carter's political voice might consider other such memoirs and treatises as Barack Obama's *The Audacity of Hope* or Al Gore's *The Assault on Reason* or *An Inconvenient Truth*.

Clarke, Richard William Barnes

🏅 *Against All Enemies: Inside America's War on Terror.* Free Press. 2004. 304 pp. ISBN 9780743260244.

In this forthright and detailed political insider's memoir, Clarke details his experiences in the George W. Bush administration, both before and after the terrorist attacks of 9/11. The author maintains that before the attacks, he pleaded with administration officials to believe in the possibility of terrorist attacks and to be ready to respond to them; after the attacks, his tale turns to one of frustration as he and his recommendations were ignored by Vice President Dick Cheney, Secretary of Defense Donald Rumsfeld, and Undersecretary of Defense Paul Wolfowitz in favor of their plan to invade Iraq. Clarke also provides historical context for the events of the early twenty-first century by exploring the presidency of Ronald Reagan in the 1980s (specifically, Reagan's response to the 1982 bombings in Beirut); he is also an adventure novelist, and his prose, while dealing with extremely serious subjects, is thrilling and quickly paced.

Subjects: 9/11, American History, George W. Bush, Foreign Relations, Government, Iraq War (2003), Memoirs, Politics, Terrorism

Awards: New York Times Notable

Now Try: Richard Clarke's fiction thrillers might appeal to his readers, including *Breakpoint* and *The Scorpion's Gate*, as might other fiction thrillers by authors including Tom Clancy, Steve Alten, and Brad Meltzer. Nonfiction titles that may appeal include Thomas Ricks's *Fiasco: The American Military Adventure in Iraq*, Michael Isikoff's *Hubris*, and Michael Gordon's *Cobra II*; also consider insider Memoirs such as Ron Suskind's *The One Percent Doctrine* and *The Price of Loyalty*, George Tenet's *At the Center of the Storm*, or Tyler Drumheller's *On the Brink: An Insider's Account of How the White House Compromised American Intelligence*.

Clinton, Bill

Giving: How Each of Us Can Change the World. Knopf. 2007. 240 pp. ISBN 9780307266743.

Former president Bill Clinton examines ways in which individuals and groups have used their dedication to volunteerism and charitable giving to change the world for the better. Using case studies (from individuals such as Dr. Paul Farmer, Bill and Melinda Gates, and Andre Agassi to groups like Heifer International) President Clinton demonstrates both how change can be achieved and the power of peoples' giving habits and issues a call to action to all readers to create change, as well as to improve and supplement government policy.

> **Subjects:** Charity, Bill Clinton, Economics, Politics, Social Action, Society

> **Now Try:** Although not a typical work of political science, there is no doubt that this book will be most popular among readers who share Clinton's democratic affiliation; as such, other political authors and memoirists might also appeal, including Madeleine Albright (*The Mighty and the Almighty*), Al Gore (*An Inconvenient Truth* and *The Assault on Reason*), or Paul Begala and James Carville. Books by Edward Kennedy, Barack Obama, John Edwards, and Hillary Clinton might also be offered. These readers might also be interested in Clinton's autobiography *My Life* or Hillary Clinton's autobiography *Living History* (as well as *A Woman in Charge*, the biography of her by Carl Bernstein). A wide variety of Change-Maker and Activists Biographies might also appeal, including Tracy Kidder's *Mountains beyond Mountains* (about Dr. Paul Farmer) or *There Is No Me without You* by Melissa Fay Greene.

Gore, Al

The Assault on Reason. Penguin Press. 2007. 308 pp. ISBN 9781594201226.

Former Vice President Gore returns to his political roots in this treatise on the current American political climate and what he sees to be its dependence on marketing and sound clips, as well as many politicians' reliance on emotional appeals at the expense of factual information.

> **Subjects:** 21st Century, American History, Government, Politics, Society

> **Now Try:** Fans of Al Gore's writing might enjoy his earlier works, *Earth in the Balance* and *An Inconvenient Truth*, as well as political works from other well-known Democrat authors: Bill Bradley's *The New American Story*, Barack Obama's *The Audacity of Hope*, Bill Richardson's *Between Worlds: The Making of an American Life*, or Edward Kennedy's *America Back on Track*.

McClellan, Scott

What Happened: Inside the Bush White House and Washington's Culture of Deception. PublicAffairs. 2008. 341 pp. ISBN 9781586485566.

Readers on both the left and right sides of the American political spectrum may find much of interest (or much to disdain) in this tell-all about the administration of President George W. Bush, as related by his former White House press secretary. Although he maintains in his text that "I still like and admire George W. Bush," the majority of his story centers on his feelings of betrayal after learning that the story he'd been told and dutifully related to the press—that Karl Rove and Scooter Libby were not involved with the revelation of Valerie Plame Wilson's CIA work—was false. In addition to that revelation, he also relates his confusion about other Bush administration assertions (particularly about the Iraq War) and his growing feeling that Bush was a "leader unable to acknowledge that he got it wrong."

Subjects: George W. Bush, Government, Iraq War (2003), Memoirs, Valerie Plame Wilson, Politics, Professions

Now Try: A wide variety of books about the George W. Bush administration have been published, including Karen Hughes's rather more positive *Ten Minutes from Normal*, Robert Draper's relatively objective *Dead Certain: The Presidency of George W. Bush*, Bob Woodward's *Plan of Attack*, and longtime Washington insider and presidential advisor Richard Clarke's *Against All Enemies: Inside America's War on Terror*. Books specifically about the Valerie Plame incident might be suggested, most notably Wilson's own *Fair Game: My Life as a Spy, My Betrayal by the White House*, or her husband Joe Wilson's *The Politics of Truth: A Diplomat's Memoir*. Books by other former White House insiders might also hold some appeal, such as Sidney Blumenthal's *How Bush Rules* and *The Clinton Wars*, Dee Dee Myers's *Why Women Should Rule the World*, and even journalist Helen Thomas's *Watchdogs of Democracy?: The Waning Washington Press Corps and How It Has Failed the Public*.

Murray, Craig

Dirty Diplomacy: The Rough-and-Tumble Adventures of a Scotch-Drinking, Skirt-Chasing, Dictator-Busting and Thoroughly Unrepentant Ambassador Stuck on the Frontline of the War against Terror. Scribner. 2007. 366 pp. ISBN 9781416548010.

Diplomats are typically known for one thing: their diplomacy. In this political and personal memoir, the former British ambassador to Uzbekistan dispenses with that convention in his subtitle, readily admitting there and in his narrative that he "enjoys a drink or three, and if it's in the company of a pretty girl, so much the better." However, Murray does not agree with the torture of government dissidents, and he spent much of his appointed time trying to expose such instances of human rights abuses in the central Asian country to which he was posted with little prior knowledge. Fast-paced, personal, and often shocking, the narrative concludes when Murray is recalled from his post because of his bosses' unhappiness with his vocal exposures of governmental corruption. Murray doesn't mince words when it comes to his disappointment with British and American leadership, concluding that "sadly, public life in the U.S. and the U.K. has come to be dominated by those driven by arrogance and by corporate greed and personal acquisitiveness."

Subjects: Government, Human Rights, Memoirs, Politics, Professions, Torture, Uzbekistan

Now Try: Other extremely personal and quickly paced narratives of foreign relations and global politics might be suggested to these readers, including John Perkins's *Confessions of an Economic Hit Man* or *The Secret History of*

the American Empire, Rob Ferguson's *The Devil and the Disappearing Sea: A True Story about the Aral Sea Disaster*, or Tom Bissell's *Chasing the Sea*, as might more straightforward political works as Samuel Huntington's *The Clash of Civilizations and the Remaking of the World Order*. The author suggests titles by Chalmers Johnson, Reza Aslan (*No God but God*), and Colin Thubron (*The Lost Heart of Asia*); fiction by authors such as Graham Greene and Alan Furst might also be suggested.

Paul, Ron

The Revolution: A Manifesto. Grand Central. 2008. 173 pp. ISBN 9780446537513.

Former presidential candidate and doctor-turned-congressman Ron Paul offers a slim treatise on his belief that many Americans want a return to a government more firmly attuned to the Constitution and the principles and framework originally envisioned by the Founding Fathers. Rather than a typical campaign book, this is indeed a soberly argued manifesto that outlines the problems in America's current two-party system, foreign policy, and economic system, complete with a reading list "for a free and prosperous America."

> **Subjects:** American History, Constitution, Economics, Foreign Relations, Founding Fathers, Government, Ron Paul, Politics, Quick Reads

> **Now Try:** Paul is kind enough to provide a bibliography of books that have influenced his political development; a few titles off that list that may appeal to his readers include Andrew Bacevich's *The New American Militarism*, Thomas Fleming's history books *The Illusion of Victory: America in World War I* and *The New Dealers War: FDR and the War Within World War II*, Chalmers Johnson's *Blowback*, Michael Seuer's *Imperial Hubris: Why the West Is Losing the War on Terror*, and even Ayn Rand's *Atlas Shrugged* (although Paul notes that he disagrees with the novelist on important matters). Books by other somewhat independently minded politicos might also be suggested, including Pat Buchanan's *Day of Reckoning: How Hubris, Ideology, and Greed Are Tearing America Apart* and his new-perspective history title *Churchill, Hitler, and the "Unnecessary War,"* Jack Cafferty's *It's Getting Ugly Out There*, and Lou Dobbs's *War on the Middle Class*.

Soros, George

The Age of Fallibility: Consequences of the War on Terror. PublicAffairs. 2006. 259 pp. ISBN 9781586483593.

Soros, financial speculator extraordinaire (in 1992 he completed a billion-dollar transaction that would make his reputation as the "man who broke the Bank of England") and bankroller of the political action group MoveOn.org, offers his opinions on what constitutes freedom, how it can be promoted in society, and the many ways in which George W. Bush's policies both domestically and abroad are eroding America's reputation for strong beliefs on human rights and an open society. Along the way, he speculates on the reasons the Democratic Party couldn't field a candidate who could succeed against Bush and how it might reclaim the high ground on so-called values issues that conservative Republicans have claimed as their own.

> **Subjects:** Business, Economics, Globalization, Memoirs, Politics, Terrorism

> **Now Try:** Other books by Soros might appeal, including *Open Society, Soros on Soros: Staying Ahead of the Curve* and *George Soros on Globalization*; Matt Bai's book about changing political norms, *The Argument: Billionaires, Bloggers, and the Battle to Remake Democratic Politics*, might also be offered. Books mixing finance concepts and

society might also be offered, including Nassim Nicholas Taleb's *Fooled by Randomness* or *The White Swan*, Lee Iacocca's personal and political manifesto *Where Have All the Leaders Gone?*, or Steven Levitt's and Stephen Dubner's *Freakonomics*.

Woodward, Bob

State of Denial: Bush at War, Part III. Simon & Schuster. 2006. 560 pp. ISBN 9780743272230.

Infamous investigative reporter Woodward turns his attention to President George W. Bush's (and his administration's) policies regarding the 2003 Iraq invasion and the Middle East. Focusing on the war's aftermath in Iraq and on the decision-making practices within Bush's White House staff, this book stands as a sequel to Woodward's *Bush at War* (2002) and *Plan of Attack* (2004); its key figures are President Bush, Dick Cheney, Donald Rumsfeld, Condoleezza Rice, Andrew Card, and Henry Kissinger.

Subjects: George W. Bush, Foreign Relations, Government, Iraq, Iraq War (2003), Middle East, Politics, Presidents

Now Try: Woodward's prior two books on the Bush administration, which some critics felt were too complimentary to Bush, might be offered: *Bush at War* and *Plan of Attack*. Readers interested in this title might consider other works on the subject, such as George Packer's *The Assassins' Gate: America in Iraq*, Thomas Ricks's *Fiasco: The American Military Adventure in Iraq*, Frank Rich's *The Greatest Story Ever Sold*, or Michael Gordon's *Cobra II: The Inside Story of the Invasion and Occupation of Iraq*. Ron Suskind's *The One Percent Doctrine* or John Dean's *Worse than Watergate*, both critical about the Bush administration, might also be suggested.

Fiction Read-Alikes

- **Baldacci, David.** Baldacci is known for his political suspense novels and has been compared to John Grisham for his inclusion of courtroom settings; his titles include *Absolute Power*, *The Simple Truth*, *Saving Faith*, *Split Second* (and its sequels *Hour Game* and *Simple Genius*), and *The Camel Club*.

- **Clancy, Tom.** Although it might seem that Clancy's books might be considered techno- rather than political thrillers, many of his adventure novels also feature historical and political machinations between governments, including his classic *The Hunt for Red October*, *Patriot Games*, *Clear and Present Danger*, and *The Teeth of a Tiger*. It should be noted that Clancy refers to his own politics as "conservative," and he may particularly appeal to readers with conservative political worldviews.

- **Flynn, Vince.** Flynn's quickly paced and suspenseful political novels include characters ranging from politicians to CIA agents; they include *Term Limits*, *Transfer of Power*, *Age of Treason*, and *Protect and Defend*.

- **Forsyth, Frederick.** Forsyth's adventure and espionage novels (he is widely considered an early definer of the "international conspiracy thriller"), many of which offer political subplots, might appeal to readers of political nonfiction; they include *The Day of the Jackal*, *The Odessa File*, *The Dogs of War*, *The Devil's Alternative*, and *The Afghan*.

- **McCullough, Colleen.** Readers interested in politicians in history might enjoy McCullough's Masters of Rome series, which began with *The First Man in Rome*, *The Grass Crown*, and *Fortune's Favorites*.

- **Meltzer, Brad.** Meltzer writes quickly paced legal and political thrillers, including *The Tenth Justice*, *The First Counsel*, *The Zero Game*, and *The Book of Fate*.

- **Patterson, Richard North.** Patterson, a former attorney, writes literary and thoughtful but still quickly paced novels that often feature characters who work in legal and political fields; his novels *The Lasko Tangent* or *Exile* or his series featuring Senator Kerry Kilcannon might particularly appeal (*No Safe Place*, *Protect and Defend*, and *Balance of Power*).

- **Richardson, Doug.** Richardson's thrillers feature political characters and plots; they include *Dark Horse* and *True Believers*.

- **Shelby, Philip.** Shelby's political thrillers, which often feature terrorism and conspiracy plots as well as female protagonists, include *Days of Drums*, *Last Rights*, *Gatekeeper*, and *By Dawn's Early Light*.

- **Vidal, Gore.** Vidal's historical novels, which feature politicians as characters and historical political and cultural events, might appeal to political readers; they include *Washington, D.C.*, *Burr*, *1876*, *Lincoln*, and *Empire*.

- **Warren, Robert Penn.** Warren's classic novel *All the King's Men* is based on the life of controversial politician Huey Long; his historical novels *At Heaven's Gate* and *World Enough and Time* (said by critics to combine "history, philosophy, politics, and passion") might also appeal.

Further Reading

Tebbel, John, and Sarah Miles Watts. 1985. *The Press and the Presidency: From George Washington to Ronald Reagan*. New York: Oxford University Press.

References

Shapiro, Bruce, ed. 2003. *Shaking the Foundations: 200 Years of Investigative Journalism in America*. New York: Thunder's Mouth Press.

Williamson, Chilton, Jr. 2004. *The Conservative Bookshelf: Essential Works That Impact Today's Conservative Thinkers*. New York: Citadel Press.

Chapter 6

Business Reporting

Definition of Business Reporting

Both the Business Reporting and Political Reporting categories of Investigative Writing owe much of their cohesiveness to their subject matter. Business Reporting, however, has a long tradition of its own, and it has most often been practiced in the pages of daily and other serial newspapers and publications. One of the earliest examples of the form could be found in seventeenth-century British papers, when lists of ships, ports, and cargos were published in British newspapers as a service to their readers involved in such business; in *A History of News: From the Drum to the Satellite*, Stephens points out that by the 1700s, numerous papers were featuring business news and what he terms "commercial intelligence" (Stephens 1988, 181). The relationship between reporters and authors and business has not always been a friendly one; Business Reporting is also related to Exposé writing, primarily because so many muckraking journalists of the early twentieth century exposed stories of corruption and incompetence in business and business leaders in their books (e.g., Ida Tarbell's *A History of the Standard Oil Company*). However, a strong tradition of writing that celebrates the progressive and innovative contributions of business also exists, and titles in that tradition can be found here. Lincoln Steffens, one of the most famous muckrakers, also recognized the importance of business in the wider American culture: "Steffens is best known for his work as a muckraker at *McClure's* magazine in the early years of the twentieth century. But throughout his career, his goal was to inspire his writers (and himself) to create 'literature' about America's most important institutions—business and politics" (Boynton 2005, xxv).

Books written about business are perpetually popular with readers, a status that is confirmed by book industry research that found in 2006 that one of the hottest categories of that year was business books; in 2006 the number of titles published was 9,006, which was up 12 percent from the previous year (Bowker 2008). The reasons for their popularity are legion, including their crisp writing and a large reading audience of business travelers who read them in airports and on planes, but it should also be noted that these titles are largely positive business stories, and narratives that assume an important place for business in the world's culture and everyday life. Those readers seeking works more critical of the processes of business might wish to consider first titles from the Biz Crit subgenre, and then Corporate Exposés from the Exposés chapter.

Business Reporting titles are often placed within the "current affairs" popular interest classification, and revolve around issues of economics and finance. Although typically produced in response to current economic events, many are solid works of reporting and history that better withstand the test of time than more ephemeral works of financial advising or personal finance books advocating the latest "get rich quick" or "stay rich now" techniques.

Appeal of Business Reporting

The subject of Business Reporting is business, and as Wyatt has pointed out in her guide *The Readers' Advisory Guide to Nonfiction*, many readers who choose nonfiction based on subject are hoping to learn something about it. But to stop there would be to do the category of Business Reporting a grave disservice. As with many other types of nonfiction, a wide variety of appeal factors can be ascribed to these titles. Much like History nonfiction, Business Histories and Profiles are often story-driven and quickly paced narratives of noteworthy companies, industries, and individuals or groups of individuals who were primarily responsible for the success (or failure) of their companies. The profiles of business personalities included in this chapter also offer what Christopher Booker has termed one of the seven basic plots: the rags to riches theme, in which characters who start out with nothing but their good character and good deeds often succeed beyond their wildest dreams. Titles in the Business Trends subgenre do not offer stories with as much narrative drive but nonetheless highlight fascinating new trends in the business world and are, in their own way, speculative stories about possibility.

In the books that I have defined as "Biz Crit" titles, authors who are willing to think critically about the business world and its influence on other human institutions and society but are not necessarily critical of business, also typically share more of their own opinions regarding the stories they're reporting.

Because these narratives offer such a wide variety of appeal, readers' advisors should be glad to find that readers who enjoy these books might enjoy numerous other fiction and nonfiction genres, subgenres, and authors. (Those in charge of merchandising at airport bookstores already know this; of course they stock a wide variety of Business Reporting and Success Guide titles for frequent business travelers, but they also offer a wide variety of magazines and novels, many of which are also purchased by those same business and corporate travelers.) Readers drawn to compelling business stories, often told in Business Histories and Profiles and Biz Crit books, might enjoy fiction page-turners and thrillers (particularly by authors such as Joseph Finder or Stephen Frey). Readers who enjoy more character-driven examples of the Business Histories and Profiles titles might also consider a wide variety of Biographies, particularly those of historical figures in business and politics (as well as Professional Biographies, about pioneers in their chosen fields, or Sports Biographies); in their lighter moods, they might also consider Biographies of Celebrities and Superstars. These readers also tend to be interested in other world and political events, so they might also consider titles from the Political Reporting category of Investigative Writing, not to mention Exposés (particularly Corporate Exposés), as well as works of History or sociological titles by authors like Robert Putnam or Jared Diamond. Don't forget about the True Adventure nonfiction titles for these readers; they might particularly enjoy high-adrenaline classics like Jon Krakauer's *Into Thin Air* or Robert Kurson's *Shadow Divers*. Advisors who work with business readers should try to keep somewhat abreast of developments in the news, financial and otherwise; these are also readers who will be interested in what other people are reading, particularly best sellers and titles receiving a lot of buzz in the national media.

Those readers drawn to technological aspects of business and culture, and future developments and possibilities, many of which are discussed in the Business Trends section, might also enjoy nonfiction Science and Math titles, including those by Henry Petroski (who writes about design and engineering questions), Michael Pollan (his current best sellers *The Omnivore's Dilemma* and *In Defense of Food* might interest these readers), or Richard Dawkins (who is making a big stir currently with *The God Delusion*, and who made a big stir historically with his idea of "memes" in *The Selfish Gene*). Don't assume that your Business Reporting readers won't read books on any other subject; and don't be afraid to ask what types of business books they particularly enjoy to better explore further reading avenues.

Organization of the Chapter

The chapter opens with one of the most recognizable of all the Business Reporting subgenres, **Business Histories and Profiles**, which offers stories of businesses and industries and often includes information about the people most responsible for their growth, success, or development. **Business Histories and Profiles** is followed by titles in which business trends and relatively objective business reporting are most on display; these are the **Business Trends** titles. The first two categories tend to be the most positive and optimistic in tone, and the least critical in coverage of business tactics and conventions. The following section, **Biz Crit**, offers titles in which the authors offer a bit more of their own opinions and analysis regarding the business stories they are telling; in addition to their slightly larger social and cultural context, the tone of these titles tends to be a bit more questioning (although on the whole they tend to be critical in a positive sense). They can be likened to literary criticism titles, in which the focus is not so much on criticizing literature as it is on discussing its many features and glories; in **Biz Crit**, the authors have questions about business but are not really seeking to lay any blame at its door. This chapter concludes with a small section of suggestions of **Success Guides**; these are included more as a service to those readers' advisors and reference staff seeking to familiarize themselves with the most popular business authors' names; they can't really be considered narrative nonfiction but are still included because of their importance to readers who enjoy Business Reporting of all types.

Business Histories and Profiles

Business Histories and Profiles are perhaps, along with the Success Guides, the most immediately recognizable and popular subgenre of Business

Reporting books. Whether it is because readers of these books are interested in the subjects of both business and history or because they hope to learn from and emulate past corporate success stories, there can be no denying that these often very narrowly focused books might appeal to a larger class of readers than is commonly thought. These histories can focus on specific companies, or on broader industries, but most of their stories are chronologically organized, and many depend quite heavily not only on research but also on numerous interviews with their subjects. Many of the authors of these books are long-time business reporters who know both their subjects and specialized industries as well as the larger business and economic picture. They tend to be, if not adulatory, at least positive in their portrayal of a wide variety of business professionals and industries.

These books are often surprisingly lively and story-driven, although their characters are often a large part of their appeal as well. The characters in question can be either individuals or companies (as is the case in business histories such as *Boeing versus Airbus* or *The Pixar Touch: The Making of a Company*), which is only fitting, as the dictionary definition of corporations maintains that each one is "a body formed and authorized by law to act as a single person." Readers who enjoy these titles might, of course, enjoy a wide variety of other Business Reporting books (particularly from the Success Guides section); they might also consider History nonfiction, particularly on economic and political subjects in American history. More personal and informal books in which jobs and professions are the main subject might also be suggested to these readers, including Professional Biographies, Working Life Memoirs, or titles from the Work World Immersion Journalism section.

Business Histories and Profiles focus on specific individuals and companies, as well as on their histories of success (most commonly) or failure. Although they feature unique characters and the authors often conduct and quote from numerous interviews and research to illuminate those characters, they are also story-driven narratives that more often than not feature straightforward narratives of complete lives or discrete events in the lives of corporations.

Bernstein, Peter W., and Annalyn Swan

All the Money in the World: How the Forbes 400 Make—and Spend—Their Fortunes. Knopf. 2007. 416 pp. ISBN 9780307266125.

This completely fascinating and historical (the list is now twenty-five years old) breakdown of the Forbes 400 richest Americans examines how the list's members make and spend their money. In three parts ("What It Takes," "Making It," and "Spending It") and illustrated with charts and supplemented with informational sidebars, the result is an educational exploration of both production and consumption and provides numerous insights on social, gender, and historical issues.

Subjects: Biographies, Business, Character Profiles, Consumerism, Economics, Trivia

Now Try: A number of biographies of previous and current members of the Forbes 400 might appeal to these readers, as might biographies of legendary business figures such as David Nasaw's *Andrew Carnegie*, David Cannadine's *Mellon*, Ron Chernow's *Titan: The Life of John D. Rockefeller, Sr.*, Robert Lacey's *Ford: The Man and the Machine*, or Bob Ortega's *In Sam We Trust*. Can money buy happiness? Other books such as Daniel Gilbert's *Stumbling on Happiness* or Gregg Easterbrook's *The Progress Paradox*, which also try to answer that question, might also be offered these readers.

Burr, Chandler

The Perfect Scent: A Year Inside the Perfume Industry in Paris and New York. Henry Holt. 2008. 306 pp. ISBN 9780805080377.

Perfume critic for the *New York Times*, Burr is no stranger to explaining the minutiae of perfume creation, marketing, and the industry as a whole. In this illuminating and lively work of reporting, the author spends a year observing and commenting on the process of creation for two fragrances, one being developed in Paris for a high-end luxury house (Hermes), the other a commercial fragrance associated with actress Sarah Jessica Parker and being made in New York by Coty, Inc. (Lovely). The industry is secretive, high-tech, and surprisingly scientific; Burr makes all the details come alive in this detailed year-in-the-life business and cultural story.

> **Subjects:** Beauty Industry, Business, Luxury, New York City, Paris, Sarah Jessica Parker, Perfume, Year in the Life

> **Now Try:** Fans of this accessible book might also enjoy Chandler Burr's earlier book *The Emperor of Scent: A Story of Perfume, Obsession, and the Last Mystery of the Senses* (about Luca Turin), as well as Turin's more science-heavy but still enlightening *The Secret of Scent: Adventures in Perfume and the Science of Smell*. Other books told from a "year in the life" standpoint include James Barron's *Steinway: The Making of a Steinway Concert Grand*, Steve Almond's *Candyfreak*, Amy Stewart's *Flower Confidential*, Lisa Takeuchi Cullen's *Remember Me*, Taylor Clark's *Starbucked*, or even Michael Ruhlman's foodie title *The Making of a Chef*. Other books on luxury and business might be considered, including a wide variety of books by James Twitchell (*Living It Up: America's Love Affair with Luxury*) and books by such literary science authors as Diane Ackerman, Rachel Carson, or Dava Sobel.

Cepuch, Randy

A Weekend with Warren Buffett: And Other Shareholder Meeting Adventures. Thunder's Mouth Press. 2007. 250 pp. ISBN 9781560259541.

Financial writer Cepuch decided to learn more about a few companies in which he owned stock. Five years and fifty shareholders' meetings later, he was able to write this amusing and actually quite informative review of their meetings. Cepuch visited all the companies you've heard about—Berkshire Hathaway, Wal-Mart, Starbucks, Playboy—and a few you probably haven't, including Otter Tail and the Chalone Wine Group. In addition to providing the inside story on these meetings ("At 9:40 Christie Hefner breezes in. You can't miss her: She's wearing a brilliant white suit and has the bearing of someone who knows she must be 'on' at all times"), he also grades their informational content, their entertainment value, and their freebies.

> **Subjects:** Business, Business Histories, Economics, Finance, Humor, Immersion Journalism, Quick Reads, Travel

Now Try: Peter Bernstein's and Annalyn Swan's *All the Money in the World: How the Forbes 400 Make—and Spend—Their Fortunes* might prove interesting to these readers, as might a number of books the author suggests, including Chris Anderson's *The Long Tail*, Roger Lowenstein's *Buffett: The Making of an American Capitalist*, or David Vise's and Mark Malseed's *The Google Story*. Other Immersion and Travel titles might also appeal to these readers, including Michael Lewis's classic *Liar's Poker*, Alex Frankel's *Punching In*, or Barbara Ehrenreich's *Bait and Switch*.

Clark, Taylor

Starbucked: A Double Tall Tale of Caffeine, Commerce, and Culture. Little, Brown. 2007. 297 pp. ISBN 9780316013482.

A small library could be stocked solely with books about Starbucks, but Clark's investigative look at the company is one of the most even-tempered and in-depth studies available. He relates the history of the company and its founders, the growth of the gourmet coffee market worldwide (and the growing interest in fair-trade coffee), and possible future developments for the company, as well as its managers' responses to critics of their corporate policies and plans. Quickly paced and personal, with fascinating insights into the company's employees and customers, this is a business book for any reader who enjoys good nonfiction.

Subjects: Book Groups, Business Histories, Caffeine, Coffee, Companies, Globalization, Seattle, Society, Starbucks

Now Try: Some of those other books on Starbucks might appeal to these readers, including Howard Schultz's *Pour Your Heart into It*, Howard Behar's *It's Not about the Coffee*, or Michael Gates Gill's *How Starbucks Saved My Life*. Other business books that may appeal to generalist readers include Amy Stewart's *Flower Confidential*, Sasha Issenberg's *The Sushi Economy*, Rachel Louise Snyder's *Fugitive Denim*, or Charles Fishman's *The Wal-Mart Effect*; Alex Frankel's *Punching In* (an Immersion business book in which Frankel worked at a Starbucks) or Jeffrey Rothfeder's *McIlhenny's Gold: How a Louisiana Family Built the Tabasco Empire*.

Echikson, William

Noble Rot: A Bordeaux Wine Revolution. W.W. Norton. 2004. 302 pp. ISBN 9780393051629.

Wall Street Journal wine columnist Echikson follows the growing season and harvest of Bordeaux grapes of 2001, illuminating the wine-making process from pruning and grape selection to the timing of the harvest to the blending of the grapes into different wines. Numerous vintners and growers, as well as luminaries from the close-knit wine world, are interviewed to give the reader the broadest possible picture of the business from the ground up.

Subjects: Business Histories, Food, France, Travel, Wine, Year in the Life

Now Try: Interest in all topics "foodie" is running high right now, and there's a wide variety of books about food and wine available, including foodie books by authors such as Michael Ruhlman, Ruth Reichl, Michael Pollan, or Marlena de Blasi; books about France and cooking, particularly Julia Child's *My Life in France* or Peter Mayle's *A Year in Provence* might be offered, as well as other books on wine such as *The Accidental Connoisseur* by Lawrence Osborne. Business histories about the hospitality industry might also be offered; these include Thomas McNamee's *Alice Waters & Chez Panisse* and Julia Flynn Siler's *The House of Mondavi: The Rise and Fall of an American Wine Dynasty*.

Greenspan, Alan

The Age of Turbulence: Adventures in a New World. Penguin Press. 2007. 531 pp. ISBN 9781594201318.

Greenspan, longtime chairman of the Federal Reserve Board and perhaps the most visible economist of the past two decades, relates his life story, focusing on life and financial lessons learned in government service and particularly in the aftermath of the 9/11 terrorist attacks. Although this book is technically an autobiography, Greenspan is not afraid to dish out the more complex aspects of finance, economic theory, and foreign relations. He also doesn't shy away from telling political anecdotes, asserting his faith in market capitalism, and making predictions for the world of 2030.

> **Subjects:** American History, Autobiographies, Economics, Finance, Government, Alan Greenspan, Politics

> **Now Try:** Fans of Greenspan's autobiography might consider a wide variety of business and political autobiographies, memoirs, and biographies, including Donald Trump's *Trump: The Art of the Deal*, Douglas Brinkley's *The Reagan Diaries*, Bill Clinton's *My Life*, Robert Dallek's *Nixon and Kissinger*, or Robert Draper's *Dead Certain: The Presidency of George W. Bush*. Numerous books on economics and economic theory might also be offered, including Nassim Nicholas Taleb's *Fooled by Randomness* or *The Black Swan*, Thomas Friedman's *The World Is Flat*, or Tim Harford's *The Undercover Economist*. Greenspan himself has been a longtime reader of Ayn Rand; readers of this autobiography might also consider her fiction titles *The Fountainhead* or *Atlas Shrugged*.

John, Daymond and Daniel Paisner

Display of Power: How FUBU Changed a World of Fashion, Branding and Lifestyle. Naked Ink. 2007. 223 pp. ISBN 9781595558534.

Daymond John, known popularly as the "Godfather of urban fashion" and the creator of the FUBU ("For Us, By Us") line relates his life story, growing up in Queens, New York, and eventually launching his own clothing line, which would become an empire. The writing is brisk, the stories personal, and the relation of business triumphs and missteps both informative and inspirational. The book also includes lengthy sidebars of personal insights and asides, as well as discussions of numbers and business trends, including such pieces of information as the fact that today more than a third of all black men in their thirties with only a high school education have been incarcerated.

> **Subjects:** African American Authors, Business Histories, Fashion, Memoirs, New York City, Professions, Quick Reads, Race Relations, YA

> **Now Try:** In addition to other business histories, books by African American authors relating the stories of their singular successes might also be offered; these include Chris Gardner's *The Pursuit of Happyness*, Russell Simmons's *Do You: 12 Laws to Access the Power in You to Achieve Happiness and Success*, Cupcake Brown's *A Piece of Cake*, or T. D. Jakes's *Reposition Yourself*. John did not start out a wealthy fashion designer; Overcoming Adversity Memoirs such as Angela Bassett's and Courtney Vance's *Friends: A Love Story*, Melba Pattillo Beals's *Warriors Don't Cry*, or James McBride's *The*

Color of Water might all be good related reads, as might Charles Barkley's fantastic book of interviews, *Who's Afraid of a Large Black Man?*

Karmin, Craig

Biography of the Dollar: How the Mighty Buck Conquered the World and Why It's Under Siege. Crown Business. 2008. 263 pp. ISBN 9780307339867.

Karmin, a reporter with the *Wall Street Journal*, offers a concise and readable explanation of the American dollar's history and its important role in global finance and economic systems. In systematic but readable chapters, he offers behind-the-scenes looks at the individuals who engage in currency trading, the Bureau of Engraving and Printing and its production and anticounterfeiting methods, the history of the dollar from the Civil War through the current day and the creation of the Federal Reserve system, use of the dollar in other countries, the South Korean institutions that hold vast dollar reserves, and new institutions that are warning that the dollar is facing many challengers for its dominant position.

> **Subjects:** American History, Business, Economics, Globalization, Money

> **Now Try:** Fans of this succinct and readable business nonfiction might consider other Business titles, particularly "behind the scenes" books like Michael Lewis's classic *Liar's Poker*, Allan Brandt's *The Cigarette Century*, or Rachel Louise Snyder's *Fugitive Denim*; business and management books by popular authors such as Ram Charan or Marcus Buckingham might also appeal. A wide variety of micro-histories might also appeal to these readers, such as Mark Kurlansky's *Salt* or *Cod*, John Micklethwait's *The Company*, or Daniel Yergin's *The Prize: The Epic Quest for Oil, Money, and Power*.

Lacy, Sarah

Once You're Lucky, Twice You're Good: The Rebirth of Silicon Valley and the Rise of Web 2.0. Penguin. 2008. 294 pp. ISBN 9781592403820.

Business writer Lacy investigates the rebirth of Silicon Valley industry and dot-com ventures, particularly as embodied by such "Web 2.0" personalities as Max Levchin and Peter Thiel (founders of PayPal), Marc Andreessen (Netscape and Ning), Reid Hoffman (LinkedIn), and Ben and Mena Trott (Six Apart), among many others (including the individuals behind YouTube, MySpace, and Facebook). Lacy provides a history of innovation and technological advances after the dot-com bubble first burst in 2000. Through personal interviews and case studies, the author provides both a compelling business history and character portraits of the innovators involved.

> **Subjects:** Business Histories, Computers, Innovation, Internet, Professions, Programmers, Silicon Valley, Technology

> **Now Try:** Other inside looks at the culture of technology and innovation might be offered to these readers, including Tracy Kidder's classic *The Soul of a New Machine*, Nicholas Carr's *The Big Switch: Rewiring the World, from Edison to Google*, or Scott Rosenberg's *Dreaming in Code*, also of interest might be more straightforward business histories such as Michael Malone's *Bill & Dave: How Hewlett and Packard Built the World's Greatest Company* or John Battelle's *The Search: How Google and Its Rivals Rewrote the Rules of Business and Transformed Our Culture*. Fiction such as Douglas Coupland's classic *Microserfs* or Neal Stephenson's science fiction title *Cryptonomicon* might also appeal.

Malone, Michael S.

Bill & Dave: How Hewlett and Packard Built the World's Greatest Company. Portfolio. 2007. 438 pp. ISBN 9781591841524.

This surprisingly enthralling business history tells the story of the venerable Hewlett-Packard company and its founders Bill Hewlett and Dave Packard. Starting from humble beginnings in a small garage in Palo Alto, California, in 1938, the pair started their business by building an audio oscillator and went on to become heads of one of the most influential and innovative technology companies of the century. Author Malone was granted full access to the founders' private archives and conducted hundreds of interviews with past and current employees to write this comprehensive business history. Between descriptions of the partners' very different personalities and the development of their "HP Way" management philosophy, Malone also provides a good overview of the larger business and technology industry history in California.

Subjects: 20th Century, Biographies, Business Histories, California, Character Profiles, Computers, Bill Hewlett, Dave Packard, Technology

Now Try: A related book about the more recent history of Hewlett Packard is Carly Fiorina's memoir *Tough Choices* (about her six years as CEO, and the end of her tenure when she was forced out by the company's board of directors in 2005). A wide variety of other business histories, particularly those including engineering or technological stories, might also be offered: John Newhouse's *Boeing versus Airbus*, Michael Malone's *Betting It All: The Technology Entrepreneurs*, John Battelle's *The Search: How Google and Its Rivals Rewrote the Rules of Business and Transformed Our Culture*, or Charles Ellis's *Joe Wilson and the Creation of Xerox*. Tracy Kidder's classic *The Soul of a New Machine* might also be suggested.

McNamee, Thomas

Alice Waters and Chez Panisse: The Romantic, Impractical, Often Eccentric, Ultimately Brilliant Making of a Food Revolution. Penguin Press. 2007. 380 pp. ISBN 9781594201158.

McNamee provides both an official history of Alice Waters's influential Berkeley restaurant, Chez Panisse, and a delightfully personal biography of Waters herself, who started a business and a food movement out of her enthusiasm and love for good, healthy food, rather than out of any real business experience or acumen. In addition to a character portrait of Waters and a business history of the restaurant's thirty-five successful years, McNamee includes stories of other unique characters and chefs involved with the enterprise, as well as insights into some of Waters's favorite food philosophies and recipes.

Subjects: Biographies, Business Histories, California, Chefs, Cooking, Food, Foodies, Professions, Restaurants, Alice Waters, Women's Contributions, Women's Nonfiction

Now Try: Readers of this homage to one of the best-known foodies in America might enjoy other books by and about chefs and foodies, including Noël Riley Fitch's *Appetite for Life: A Biography of Julia Child*, Anthony Bourdain's *Kitchen Confidential*, Bill Buford's *Heat*, Robert Clark's *The Solace of Food: A*

Life of James Beard, and M. F. K. Fisher's *The Measure of Her Powers.* Books by other dedicated food critics and writers such as Michael Ruhlman, Ruth Reichl, Laurie Colwin, Calvin Trillin, and Amanda Hesser might appeal, as might more environmentally or politically motivated books by such authors as Frances Moore Lappe or Marion Nestle. Other professional biographies such as Mark Arax's *The King of California* or Charles Slack's *Hetty: The Genius and Madness of America's First Female Tycoon* might also appeal.

Mezrich, Ben

Rigged: The True Story of an Ivy League Kid Who Changed the World of Oil, from Wall Street to Dubai. William Morrow. 2007. 294 pp. ISBN 9780061252723.

Mezrich tells the life and business story of Harvard graduate "David Russo" (in reality: John D'Agostino), who went from Brooklyn to the high-stakes world of the petroleum and oil industry. Russo, who became hugely successful trading in the testosterone-heavy and high-risk "Merc" (the New York Mercantile Exchange), then joined forces with a mysterious young Muslim, traveled to Dubai, and became involved with the Dubai Mercantile Exchange. In addition to business stories, Mezrich doesn't hold back on the glitzy details of life lived in the oil fast lane, complete with yachts, hotel palaces, and massive amounts of money.

Subjects: Biographies, Book Groups, Business, Character Profiles, Dubai, Economics, Finance, New York City, Oil, Professions, United Arab Emirates

Now Try: Fans of Mezrich's fast-paced storytelling might consider his earlier title *Bringing Down the House,* as well as a wide variety of Cons and Card Games True Adventure narratives, such as Mitchell Zuckoff's *Ponzi's Scheme* and Frank Abagnale's *Catch Me If You Can.* Michael Lewis's *Liar's Poker,* or *Freakonomics* by Stephen Dubner and Steven Levitt, might also be offered, as might financial thrillers by authors such as Joseph Finder, Stephen Frey, or Michael M. Thomas (*Baker's Dozen* or *Black Money*).

Newhouse, John

Boeing versus Airbus: The Inside Story of the Greatest International Competition in Business. Knopf. 2007. 254 pp. ISBN 9781400043361.

Not a lot of business histories can be described as "thrilling," but the high-stakes competition between rival commercial aircraft manufacturer Boeing and their European competitor Airbus can arguably lay claim to that descriptor. By detailing the manufacturing innovations, management cultures, and market dominance that went back and forth between the two companies, Newhouse offers personal insights gained from interviews and draws a vivid picture of a formerly glamorous industry that has struggled of late to meet production deadlines and profit expectations.

Subjects: Business Histories, Companies, Economics, Flying, Globalization, Management, Manufacturing

Now Try: In addition to other business histories from this section, these readers might consider books on flight and the history of flight, such as William Langewiesche's *Inside the Sky: A Meditation on Flight,* Mariana Gosnell's *Zero 3 Bravo: Across America in a Small Plane,* or Dominick Pisano's *Chuck Yeager and the Bell X-1.*

Price, David A.

The Pixar Touch: The Making of a Company. Random House. 2008. 308 pp. ISBN 9780307265753.

In this straightforward business history, journalist David Price details the tumultuous financial and technological beginnings of the Pixar Animation Studios. In addition to interviewing the individuals most responsible for the company's success, including the founding CEO Ed Catmull and the innovative animator John Lasseter (not to mention the always enigmatic Steve Jobs and George Lucas, who also play a part in the story), Price examines the making of each of Pixar's films, including *Toy Story*, *A Bug's Life*, *Monsters Inc.*, *The Incredibles*, and *Cars*.

Subjects: Animation, Business Histories, Companies, Computers, Steve Jobs, Movies, Technology

Now Try: Fans of this quickly paced business history might enjoy other works of Business Reporting about particularly innovative companies, including Michael Malone's **Bill & Dave: How Hewlett and Packard Built the World's Greatest Company**, John Battelle's **The Search** (about Google), **Amazonia** (James Marcus's insider Memoir about Amazon.com), or even Tracy Kidder's classic **The Soul of a New Machine**; novels about corporate dynamics might also appeal, such as Douglas Coupland's classic **Microserfs** or Joshua Ferris's **Then We Came to the End**. Price also provides an extensive bibliography listing titles that may be of interest to these readers, such as Andy Hertzfeld's **Revolution in the Valley: The Insanely Great Story of How the Mac Was Made** and Owen Linzmayer's **Apple Confidential**.

Rothfeder, Jeffrey

McIlhenny's Gold: How a Louisiana Family Built the Tabasco Empire. Collins. 2007. 251 pp. ISBN 9780060721848.

This well-researched and entertainingly told family business history, undertaken without the permission or cooperation of the McIlhenny family, focuses on the history and production of the McIlhenny company's single product: Tabasco sauce. The author not only provides business details and background but also tells the social history of the product and its creation in the South, going back to the mid-1800s and touching on both company town and slavery issues. Rothfeder also did his homework as far as the company and the sauce were concerned, interviewing company executives, factory workers, southern Louisiana historians, and even the pepper pickers.

Subjects: American History, Business Histories, Companies, Community Life, Family Relationships, Food, Louisiana, Slavery, Work Relationships

Now Try: Other books about family businesses might be offered, such as Bob Ortega's **In Sam We Trust: The Untold Story of Sam Walton and How Wal-Mart Is Destroying America**; business family biographies might also appeal, such as Ron Chernow's **The House of Morgan** or **Titan: The Life of John D. Rockefeller, Sr.**, David Nasaw's **Andrew Carnegie**, or David Cannadine's **Mellon: An American Life**. Other broader interest business books by authors such as Jim Collins or Marcus Buckingam might be suggested, as might micro-histories such as Mark Kurlansky's **Salt** or **Cod**. Works of social history might also appeal, particularly those about the American South, such as Larry

Tye's *Rising from the Rails: Pullman Porters and the Making of the Black Middle Class* or Edward Ball's *Slaves in the Family*.

Schroeder, Alice

The Snowball: Warren Buffett and the Business of Life. Bantam Dell. 2008. 960 pp. ISBN 9780553805093.

Author Schroeder leaves no story untold and no stone unturned in this massive biography of investor extraordinaire and CEO of Berkshire Hathaway: Warren Buffett. In addition to telling his life story, complete with comprehensive details about his family, upbringing, childhood, and more recent family life, Schroeder also details a professional career spent making ever-more successful financial deals. In addition to providing direct quotes from Buffett (as well as interview materials from many others), the author also provides a staggering amount of historical and financial context that could only have come from extensive business knowledge and research.

> **Subjects:** 20th Century, Warren Buffett, Business, Epic Reads, Family Relationships, Finance, Nebraska, Work Relationships
>
> **Now Try:** Other definitive books in the twentieth century might also be suggested to these readers, including T. Boone Pickens's *The First Billion is the Hardest*, Charles Ellis's *Joe Wilson and the Creation of Xerox*, or Ron Chernow's *The House of Morgan: An American Banking Dynasty and the Rise of Modern Finance*. There is also a cottage industry's worth of books about the financial theories of Buffett, including Mary Buffett's *Warren Buffett and the Interpretation of Financial Statements*, Robert Hagstrom's *The Warren Buffett Way*, and Vahan Janjigian's *Even Buffett Isn't Perfect: What You Can—and Can't—Learn from the World's Greatest Investor*.

Thomas, Dana

Deluxe: How Luxury Lost Its Luster. Penguin Press. 2007. 375 pp. ISBN 9781594201295.

Has the concept of luxury truly lost its luster? That is the question Thomas, the cultural and fashion writer for *Newsweek* magazine in Paris, seeks to answer by investigating the birth and growth of the luxury industry. Organized in three sections, the book offers a broad history of the birth and growth of the "luxury industry" (which used to mean items that offered high-quality construction and name recognition); an investigation of two very specific luxury industries, high fashion and fragrance; and modern-day advances in manufacturing and production that have made more luxury goods available to a broader spectrum of individuals than previously thought possible. The text is dense but readable and Thomas's clean writing style offers insights that might appeal to general readers as well as to more dedicated readers of social histories and business books; anyone with an interest in the shift of the nature of prosperity (from buying something because of its quality to buying it because it's the "right thing") will find much of interest here.

> **Subjects:** Business Histories, China, Consumerism, Economics, Exposés, Fashion, France, Retail, Shopping, Travel
>
> **Now Try:** Books on consumerism and luxury goods might appeal to these readers, including James Twitchell's more scholarly but still fascinating *Living It Up: America's Love Affair with Luxury*, Matthew Hart's *Diamond*, Amy Stewart's *Flower Confidential*, and even Daymond John's business memoir *Display of Power* or Pamela

Danziger's business how-to book, *Marketing Luxury to the Masses*. Other books about shopping might also appeal to these readers, such as Paco Underhill's *Why We Buy* and *The Call of the Mall* or Pamela Klaffke's *Spree*. Novels in which fashion plays a role might also appeal to these readers, such as Lauren Weisberger's *The Devil Wears Prada* or Sophie Kinsella's *Confessions of a Shopaholic*.

Tungate, Mark

Adland: A Global History of Advertising. Kogan Page. 2007. 278 pp. ISBN 9780749448370.

British journalist Tungate provides a balanced and still quickly paced global history of modern advertising from the nineteenth century to the present day. Arranged in short and interesting chapters and bolstered with interviews with such advertising world notables as Phil Dusenberry, George Lois, Washington Olivetto, and Kevin Roberts, Tungate provides a vivid picture of life inside global advertising agencies such as Ogilvy and Dentsu, as well as considerations of why and how advertising has developed and will continue to develop into our digital age.

Subjects: 19th Century, 20th Century, Advertising, Business Histories, Pop Culture, Technology

Now Try: A surprising amount of nonfiction has been produced in recent years about advertising, marketing, branding, and sales; books that might particularly appeal to these readers include James Twitchell's *Twenty Ads That Shook the World*, *Lead Us into Temptation*, or *Shopping for God*; Paco Underhill's *Why We Buy* and *The Call of the Mall*, or even David Brooks's slightly more political *Bobos in Paradise* or *On Paradise Drive*. Tungate also provides a handy bibliography for the advertising world in his book, listing such titles as David Ogilvy's *Confessions of an Advertising Man* or Vance Packard's classic *The Hidden Persuaders* (even Augusten Burroughs's novel *Sellevision* might be offered).

Business Trends

Walk into any airport bookstore and you will most likely find a large and well-stocked business book collection, ready to be purchased by some of the most frequent flyers there are: business travelers. In this section you'll find the books that, along with Success Guides (another popular airport staple), are most likely to be found grouped together under subject headings such as Business, Economics, and Globalization. These are the books in which authors, even if they are not completely objective in their viewpoints, tend to offer the most balanced and well-researched narratives on a wide variety of business subjects. Because globalization is becoming an increasingly important topic in Business Reporting in general, many of the books here focus on that subject; these are also titles in which larger business and economic trends can be discerned more easily than in Business Histories and Profiles.

These are titles about the business of business, in much the same way that the Politics in Practice books in the Political Reporting chapter are about the operating procedures of politics; as such, those who enjoy these books might also enjoy those (particularly if they have any interest in current and political affairs). A wide variety of In-Depth Reporting titles might also appeal to these readers, as might other epic works of History and popular Biographies.

Business Trends books are upbeat in tone and feature stories about business innovations and techniques, as well as societal trends, that have an effect both on the corporate bottom line and on the lives of individuals either employed by or otherwise involved in specific industries and jobs. They are not typically story-driven, but instead their authors offer enthralling anecdotes and chapters based on extensive research and personal interviews.

Anderson, Chris

The Long Tail: Why the Future of Business Is Selling Less of More. Hyperion. 2006. 238 pp. ISBN 9781401302375.

> Anderson, editor of *Wired* magazine, offers his treatise on what he terms the "long tail" of Internet commerce, wherein fewer huge hits make big splashes in the marketplace, but the broad availability of the millions of books, songs, CDs and other products makes it possible for more people to make more money by selling fewer copies of more items. Using case studies like Amazon's relational database linking Joe Simpson's book *Touching the Void* with Jon Krakauer's *Into Thin Air* (making Simpson's book a best seller as well) and other online sales databases such as iTunes and Netflix, Anderson suggests that the way we produce items and make purchases may be changing but might actually be helping us to diversify our entertainment and commodity choices.
>
> **Subjects:** Book Groups, Classics, Consumerism, Economics, Quick Reads, Retail, Society, Technology
>
> **Now Try:** Books with differing perspectives on the brave new world of Internet commerce and the organization of information might be suggested, including David Weinberger's *Everything Is Miscellaneous* and Andrew Keen's opposing *The Cult of the Amateur.* Other business books about marketing and society might appeal, including Seth Godin's *Small Is the New Big*, James Surowiecki's *The Wisdom of Crowds*, Don Tapscott's *Wikinomics*, or even Mark Penn's *Microtrends*.

Ariely, Dan

🐦 *Predictably Irrational: The Hidden Forces That Shape Our Decisions.* Harper. 2008. 280 pp. ISBN 9780061353239.

> Ariely, a behavioral economics researcher at MIT, offers his take on the irrationality of most of our human decision-making processes, as well as offering suggestions for how those irrationalities can actually be predicted! Although the author's background is scholarly, this is a highly readable text that combines facets of psychology, business, and economics and includes lively examples such as people's thinking expensive medications actually work better than their generic counterparts and why otherwise honest people might not be above stealing a few office supplies.
>
> **Subjects:** Book Groups, Choice, Decisions, Economics, Mathematics, Society
>
> **Awards**: New York Times Notable

Now Try: Fans of Ariely's very accessible book might consider other such popular business and cultural books as Malcolm Gladwell's *The Tipping Point* or *Blink*, Nassim Nicholas Taleb's *Fooled by Randomness* or *The Black Swan*, Ian Ayres's *Super Crunchers*, Stephen Dubner's and Steven Levitt's *Freakonomics*, or Chris Anderson's *The Long Tail*. Other business books might be suggested, including Jim Collins's classic *Good to Great* or other titles by Marcus Buckingham, David Weinberger, or Dan Heath and Chip Heath (*Made to Stick*); the political title *The Political Brain: The Role of Emotion in Deciding the Fate of the Nation* by Drew Westen might also be suggested.

Ayres, Ian

🎗 *Super Crunchers: Why Thinking-by-Numbers Is the New Way to Be Smart.* Bantam Books. 2007. 260 pp. ISBN 9780553805406.

A law school professor and econometrician at Yale University, Ayres suggests that the massive sets of data now becoming available to analysts in numerous fields, including medicine, will allow individuals to make better and faster decisions than ever before. Although Ayres makes allowances that there will always be a place in our decision-making processes for intuition, his much more strident point is that allowing experts to crunch the numbers will help us but also that we will become increasingly able to use technology to process our own data and rely less on "experts'" predictions and suggestions.

> **Subjects:** Business, Mathematics, Probability, Statistics, Technology
>
> **Awards:** ALA Notable
>
> **Now Try:** Other books in which numbers and probability play a large part are Michael Lewis's *Moneyball*, Steven Levitt's and Stephen Dubner's *Freakonomics*, Nicholas Nassim Taleb's *Fooled by Randomness* or *The Black Swan*, James Surowiecki's *The Wisdom of Crowds*, or Mark Penn's *Microtrends*.

Barnes, Peter

Capitalism 3.0: A Guide to Reclaiming the Commons. Berrett-Koehler. 2006. 195 pp. ISBN 9781576753613.

Using the extended metaphor of software going through its various versions, Barnes refers to capitalism and the free market system as an operating system that worked well shortly after its inception but is becoming increasingly complex, clunky, and unsustainable (or, to quote Barnes, that is "packed with proprietary features that benefit a lucky few while threatening to crash the system for everyone else"). In addition to providing a history and investigation into our current economic and political system, the author also suggests alternatives to our current corporate-driven economic model and maintains that it is still possible to change laws and society to reinvent the commons.

> **Subjects:** Business, Capitalism, Economics, Government, Law and Lawyers, Making Sense . . ., Scholarly, Society
>
> **Now Try:** Books on the changing circumstances surrounding economic, political, and cultural systems might all appeal to these readers, such as Lawrence Lessig's *Free Culture*, Jeremy Rifkin's *The Age of Access*, or David

Weinberger's *Everything Is Miscellaneous*. Barnes also has some heavy hitters providing blurbs for his book, including Bill McKibben, George Lakoff, and Michael Pollan; authors to whom he refers in his bibliography include Gar Alperovitz, Jared Diamond, John Kenneth Galbraith, Malcolm Gladwell, Ronald Wright, and William Greider.

Fishman, Ted C.

China, Inc.: How the Rise of the Next Superpower Challenges America and the World. Scribner. 2005. 342 pp. ISBN 9780743257527.

China is currently the largest maker of toys, clothing, and consumer electronics in the world, and Fishman argues that the nation's productive dominance and abundant labor pool will make the twenty-first century the "Chinese Century." Using both quantitative data and anecdotes, Fishman illuminates China's business history over the past three decades, and speculates about the nation's (and, by extension, the world's) business future.

Subjects: Business, China, Economics, Globalization, Politics, Technology

Now Try: There is no shortage of books about China and its growing influence on global business; related titles include James Kynge's *China Shakes the World: A Titan's Rise and Troubled Future—and the Challenge for America*, Antoine van Agtmael's *The Emerging Markets Century*, and Robyn Meredith's *The Elephant and the Dragon*. Richard Florida's *The Rise of the Creative Class: And How It's Transforming Work, Leisure, Community, and Everyday Life* provides another viewpoint on the ever-changing world of workplace and societal demographics and how those changes affect both our business and personal lives, while Sara Bongiorni's memoir *A Year without "Made in China"* might also provide yet another part of the story.

Florida, Richard

Who's Your City?: How the Creative Economy Is Making Where to Live the Most Important Decision of Your Life. Basic Books. 2008. 374 pp. ISBN 9780465003525.

Author, researcher, and speaker Florida offers a thoughtful treatise on not only how we live and who we live with in our new global age, but also where we live. Arguing that the dynamics of population distribution are changing to favor large "superstar" cities, a person's proximity to which may have a great effect on his or her career and livelihood prospects, Florida also describes how individuals choose their cities and places of residence based on their stage of life. Also included are city rankings that suggest the best community matches for singles, families, and empty-nesters. In addition to broad descriptions of globalization, the author also offers a wealth of statistics and research on changing demographics and technologies.

Subjects: Business, Demographics, Geography, Homes, Scholarly, Society, Urban Life

Now Try: Richard Florida's earlier book, *The Rise of the Creative Class*, is often cited as a classic of business literature; that book might be offered, as might other sociological classics including Robert Putnam's *Bowling Alone*, Jane Jacobs's *The Death and Life of Great American Cities*, James Howard Kunstler's *The Geography of Nowhere*, Thomas Friedman's *The World Is Flat*, Malcolm Gladwell's *The Tipping Point*, or even Jared Diamond's *Guns, Germs, and Steel* or *Collapse*.

Friedman, Thomas

The World Is Flat: A Brief History of the Twenty-First Century. Farrar, Straus & Giroux. 2005 (Updated and expanded edition, Picador 2007). 488 pp. ISBN 9780312425074.

Journalist Friedman presents a "history" of the world as we are coming to know it in the twenty-first century, complete with measured thoughts on globalization, business, culture, and technology. Much of the book is informed by his "flat world" analogy, which posits that communications and other technological advances have made the global marketplace a true and unstoppable reality, and one that offers the possibility for inequality but also for prosperity.

> **Subjects:** Alternate Histories, Book Groups, Business, China, Classics, Economics, Geography, Globalization, Government, India, Politics, Technology

> **Now Try:** Before publishing this book, Friedman was most well known for his best-selling classic *The Lexus and the Olive Tree*, also about globalization and its proponents and detractors. Readers might also consider other popular economic works such as Levitt and Dubner's *Freakonomics* or Evans's and Wurster's *Blown to Bits: How the New Economics of Information Transforms Strategy*. Richard Florida's *The Rise of the Creative Class* and sociology best sellers like Jared Diamond's *Guns, Germs, and Steel* or *Collapse*, Malcolm Gladwell's *The Tipping Point* or *Blink* might also appeal to these readers, as might closer looks at globalization including Sasha Issenberg's *The Sushi Economy* or Rachel Louise Snyder's *Fugitive Denim*.

Gross, Daniel R.

Pop!: Why Bubbles Are Great for the Economy. Collins. 2007. 232 pp. ISBN 9780061151545.

Gross makes the argument that economic "bubbles," typically seen or discussed as a problem (particularly when they pop!) in the economy, are actually part of the process that drives innovation and progress in economic growth. Among the case studies he cites are the nineteenth- and twentieth-century booms in industries such as railroads and communications (the telegraph) that were followed by crashes but then leveled out into an overall higher level of prosperity.

> **Subjects:** American History, Business, Economics, Technology

> **Now Try:** Gross is a writer for *Slate* and *Wired* magazine; other writers from those publications include Chris Anderson (*The Long Tail*) and Arthur Allen (*Vaccine: The Controversial Story of Medicine's Greatest Lifesaver*). Gross also lists a number of related reads in his references, including David Denby's *American Sucker*, John Gartner's *The Hypomanic Edge*, or *Irrational Exuberance* by Robert Shiller. Stephen Ambrose's *Nothing Like It in the World* (about the railroad) might also be offered, as might Erik Larson's true crime/history *Thunderstruck* (about wireless telegraphy).

6

Kynge, James

China Shakes the World: A Titan's Rise and Troubled Future—and the Challenge for America. Houghton Mifflin. 2006. 270 pp. ISBN 9780618705641.

Kynge examines the effects that the country of China and its many residents have already had and will continue to have on world trade and politics. Making the case that most of the goods purchased by Americans and other nations are already made in China, he also strives to make his reader understand how that dependence on China could eventually have huge repercussions—particularly by illustrating how China itself faces many challenges in the form of environmental crises and faltering governmental controls. As a reporter and Asian correspondent for the venerable financial newspaper the *Financial Times*, Kynge brings an insider's grasp of details to his narrative.

> **Subjects:** Business, China, Consumerism, Economics, Foreign Relations, Globalization, Government

> **Now Try:** Other books on globalization and particularly books on China and India might be suggested to these readers, including Robyn Meredith's *The Elephant and the Dragon*, Edward Luce's *In Spite of the Gods: The Rise of Modern India*, or Ted Fishman's *China, Inc.* Other books on China might also particularly appeal to these readers, such as Simon Winchester's *The River at the Center of the World*, Peter Hessler's *Oracle Bones*, or Jonathan Spence's *The Search for Modern China*.

McGinn, Daniel

House Lust: America's Obsession with Our Homes. Currency Doubleday. 2008. 264 pp. ISBN 9780385519298.

Newsweek correspondent McGinn follows up his own interest in real estate and the housing market boom (and subsequent slowdown) of the early twenty-first century by interviewing individuals who themselves yearn for bigger and better homes; the workers who build, decorate, and renovate homes; the financial professionals who facilitate home ownership and mortgages; and those who dream of making their fortunes through "flipping" properties. McGinn also offers an impressive national take on the subject by traveling to communities in Maryland, Las Vegas, New York City, Idaho, and Florida.

> **Subjects:** Business, Economics, Homes, Psychology, Real Estate, Society

> **Now Try:** A number of books on homes and communities might be offered to these readers, including *House* by Tracy Kidder, *Who's Your City?* by Richard Florida, *Gutted: Down to the Studs in My House, My Marriage, My Entire Life* by Lawrence LaRose, Witold Rybczynski's *City Life*, *House: A Memoir* by Michael Ruhlman, and *A Place of My Own* by Michael Pollan. Books about society and economics, particularly as they relate to our living situations, might also be of some appeal: these include Robert Frank's *Richistan*, David Brooks's *Bobos in Paradise* or *On Paradise Drive*, or Robert Putnam's *Bowling Alone*.

McKibben, Bill

Deep Economy: The Wealth of Communities and the Durable Future. Times Books. 2007. 261 pp. ISBN 9780805076264.

Environmental writer McKibben offers his manifesto for communities to engage in more local production and consumption cycles (meaning we must more carefully think about the food we eat, the energy we use, and how we make the money to pay for all of it). Also of tantamount importance in this text is McKibben's argument that constant "growth" in our economies is not really sustainable, and we must find new ways to measure societal and business health.

> **Subjects:** Book Groups, Business, Capitalism, Community Life, Economics, Environmental Writing, Politics, Society, Sustainability

> **Now Try:** McKibben is most well known as an environmental writer; his earlier titles *The End of Nature* and *Enough: Staying Human in an Engineered Age* might also appeal to these readers, as well as books by other such environmental and social commentators as Wendell Berry, Edward Abbey, Jonathan Schell, and Edward Hoagland. Other books about new economic and community lifestyles might also be suggested, such as Barbara Kingsolver's *Animal, Vegetable, Miracle* or Judith Levine's *Not Buying It*, as well as books by other science writers including Michael Pollan or Rachel Carson.

Meredith, Robyn

The Elephant and the Dragon: The Rise of India and China and What It Means for All of Us. Norton. 2007. 252 pp. ISBN 9780393062366.

Meredith, who covers business and news events in China and India for *Forbes* magazine, illustrates how India and China have each followed their own economic path, considers how they are similar, and never loses sight of the truth that their growing involvement in the world market will have repercussions, good and bad, for America and other nations worldwide. Positing that "China became the factory of the world, the United States became buyer to the world, and India became back office to the world," Meredith not only explains how China and India might develop their own infrastructure and educational systems but also suggests that Americans should pay more attention to their own educations and promote innovation to take advantage of the shifting world order.

> **Subjects:** Business, China, Economics, Globalization, India

> **Now Try:** Meredith is of the opinion that further development in China and India can actually help America's economic bottom line; other similarly positive takes on globalization might appeal to these readers, such as Thomas Friedman's *The World Is Flat* or *The Lexus and the Olive Tree*, Antoine van Agtmael's *The Emerging Markets Century*, or Ted Fishman's *China, Inc.*; other more informational books like Joseph Stiglitz's *Globalization and Its Discontents* might be suggested, as might Edward Luce's *In Spite of the Gods: The Rise of Modern India*.

Penn, Mark, and E. Kinney Zalesne

Microtrends: The Small Forces behind Tomorrow's Big Changes. Twelve. 2007. 425 pp. ISBN 9780446580960.

In this thoroughly fascinating compendium of seventy-five "microtrends," political pollster Penn touches on the subjects of relationships, work, race, religion, health and wellness, politics, technology, lifestyle, and education (among others). In addition to considering how trends and statistical findings affect society and the economy in the United States, Penn also offers sidebars on those same trends and their global impact. Each chapter focuses on one microtrend and comprises five to ten pages; although there is no narrative to follow here, there is a wealth of skillfully told anecdotes and predictions for the future.

> **Subjects:** Business, Causality, Economics, Politics, Society, Trivia
>
> **Now Try:** Other books about causality and futurism might be suggested, such as Malcolm Gladwell's *The Tipping Point*, Nassim Nicholas Taleb's *The Black Swan: The Impact of the Highly Probable*, Thomas Friedman's *The World Is Flat*, Chris Anderson's *The Long Tail*, or Alvin Toffler and Heidi Toffler's *Revolutionary Wealth*. This book was also reviewed favorably by Jim Cramer, a popular financial commentator and author, whose finance self-help titles *Jim Cramer's Real Money* and *Jim Cramer's Mad Money* might also hold some appeal for these readers. Mark Penn was also a political strategist for Hillary Clinton, and other books from the Political Reporting chapter might be good related reads as well.

Rifkin, Jeremy

The End of Work: The Decline of the Global Labor Force and the Dawn of the Post-Market Era. Putnam. 1995. 350 pp. ISBN 9780874777796.

Rifkin has long been a liberal activist, and as the founder of the Foundation on Economic Trends, he has sounded so many alarms about technological and genetic engineering advances (and the deleterious effects he believes those advances will cause) that he is sometimes referred to as a "postmodern Chicken Little." In this book, he argues that technology and computers have advanced to the point where they are displacing large sectors of workers and will eventually lead to devastating levels of unemployment. Rifkin is not all doom and gloom; he also makes concrete suggestions for the creation of a new sector of the economy that will comprise voluntary and community-funded organizations, which will help provide needed social services.

> **Subjects:** Capitalism, Economics, Globalization, Making Sense . . ., Postmodernism, Professions, Scholarly, Society, Technology
>
> **Now Try:** A number of Rifkin's other books might also appeal to these readers, including *The Age of Access* and *The European Dream*; other cultural critics might also appeal, such as Christopher Lasch or Jacques Barzun, or techies and futurists like Esther Dyson or Alvin Toffler. Authors from the left side of the political spectrum might also appeal, such as Naomi Klein, Juliet Schor, or Paul Krugman, as might books about the darker side of globalization, such as John Bowe's *Nobodies* or Louis Uchitelle's *The Disposable American*.

Shapiro, Robert J.

Futurecast: How Superpowers, Population, and Globalization Will Change the Way You Live and Work. St. Martin's Press. 2008. 358 pp. ISBN 9780312352424.

In this comprehensive but well-written book about future trends, Shapiro outlines what he thinks the next few decades will bring in our economic, political, and social lives. Using statistics and research, as well as his former experiences as an economic advisor to Bill Clinton and an undersecretary of commerce from 1998 to 2001, he describes the changing demographics, globalization and its effect on business, and the rise of new superpowers worldwide (all of which will shape life in the twenty-first century).

Subjects: Demographics, Economics, Futurism, Globalization, Government, Scholarly, Society

Now Try: Fans of this brisk book of predictions might consider other books about the future, such as Alvin Toffler and Heidi Toffler's *Revolutionary Wealth*, Fareed Zakaria's *The Post-American World*, Jeffrey Sachs's *Common Wealth: Economics for a Crowded Planet*, William Greider's *The Soul of Capitalism*, or Alan Weisman's more science-oriented *The World without Us*. Business Reporting books about globalization might also be offered (these include Ted Fishman's *China, Inc.* and Edward Luce's *In Spite of the Gods: The Rise of Modern India*). More popular nonfiction by such authors as Jared Diamond (*Guns, Germs, and Steel* and *Collapse*), Robert Reich (*Supercapitalism*), and Robert Kagan (*Of Paradise and Power*) might also appeal.

Tapscott, Don, and Anthony Williams

Wikinomics: How Mass Collaboration Changes Everything. Portfolio. 2006. 324 pp. ISBN 9781591841388.

Tapscott and Williams make the argument that the way of the future is not only group collaboration but collaboration on a scale previously not thought possible. The authors explore how individuals worldwide participate in and create collaborative products for a wide variety of educational and entertainment reasons (from online encyclopedias to fan videos and music remixes). Rather than being threatened by this trend, companies and managers need to act to harness the collective capabilities both within their own organizations and in the public at large. Using such case studies as the continuing popularity of open source programming, online social networks like YouTube and Flickr, and seasoned corporations like Procter & Gamble working with outside collaborators on product development, Tapscott makes the brave new world of mass collaboration a little more personal.

Subjects: Business, Economics, Making Sense . . ., Scholarly, Society, Technology

Now Try: David Weinberger's *Everything Is Miscellaneous* and *The Cluetrain Manifesto* might appeal to these readers, as might other collaboration and social networking books such as Chris Anderson's *The Long Tail*, Ori Brafman's *The Starfish and the Spider*, James Surowiecki's *The Wisdom of Crowds*, Malcolm Gladwell's *The Tipping Point*, or Keith Sawyer's *Group Genius: The Creative Power of Collaboration*.

Toffler, Alvin, and Heidi Toffler

Revolutionary Wealth. Knopf. 2006. 492 pp. ISBN 9780375401749.

Husband-and-wife team Alvin and Heidi Toffler explore trends in our society and economy, forecasting that many such factors as increasing globalization, the rise of China as an economic power, and our own personal consumption and buying habits will all affect the way that wealth is held and distributed in the coming years. They also explore such trends as the increasing speed and transience in all facets of our lives and offer their predictions for a richer and faster future.

Subjects: Business, Economics, Futurism, Government, Society, Sociology

Now Try: Readers who enjoy this title should also be offered Alvin Toffler and Heidi Toffler's earlier classic, *Future Shock*. Other authors who might appeal to these readers include Jared Diamond (*Guns, Germs, and Steel* and *Collapse*), Malcolm Gladwell (*The Tipping Point* and *Blink*), Philip Evans and Thomas Wurster (*Blown to Bits*), Lawrence Lessig (*Free Culture*), and Steven Levitt and Stephen Dubner (*Freakonomics*). Other futurist authors who might be offered include Ray Kurzweil, Paul Ehrlich, and David Weinberger (*Everything Is Miscellaneous*); James Gleick's science classic *Faster* might also be suggested.

Weinberger, David

Everything Is Miscellaneous: The Power of the New Digital Disorder. Times Books. 2007. 277 pp. ISBN 9780805080438.

Weinberger argues that we are in a whole new age, where end-users rather than producers and organizers of information will determine the information they ultimately look at and make use of by defining their own search parameters and filters. Weinberger contrasts former organizational schemes like the Dewey decimal system and physical structures like retail establishments with the new digital environment where "everything is miscellaneous" and can be found in a variety of locations. This shift, the author concludes, will affect all aspects of society, from education and politics to science and culture, bringing us into the age of the "third order," in which items don't have one physical location or one card catalog describing where they are but rather have countless tags and masses of information explaining where they might be.

> **Subjects:** Book Groups, Business, Making Sense . . ., Society, Taxonomies, Technology

> **Now Try:** Weinberger is also the author of the bestseller *The Cluetrain Manifesto*; other best-selling business books which may appeal to these readers include Chris Anderson's *The Long Tail*, Chip Heath and Dan Heath's *Made to Stick*, Nassim Nicholas Taleb's *The Black Swan: The Impact of the Highly Probable*, Don Tapscott's *Wikinomics*, or Seth Godin's *Small Is the New Big*. Other books on the cultural impact of information technologies might appeal, including Andrew Keen's *The Cult of the Amateur: How Today's Internet Is Killing Our Culture* (Keen is much less optimistic in tone than Weinberger), or books by futurists Ray Kurzweil or Alvin Toffler. Science fiction with technological and social themes might also appeal, such as Geoff Ryman's *Air* or Max Barry's *Jennifer Government*.

Wurster, Thomas S., and Philip Evans

Blown to Bits: How the New Economics of Information Transforms Strategy. Harvard Business School Press. 2006. 261 pp. ISBN 9780875848778.

Business consultants Evans and Wurster weigh in on what they feel are the main issues shaping and affecting the information economy today. Using numerous business case studies ranging from the general (newspapers, retail banking) to the specific (Dell, Microsoft), question-and-answer sections to help readers understand new information economy strategies, and end-of-chapter recaps, the authors provide a readable, thought-provoking, and ultimately practical treatise on new business opportunities and technologies.

> **Subjects:** Business, Computers, Economics, Small Press, Society, Technology

> **Now Try:** Lawrence Lessig's *Free Culture: How Big Media Uses Technology and the Law to Lock Down Culture and Control Creativity* might also appeal to readers interested in the interplay between technology and business. Another best-selling business book that uses case studies of companies and chapter summaries and key findings at the end of every chapter is Jim Collins's *Good to Great: Why Some Companies Make*

the Leap . . . and Others Don't. Although less business-oriented, Steven Levitt's and Stephen Dubner's *Freakonomics: A Rogue Economist Explores the Hidden Side of Everything* also makes some interesting connections between economic principles and societal phenomena.

Biz Crit

Okay, the heading's a bit cutesy. It's not meant to be, really. It just seemed like the best heading for the job of describing business titles in which authors explore the darker aspects of business, without necessarily wanting to throw in the towel on business principles and principles themselves. That is, these are books in which investigative authors spend a great deal of time and energy following business stories, not to criticize business itself but rather to analyze how current business practices are affected by larger societal and cultural concerns, as well as how the business world has a great impact on our society, both locally and globally. A great many of the titles listed in this section might also strike readers and readers' advisors as being very similar indeed to Exposés, particularly Corporate Exposés. Although it is true that in some of these books the authors reveal previously hidden facts and secrets about businesses and industries, their overall tone still tends to be more positive about the role of business and capitalism than do most Exposés. Many of these titles, in fact, are written by authors who are optimistic about the state and developments in business and society and editorialize on their theories (e.g., Richard Florida's *The Creative Class*). These books often showcase the very definite opinions of their authors but tend to be written in a more sedate style than are most true Exposés.

Readers who enjoy these titles and also have political interests might consider their stylistic counterpart in that chapter, the Hot-Button Issues titles. A wide variety of Business Histories and Profiles and Business Trends titles might also appeal, as many of those books are also written with a very level tone; more scholarly books on economics and History nonfiction might also be suggested to fans of these books.

> Biz Crit books feature stories about business and economic trends and narratives about specific companies and industries, but their authors often adopt a more analytical (sometimes edging closer to critical) tone than do the authors in Business Trends book. The overall atmosphere here is still positive about the capacity of the business system to do good, but these authors offer a variety of viewpoints and research regarding specific issues in these more reflective but still very sharply written books.

Bakan, Joel

The Corporation: The Pathological Pursuit of Profit and Power. Free Press. 2004. 228 pp. ISBN 9780743247443.

> Bakan offers a history not of any specific business but rather of the "corporation" as the institution and entity we have come to know over the past century. This is not an unbiased history; Bakan states in his introduction that "the corporation is a pathological institution, a dangerous possessor of the great power it wields over people and societies." In addition to providing a history of the development of the corporation, Bakan also interviews economists and other business leaders about the twentieth-century development of corporations, including Milton Friedman.

> **Subjects:** Business, Companies, Corruption, Economics, Exposés, Law and Lawyers

> **Now Try:** Other Exposés such as Eric Schlosser's *Fast Food Nation*, Michael Moore's *Stupid White Men*, or John Bowe's *Nobodies* might appeal to these readers; in Bakan's bibliography, he lists other similar authors, including Thomas Frank, John Kenneth Galbraith, William Greider, Naomi Klein, Jeremy Rifkin, Paul Krugman, and Greg Palast.

Barber, Benjamin R.

Consumed: How Markets Corrupt Children, Infantilize Adults, and Swallow Citizens Whole. Norton. 2007. 406 pp. ISBN 9780393049619.

> Barber examines the current state of globalization as he sees it: a situation in which producers overproduce and therefore have to overbrand and oversell their products to every individual in the market they possibly can, including children worldwide. Offering in-depth research, statistics, and descriptions of such current phenomena as twenty-four hour conveniences, declining voter participation, increased privatization of public concerns, and branding, the author speculates that individuals worldwide are now being seduced into near-constant consumption, encouraged at every step by the purveyors and advertisers of capitalism's many goods.

> **Subjects:** Advertising, Business, Consumerism, Economics, Exposés, Globalization, Mass Media, Shopping, Society

> **Now Try:** Other books about how buying and selling are done in our society, including Paco Underhill's *Why We Buy* and *The Call of the Mall*, Naomi Klein's *No Logo* or *The Shock Doctrine*, Juliet Schor's *The Overspent American*, James Twitchell's *Living It Up: America's Love Affair with Luxury*, John de Graaf's *Affluenza*, Neil Postman's *Amusing Ourselves to Death*, or John Perkins's *The Secret History of the American Empire* might all appeal to these readers. Dystopian fiction by such authors as George Orwell, Kurt Vonnegut, or Aldous Huxley might also appeal.

Brandt, Allan M.

The Cigarette Century: The Rise, Fall, and Deadly Persistence of the Product That Defined America. Basic Books. 2007. 600 pp. ISBN 9780465070473.

> Brandt offers a comprehensive history of not only the industry that produces cigarettes but the cigarette itself, relating stories of how cigarettes found their way into groundbreaking advertising and marketing ploys, the cinema and pop culture, and, eventually, a large chunk of American case law. In addition to describing most of the business and cultural history of the cigarette and the companies that make them, Brandt also speculates on the still-booming worldwide marketplace

for cigarettes. Comprehensive and engagingly written, the book unfolds over five sections, highlighting the role of smoking in culture, science, politics, law, and globalization.

> **Subjects:** Advertising, Business Histories, Cigarettes, Health Issues, Law and Lawyers, Smoking

> **Now Try:** If readers can stand to learn any more about the cigarette industry, consider offering Richard Kluger's history *Ashes to Ashes* or Bryan Burrough's *Barbarians at the Gate: The Fall of RJR Nabisco*. (Emily Flake's smoking memoir *These Things Ain't Gonna Smoke Themselves* might also provide the other side of the story.) Other business histories such as Kurt Eichenwald's *Conspiracy of Fools*, Constance Hays's *The Real Thing: Truth and Power at the Coca-Cola Company*, or Robert Lacey's *Ford: The Men and the Machine* might also be enjoyed by these readers.

Brook, Daniel

The Trap: Selling Out to Stay Afloat in Winner-Take-All America. Times Books. 2007. 274 pp. ISBN 9780805080650.

> Journalist Brook examines a financial catch-22 facing a large number of young, professional, urban dwellers: to use their education and pay off their school debt, many new professionals must move to expensive urban areas to live, and once they get there, very few of them can then afford to buy a house or send their children to school anywhere near where they work. Brook also examines the strange new economic truism that many corporate elites are struggling to enjoy what were once considered the most basic of middle-class lifestyle comforts, as well as the conflict faced by many members of Generations X and Y who are finding that to pay off their debts, they must "sell out" and take jobs with large corporations rather than with nonprofits or in the social or public sector. In various chapters, Brook outlines the history of the growing income gap, political policies, lifestyle choices and the costs of raising families, the increasingly elusive dream of business ownership, and possible solutions to all these problems.

> **Subjects:** Business, Community Life, Economics, Education, Finance, Society

> **Now Try:** Other books about the middle class and even the upper middle class feeling increasingly squeezed by debt and financial concerns include Tamara Draut's *Strapped: Why America's 20- and 30-Somethings Can't Get Ahead*, Anya Kamenetz's *Generation Debt*, Louis Uchitelle's *The Disposable American*, and Robert H. Frank's *Falling Behind*, while books about the lower middle classes might also be unsettling read-alikes, including Katherine Newman's and Victor Tan Chen's *The Missing Class* and David Shipler's *The Working Poor*. Other books by business and political authors such as David Cay Johnston, Richard Florida (whose take on the situation is a bit more optimistic), David Brooks (*Bobos in Paradise*), and Kevin Phillips might be suggested, as might Douglas Coupland's novel *Microserfs* or Joshua Ferris's modern workplace tale, *Then We Came to the End*.

Brooks, David R.

Bobos in Paradise: The New Upper Class and How They Got There. Simon & Schuster. 2000. 284 pp. ISBN 9780684853772.

> In this influential book Brooks argues that the people he terms the "Bobos" (deriving their name from mixing "bourgeois" with "bohemians") have somehow combined the values of the 1960s counterculture with the materialism that was present in 1980s culture. The author worked previously as a senior editor at the conservative *Weekly Standard*, and offers a mix of cultural and economic reporting and writing in this volume.
>
> > **Subjects:** 1960s, 1980s, Classics, Classism, Economics, Making Sense. . ., Politics, Society
> >
> > **Now Try:** Brooks's subsequent title, the related *On Paradise Drive*, might also be offered to these readers, as might Robert Frank's *Richistan* or James Twitchell's *Living It Up: America's Love Affair with Luxury*. Authors who provided blurbs for this title might be suggested, including conservative humorist and political commentator P. J. O'Rourke and novelist and new journalist Tom Wolfe. Other books about changing ideas of community in America, such as Robert Putnam's *Bowling Alone* or Alain de Botton's *Status Anxiety* might be suggested, as might books by other *Weekly Standard* contributors such as Stephen F. Hayes (*Cheney*), William Kristol, or John Podhoretz.

Cycon, Dean

Javatrekker: Dispatches from the World of Fair Trade Coffee. Chelsea Green. 2007. 239 pp. ISBN 9781933392707.

> Cycon explores the global coffee trade, which culminates in as domestic and everyday an occurrence as our morning cup of coffee, by traveling to the places where coffee is grown and meeting the people who have grown it. Grown in fifty countries worldwide by some twenty-eight million growers, the industry also supports a complex web of traders, sellers, and other middlemen who get the coffee into stores, coffee shops, and our cups. In this narrative, part investigation and part travelogue, Cycon takes his readers on a tour of ten countries and along the way explains such concepts as cooperation, fair trade, and profit sharing.
>
> > **Subjects:** Business, Coffee, Economics, Food, Globalization, Small Press, Travel
> >
> > **Now Try:** Other books in which authors take a closer look at specific companies and industries might be offered to these readers, including Taylor Clark's *Starbucked*, Rachel Louise Snyder's *Fugitive Denim*, or Amy Stewart's *Flower Confidential*. Other books about globalization might be suggested, from the more positive, such as Thomas Friedman's *The World Is Flat*, to the more questioning *Nobodies: Modern American Slave Labor and the Dark Side of the New Global Economy*, as might a selection of travel books, such as Pico Iyer's *Sun after Dark* or Paul Theroux's *The Old Patagonian Express: By Train through the Americas*. Fans of books published by Chelsea Green might also consider sustainability titles by authors including Bill McKibben and Wendell Berry.

Eichenwald, Kurt

🌸 *Conspiracy of Fools: A True Story.* Broadway Books. 2005. 742 pp. ISBN 9780767911788.

> *New York Times* financial journalist Eichenwald provides nearly a minute-by-minute account of Enron's rise to glory and subsequent fall to disgrace and ruin.

Based on numerous interviews and in-depth reporting, Eichenwald describes the company's philosophy, leadership, and, most important, the illegal accounting practices that would eventually cause its downfall.

Subjects: Accounting and Accountants, Business Histories, Companies, Economics, Energy, Epic Reads, Exposés, Politics, Work Relationships

Awards: ALA Notable, New York Times Notable

Now Try: Fans of this lengthy Exposé might enjoy a wide variety of other Corporate Exposés or business histories, including Bryan Burroughs's and John Helyar's *Barbarians at the Gate*, Richard Johnson's *Six Men Who Built the Modern Auto Industry*, Constance Hays's *The Real Thing: Truth and Power at the Coca-Cola Company*, Robert Lacey's *Ford: The Men and the Machine*, or Bob Ortega's *In Sam We Trust: The Untold Story of Sam Walton and Wal-Mart*. Titles featuring financial True Crime stories, including *Ponzi's Scheme* by Mitchell Zuckoff and *American Roulette* by Richard Marcus, as well as James B. Stewart's *Disney War* and *Den of Thieves* might also be offered to these readers, as might a broad variety of financial thrillers by authors such as Jeffrey Archer, Joseph Finder, and James Grippando.

Florida, Richard L.

The Rise of the Creative Class: And How It's Transforming Work, Leisure, Community and Everyday Life. Basic Books. 2002. 404 pp. ISBN 9780465024766.

Florida explores the work performed by members of the "creative class," which he estimates comprises more than thirty-eight million Americans and includes individuals from the widely varied fields of engineering, business and finance, law, health care, and many other fields. Positing that America is becoming a nation of three classes (the Creative, Working, and Service classes), he further suggests that individuals hoping to make themselves more marketable as "Creatives" need to broaden their skill sets, become more comfortable working as part of collaborative groups, and increase their leadership skills to become a more cohesive and powerful group in their own right.

Subjects: Business, Companies, Creativity, Economics, Professions, Sociology, Work Relationships

Now Try: Florida's fans might consider his subsequent title, *Who's Your City?* Other authors optimistic about new work organizations and opportunities might be offered, including David Weinberger (*The Cluetrain Manifesto* and *Everything Is Miscellaneous*), Peter Barnes (*Capitalism 3.0*), and Thomas Wurster (*Blown to Bits*). Authors suggested by Florida himself include Daniel Pink (*A Whole New Mind* and *Free Agent Nation*), John Seely Brown (*The Social Life of Information*), and Robert Putnam.

Frank, Robert H.

Falling Behind: How Rising Inequality Harms the Middle Class. University of California Press. 2007. 148 pp. ISBN 9780520251885.

In this short, readable treatise on the changing economics of America's middle class, Frank posits that out-of-control spending habits and the carrying of huge loads of credit debt stem primarily from the very human desire to see what the upper classes can buy and then seeking to "keep up with the Joneses." By citing such statistics as the growing sizes of American homes and the increases in price of other goods, the author makes a persuasive case that if this situation persists, it will have dire consequences for the broader economy. Also included are the author's suggestions to correct the situation, at least partly through a progressive tax and other reforms.

> **Subjects:** Classism, Consumerism, Economics, Government, Homes, Public Policy, Small Press, Sociology

> **Now Try:** Any number of investigative works might appeal to readers who enjoy Frank's slim volume on consumerism and American culture; these include Paco Underhill's *Why We Buy*, Alissa Quart's *Branded: The Buying and Selling of Teenagers*, or Naomi Klein's *No Logo*. Other books on community life, such as Robert Putnam's *Bowling Alone: The Collapse and Revival of American Community* might appeal, as might books about class distinctions in America, such as David Shipler's *The Working Poor*, Katherine Newman's and Victor Tan Chen's *The Missing Class: Portraits of the Near Poor in America*, Daniel Brook's *The Trap: Selling Out to Stay Afloat in Winner-Take-All America, Class Matters*, or Joe Bageant's more politically motivated *Deer Hunting with Jesus*. Frank himself provides a stellar list of related reading in his references, citing works by Juliet Schor (*The Overspent American*) and John Kenneth Galbraith (*The Affluent Society*).

Frank, Thomas S.

One Market under God: Extreme Capitalism, Market Populism, and the End of Economic Democracy. Doubleday. 2000. 414 pp. ISBN 9780385495035.

> Best known for his best-selling political book *What's the Matter with Kansas?*, Frank is also a skilled writer when considering the complex processes of market capitalism and how they collide with the principles and values of democracy. By looking at such various business subjects as management theory, marketing, and advertising, Frank makes the case that equating the free market with free democracy, as we tend to do in America, is simplistic at best and a dangerous delusion at worst.

> **Subjects:** Business, Capitalism, Economics, Exposés, Government, Politics, Scholarly, Sociology

> **Now Try:** Books by writers similar in style and subject matter to Frank might be offered; these include William Greider (*One World, Ready or Not* or *The Soul of Capitalism*), Paul Krugman (*The Great Unraveling*), or Robert B. Reich (*Supercapitalism*). Other books about economics and globalization by authors such as Kevin Phillips (*American Theocracy* and *Bad Money*) might be suggested, as might books about American economics and classism, such as David Shipler's *The Working Poor* or Louis Uchitelle's *The Disposable American*.

Greenhouse, Steven

The Big Squeeze: Tough Times for the American Worker. Knopf. 2008. 365 pp. ISBN 9781400044894.

> Longtime labor and workplace correspondent for the *New York Times* Greenhouse examines, in dense but short and compelling chapters, the many ways in which members of the American labor force are being squeezed on all sides, in the form of lower wages, higher health care costs and costs of living, globalization and immigration issues, and fewer government assistance programs. Greenhouse pulls no punches when exposing how many companies take advantage of their workers

(particularly retail giants like Wal-Mart and Family Dollar), but he also describes many employers treating their workers well and offers suggestions for other companies to follow their examples.

Subjects: Business, Companies, Economics, Globalization, Labor History, Unions

Now Try: Works similar to Greenhouse's in tone include Jared Bernstein's *Crunch: Why Do I Feel So Squeezed?*, Louis Uchitelle's *The Disposable American*, Barbara Ehrenreich's *Nickel and Dimed*, and *Class Matters* (a collection by *New York Times* correspondents). A number of other Corporate Exposés (not to mention Government Exposés and Social Exposés) might also be suggested, such as Jonathan Cohn's *Sick: The Untold Story of America's Health Care Crisis*, Alexandra Harney's *The China Price*, and David Shipler's *The Working Poor*.

Greider, William

One World, Ready or Not: The Manic Logic of Global Capitalism. Simon & Schuster. 1997. 528 pp. ISBN 9780684811413.

Using the metaphor of a wondrous new machine that "throws off enormous mows of wealth and bounty while it leaves behind great furrows of wreckage," Greider suggests that capitalism, as the machine, is simultaneously making great accumulations of wealth possible for the very few, while making it necessary on the other side to force more and more workers into indentured servitude and even slavery worldwide. This is a complex title, offering nuanced explanations of the possibilities of widespread industrialized production, which leads to excess goods and labor and further reduces prices and ages, but Greider is a skillful writer (and former national editor of *Rolling Stone* magazine) and excels at making even the most complex of economic and global processes and theories accessible.

Subjects: Business, Capitalism, Economics, Globalization, Politics, World History

Now Try: Greider mentions numerous names and events from world history; histories or biographies of Mahatma Gandhi, Karl Marx, or early economic and consumerism theorist Thorstein Veblen might appeal to these readers. Greider's other books, *Secrets of the Temple* and *Who Will Tell the People?* might be offered, as might other books about classism and globalization such as John Bowe's *Nobodies: Modern American Slave Labor and the Dark Side of the Global Economy*, Joe Bageant's more politically motivated *Deer Hunting with Jesus*, or Louis Uchitelle's *The Disposable American*.

Issenberg, Sasha

The Sushi Economy: Globalization and the Making of a Modern Delicacy. Gotham Books. 2007. 323 pp. ISBN 9781592402946.

Issenberg describes the concept of global trade by describing how all the pieces of the globalization puzzle had to come together to create both the demand for and the fulfillment of one of sushi's main ingredients: tuna. The book is organized into four parts, in which the author provides a worldwide tour of the new sushi industry from the fishing and transportation industries to the artistry and marketing of the final product, traveling from Toronto to Japan to Gloucester to Australia in the process.

Subjects: Business, Food, Globalization, Japan, Sushi, Travel

Now Try: Other books about globalization and its processes, both positive and negative, might be suggested; on the positive side, Thomas Friedman's *The World Is Flat* or *The Lexus and the Olive Tree* or Antoine van Agtmael's *The Emerging Markets Century* might be offered, while neutral or less positive books such as Amy Stewart's *Flower Confidential*, Rachel Louise Snyder's *Fugitive Denim*, or John Bowe's *Nobodies: Modern American Slave Labor and the Dark Side of the New Global Economy* might also appeal. Other books about global commodities, such as Richard Ellis's *The Empty Ocean* or Mark Kurlansky's *Salt* or *Cod* might appeal, while food books by authors such as Michael Pollan, Anthony Bourdain (particularly his book about international travel, *No Reservations*), Julia Child, or Thomas McNamee's business biography, *Alice Waters and Chez Panisse*, might also be good related reads.

Lardner, James, and David A. Smith, editors

Inequality Matters: The Growing Economic Divide in America and Its Poisonous Consequences. Norton. 2005. 328 pp. ISBN 9781565849952.

Leading scholars, activists, and writers address the question of the trend, since the 1970s, for more and more of the resources and wealth of the American economic system to go to fewer and fewer people. Growing inequalities between the very rich and the rest of society, in both wages and opportunities, are described in this collection of essays with statistics, research, and case studies. The book also includes a section suggesting ways in which a more "just and humane economy" may still be achieved through plausible policy choices.

Subjects: Classism, Economics, Essays, Government, Politics, Society

Now Try: This collection features a foreword by Bill Moyers; likewise, books by other contributors, including Barbara Ehrenreich, William Greider, Christopher Jencks, Davd Cay Johnston, Robert Kuttner, Miles Rapoport, Joel Bakan, and Theda Skocpol might also be offered. A number of business and government Exposés might also be suggested, as might a wide variety of related titles from this and the Political Reporting chapters.

Levitt, Steven D., and Stephen J. Dubner

Freakonomics: A Rogue Economist Explores the Hidden Side of Everything. William Morrow. 2005. 242 pp. ISBN 9780060731328.

"Rogue economist" Levitt presents a number of economic, financial, and sociological studies and theories based on his practice of asking the questions no one else asks and making the connections no one else makes. The most famous case study in the book is the one in which Levitt posits that lower crime rates can be attributed to the legalization of abortion, although he also offers theories about gangs and the drug trade, how much parenting skills really matter, and baby naming patterns.

Subjects: Book Groups, Business, Classics, Economics, Pop Culture, Quick Reads, Sociology, True Crime

Now Try: Readers who enjoy *Freakonomics* might also like Malcolm Gladwell's *The Tipping Point* or *Blink*; as well as Jared Diamond's *Guns, Germs, and Steel* (as well as *Collapse*). They might also consider other economics titles that offer the "inside scoop," such as John Perkins's *Confessions of an Economic Hit Man* or Tim Harford's *The Undercover Economist*. Other authors who might appeal to Levitt's fans include Nassim Nicholas Taleb and Ian Ayres.

Lewis, Michael D.

Liar's Poker: Rising through the Wreckage on Wall Street. Norton. 1989. 249 pp. ISBN 9780393027501.

Although closer in writing style and tone to Immersion Journalism (Lewis himself was a Wall Street bond trader) and Memoir, Lewis's story is nonetheless an important investigation into the world of high finance. The events described took place in the heady mid-1980s and culminated with the market crash of October 1987; this book will appeal to readers who enjoy a dash of the personal "insider's look" perspective about the world of investment banking. The game named in the title refers to a bet in which traders bet each other on the serial numbers listed on dollar bills only they can see.

Subjects: 1980s, Business, Classics, Finance, Immersion Journalism, Memoirs, Professions, Work Relationships

Now Try: Michael Lewis is one of the most well-known practitioners of recent investigative journalism; his other popular books *Moneyball*,*The Blind Side*, or *Panic: The Story of Modern Financial Insanity* might also be suggested, as might other books about finance, such as Charles Slack's biography *Hetty: The Genius and Madness of America's First Female Tycoon* or Mitchell Zuckoff's *Ponzi's Scheme*. Nomi Prins's less personal but rigorously reported *Other People's Money: The Corporate Mugging of America* might also appeal to Lewis's readers, as might Kurt Eichenwald's best-selling *Conspiracy of Fools*, about Enron's financial implosion.

Margonelli, Lisa

🌷 *Oil on the Brain: Adventures from the Pump to the Pipeline.* Doubleday. 2007. 324 pp. ISBN 9780385511452.

Margonelli, who realized she had really only ever seen oil in any form whenever she gassed up her car, decided to follow the commodity back from its delivery to her at her local gas station through its various shipping and production routes. The result is a personable and compellingly told story of how oil is extracted from the earth, refined, sold, and transported to its various sales outlets. She traveled to such locations as Chad, China, and the salt caverns in Texas where the U.S. Strategic Petroleum Reserve stores millions of barrels to help regulate supply; she also observed the action at her local gas station, on an oil rig, and even in the oil trading pit on the New York Stock Exchange floor.

Subjects: Business, Chad, China, Economics, Globalization, Oil, World Travel

Awards: ALA Notable

Now Try: Other books about oil and other fuels might be suggested, including Daniel Yergin's *The Prize*, Dilip Hiro's *Blood of the Earth*, Jeff Goodell's *Big Coal*, or Howard Kunstler's more environmentally minded *The Long Emergency*. Other books in which intrepid reporters look more carefully at other industries include Amy Stewart's *Flower Confidential*, Sasha Issenberg's *The Sushi Economy*, William Langewiesche's *The Outlaw Sea*, Taylor Clark's *Starbucked*, and Rachel Louise Snyder's *Fugitive Denim*. Classics by John McPhee might also appeal to these readers, including his *Uncommon Carriers* and *Annals of the Former World*.

Mitchell, Stacy

Big-Box Swindle: The True Cost of Mega-Retailers and the Fight for America's Independent Businesses. Beacon Press. 2006. 318 pp. ISBN 9780807035009.

This is not a disinterested business manual; Mitchell, the chairperson of the American Independent Business Alliance, sets out very systematically to prove that mega-retailers have a negative effect on American business, economics, and the society as a whole. In the first segment of the book, she explores how retailers such as Wal-Mart, Lowe's, Costco, Home Depot, and others affect not only consumer behavior and global manufacturing patterns, but also the environment. In the second half of the narrative, Mitchell offers concrete strategies for individuals and communities seeking to protest the arrival or presence of big-box stores in their communities.

> **Subjects:** Business, Community Life, Consumerism, Exposés, Retail, Shopping, Wal-Mart

> **Now Try:** Mitchell is writing on a popular topic; other polemics questioning the dominance of Wal-Mart have been published in great numbers. These include Anthony Bianco's *The Bully of Bentonville*, Bill Quinn's classic *How Wal-Mart Is Destroying America and the World*, and Sam Ortega's biography of the company's founder, *In Sam We Trust*. (Charles Fishman's *The Wal-Mart Effect* is more of a straightforward business book, if your readers have an interest in that aspect of the story.) These readers might also find a lot to like in the recent wave of books questioning unchecked consumerism, such as Naomi Klein's *No Logo*, Juliet Schor's *Born to Buy* and *The Overspent American*, Bill McKibben's *Deep Economy*, or Benjamin Barber's *Consumed: How Markets Corrupt Children, Infantilize Adults, and Swallow Citizens Whole*; other business and industry histories might also be offered, such as Taylor Clark's *Starbucked* or even William Greider's broader *One World, Ready or Not: The Manic Logic of Global Capitalism*.

Newman, Katherine S., and Victor Tan Chen

The Missing Class: Portraits of the Near Poor in America. Beacon Press. 2007. 258 pp. ISBN 9780807041390.

Newman and Chen offer a thoroughly researched and compelling narrative on the individuals in American society who fall through the crack between the middle class and the individuals living below the poverty line. Arguing that this class of people is currently making it, financially, but is only one small health or accidental problem away from complete ruin, the authors present case studies and examples they garnered over the course of several years of personal interviews to conclude that the individuals in this class, and particularly their children, are very much in danger of slipping ever downward on the economic and class ladder.

> **Subjects:** Business, Classism, Economics, Poverty, Scholarly, Society

> **Now Try:** A wide variety of class and economic titles might also be suggested to these readers, including Barbara Ehrenreich's best seller *Nickel and Dimed* or *Bait and Switch*, David Shipler's *The Working Poor*, the anthology *Class Matters*, Louis Uchitelle's *The Disposable American*, Jason DeParle's *American Dream: Three Women, Ten Kids, and a Nation's Drive to End Welfare*; also of interest might be books like Anya Kamenetz's *Generation Debt*, Tamara Draut's *Strapped*, or Joe Bageant's more political memoir *Deer Hunting with Jesus*.

O'Rourke, P. J.

On the Wealth of Nations. Atlantic Monthly Press. 2007. 242 pp. ISBN 9780871139498.

Humorist and political satirist O'Rourke read Adam Smith's classic *The Wealth of Nations* so his readers didn't have to—all 900-plus pages of it—as well as Smith's earlier volume, *The Theory of Moral Sentiments.* In this recap of Smith's basic ideas, O'Rourke defends Smith's tenets of freedom of trade, the healthy pursuit of self-interest, and the importance of being a person who "adheres, on all occasions, steadily and resolutely to his maxims." Part of the Books That Changed the World series, published by the Atlantic Monthly Press, this small book combines history, economics, and humor to great effect.

Subjects: 18th Century, Book Groups, Books and Learning, Business, Capitalism, Economics, History, Humor, Quick Reads, Adam Smith

Now Try: This is one of the books in the Atlantic Monthly Press's Books That Changed the World series; other titles from that series might be offered, such as Bruce Lawrence's *The Qur'an: A Biography*, Christopher Hitchens's *Thomas Paine's Rights of Man*, or Francis Wheen's *Marx's Das Kapital: A Biography*, as might other books by political humorist and commentator O'Rourke. Numerous other books on business from this chapter might be suggested, as might books by and about more economists who were also strong believers in the processes of the capitalist marketplace, including those by Alan Greenspan, Milton Friedman, John Maynard Keynes, Joseph Schumpeter, or Friedrich von Hayek.

von Rothkopf, David

Superclass: The Global Power Elite and the World They Are Making. Farrar, Straus & Giroux. 2008. 376 pp. ISBN 9780374272104.

Rothkopf provides an illuminating consideration of the identities and influence of the world's richest, most powerful individuals (the "superclass") and how their opinions, beliefs, and actions are shaping the business and cultural trends affecting the rest of the world's population. Drawing on numerous interviews and comprehensive research, Rothkopf excels at providing both a historical and economical context for our current global society, as well as telling stories of the members of the superclass and examining how they both achieved their wealth and power and how they wield it.

Subjects: Business, Classism, Economics, Globalization, Scholarly, Society

Now Try: Readers of this volume might consider a wide variety of other Business Reporting narratives, as well as Making Sense . . . titles such as Malcolm Gladwell's *The Tipping Point*, Alain de Botton's *Status Anxiety*, Gregg Easterbrook's *The Progress Paradox*, or even Jared Diamond's *Collapse*. Specific business, economics, and cultural titles that may appeal to these readers include Peter Bernstein's and Annalyn Swan's *All the Money in the World: How the Forbes 400 Make—and Spend—Their Fortunes*, Christopher Lasch's *The Revolt of the Elites*, or titles by Thomas Friedman such as *The World Is Flat* and *The Lexus and the Olive Tree*.

6

Scurlock, James

Maxed Out: Hard Times, Easy Credit and the Era of Predatory Lenders. Scribner. 2007. 248 pp. ISBN 9781416532514.

Scurlock presents a disturbing picture showing the full and disastrous extent to which Americans owe money to a variety of credit card companies and other institutions, as well as the rising number of foreclosures, college debts, bankruptcies, and even debtor suicides. This book was originally produced as a movie of the same name; as a result, the book displays an easy conversational tone that belies the seriousness of the topic, and Scurlock even employs readable footnotes that provide hard numbers and facts to augment the interviews and assertions shared in the text.

Subjects: Banks, Business, Credit, Debt, Economics, Exposés, Finance, Globalization

Now Try: Other readable books on personal finance might be suggested to these readers, including Tamara Draut's *Strapped*, Anya Kamenetz's *Generation Debt*, Daniel Brook's *The Trap: Selling Out to Stay Afloat in Winner-Take-All America*, Barbara Ehrenreich's *Nickel and Dimed: On (Not) Getting by in America*, Louis Uchitelle's *The Disposable American*, David Shipler's *The Working Poor*, or Katherine Newman's and Victor Tan Chen's *The Missing Class: Portraits of the Near Poor in America*. Other Exposés by authors such as Morgan Spurlock, Michael Moore, and Eric Schlosser might also appeal.

Snyder, Rachel Louise

Fugitive Denim: A Moving Story of People and Pants in the Borderless World of Global Trade. Norton. 2008. 352 pp. ISBN 9780393061802.

Do you know where the jeans you're wearing came from? Chances are good, according to Snyder, that they traveled through several countries and the operations of many individuals in the process of being grown, sewn, and shipped. Snyder illuminates the unbelievably complex world of cotton production, the fashion world, and denim production in this dense but readable primer on globalization and its processes. Although she keeps herself largely out of the story, her tone of wonder at what it takes to get something as simple as a pair of pants from producer to consumer stays constant and observable throughout.

Subjects: Azerbaijan, Business, Cotton, Economics, Environmental Writing, Fashion, Globalization, World Travel

Now Try: Other books about businesses, industries, and the processes of globalization might be offered to these readers, including Lisa Margonelli's *Oil on the Brain*, Taylor Clark's *Starbucked*, Amy Stewart's *Flower Confidential*, Thomas Pawlick's *The End of Food*, Dean Cycon's *Javatrekker: Dispatches from the World of Free Trade Coffee*, Sasha Issenberg's *The Sushi Economy*, Fred Pearce's *Confessions of an Eco-Sinner: Tracking Down the Sources of My Stuff*, or even John Bowe's *Nobodies: Modern American Slave Labor and the Dark Side of the New Global Economy*. Snyder also refers to Stephen Yafa's book *Big Cotton* in her notes; other books on China and India and their rises in the marketplace might also be considered, such as Robyn Meredith's *The Elephant and the Dragon* or Ted Fishman's *China, Inc.*

Twitchell, James B.

Living It Up: Our Love Affair with Luxury. Columbia University Press. 2002. 309 pp. ISBN 9780231124966.

Social researcher and academic Twitchell examines the American love affair with luxury, or, more specifically, the American desire to engage in the wholehearted consumption of luxury goods. Sprinkled throughout the text are a wide variety of photographs and examples of advertisements from various periods in American history, and Twitchell provides a cultural snapshot of what Americans consider luxury goods, how we shop, how companies study our consumption patterns and use them to their advertising and selling advantage, and even how tourist communities like Las Vegas use the principles developed from that research to encourage spending. Twitchell is a professor and his book can be a bit academic in tone, but it is still a readable and even lively consideration of the pursuit of the finer things in life.

Subjects: 20th Century, Advertising, American History, Consumerism, Economics, Marketing, Psychology, Scholarly, Shopping, Small Press

Now Try: Fans of Twitchell's academic but accessible books might consider similar authors such as Juliet Schor (although Twitchell does not agree with many of her conclusions in such books as *The Overspent American*), Gregg Easterbrook, Alain de Botton, Malcolm Gladwell, Christopher Lasch, and Earl Shorris. Another illustrated book about consumerism and advertising, Jean Kilbourne's *Can't Buy My Love*, would provide another perspective, as might business histories such as Dana Thomas's *Deluxe*, Mark Tungate's *Adland*, or Taylor Clark's *Starbucked*.

Uchitelle, Louis

The Disposable American: Layoffs and Their Consequences. Knopf. 2006. 283 pp. ISBN 9781400041176.

Uchitelle, a financial journalist with the *New York Times*, enumerates what he believes are the three main factors that have led to widespread worker layoffs becoming the accepted order of the day in American business: that layoffs revitalize corporate America, that employees who are laid off can simply further their education or learn different skills to go and obtain better jobs, and that layoffs only affect the financial bottom line of the companies and workers affected. Instead, Uchitelle argues, being laid off is a serious blow to most people's finances and future job prospects, and it also undermines future productivity in those workers who have previously lost their jobs and fear losing them again. This is a sympathetic portrait of a workforce under pressure, although Uchitelle also provides historical research, statistical analysis, and case studies of companies like Stanley Works (makers of Stanley tools) and United Airlines.

Subjects: Business, Economics, Globalization, Government, Poverty, Psychology, Society

Now Try: Any number of books about lost jobs and lost prosperity in the American business world might appeal to these readers, including David Shipler's *The Working Poor*, Anya Kamenetz's *Generation Debt*, Tamara Draut's *Strapped*, Richard Longworth's *Caught In the Middle: America's Heartland in the Age of*

Globalism, Katherine Newman's and Victor Tan Chen's *The Missing Class*, Robert Frank's *Falling Behind*, or the journalism anthology *Class Matters*; the slightly more political *Deer Hunting with Jesus* by Joe Bageant might also be suggested.

Underhill, Paco

Why We Buy: The Science of Shopping. Simon & Schuster. 1999. 255 pp. ISBN 9780684849133.

Ostensibly a manual for those retail and sales professionals who are in charge of organizing their merchandise and stores to entice shoppers to spend money, Underhill's extensive insight into shopping behavior, gleaned from years of research in the field he calls retail anthropology (of which he and his firm Envirosell were the first practitioners) is fascinating reading for both sellers and shoppers. Underhill's information is delivered in rapid-fire business style and is enjoyable in its brisk clarity, although the main focus here is the statistical and quantitative findings from his research. References to this work and to Underhill in general abound in a surprising number of other, even nonbusiness works, as well as newspaper and magazine articles.

Subjects: Business, Classics, Consumerism, Professions, Retail, Shopping

Now Try: Paco Underhill's follow-up title, *The Call of the Mall*, is also interesting but not as broadly based. On the other hand, Douglas Atkin's *The Culting of Brands: When Customers Become True Believers* is a similarly crisp and well-researched exposition of the phenomenon of brand loyalty and how it is has been used by various companies (as is Juliet Schor's *Born to Buy: The Commercialized Child and the New Consumer Culture*). Dana Thomas's *Deluxe: How Luxury Lost Its Luster* might appeal, as might a number of James Twitchell's more scholarly but still fascinating consumerism titles. Readers more interested in the shopping end of Underhill's work, rather than the business applications, might also appreciate Pamela Klaffke's enjoyable whirlwind tour through the history of consumption, *Spree: A Cultural History of Shopping*.

Success Guides

I'll be the first to admit that we're veering into dangerously subject-matter-only waters with the inclusion of this category of books in the Business Reporting chapter. For one thing, these types of books tend to be written just as often by business practitioners, consultants, and other insiders as they do by business journalists (but not always). They also tend to offer the least in the way of narrative flow; although their authors often use examples, extended metaphors, fables, and shorter stories to make their points, these are not books in which start-to-finish accounts unfold. Their appeal also tends to rest squarely on the shoulders of their subject matter, which is how most readers find them and decide to read them. They are often the most jargon-filled of all business books, assuming that their readers bring to the book a certain level of business and economics knowledge. So why are they here?

For one thing, although many of these titles are written by business professionals, a surprising number of them are also written by the business reporters, journalists, and reviewers who have made a career out of observing and interviewing the businesspeople. As such, they can provide a valuable overview of the trends and accepted tenets and habits of the market and businesses in general, which might always be useful to librarians and readers' advisors who strive to provide advisory and reference services from a more generalist standpoint. Also, although they, along with the Business Histories and Profiles, are often found and purchased in airport bookstores (and other outlets where business travelers congregate), these books are surprisingly ubiquitous in the culture. Everyone who works with readers, and particularly with nonfiction readers, should at least be familiar with titles such as Jim Collins's *Good to Great* or Chip and Dan Heath's *Made to Stick*. These books not only sell well and get read, they are referred to often in such publications as *Business Week, The Economist, Fortune, Forbes,* and *Smart Money* (to name just a few); because the process of journalism and reporting can be such a cannibalistic one, that means that eventually other news and general interest magazines such as *Time, Newsweek,* and even *USA Today* will start referring to them as well. They are, in the end, simply good titles with which to be familiar.

"Success Guides" has been chosen as a heading because these books are not really examples of your more typical "how-to" guides (many of which are much more specific, feature specific action plans, and can be found easily in most library catalogs under their subjects, including, for example, management theory, human resources, finances, and retirement planning, to name a very view). Nor are they all "motivational" books, most of which are familiar to business readers but which tend to be viewed more as self-help nonfiction (including titles like Dale Carnegie's classic *How to Make Friends and Influence People*).

Readers who read a lot of these books might also consider a wide variety of Business Histories and Profiles books. It is important to note that although the appeal of these titles is primarily their subjects; it cannot be assumed that these readers are exclusively readers of nonfiction. They might very well also consider a wide variety of fiction titles (particularly page-turners of any type, in my experience), especially for more recreational reading purposes.

Success Guides are business- and economics-oriented books that do not typically offer story-driven narratives but that do feature succinct writing, recommendations from the authors for better business or personal success techniques, and often short anecdotes, sidebars, or bulleted lists further outlining their authors' contentions. They can be written by business journalists, but more often are written by business world insiders, consultants, and experts.

Beckstrom, Rod A., and Ori Brafman

The Starfish and the Spider: The Unstoppable Power of Leaderless Organizations. Portfolio. 2006. 230 pp. ISBN 9781591841432.

For many years, the accepted business wisdom was that successful and prosperous organizations needed strong, top-down leadership, typically in the persona of a charismatic CEO, but Beckstrom and Brafman make the case that business structures in the twenty-first century would benefit from being more decentralized (using the metaphor that spiders who lose limbs are disabled, while starfish, who can regenerate lost legs, can adapt and continue); in their narrative, they explore the structures of organizations like Wikipedia, Craigslist, and Skype and contrast more traditional corporations like GM and Toyota against one another. With a style that's been described by reviewers as "breezy," the authors compress their more than five years of research into a very readable book on business and management.

> **Subjects:** Business, Companies, Management, Technology
>
> **Now Try:** Books about new organizational and technological advances in the business world might appeal, such as Keith Sawyer's *Group Genius: The Creative Power of Collaboration*, Alan Murray's *Revolt in the Boardroom*, or Phil Rosenzweig's *The Halo Effect: And the Eight Other Business Delusions That Deceive Managers*; books like Chris Anderson's *The Long Tail*, David Weinberger's *Everything Is Miscellaneous*, James Surowiecki's *The Wisdom of Crowds*, or Dan Tapscott's *Wikinomics* might also be offered. Closer looks at technology companies and individuals might also appeal, such as Scott Rosenberg's *Dreaming in Code* or Tracy Kidder's *The Soul of a New Machine*.

Bing, Stanley

Throwing the Elephant: Zen and the Art of Managing Up. HarperBusiness. 2002. 201 pp. ISBN 9780060188610.

Books by Bing would probably fit more comfortably in the Business How-To Category, but he is such an institution in the field of business publishing (not to mention in the business world; "Stanley Bing" is the pen name of Gil Schwartz, who is actually a public relations executive for CBS and has long been a column writer for *Fortune* magazine) and his books are in a class of their own for his use of humor, satire, and yes, even some business strategy, that he has a rightful place in this section. This title is no exception; in it, Bing offers advice gleaned from Zen Buddhist tenets (not really) for the businessperson seeking to get ahead. An example is his sutra on the importance of proper office furniture: "He whose lower back is messed up from cheap or inadequate seating cannot leave his body for more important work."

> **Subjects:** Business, Humor, Quick Reads, Satire
>
> **Now Try:** Bing is a popular and prolific writer; his other titles, including *Crazy Bosses, Rome, Inc., What Would Machiavelli Do? The Ends Justify the Meanness, Sun Tzu Was a Sissy*, or *100 Bullshit Jobs—and How to Get Them* might all appeal to these readers. Any books in which humor plays a major part, including Humorous Memoirs and essay collections or novels by Christopher Moore (including *The Stupidest Angel* and *Lamb: The Gospel According to Biff, Christ's Childhood Pal*) might also be suggested, as might a wide variety of Business Reporting books, particularly those from the Business Trends and Biz Crit categories.

Blanchard, Kenneth, and Spencer Johnson

The One Minute Manager. Morrow. 1981. 111 pp. ISBN 9780688014292.

Yes, it's more than two decades old. That doesn't matter; this is one of the first and foremost titles that business students, employees, and new managers are asked to read before they begin new positions or take on managerial duties. Written in accessible language, with short chapters, the entire aim of this book is to help its readers learn managerial lessons, including how to set goals, be concise, provide employees and colleagues with emotional support, and develop productive work habits, all in lessons that are meant to be read and absorbed in one minute.

Subjects: Business, Classics, Management, Quick Reads

Now Try: Johnson and Blanchard are cottage industries by themselves; fans of this slim volume might enjoy other best-selling business books by these authors, including Blanchard's *Leadership and the One Minute Manager*, *The Power of Ethical Management*, and *Managing by Values*, or Johnson's popular fables *Who Moved My Cheese?* or *The Present*. Other business classics by authors such as Norman Vincent Peale, Jeffrey Gitomer, Stephen Covey, or even fables by Patrick Lencioni can also be suggested.

Buckingham, Marcus, and Curt Coffman

First, Break All the Rules: What the World's Greatest Managers Do Differently. Simon & Schuster. 1999. 271 pp. ISBN 9780684852867.

In this landmark business title, which is still required reading in many corporate workplaces, research consultants Buckingham and Coffman distill years of Gallup polling and interviews into seven chapters that debunk what the authors view as the biggest misconceptions in management, including the idea that managers' roles are diminishing in today's economy. They suggest instead that managers spend time developing their best people, hire carefully to fill organizational needs, and seek out talent rather than experience.

Subjects: Business, Classics, Companies, Management

Now Try: Fans of Buckingham's first title might also consider his subsequent best sellers: *Now, Discover Your Strengths* and *Go Put Your Strengths to Work*. Other authors who might appeal to these readers include Jim Collins, John C. Maxwell, Seth Godin, and Tom Rath.

Collins, Jim

Good to Great: Why Some Companies Make the Leap—And Others Don't. HarperBusiness. 2001. 300 pp. ISBN 9780066620992.

In this research-based business how-to, Collins explains how he and his team started with a list of 1,435 companies, studied them for performance and improvements, and eventually came up with a set of eleven companies that they felt had succeeded in making the move from good companies to great companies. By combining research with case studies and drawing conclusions about the methods used by the companies they profile (including Gillette and Walgreens), Collins and his team wrote one of the seminal business texts of the past decade.

Subjects: Book Groups, Business, Classics, Companies

Now Try: Collins's other best-selling book, *Built to Last*, might also appeal to these readers, as might *The Breakthrough Company* by Keith McFarland. Other authors who might be suggested include Marcus Buckingham, Tom Rath, John C. Maxwell, Larry Bossidy, and Ram Charan.

Dowd, Matthew, Ron Fournier, and Douglas Sosnik

Applebee's America: How Successful Political, Business, and Religious Leaders Connect with the New American Community. Simon & Schuster. 2006. 260 pp. ISBN 9780743287180.

Political strategists Sosnik and Dowd team up with investigative reporter Fournier to provide this insider's look at how political, business, and religious leaders are seeking new ways to connect with American communities, which are typically outwardly less cohesive than they have been in past decades but which still can be approached as groups of individuals with distinct needs for belonging and acceptance. Part investigation, part how-to, this business book contains many surprising statistics and studies regarding human behavior, and its authors suggest that successful leaders in any field must recognize that people make choices with their hearts, not their heads, and that Americans are still searching for common themes of community and authenticity.

Subjects: Advertising, Business, Marketing, Politics, Religion, Society

Now Try: Although written as a how-to for businesspeople wanting to emulate the lifestyle-marketing success, this book also provides a valuable inside look at the subjects of community life, marketing, and society. Other thoughtful business books that might appeal include Taylor Clark's *Starbucked*, James Twitchell's *Shopping for God* or *Living It Up*, or even Drew Westen's more political title *The Political Brain: The Role of Emotion in Deciding the Fate of the Nation*. Those readers particularly interested in the success story of mega-church marketing methods might also enjoy Rick Warren's huge best seller *The Purpose-Driven Life* or Joel Osteen's equally popular *Your Best Life Now*.

Godin, Seth

Purple Cow: Transform Your Business by Being Remarkable. Portfolio. 2003. 145 pp. ISBN 9781591840213.

Marketing guru Godin's books are always breezy and helpful reads on a wide variety of marketing topics, from making your company remarkable and memorable, tossing out the "accepted knowledge" about marketing and advertising in the stereotypical media sources, and never, ever settling for "good enough" in your company's performance or your own.

Subjects: Business, Classics, Marketing, Quick Reads

Now Try: Godin is a prolific author; his readers might consider his other titles including *All Marketers Are Liars*, *Permission Marketing*, *Small Is the New Big*, *The Dip*, or *Meatball Sundae*. Other books about the new world of marketing and sales might also appeal to these readers, including *Made to Stick* by Chip and Dan Heath. *The Long Tail* by Chris Anderson, or *Everything Is Miscellaneous* by David Weinberger; popular business authors Daniel Pink and Jeffrey Gitomer might also be suggested.

Heath, Chip and Dan Heath

Made to Stick: Why Some Ideas Survive and Others Die. Random House. 2007. 291 pp. ISBN 9781400064281.

Borrowing the concept of "stickiness" from Malcolm Gladwell's book *The Tipping Point*, brothers Chip and Dan Heath expand on eight principles marketers can use to make their ideas and branding efforts resonate with consumers. Exploring and explaining such phenomena as urban legends and conspiracy theories, the brothers (one an academic, the other a textbook publisher) offer suggestions for improving advertising, marketing, persuasion, sales, and other situations in which individuals might wish to make a truly unforgettable impression. Accessible and fast-paced, this well-reviewed book is its own best advertisement: it's one of business reporting's "stickiest" titles.

> **Subjects:** Branding, Business, Causality, Classics, Marketing, Self-Help, Society

> **Now Try:** A wide number of other business "classics" might be suggested to these readers, including Malcolm Gladwell's *The Tipping Point*, Chris Anderson's *The Long Tail*, Jim Collins's *Good to Great*, Nassim Nicholas Taleb's *Fooled by Randomness* or *The Black Swan*, Seth Godin's *Purple Cow* or *All Marketers are Liars*, or Jay Conrad Levinson's *Guerrilla Marketing*.

Meyer, Danny

Setting the Table: The Transforming Power of Hospitality in Business. HarperCollins. 2006. 320 pp. ISBN 9780060742751.

Part foodie manual, part business and management self-help, Danny Meyer's engaging business memoir is all fascinating reading. In relating his stories of restaurant entrepreneurship (including the opening of New York City's revered Union Square Cafe, Meyer also shares lessons learned the hard way about work relationships and customer service, culminating in the ideals of "enlightened hospitality." As long as you take care of the people who work for you, yours guests, your community, and your suppliers (in that order), Meyer argues, your bottom line will always be healthy, which will mean you're taking good care of your shareholders as well.

> **Subjects:** Business, Business Histories, Customer Service, Family Relationships, Friendships, Food, Foodies, Management, Memoirs, Professions, Restaurants, Self-Help, Work Relationships

> **Now Try:** Other business titles on customer service might be suggested to fans of Meyer's huge bestseller, including Joseph Michelli's *The Starbucks Experience*, Jim Collins's *Good To Great*, or Ron Zemke's *Delivering Knock Your Socks Off Service*. Other foodie books by authors such as Ruth Reichl, Anthony Bourdain, Michael Ruhlman, or Michael Pollan might appeal; other business histories or professions memoirs might also be suggested, such as Thomas McNamee's *Alice Waters and Chez Panisse*, Debra Ginsberg's *Waiting*, or Patricia Volk's *Stuffed: Adventures of a Restaurant Family*. Novels featuring restaurants as settings might also provide fun related reads, like Anne Tyler's *Dinner at the Homesick Restaurant*, Julia Glass's *The Whole World Over*, or Timothy Taylor's *Stanley Park*.

Murray, Alan

Revolt in the Boardroom: The New Rules of Power in Corporate America. Collins. 2007. 247 pp. ISBN 9780060882471.

Murray traces the rise to power of such "imperial CEOs" as Michael Eisner, Franklin Raines, and Carly Fiorina, but then tells the stories of their equally impressive falls from grace, in which they were all removed against their wills from their positions of power. The author then goes on to argue that in the absence of CEO rule, a new system of board rule—using input from shareholders, regulators, labor unions, and even employees—is poised to usher in a new age in business. The author, enthusiastic about this prospect and the future of American business and economics in general, offers chapters on the dynamics of corporations, the coming of the new order, and how new CEOs and managers will adapt to these circumstances.

> **Subjects:** Business, Character Profiles, Companies, Economics, Management, Politics, Self-Help
>
> **Now Try:** Readers looking for more information on the lives and work of infamous CEOs might enjoy a wide variety of business memoirs and biographies, including Carly Fiorina's *Tough Choices* or Jack Welch's *Straight from the Gut*, as well as business histories like Patricia Beard's *Blue Blood and Mutiny: The Fight for the Soul of Morgan Stanley*, Kurt Eichenwald's *Conspiracy of Fools*, and Bryan Burrough's *Barbarians at the Gate: The Fall of RJR Nabisco*. One of the most infamous CEOs of all time, Lee Iacocca, has recently written a memoir/political book called *Where Have All the Leaders Gone?*, while other optimistic business books might also be offered, such as Chris Anderson's *The Long Tail* or David Weinberger's *Everything Is Miscellaneous*.

Sawyer, Keith

Group Genius: The Creative Power of Collaboration. Basic Books. 2007. 274 pp. ISBN 9780465071920.

Sawyer reveals how businesses and organizations can foster a spirit of collaboration to encourage creativity and innovation among their individual members. Although popular myths tend to ascribe creativity primarily to individuals, the author, a professor of psychology, demonstrates how breakthroughs, even when made by individuals, frequently follow periods of discussion, argumentation, and group activities (if not brainstorming). He further illustrates his points by offering case histories of the inventors of ATMs, mountain bikes, and open source operating systems.

> **Subjects:** Business, Companies, Creativity, Management, Psychology, Self-Help
>
> **Now Try:** A number of business and management self-help titles, particularly those that deal with collaboration and group dynamics, might appeal to these readers. These include Don Tapscott's *Wikinomics*, David Weinberger's *The Cluetrain Manifesto* or *Everything is Miscellaneous*, Ori Brafman's *The Starfish and the Spider*, James Surowiecki's *The Wisdom of Crowds*, Malcolm Gladwell's *The Tipping Point*, or Ian Ayres's *Super Crunchers*.

Sutton, Robert I.

The No Asshole Rule: Building a Civilized Workplace and Surviving One That Isn't. Warner Business Books. 2007. 210 pp. ISBN 9780446526562.

In a book that first saw life as an essay in the *Harvard Business Review*, Stanford professor Sutton lays on the line what he feels is the biggest problem in the American workplace today: the prevalence of assholes. Positing that the TCA (total cost of assholes) is wreaking havoc with corporate profits and worker satisfaction, Sutton provides hints on how to deal with assholes in the workplace, starting with spotting them (he also offers a self-test so you can make sure you're not the offender in your business). Lighthearted and informal in tone, this is nonetheless a serious business and management treatise on how to better your business by making sure there are fewer jerks on your staff; as a business writer, Sutton also knows how to make the most of the case study as an example, explaining how Google's company maxim of "don't be evil" helped lead to its massive growth and success.

Subjects: Business, Humor, Leadership, Management, Profanity, Work Relationships

Now Try: Other admirably forthright business writers might appeal to Sutton's readers, such as Stanley Bing (*What Would Machiavelli Do?*, *Crazy Bosses*, *100 Bullshit Jobs . . . And How to Get Them*) or the contributors to John Bowe's oral history *Gig*. Other offbeat humor books, such as novels by Christopher Moore (*Lamb* or *The Stupidest Angel*) or Calvin Trillin (*Tepper Isn't Going Out*, or his book of verse *Obliviously On He Sails: The Bush Administration in Rhyme* may please, although the latter title may not be right for readers whose politics align along the right side of the spectrum).

Trump, Donald

Trump: The Art of the Deal. Random House. 1987. 246 pp. ISBN 9780394555287.

Arguably one of the best-known business professionals in America (thanks to his sheer staying power and his own successful foray into reality television with his series *The Apprentice*), this is Trump's seminal work, in which he describes his early career in real estate in New York City in the 1980s, as well as dishing on his own personal history and celebrity status. The book remains a perennial favorite with readers, although it was first published in 1987, and Trump has since passed through several cycles of boom and bust in his own business dealings and finance.

Subjects: Business, Classics, Finance, New York City, Real Estate, Donald Trump

Now Try: Fans of Trump have no shortage of his other titles from which to choose, including *How to Get Rich*, *The Art of the Comeback*, *Think Like a Billionaire*, and *Think Big and Kick Ass in Business and Life*, as well as the book he coauthored with popular investing author Robert Kiyosaki, *Why We Want You to Be Rich*. Other books by business and self-help gurus including Jim Cramer, Jack Welch, Stephen Covey, and Norman Vincent Peale might also appeal.

Welch, Jack

Winning. HarperBusiness. 2005. 372 pp. ISBN 9780060753948.

Few CEOs in history have attracted as much simultaneous hero-worship and vitriol as Jack Welch, who is widely regarded as one of the last "celebrity CEOs," mainly from his reputation as the head of the General Electric corporation. In this book, he teams up with his wife Suzy Welch (herself a former editor at the *Harvard Business Review*) to provide answers to a wide variety of business and management questions; he also suggests personal qualities that help foster success, including candor and logical and widely disseminated decision-making processes.

Subjects: Business, Character Profiles, Management, Memoirs, Self-Help, Jack Welch

Now Try: Welch is also the author of a business memoir, *Jack: Straight from the Gut*; readers interested in his thoughts on management might consider a wide variety of other business management theorists and authors, including the infamous Peter Drucker, John C. Maxwell, Jim Collins, and Marcus Buckingham, as well as fables by authors such as Spencer Johnson or Patrick

Lencioni. Books by other well-known corporate executives including Lee Iacocca or Starbucks's Howard Schultz might also be suggested.

Other Authors

Although their titles have not been annotated here, business books by personal finance gurus Jim Cramer, Robert Kiyosaki, and Suze Orman might appeal to these readers, as might management books by John C. Maxwell and sales books by Jeffrey Gitomer.

Fiction Read-Alikes

- **Archer, Jeffrey.** Finance and investments gone wrong play a large part in many of Archer's thrillers, including *Not a Penny More, Not a Penny Less*, *Kane and Abel*, *Total Control*, and *False Impression*.

- **Bing, Stanley.** Bing is, of course, a popular and prolific author of nonfiction business books but has also produced the novels *Lloyd—What Happened: A Novel of Business* and *You Look Nice Today*.

- **Coupland, Douglas.** Coupland's novels are quirky and character-driven, but many of them are set in the workplace (particularly IT companies) and might be of some interest to these readers; they include his classics *Generation X* and *Microserfs*, as well as *JPod* and *The Gum Thief*.

- **Ellis, Bret Easton.** Ellis's violent and satirical novel *American Psycho* features a main character who works on Wall Street by day and murders homeless and other people not likely to be missed by night. This book may not be for all business readers, but there can be no doubt that the culture of Wall Street plays a large part in the novel.

- **Erdman, Paul.** Although Erdman has been writing since the 1970s, his financial thrillers might still prove interesting to business readers who enjoy fast-paced novels; they include *The Billion Dollar Sure Thing*, *The Swiss Account*, and *The Set-Up*.

- **Ferris, Joshua.** Ferris's first and well-reviewed novel *Then We Came to the End* is related to Business Reporting largely through its subject matter, but his masterful portrayal of office life, relationships, and ennui at the beginning of the twenty-first century might particularly appeal to Business Reporting readers.

- **Finder, Joseph.** Finder combines his copious political and financial expertise to write tautly plotted thrillers including *The Zero Hour*, *Paranoia*, *Company Man*, and *Killer Instinct*.

- **Frey, Stephen.** Frey is famous for his Wall Street thrillers and is himself a former Wall Street banker; his titles *The Takeover* or his series featuring Christian Gillette (a financier in his mid-thirties), which began with *The Chairman* and continued with *The Protégé*, *The Power Broker*, and *The Successor* may be of interest to business readers.

- **Liss, David.** Liss combined research interests in early English novels and the history of capitalism to write the historical thrillers *A Conspiracy of Paper* (and its sequel *A Spectacle of Corruption*) and *The Coffee Trader*. His work is rich with period detail and economic understanding.

- **Vachon, Dana.** Vachon's 2007 novel *Mergers & Acquisitions* also follows the lives of a group of Manhattanites who work in finance and investment banking.

Further Reading

Quirt, John. 1993. *The Press and the World of Money: How the News Media Cover Business and Finance, Panic and Prosperity, and the Pursuit of the American Dream.* Byron, CA: Anton/California Courier.

Surowiecki, James, ed. 2002. *Best Business Crime Writing of the Year.* New York: Anchor Books.

References

Bowker Book Statistics. 2008. http://www.bowker.com/press/bowker/2007_0531_bowker.htm (accessed 6 March 2008).

Boynton, Robert S., ed. 2005. *The New New Journalism: Conversations with America's Best Nonfiction Writers on Their Craft.* New York: Vintage.

Stephens, Mitchell. 1988. *A History of News: From the Drum to the Satellite.* New York: Viking.

Wyatt, Neal. 2007. *The Readers' Advisory Guide to Nonfiction.* Chicago: American Library Association.

1

2

3

4

5

6

Appendix A

Investigative Writing Book Awards

The standard disclaimer applies: this is a highly selective list of popular and well-known awards that focus on nonfiction and investigative and journalistic titles. Representative Investigative Writing books that have won the awards in recent years are listed at the end of each of the award annotations.

American Library Association Notable Nonfiction Books

History

Web site: www.ala.org/ala/rusa/rusaprotools/rusanotable/notablebooks.htm

Lists of Notable Books:

Web site: www.ala.org/ala/rusa/rusaprotools/rusanotable/ thelists/notablebooks. htm

Each year a twelve-member committee from the CODES (Collection Development and Evaluation Section) of the association selects twenty-five titles each of fiction, poetry, and nonfiction that are "very good, very readable, and at times very important." The Notable Books listings have existed, in various forms, since 1944.

2008 Winners: *Animal, Vegetable, Miracle: A Year of Food Life* by Barbara Kingsolver; *Oil on the Brain: Adventures from the Pump to the Pipeline* by Lisa Margonelli.

The Charles Taylor Prize for Literary Nonfiction

Web site: www.thecharlestaylorprize.ca

Awarded annually, this Canadian award is given to nonfiction authors whose books combine a "superb command of the English language, an elegance of style, and a subtlety of thought and perception."

2005 Finalist: *A War Against Truth: An Intimate Account of the Invasion of Iraq* by Charles Montgomery.

Edgar Awards for Fact Crime

Web site: www.theedgars.com

The Edgar Awards, although known more for their fiction awards celebrating mysteries, also have categories for nonfiction titles, including Criticism and Best Fact Crime. The awards are sponsored by the Mystery Writers of America organization and have been awarded since 1948.

2006 Winner: *The Rescue Artist: A True Story of Art, Thieves, and the Hunt for a Missing Masterpiece* by Edward Dolnick

2001 Winner: *Black Mass: The Irish Mob, the FBI, and a Devil's Deal* by Dick Lehr and Gerard O'Neill.

The Governor General's Literary Awards

Web site: www.canadacouncil.ca/prizes/ggla/default.htm

Awarded annually in seven categories (Fiction, Literary Nonfiction, Poetry, Drama, Children's Literature—text, Children's Literature—illustration, and Translation), these awards are given to recognize the best titles published each year in Canada.

2005 Winner: *The Golden Spruce: A True Story of Myth, Madness and Greed* by John Vaillant.

James Beard Foundation Awards

About the Awards: jbfawards.com/content/about-awards

The James Beard Foundation offers annual awards in a variety of categories about food writing, including "Writing on Food" and Journalism Awards. Rich in prestige, these awards are often referred to as the "Oscars of the food world."

2008 Winner of the "Writing on Food" category: *Animal, Vegetable, Miracle: A Year of Food Life*, by Barbara Kingsolver.

The John Burroughs Medal

List of Winners: research.amnh.org/burroughs/medal_award_list.html

Although not all of the environmental books that have won the John Burroughs Medal (awarded to works of outstanding natural history writing) are investigative in tone, many of them are classics that display journalistic tendencies, including classics by Rachel Carson and John McPhee.

2004 Winner: *Liquid Land: A Journey through the Florida Everglades* by Ted Levin.

The Los Angeles Times Book Awards

About the Awards: www.latimes.com/extras/bookprizes/prizes2003.html

Winners Lists: www.latimes.com/extras/bookprizes/winners.html

> The *Los Angeles Times* has distributed a variety of both fiction and nonfiction awards (including biography, current interests, and science and technology) annually since 1980.

> 2007 Finalist: *The Shock Doctrine: The Rise of Disaster Capitalism* by Naomi Klein.

> 2006 Finalist: *Imperial Life in the Emerald City: Inside Iraq's Green Zone* by Rajiv Chandrasekaran.

Lukas Book Prize

History: www.jrn.columbia.edu/events/lukas/

Awards List: www.jrn.columbia.edu/events/lukas/winners/

> The Lukas Prize was established in 1998 with the simple charge of honoring the best American nonfiction. It is administered jointly by the Columbia University Graduate School of Journalism and the Nieman Foundation at Harvard University.

> 2007 Winner: *The Looming Tower: Al-Qaeda and the Road to 9/11* by Lawrence Wright.

Martha Gellhorn Prize

Web site: www.marthagellhorn.com

> The Martha Gellhorn Prize, named for the intrepid reporter who inspired it, is awarded annually to "a journalist whose work has penetrated the established version of events and told an unpalatable truth, validated by powerful facts, that exposes establishment propaganda." Although it is not awarded for specific books, its past recipients (including Robert Fisk and Patrick Cockburn) also write books in addition to newspaper journalism.

NASW Science in Society Journalism Awards

About the Awards: www.nasw.org/awards/society.htm

> Awarded by the National Association of Science Writers, these awards are dedicated to "honoring and encouraging outstanding investigative and interpretive reporting about the sciences and their impact for good and ill."

> 2005 Winner: *Pandora's Baby: How the First Test-Tube Babies Sparked the Reproductive Revolution* by Robin Marantz Henig.

National Academies Communications Awards (Keck Futures Initiative)

About the Awards and Winners: www.keckfutures.org/site/PageServer?pagename=Communication_Award_Winners

The National Academies annually present awards in three areas of publishing: books; magazine, newspaper, or online journalism; and television and radio broadcasting. These awards reflect the educational missions of the National Academies of Science, Engineering, the Institute of Medicine, and the National Research Council. The National Academy first presented these three awards in 2003.

2007 Winner in the "Newspaper/Magazine/Internet" category: Carl Zimmer (author of *Parasite Rex* and *Soul Made Flesh: The Discovery of the Brain*).

2005 Finalist: *Out of Gas: The End of the Age of Oil* by David Goodstein.

The National Book Award

About the National Book Foundation: www.nationalbook.org/history.html

Awards Archives: www.nationalbook.org/nba2007.html

The National Book Award has been awarded since 1950, but the National Book Foundation, which helps to support its choices, was established in 1989 to "raise the cultural appreciation of great writing in America." Each year it names one award winner based on literary merit in the categories of fiction, nonfiction, and poetry.

2007 Winner: *Legacy of Ashes: The History of the CIA* by Tim Weiner.

2004 Finalist: *Life on the Outside: The Prison Odyssey of Elaine Bartlett* by Jennifer Gonnerman.

The National Book Critics Circle Award

Web site: www.bookcritics.org/

The National Book Critics Circle was founded in 1974 and currently consists of more than 700 active book reviewers. Its Board of Directors nominates and selects the winners of its annual award in the categories of fiction, general nonfiction, biography/autobiography, poetry, and criticism.

2006 Finalist: *The Lemon Tree: An Arab, a Jew and the Heart of the Middle East* by Sandy Tolan.

2005 Finalist: *Voices from Chernobyl: The Oral History of Nuclear Disaster* by Svetlana Alexievich.

National Magazine Awards

Winners and Finalists: www.magazine.org/Editorial/National_Magazine_Awards/Winners_and_Finalists/

Presented annually for the last half-century, the National Magazine Awards recognize excellence in print and online journals, particularly focusing on editorial objectives and techniques, as well as journalistic enterprise and notable design. Those readers looking for new magazines to peruse (as well as new nonfiction authors to discover in their pages) might consider any of the award-winners as chosen by the American Society of Magazine Editors.

Award-winning Authors: Michael Isikoff, Jon Krakauer, William Langewiesche, Samantha Power, Eric Schlosser

New York Times Notable Books

2008 List: http://www.nytimes.com/2008/12/07/books/review/100Notable-t.html?ref=books

At the end of every year, the *New York Times* lists the notable fiction, nonfiction, and poetry books that were published over the previous year, as culled from favorable reviews in the *New York Times Book Review*. The nonfiction titles on the list almost always represent a diverse mix of history, biography, memoir, science, investigative, and political titles from the previous year in publishing. (The link provided goes to the most recent list, for 2008; an Internet search of "new york times notable" and any year will retrieve the annual lists.)

2007 Notables: *The Argument: Billionaires, Bloggers, and the Battle to Remake Democratic Politics*, by Matt Bai; *Cleopatra's Nose: 39 Varieties of Desire*, by Judith Thurman; *The Nine: Inside the Secret World of the Supreme Court*, by Jeffrey Toobin.

2008 Notables: *The Dark Side: The Inside Story of How the War on Terror Turned Into a War on American Ideals*, by Jane Mayer; *The Forever War*, by Dexter Filkins.

Orwell Prize

Information and Archive: www.theorwellprize.co.uk/home.aspx

The Orwell Prize is the "pre-eminent British award for political writing." Two awards are given annually, a Book Prize and a Journalism Prize, and are intended to encourage the publication of books and shorter pieces about public policy, politics, social and cultural concerns, and the quality of public life. Most winners are nonfiction, but novels have won the award in the recent past as well.

2008 Winner: *Palestinian Walks* by Raja Shehadeh.

The Pulitzer Prizes

History of the Pulitzer Prizes and Awards Archives: www.pulitzer.org

Pulitzer Prizes are awarded annually to "distinguished" works in three major areas of nonfiction: biography or autobiography, history, and general nonfiction. The awards for the first two categories have been given since

1917, and the award for the latter was instituted in 1962. Pulitzers are also given for journalistic excellence in a wide variety of categories, including Beat Reporting, Commentary, Investigative Reporting, and Criticism; by searching the Pulitzer archive by category, interested readers can find the names of award winners (many of whom have gone on to write book-length works of reporting).

2007 Winner: *The Looming Tower: Al-Qaeda and the Road to 9/11* by Lawrence Wright.

2005 Winner: *Ghost Wars* by Steve Coll.

Samuel Johnson Prize for Nonfiction

About the Prize and List of Winners: www.thesamueljohnsonprize.co.uk

The Samuel Johnson Prize for Nonfiction is a British award that has been awarded annually since 1989. It recognizes nonfiction of all types, but many investigative works have been among its contenders.

2007 Winner: *Imperial Life in the Emerald City: Inside Iraq's Green Zone* by Rajiv Chandrasekaran

William Hill Sports Book of the Year Award

2007 Longlist and Home Page: www.williamhillmedia.com/sportsbook_longlist2007.asp

Sponsored by the British bookmakers firm William Hill, this annual award is given to book-length works about sports. Many are about British sports and topics, but a wide variety of sports reporting titles from America and other countries also appear on each year's longlists of contenders.

2001 Winner: *Seabiscuit* by Laura Hillenbrand.

1999 Finalist: *The Miracle of Castel di Sangro* by Joe McGinniss.

Appendix B

Documentary Films

Fans of Investigative Writing might also be interested in a wide variety of documentary films, which have experienced a renaissance of sorts in both coverage and numbers of subjects documented, as well as in popularity and notoriety. Pioneers like Michael Moore, regardless of how you feel about his politics, deserve much of the credit for taking documentaries mainstream and paving the way for such popular and award-winning recent films as Al Gore's Academy Award–winning *An Inconvenient Truth* and Morgan Spurlock's hugely popular *Super Size Me*.

One charge that is sometimes leveled against documentary films, particularly those with political subjects, is that many more movies from the leftist perspective are available than those from the perspective of the conservative right. A discussion of possible reasons for this discrepancy, if it does indeed exist, is beyond the scope of this primarily informational list. I have sought to provide as near an equal number of each as possible. Readers who are interested in possible reasons for the imbalance might find informative John Hayes's online article "Do Documentaries Ever Focus on the Conservative Point of View?"; it can be accessed at www.post-gazette.com/pg/06174/700500-254.stm.

The list that follows is by no means exhaustive but rather provides a sampling of popular and award-winning feature-length documentaries from the past fifteen years.

Born into Brothels. Thinkfilm, 2004.

> Winner of the 2004 Academy Award for best documentary, this movie is set in the red-light district of Calcutta and follows the lives of several young children whose mothers work as prostitutes and who may be forced into the practice soon as well. The directors gave the children cameras so that they could photograph their lives inside the brothels; the inclusion of these still photographs in the film contributes to its realism and tragedy.

Bowling for Columbine. MGM Home Entertainment, 2003.

> Michael Moore is no stranger to controversy, and in this film he sets out to explore factors which might contribute, particularly in America, to incidents like the Columbine High School shootings. Focusing on the availability of firearms and the vehemence with which supporters of gun rights make their case, Moore even shows up on Charlton Heston's doorstep to interrogate him about the National Rifle Association. This film won the 2002 Academy Award.

Buena Vista Social Club. Artisan Home Entertainment, 1999.

Directed by Wim Wenders, this classic documentary follows guitar legend Ry Cooder as he travels to Cuba and makes and records music with some of that nation's great artists, including Ibrahim Ferrer; also included are interviews with the Cuban artists about their country's complex political past and their thoughts about the future, as well as concert performances of their songs.

Cochise County, USA: Cries from the Border. Genius Entertainment, 2005.

Filmmaker Mercedes Maharis offers an in-depth look at the effect of illegal immigration on Cochise County, Arizona, which has a legal population of 130,000 (although it is speculated that more than 200,000 illegal aliens passed through the county in 2004). Although many documentaries offer a progressive or "liberal" point of view, this one has been cited for its adherence to conservative tenets of thought.

Common Threads: Stories from the Quilt. New Yorker Video, 1989 (2004).

Originally filmed in 1989 (and winner of the Academy Award for that year) and consisting of interviews with those suffering from AIDS, along with their families and friends, this movie not only highlights the struggle to combat and treat AIDS but also acts as a piece of history in which attitudes and events from the 1980s can be contrasted with today's society. The title refers to the making and displaying of the AIDS quilt, and many individuals interviewed tell stories of the individuals whose stories were commemorated in squares of the NAMES Project AIDS memorial quilt.

The Corporation. Zeitgeist Films, 2005.

Although only about 150 years old in the form in which we know it, the "corporation" has rapidly become one of the most recognizable and dominant of all institutions. Based on the best-selling book of the same title by Joel Bakan, the producers of this documentary strive not to leave any doubt that the corporation is alive, mutating constantly, and becoming more influential and powerful all the time. Interview subjects include CEOs, other business figures, and other media and cultural commentators such as Naomi Klein, Noam Chomsky, Howard Zinn, and Michael Moore.

Crumb. Columbia TriStar Home Video, 1994.

Part biography, part cultural history of comix and graphic novels, this documentary focuses on the life and work of iconic and reclusive artist R. Crumb (the creator of Felix the Cat and Mr. Natural), and includes many interviews with his family members (many of whom struggled with their own obsessions and reclusiveness) and other influential artists and illustrators.

Dirty Jobs. Image Entertainment, 2007.

Dirty Jobs is a television series hosted by Mike Rowe and aired on the Discovery Channel; in each episode, Rowe meets different individuals and learns more about (as well as helps perform) their "dirty jobs." As of 2008, three seasons were available on DVD.

Encounters at the End of the World. Image Entertainment, 2008.

Described in a review in the *Christian Science Monitor* as both "cranky" and "lyrical," this is a documentary for the environmentalists among you. Famed director Werner Herzog travels to Antarctica and films its unique beauty, combining his landscape footage with both music and natural sound effects.

Enron: The Smartest Guys in the Room. Magnolia Home Entertainment, 2005.

Based on the book of the same name by Bethany McLean and Peter Elkind, this investigation into the fraudulent business and accounting practices scandal at Enron is both fast-paced and subtly disquieting. In addition to exposing the activities of Enron's highest members of management (including Ken Lay and Jeffrey Skilling) and their walking away with millions while their employees and stockholders lost money, the directors also provide a fascinating closer look into the energy business and its recent deregulation activities.

Fahrenheit 9/11. Columbia TriStar Home Entertainment, 2004.

In this incendiary political documentary, popular liberal author and commentator Michael Moore levels criticism at the George W. Bush administration for a variety of charges from their close ties to Saudi oil magnates to their handling of the 9/11 terrorist attacks and the subsequent Iraq War.

*NOTE: For those readers and viewers on the opposite side of the political spectrum from Moore, a documentary titled **Fahrenhype 9/11: Unraveling the Truth about Michael Moore's Fahrenheit 9/11** is also available.*

The Farmer's Wife. PBS Home Video, 1998 (2005).

In this in-depth and deeply empathetic view of modern rural life and agribusiness, the filmmakers tell the story of the challenges facing a small family farmer from the point of view of his wife, struggling to help him make ends meet, make time for their children, and maintain their own relationship.

Farmingville. New Video, 2004.

In this sobering story, the filmmakers relate the tale of the race-based hate crimes that took place in the small agricultural town of Farmingville, New York, during the late 1990s. In addition to telling the story of the murders of two Mexican day laborers, the story of the conflicts in the town between its longtime residents and its new residents, primarily immigrants from Mexico, is also explored.

Fast, Cheap, and Out of Control. Columbia TriStar Home Entertainment, 1996 (2002).

Directed by Errol Morris, a prolific and opinionated filmmaker (he also directed *The Fog of War*), this documentary offers character profiles of four very unique characters: a topiary gardener, a retired lion tamer, a robotics researcher, and a man fascinated by mole rats. In the process of telling their unique stories, Morris also somehow manages to relate the four stories to one another and to ask the larger question of where our humanity will take us in the future.

The Fog of War. Columbia TriStar Home Entertainment, 2003.

Filmmaker Errol Morris (who also directed the documentary *Fast, Cheap, and Out of Control*) won the 2003 Academy Award for this chilling documentary about the effects of war and American foreign policy, particularly during the administrations of John F. Kennedy and Lyndon B. Johnson. Subtitled "eleven lessons from the life of Robert S. McNamara," the movie features archival materials and in-depth interviews with former Secretary of Defense McNamara, who reveals the "what-ifs" he feels about his role in American history.

The Great Global Warming Swindle. Wag TV, 2007.

Director Mike Durkin sets out to prove that all the doomsday predictions you've heard about the causes and severity of global warming, in such other films as Al Gore's *An Inconvenient Truth*, are at best misleading and at worst perpetrating a "swindle." Offering testimony and proof from scientists who refuse to bend to "political or philosophical pressure," this film promises that the global climate situation is not nearly as dire as we are told.

The Heart of the Game. Buena Vista Home Entertainment, 2007.

In this story of the Roosevelt Roughriders, a girls' basketball team in Seattle, the action primarily follows one girl's fight to regain her eligibility to play for the team she loves. Both this movie and *Hoop Dreams* (see below) might particularly appeal to fans of sports movies and sports reporting alike.

Hoop Dreams. New Line Home Video, 1994 (2005).

This inspiring and lengthy documentary (clocking in at nearly three hours) follows the lives of two inner-city Chicago teenagers, William Gates and Arthur Agee, through their time in high school and their struggles to develop their basketball skills to achieve their dreams of careers playing professional basketball.

An Inconvenient Truth. Paramount, 2006.

Al Gore's well-received documentary about the encroaching dangers of global warming won the Academy Award in 2006. In it, Gore weaves together stories of his personal commitment to environmental change and policy making, as well as stirring commentary and scientific statements about the processes of global warming and what they mean to all areas of the earth.

Jesus Camp. Magnolia Home Entertainment, 2006.

A summer camp of a slightly different sort, Kids on Fire draws children who are hoping to one day become evangelical Christian ministers. By following the children and a woman named Becky Fisher, who works at the camp, the filmmakers ostensibly show a regular youth camp experience, but also provide an inside look into a world of unswerving belief and fundamentalism.

Lost Boys of Sudan. New Video Group, 2003.

The brutal civil war in Sudan at the end of the 1980s created more than 20,000 "lost boys," or orphans; this documentary follows the trail of two such young men as they struggle to make their way from Sudan to America. Even after the two arrive in America, they find that they may have found physical safety but still have many cultural and personal difficulties with which to contend.

Manufacturing Consent: Noam Chomsky and the Media. Zeitgeist Video, 2002.

This documentary about political writer and social commentator Noam Chomsky explores the thought process used in his classic works, the books *Manufacturing Consent* and *Hegemony or Survival*, and includes interviews with other journalists and commentators such as William F. Buckley, Jr., Tom Wolfe, and Bill Moyers offering their opinions of the man and his work.

March of the Penguins. Warner Home Video, 2005.

This popular (even with the kids!) documentary features beautiful footage from the South Pole and focuses on some of its most fascinating inhabitants:

Antarctica's Emperor penguins. The movie was narrated by Morgan Freeman and won the 2005 Academy Award.

Maxed Out. Magnolia Home Entertainment, 2007.

Based on James Scurlock's book of the same title, this documentary uses research and interviews to make the point that credit card companies are for-profit entities whose profits depend on getting their customers to rack up as much debt as possible, at as high an interest rate as possible. Offering interviews with individuals who have become trapped in debt, as well as with financial experts, this movie is not only an exposé but also an education in using credit wisely.

Murderball. Lions Gate Home Entertainment, 2005.

The violence and competitiveness of quadriplegic rugby can be made clear from its nickname: "kill the man with the ball." In this character-driven documentary, the filmmakers interview the players and coaches from the U.S. and Canadian teams and offer plenty of footage of the high adrenaline game being played.

My Flesh and Blood. New Video, 2003.

Single mother Susan Tom has her hands full—having adopted eleven special needs children and receiving limited aid from the government, Tom and her kids mainly spend their time trying to make it through each day, depending on life's routines and small pleasures, as well as a good measure of hope and love, to get them through.

Mythbusters. Image Entertainment, 2007.

Originally shown on the Discovery network, this series endeavors to help viewers "debunk, decode, and demystify" all manner of myths, urban legends, and pop culture mysteries. Not only information is presented; the hosts of the show regularly offer their debunking proof in the form of experiments; if you've ever wondered if silicone implants really do explode at high altitudes, this is the show for you. As of 2008, there were three series of this show available.

No End in Sight. Magnolia Home Entertainment, 2007.

Embroiled in a war that may end up costing the nation trillions of dollars, George W. Bush's administration is coming under increasing fire for not adequately planning for the war or its execution. Filled with interviews with mid-level bureaucrats and other individuals who are just far enough inside to see what's happening in Iraq but not far enough to be able to make any real changes, this is a chilling history and exposé of a war that has been mishandled from the start, and which is rife with corruption (particularly in the form of "pretty boys," who are political insiders with no real job skills who are being awarded plum titles and responsibilities in postwar Iraq).

Okie Noodling. ITVS, 2002.

This thoroughly enjoyable and delightfully quirky documentary details the practice of fishing entirely by hand, also known as "noodling." Only legal in four states (Oklahoma, Louisiana, Tennessee, and Mississippi), the practice is held dear by its practitioners, who proudly display their skills in this earthy, honest film.

Outfoxed: Rupert Murdoch's War on Journalism. Disinformation, 2004.

Ever wondered what it's really like to work for the Fox network's "fair and balanced" newsroom? Former employees, including reporters, bookers, and producers, all provide the inside take on working for Rupert Murdoch; also interviewed are media and communications experts who discuss Murdoch's (and that of his company, News Corp.) influence on the media in general.

Promises. New Yorker Video, 2004.

Between the years of 1995 and 1998, the directors of this film followed several Israeli and Palestinian children in the Middle East, documenting their lives but also introducing them to one another. In addition to footage from the three years they were filmed, the children were also taped speaking their thoughts on the continuing conflict in the region in an epilogue.

The Real Dirt on Farmer John. Gaiam Media, 2005.

Third-generation farmer John Peterson is profiled in this engaging documentary that explores his work as a farmer, artist, and writer (of *Farmer John's Cookbook*). Also included are recipes, anecdotes from Peterson's life, and information on organic farming and community sponsored agriculture.

Roger and Me. Warner Home Video, 1989 (2003).

In Michael Moore's first and still hugely popular documentary, he set out to interview then-chairman of General Motors, Roger Smith, to get some answers regarding the GM plant closure in Moore's hometown of Flint, Michigan. Equal parts pathos and humor, the story here is Moore trying desperately to get Smith to tell him the story.

Sicko. Weinstein Co. Home Entertainment, 2007.

Filmmaker Michael Moore strikes again in this exposé about the American health care system, in which he is less interested in speaking with CEOs and experts and focuses on individuals whom the American health care system has failed. Although it is much quieter in tone than most Moore documentaries, it is every bit as effective.

Spellbound. Columbia TriStar Home Entertainment, 2002.

The makers of the film *Spellbound* followed eight teenagers from the beginning of the National Spelling Bee process, at their local and regional competitions, all the way to the podium at the national competition. Although the competition provides the tense backdrop for the action, the real story is in the eight very different teenagers, who come from different states and different socioeconomic statuses but are all driven in their own way to achieve the championship.

The Story of the Weeping Camel. New Line Home Entertainment, 2005.

Although this film blurs the lines between documentary and fiction, it is still a compelling portrait of the lives of a shepherd family in the Gobi Desert of southern Mongolia and their struggle to care for a camel colt that is rejected by its mother shortly after its birth.

Super Size Me. Hart Sharp Video, 2004.

Morgan Spurlock set out to eat all of his meals at McDonald's for one month—further opting to accept any McDonald's employee's offer to "super size" his meal. Spurlock (and his girlfriend) were unpleasantly surprised to find that it only took a week for him to gain weight, to watch his cholesterol skyrocket and his mood plummet, and to lose his libido.

Taxi to the Dark Side. Thinkfilm, 2007.

By telling the story of a young Afghani taxi driver who was tortured and killed in 2002, the filmmakers explore the broader ramifications of the United States' interrogation and torture practices and policies in Afghanistan, Iraq, and Guantanamo Bay. This film was the winner of the 2007 Academy Award.

Touching the Void. MGM Home Entertainment, 2003.

In 1985 two mountain climbers (Brits Joe Simpson and Simon Yates) set out to conquer the previously unconquered Siula Grande in the Peruvian Andes and promptly found out about the treacherous peak's many hazards. In this nail-biter, the story of their successful climb to the summit is followed by the unbelievable narration and reenactment of their disastrous descent, during which Simpson shattered his leg and the friends were separated.

The Tragedy of the Munich Games. ESPN, 2005.

This historical compilation examines the events of September 5, 1972, when Israeli athletes were killed by Palestinian assassins at the Olympic Games in Munich. Consisting largely of footage compiled during the day by ABC, it also alternates the historical footage with present-day interviews of many individuals involved in the events of that tragic day.

Trekkies. Paramount, 1998.

It's a decade old, but this classic of documentary filmmaking remains as enjoyable as ever, with its focus on dedicated and even obsessed *Star Trek* fans (Trekkies) who congregate at annual conventions, fan meetings, and other events. Also included are interviews with the original *Star Trek* cast members; making this a sure bet for William Shatner's ever-present fan base. A sequel, *Trekkies 2*, is also available.

Tupac: Resurrection. Paramount, 2003.

Tupac Shakur was a hugely popular rap star when he was alive, and his 1996 death as the victim of a drive-by shooting in Las Vegas only served to make him more popular in death. In this documentary, produced by the rapper's mother, the story is told entirely through Tupac's music and recordings made of his voice during other interviews.

The Up Series. First Run Features, 2004.

The original concept behind this documentary series was both brilliant and simple: meet and interview fourteen children from diverse backgrounds and in different locations in Britain and ask them about their ideas, plans, and dreams for the future. The original film, done in 1964, was interesting, but what has truly made the "Seven Up" series unique is that the director, Mike Apted, has refilmed and reinterviewed the original participants every seven years since; this latest installment (*49 Up*) finds his subjects entering middle age.

Wal-Mart: The High Cost of Low Price. Retail Project LLC, 2005.

Director Robert Greenwald takes you behind Wal-Mart's promise of low prices and interviews employees of the company and their families, business owners who relate tales of what happened to their businesses when Wal-Mart moved into town, and many others who discuss the effect of the retail behemoth on other companies and on communities.

What Would Jesus Buy? Visual Material, 2008.

Reverend Billy and his Stop Shopping Choir want you to let the spirit of non-commercialism move you! Can we get an Amen? In this lighthearted but still serious satire, the Reverend and his choir take their show on the road to help save you from the fires of eternal debt—and maybe have a little fun staging anti-consumerism shows in retail outlets across the country while they're at it.

When We Were Kings. PolyGram Video, 1996.

In 1974 Muhammad Ali and George Foreman were matched up for boxing promoter Don King's master stroke of genius: the "Rumble in the Jungle." When the boxers arrived in Kinshasa, Zaire, delays kept them there longer than planned; in the interim the vivacious Ali went out to meet and train among the African people while Foreman, more reclusive by nature, kept to himself. The result is a fascinating documentary about two unique men and world-class athletes, as well as the business of the boxing business, complete with insights from Norman Mailer and George Plimpton (who were both on hand to report on the bout).

Who Killed the Electric Car? Sony Pictures Home Entertainment, 2006.

Electric cars are not new innovations; one had been engineered before the advent of the age of the internal combustion engine. Fast forward one hundred years to 1996, when electric cars began popping up in California, and then, just as quietly as they had appeared, began to disappear. Director Chris Paine set out to find out why, and interviews a number of people involved with GM's battery-powered EV1, as well as politicians, race drivers, protestors, and petroleum spokespeople.

Why Wal-Mart Works, and Why That Makes Some People Crazy. Hanover House, 2005.

Producers Ron and Robert Galloway provide an inside look at the workings of Wal-Mart, citing its many efficiencies in technology and distribution methods as a great boon not only to its million-plus workers but also the nearly 140 million shoppers who shop there every week to take advantage of its bargains, on which many of them depend to make their paychecks go further.

Why We Fight. Sony Pictures Home Entertainment, 2005.

Although described in reviews as "decidedly leftist," this is nonetheless a fascinating look at Eisenhower's warning half a century ago about the growing influence of the "military industrial complex" (the movie opens with Eisenhower's speech on the subject) and the various ways in which that prophecy has come to fruition through America's military interventions of the last fifty years. The overriding theme of the film is that the business of war is business—and good business at that—and includes interview material with John McCain, Gore Vidal, Dan Rather, and a Vietnam veteran whose son died in the 9/11 attacks on the World Trade Center.

Wordplay. Weinstein Co. Home Entertainment, 2006.

Like its counterpart *Spellbound, Wordplay* is a treatise on all things crossword puzzle, from creation to completion to obsession. Including interviews with crossword puzzle creators Will Shortz and Merl Reagle, there are also a number of cameo appearances from notables including Bill Clinton and Jon Stewart, and the plot is structured around the American Crossword Puzzle Tournament, even lending an air of action to this lighthearted film.

The Yes Men. MGM Home Entertainment, 2005.

Equal parts activists and pranksters, Mike Bonanno and Andy Bichlbaum spend their time throughout this film pulling ever greater stunts to raise political awareness (including their bid to represent the World Trade Organization at conferences and to float the idea of disbanding the organization) only to find that most of their audiences weren't realizing they were participating satirically. The result is a hilarious and nearly unbelievable foray into meetings, conferences, and other restricted-access events, often with surprising results.

Young @ Heart. 20th Century Fox Entertainment, 2008.

In this documentary the stars are members of the Minneapolis-based choral group "Young at Heart," who have achieved homegrown fame and are now sufficiently well known that they tour in the United States and Europe. There's one twist, but it's a doozy: all the members of the choir are seventy years old (and up!), and they emphatically don't bother with typical "choral" music, opting instead to perform such songs as James Brown's "I Feel Good" and Coldplay's "Fix You."

SOURCES

Academy Awards Database: www.oscars.org/awardsdatabase/index.html

Amazon.com

Box Office Mojo Documentaries: www.boxofficemojo.com/genres/chart/?id=documentary.htm

GreenCine: www.greencine.com/central/

Internet Movie Database: imdb.com

Appendix C

Internet Resources

General Nonfiction Resources

Bestseller Lists 1900 to 1998

www.caderbooks.com/bestintro.html

Provided by Cader Books, a book packager, this list of twentieth-century best-seller lists is compiled from the *Publishers Weekly* hardcover best-seller lists.

Book List from The Daily Show with Jon Stewart

www.squidoo.com/DailyShowBookList

Compiled by a dedicated fan, this site lists all the books (almost exclusively nonfiction) featured on *The Daily Show with Jon Stewart*. Also linked to this page is a similar listing of books from *The Colbert Report*, a spin-off from *The Daily Show* featuring Stephen Colbert.

Book Sense Picks Archives

www.bookweb.org/booksense/picks/archives.html

The American Booksellers Association ran a program called Book Sense to provide support for independent booksellers and to provide access to word-of-mouth and hand-sold best sellers to readers for a decade; the program recently morphed into the organization known as IndieBound, but the previous Book Sense picks from independent booksellers across the United States are available through this archive.

Bookslut.com

www.bookslut.com

One of the oldest and most venerable litblogs available, this site, founded by Jessa Crispin, features both nonfiction and fiction book reviews and book news columns on a monthly basis, as well as a daily blog filled with book news, links, commentary, and author and publisher interviews.

Bruce Dobler's Creative Nonfiction Compendium

www.pitt.edu/~bdobler/readingnf.html

This is one of the best sites I've found listing creative nonfiction definitions, as well as a list of suggested titles to start with, that is currently available. It was written by Bruce Dobler, an associate professor of English at the University of Pittsburgh.

Citizen Reader

www.citizenreader.com

I'm not a disinterested party in this Web site; at this blog, I review primarily nonfiction books, a large percentage of which are investigative, as well as some novels. Because I love to think and ask questions about reading, I'll also frequently post questions about reading habits and seek to foster reading discussions in the comments section.

Court TV's Crime Library

www.crimelibrary.com

The comprehensive and detailed Crime Library site contains nutshell descriptions of numerous true crime cases (in short articles that include bibliographies listing book titles), in case you're looking for the details before recommending true crime and true crime reporting books.

Creative Nonfiction (journal)

www.creativenonfiction.org

Creative Nonfiction is a journal devoted exclusively to the creative nonfiction genre and was founded by author and academic Lee Gutkind in 1993. The site offers descriptions of creative nonfiction and suggestions for popular authors in the genre.

Dear Reader

www.dearreader.com

Dear Reader is a great and personable site where you can sign up to receive daily excerpts of nonfiction (and other) titles through your email. Of particular interest are their "Business" and "Nonfiction" categories.

The Early Word

www.earlyword.com

Featuring "news for collection development and readers advisory librarians," this title-awareness site offers news about forthcoming fiction and nonfiction titles, as well as publishing and book world news and commentary.

Fiction_L

www.webrary.org/rs/Flmenu.html

Fiction_L is a listserv devoted to readers' advisory and fiction (although the collective brain is great at answering nonfiction questions as well). The Morton Grove Public Library site (where Fiction_L is archived) also provides booklists periodically culled from the listserv, many of which feature both fiction and nonfiction titles.

IndieBound

www.indiebound.org

Previously known as the Book Sense program for independent booksellers, IndieBound provides resources to help readers find those bookstores in their areas, as well as lists of "indie bestsellers" from smaller and independent booksellers nationwide.

National Public Radio Books Page

www.npr.org/books

The National Public Radio site offers book recommendations, book reviews, and author information. In an age when major publications and news sources cull their book review sections and resources, NPR stands alone in increasing its book coverage and programs.

100+ Narrative Nonfiction Authors

www.wrl.org/bookweb/booklists/nonfiction.html

Published by the Williamsburg Public Library, this list provides a great starting point for readers looking for primarily story-driven, "narrative" nonfiction. Among the popular authors on this list are Mark Bowden, Joan Didion, Christopher Hitches, and William Langewiesche.

Overbooked

www.overbooked.org

Overbooked's tagline says it all: "a resource for readers, providing timely information about fiction (all genres) and readable nonfiction." Ann Chambers Theis, the collection management administrator for the Chesterfield County Public Library (Virginia), is the coordinator of this very helpful site, which provides book news, booklists, and access to books which have received "starred reviews" from the main review sources of *Publishers Weekly*, *Library Journal*, *BookList*, and *Kirkus*.

The Reader's Advisor Online Blog

www.readersadvisoronline.com/blog

Although the Reader's Advisor Online is a subscription database, the blog is freely available and caters to readers' advisors, library staff, and readers alike. Edited by Cynthia Orr, it features weekly lists of nonfiction and fiction best sellers, new titles, and "under the radar" titles, as well as a wide variety of articles about books, publishing trends, reading, and readers' advisory tips and tricks.

General Journalism and News Resources

American Journalism Review

www.ajr.org

The Web page of the *American Journalism Review*, published six times a year by the University of Maryland Foundation, offers not only fascinating articles about the practice (and practitioners) of journalism but also links to online news services, journalism awards, and journalism organizations. Particularly helpful are their lists of newspapers and magazines published, organized by subject area (particularly the "news/opinion" magazines list).

American Society of Journalists and Authors (ASJA)

www.asja.org/links/links.php

This ASJA Web site provides a true "inside look" at the tools and Web sites that investigative authors use for their own research and might provide valuable insight into the style of writing, as well as resources to use at the reference desk, for the intrepid reference librarian.

Columbia Journalism Review

www.cjr.org/index.php

This superlative Web site, the companion to the venerable print version of the *Columbia Journalism Review*, seeks to "encourage and stimulate excellence in journalism." In addition to providing reviews of daily journalism, as well as investigative books, the site also features a handy "Who Owns What" feature, which allows readers to learn which companies are owned by which major media companies.

Drudge Report

www.drudgereport.com

Infamous for being the journalist who officially broke the President Clinton and Monica Lewinsky story, Matt Drudge has been providing an aggregated site of news headlines and links since 1997 (before that, he published e-mail-based reports that were sent to subscribers). In addition to political links, Drudge lists a variety of other news stories (including international, human-interest, and entertainment news); his site can be both a valuable overview of the day's popular headlines and a place to discover other popular media outlets and blogs.

The Huffington Post

www.huffingtonpost.com

Founded by Arianna Huffington, a former contributor to the conservative magazine *National Review* who has, in recent years, moved to the left politically, *The Huffington Post* bills itself as "The Internet Newspaper: News Blogs Videos Community" and offers a variety of news headlines, columns, and feature sections on politics, business, entertainment, science, style, and green living.

Talking Points Memo (TPM)

www.talkingpointsmemo.com/

Maintained by award-winning journalist Josh Marshall, this Web site features news stories and commentary on reporting and politics. TPM provides insight into the news, as well as a model for how daily journalism and blogging might evolve over the next few years; it is also the jump-off point for the related Web sites of TPM Café, which provides a forum for policy and culture debates, and TPM Muckraker, which provides news about political scandals.

Top 100 Works of Journalism in the United States in the 20th Century

www.nyu.edu/classes/stephens/Top%20100%20page.htm

A list of the top 100 works of journalism (most of them book-length), as selected by journalists and New York University's journalism faculty, including David Brinkley, Pete Hamill, Mitchell Stephens, and many others.

Business and Political Resources

800 CEO Read.com

www.800ceoread.com

Although this is a bookselling Web site, it offers up-to-date business best-seller lists, reviews, and recommendations; for business "title awareness" this site is second to none.

Classic Business Books

www.uflib.ufl.edu/cm/business/books/classbks.htm

A list of classic business books as selected by the staff of the University of Florida (at Gainesville) business school library.

Novel Ideas

www.entrepreneur.com/management/leadership/article177286.html

In this Entrepreneur.com article, the author selects the nine best classic business books of the past thirty years and discusses why they still matter.

Powell's Bookstore—Business

www.powells.com/psection/Business.html

A thorough and aesthetically pleasing site listing current business best sellers at Powell's (the venerable bookstore based in Portland, Oregon) and offering current titles in such areas as strategy, marketing, biographies, management, personal skills, and many more.

Powell's Bookstore—Politics

www.powells.com/psection/Politics.html

The political section of the Powell's Web site also offers best-selling and current titles in such areas as political science, conspiracy theories, international studies, and many more.

Seattle Public Library Recommended Classic Business Books

www.spl.org/default.asp?pageID=collection_readinglists_category_detail&cid=1200700423676

A list of a "few time-tested titles to increase your business savvy."

Appendix D

Magazines Offering Investigative Writing and Authors

General Interest Magazines

The Atlantic Monthly: The first issue of this general interest, culture, and political magazine was published in November 1857, and well-known Americans who took part in its founding include Oliver Wendell Holmes, Ralph Waldo Emerson, and Henry Wadsworth Longfellow. The magazine still attempts to be a forum for many different voices and viewpoints, and although it used to regularly publish fiction, it now publishes one dedicated "fiction issue" per year.

Representative authors: Mark Bowden, Nicholas Carr, Gregg Easterbrook, James Fallows, Caitlin Flanagan, Christopher Hitchens, Robert Kaplan.

Web site: www.theatlantic.com

Essence: *Essence* is a monthly magazine for which the target audience is African American women and which offers articles on fashion, lifestyle, entertainment, and culture as well as character profiles and columns on money and relationships. The magazine depends more on freelance magazine writers, with fewer articles being contributed by book authors. Nonetheless, it is an important source for news, entertainment reviews, and pop culture knowledge.

Web site: www.essence.com/essence

Good: *Good* magazine offers features and character portraits about people "doing things that matter." The magazine offers a variety of interest areas, including business and money, the environment, health, and culture. The magazine's Web site is also a very helpful place to keep up with environmental trends, as well as reviews of music and art.

Web site: www.goodmagazine.com

The New Yorker: *The New Yorker* is a weekly publication offering sections on "reporting & essays," "arts & culture," "humor," "fiction & poetry," and the "talk of the town" (focusing on New York City happenings and events). It was first published in 1925 and has long been considered an important journal for political and cultural awareness.

Representative authors: Steve Coll, Atul Gawande, Malcolm Gladwell, Paul Goldberger, Seymour Hersh, Elizabeth Kolbert, John McPhee, Susan Orlean, George Packer, David Sedaris, Calvin Trillin, and Lawrence Wright.
Web site: www.newyorker.com

New York Times Magazine: Published every week along with the Sunday edition of the *New York Times*, the magazine offers lively and opinionated reporting on such topics as politics, social trends, art, business, lifestyle, and culture. **Representative authors:** David Brooks, Zev Chafets, Frank Rich.
Web site: www.nytimes.com/pages/magazine/index.html

Rolling Stone Magazine: *Rolling Stone* is a magazine known for its coverage of music, culture, and political news. Although many librarians might be used to perusing it for its in-depth movie and film reviews, its current affairs reporting staff also provides different viewpoints on issues of the day.
Representative authors: Greil Marcus, P. J. O'Rourke, Matt Taibbi, Hunter S. Thompson.

Salon (online only): *Salon* is a freely available online magazine that is updated daily and features short articles on politics, opinion, technology and business, arts and entertainment, life, books, and comics (a true "general interest" magazine). Written primarily by staffers who don't yet have books to their credit, *Salon* is nonetheless an important source of reviews about political and investigative books.
Web site: www.salon.com

Slate (online only): Another entirely electronic offering, *Slate* magazine is also freely available online and offers, in their own words, a "strong editorial voice and witty take on current events." Major categories for feature writing include news and politics, art and life, business and tech, health and science, style and shopping, travel and food, and sports.
Representative authors: Anne Applebaum, Paul Collins, Christopher Hitchens, Farhad Manjoo, Jacob Weisberg.
Web site: www.slate.com

Utne Reader: The *Utne Reader* is published six times a year and comprises reprints from other magazines and books; it is generally considered to be progressive in its political leanings, but it contains more articles on cultural and lifestyle issues than it does on politics.
Web site: www.utne.com/daily.aspx

Vanity Fair: Although *Vanity Fair* looks more like an entertainment and fashion glossy magazine than a general-interest one, its many well-known contributors keep it consistently stocked with in-depth articles on true crime, business, politics, society figures, and other news and culture stories.

Representative authors: Buzz Bissinger, Douglas Brinkley, Bryan Burrough, Dominick Dunne, William Langewiesche, Seth Mnookin.

Web site: www.vanityfair.com

Lifestyle Magazines

Details: *Details* is a monthly lifestyle magazine marketed to men, offering articles on culture, fashion, relationships, and politics. Although most of it is written by its staff writers and it doesn't feature many contributors who are also book authors, its book-review page always offers unique selections, and the magazine also offers character profiles and essays.

Web site: men.style.com/details

Esquire: *Esquire* magazine is also a monthly publication marketed to men and was first published in the 1930s as a quarterly fashion magazine for men. It still offers fashion and lifestyle information but increasingly features cultural commentary and character profiles, as well as articles about social and political issues.

Representative authors: A. J. Jacobs, Chuck Klosterman, Robert Kurson, Charles Pierce, Mike Sager.

Web site: www.esquire.com

GQ: Similar in style and coverage to *Details* magazine, *GQ* also offers articles on men's fashion, lifestyle, and other cultural issues, as well as brief book and music reviews. Published monthly, the magazine also frequently offers character profiles of notables in the entertainment world.

Representative authors: Jeanne Marie Laskas, Michael Paterniti, Alan Richman, Davy Rothbart.

Web site: men.style.com/gq

Political Magazines—Left

The American Prospect: By its own definition, *The American Prospect* is a "biweekly magazine covering politics, culture, and policy from a liberal perspective." It was initially launched as a quarterly publication in 1990, and was founded by Robert Kuttner, Robert Reich, and Paul Starr.

Representative authors: Eric Alterman, Ann Crittenden, Susan Jacoby, Robert Kuttner, Chris Mooney, Robert Putnam, Jeffrey Sachs.

Web site: www.prospect.org

Harper's: *Harper's* is a monthly magazine with a long historical tradition (first launched in 1850), and offers many popular and well-known features, including their "Index" (a compilation of startling statistics), short essays and works of poetry, and longer feature articles on environmental, cultural, and political issues, as well as in-depth reviews of both fiction and nonfiction books. The magazine is decidedly left; a recent issue featured an article titled "Why the G.O.P. Must Die."

Representative authors: Thomas Frank, Seymour Hersh, Edward Hoagland, Naomi Klein, Kevin Phillips, Ken Silverstein.

Web site: www.harpers.org

Mother Jones: Although it identifies itself as a publication that is more independent and progressive than liberal, the historical tradition of *Mother Jones* reveals many influences often thought of as more "left" (it is named, after all, for Mary Harris "Mother" Jones, a labor activist in the early twentieth century). Its tagline is "smart, fearless journalism," and that seems accurate enough when considering recent headlines such as "Slammed: Welcome to the Age of Incarceration" and "Recession be Damned: Rich Still Getting Richer." It is published six times a year.

Representative authors: Barbara Ehrenreich, Jennifer Gonnerman.

Web site: www.motherjones.com

The Nation: Published weekly, this "flagship of the American left" provides the most reliably Democratic and liberal viewpoints of any of the left-leaning publications. It is devoted primarily to news and politics, although it does include social commentary and media reviews.

Representative authors: Slavenka Drakulic, Naomi Klein, Katha Pollitt, I. F. Stone, Calvin Trillin.

Web site: www.thenation.com

The New Republic: Published twice a month, *The New Republic* offers left-leaning news and political stories, as well as a good deal of cultural commentary and general-interest features. It is not as reliably liberal as *The Nation*, however; one example of its more independent positions was its early support for the 2003 Iraq War.

Representative authors: Niall Ferguson, Tony Judt, Camille Paglia, Lee Siegel, Charles Wohlforth, James Wood.

Web site: www.tnr.com

New Statesman: The *New Statesman* is a left-leaning political journal published in Great Britain. Nonetheless, it can be an important source for international news and commentary and publishes a variety of columns on food, sport, fashion, and environmental issues.

Web site: www.newstatesman.com

The Progressive: The Web site of *The Progressive* proudly proclaims that it has championed "peace and social justice since 1909." The magazine is published once a month and features primarily political news and commentary, as well as columns and features by such popular authors as Edwidge Danticat, Barbara Ehrenreich, Jim Hightower, and Howard Zinn.

Web site: www.progressive.org

Political Magazines—Right

The American Spectator: A monthly conservative magazine edited by R. Emmett Tyrell Jr. and published by Alfred Regnery, this magazine is known for its provocative articles and strong conservative stances. A list of contributors to the magazine is available at its Web site.

Web site: www.spectator.org

National Review: Founded by icon of the right William F. Buckley, Jr. and published twice a month, the *National Review* can be depended on for the conservative viewpoint. It offers primarily news, political, and business commentary.

Representative authors: Jed Babbin, Mona Charen, Dinesh D'Souza, Jonah Goldberg, Thomas Sowell, George F. Will, Byron York.

Web site: www.nationalreview.com

The Weekly Standard: *The Weekly Standard* is perhaps the most staunchly conservative of all the magazines listed here (it is edited by Fred Barnes and William Kristol, the latter of whom frequently appears as an arch-conservative commentator on news programs). It was founded in 1995.

Representative authors: David Frum, Stephen Hayes, Robert Kagan, P. J. O'Rourke.

Web site: www.weeklystandard.com

Science and Technology

Discover: *Discover* magazine is published once a month and offers articles on science written for the "general audience." It is intended to be more accessible than *Scientific American* and features articles on all branches of the sciences.

Representative authors: Jared Diamond, John Horgan, Walter Isaacson, Jessica Snyder Sachs, Carl Zimmer.

Web site: discovermagazine.com

Orion: *Orion* is a monthly magazine that offers stories primarily on environmental issues, culture, and society. In addition to offering essays and short features, it also offers interviews, in-depth articles, and photojournalism essays, as well as book reviews.

Representative authors: Rick Bass, Wendell Berry, Bill McKibben, Janisse Ray, Rebecca Solnit, Terry Tempest Williams.

Web site: www.orionmagazine.org

Wired: *Wired* is a monthly magazine that features stories on culture and society, albeit with an emphasis on technology and scientific advances. It also features stories on business and future trends, and can be useful for librarians seeking to learn about the newest technologies and tools, as well as about technology writers.

Representative authors: Chris Anderson, Steven Johnson, Lawrence Lessig, Daniel Pink.

Web site: www.wired.com

Journalism

Columbia Journalism Review: Although it exists primarily as a magazine about journalism for journalists, the *CJR* is a valuable source of news about the mass media and provides an inside look at how news and feature stories are typically crafted. The magazine's Web site also offers an invaluable tool to librarians: a "Who Owns What" database that shows exactly which publishers and companies are owned by which media conglomerates.

Web site: www.cjr.org

Author/Title Index

Aaron, Hank, 55, 56
Abagnale, Frank, 93, 154, 199, 203, 294
Abbey, Edward, 13, 108, 111, 132, 167,
    195, 203, 303
About a Boy, 77
About Alice, 158
Abramsky, Sasha, 114
Absolutely American, 211–12, 218
An Abundance of Katherines, 129
Abuse of Power, 245
The Accidental Connoisseur, 20, 290
Achebe, Chinua, 38, 79, 155
Ackerman, Diane, 48, 128, 155, 289
Adamson, Joy, 22, 151
Adcult USA, 133
Adichie, Chimamanda Ngozi, 198
Adland: A Global History of Advertising,
    125, 297, 319
The Affluent Society, 252, 312
Affluenza, 308
Afghanistan: The Mirage of Peace, 185
Aftermath, Inc., 62, 168
Against All Enemies, 89, 243, 258, 270,
    279–80, 281
Against Interpretation, 200
Against Love, 104
Against the Machine, 79
Agee, James, 40, 159, 170–71, 248
Agee, Jonis, 255
The Age of Abundance, 274
The Age of Access, 115, 299, 304
The Age of American Reason, 96
The Age of Fallibility, 271, 282–83
The Age of Narcissism, 48
The Age of Reagan, 238
The Age of Spiritual Machines, 118
The Age of Turbulence, 89, 291
Agin, Dan, 101, 114–15
Agtmael, Antoine van, 300, 303, 314
Air, 115, 306
Albrecht, Katherine, 90, 115, 139
Albright, Madeleine, 261, 277–78, 280
Alexander, Brian, 6, 46
Alexievich, Svetlana, 70, 96, 100, 134, 137,
    140, 142, 184, 198, 222

Ali, Ayaan Hirsi, 9
Ali, Monica, 9, 187
Alice, Let's Eat, 51, 158, 162
Alice Waters & Chez Panisse, 14, 290,
    293–94, 314, 325
All Creatures Great and Small, 20
Allen, Arthur, 43, 45, 111, 301
Allende, Isabel, 152, 208
All Familes Are Psychotic, 219
All God's Children, 60–61, 211
All I Did Was Ask, 76
Allison, Graham, 258
All Marketers Are Liars, 324, 325
All Over but the Shoutin', 212, 218
All the Money in the World, 122, 174, 232,
    262, 288–89, 290, 317
All the President's Men, 87–88, 264, 273
All Things Bright and Beautiful, 20
All Things Wise and Wonderful, 20
Almond, Steve, 6–7, 10, 13, 19, 41, 77, 106,
    289
Almost Human: Making Robots Think, 42
Alperovitz, Gar, 300
Alten, Steve, 279
Alterman, Eric, 242
Alvarez, Julia, 140, 152, 173, 208
The Amateurs, 54
Amazonia, 98, 295
Ambrose, Stephen, 73, 185, 211, 245, 301
America: The Book, 98, 244, 253
America: The Last Best Hope, 238, 240
America Alone, 232, 233, 234, 236
America at the Crossroads, 261, 263
America Back on Track, 243
America Behind the Color Line, 37
Americana, 266
American Crescent, 278
*American Dream: Three Women, Ten Kids,
    and a Nation's Drive to End Welfare*,
    119–20, 121, 164, 210, 211, 262, 316
American Dreams: Lost and Found, 39
American Fascists, 71, 109, 245, 248, 251
American Fictions, 76
American Furies, 114
American Green, 23, 26

American Ground, 8, 23, 24–25, 29, 33, 43, 70, 91, 117, 270

The American House of Saud, 138

American Jesus, 248

American Mania: When More Is Not Enough, 120, 162

American Project: The Rise and Fall of a Modern Ghetto, 34–35, 126, 209

American Roulette, 154, 311

American Sphinx, 245

American Studies, 200

American Sucker, 301

American Terrorists, 198

American Theocracy, 249, 256, 264, 267, 269, 278, 312

The American Way of Birth, 104, 116

The American Way of Death Revisited, 10, 44, 47, 103, 104, 125, 221

America Unzipped, 6, 46

Amiry, Suad, 135, 138, 183–84

Among Schoolchildren, 12, 14, 35, 57, 63, 125, 129, 171, 172, 207, 208, 209, 211, 214, 218, 220

Among the Thugs, 162

Amusing Ourselves to Death, 308

Anderson, Bonnie, 98

Anderson, Chris, 17, 101, 166, 290, 298, 299, 301, 304, 305, 306, 322, 324, 325, 326

Anderson, Sherwood, 63

Anderson, Thorne, 256

Andrew Carnegie, 288, 295

And the Band Played On, 31, 136, 196

And the Dead Shall Rise, 124

Angell, Marcia, 102, 107

Angell, Roger, 49–50, 52, 56

Angier, Natalie, 47

The Angry Right: Why Conservatives Keep Getting It Wrong, 251

Animal, Vegetable, Miracle, 16, 18, 41, 107, 111, 130, 174, 180, 303

Annals of the Former World, 117, 315

Another Bullshit Night in Suck City, 218

Another Day in Paradise, 67

Ansay, A. Manette, 64

Answering 911, 10

Apologizing to Dogs, 201

Appetite for Life: A Biography of Julia Child, 14, 293

Appetite for Profit, 105, 107, 111, 132

Applebaum, Anne, 114, 134, 142

Applebee's America, 276, 324

Apple Confidential, 295

Arab and Jew, 30, 135, 138

Arax, Mark, 62, 65, 100, 294

Archer, Jeffrey, 90, 144, 311, 328

The Archimedes Codex, 31, 216

Arc of Justice, 124

The Areas of My Expertise, 176, 244

Are Men Necessary?, 247

Arenas, Reinaldo, 178

Arendt, Hannah, 71

The Argument: Billionaires, Bloggers, and the Battle to Remake Democratic Politics, 271, 276, 282

Ariel Sharon: A Life, 138

Ariely, Dan, 123, 298–99

Armed America, 118

Armed Madhouse, 141, 248, 253

The Armies of the Night, 29, 175

Armstrong, Jerome, 243

Armstrong, Karen, 34, 248

Armstrong, Lance, 49, 197

Arnold, Eric, 20

Arrogance, 235

Arsenals of Folly, 46

Articles of Faith, 11, 30, 31

The Art of the Comeback, 327

Ashe, Arthur, 215

Ashes to Ashes, 103, 108, 119, 125, 309

Asian Godfathers, 99

Asimov, Isaac, 128

Aslan, Reza, 188, 282

As Nature Made Him, 45, 202, 203–4, 206

The Assassins' Gate, 8, 32, 34, 68, 69, 90, 109, 135, 187, 250, 254, 260, 264, 268, 269, 273, 283

The Assault on Reason, 279, 280

Assembling California, 166–67

At Any Cost, 238

At Dawn We Slept, 33

Atkins, Douglas, 320

Atkinson, Kate, 79, 219

The Atlas, 40, 159

Atlas Shrugged, 282, 291

The Atomic Bazaar, 25, 45, 96, 117, 139–40, 258, 278

At the Center of the Storm, 89, 269, 280

At the Same Time, 247, 256

Atwood, Margaret, 61, 76, 78, 79, 144

The Audacity of Hope, 243, 279, 280

Ault, James M., Jr., 152

Auslander, Shalom, 154

Austen, Jane, 79

Ayres, Ian, 55, 299, 314, 326

Babbin, Jed, 259
The Baby Business, 155
Bacevich, Andrew, 246, 250, 282
Back from the Dead, 216
Back on Track, 280
The Backwash Squeeze and Other Improbable Feats, 154, 156, 166
Backyard Giants, 18, 19, 23, 151, 158
Bad Money, 267, 312
Baer, Robert, 29, 89, 139
Bagdikian, Ben, 97, 142
Bageant, Joe, 14, 118, 130, 164, 220, 242, 253, 263, 266, 312, 313, 316, 320
Baggott, Julianna, 7
Baghdad without a Map, 9
Bai, Matt, 271, 276, 283
Bait and Switch, 130, 164, 166, 242, 246, 290, 316
Bakan, Joel, 98, 308, 314
Baker's Dozen, 294
Bakhash, Shaul, 269
Baldacci, David, 199, 274, 283
Balfe, Kevin, 231–32
The Balkan Express, 136
Ball, Edward, 180, 202, 204, 205, 296
Ballard, J. G., 28, 33, 61
Bamberger, Michael, 129, 171, 177, 211, 214, 218, 220
Banana: The Fate of the Fruit That Changed the World, 16
Bananas!, 105
Bangs, Lester, 179
Bank, Melissa, 163, 176, 177, 223
Banks, Russell, 79–80, 121
Barbarians at the Gate, 103, 309, 311, 326
Barber, Benjamin R., 308, 316
Barber, Charles, 95–96, 107, 119
Barkley, Charles, 37, 215–16, 292
Barnes, John, 28, 33
Barnes, Julian, 264
Barnes, Kim, 64, 152
Barnes, Peter, 299–300, 311
Barron, James C., 7–8, 51, 289
Barry, Dave, 132
Barry, John, 43, 45, 218
Barry, Max, 87, 115, 144, 161, 306
Barsamian, David, 244
Barthelme, Donald, 200
Barthes, Roland, 75
Barzun, Jacques, 274, 304
Bascomb, Neal, 23
Basin and Range, 167

Bassett, Angela, 291
Batt, Marissa, 63, 276
Battelle, John, 292, 293, 295
The Battle for God, 248
Beah, Ishmael, 38, 136, 137, 141, 155, 182, 196, 198, 218
Beals, Melba Pattillo, 37, 126, 215, 220, 291
Beam, Alex, 21
The Bean Trees, 174
Beard, James, 14
Beard, Patricia, 326
Beaumier, Michael, 9
Beautiful Boy, 96
The Beauty Myth, 247, 256
Bechdel, Alison, 10
Beck, Glenn, 231–23, 238, 239
Beckstrom, Rod A., 321–22
Become a Better You, 235
Before Night Falls, 178
Begala, Paul, 243, 280
Behar, Howard, 290
Being Dead, 47
Being Right Is Not Enough, 243
Belfer, Lauren, 112
Belkin, Lisa, 155, 208–9, 265
A Bell for Adano, 137
Bellow, Saul, 79
Benjamin, David, 220
Bennett, William, 238, 240
Bennetts, Leslie, 39, 115–16
Beowulf, 22
Berendt, John, 23, 61, 65, 186, 199, 202, 209
Bergal, Jenni, 27–28, 88
Berger, John, 75, 272
Bergman, Carol, 67
Bergreen, Laurence, 25
Bernstein, Carl, 87–88, 264, 273, 277–78, 280
Bernstein, Jared, 313
Bernstein, Peter, 122, 174, 232, 262, 288–89, 290, 317
Berry, Wendell, 18, 24, 38, 108, 127, 174, 180, 212–13, 217, 242, 259, 266, 303, 310
Beschloss, Michael, 267
The Best and the Brightest, 71, 90, 197, 273
The Best Creative Nonfiction, 42
The Best Democracy Money Can Buy, 141, 248, 249
Betrayal of Trust: The Collapse of Global Public Health, 42
Betting It All, 293

Between a Rock and a Hard Place, 202, 204
Between Worlds, 280
Beyer, Rick, 132
Beyond the Green Zone, 187
Bhutto, Benazir, 278
Bianco, Anthony, 106, 316
Bias, 97, 235, 238, 267
Bibeau, Paul, 9, 153, 221
Big-Box Swindle, 102, 106, 316
Big Coal, 112, 315
The Big Con, 89, 252, 253
Big Cotton, 318
Bigger Deal: A Year Inside the Poker Boom, 166
The Big Squeeze: Tough Times for the American Worker, 312–13
The Big Switch, 292
Bill & Dave: How Hewlett and Packard Built the World's Greatest Company, 292, 293, 295
The Billionaire's Vinegar, 20
Bill of Wrongs, 93, 245, 249
Bing, Stanley, 95, 322, 327, 328
The Bin Ladens, 93, 188
Biography of the Dollar, 292
The Biotech Century, 127
Birkerts, Sven, 76, 78
Birkett, Dea, 221
Birth: The Surprising History of How We Are Born, 116
Bissell, Tom, 29, 67, 91, 182, 184, 186, 282
Bissinger, H. G. ("Buzz"), 19, 35, 50–51, 52, 54, 55, 56, 157, 160, 172, 197, 206, 209, 213, 218
Bitter Chocolate, 105–6
Bitter Friends, Bosom Enemies, 268–69, 278
Bitter Harvest, 61, 64
Black, George, 51, 55, 151
Black, Jonathan, 156, 161–62
Black, Lewis, 178, 244
Blackburn, Simon, 178
The Black Echo, 60
Black Girl/White Girl, 78
Black Hawk Down, 8, 59, 72, 73, 90, 182, 203, 211
The Black Ice, 60
Black Lamb and Grey Falcon, 143, 222
Black Like Me, 180
Blacklisted by History, 235–36
Black Money, 294
Blackout: How the Electric Industry Exploits America, 96, 112, 121

Black Rednecks and White Liberals, 239
The Black Swan, 123, 291, 299, 304, 306, 325
Blacktop Cowboys, 175, 212
Blackwater, 52, 108–9, 137, 144, 180, 217, 250–51, 256
Blais, Madeleine, 50
Blanchard, Kenneth, 322–23
Blasphemy: How the Religious Right Is Hijacking Our Declaration of Independence, 245, 254
Bleachy-Haired Honky Bitch, 156, 163
Blehm, Eric, 132, 195, 202–3, 212
Blind Ambition, 245
Blind into Baghdad, 266
The Blind Side, 50, 55, 157, 196, 197, 205–6, 207, 213, 315
Blink, 120, 123, 299, 301, 306
Block, Jennifer, 116, 155
Block, Robert C., 88
Blodgett, Lynn, 171
Blood and Oil, 117, 251
Blood Diamonds, 43, 134–35, 137, 138
Blood Done Sign My Name, 209
Blood from Stones, 117, 136–37, 144
Bloodless Revolution, 26
Blood of the Earth, 138, 315
Blood of the Liberals, 266
Blood Stripes, 73
Bloodthirsty Bitches and Pious Pimps of Power, 254
Bloom, Allan, 274
Bloom, Amy, 204, 205
Bloom, Stephen G., 24, 35, 173
Blowback, 250, 282
Blown to Bits, 15, 301, 306–7, 311
Blow the House Down, 29
The Blue Bear, 202
Blue Blood, 43, 57, 58, 60, 62, 165, 168, 216
Blue Blood and Mutiny, 326
The Blue Death, 42, 48, 127
Blumenthal, Ralph, 114, 163, 216
Blumenthal, Sidney, 89, 242–43, 246, 252, 256, 272, 278–79, 281
Bly, Robert, 203
Bobos in Paradise, 30, 122, 232, 266, 297, 302, 309, 310
The Body Hunters, 110–11, 136
The Body Project, 208
Boehlert, Eric, 271
Boeing vs. Airbus, 15, 293, 294
The Bogey Man, 54, 167

Bogira, Steve, 30, 58, 63, 165, 168, 199, 274, 276
Bohjalian, Chris, 45
Bomb Squad: A Year Inside the Nation's Most Exclusive Police Unit, 165
Bond, Larry, 72
Bone in the Throat, 162
The Bonfire of the Vanities, 178
Bongiorni, Sara, 99, 117, 156, 300
Bonk: The Curious Coupling of Science and Sex, 6, 46–47
Book by Book, 76
Bookchin, Denise, 111, 204
The Book of General Ignorance, 132
The Bookseller of Kabul, 9, 69, 185, 186–87, 222
Boom!, 34
Born Free, 22, 151
Born to Buy, 316, 320
Bortolotti, Dan, 66–67, 141
Bossidy, Larry, 323
The Botany of Desire, 18, 23, 130
Bound to Please, 75–76, 79
Bourdain, Anthony, 14, 18, 153, 162, 168, 169–70, 216, 293, 314, 325
Bowden, Charles, 58–59, 108
Bowden, Mark, 8, 10, 25, 30, 32, 51–52, 54, 57, 59, 72, 73, 78, 90, 144, 182, 203, 207, 211, 218, 269, 278
Bowe, John, 18, 36–37, 38, 39, 92, 94, 99, 106, 109, 112, 116–17, 137, 140, 141, 144, 169, 171, 173, 210, 216, 304, 308, 313, 314, 318, 327
Bowe, Marisa, 36–37, 39
Bowling Alone, 26, 120, 220, 232, 242, 266, 275, 300, 302, 310, 312
Boylan, Jennifer Finney, 202, 205
Boyle, Kevin, 124
The Boys of Winter, 49, 52, 54, 57, 172, 206, 218
Bradley, Bill, 280
Bradley, James, 72, 73, 185
Brady, James, 66
Brafman, Ori, 305, 321–22, 326
Bragg, Rick, 212, 218
The Brain That Changes Itself, 123
Brainwash, 35, 90, 92, 93, 94, 114, 131–32, 139
Branded, 312
Brandt, Allan, 103, 107, 208–9, 292
Brasco, Donnie, 59, 60, 64
Brave New Ballot, 275, 276
Brave New War, 261

Bravo, Ellen, 116
Breach of Faith, 28, 68, 88, 213, 218
Breakfast at Tiffany's, 75
Breaking the News, 266
Breaking the Spell, 264
Breakpoint, 279
The Breaks of the Game, 54, 57
The Breakthrough Company, 323
The Breast Cancer Wars, 11, 30, 119
Breitling, Tom, 93
Breitweiser, Kristen, 29, 91, 270
Brenner, Joel Glenn, 106
Breslin, Jimmy, 59–60
Brick Lane, 9, 187
Bright, Susie, 178
A Bright Shining Lie, 71, 91, 186
Bringing Down the House, 154, 156, 166, 199, 294
Bringing the Heat, 51–52, 54, 57
Brinkley, Douglas, 28, 33, 88, 218, 254, 267, 291
Brizendine, Louann, 128
Brkic, Courtney Angela, 136
Broad, William, 41–42, 45
Brockman, John, 42
Brokaw, Tom, 34
Broken, 96
Broken Government, 245, 260
Brook, Daniel, 122, 262, 309, 312, 318
Brookhiser, Richard, 240
Brooklyn Boy, 55
Brooks, David, 30, 116, 122, 232, 262, 266, 274, 297, 302, 309, 310
Brooks, Geraldine, 8–9, 67, 69, 80, 186
Brooks, Robin, 216
Brown, Cupcake, 291
Brown, Dale, 49, 72, 212
Brown, Dee, 124
Brown, John Seely, 311
Browne, Mick, 61
Brownlee, Shannon, 97, 107
Brox, Jane, 23, 259
Broyard, Bliss, 202
Brumberg, Joan Jacobs, 208
Bryant, Howard, 52
Bryce, Robert, 117
Bryson, Bill, 19, 132, 157, 220
Buchanan, Mark, 122
Buchanan, Patrick, 234, 236, 259–60, 263, 267, 282
Buckingham, Marcus, 292, 295, 299, 323, 327

Buckley, Christopher, 232
Buckley, William F., Jr., 232, 234, 237, 240, 275
The Buffalo Creek Disaster, 206
Buffett, Mary, 296
Buffett: The Making of an American Capitalist, 122, 290
Buford, Bill, 16, 17, 20, 105, 158, 159, 162, 165, 169, 186, 293
Bugliosi, Vincent, 69
Building Red America, 266, 273
Built to Last, 323
Bukowski, Charles, 175
The Bulldozer and the Big Tent, 251, 273
The Bullfighter Checks Her Makeup, 199, 220
The Bully of Bentonville, 106, 316
Burau, Caroline, 10
Burbick, Joan, 117–18, 180
Burgess, Anthony, 61
The Buried Book, 31
Buried in the Bitter Waters, 124
Burke, Jason, 67
Burke, Monte, 150–51
Burnett, John F., 67, 68, 72, 182, 187
Burnett, John S., 141, 181–82, 183, 184
Burr, Chandler, 289
Burrough, Bryan, 59, 103, 309, 311, 326
Burroughs, Augusten, 96, 178, 297
Buruma, Ian, 67
Bury My Heart at Wounded Knee, 124
Bush at War, 88, 283
The Bush Tragedy, 69, 245
Bushwhacked, 243, 246, 249, 253
Bushworld, 243, 245–46, 252
But Enough about Me, 163
Butler, Octavia, 61
Buying In, 132–33
Byatt, A. S., 223
Byer, Heather, 163

The Cadence of Grass, 55
Cafferty, Jack, 88, 93, 235, 242, 248, 249, 253, 260, 263, 282
Cahill, Tim, 159
Cain, Kenneth, 67, 183, 187
Calamities of Exile, 223
Caldicott, Helen, 96, 108
Callahan, David, 99
The Call of the Mall, 104, 297, 308, 320
The Call of the Weird, 175
Campbell, Bebe Moore, 216
Campbell, Greg, 43, 134–35, 137, 138

Campbell, Tracy, 275
Cancel Your Own Goddamn Subscription, 232
Candyfreak, 6–7, 10, 19, 41, 106, 289
Candy Girl, 6
Cannadine, David, 288, 295
Canon: A Whirligig Tour of the Beautiful Basics of Science, 47
Canseco, Jose, 52, 99
Can't Buy My Love, 125, 132, 180, 319
Canton, James, 118
Can You Trust a Tomato in January?, 41, 119, 130–31
Capa, Robert, 70
Capitalism 3.0: A Guide to Reclaiming the Commons, 299–300, 311
Capote, Truman, 57, 64, 75, 76, 200, 214, 221
Caputo, Philip, 22, 28–29, 71, 151, 182
Carhart, Thad, 7
Carnegie, Dale, 321
Carnivorous Nights, 151, 182
Caro, Robert, 273
Carr, Nicholas, 292
Carroll, James, 139, 244, 246, 251
Carson, Rachel, 23, 44, 46, 48, 107, 108, 122, 123, 126–27, 167, 289, 303
Carter, Jimmy, 135, 183, 262, 278, 279
Carucci, Vic, 197
Carville, James, 243, 280
The Case for Israel, 245, 261
The Cases That Haunt Us, 65
Cassidy, Kyle, 118
Cassidy, Tina, 116
Casting a Spell, 51, 55, 151
Catch-22, 186
Catch Me If You Can, 93, 154, 199, 203, 294
Cather, Willa, 75
Caudron, Sheri, 6, 9, 13, 18, 19, 56, 118, 151, 153, 158, 214, 219, 220
Caught in the Middle: America's Heartland in the Age of Globalism, 266, 319–20
Cecchini, Toby, 163
Cepuch, Randy, 289–90
Chabon, Michael, 188, 219
Chafets, Zev, 30, 260–61, 262
Chaikin, Andrew, 214
Chain of Command, 91, 139, 264
Chait, Jonathan, 89, 252, 253
Chandler, Raymond, 60
Chandrasekaran, Rajiv, 68–69, 70, 187, 250, 264, 268

Chang, Iris, 91
Chapman, Peter, 105
Character Studies, 9, 13, 118, 153, 222, 266
Charan, Ram, 292, 323
Charen, Mona, 131
Charlie Wilson's War, 89
Chase, Alston, 198
Chasing Kangaroos, 151
Chasing the Sea, 67, 182, 183, 184, 282
Chatter, 90, 115, 139
Chatwin, Bruce, 221
The Cheating Culture, 99
*Cheer! Three Teams on a Quest for
        Cheerleading's Ultimate Prize*, 18–19
Cheever, Joan, 216
Chehab, Zaki, 135
Chen, Pauline, 11
Chen, Victor Tan, 119, 120, 130, 242, 309,
        312, 316, 318, 320
Cheney, 238, 250, 310
Chernow, Ron, 288, 295, 296
Chevalier, Tracy, 216
Child, Julia, 158, 162, 170, 290, 314
*China, Inc.: How the Rise of the Next
        Superpower Challenges America and
        the World*, 99, 259, 300, 302, 303, 305,
        318
The China Price, 99, 313
China Shakes the World, 99, 300, 302
The Choice, 272
Chomsky, Noam, 142, 175, 184, 243–44,
        246, 251, 255, 257, 262, 279
Chopin's Funeral, 8
Christine Jorgensen, 205
Christy, Bryan, 16
Chua, Amy, 139, 250
Chuck Yeager and the Bell X-1, 294
*Churchill, Hitler, and the "Unnecessary
        War,"* 282
The Cider House Rules, 45
The Cigarette Century, 103, 107, 292, 308–9
Ciresi, Rita, 163, 223
Cisneros, Sandra, 140, 173
City Adrift, 27–28, 88
The City in History, 24
City Life, 23, 26, 302
The City of Falling Angels, 23, 186
City of Light, 112
A Civil Action, 30, 63, 99–100, 107, 128, 199,
        209, 265, 274
Civil Disobedience, 90, 115

Clancy, Tom, 50, 59, 72, 90, 140, 212, 279,
        283
Clark, Robert, 293–94
Clark, Taylor, 14, 103–4, 166, 289, 290, 310,
        315, 316, 318, 319, 324
Clarke, Jonathan, 251, 261, 263, 270
Clarke, Richard, 89, 243, 258, 270, 279–80,
        281
*The Clash of Civilizations and the Remaking
        of the World Order*, 282
Class Matters, 119, 130, 164, 196, 220, 242,
        261–62, 266, 312, 313, 316, 320
Class Warfare, 244
Clear and Present Danger, 59
A Clearing in the Distance, 23, 26
Clegg, Douglas, 131
Clemente, 55, 197
Cleopatra's Nose, 200
Clinton, Bill, 120, 242, 243, 277, 278, 280,
        291
Clinton, Hillary, 243, 277, 278, 280
The Clinton Wars, 272, 278–79, 281
The Closing of the American Mind, 274
Closing the Food Gap, 38
*Closure: The Untold Story of the Ground Zero
        Recovery Mission*, 270
The Cloud Garden, 59, 184, 199
The Cloudspotter's Guide, 26
The Cluetrain Manifesto, 305, 306, 311, 326
Coal, 108, 138
Cobb, 56
Coben, Harlan, 50, 54
*Cobra II: The Inside Story of the Invasion and
        Occupation of Iraq*, 32, 68, 69, 72, 90,
        117, 250, 260, 269, 270, 280, 283
Cockburn, Patrick, 69, 187, 217
The Cockroach Papers, 44
Cod, 16, 26, 105, 292, 295, 314
Codrescu, Andrei, 28, 88, 218
Cody, Diablo, 6
Coffey, Wayne, 49, 52, 54, 57, 172, 206, 218
Coffman, Curt, 323
Cohen, Leah Hager, 151–52
Cohn, Jonathan, 44, 48, 97, 102, 108, 115,
        116, 313
Colapinto, John, 45, 202, 203–4, 206
Colbert, Stephen, 98, 244, 253
A Cold Case, 60, 62, 70
The Coldest Winter, 273
Cold New World, 121, 130, 209, 219, 242,
        262
Coll, Steve, 89–90, 93, 188

Collapse, 300, 305, 306, 314, 317
Collateral Damage, 71
Collins, Catherine, 134, 143
Collins, Jim, 55, 99, 295, 299, 306–7, 323, 325, 327
The Colombo Bay, 25
Colored People, 37
The Color of Water, 37, 126, 202, 212, 219, 291–92
Coloroso, Barbara, 144
The Color Purple, 185
Colossus: The Rise and Fall of the American Empire, 234
The Colossus of New York, 176
Colwin, Laurie, 158, 162, 294
Comeback: Conservatism That Can Win Again, 234, 240
Comfortably Numb, 95–96, 107, 119
Comfort Me with Apples, 158
Coming of Age in the Milky Way, 46
The Coming Plague, 41–42
The Commitment, 31
The Common Good, 244
Common Ground, 140, 219–20
Common Wealth: Economics for a Crowded Planet, 270, 305
Communities without Borders, 38
The Company, 161, 292
Company C, 186
Complications, 11, 43, 169
Confederates in the Attic, 9, 19, 181
Confessions of a Master Jewel Thief, 154
Confessions of a Memory Eater, 205, 219
Confessions of an Advertising Man, 297
Confessions of an Economic Hit Man, 35, 59, 93, 117, 138, 141, 144, 249, 267, 276, 281, 314
Confessions of an Eco-Sinner, 123, 318
Confessions of a Political Hitman, 92–93
Confessions of a Shopaholic, 297
Confessions of a Tax Collector, 17, 93, 276
Conlon, Edward, 43, 57, 58, 60, 62, 165, 168, 216
Connelly, Michael, 10, 57–58, 60, 62, 165, 168
Conover, Ted, 37, 43, 44, 49, 57, 114, 124, 141, 159, 162, 163, 165, 172, 176–77, 179, 180, 188, 196
Conrad, Joseph, 71
Conroy, John, 35, 70, 92, 93
The Conscience of a Conservative, 240

The Conscience of a Liberal, 242, 249, 251–52, 267
Conservatives without Conscience, 245, 263, 264
Consider the Lobster, 156, 176
Conspiracy of Fools, 15, 52, 96, 99, 103, 112, 309, 310–11, 315, 326
Consumed: How Markets Corrupt Children, Infantilize Adults, and Swallow Citizens Whole, 308, 316
Continental Drift, 121
Continetti, Matthew, 94
Cook, Robin, 45, 102, 111, 144
Cookoff: Recipe Fever in America, 151, 157–58
A Cook's Tour, 162
Coomer, Joe, 201
Coontz, Stephanie, 48, 120, 274
Cooper, Christopher, 28, 88, 218
Cooper, Cynthia, 141
Corera, Gordon, 140
Corn, David, 250
Cornwell, Bernard, 66
Cornwell, Patricia, 58, 168
Coronary: A True Story of Medicine Gone Awry, 52, 96, 102, 107, 111, 204
The Corporation, 98, 308
Corporation Nation, 98, 102, 180
Cosmopolitan, 163
Cosmos, 46
Coulter, Ann, 131, 232, 233, 234, 235, 236, 238, 239, 260
A Country Practice, 20
Coupland, Douglas, 95, 161, 219, 292, 295, 309, 328
Courtroom 302, 30, 58, 62, 165, 168, 199, 274, 276
Coverdale, Linda, 37–38
Cover-Up: Mystery at the Super Bowl, 53
Cover-up: The Army's Secret Investigation of the Massacre at My Lai 4, 91
Covey, Stephen, 323, 327
Covington, Dennis, 152, 154
Coyotes: A Journey through the Secret World of America's Illegal Aliens, 141, 163, 172–73, 179
Coyote Warrior, 206
Crace, Jim, 47
Cracking the Code, 247
A Crack in the World, 28
Cramer, Jim, 304, 327, 328

Cramer, Richard Ben, 129, 135, 261, 262, 272, 279
Crashing the Gate, 243, 271
Crashing Through, 45, 205
Crawford, John, 68
Crazies to the Left of Me, Wimps to the Right, 238, 267
Crazy: A Father's Search through America's Mental Health Madness, 21, 96
Crazy Bosses, 322, 327
Crewdson, Michael, 151, 182
Crichton, Michael, 45, 80
Crile, George, 89
Crime Beat, 57–58, 60, 62, 165, 168
The Crime of Sheila McGough, 198–99
A Crime So Monstrous, 144
Critser, Greg, 105, 118–19
Crittenden, Ann, 116
Cronies: Oil, the Bushes, and the Rise of Texas, 117
Crossing Over, 59, 92, 117, 140, 141, 169, 173
Crossing the Line, 121
Cruising Speed, 232
Crunch: Why Do I Feel So Squeezed?, 313
Crusade: Chronicles of an Unjust War, 244, 251
Cryptonomicon, 292
Cuadros, Paul, 172, 173, 186
Cubs Nation, 19, 54, 56, 99, 157, 160
Cullen, Lisa Takeuchi, 6, 9–10, 18, 47, 103, 104, 221, 289
The Culting of Brands, 320
The Cult of the Amateur, 298, 306
The Culture of Fear, 98, 123, 142
Culture Warrior, 232, 233, 234, 238
Cummins, Jeanine, 62, 65
Curtis, Drew, 97–98, 101, 104, 142
Cussler, Clive, 49, 155
Cutting for Sign, 25, 59, 117, 140, 141, 169, 173
Cycon, Dean, 310, 318

Dallek, Robert, 261, 291
Dalrymple, Theodore, 235
Damrosch, David, 31
Danelo, David, 73
The Dangerous Joy of Dr. Sex and Other True Stories, 219
Daniels, Susanne, 102
Danner, Mark, 35, 70, 92, 264, 272
Danziger, Danny, 216

Danziger, Pamela, 296–97
The Dark Side, 93
The Dark Side of Camelot, 91
Darwin and Design, 265
Dash, Leon, 61, 63, 65, 120, 121, 129, 209–10, 211
The Daughters of Juarez, 58
Davidson, Miriam, 92
Davis, Devra, 119
Davis, Joshua, 152–53
Dawkins, Richard, 40, 48, 72, 264, 287
Day of Empire, 139, 250
Day of Reckoning, 260, 263, 282
Days of Grace, 215
Dead Center: Behind the Scenes at the World's Largest Medical Examiner's Office, 168–69
Dead Certain, 250, 272, 281, 291
Dead Man Walking, 114, 216
Dead Wood, 10
Deal Breaker, 50
Dean, John, 244–45, 260, 263, 264, 283
Dear G-Spot, 178
The Death and Life of Great American Cities, 24, 300
Death at an Early Age, 126
A Death in Belmont, 65
The Death of the West, 260
Death on the Black Sea, 134, 143
Deaver, Jeffery, 58
De Blasi, Marlena, 290
DeBlieu, Jan, 32
De Botton, Alain, 26, 48, 74, 75, 120, 154, 310, 317, 319
Deep Economy, 18, 111, 130, 174, 259, 302–3, 316
Deer Hunting with Jesus, 14, 118, 130, 164, 220, 242, 253, 263, 266, 312, 313, 316, 320
Defining the Wind, 32
Deford, Frank, 49–50, 53, 80
De Graaf, John, 308
Deighton, Len, 139
DelCorso's Gallery, 29
DeLillo, Don, 29, 40, 221, 223
Delivering Knock Your Socks Off Service, 325
Deliver the Vote, 275
Deliver Us from Evil, 238
Deluxe: How Luxury Lost Its Luster, 176, 180, 296–97, 319, 320
DeMarco, Susan, 248–49
DeMille, Nelson, 90, 212

The Demon in the Freezer, 41, 45, 46
Denby, David, 74, 76, 301
Denfeld, Rene, 60–61, 211
Dennett, Daniel, 72, 264
Den of Thieves, 311
DeParle, Jason, 119–20, 121, 164, 210, 211, 262, 316
The Depths of Space, 214
Derber, Charles, 98, 102, 180
Dershowitz, Alan, 239, 245, 254, 261
The Deserter's Tale, 256
Desert Solitaire, 13, 111, 195, 203
The Devil and the Disappearing Sea, 67, 183, 184, 282
De Villiers, Marq, 155, 183
Devil's Game, 244
The Devil Wears Prada, 297
Dexter, Pete, 8, 10, 17, 52, 60, 203, 218
DeYoung, Karen, 234
The Dharma Bums, 159
Diamant, Jeff, 203
Diamond, 43, 104, 105, 135, 137, 296
Diamond, Jared, 74, 118, 265, 274, 286, 300, 301, 305, 306, 314, 317
The Diary of a Young Girl, 143
Dick, Philip K., 128
Dickens, Charles, 75, 78
Didion, Joan, 35, 59, 60, 68, 76, 77, 100, 144, 155, 167, 247, 272, 273
Did Monkeys Invent the Monkey Wrench?, 132
Diet for a Poisoned Planet, 122
Diffee, Matthew, 112
Dillard, Annie, 23, 215, 259
Dillon, Katherine V., 137
The Din in the Head, 78
Dinner at the Homesick Restaurant, 207, 325
Dinner at the New Gene Cafe, 127
The Dip, 324
Dirda, Michael, 75–76, 79
Dirt, 47
Dirty Diplomacy, 94, 183, 184, 281–82
Disaster: Hurricane Katrina and the Failure of Homeland Security, 28, 88, 218
Dishwasher, 37, 166
Disney War, 311
Disobedience and Democracy, 257
Dispatches, 29, 71, 186
Display of Power: How FUBU Changed a World of Fashion, Branding and Lifestyle, 291–92, 296

The Disposable American, 92, 130, 164, 242, 248, 249, 304, 309, 312, 313, 316, 318, 319–20
Divine Secrets of the Ya-Ya Sisterhood, 207
Divining Women, 185
Dixie, 28
Do as I Say (Not as I Do), 235, 238
Do Bald Men Get Half-Price Haircuts?, 132
Dobbs, Lou, 248, 260, 262–63, 282
The Doctor's Plague, 111, 116
Does Measurement Measure Up?, 115
The Dogs of War, 144
Dog Years, 196
Doidge, Norman, 123
Dolittle, Sean, 47
Do Me Twice: My Life after Islam, 64
Don't Eat This Book, 119, 188
Don't Get Too Comfortable, 156, 176
Don't Let's Go to the Dogs Tonight, 22, 155, 195
Don't Think of an Elephant, 243, 256, 273
Do Pharmacists Sell Farms?, 132
Dos Passos, John, 204
Doty, Mark, 196
Double or Nothing, 93
Douglas, Susan, 39
Dowd, Matthew, 276, 324
Dowd, Maureen, 243, 244, 245–46, 247, 252
Down By the River, 58–59, 125
Down from Troy, 169
Downtown: My Manhattan, 176
Doyle, Roddy, 223–24
Do You: 12 Laws to Access the Power in You to Achieve Happiness and Success, 291
The Dragonhead, 186
Drakulic, Slavenka, 135–36, 143
Drape, Joe, 52–53, 160
Draper, Robert, 69, 250, 256, 272, 281, 291
Draut, Tamara, 309, 316, 318, 319
Dreaming in Code, 15, 16–17, 42, 292, 322
Dreaming in Cuban, 208
Dress Your Family in Corduroy and Denim, 176
Drew, Elizabeth, 272
Dreyfuss, Robert, 244
Drinking the Sea at Gaza, 142, 184
The Drowned World, 28, 33
Drucker, Peter, 327
Drudge, Matt, 98
Drudge Manifesto, 98
Drumheller, Tyler, 280

Dry, 96
D'Souza, Dinesh, 233–34
Dubner, Stephen, 101, 123, 283, 294, 299,
   301, 306, 307, 314
Dubose, Lou, 94, 260
Dude, Where's My Country?, 252
Due Considerations, 79, 200
Duke, Lynne, 144
Duneier, Mitchell, 126
Dungy, Tony, 52, 197
Dunn, Jancee, 163
Dunn, Katherine, 9
Dunne, Dominick, 61, 168, 174
Dunne, John Gregory, 79
Duty, Honor, Country, 211
Dworkin, Andrea, 180
Dwyer, Jim, 25, 29, 33, 169
Dyer, Geoff, 222
Dyke, Tom Hart, 59, 184, 199
Dyson, Esther, 304
Dyson, Freeman, 46

Earley, Pete, 21, 66, 96
Earth in the Balance, 280
The Earth Moved, 18, 23, 130
Easterbrook, Gregg, 120, 123, 232, 289,
   317, 319
East of Eden, 171
Eat, Pray, Love, 18, 20, 105, 152
Eberhart, Mark, 25, 120–21
Echikson, William, 20, 290
Economic Facts and Fallacies, 234, 237, 239
The Economics of Innocent Fraud, 252
Edsall, Thomas, 266, 273
The Education of a Coach, 50, 54, 197
The Education of a Poker Player, 154, 166
Edwards, John, 280
Egan, Jennifer, 188
Eggers, Dave, 135, 151, 182, 188, 198
Ehlers, Tracy Bachrach, 210
Ehrenreich, Barbara, 37, 44, 63, 72, 97, 114,
   116, 120, 125, 126, 130, 156, 161, 162,
   164, 165, 166, 169, 176, 179, 180, 188,
   196, 209, 210, 220, 242, 246, 249, 261,
   266, 290, 314, 316, 318
Ehrlich, Gretel, 44, 221
Ehrlich, Paul, 306
Ehrman, Bart, 31, 248
Eichenwald, Kurt, 15, 52, 96, 99, 103, 112,
   309, 310–11, 315, 326
Eig, Jonathan, 51, 56, 197
Eight Ways to Run the Country, 273, 274–75

Einstein's Dream, 46
Eisler, Benita, 8
Elder, Larry, 239
The Elephant and the Dragon, 259, 300, 302,
   303, 318
The Elephant in the Room, 263
Elkind, Peter, 141
Elliot, Jason, 67, 184, 185, 187
Ellis, Bret Easton, 328
Ellis, Charles, 293, 296
Ellis, Joseph, 245
Ellis, Richard, 314
Ellroy, James, 60
Ellsberg, Daniel, 273
Elon, Amons, 262
Embryo Culture, 116, 154–55
Emergency Sex and Other Measures, 67, 183,
   184, 187
The Emerging Markets Century, 300, 303,
   314
Emerson, Steven, 138
Emotionally Weird, 219
The Emperor of Scent, 289
The Emperors of Chocolate, 106
*Empire: The Rise and Demise of the British
   World Order*, 270
The Empty Ocean, 314
Endangered Pleasures, 75
The End of America, 249, 251, 252, 256
The End of Faith, 245, 248, 264
The End of Food, 41, 105, 106–7, 111, 119,
   122, 127, 132, 265, 318
The End of History and the Last Man, 263
The End of Medicine, 43–44, 97, 108, 122
The End of Nature, 13, 44, 259, 303
The End of Oil, 117
The End of Racism, 234
The End of Work, 304
The Enemy at Home, 233–34
The Enemy Within, 238
Engelberg, Stephen, 45
Engelhardt, Tom, 98, 244, 246
English, Deirdre, 164
The English Patient, 151, 155
*Enough: Staying Human in an Engineered
   Age*, 303
Envy, 178
Ephron, Nora, 156, 246
Epstein, Helen, 136
Epstein, Joseph, 178, 222
Erdman, Paul, 328
Erickson, Carolly, 212

Erlich, Reese, 268
Ernie Pyle's War, 68
Escape, 64
Esposito, Richard, 165
Esquivel, Laura, 173, 208
Estess, Jenifer, 205
Ettlinger, Steve, 7, 41
The European Dream, 109, 304
The Europeans, 109
Europe Central, 40, 159
The Evangelical President, 237–38
Evans, M. Stanton, 235–36
Evans, Philip, 15, 301, 306–7
Evans, Walker, 170–71, 248
Even Buffett Isn't Perfect, 296
Everything Is Miscellaneous, 15, 17, 101,
    118, 128, 299–300, 305, 306, 311, 322,
    324, 326
Everything That Rises, 223
The Evil B. B. Chow, 7
*Evolution: The Remarkable History of a
    Scientific Theory*, 265
The Evolution of Useful Things, 51
The Executioner's Song, 64, 175, 216
Ex-Friends, 237
Ex Libris, 76, 78
Explaining Hitler, 129, 221
Exposed, 48, 101, 107, 109, 122, 127
Extraordinary Circumstances, 141
Extraordinary Evil, 144
The Extreme Future, 118
Exuberance, 120

*F5: Devastation, Survival, and the Most
    Violent Tornado Outbreak of the 20th
    Century*, 28, 31–32, 33, 88, 218
The Face of War, 69–70
Fadiman, Anne, 10–11, 30, 43, 44, 76, 78,
    102, 107, 122, 136, 204, 208
Fagone, Jason, 11–12, 19, 153, 158, 165, 220
Fainaru-Wada, Mark, 51, 52, 98–99
Fair Game, 250, 281
Fairstein, Linda, 168
The Faith of a Writer, 78
Falling Behind, 120, 130, 232, 309, 311–12,
    320
Falling Man, 29
Falling Upwards, 78–79
The Fall of the House of Bush, 217, 255–56
Fallout, 140
Fallows, James, 266
The Falls, 78

Faludi, Susan, 39, 125, 180, 246–47, 256
Fame and Obscurity, 78
Fame Junkies, 12–13
Family Linen, 242
Family of Spies, 66
Fanon, 252
Fantasyland, 56, 151, 153, 159–60, 166
Farah, Douglas, 117, 136–37, 144
Farah, Joseph, 236
Fargo Rock City, 17, 77, 174
Faster, 118, 306
Fast Food Nation, 41, 104, 105, 106, 107,
    110, 111, 119, 127, 174, 180, 308
Fatal Vision, 61, 64, 186, 199
The Fateful Triangle, 184, 244, 262, 279
Fat Envelope Frenzy, 218–19
The Father of All Things, 29, 91, 186
Fat Land, 105, 118–19
Fatsis, Stefan, 12, 18, 19, 118, 153, 156, 160,
    166, 214
The Fattening of America, 105
Faulkner, William, 55, 204
*Fear and Loathing in George W. Bush's
    Washington*, 272
Fear and Loathing in Las Vegas, 17, 174,
    178–79
Fear of Falling, 164
Featherstone, Lisa, 106
Feeding a Yen, 7, 12, 19, 51, 158, 162, 266
Feeding the Fire, 120–21
Feeding the Green Monster, 55
Feeding the Monster, 51, 55, 56, 99, 160
Feige, David, 63
Feiler, Bruce S., 34, 165
Feinstein, John, 19, 49, 52, 53–54, 157, 167
Feldman, Richard, 118
The Female Thing, 104, 247
The Feminine Mystique, 39
The Feminist Mistake, 39, 115–16
Ferguson, Craig, 221
Ferguson, Niall, 71, 144, 234, 270
Ferguson, Rob, 67, 183, 184, 282
Ferner, Mike, 217
Ferris, Joshua, 95, 160, 295, 309, 328
Ferris, Timothy, 40, 46
Fever Trail, 181
*Fiasco: The American Military Adventure in
    Iraq*, 32, 68, 69, 90, 187, 243, 250, 256,
    267–68, 269, 280, 283
Fidelity, 259
Fielding, Helen, 177
Field Notes from a Catastrophe, 44, 115

Fies, Brian, 45, 100, 112, 119
Fifty Acres and a Poodle, 174
Figes, Orlando, 134, 142, 246
Fight Club, 61
Fighting Back, 238
Fighting for Air, 97–98, 101, 102
Final Exam, 11
Finder, Joseph, 90, 102, 286, 294, 311, 328
Finders Keepers, 59, 203
Finding Grace, 171
Finding Jefferson, 245
Finkelstein, Eric, 105
Finnegan, William, 121, 130, 209, 219, 223, 242, 262
Fiorina, Carly, 293, 326
First Big Crush, 20
The First Billion Is the Hardest, 296
First, Break All the Rules, 323
First, Do No Harm, 209
First in His Class, 278
First Light: The Search for the Edge of the Universe, 46
The First Man-Made Man, 46–47, 180, 202, 204–5, 219
Fish: A Memoir of a Boy in a Man's Prison, 114
Fisher, Len, 25
Fisher, M. F. K., 76, 158, 162, 294
Fishing on the Edge, 151
Fishman, Charles, 106, 290, 316
Fishman, Ted C., 99, 259, 300, 302, 303, 305, 318
Fisk, Robert, 30, 135, 142
Fitch, Noël Riley, 293
Fitzgerald, F. Scott, 55
Fitzgerald, Randall, 48, 101, 107, 109, 111, 116, 121–22, 265
Fixed Ideas, 247, 272
The Fixer: A Story from Sarajevo, 68, 143, 199–200
Flake, Emily, 309
Flanagan, Caitlin, 72, 246
The Flanders Panel, 31, 216
Flannery, Tim, 13, 33, 151, 182
Flat Broke with Children, 120
Flaubert, Gustave, 75
Fleming, Thomas, 282
Flinn, Kathleen, 16
Florida, Richard, 300, 301, 302, 309, 311
Flower Confidential, 7, 9, 10, 14, 18, 47, 105, 109, 117, 118, 130, 199, 289, 290, 296, 310, 314, 315, 318

Flux: Women on Sex, Work, Love, Kids, and Life in a Half-Changed World, 39
Flying Over 96th Street, 35
Flynn, Kevin, 25, 29, 33, 63
Flynn, Nick, 218
Flynn, Vince, 283
Foden, Giles, 155, 196
Foer, Franklin, 172, 186
Fontana, Marian, 29, 33
Food, Inc., 110, 111, 127, 174
Food Fight: The Citizen's Guide to a Food and Farm Bill, 265
Food Politics, 105
Fooled by Randomness, 55, 283, 291, 299, 325
For Common Things, 275
Ford, Richard, 15, 55, 121, 195, 224
Ford: The Man and the Machine, 288, 309, 311
Foreskin's Lament, 154
Forever Fat, 42
The Forgotten Man, 235
For Her Own Good, 164
Forsyth, Frederick, 90, 131, 140, 144, 283–84
The Fortune Cookie Chronicles, 15–16
Forty Acres and a Fool, 24
For Whom the Bell Tolls, 70
Fossey, Dian, 22, 46, 182
The Founding Fish, 167
The Fountainhead, 291
Fournier, Ron, 276, 324
Francis, Dick, 53
Frank, Anne, 143
Frank, Robert H., 120, 122, 130, 174, 176, 232, 252, 262, 302, 309, 310, 311–12, 320
Frank, Thomas, 89, 97, 98, 130, 244, 246, 248, 252, 255, 256, 262, 266, 273, 274, 275, 308, 312
Frankel, Alex, 39, 161, 165–66, 290
Franken, Al, 247, 252, 254
Franklin and Winston, 207
Franzen, Jonathan, 200
Fraud, 176
Frayn, Michael, 118
Freakonomics, 101, 123, 283, 294, 299, 301, 306, 307, 314
Free Agent Nation, 311
Free Culture, 17, 299, 306
Freedom Next Time, 142

Freedomnomics: Why the Free Market Works and Other Half-Baked Theories Don't, 236–37
Freese, Barbara, 108, 138
The French Laundry Cookbook, 169
French Revolutions, 167
Frey, Darcy, 54, 57, 206, 213
Frey, Stephen, 102, 286, 294, 328
Friday Night Lights, 19, 50, 54, 157, 172, 197, 206, 209, 213
Friedan, Betty, 39, 116, 180, 278
Friedman, Milton, 89, 317
Friedman, Robert, 59, 134
Friedman, Thomas L., 29–30, 101, 117, 138, 237, 261, 270, 291, 300, 301, 303, 304, 310, 314, 317
Friends: A Love Story, 291
From Baghdad, with Love, 73
From Beirut to Jerusalem, 29–30, 138, 261
Fromkin, David, 279
From Our House, 255
From the Farm to the Table, 38
From the Ground Up, 18, 23, 26
Frum, David, 234, 235, 240
Frump, Robert, 22, 151
FUBAR: America's Right-Wing Nightmare, 247, 252, 271
Fugitive Denim, 99, 117, 166, 290, 292, 301, 310, 314, 315, 318
Fukuyama, Francis, 261, 263
Fuller, Alexandra, 22, 155, 194–95
Fun Home, 10
Furst, Alan, 140, 282
Fussell, Paul, 71
Fussman, Cal, 93
Futurecast: How Superpowers, Population, and Globalization Will Change the Way You Live and Work, 304–5
The Future of Freedom, 270
The Future of the Race, 37
Future Shock, 118

Gag Rule, 252
Gaitskill, Mary, 177
Galbraith, John Kenneth, 252, 300, 308, 312
Game of Shadows, 51, 52, 98–99
Gaming the Vote, 275, 276
Gang Leader for a Day, 35, 120, 126, 172, 180, 262
The Gang That Couldn't Shoot Straight, 59
Garbage Land, 48, 123, 129–30
García, Cristina, 208

Gardner, Chris, 291
Gardner, Daniel, 123
Garlic and Sapphires, 158, 162, 170
Garrett, Laurie, 41–42
Gartner, John, 301
Gaskell, Elizabeth, 145
Gass, Thomas Edward, 43, 102, 108
Gates, David, 195
Gates, Henry Louis, Jr., 37
Gawande, Atul, 11, 43, 97, 169
The Gawker Guide to Conquering All Media, 98
The Gay Talese Reader, 75, 178, 221
Gee, Henry, 127
Geek Love, 9
Gellhorn: A Twentieth Century Life, 70, 141, 185
Gellhorn, Martha, 69–70, 73, 204
The Generals' War, 90
Generation Debt, 122, 130, 262, 309, 316, 318, 319
The Geography of Bliss, 16
The Geography of Nowhere, 26, 126, 300
George, Nelson, 37, 124, 215
George Soros on Globalizaton, 282
Germs: Biological Weapons and America's Secret War, 41–42, 45, 258
Gerritsen, Tess, 102, 111
Gerstein, Ted, 165
Get to Work, 116
Ghost, 46
The Ghostly Lover, 76
The Ghost Map, 42, 48
Ghosts of Tsavo, 22, 151, 182
Ghost Soldiers, 73
Ghost Wars, 89–90, 93
Gibbons, Kaye, 185
Gibson, William, 61, 115, 128, 139
Gig, 36–37, 39, 117, 216, 327
Gilbert, Daniel, 120, 289
Gilbert, Elizabeth, 11, 18, 20, 56, 105, 132, 152, 157, 159, 175, 177, 195, 197–98, 200–201, 203, 212
Gill, Michael Gates, 290
Gillespie, Hollis, 156, 163, 178
Gilmore, Mikal, 64
Gingrich, Newt, 234–35, 240
Ginsberg, Debra, 21, 37, 165, 325
Girl, Interrupted, 21
The Girl from Botany Bay, 212
A Girl Named Zippy, 152
Girl with a Pearl Earring, 216

Gitlin, Todd, 251, 273
Gitomer, Jeffrey, 323, 324, 328
Give Me a Break, 131, 235, 263, 267
Give Me Liberty, 254
Giving: How Each of Us Can Change the World, 120, 242, 243, 280
Gjeltsen, Tom, 136
Gladwell, Malcolm, 26, 74, 118, 120, 123, 215, 299, 300, 301, 304, 305, 306, 314, 317, 319, 325, 326
Glass, Julia, 325
Glass, Paper, Beans, 152
Glassner, Barry, 98, 123, 142
Gleick, James, 118, 123, 306
Globalization and Its Discontents, 303
Gluttony, 178
God: The Failed Hypothesis, 264
God and Man at Yale, 232, 240, 275
The God Delusion, 264, 287
The Godfather, 60
God Has Ninety-Nine Names, 8–9, 69, 187
Godin, Seth, 101, 298, 306, 323, 324, 325
God Is Not Great, 72, 245, 248, 264
Godless: The Church of Liberalism, 232, 233, 234, 235, 238
God on Trial: Dispatches from America's Religious Battlefields, 274
God's Politics, 243, 251, 266, 273, 278
God's War: A New History of the Crusades, 279
Going after Cacciato, 29, 71
Going Up the River: Travels In a Prison Nation, 114, 124, 196, 216
Goldberg, Bernard, 97, 131, 233, 235, 236, 238, 239, 260, 267
Goldberg, Jonah, 235–36, 238, 240
Goldberger, Paul, 22–23, 25, 29
The Golden Spruce, 108, 132, 157
Goldstein, Donald, 137
Goldwater, Barry, 240
Goleman, Daniel, 120
Golway, Terry, 165
Gomorrah, 64, 144
Gone Bamboo, 162
Gonick, Larry, 112
Gonnerman, Jennifer, 35, 114, 124, 195–96, 210
Gonzalez-Crussi, F., 116
Goodall, Jane, 182
Goodell, Jeff, 112, 315
Good Germs, Bad Germs, 47–48, 115
The Good Life, 29

Goodnough, Abby, 12, 14, 126, 129, 177, 218
Good Rat, 59–60
Good to Great, 299, 306–7, 323, 325
Goodwin, Doris Kearns, 207
The Google Story, 290
Gopnik, Adam, 221
Go Put Your Strengths to Work, 323
Gordon, Michael, 32, 68, 69, 72, 90, 117, 250, 260, 269, 270, 280, 283
Gore, Al, 44, 117, 126, 130, 279, 280
Gorillas in the Mist, 22, 46
Gorney, Cynthia, 11, 30, 31
Gosling, Sam, 133
Gosnell, Mariana, 294
The Gospel of Judas, 31
The Gospel of Judas (Mawer), 31
Gourevitch, Philip, 38, 60, 62, 70, 93, 121, 134, 182, 196, 198
Gracefully Insane, 21
Graham, Katharine, 34, 88, 104, 278
Gralish, Tom, 10, 12, 52, 209, 217–18
The Grapes of Wrath, 171
The Gravedigger's Daughter, 78
Graves, Robert, 71
The Great Awakening, 243, 251
Great Books, 76
The Great Bridge, 7
The Great Deluge, 28, 33, 88, 218, 254, 267
The Great Derangement, 188
The Greatest Stories Never Told, 132
The Greatest Story Ever Sold, 28, 68, 88, 94, 250, 254, 256, 268, 283
The Great Improvisation, 261
The Great Influenza, 43, 45
The Great Transformation, 248
The Great Unraveling, 89, 252, 267, 312
Green, Jane, 177
Green, John, 129, 177
Greene, Graham, 22, 135, 144, 204, 232, 282
Greene, Melissa Fay, 128, 134, 136, 183, 196, 219, 222, 280
Greenhouse, Steven, 312–13
Green River, Running Red, 60
Greenspan, Alan, 89, 290, 317
Greenspan, Jay, 12, 153–54, 156, 166
Greider, William, 98, 249, 252, 266, 300, 305, 308, 312, 313, 314, 316
Griffin, John Howard, 180
Griffin, W. E. B., 66, 72, 212
Grippando, James, 311

Grisham, John, 30, 52, 62, 100, 145, 199, 274, 276
Groopman, Jerome, 11, 43, 97, 107, 108, 169
Gross, Daniel, 122, 237, 301
Gross, Terry, 76
Grossman, Elizabeth, 123
Group Genius: The Creative Power of Collaboration, 305, 322, 326
Growing Up Fast, 61, 211
Grub, 111
Gruen, Sara, 165
Guantánamo and the Abuse of Presidential Power, 35, 70, 92, 93, 94, 217, 254
Guerrilla Marketing, 325
Guests of the Ayatollah, 8, 30, 144, 269, 278
Gulag: A History, 114, 134, 142
The Gulag Archipelago, 134
Guns, Germs, and Steel, 300, 301, 305, 306, 314
Gun Show Nation, 117–18, 180
Gup, Ted, 90, 93, 115
Gusher of Lies, 117
Gutkind, Lee, 42–43, 167
Gutted, 302

Haddon, Mark, 224
Hafvenstein, Joel, 183
Hagstrom, Robert, 296
Hakakian, Roya, 269
Halberstam, David, 50, 53, 54, 55, 56, 57, 71, 90, 99, 197, 272, 273
Haley, Vince, 234–35
Half of a Yellow Sun, 198
Hallinan, Joseph, 114, 124, 196, 216
The Halo Effect, 322
Halper, Stefan, 251, 258, 261, 263, 270
Halpern, Jake, 12–13
Hamill, Pete, 51, 79, 176, 221
Hamilton, Lee H., 91
The Hammer, 94
Handler, Chelsea, 6
Handling Sin, 201
Hannity, Sean, 238, 260
The Happiest Man in the World, 200–201, 219
Happy Days Were Here Again, 232
Hard News, 34, 102, 104–5
Hard Sell, 97, 98, 107, 108
Hard Times, 39, 134
Hardwick, Elizabeth, 76
Harford, Tim, 291, 314

Harline, Craig, 220
Harney, Alexandra, 99, 313
Harr, Jonathan, 30, 31, 63, 99–100, 107, 128, 199, 209, 265, 274
Harris, Sam, 72, 245, 248, 264
Harrison, Jim, 55, 167, 212
Hart, Matthew, 31, 43, 104, 105, 135, 137, 216, 296
Hartmann, Thom, 247–48, 254
Hartocollis, Anemona, 12
Haruf, Kent, 55, 170, 195, 203, 212, 242
Harvard and the Unabomber, 198
Harwood, Gean, 31
Hass, Amira, 142, 184–85
Hatzfeld, Jean, 37–38, 91, 134, 135, 136, 137, 141, 143, 198, 222
Hawks, Tony, 7, 153, 157, 159
Hayden, Thomas, 73
Hayek, Friedrich von, 89, 237, 239, 317
Hayes, Stephen, 238, 250, 310
Haynes, John Earl, 236
Hays, Constance, 106, 309, 311
Hays, John, 259
Hays, Sharon, 120
Headley, Maria Dahvana, 153, 180
Healy, David, 96
Heaney, Seamus, 22
Heart, You Bully, You Punk, 152
The Heartless Stone, 43, 137
Heat, 16, 17, 20, 105, 158, 159, 162, 165, 169, 186, 293
Heath, Chip, 299, 306, 324–25
Heath, Dan, 299, 306, 324–25
Hedges, Chris, 31, 67, 70–71, 72, 91, 109, 186, 245, 248, 251
Hefez, Nir, 138
Hegemony or Survival, 142, 243–44
Heinrich, Bernd, 46
Heist!, 203
Heist: Superlobbyist Jack Abramoff, His Republican Allies, and the Buying of Washington, 94, 247, 253
Heller, Joseph, 186
Heller, Peter, 13
Hell or High Water, 13
Hell's Angels, 17, 174, 178, 179
Helping Me Help Myself, 155–56, 161
Helyar, John, 103, 311
Hemingway, Ernest, 55, 70, 80, 204
Hendrickson, Paul, 273
Henig, Robin Marantz, 116, 155, 205
Henshaw, John, 115

Here to Stay, 204
Herr, Michael, 29, 70, 71, 185, 186
Herriot, James, 20
Hersey, John, 69, 71, 134, 137, 140, 167, 184–85, 186, 204
Hersh, Seymour, 71, 91, 137, 139, 186, 264
Her Sister's Keeper, 45
Hertzfeld, Andy, 295
Hesser, Amanda, 294
Hessler, Peter, 302
Hetty: The Genius and Madness of America's First Female Tycoon, 294, 315
Hiaasen, Carl, 10, 80, 178
The Hidden Persuaders, 297
Higgins, Marguerite, 70
Higher: A Historic Race to the Sky and the Making of a City, 23
High Fidelity, 77
High Tech Trash, 123
Hightower, Jim, 246, 248–49, 253
Hillenbrand, Laura, 49, 50, 53, 54, 172, 218
Hiro, Dilip, 138, 262, 315
Hiroshima, 134, 137, 140, 184
Hirsch, James, 73
Hirshman, Linda, 39, 116
His Brother's Keeper, 205
His Holiness, 88
The History of the Standard Oil Company, 171
Hitchcock, Jane Stanton, 177
Hitchens, Christopher, 32, 71–72, 162, 245, 248, 256, 260, 264, 317
Hoagland, Edward, 303
Hochschild, Adam, 106, 134, 196
Hockenberry, John, 68, 205
Hodgman, John, 176, 244
Holden, Anthony, 166
Hold Everything Dear, 75, 272
Hold the Enlightenment, 159
Holland, Barbara, 75
Hollinghurst, Alan, 79
Holmes, Hannah, 19, 23, 26
Holthaus, Gary H., 38
Holtz, Lou, 197
Home: A Short History of an Idea, 26
Homecoming, 208
Home Cooking, 158
Home from Nowhere, 126
Homegrown Democrat, 242, 246, 252
A Home on the Field, 172, 173, 186
Home Town, 24, 26, 172, 173, 242
Homicide Special, 165

Honigsbaum, Mark, 181
Hons and Rebels, 104
Hope in Hell: Inside the World of Doctors without Borders, 66–67, 141
A Hope in the Unseen, 14, 35, 57, 125–26, 196, 206–7, 210, 215, 218
Horn, Stacy, 58, 61–62, 165, 168, 169
Hornby, Nick, 17, 77, 159, 224
Horne, Alistair, 268
Horne, Jed, 28, 68, 88, 213, 218
Horn of Africa, 29
Horowitz, Joy, 100, 107, 128, 206
Horse Heaven, 53
Horsemen of the Esophagus, 11–12, 19, 153, 158, 165, 220
Horwitz, Tony, 9, 19, 181
Hosseini, Khaled, 9, 67, 184, 185, 187, 212
The Hotel Alleluia, 196
The Hot Zone, 41, 45, 46, 205
House, 302
House: A Memoir, 302
The Housekeeping Book, 208
Housekeeping vs. the Dirt, 77
House Lights, 152
House Lust: America's Obsession with Our Homes, 302
The House of Mondavi, 20, 290
The House of Morgan, 295, 296
The House of the Spirits, 208
House of War, 139, 246
The House on Mango Street, 140, 173
Howarth, David, 66, 73, 187, 200
How Bush Rules, 89, 242–43, 246, 252, 279, 281
How Doctors Think, 11, 43, 107, 108, 169
How Israel Lost, 135, 262, 272, 279
How Reading Changed My Life, 76
How Soccer Explains the World, 172, 186
How Starbucks Saved My Life, 290
How the García Girls Lost Their Accents, 208
How the Good Guys Finally Won, 59–60
How the Other Half Lives, 171
How to Be Alone, 200
How to Get Rich, 327
How to Make Friends and Influence People, 321
How to Make Love Like a Porn Star, 6
How to Rig an Election, 275, 276
How to Tell When You're Tired, 18, 39, 165, 166, 169
How Tough Could It Be, 155
How Wal-Mart Is Destroying the World, 316

How We Choose, 16
How We Got Here, 44
Huberman, Jack, 253
*Hubris: The Inside Story of Spin, Scandal,
    and the Selling of the Iraq War*, 68,
    217, 243, 250, 254, 256, 268, 280
Huffington, Arianna, 239, 249, 271
Hugging the Shore, 79
Hughes, Karen, 281
Huler, Scott, 32
Human Cargo, 140–41
Human Touch, 118
Humes, Edward, 30, 58, 62–63, 126, 199,
    264–65, 274
The Hundred-Year Lie, 48, 101, 107, 109,
    111, 121–22, 265
*Hunting Fish: A Cross-Country Search for
    America's Worst Poker Players*, 12,
    153–54, 156, 166
Huntington, Samuel, 282
Hurley, Dan, 100–101, 115
Huxley, Aldous, 308
The Hypomanic Edge, 301

Iacocca, Lee, 263, 283, 326, 328
Iaconelli, Mike, 151
I Am America (And So Can You!), 98, 244,
    253
I Am a Pencil, 12, 14, 126, 129, 177, 211, 214
I Am Charlotte Simmons, 178
Ideas Matter, 246
I Don't Believe in Atheists, 248
I'd Rather Eat Chocolate, 178
*If Democrats Had Any Brains, They'd Be
    Republicans*, 233, 236, 238, 239
I Feel Bad about My Neck, 156, 246
If I Am Missing or Dead, 61
If I Did It, 61
*If the Gods Had Meant Us to Vote, They'd
    Have Given Us Candidates*, 249
If You Lived Here, I'd Know Your Name, 24,
    33, 50, 170, 173
Ignatieff, Michael, 71
I Had a Hammer, 55, 56
I Know You're Out There, 9
I Like You, 244
*The Illusion of Victory: America in World
    War I*, 282
I Loved You All, 64
Imhoff, Daniel, 265
I'm Looking Through You, 202, 205
Imperial Ambitions, 251

Imperial Grunts, 72, 73
Imperial Hubris, 282
Imperial Life in the Emerald City, 68–69, 70,
    187, 250, 264, 268
In An Instant, 73
In Cold Blood, 57, 64
An Inconvenient Book, 231–32, 238, 279, 280
An Inconvenient Truth, 44, 117, 126, 130,
    279, 280
In Defense of Food, 38, 105, 107, 110, 111,
    119, 127, 132, 174, 265, 287
Indefensible, 63
*In Denial: Historians, Communism, and
    Espionage*, 236
Independents Day, 248, 260, 262–63
*Inequality Matters: The Growing Economic
    Divide in America and Its Poisonous
    Consequences*, 314
In Fact: The Best of Creative Nonfiction, 42
Infidel, 9
Ingraham, Laura, 232, 233, 234, 236, 237,
    240, 259
Inherited Risk, 71
In My Father's Name, 62, 65, 100
An Innocent, a Broad, 155
In Our Hearts We Were Giants, 198
In Pharaoh's Army, 71
In Retrospect, 273
In Sam We Trust, 106, 289, 295, 311, 316
In Search of Anti-Semitism, 232
In Search of King Solomon's Mines, 22
In Search of Our Mothers' Gardens, 247
In Service to the Horse, 20
Inside Hamas, 135
Inside Rikers, 63, 114, 124, 196, 216
Inside the Bush White House, 69
Inside the Red Zone, 217
Inside the Resistance, 135
Inside the Sky, 214, 294
In Spite of the Gods, 99, 302, 303, 305
In Suspect Terrain, 167
In the Lake of the Woods, 63
In the Shadow of No Towers, 29, 169, 200
In the Time of the Butterflies, 140, 173, 208
In the Wilderness, 64, 152
In the Words of Our Enemies, 259
In These Girls, Hope Is a Muscle, 50
Into the Heart of Borneo, 67
Into the Valley, 184–85, 186
Into the Wild, 64, 132, 157, 159, 195, 201,
    202, 212
Into Thin Air, 64, 132, 202, 287

The Invisible Cure, 136
IQ: A Smart History of a Failed Idea, 131
The Iran Agenda, 268
The Iranian Labyrinth, 138
Iraq Confidential, 268
The Irish Game, 31, 43, 216
Iron John, 203
Irons, Peter H., 274
Irrational Exuberance, 301
Irving, John, 9, 15, 17, 45, 55, 178
Isaac's Storm, 28, 32, 33, 88, 218
Isak Dinesen: The Life of a Storyteller, 200
Ishiguro, Kazuo, 78, 188
Isikoff, Michael, 68, 69, 109, 217, 243, 250,
    254, 256, 268, 280
Issenberg, Sasha, 16, 290, 301, 313–14, 315,
    318
I Thought My Father Was God, 76
It's Getting Ugly Out There, 88, 93, 235, 242,
    248, 249, 253, 260, 263, 282
It's Not about the Bike, 49, 197
It's Not about the Coffee, 290
It's Not News, It's Fark, 97–98, 101, 102,
    104, 142
It Takes a Village Idiot, 174
Ivins, Molly, 93, 243, 244, 245, 246, 249, 253
Iyengar, Sheena, 16
Iyer, Pico, 133, 223, 310

Jack: Straight from the Gut, 326, 327
Jackie Robinson, 55
Jackson, Wes, 38, 259
Jacobs, A. J., 13, 44, 49, 76, 132, 154, 156,
    159, 160, 188
Jacobs, Jane, 24, 300
Jacob's Ladder, 127
Jacoby, Susan, 96
Jadick, Richard, 73
Jager-Hyman, Joie, 218–19
Jakes, T. D., 291
Jamail, Dahr, 187
Jameson, Jenna, 6
Jamison, Kay Redfield, 96, 120
Janjigian, Vahan, 296
Jansen, Hanna, 196
Jarhead, 73
Jaspin, Elliot, 124
*Javatrekker: Dispatches from the World of Fair
    Trade Coffee*, 310, 318
Jayber Crow, 24, 108, 213, 242, 259
Jencks, Christopher, 314
Jenkins, Jerry, 235

Jennifer Government, 87, 115, 306
Jerusalem, 34
Jessop, Carolyn, 64
Jesus Freaks, 61
Jewett, Sarah Orne, 75
Jim Cramer's Mad Money, 304
Jim Cramer's Real Money, 304
Joe College, 219
Joe Gould's Secret, 200
Joe Wilson and the Creation of Xerox, 293,
    296
John, Daymond, 291–92, 296
Johnson, Chalmers, 71, 109, 139, 142, 244,
    246, 250–51, 282
Johnson, Chris, 185
Johnson, Denis, 71
Johnson, Richard, 311
Johnson, Spencer, 322–23, 327
Johnson, Steven, 42, 48
Johnston, David Cay, 309, 314
Join Me!, 153, 159
Jonas, George, 8, 135, 138, 184
Jones, Ann Rosalind, 185
Jones, Chris, 205, 214
Jordan, E. Vernon, 35
Jordan, Pete, 37, 166
Jordan Can Read!, 35
Jorgensen, Christine, 205
Joshi, S. T., 251
The Journalist and the Murderer, 199
Journey beyond Selene, 46, 214
Journey from the Land of No, 269
Journey without Maps, 22, 135
Joyce Carol Oates: Conversations, 78
The Joy of Drinking, 75
Jpod, 161
Juiced, 52, 99
Juicing the Game, 52
Julie and Julia, 158, 163
Junger, Sebastian, 13, 28, 32, 65, 202, 204,
    218
The Jungle, 110, 171
Junk Science, 101, 114–15
Just, Ward, 198
Justice: Crimes, Trials, and Punishments, 61,
    168, 174

Kabul Beauty School, 9
Kabul in Winter, 185
Kagan, Robert, 270, 275, 305
Kamenetz, Anya, 122, 130, 262, 309, 316,
    318, 319

Kamp, David, 13–14
Kanigel, Robert, 46, 274
Kanner, Bernice, 101, 102
Kaplan, Robert M., 72, 73, 183
Kapuscinski, Ryszard, 198
Karmin, Craig, 292
Karnow, Stanley, 29, 273
Kasser, Rodolphe, 31
Katzen, Mollie, 14
Kaufman-Lacusta, Maxine, 183–84
Kaysen, Susanna, 21
Kean, Thomas H., 91
Keefe, Patrick Radden, 90, 115, 139
Keegan, William, 270
Keen, Andrew, 298, 306
Keillor, Garrison, 242, 246, 252
Kellerman, Jonathan, 58, 168
Kelton, Elmer, 195, 212
Kennedy, Edward, 243, 280
Kennedy, Michelle, 164
Kennedy, Pagan, 46–47, 180, 202, 204–5, 219
Kennedy, Randy, 23–24
Kerouac, Jack, 159, 175, 201
Kessler, Andy, 43–44, 97, 108, 122
Kessler, Ronald, 61, 122, 173–74
Key, Joshua, 256
Keynes, John Maynard, 317
Khadra, Yasmina, 185
Khomeini: Life of the Ayatollah, 269
The Kid: What Happened after My Boyfriend and I Decided to Get Pregnant, 155
Kidd, Sue Monk, 185
Kidder, Tracy, 7, 12, 14, 15, 17, 24, 26, 35, 42, 57, 63, 67, 121, 125, 129, 136, 171, 172, 173, 182, 196, 207, 208, 209, 210, 211, 214, 218, 219, 220, 242, 280, 292, 293, 295, 302, 322
Kilbourne, Jean, 125, 132, 180, 319
Killed: Great Journalism Too Hot to Print, 112
Killed Cartoons, 111–12
Killing Pablo, 59
Kimmel, Haven, 152
The Kingdom, 138
The Kingdom and the Power, 33–34, 104
King Leopold's Ghost, 106, 134, 196
The King of California, 294
King of the Cowboys, 212
King of the World, 49
The Kings of New York, 19, 129, 153, 156, 166, 213–14

Kingsolver, Barbara, 16, 18, 41, 107, 111, 130, 152, 174, 180, 196, 224, 303
Kinsella, Sophie, 177, 297
Kinsella, W. P., 51, 55
Kipnis, Laura, 104, 180, 247
Kirk, Donald, 71, 73, 90, 185
Kitchen Confidential, 18, 162, 168, 169–70, 216, 293
The Kite Runner, 67, 184, 185, 187
Kiyosaki, Robert, 327, 328
Klaffke, Pamela, 297, 320
Klaidman, Stephen, 52, 96, 102, 107, 111, 204
Klare, Michael, 117, 135, 251
Klein, Naomi, 48, 89, 93, 96, 98, 109, 125, 133, 141, 144, 180, 244, 247, 248, 250, 256, 304, 308, 312, 316
Klinenberg, Eric, 97–98, 101, 102
Klosterman, Chuck, 13, 17, 77, 79, 153, 154, 159, 174, 177, 222
Klucas, Gillian, 100, 128, 265
Kluger, Jeffrey, 46, 214
Kluger, Richard, 103, 108, 119, 125
Kluger, Steve, 55
Knipfel, Jim, 10, 77, 104, 153, 156, 162, 176, 178, 205
The Know-It-All, 76, 154, 159
Knowledge and Decisions, 239
Koch, Doro Bush, 233
Koehler, Steven, 62
Koeppel, Dan, 16
Kohl, Beth, 116, 154–55
Kolbert, Elizabeth, 44, 46, 115, 221
Koontz, Dean, 131
Kopelman, Jay, 73
Kotlowitz, Alex, 14, 25, 35, 59, 62, 63, 121, 125–26, 164, 196, 207, 209, 210, 211, 220
Kozol, Jonathan, 14, 63, 120, 125, 126, 129, 164, 169, 196, 207, 209, 210, 214, 220
Krakauer, Jon, 50, 63–64, 132, 157, 159, 195, 201, 202, 212, 287
Kramer, Jane, 109, 177, 195, 203, 212
Kramer, Jerry, 56, 197–98
Krantz, Judith, 61, 174
Kraus, Harry Lee, 111
Kriegel, Mark, 50–51, 52, 54, 57, 197, 206, 214
Kristol, Bill, 237, 310
Krosney, Herbert, 30–31, 216
Krugman, Paul, 89, 242, 249, 251–52, 267, 304, 308, 312

The K Street Gang, 94
Kunstler, James Howard, 23, 26, 117, 121, 126–27, 138, 265, 300, 315
Kupelian, David, 236
Kurlansky, Mark, 16, 26, 34, 41, 105, 266, 292, 295, 314
Kurson, Robert, 27, 32, 45, 154, 205, 287
Kurzweil, Ray, 17, 42, 118, 128, 306
Kutler, Stanley, 245
Kuttner, Robert, 252, 265–66, 270, 314
Kynge, James, 99, 300, 302

LaBastille, Anne, 195
Lacey, Robert, 138, 288, 309, 311
Lacy, Sarah, 292
Laderman, Gary, 47
LaHaye, Tim, 235
Lakoff, George, 243, 256, 266, 273, 276, 300
Lamb: The Gospel According to Biff, 322, 327
Lambrecht, Bill, 127
Lamott, Anne, 152
Lane, Anthony, 77
Langewiesche, William, 8, 13, 16, 17, 23, 24–25, 29, 32, 33, 38, 43, 45, 59, 65, 67, 69, 70, 72, 91, 96, 108, 109, 117, 129, 139–40, 141, 155, 169, 173, 207, 214, 252, 258, 270, 278, 294, 315
Lansky, Doug, 157
Lapdogs: How the Press Rolled Over for Bush, 271
Lapham, Lewis, 31, 252, 255
Lappé, Anna, 38, 105, 107, 111, 119
Lappé, Frances Moore, 14, 38, 105, 107, 111, 119, 122, 294
Lardner, James, 314
Lardner, Ring, 49
Larner, Jesse, 238
LaRose, Lawrence, 302
Larson, Edward, 265, 274
Larson, Erik, 28, 32, 33, 88, 218, 301
Lasch, Christopher, 48, 71, 98, 304, 317, 319
Laskas, Jeanne Marie, 174
The Last American Man, 11, 56, 132, 157, 159, 175, 177, 195, 197–98, 200–201, 203, 212
The Last Best League, 55, 99
The Last Cowboy, 195, 203, 212
Last Dance, 52, 53, 54, 157
Last Days of Summer, 55
Last Harvest, 25–26
The Last King of Scotland, 155, 196

The Last Run, 13
The Last Season, 132, 195, 202–3, 212
Last Shot: A Final Four Mystery, 53
Last Shot (Frey), 54, 57, 206, 213
The Last True Story I'll Ever Tell, 68
Lattin, Don, 61
Latus, Janine, 61
Lawrence, Bruce, 317
Lawson, Mary, 224
Lax, Eric, 45
Leadership and the One Minute Manager, 323
Lead Us into Temptation, 125, 133, 297
Leadville, 100, 128, 265
Learning to Eat Soup with a Knife, 268
Leary, Ann, 155
LeBlanc, Adrian Nicole, 35, 61, 63, 120, 121, 124, 126, 164, 196, 201, 209, 210, 211, 219
Le Carré, John, 131
LeDuff, Charlie, 13, 24, 153, 174–75, 179, 222
Lee, Jennifer 8, 15–16
Legacy: Paying the Price for the Clinton Years, 240
Legacy of Ashes, 89, 131, 140, 276
The Legend of Colton H. Bryant, 194–95
Lelchuk, Alan, 55
The Lemon Tree, 34, 135, 261, 279
Lencioni, Patrick, 323, 327–28
Lende, Heather, 24, 33, 50, 170, 173
Lenin's Tomb, 142, 264
Leonard, John, 77
Leopold, Aldo, 108, 259
Lerner, Barron, 11, 30, 119
Lescroart, John, 62
Lessig, Lawrence, 17, 74, 299, 306
Let Freedom Ring, 238
Let's Stop Beating around the Bush, 246
Letters to a Christian Nation, 245, 264
Letters to a Young Contrarian, 256
Letters to a Young Patriot, 109
Letters to a Young Teacher, 14
Let Them Eat Prozac, 96
Let Us Now Praise Famous Men, 40, 159, 170–71, 248
Leveridge, Brett, 153
Levine, Judith, 48, 125, 156, 180, 303
Levine, Mark, 28, 31, 33, 88, 218
Levine, Steve, 268
Levinson, Jay Conrad, 325
Levison, Iain, 37, 166

Levitt, Steven, 101, 123, 283, 294, 299, 301,
    306, 307, 314
Lewan, Todd, 13
Lewis, Bernard, 237
Lewis, Michael, 25, 49, 50, 52, 54–55, 56,
    99, 122, 157, 160, 196, 197, 205–6,
    207, 213, 290, 292, 294, 299, 315
The Lexus and the Olive Tree, 30, 237, 301,
    303, 314, 317
Liar's Poker, 52, 55, 122, 290, 292, 294, 315
Liberal Fascism, 235–36, 238, 240
Liberalism Is a Mental Disorder, 238
Lieb, Fred, 56
Liebling, A. J., 50, 176
Lies and the Lying Liars Who Tell Them, 247
Lieve, Joris, 198
The Life and Times of the Last Kid Picked, 220
The Life and Times of the Thunderbolt Kid,
    220
Life Laid Bare, 38, 91, 135, 136, 141, 143,
    198, 222
Life on the Line, 92
Life on the Outside, 35, 114, 124, 195–96, 210
Life So Far, 278
Life Stories, 176
Life's Work, 155
Lightman, Alan, 46
Like Water for Chocolate, 173, 208
Limbaugh, Rush, 233
Lindsey, Brink, 274
Linzmayer, Owen, 295
Lipper, Joanna, 61, 211
Lipsky, David, 211–12, 218
Lisick, Beth, 155–56, 161
Liss, David, 328
Littleton, Cynthia, 102
The Living and the Dead, 273
Living Blue in the Red States, 254–55, 266
Living History, 243, 277, 278, 280
*Living It Up: America's Love Affair with
    Luxury*, 274, 289, 296, 308, 310, 319,
    324
Living on the Black, 53
The Lizard King, 16
Lloyd, John, 132
Loewen, James, 112
Logan, Ben, 38
Logan, William, 157
Lohr, Steve, 17
*Lone Patriot: The Short Career of an
    American Militiaman*, 177, 195,
    197–98

Lonesome Rangers, 77
Lone Survivor, 72, 73, 211
The Long Emergency, 26, 117, 121, 126–27,
    138, 315
The Long-Legged House, 18, 127, 180
The Long Road Home, 72, 73
A Long Short War, 32
The Long Tail, 17, 101, 166, 290, 298, 299,
    301, 304, 305, 306, 322, 324, 325, 326
A Long Way Gone, 38, 136, 137, 141, 155,
    182, 196, 198, 218
Longworth, Richard C., 266, 319
Looking for Alaska, 129, 177
The Looming Tower, 65, 67, 70, 89, 91, 109,
    188, 256, 260, 264, 269–70
Lopate, Phillip, 24, 221, 222
The Lord God Made Them All, 20
Losing Moses on the Freeway, 248
The Lost Gospel, 30–31, 216
The Lost Heart of Asia, 282
Lost in America, 169
Lost Mountain, 107–8, 132
The Lost Painting, 31, 100
Lott, John R., 236–37
Love, Dennis, 100, 108, 127–28
Love, Poverty, and War, 71–72
Love in the Driest Season, 196
Lovenheim, Peter, 110
Lowell, Robert, 175
Lowenstein, Roger, 122, 290
Lowry, Rich, 240
Luce, Edward, 99, 302, 303, 305
The Lucifer Effect, 92, 94
Ludlum, Robert, 50, 131, 139, 140
Lukas, J. Anthony, 140, 219–20
Luntz, Frank, 276
Lupica, Mike, 52
Lust, 178
Lutes, Jason, 257
Luttrell, Marcus, 72, 73, 211

M, 186
Maas, Peter, 59, 60, 64
MacArthur, John, 92
Machete Season, 37–38, 91, 134, 135, 136,
    137, 141, 143, 198, 222
Mack, William P., 66
Maclean, Norman, 51
Macmillan, Margaret, 33, 261
Madam Secretary, 278
Made to Break, 48, 123, 130
Made to Stick, 299, 306, 324–25

Madigan, Charles, 104
Madonna, Paul, 112
Maggie Darling, 126
Magnificent Corpses, 221
Mailer, Norman, 29, 60, 64, 175, 179, 214, 216
Makers and Takers: How Conservatives Do All the Work while Liberals Whine and Complain, 238
The Making of a Chef, 7, 51, 105, 158, 162, 169–70, 289
The Making of a Country Lawyer, 254
The Making of the Atomic Bomb, 45, 46, 140
The Making of the President, 272
Malan, Rian, 63
Malcolm, Janet, 198–99
Malkin, Michelle, 131, 235, 236, 238
Malone, Michael, 201, 292, 293, 295
Malseed, Mark, 290
Managing by Values, 323
Mandela, Mobutu, and Me, 144
The Man-Eaters of Eden, 22, 151
The Man-Eaters of Tsavo, 151
Manguel, Alberto, 74
Manhattan Passions, 173, 220–21
Mankoff, Robert, 112
Mann, Brian, 266
Manning, Richard, 123
A Man on the Moon, 214
Manufacturing Consent, 244
The Man Who Mistook His Wife for a Hat, 45
The Man Who Pushed America to War, 144
Man without a Country, 255
Many Sleepless Nights, 42–43
Maraniss, David, 29, 55, 197, 278
Marcus, James, 98, 295
Margolin, Phillip, 30, 62, 80, 100, 274, 276
Margonelli, Lisa, 100, 112, 117, 121, 127, 138, 315, 318
Margulies, Joseph, 35, 70, 92, 93, 94, 217, 254
Marketing Luxury to the Masses, 296–97
The Marketing of Evil, 236
Marks, Stephen, 92–93
Maron, Margaret, 58
Márquez, Gabriel García, 79
Martin, Lee, 255
Martinez, Ruben, 59, 92, 117, 140, 141, 169, 173
Marx's Das Kapital: A Biography, 317
Mason, Bill, 154
Masson, Jeffrey Moussaieff, 182

Masters, Edgar Lee, 213
Masters of Chaos, 89, 140, 211–12
A Match Made in Heaven, 30, 260–61, 262
Matthiessen, Peter, 46, 151, 182
Maus, 143
Mawer, Simon, 31
Maxed Out: Hard Times, Easy Credit and the Era of Predatory Lenders, 318
Maximum City, 142
Maxwell, John C., 323, 327, 328
Mayer, Jane, 93
Mayes, Frances, 75
Mayle, Peter, 75, 290
McBride, James, 37, 126, 202, 212, 219, 291–92
McCall Smith, Alexander, 151
McCarthy, Cormac, 212
McCarthy, Mary, 76, 104, 154
McCarthy, Michael, 43, 44–45, 205, 206
McChesney, Robert, 98
McClellan, Scott, 280–81
McCourt, Frank, 12, 177
McCoy, Alfred, 70, 92, 244, 251
McCullers, Carson, 78
McCullough, Colleen, 284
McCullough, David, 7, 33
McCumber, David, 163
McFarland, Keith, 323
McGann, Eileen, 93, 234, 266–67
McGinn, Daniel, 302
McGinniss, Joe, 61, 64, 157, 172, 185–86, 199, 272, 273
McGuane, Thomas, 55
McIlhenny's Gold, 124, 290, 295–96
McInerney, Jay, 29, 170
McIntyre, Liz, 90, 115, 139
McKibben, Bill, 13, 18, 44, 46, 96, 108, 111, 121, 127, 130, 174, 202, 259, 300, 302–3, 310, 316
McLean, Bethany, 141
McManus, James, 12, 154, 156, 166
McMasters, Kelly, 119, 128
McMillan, Terry, 216
McMurtry, Larry, 212
McNamara, Robert, 273
McNamee, Thomas, 14, 290, 293–94, 314, 325
McPhee, John, 9, 16, 25, 26, 51, 117, 155, 166–67, 315
McPherson, Edward, 154, 156, 166
McQuaid, John, 28
Meacham, Jon, 207

Mead, Rebecca, 14, 103–4, 132, 176
Me against My Brother, 182
Mean Justice, 62
Means of Escape, 29
The Measure of a Man, 215
A Measure of Endurance, 30, 45, 100, 128, 195, 201, 204, 205, 206, 218
The Measure of Her Powers, 294
Meatball Sundae, 324
The Meat You Eat, 110
Mehta, Suketu, 142
Meir, Golda, 138
Mellon, 288, 295
Meltzer, Brad, 279, 284
Memories of a Catholic Girlhood, 154
Menand, Louis, 200
Men at Work, 240
Men My Mother Dated, 153
The Men Who Stare at Goats, 13, 35, 92, 93, 94, 131, 139, 177, 188, 197
Merchant of Death, 137
Meredith, Robyn, 259, 300, 302, 303, 318
Me Talk Pretty One Day, 156, 176
Meyer, Danny, 325
Meyers, Jeffrey, 71
Mezrich, Ben, 50, 93, 154, 156, 166, 199, 294
Michel, Lou, 198
Michelli, Joseph, 325
Micklethwait, John, 263, 292
Microcosm: E. Coli and the New Science of Life, 47
Microserfs, 95, 161, 292, 295, 309
Microtrends: The Small Forces behind Tomorrow's Big Changes, 118, 298, 299, 303–4
Midkiff, Ken, 110
Midnight in the Garden of Good and Evil, 61, 65, 199, 202, 209
Midwives, 45
The Mighty and the Almighty, 261, 277–78, 280
Miles Gone By, 232
Miller, Aaron David, 268
Miller, Judith, 8–9, 41–42, 45, 69, 187, 258
Miller, Mark Crispin, 255
Miller, Sue, 224
Millet, Catherine, 6
Mills, Kay, 278
Mills, Magnus, 104, 178, 221
Mind of the Raven, 46
Miracle at Sing Sing, 114, 163, 216

A Miracle, a Universe, 35
The Miracle of Castel di Sangro, 157, 172, 185–86
The Miracle of St. Anthony, 54, 56–57
Mirrors of the Unseen: Journeys in Iran, 67
Misconceptions, 256
Mishler, William, 30, 45, 100, 128, 195, 201, 204, 205, 206, 218
Misquoting Jesus, 31, 248
The Missing Class: Portraits of the Near Poor in America, 119, 120, 130, 242, 309, 312, 316, 318, 320
Mission Unaccomplished, 246
Mississippi Mud, 62
Misunderestimated, 234, 238
Mitchell, Brian Patrick, 273, 274–75
Mitchell, Joseph, 10, 16, 50, 78, 175–76, 200, 204, 221, 222
Mitchell, Stacy, 102, 106, 316
Mitford, Jessica, 10, 44, 47, 103, 104, 116, 125, 221
Mittelbach, Margaret, 151, 182
Mnookin, Seth, 34, 51, 55, 56, 99, 102, 104–5, 160
Moats, David, 31–32
Moehringer, J. R., 153
Moin, Baqer, 269
Moir, John S., 45–46
The Mold in Dr. Florey's Coat, 45
Molly Ivins Can't Say That, Can She?, 246, 249, 253
The Mommy Myth, 39
Mommy Wars, 155
The Mommy Wars, 116
Mom's Cancer, 45, 100, 119
Moneyball, 50, 52, 54–55, 56, 99, 160, 206, 299, 315
Money for Nothing, 203
Monkey Girl: Evolution, Education, Religion, and the Battle for America's Soul, 62, 264–65, 274
Monster of God, 22, 182
Montana 1948, 195
Montville, Leigh, 55
Mooney, Chris, 115
Moore, Christopher, 322, 327
Moore, Michael, 98, 244, 247, 252, 308, 318
Moore, Tim, 167
Moorehead, Caroline, 70, 140–41
More Guns, Less Crime, 237
Morrell, David, 90
Morrill, Donald, 255

Morris, Dick, 93, 233, 236, 266–67
Morris, Errol, 70
Morris, Robert, 42, 48, 127
Mortenson, Greg, 67, 185, 222, 278
Mosley, Walter, 60, 188, 215–16
The Most of A. J. Liebling, 176
Mother of Storms, 28, 33
Mountains Beyond Mountains, 14, 15, 67, 136, 182, 196, 219, 280
Moving Violations, 68, 205
Mowat, Farley, 13, 22, 46, 132, 151, 182
Moyers, Bill, 266, 272, 314
Moyers, William Cope, 96
Mozart's Brain and the Fighter Pilot, 128
Mr. Personality, 222
Mr. Wilson's Cabinet of Wonders, 223
Ms. Moffett's First Year, 12, 14, 126, 129, 177, 218
The Much Too Promised Land, 268
Muir, John, 159
Mullen, Jim, 174
Mumford, Lewis, 24, 209
The Mummy Congress, 47
Munro, Alice, 79
Murdoch, Stephen, 131
Murphy, Austin, 155
Murphy, Robert, 237
Murray, Alan, 322, 325–26
Murray, Craig, 94, 183, 184, 281–82
Murray, Ty, 212
Museum: Behind the Scenes at the Metropolitan Museum of Art, 216
Muzzled: From T-Ball to Terrorism, 233, 238, 239
My City Was Gone, 100, 108, 127–28
My Detachment, 15
Myers, Dee Dee, 281
My Father, My President, 233
My Grandfather's Son, 234, 238, 274
My Horizontal Life, 6
My Kind of Place, 199
My-Lai 4, 71, 137, 186
My Life, 138
My Life (Clinton), 243, 277, 278, 280, 291
My Life in France, 162, 170, 290
My Love Affair with America, 237
My Own Country, 11
The Myth of Solid Ground, 32, 33, 167
Mythologies, 75
Myths, Lies, and Downright Stupidity, 130, 232, 233, 236, 239, 263
My Traitor's Heart, 63

Nabokov, Vladimir, 74
Nadelson, Theodore, 91
Nafisi, Azar, 9, 34, 185, 187, 222, 269
Nagl, John, 268
Naipaul, V. S., 198
The Naked and the Dead, 175
The Naked Brain, 128
Naked Pictures of Famous People, 244
Namath, 51, 52, 54, 57, 197, 206, 214
Nance, John, 49
Nasaw, David, 288, 295
The Nasty Bits, 162
Nation of Secrets, 90, 93, 115
Natural Causes, 100–101, 115
Nearer, My God to Thee, 232
Negev, Eilet, 198
Nemesis: The Last Days of the American Republic, 250–51
Nestle, Marion, 14, 38, 105, 107, 111, 119, 122, 265, 294
Netz, Reviel, 31, 216
Neuromancer, 115
Never Cry Wolf, 13, 22, 46, 151
The New American Militarism, 246, 250, 282
The New American Story, 280
Newby, Eric, 133, 159
The New Dealers War, 282
Newhouse, John, 15, 293, 294
Newjack: Guarding Sing Sing, 37, 43, 49, 57, 114, 124, 163, 165, 176–77, 188, 196
Newman, Katherine, 119, 120, 130, 242, 309, 312, 316, 318, 320
The New Media Monopoly, 97, 142
New Orleans, Mon Amour, 28, 88, 218
News Flash, 98
Next Man Up, 19, 53
Neyer, Rob, 55
Nicholas, Lynn H., 216
Nickel and Dimed, 37, 120, 126, 130, 156, 161, 164, 165, 166, 169, 176, 179, 188, 196, 209, 220, 242, 246, 261, 266, 316, 318
Night, 91, 143
Night Chills, 131
Night Draws Near, 32, 68, 187, 217, 264, 268
The Nightmare Chronicles, 131
9 Highland Road, 20–21, 209
The Nine: Inside the Secret World of the Supreme Court, 31, 104–5, 274, 275–76
Nine Parts of Desire, 8–9, 67, 69, 186
1984, 87

1968, 34
Nixon and Kissinger, 261, 291
Nixon and Mao, 33, 261
Nixonland, 88
The No Asshole Rule: Building a Civilized Workplace and Surviving One That Isn't, 326–27
Noble Rot: A Bordeaux Wine Revolution, 20, 290
Nobodies, 18, 37, 38, 92, 94, 99, 106, 109, 112, 116–17, 137, 140, 141, 144, 169, 171, 173, 304, 308, 310, 313, 314, 318
Nobody's Fool, 121, 219
Nobody's Home, 43, 102, 108
Nobody's Perfect, 77
Noel, William, 31, 216
No Excuses, 197
No God but God, 188, 282
Nolan, Stephanie, 136
Nollman, Jim, 18, 23
No Logo, 48, 109, 125, 133, 180, 308, 312, 316
No Matter How Loud I Shout, 30, 58, 62–63, 126, 199
Noonan, Peggy, 235
The Noonday Demon, 96
No Reservations, 314
Normal, 204, 205
Not Buying It, 48, 125, 156, 180, 303
Nothing but Blue Skies, 55
Nothing Like It in the World, 301
Nothing Sacred, 244
Nothing to Be Frightened Of, 264
Not-Knowing, 200
Not Much Just Chillin', 171
Not Remotely Controlled, 79
No True Glory, 72
Not That You Asked, 7, 77
Novak, Robert, 250, 260
Now, Discover Your Strengths, 323
Nuclear Power Is Not the Answer, 96, 108
Nuclear Terrorism, 258
Nuland, Sherwin, 48, 111, 116, 169
Nusser, Susan, 20

Oak: The Frame of Civilization, 157
Oates, Joyce Carol, 76, 77–78, 79
Obama, Barack, 243, 279, 280
Obliviously On He Sails, 327
O'Brien, Tim, 29, 63, 71, 188–89, 273
Occidentalism, 67

The Occupation: War and Resistance in Iraq, 69, 187, 217
O'Connor, Flannery, 204
October 1964, 53
Odd Jobs, 79
O'Donnell, Patrick, 72–73
Off, Carol, 105–6
Off Ramp, 19, 153, 174, 266
Off the Books, 35
Of Paradise and Power, 270, 275, 305
Ogilvy, David, 297
O'Hanlon, Redmond, 67
The OId Patagonian Express, 16
The Oil and the Glory, 268
Oil on the Brain, 100, 112, 117, 121, 127, 138, 315, 318
Olbermann, Keith, 249, 252, 253, 254
The Oldest Gay Couple in America, 31
The Old Patagonian Express, 159, 310
Olsen, Jack, 64
Olshaker, Mark, 65
The Omnivore's Dilemma, 18, 38, 41, 107, 109, 110, 111, 130, 174, 265, 287
On Being Born, 116
On Call in Hell, 73
Once Upon a Quinceañara, 208
Once You're Lucky, Twice You're Good, 292
Ondaatje, Michael, 79, 151, 155
The One Best Way, 274
One Drop: My Father's Hidden Life, 202
One Great Game, 206, 213
100 Bullshit Jobs, 322, 327
100 People Who Are Screwing Up America, 233, 235, 236, 238
101 People Who Are Really Screwing Up America, 253
100 Ways America Is Screwing Up the World, 255
102 Minutes: The Untold Story of the Fight to Survive inside the Twin Towers, 25, 29, 33, 169
One Man's America, 239–40
One Man's Meat, 176
One Man's Wilderness, 195
One Market under God, 130, 248, 252, 262, 274, 312
The One Minute Manager, 322–23
The One-Percent Doctrine, 89, 90, 243, 250, 267, 268, 269, 270, 280, 283
One Perfect Day: The Selling of the American Wedding, 14, 103–4, 132, 176

One World, Ready or Not: The Manic Logic of Global Capitalism, 266, 312, 313, 316
Oney, Steve, 124
On Neoliberalism, 244
On Paradise Drive, 122, 232, 262, 266, 274, 297, 302, 310
On Photography, 200
On Power and Prospects, 244
On the Brink, 280
On the Road, 159, 201
On the Road to Kandahar, 67
On the Water: Discovering America in a Rowboat, 51
On the Wealth of Nations, 237, 317
On Travel, 75
Open: Inside the Ropes at Bethpage Black, 54
An Open Book, 76
Opening Day, 51, 56, 197, 215
Open Net, 167
Open Society, 282
Opium Season, 183
Opting Out?, 38–39, 116, 155
Oracle Bones, 302
The Orchid Thief, 12, 18, 151, 199, 220
An Ordinary Person's Guide to Empire, 247
O'Reilly, Bill, 131, 232, 233, 234, 238, 239, 260
Orenstein, Peggy, 39
Orientalism, 142
Orlean, Susan, 12, 18, 56, 78, 151, 173, 199, 220, 222
Orman, Suze, 328
O'Rourke, P. J., 237, 310, 317
Ortega, Bob, 106, 289, 295, 311, 316
Orwell, George, 87, 308
Osborne, Lawrence, 20, 290
Oshinsky, David, 43, 111
Osteen, Joel, 235, 324
Other People's Dirt, 164
Other People's Money, 315
The Other Side of the River, 59, 62, 63, 126, 196, 209
Other Voices, Other Rooms, 75
Otherwise Normal People, 17–18, 19
Ottaviani, Jim, 140
Our Daily Meds, 97, 107, 119, 132
The Outlaw Sea, 8, 13, 17, 25, 43, 108, 315
Out of My League, 53, 54, 167
Outrage, 93, 233, 234, 236, 266–67
An Outside Chance: Classic & New Essays on Sport, 55
The Overachievers, 128–29, 171, 176, 211, 214

Over a Thousand Hills I Walk with You, 196
Overbye, Dennis, 46
Overdrive, 232
The Overspent American, 48, 125, 133, 180, 308, 312, 316, 319
Over the Edge of the World, 25
Overtreated, 97, 107
Owen, Wilfred, 71
Ozeki, Ruth, 145
Ozick, Cynthia, 78

Packard, Vance, 297
Packer, George, 8, 32, 34, 68, 69, 90, 109, 135, 155, 187, 250, 254, 260, 264, 266, 268, 269, 273, 283
Pagels, Elaine, 31
Paglia, Camille, 180
Paisner, Daniel, 291–92
Palahniuk, Chuck, 61, 145
Palast, Greg, 141, 248, 249, 253, 255, 308
Palestine, 200
Palestine: Peace Not Apartheid, 135, 183, 262, 278, 279
Palmer, Michael, 102, 145
Pamuk, Orhan, 79
Pandora's Baby, 116, 155, 205
Panic: The Story of Modern Financial Insanity, 315
The Paperboy, 8, 203
Paper Lion, 19, 50, 52, 53, 54, 167
Paper Trails, 8, 10, 17, 52, 203
The Paradox of Choice, 120
Parasite Rex, 47
Paretsky, Sara, 247
Paris Trout, 8, 10, 203
Park, Robert, 60
Parsell, T. J., 114
The Partly Cloudy Patriot, 105, 176
Parts Per Million, 100, 107, 128, 206
Party of One: A Loner's Manifesto, 221
Passage to Juneau, 132
Path of Destruction, 28
Pattern Recognition, 139
Patterson, James, 168
Patterson, John Henry, 151
Patterson, Richard North, 284
Paul, Ron, 282
Paula, 152
Pawlick, Thomas, 41, 105, 106–7, 111, 119, 122, 127, 132, 265, 318
A Peace to End All Peace, 279
Peale, Norman Vincent, 323, 327

Pearce, Fred, 123, 318
Peck, Dale, 79
Peninsula of Lies, 180, 202, 204, 205
Penn, Mark, 118, 298, 299, 303–4
People of the Book, 8
A People's History of American Empire, 257
The People's History of the United States, 141, 246, 249, 255, 257
A People's Tragedy, 134, 142
Percy, Walker, 195
Peretti, Frank E., 235
Pérez-Reverte, Arturo, 31, 216
Perfect Murder, Perfect Town, 62, 65
The Perfect Scent: A Year Inside the Perfume Industry in Paris and New York, 289
The Perfect Storm, 13, 28, 32, 202, 204, 218
Perkins, John, 35, 59, 93, 99, 117, 138, 141, 144, 249, 250, 267, 276, 281, 308, 314
Perlstein, Linda, 171
Perlstein, Rick, 88
Permission Marketing, 324
Perrotta, Tom, 219
Perry, Michael, 10, 24, 33, 50, 154, 173, 220
Persepolis, 200, 269
Persepolis II, 269
Persian Mirrors, 269
Personal History, 34, 88, 104, 278
Pessl, Marisha, 129, 219
Petersen, Melody, 97, 107, 119, 132
Peterson, Scott, 182
Petroski, Henry, 15, 25, 40, 51, 123, 287
Phillips, Kevin, 249, 256, 264, 267, 269, 278, 309, 312
Phillips, Ty, 175, 212
Piano: The Making of a Steinway Concert Grand, 7–8, 51
The Piano Man, 7–8
Piano Notes, 7
The Piano Shop on the Left Bank, 7
Pickens, T. Boone, 296
Picoult, Jodi, 45
A Piece of Cake, 291
Pigs at the Trough, 249
Pileggi, Nicholas, 60
Pilger, John, 142
Pilgrim at Tinker Creek, 259
Pilgrims, 195
Pinhook: Finding Wholeness in a Fragmented Land, 157
Pink, Daniel, 311, 324
Pipe Dreams, 117
Pipher, Mary, 208

Pisano, Dominick, 294
Pistol: The Life of Pete Maravich, 51, 54, 57, 197, 206, 214
Pitching around Fidel, 213
Pity the Nation: The Abduction of Lebanon, 30, 135, 142
The Pixar Touch: The Making of a Company, 295
A Place of My Own, 302
Plainsong, 242
Planck, Nina, 38, 107, 119, 122, 265
The Planets, 46
Plan of Attack, 88, 117, 281, 283
The Playboy Book of True Crime, 64
Playboy Enterprises, 64
Playing for Pizza, 52
Playing Off the Rail, 163
Playing the Moldovans at Tennis, 7, 153, 157, 159
Pledged: The Secret Life of Sororities, 129, 171, 176–77, 211
Plimpton, George, 19, 50, 52, 53, 54, 167
Podhoretz, John, 310
Podhoretz, Norman, 237
Poe's Heart and the Mountain Climber, 128
The Poisonwood Bible, 152, 174, 196
Poitier, Sidney, 215
Polio, 43, 111
The Political Brain, 275, 276, 299, 324
Political Fictions, 272, 273
The Politically Incorrect Guide to Capitalism, 237
The Political Zoo, 233, 238
The Politics of Truth, 250, 281
Politkovskaya, Anna, 142, 222
Pollack, Neal, 159
Pollak, Richard, 25
Pollan, Michael, 18, 23, 38, 41, 105, 107, 109, 110, 111, 119, 122, 127, 130, 132, 174, 215, 265, 287, 290, 300, 302, 303, 314, 325
The Polysyllabic Spree, 77
Ponzi's Scheme, 154, 199, 294, 311, 315
Poor People, 39–40, 68, 159
Population 485, 10, 24, 33, 50, 173, 220
Pop! Why Bubbles Are Great for the Economy, 122, 237, 301
The Portland Vase, 216
Portrait of a Burger as a Young Calf, 110
Portraits and Observations: The Essays of Truman Capote, 75, 76, 200
Positively Fifth Street, 12, 154, 156, 166

The Post-American World, 268, 270, 305
Postlewait, Heidi, 184
Postman, Neil, 308
Postmortem, 62
Post-Soul Nation, 37, 124, 215
*Postville: A Clash of Cultures in Heartland
    America*, 24, 35, 173
Poundstone, William, 275, 276
Pour Your Heart into It, 290
Powell, Julie, 158, 163
A Power Governments Cannot Suppress, 257
The Power of Ethical Management, 323
Power, Samantha, 32, 109, 136, 143, 222
The Powers that Be, 272, 273
Power to the People, 232, 233, 234, 236, 240,
    259
Prange, Gordon, 33
Pratchett, Terry, 178
A Prayer for Owen Meany, 9
A Prayer for the City, 35, 52, 56, 209
Praying for Sheetrock, 128
Predictably Irrational, 123, 298–99
Prejean, Helen, 114, 216
Prep, 129, 171, 177
The Present, 323
Presidential Courage, 267
President Reagan, 233
Preston, Marcia, 7–8
Preston, Richard, 41, 45, 46, 132, 156–57,
    182, 205
*Pretensions to Empire: Notes on the Criminal
    Folly of the Bush Administration*, 252
Pretor-Pinney, Gavin, 26
Price, David A., 295
Price, S. L., 213
The Price of Loyalty, 280
Prime Green, 34
The Prince of Darkness, 250
Pringle, Heather, 47
Pringle, Peter, 110, 111, 127, 174
Prins, Nomi, 315
The Prize, 100, 117, 121, 138, 292, 315
"*A Problem from Hell*," 32, 136, 143, 222
Proenneke, Richard, 195
Profit Over People, 244
The Progress Paradox, 120, 123, 232, 289,
    317
The Proper Care and Feeding of Husbands,
    236
*The Prophet of Love and Other Tales of Power
    and Deceit*, 221
The Prophets, 237

Prose, Francine, 178
*The Prosecution of George W. Bush for
    Murder*, 69
Prothero, Stephen, 248
Proust, Marcel, 75
Provost, Gary, 61
Public Enemies, 59
Punching In, 39, 161, 165–66, 290
Purdy, Jedediah, 275
*Purple Cow: Transform Your Business by
    Being Remarkable*, 324, 325
The Purpose-Driven Life, 324
The Pursuit of Happyness, 291
*Pushed: The Painful Truth about Childbirth
    and Modern Maternity Care*, 116, 155
Pushing the Limits, 15
Putin's Russia, 142
Putnam, Robert, 26, 120, 220, 232, 242, 266,
    275, 286, 300, 302, 310, 311, 312
Puzo, Mario, 60
Pyle, Ernie, 68, 69, 71, 72, 73, 185, 186
Pynchon, Thomas, 40, 74, 78, 223

Qazwini, Imam Hassan, 278
Quammen, David, 22, 182
Quart, Alissa, 312
A Question of Torture, 70, 92, 244, 251
The Quiet American, 232
Quiet Strength, 52, 197
Quindlen, Anna, 76
Quinn, Bill, 316
The Qur'an: A Biography, 317

Raab, Scott, 154
Raban, Jonathan, 132
Rabbit, Run, 121
Race, 39, 215
The Race for the Triple Crown, 52–53, 160
Raddatz, Martha, 72, 73
Rafkin, Louise, 164
Rain, Patricia, 16
Rain of Ruin, 137
Raising Blaze, 21
Rakoff, David, 7, 77, 79, 156, 162, 176
Rall, Ted, 112
Ralston, Aron, 202, 204
Rammer, Jammer, Yellow, Hammer, 56, 157
Rand, Ayn, 282, 291
Random Family, 35, 61, 63, 120, 121, 124,
    126, 164, 196, 201, 209, 210, 211, 219
Rankin, Ian, 58
The Rape of Europa, 216

The Rape of Nanking, 91
Rapoport, Miles, 314
The Rapture of Canaan, 64
Rath, Tom, 323
Rats, 26, 130
Ray, Janisse, 157
Ray, Rachael, 14
Raymond, Allen, 275, 276
The Reach of a Chef, 169
Reading Judas, 31
Reading Life, 78
Reading Lolita in Tehran, 9, 34, 185, 187, 222, 269
Readings, 76
"Ready for the People," 63, 276
The Reagan Diaries, 267, 291
Real Change, 234–35, 240
The Real Thing, 106, 309, 311
Reasons: Why Liberals Will Win the Battle for America, 252
Reavill, Gil, 62, 168
The Rebels' Hour, 198
Reconciliation: Islam, Democracy, and the West, 278
Red Mafiya, 59, 134
Red River Rising, 28, 32–33, 213, 218
Reece, Erik, 107–8, 132
Reed, Cheryl, 154
Reeves, Richard, 233
Refuge, 100, 119, 128
Regards: The Collected Nonfiction of John Gregory Dunne, 272
Reich, Robert, 98, 141, 252, 305, 312, 325
Reichl, Ruth, 14, 105, 158, 162, 170, 290, 294
Reichs, Kathy, 58, 168
Reidy, Jamie, 97, 98, 107, 108
The Reign of the Ayatollahs, 269
The Rejection Collection, 112
The Rejection Collection Volume 2, 112
Relentless Pursuit, 63
Religion of Peace?, 259
Remembering Satan, 64–65
Remember Me, 6, 9–10, 18, 47, 103, 104, 221, 289
Remnick, David, 49, 79, 121, 142, 176, 200, 264
Reporting: Writings from the New Yorker, 79, 176, 200, 264
Reposition Yourself, 291
The Republican War on Science, 115
Rereadings, 78

Resource Wars, 135
Restak, Richard M., 128
Rest in Peace, 47
The Restless Sleep, 58, 61–62, 165, 168, 169
The Return of History and the End of Dreams, 275
Return of the Condor, 45–46
Revenge of the Donut Boys, 17
Reviving Ophelia, 208
Revolt in the Boardroom: The New Rules of Power in Corporate America, 322, 325–26
The Revolt of the Elites, 317
The Revolution: A Manifesto, 282
Revolutionary Wealth, 118, 304, 305–6
Revolution in the Valley, 295
Rewriting History, 233, 267
Reynolds, Sheri, 64
Rhodes, Benjamin D., 91
Rhodes, Richard, 45, 46, 140
Ribowsky, Shiya, 168–69
Rich, Frank, 28, 68, 69, 88, 94, 250, 254, 256, 268, 283
Richard, Marcus, 154
Richardson, Bill, 280
Richardson, Doug, 284
Richistan, 122, 174, 176, 232, 262, 302, 310
Ricks, Thomas, 32, 68, 69, 90, 187, 243, 244, 250, 256, 267–68, 269, 280, 283
Ricochet: Confessions of a Gun Lobbyist, 118
Riding toward Everywhere, 159
Rieff, David, 79
Rifkin, Jeremy, 109, 115, 127, 299, 304, 308
Rigged: The True Story of an Ivy League Kid Who Changed the World of Oil, 93, 294
Right from the Beginning, 234
Right Is Wrong, 249, 271
The Right Nation, 263
Rights from Wrongs, 245
The Right Stuff, 17, 214
Riis, Jacob, 171
Rinella, Steven, 162
A Rip in Heaven, 62, 65
Risen, James, 32, 69, 89, 109, 131, 250, 260, 267, 269, 270, 276
The Rise of the Counter-Establishment, 279
The Rise of the Creative Class, 300, 301, 311
Rising from the Plains, 167, 295–96
Rising from the Rails, 37, 124
Rising Tide, 218
Rising Up and Rising Down, 40, 159

Ritter, Scott, 268
The River at the Center of the World, 302
A River Runs through It, 51
The River Wife, 255
Roach, Mary, 6, 10, 44, 46–47, 104, 155, 169, 221
Roadfood, 158
The Road to Serfdom, 89, 237, 239
Road Work, 8, 78, 203
Robb, John, 261
Robbins, Alexandra, 128–29, 171, 176–77, 180, 211, 214
Robbins, Tom, 189
Roberts, Adam, 143–44
Roberts, Paul, 117
Robinson, Linda, 89, 140, 211
Robinson, Rachel, 55
Rockman, Alexis, 182
Rocky Stories, 10, 12, 52, 209, 217–18
Rodriguez, Deborah, 9
Rodriguez, Teresa, 58
Rogue States, 244
Rolling Nowhere, 159, 163
Rome, Inc., 322
Ronald Reagan: How an Ordinary Man Became an Extraordinary Leader, 234
Ronson, Jon, 13, 35, 92, 93, 94, 131, 139, 162, 174–75, 177, 188, 197, 222
Rosa Lee, 61, 120, 121, 209–10, 211
Rose, David, 9
Rosen, Charles, 7
Rosenbaum, Ron, 78, 129, 173, 220–21
Rosenberg, Scott, 15, 16–17, 42, 292, 322
Rosenthal, A. M., 62
Rosenzweig, Phil, 322
Rossmiller, A. J., 271
Rost, Peter, 48, 96, 97, 98, 100, 102, 107, 108, 111, 115, 141
Roston, Aram, 144
Roth, Kenneth, 94
Rothenberg, Daniel, 130, 169
Rothfeder, Jeffrey, 124, 290, 295–96
Rothkopf, David, 270, 317
Round Ireland with a Fridge, 7, 153, 159
Roy, Arundhati, 247
Roy, Lucinda, 196
The Royal Family, 40
Royte, Elizabeth, 48, 123, 129–30
Rubin, Aviel D., 275, 276
Ruff, Matt, 21, 221
Rufus, Anneli, 221

Ruhlman, Michael, 7, 14, 51, 105, 158, 162, 169–70, 289, 290, 294, 302, 325
Ruining It for Everybody, 10, 156, 176
Rule, Ann, 57, 60, 61, 64
Rumbles Left and Right, 232
A Rumor of War, 29, 71
Running Money, 44
Ruse, Michael, 265
Rush Limbaugh Is a Big Fat Idiot, 247
A Russian Diary, 142, 222
Russo, Richard, 15, 17, 55, 80, 121, 219, 242
The Rustle of Language, 75
Rybczynski, Witold, 23, 25–26, 302
Ryman, Geoff, 115, 306

S: A Novel about the Balkans, 136
Sabotage: America's Enemies within the CIA, 259
Sacco, Joe, 34, 68, 143, 199–200, 257, 262
Sachs, Jeffrey, 270, 305
Sachs, Jessica Snyder, 47–48, 115
Sack, John, 186
Sacks, Oliver, 40, 45, 128
Safe Area Gorazde, 200
Sagan, Carl, 46
Sager, Mike, 17
Sager, Ryan, 263
Sahara, 155
Sahara Unveiled, 25, 38, 67, 155
Said, Edward, 34, 142, 262
Salinger, J. D., 78, 224
Salt, 16, 26, 41, 105, 292, 295, 314
Salt of the Earth, 64
Salvador, 35, 59, 68, 144
Salvation on Sand Mountain, 152, 154
Salzman, Mark, 8
Sammon, Bill, 234, 235, 237–38
Sanders, Lawrence, 60
Sanders, Scott Russell, 38
Sarajevo Daily, 136
Saramago, Jose, 40
Satrapi, Marjane, 200, 269
Saturday Night, 12, 56, 78, 173, 220
Savage, Dan, 31, 155, 177–78
Savage, Michael, 233, 235, 237, 238
Savage Inequalities, 14, 63, 120, 125, 126, 129, 164, 169, 196, 207, 209, 214, 220
The Savage Nation, 238
A Savage War of Peace: Algeria, 1954–1962, 268
Saviano, Robert, 64, 144
Saving the Queen, 232

Sawyer, Keith, 305, 322, 326
Scahill, Jeremy, 52, 108–9, 137, 144, 180, 217, 250–51, 256
Scarborough, Roman, 259
Scary Monsters and Super Freaks, 17
The Scavenger's Guide to Haute Cuisine, 162
Schachtman, Tom, 168–69
Schapiro, Mark, 48, 100, 107, 109, 122, 123, 127
Schell, Jonathan, 46, 252, 303
Schiller, Lawrence, 62, 64, 65
Schlosser, Eric, 38, 41, 104, 105–6, 107, 110, 111, 114, 119, 127, 174, 180, 308, 318
Schooler, Lynn, 202
Schor, Juliet, 39, 48, 98, 125, 133, 180, 304, 308, 312, 316, 319, 320
Schroeder, Alice, 296
Schulian, John, 50, 55, 56
Schultz, Howard, 290, 328
Schumacher, Jim, 111, 204
Schumpeter, Joseph, 89, 317
Schwartz, Barry, 120
Schweid, Richard, 44
Schweizer, Peter, 235, 238
The Science of Fear, 123
The Science of Secrecy, 90, 115
Sciff, Stacy, 261
Sciolino, Elaine, 269
Sclessinger, Laura, 236
The Scorpion's Gate, 279
Scott, Aurelia C., 17–18, 19
Scotti, R. A., 32
Scottoline, Lisa, 30
Screwed: The Undeclared War against the Middle Class, 247–48, 254
Scribbling the Cat, 195
Scurlock, James, 318
Seabiscuit, 49, 50, 53, 54, 172, 218
Seaman, Donna, 76
The Search, 292, 293, 295
The Search for Modern China, 302
Searching for Bobby Fischer, 214
Searching for Caleb, 7
The Season: Inside Palm Beach, 61, 122, 173–74
Season Finale, 102
A Season on the Brink, 52, 53, 54, 157
Sebold, Alice, 78
Secret Diary of a Call Girl, 6
The Secret History of the American Empire, 99, 117, 141, 144, 250, 267, 276, 281–82, 308

The Secret History of the War on Cancer, 119
The Secret Life of Bees, 185
The Secret Man, 88
The Secret of Scent, 289
The Secret Parts of Fortune, 78, 129, 221
Secrets: A Memoir of Vietnam and the Pentagon Papers, 273
Secrets, Lies, and Democracy, 244
Secrets of the Temple, 313
The Secret Way to War, 272
Sedaris, Amy, 244
Sedaris, David, 7, 153, 156, 176, 177
Seder, Sam, 247, 252, 271
Seierstad, Åsne, 9, 69, 184, 185, 186–87, 200, 222
Selected Essays of John Berger, 75
The Selected Letters of Martha Gellhorn, 70
The Selfish Gene, 287
Self-Made Man, 153, 176, 179, 180, 205
Sellevision, 297
The Selling of "Free Trade," 92
The Selling of the President, 272, 273
Selling Women Short, 106
Selzer, Richard, 169
A Sense of the Mysterious, 46
Serpent in Paradise, 221
Set This House in Order, 21
Setting the Table: The Transforming Power of Hospitality in Business, 325
Seuer, Michael, 282
Seven Days of Possibilities, 12
1776, 33
The Seventh Decade, 252
Sewell, Joan, 178
Sex, Drugs, and Cocoa Puffs, 17
Sex, Economy, Freedom, and Community, 174, 259
The Sexual Life of Catherine M, 6
Sexy, 78
Shadid, Anthony, 32, 68, 187, 217, 264, 268
Shadow Box, 167
Shadow Divers, 27, 32, 287
Shah, Sonia, 110–11, 136
Shah, Tahir, 22
The Shakespeare Wars, 221
The Shame of the Nation, 126, 214, 220
Shapiro, Robert J., 304–5
Sharing the Promised Land, 138
Sharon and My Mother-in-Law, 135, 138, 183–84
Sharp, Paula, 64
The Sharper Your Knife, 16

Sheehan, Neil, 71, 91, 186
Sheff, David, 96
Shelby, Ashley, 28, 32–33, 213, 218
Shelby, Philip, 284
Sheldon, Sidney, 61, 174
Shermer, Michael, 244
Sherrill, Stephen, 247, 252
She's Not There, 202, 205
Shields, Carol, 212
Shiller, Robert, 301
Shilts, Randy, 31, 136, 196
Shipler, David, 14, 30, 35, 97, 120, 121, 126,
        130, 135, 138, 164, 196, 209, 210, 211,
        220, 248, 262, 309, 312, 313, 316, 318,
        319
Shlaes, Amity, 235
The Shock Doctrine, 89, 93, 98, 109, 141, 144,
        180, 247, 248, 250, 256, 308
Shoeless Joe, 51, 55
Shopping for Bombs, 140
Shopping for God, 179–80, 297, 324
Shopping Our Way to Safety, 109
Shorris, Earl, 319
Shot in the Heart, 64
*Showdown: Why China Wants War with the
        United States,* 259
Show Me a Hero, 208–9, 265
Shteyngart, Gary, 145
Shut Up & Sing, 233, 240
*Sick: The Untold Story of America's Health
        Care Crisis,* 44, 48, 97, 102, 108, 115,
        116, 313
Sides, Hampton, 73, 222, 266
Sidewalk, 126
Siegel, Lee, 77, 78–79
Silence of the Rational Center, 251, 258, 261,
        263, 270
Silent Spring, 44, 46, 107, 122, 123, 126–27
Siler, Julia Flynn, 20, 290
Simmons, Russell, 291
Simon, Michele, 105, 107, 111, 132
Simon, Scott, 142
Simple Justice, 103
A Simple Plan, 203
Simple Truth, 76
Sinclair, Upton, 110, 145, 171
Singer, Mark, 9, 13, 118, 153, 156, 174, 177,
        222, 266
Singh, Simon, 90, 115
The Singularity Is Near, 128
Sittenfeld, Curtis, 129, 163, 171, 177

*Six Men Who Built the Modern Auto
        Industry,* 311
Skinner, E. Benjamin, 144
Skipping towards Gomorrah, 177–78
Skocpol, Theda, 314
Slack, Charles, 294, 315
Slackjaw, 10, 205
Slade, Giles, 48, 123, 130
Slatalla, Michelle, 24, 33, 108, 212–13
Slater, Robert, 106
Slaves in the Family, 202, 296
Slavin, Barbara, 268–69, 278
Sleepaway School, 126
Sleeping with the Devil, 89
Sleepless Nights, 76
Sloth, 178
Slouching Towards Bethlehem, 272
Slowly Down the Ganges, 159
A Small Corner of Hell, 142
Small Is the New Big, 298, 306, 324
Smartest Guys in the Room, 141
Smerconish, Michael, 233, 238, 239
Smiley, Jane, 53
Smith, Adam, 237
Smith, David A., 314
Smith, Gary, 56
Smith, Lee, 242
Smith, Scott, 203
Smith, Zadie, 9, 187
The Smoking Gun, 254
Snoop: What Your Stuff Says about You, 133
*The Snowball: Warren Buffett and the
        Business of Life,* 296
Snow in August, 51
The Snow Leopard, 151, 182
Snyder, Rachel Louise, 99, 117, 166, 290,
        292, 301, 310, 314, 315, 318
Sobel, Dava, 40, 46, 289
The Social Atom, 122
Social Intelligence, 120
The Social Life of Information, 311
Sokolove, Michael, 50, 52, 55, 56, 57, 99,
        196, 201, 206, 207, 213, 218
The Solace of Food, 14, 293–94
Soldier: The Life of Colin Powell, 234
The Soloist, 8
Solomon, Andrew, 96
Solzhenitsyn, Aleksandr, 134
Somewhere in America, 174, 222
Songbook, 77
The Songlines, 221
Sontag, Susan, 78, 200, 217, 247, 256

Soos, Frank, 255
So Others Might Live, 165
Soros, George, 271, 282–83
Soros on Soros, 282
The Sorrows of Empire, 109, 142, 246, 250
Sosnik, Douglas, 276, 324
The Soul of a Chef, 169
The Soul of a New Machine, 7, 14, 15, 17, 42, 292, 293, 295, 322
The Soul of Capitalism, 249, 305, 312
Sowbelly, 150–51
Sowell, Thomas, 234, 237, 239
Spar, Debora, 155
Special Topics in Calamity Physics, 129, 219
Spence, Gerry, 254
Spence, Jonathan, 302
Spencer, Lynn, 33
Spencer, Robert, 234, 259
Spice, 16, 105
Spiegelman, Art, 29, 143, 169, 200
Spinsters, 205, 219
Spirit and Flesh, 152
The Spirit Catches You and You Fall Down, 10–11, 30, 43, 44, 102, 107, 122, 136, 204, 208
Spook: Science Tackles the Afterlife, 46, 47, 221
Spoon River Anthology, 213
The Sportswriter, 121
Spree, 297, 320
Spurlock, Morgan, 119, 187–88, 318
Spychips, 90, 115, 139
The Squandering of America, 252, 265–66, 270
St. John, Warren, 56, 157
Standard Operating Procedure, 70, 93
Stanley Park, 325
Starbucked, 14, 103–4, 166, 289, 290, 310, 315, 316, 318, 319, 324
The Starbucks Experience, 325
The Starfish and the Spider, 305, 321–22, 326
Starkey, David, 254–55
Statecraft as Soulcraft, 240
Staten, Vince, 41, 119, 130–31
State of Denial, 90, 250, 254, 256, 268, 283
State of Emergency, 236, 259–60, 267
State of War, 32, 69, 89, 109, 131, 250, 260, 267, 269, 270, 276
Status Anxiety, 26, 48, 75, 120, 310, 317
Steel, Danielle, 61, 174
Steele, Shelby, 239
Stegner, Wallace, 167, 203, 212

Stein, Gertrude, 76
Steinbeck, John, 170, 171, 189, 203, 204
Steinberg, Ted, 23, 26
Steinem, Gloria, 116
Steiner, Leslie Morgan, 155
Steingarten, Jeffrey, 158
Steinway, 289
Stenger, Victor, 264
Stephenson, Neal, 128, 292
Stern, Jane, 158
Stern, Michael, 158
Stern Men, 195
Stewart, Amy, 7, 9, 10, 14, 18, 23, 26, 47, 105, 109, 117, 118, 130, 199, 289, 290, 296, 310, 314, 315, 318
Stewart, James B., 311
Stewart, Jon, 98, 244, 252, 253
Steyn, Mark, 232, 233, 234, 236, 260
Stiff: The Curious Lives of Human Cadavers, 10, 44, 46, 47, 104, 169, 221
Stiglitz, Joseph, 303
Still Broken, 271
Stone, Nathaniel, 51
Stone, Pamela, 38–39, 116, 155
Stone, Peter Bennet, 94, 247, 253
Stone, Robert, 34, 175
The Stone Diaries, 212
The Stone Fields, 136
Storming the Valley, 137
Stossel, John, 131, 232, 233, 235, 236, 239, 260, 263, 267
Strapped, 309, 316, 318, 319
Strategery, 238
Streatfeild, Dominic, 35, 90, 92, 93, 94, 114, 131–32, 139
Streeter, Sabin C., 36–37, 39
Stringer, Lee, 126
Stuart, Tristram, 26
Studwell, Joe, 99
Stuever, Hank, 19, 153, 156, 174, 175, 222, 266
Stuffed: Adventures of a Restaurant Family, 325
The Stuff of Dreams, 152
Stumbling on Happiness, 120, 289
Stump, Al, 56
Stupid Black Men, 239
The Stupidest Angel, 322, 327
Stupid White Men, 252, 308
Suburban Safari, 19, 23, 26
Subwayland, 23–24
Sudden Sea, 32

Sugar's Life in the Hood, 210
Sullivan, Robert, 13, 26, 130, 132, 154, 221
Summer for the Gods, 265, 274
The Summer Game, 49–50, 56
Summer of '49, 53, 55, 56, 99, 197
The Sum of Our Days, 208
Sun after Dark, 310
Sunday: A History of the First Day, 220
Sundays with Vlad, 9, 153, 221
The Sun Farmer, 43, 44–45, 205, 206
Sun Tzu Was a Sissy, 322
Supercapitalism, 98, 141, 252, 305, 312
Superclass: The Global Power Elite and the World They Are Making, 270, 317
Super Crunchers, 55, 299, 326
Supernation at Peace and War, 91, 175
A Supposedly Fun Thing I'll Never Do Again, 176
Surowiecki, James, 298, 299, 305, 322, 326
The Sushi Economy, 16, 290, 301, 313–14, 315, 318
Suskind, Ron, 14, 32, 35, 57, 88, 90, 125–26, 196, 206–7, 210, 215, 218, 243, 250, 267, 268, 269, 270, 280, 283
Sutherland, Amy, 151, 157–58
Sutton, Robert I, 326–27
The Swallows of Kabul, 185
Swan, Annalyn, 122, 232, 262, 288–89, 290, 317
Sweet: An Eight-Ball Odyssey, 163
Swim Against the Current, 248–49, 253
Swofford, Anthony, 73
Swope, Sam, 12, 14, 126, 129, 177, 211, 214
Szasz, Andrew, 109

Taibbi, Matt, 188
Tait, Arch, 142
Take It Back: Our Party, Our Country, Our Future, 243
Take the Cannoli, 105, 176
Taking America Back, 236
Taking On the Big Boys, 116
Taleb, Nassim Nicholas, 55, 123, 283, 291, 299, 304, 306, 314, 325
Talese, Gay, 6, 16, 33–34, 46, 60, 75, 78, 104, 178, 179, 214, 221, 222
Tales from Q School, 19, 53–54
Tales from the Bed, 205
Tapscott, Don, 298, 305, 306, 322, 326
Tarbell, Ida, 171
Target Iran, 268
Tarte, Bob, 132

Tate, Sonsyrea, 64
Taylor, Timothy, 325
Teacher Man, 12, 177
The Teammates, 56, 197
Team of Rivals, 207
Tearing Down the Wall of Sound, 61
Ted Williams, 55
Tefertiller, Casey, 212
Tell It To the Dead, 90
Tender at the Bone, 105, 158, 170
The Tender Bar, 153
Tenet, George, 89, 269, 280
Ten Minutes from Normal, 281
The Ten Things You Can't Say in America, 239
Tepper Isn't Going Out, 327
Terkel, Studs, 16, 37, 39, 76, 134, 169, 171, 185, 215, 216
The Terror Dream, 246–47, 256
Thank You for Not Reading, 76
That Distant Land, 259
The Devil's Playground, 23
Them: Adventures with Extremists, 13, 94, 174–75, 177, 188, 197
Then We Came to the End, 95, 160, 295, 309
There Are No Children Here, 14, 35, 62, 63, 125–26, 164, 207, 210, 211, 220
There Is No Me without You, 134, 136, 183, 196, 219, 222, 280
Theriault, Reg, 18, 39, 165, 166, 169
Theroux, Louis, 156, 175
Theroux, Paul, 16, 159, 310
These Things Ain't Gonna Smoke Themselves, 309
These United States, 77
They Call Me Naughty Lola, 9
They Marched into Sunlight, 29
They Went Whistling, 75
They Would Never Hurt a Fly, 135–36, 143
Thieves in High Places, 249, 253
Things Fall Apart, 38, 155
The Things They Carried, 29, 71
Think Like a Billionaire, 327
13 Seconds: A Look Back at the Kent State Shootings, 28–29
Thirteen Ways of Looking at a Black Man, 37
30: The Collapse of the Great American Newspaper, 104
Thirty-Eight Witnesses: The Kitty Genovese Case, 62
This Cold Heaven, 44, 221
This Is New York, 176

This Is Your War, 186
This Land Is Their Land, 249
This Little Light of Mine, 278
Thoene, Bodie, 235
Thoene, Brock, 235
Thomas, Clarence, 234, 238, 274
Thomas, Dana, 176, 180, 296–97, 319, 320
Thomas, Helen, 281
Thomas, Michael M., 294
Thomas Paine's Rights of Man, 317
Thompson, Hunter S., 17, 105, 174, 175, 178–79, 214
Thoreau, Henry David, 16, 26, 90, 108, 115, 167
A Thousand Splendid Suns, 9, 67, 185, 187, 212
Three Cups of Tea, 67, 185, 222, 278
Three Nights in August, 50–51, 55, 56, 160, 209
Throwing the Elephant: Zen and the Art of Managing Up, 322
Thubron, Colin, 133, 183, 282
Thunderstruck, 301
Thurman, Judith, 200
Thy Neighbor's Wife, 6, 34, 46, 178
The Ticket Out, 50, 52, 55, 56, 57, 99, 196, 201, 206, 207, 213, 218
The Ties that Bind, 195
Tigers in the Snow, 46
Timmerman, Kenneth, 235
Timperlake, Edward, 259
The Tipping Point, 118, 120, 123, 215, 299, 300, 301, 304, 305, 306, 314, 317, 325, 326
Tirman, John, 255
Titan: The Life of John D. Rockefeller, Sr., 288, 295
To Air Is Human, 158–59
Tobin, James, 68
Toffler, Alvin, 42, 118, 266, 304, 305–6
Toffler, Heidi, 304, 305–6
To Have or Have Not, 70
To Hell with All That, 246
Tolan, Sandy, 34, 135, 261, 279
Toobin, Jeffrey, 31, 104–5, 244, 274, 275–76
Too Far from Home, 205, 214
Torgovnick, Kate, 18–19
Torture, 94
Torture and Truth, 35, 70, 92, 264
Touching History, 33
Tough Choices, 293, 326

The Town on Beaver Creek, 24, 33, 108, 212–13
Trained to Kill, 91
Train Go Sorry, 152
Trainor, Bernard, 90, 117
The Trap: Selling Out To Stay Afloat in Winner-Take-All America, 122, 262, 309, 312, 318
Traub, James, 23
Traveling Mercies, 152
Travels with Dr. Death, 129
Travels with Myself and Another, 70
Tree of Smoke, 71
Trillin, Calvin, 7, 12, 14, 16, 19, 51, 78, 79, 158, 162, 222, 266, 294, 327
Trollope, Anthony, 145
Trotter, Charlie, 14
Trudeau, Garry, 112
Trump, Donald, 291, 327
Trump: The Art of the Deal, 291, 327
The Truth: With Jokes, 247
The Truth about the Drug Companies, 102, 107
Truth and Consequences, 249
Tucker, Neely, 196
The Tummy Trilogy, 158
Tungate, Mark, 125, 297, 319
Turin, Luca, 289
Turner, Jack, 16, 105
Turner, Sugar, 210
Türoque, Björn, 158–59
Turow, Scott, 100, 276
Twain, Mark, 159
Twenty Ads That Shook the World, 297
28: Stories of AIDS in Africa, 136
Twilight of the Long-ball Gods, 55, 56
Twinkie, Deconstructed, 7, 41
Twins, 65
Twitchell, James, 125, 133, 179–80, 274, 276, 289, 296, 297, 308, 310, 319, 320, 324
Two for the Road, 158
Two Souls Indivisible, 73
Tye, Larry, 37, 124, 295–96
Tyerman, Christopher, 279
Tyler, Anne, 7, 152, 207, 224, 325
Tyler, Rick, 234–35
Tyson, Timothy, 209

Uchitelle, Louis, 92, 130, 164, 242, 248, 249, 304, 309, 312, 313, 316, 318, 319–20
Ugel, Edward, 203

Ugresic, Dubravka, 76
Ulin, David, 32, 33, 167
Uncensored: Views & (Re)views, 77–78, 79
Uncivilized Beasts and Shameless Hellions, 67, 68, 72, 182, 188
Uncommon Carriers, 9, 16, 51, 117, 167, 315
Undaunted Courage, 245
Underboss, 59, 60, 64
The Undercover Economist, 291, 314
The Underdog: How I Survived the World's Most Outlandish Competitions, 152–53
Underhill, Paco, 48, 104, 297, 308, 312, 320
Under the Banner of Heaven, 63–64, 132
Under the Big Top, 165
Under the Tuscan Sun, 75
Unembedded: Four Independent Photojournalists on the War in Iraq, 68, 187, 256
Unequal Protection, 247
An Unexpected Light, 67, 184, 185, 187
Unforgivable Blackness, 197
Unger, Craig, 217, 255–56
Unhinged, 235, 236
Unified Field Theory, 255
The United States of Arugula, 13–14
Unless, 212
The Unquiet Mind, 96
The Unraveling of the Bush Presidency, 257
The Unsettling of America, 259
Unspeakable Acts, Ordinary People, 35, 70, 92, 93
Unto the Sons, 178
The Untouched Minutes, 255
Unveiled: The Hidden Lives of Nuns, 154
Updike, John, 15, 78, 79, 121, 195, 200, 221
Up from Zero, 22–23, 25, 29
Up in the Old Hotel, 78, 175–76, 222
Up the Amazon without a Paddle, 157
US Guys, 153, 174–75

Vaccine, 43, 45, 111, 301
Vachon, Dana, 329
The Vagabond, 200
Vaillant, John, 108, 132, 157
Vance, Courtney, 291
vanden Heuvel, Katrina, 246
VanDevelder, Paul, 206
Vanilla, 16
The Vast Left Wing Conspiracy, 240
Vengeance: The True Story of an Israeli Counter-Terrorist Team, 8, 135, 138, 184

Venkatesh, Sudhir Alladi, 34–35, 63, 120, 126, 172, 180, 209, 262
Verghese, Abraham, 11
Verklin, David, 101, 102
Veronica, 177
A Very Good Year, 19–20
The Veterinarian's Touch, 20, 42
Vidal, Gore, 284
Vietnam: A History, 29
Vincent, Fay, 52
Vincent, Norah, 153, 176, 179, 180, 205
Vinegar Hill, 64
The Virus and the Vaccine, 111, 204
Vise, David, 290
Vitez, Michael, 10, 12, 52, 209, 217–18
Voices from Chernobyl, 70, 96, 100, 134, 137, 140, 142, 184, 198, 222
Volk, Patricia, 325
Vollmann, William T., 39–40, 68, 71, 72, 159, 171, 223
Vonnegut, Kurt, 40, 255, 308
Vowell, Sarah, 105, 176, 177

Waiting: The True Confessions of a Waitress, 37, 165, 325
Waiting for the Barbarians, 252
Wakefield, Dan, 91, 175
Wake-Up Call, 29, 91, 270
Waldman, Paul, 243
Walker, Alice, 185, 247
Walker, Rob, 132–33
Walker, Sam, 56, 151, 153, 159–60, 166
Walking to Connecticut, 16, 51
A Walk in the Woods, 19, 157
The Wall, 137
Wallace, Benjamin, 20
Wallace, Danny, 153, 159
Wallace, David Foster, 74, 156, 176
Wallace, Don, 206, 213
Wallis, David, 111–12
Wallis, Jim, 243, 251, 266, 273, 278
Wall Street Meat, 44
The Wal-Mart Decade, 106
The Wal-Mart Effect, 106, 290, 316
A Wanderer in the Perfect City, 223
Ward, Geoffrey C., 197
War Is a Force That Gives Us Meaning, 67, 70–71, 72, 91, 186, 248
War on the Middle Class, 248, 260, 282
Warren, Edith, 75
Warren, Rick, 324
Warren, Robert Penn, 284

Warren, Susan, 18, 19, 23, 151, 158
Warren Buffett and the Interpretation of Financial Statements, 296
The Warren Buffett Way, 296
Warriors Don't Cry, 37, 126, 215, 220, 291
Wars of Watergate, 245
Wasserstein, Wendy, 178
Watchdogs of Democracy, 281
Watch This, Listen Up, Click Here, 101, 102
Water for Elephants, 165
Waterfront: A Journey around Manhattan, 24
Waters, Liz, 198
Watson, Larry, 195
The Way of Ignorance, 259
The Way of the Wise Guy, 59, 60, 64
The Way Things Ought to Be, 233
The Way We Lived Then, 174
The Way We Never Were, 48, 120, 274
The Way You Wear Your Hat, 221
The Wealth of Nations, 237
The Weather Makers, 13, 33
Webber, Thomas L., 35
We Die Alone, 66, 73, 187, 200
A Weekend with Warren Buffett, 289–90
Weigel, George, 235
The Weight of Dreams, 255
Weil, Gordon Lee, 96, 112, 121
Weinberger, David, 15, 17, 101, 118, 128, 298, 299–300, 305, 306, 311, 322, 324, 326
Weiner, Eric, 16
Weiner, Jonathan, 42, 48, 205
Weiner, Tim, 89, 131, 140, 276
Weinreb, Michael, 19, 129, 153, 156, 166, 213–14
Weis, Charlie, 197
Weisberg, Jacob, 69, 245, 256
Weisberger, Lauren, 297
Weisman, Alan, 25, 42, 127, 305
Weiss, Mike, 19–20
Welch, Jack, 326, 327–28
Welcome to Doomsday, 266, 272
Welcome to Shirley, 119, 128
Welcome to the Homeland, 266
Wells, Rebecca, 152, 207
Welsch, Roger, 24
Wenger, J. Michael, 137
Weschler, Lawrence, 35, 65, 129, 198, 223
Wesley, Elana, 183–84
West, Bing, 72
West, Cornell, 244
West, Rebecca, 143, 222

Westen, Drew, 275, 276, 299, 324
We Were One, 72–73
We Wish to Inform You That Tomorrow We Will Be Killed with Our Families, 38, 70, 134, 182, 196, 198
The Whale and the Supercomputer, 13, 33, 44
A Whale Hunt, 13, 132
The Whale Warriors, 13
What Are People For?, 259
What Do You Think of Ted Williams Now?, 272
What Every Person Should Know about War, 71
What Happened: Inside the Bush White House and Washington's Culture of Deception, 280–81
What Is the What, 38, 135, 151, 182, 198
What It Takes: The Way to the White House, 262, 272
What's So Great about America, 234
What's the Matter with Kansas?, 89, 248, 252, 255, 266, 273, 275
What to Eat, 14
What We Say Goes, 244
What Would Machiavelli Do?, 322, 327
What Would the Founders Do, 240
Wheen, Francis, 317
When Smoke Ran Like Water, 119
Where Have All the Leaders Gone?, 263, 283, 326
Where In the World Is Osama Bin Laden?, 187–88
Where I Was From, 100
Where Soldiers Fear to Tread, 141, 181–82, 183, 184
Which Brings Me To You, 7
The Whistleblower, 48, 96, 97, 98, 100, 102, 107, 108, 111, 115, 141
White, E. B., 10, 16, 49, 78, 176, 204
White, Theodore, 272
White Guilt, 239
Whitehead, Colson, 176, 216, 224
Whiteout: Lost in Aspen, 163, 172–73
The White Swan, 283
White Teeth, 9, 187
Who Are You People?, 6, 9, 13, 18, 19, 56, 118, 151, 153, 158, 214, 219
A Whole New Mind, 311
The Whole World Over, 325
Who Moved My Cheese?, 323
Who's Afraid of a Large Black Man?, 37, 215–16, 292

Who's Your City?, 300, 302, 311
Who Will Tell the People?, 266, 313
Whybrow, Peter, 120, 162
Why Israel Lost, 261
Whynott, Douglas, 20
Why Things Break, 25, 121
Why We Buy, 48, 104, 297, 308, 320
Why We Garden, 18, 23
Why We're Liberals, 242
Why We Want You To Be Rich, 327
Why Women Should Rule the World, 281
Wideman, John Edgar, 252
A Widow's Walk, 29, 33
Wiesel, Elie, 34, 91, 143
Wigfield, 244
*Wikinomics: How Mass Collaboration
    Changes Everything*, 298, 305, 306,
    322, 326
The Wild Trees, 132, 156–57
Wilentz, Sean, 238
Wilkie, Curtis, 28
Wilkinson, Alec, 200–201, 219
Will, George, 237, 239–40
Williams, Anthony, 305
Williams, Terry Tempest, 100, 119, 128
Will They Ever Trust Us Again?, 252
Wilson, Joseph, 250, 281
Wilson, Valerie Plame, 250, 281
Winchester, Simon, 28, 114, 302
Wind, 32
Winder, Paul, 59, 199
Winerip, Michael, 20–21, 209
Winesburg, Ohio, 63
Winne, Mark, 38
Winning, 327–28
Wins, Losses, and Lessons, 197
The Wisdom of Crowds, 298, 299, 305, 322,
    326
Without a Net, 164
Without Apology, 151–52
Without Mercy, 61
Without Precedent, 91, 270
With Their Backs to the Wall, 184, 200, 222
With These Hands, 130, 169, 173
Wohlforth, Charles, 13, 33, 44
Wojciechowski, Gene, 19, 54, 56, 99, 157,
    160
Wojnarowski, Adrian, 54, 56–57
Wolf, Naomi, 109, 180, 217, 244, 247, 249,
    251, 252, 256
Wolfe, Thomas, 159

Wolfe, Tom, 17, 60, 175, 178, 179, 214, 274,
    310
Wolff, Tobias, 71
Wolverton, Mark, 214
Woman: An Intimate Geography, 47
The Woman I Kept to Myself, 208
A Woman in Charge, 88, 277–78, 280
Wonder Boys, 219
Wonderland, 129, 171, 177, 211, 214, 218,
    220
The Wonder Spot, 176, 177
The Wonga Coup, 143–44
Woodruff, Lee, 73
Woodswoman, 195
Woodward, Bob, 87–88, 90, 117, 245, 250,
    254, 256, 264, 268, 272, 273, 281, 283
Woodward, William, 277–78
Wooldridge, Adrian, 263
Woolf, Virginia, 76
Worden, Minky, 94
Word Freak, 12, 18, 19, 118, 153, 156, 160,
    166, 214
Words That Work, 276
Work and Other Sins, 24
Working, 37, 39, 76, 134, 216
The Working Poor, 14, 35, 120, 121, 126, 130,
    164, 196, 209, 210, 211, 220, 248, 262,
    309, 312, 313, 316, 318, 319
A Working Stiff's Manifesto, 37, 166
The World According to Breslin, 60
The World Is Flat, 30, 101, 117, 270, 291,
    300, 301, 303, 304, 310, 314, 317
World Made by Hand, 126
*World War IV: The Long Struggle against
    Islamofascism*, 237
The World without Us, 25, 127, 305
Worse than Watergate, 244–45, 283
The Worst Person in the World, 253, 254
The Woven Figure, 240
Wren, Christopher, 16, 51
Wright, Lawrence, 64–65, 67, 70, 89, 91,
    109, 188, 256, 260, 264, 269–70
Wright, Ronald, 300
Wright, William, 42, 128
A Writer's Life, 34, 178
Writers on the Air, 76
Writing in an Age of Silence, 247
Writing with Intent, 78, 79
Wurster, Thomas, 15, 301, 306–7, 311
Wyatt Earp, 212
Wynn, Jennifer, 63, 114, 124, 196, 216

Yafa, Stephen, 318
Yancey, Richard, 17, 93, 276
Yardley, Herbert, 154, 166
A Year in Provence, 75, 290
The Year of Living Biblically, 49, 154, 156, 159, 160, 188
The Year of Magical Thinking, 272
Year of Wonders, 8
The Year of Yes, 153, 180
A Year without "Made in China," 99, 117, 156, 300
Yergin, Daniel, 100, 117, 121, 138, 292, 315
Yes Man, 153, 159
Yes You Can!, 156, 161–62
York, Byron, 240
You Can't Be Neutral on a Moving Train, 257

You Look Lovely Today, 95
Young, Toby, 13
Your Best Life Now, 324

Zakaria, Fareed, 268, 270, 305
Zane, 178
Zehme, Bill, 221, 222
Zemke, Ron, 325
Zero 3 Bravo, 294
Zimmer, Carl, 47, 128
Zinn, Howard, 112, 141, 244, 246, 249, 255, 257, 266
Zoellner, Tom, 43, 137
Zombardo, Phillip, 92, 94
Zuckerman, Laurie, 105
Zuckoff, Mitchell, 154, 199, 294, 311, 315

Subject Index

9/11
  Against All Enemies, 279–80
  American Ground: Unbuilding the World Trade Center, 24–25
  Blood from Stones, 136–37
  Chain of Command, 264
  The Dark Side, 93
  Dead Center, 168–69
  The End of America, 256
  The Enemy at Home, 233–34
  The Evangelical President, 237–38
  Ghost Wars, 89–90
  The Greatest Story Ever Sold, 254
  The Looming Tower, 269–70
  Love, Poverty, and War, 71–72
  102 Minutes: The Untold Story of the Fight to Survive inside the Twin Towers, 29
  The Terror Dream, 246–47
  Touching History, 33
  Up from Zero, 22–23
  Where in the World Is Osama Bin Laden?, 187–88
  Without Precedent, 91
  World War IV: The Long Struggle against Islamofascism, 237
  See also Terrorism
1930s
  The Town on Beaver Creek, 212–13
  Up in the Old Hotel, 175–76
1940s
  The First Man-Made Man, 204–5
  Hiroshima, 137
  Up in the Old Hotel, 175–76
1950s
  The First Man-Made Man, 204–5
1960s
  The Armies of the Night, 175
  The Best and the Brightest, 273
  Bobos in Paradise, 310
  Cover-up: The Army's Secret Investigation of the Massacre at My Lai 4, 91
  Dispatches, 71
  The Kingdom and the Power, 33–34

  M, 186
1970s
  Articles of Faith: A Frontline History of the Abortion Wars, 30
  Common Ground, 219–20
  Dispatches, 71
  F5: Devastation, Survival, and the Most Violent Tornado Outbreak of the 20th Century, 31–32
  From Beirut to Jerusalem, 29–30
  A Miracle, A Universe: Settling Accounts with Torturers, 35
  The Secret Parts of Fortune, 78
  The Soul of a New Machine, 15
  13 Seconds: A Look Back at the Kent State Shootings, 28–29
  Vengeance, 138
1980s
  Articles of Faith: A Frontline History of the Abortion Wars, 30
  Bobos in Paradise, 310
  Common Ground, 219–20
  From Beirut to Jerusalem, 29–30
  Ghost Wars, 89–90
  Liar's Poker, 315
  A Miracle, A Universe: Settling Accounts with Torturers, 35
  The Secret Parts of Fortune, 78
  Voices from Chernobyl, 134
1990s
  Articles of Faith: A Frontline History of the Abortion Wars, 30
  Bringing the Heat, 51–52
  The Clinton Wars, 278–79
  Ghost Wars, 89–90
  Machete Season, 37–38
  The Mighty and the Almighty, 277–78
  Red River Rising, 32–33
  The Secret Parts of Fortune, 78
  The Selling of "Free Trade," 92
18th Century
  On the Wealth of Nations, 317
19th Century
  Adland, 297
  Blood of the Earth, 138

20th Century
    Adland, 297
    The Age of Abundance, 274
    The Atomic Bazaar, 139–40
    The Big Con, 89
    Bill & Dave, 293
    Blood of the Earth, 138
    Buried in the Bitter Waters, 124
    Civil Wars: A Battle for Gay Marriage, 31
    The Conscience of a Liberal, 251–52
    Friday Night Lights, 50
    Inside Hamas, 135
    Living It Up, 319
    Machete Season, 37–38
    Made to Break, 48
    A Miracle, A Universe: Settling Accounts
        with Torturers, 35
    Palestine: Peace Not Apartheid, 279
    Peninsula of Lies, 202
    Political Fictions, 272
    Portraits and Observations: The Essays of
        Truman Capote, 75
    The Snowball: Warren Buffett and the
        Business of Life, 296
21st Century
    The Assault on Reason, 280
    102 Minutes: The Untold Story of the
        Fight to Survive inside the Twin
        Towers, 29
    The Science of Fear, 123

Abortion
    Articles of Faith: A Frontline History of the
        Abortion Wars, 30
Abramoff, Jack
    Heist, 94
Abu Ghraib
    Chain of Command, 264
    Standard Operating Procedure, 70
Abuse
    Remembering Satan, 64–65
    Standard Operating Procedure, 70
Accidents
    The Last Season, 202–3
    The Legend of Colton H. Bryant, 194–95
    A Measure of Endurance, 206
    The Sun Farmer, 44–45
Accounting and Accountants
    Conspiracy of Fools, 310–11
Activism
    Dinner at the New Gene Cafe, 127
    Swim Against the Current, 248–49

Activists
    Inside the Red Zone, 217
Addiction
    Can't Buy My Love, 125
    Adventure
    Killing Pablo, 59
    Advertising
    Adland, 297
    Appetite for Profit, 111
    Applebee's America, 324
    Buying In, 132–33
    Can't Buy My Love, 125
    The Cigarette Century, 308–9
    Consumed, 308
    Living It Up, 319
    Shopping for God, 179–80
    Watch This, Listen Up, Click Here, 101
Afghanistan
    Blackwater, 108–9
    The Bookseller of Kabul, 186–87
    Freedom Next Time, 142
    Ghost Wars, 89–90
    Kabul in Winter, 185
    Opium Season, 184
    On the Road to Kandahar, 67
    Road Work, 8
    Uncivilized Beasts and Shameless Hellions,
        68
    World War IV: The Long Struggle against
        Islamofascism, 237
Africa
    Blood from Stones, 136–37
    The Body Hunters, 110–11
    Ghosts of Tsavo, 151
    Hope in Hell, 66–67
    Human Cargo, 140–41
    The Invisible Cure, 136
    Machete Season, 37–38
    The Man-Eaters of Eden, 22
    The Rebels' Hour, 198
    Sahara Unveiled, 155
    The Secret History of the American
        Empire, 141
    There Is No Me without You, 196
    Where Soldiers Fear to Tread, 181–82
    The Wonga Coup, 143–44
African American Authors
    America Behind the Color Line, 37
    Display of Power, 291–92
    Economic Facts and Fallacies, 239
    Rosa Lee, 209–10
    Who's Afraid of a Large Black Man?, 215–16

Agribusiness
  Food Politics, 105
Agriculture
  Animal, Vegetable, Miracle, 174
  Dinner at the New Gene Cafe, 127
  The End of Food, 106–7
  From the Farm to the Table, 38
  Flower Confidential, 18
  Food Fight, 265
  Food Politics, 105
  Let Us Now Praise Famous Men, 170–71
  A Measure of Endurance, 206
  The Sun Farmer, 44–45
  With These Hands, 169
  Twinkie, Deconstructed, 41
  A Very Good Year, 19–20
  See also Food
AIDS
  The Invisible Cure, 136
  There Is No Me without You, 196
Alabama
  *F5: Devastation, Survival, and the Most
      Violent Tornado Outbreak of the
      20th Century,* 31–32
  Let Us Now Praise Famous Men, 170–71
  My City Was Gone, 127–28
  Rammer, Jammer, Yellow, Hammer, 157
ALA Notable
  Animal, Vegetable, Miracle, 174
  *Articles of Faith: A Frontline History of the
      Abortion Wars,* 30
  The Assassins' Gate, 32
  Blood Diamonds, 134–35
  Breach of Faith, 218
  Chain of Command, 264
  Civil Wars: A Battle for Gay Marriage, 31
  Conspiracy of Fools, 310–11
  Crossing Over, 140
  Fast Food Nation, 110
  Field Notes from a Catastrophe, 44
  Going Up the River, 124
  A Hope in the Unseen, 206–7
  Human Cargo, 140–41
  *9 Highland Road: Sane Living for the
      Mentally Ill,* 20–21
  Nine Parts of Desire, 8–9
  Oil on the Brain, 315
  The Orchid Thief, 199
  Random Family, 210
  Salvation on Sand Mountain, 152
  Selected Essays of John Berger, 75
  Show Me a Hero, 208–9

  Super Crunchers, 299
  There Is No Me without You, 196
  The Ticket Out, 213
  Under the Banner of Heaven, 63–64
  Voices from Chernobyl, 134
Alaska
  Field Notes from a Catastrophe, 44
Albright, Madeleine
  The Mighty and the Almighty, 277–78
Alcoholics and Alcoholism
  Fear and Loathing in Las Vegas, 178–79
al-Qaeda
  The Dark Side, 93
  The Looming Tower, 269–70
  Where in the World Is Osama Bin Laden?,
      187–88
Alternate Histories
  The World Is Flat, 301
American History
  The Age of Abundance, 274
  The Age of Turbulence, 291
  Against All Enemies, 279–80
  All the President's Men, 87–88
  America Behind the Color Line, 37
  *American Green: The Obsessive Quest for
      the Perfect Lawn,* 26
  The Angry Right, 251
  *Articles of Faith: A Frontline History of the
      Abortion Wars,* 30
  The Assault on Reason, 280
  The Best and the Brightest, 273
  Biography of the Dollar, 292
  *Blasphemy: How the Religious Right Is
      Hijacking Our Declaration of
      Independence,* 245
  Buried in the Bitter Waters, 124
  Candyfreak, 6–7
  Can You Trust a Tomato in January?,
      131–32
  Casting a Spell, 51
  The Clinton Wars, 278–79
  *Cover-up: The Army's Secret Investigation
      of the Massacre at My Lai 4,* 91
  Dispatches, 71
  *F5: Devastation, Survival, and the Most
      Violent Tornado Outbreak of the
      20th Century,* 31–32
  The Face of War, 69–70
  Feeding the Fire, 120–21
  God on Trial, 274
  The Great Deluge, 28
  Gun Show Nation, 117–18

American History (*Cont.*)
  Gusher of Lies, 117
  Into the Valley, 184–85
  Killed Cartoons, 111–12
  Let Us Now Praise Famous Men, 170–71
  Living It Up, 319
  M, 186
  Made to Break, 48
  McIlhenny's Gold, 295–96
  Mission Unaccomplished, 246
  Nation of Secrets, 90
  Nobodies, 117–18
  *100 Ways America Is Screwing Up the
    World*, 255
  *102 Minutes: The Untold Story of the
    Fight to Survive inside the Twin
    Towers*, 29
  One Man's America, 239–40
  A People's History of American Empire, 257
  Political Fictions, 272
  *Pop! Why Bubbles Are Great for the
    Economy*, 301
  The Revolution: A Manifesto, 282
  *Screwed: The Undeclared War against the
    Middle Class*, 247–48
  *Showdown: Why China Wants War with
    the United States*, 259
  The Summer Game, 49-50
  *13 Seconds: A Look Back at the Kent State
    Shootings*, 28-29
  Touching History, 33
  The Town on Beaver Creek, 212–13
  Travels with Dr. Death, 129
  Up in the Old Hotel, 175–76
  See also World History
American Indians
  The Happiest Man in the World, 200–201
American South
  Buried in the Bitter Waters, 124
  *F5: Devastation, Survival, and the Most
    Violent Tornado Outbreak of the
    20th Century*, 31–32
  Let Us Now Praise Famous Men, 170–71
  Peninsula of Lies, 202
  Rammer, Jammer, Yellow, Hammer, 157
  Salvation on Sand Mountain, 152
American West
  Blacktop Cowboys, 212
  The Legend of Colton H. Bryant, 194–85
  Riding toward Everywhere, 159
Ancient History
  The Lost Gospel, 30–31

Animals
  Carnivorous Nights, 182
  A Country Practice, 20
  Ghosts of Tsavo, 151
  The Man-Eaters of Eden, 22
  The Men Who Stare at Goats, 94
  The Race for the Triple Crown, 52–53
  Return of the Condor, 45–46
  Under the Big Top, 165
Animation
  The Pixar Touch, 295
Antarctica
  The Whale Warriors, 13
Antiquities
  The Lost Gospel, 30–31
Apartheid
  Calamities of Exile, 223
Appalachian Mountains
  Animal, Vegetable, Miracle, 174
  The Last American Man, 195
  Lost Mountain, 107–8
  Salvation on Sand Mountain, 152
  The Town on Beaver Creek, 212–13
Arab-Israeli Conflict
  Drinking the Sea at Gaza, 183–84
  From Beirut to Jerusalem, 29–30
  How Israel Lost, 262
  Inside Hamas, 135
  The Lemon Tree, 34
  A Match Made in Heaven, 260–61
  Palestine: Peace Not Apartheid, 279
  Vengeance, 138
Aral Sea
  The Devil and the Disappearing Sea, 183
Archaeology
  The Lost Gospel, 30–31
Architecture
  *American Ground: Unbuilding the World
    Trade Center*, 24–25
  Last Harvest, 25–26
  *102 Minutes: The Untold Story of the
    Fight to Survive inside the Twin
    Towers*, 29
  Up from Zero, 22–23
Arctic
  Field Notes from a Catastrophe, 44
Arkansas
  In Sam We Trust, 106
Art and Artists
  All I Did Was Ask, 76
  *Museum: Behind the Scenes at the
    Metropolitan Museum of Art*, 216

Selected Essays of John Berger, 75
Artificial Intelligence
    Almost Human: Making Robots Think, 42
Asia
    *The Secret History of the American
        Empire*, 141
Aspen
    Whiteout: Lost in Aspen, 172–73
Assassinations
    Vengeance, 138
Astronauts
    The Right Stuff, 214
Astronomy
    First Light, 46
Atheism
    God Is Not Great, 264
Athletes
    The Ticket Out, 213
Atomic Bomb
    The Atomic Bazaar, 139–40
    Hiroshima, 137
Atrocities
    Chain of Command, 264
    *Cover-up: The Army's Secret Investigation
        of the Massacre at My Lai 4*, 91
    Hiroshima, 137
    Machete Season, 37–38
    "A Problem from Hell," 143
    The Rebels' Hour, 198
Australia
    Carnivorous Nights, 182
Authors
    American Fictions, 76
Autobiographies
    The Age of Turbulence, 291
Aviation
    Touching History, 33
Azerbaijan
    Fugitive Denim, 318

Baghdad
    Night Draws Near, 187
Bakersfield, California
    Mean Justice, 62
Baltimore
    Next Man Up, 53
Banks
    Maxed Out, 318
Barkley, Charles
    Who's Afraid of a Large Black Man?,
        215–16

Baseball
    Cubs Nation, 56
    Fantasyland, 159–60
    Feeding the Monster, 55
    Game of Shadows, 98–89
    Juicing the Game, 52
    Moneyball, 54–55
    The Summer Game, 49–50
    Three Nights in August, 50–51
    The Ticket Out, 213
    Twilight of the Long-ball Gods, 56
    See also Sports
Basketball
    The Breaks of the Game, 54
    The Miracle of St. Anthony, 56–57
    Who's Afraid of a Large Black Man?,
        215–16
    See also Sports
Batali, Mario
    Heat, 162
Beane, Billy
    Moneyball, 54–55
Beard, James
    The United States of Arugula, 13–14
Beauty Industry
    The Perfect Scent, 289
Belarus
    Voices from Chernobyl, 134
Belichick, Bill
    The Education of a Coach, 197
Beverly Hills
    Parts Per Million, 100
Bhutto, Benazir
    *Reconciliation: Islam, Democracy, and the
        West*, 278
Bible
    The Lost Gospel, 30–31
Billiards
    Sweet: An Eight-Ball Odyssey, 163
bin Laden, Osama
    Where in the World Is Osama Bin Laden?,
        187–88
Biographies
    Alice Waters and Chez Panisse, 292–83
    All the Money in the World, 288–89
    As Nature Made Him, 203–4
    Bill & Dave, 293
    The Clinton Wars, 278–79
    Crashing Through, 205
    The Education of a Coach, 197
    Finders Keepers, 203

Biographies (*Cont.*)
  The First Man-Made Man, 204–5
  The Happiest Man in the World, 200–201
  In Sam We Trust, 106
  Killing Pablo, 59
  The Last American Man, 195
  Rigged, 294
  The Ticket Out, 213
  See also Memoirs
Biology
  *American Green: The Obsessive Quest for
      the Perfect Lawn*, 26
  *Bonk: The Curious Coupling of Science and
      Sex*, 46–47
  *The Dangerous Joy of Dr. Sex and Other
      True Stories*, 219
  *Germs: Biological Weapons and America's
      Secret War*, 45
  The Science of Fear, 123
  See also Science
Birds
  Return of the Condor, 45–46
Blair, Jayson
  Hard News, 104–5
Blogs
  *The Argument: Billionaires, Bloggers, and
      the Battle to Remake Democratic
      Politics*, 271
Bonds, Barry
  Game of Shadows, 98–89
Book Groups
  The Blind Side, 205–6
  The Bookseller of Kabul, 186–87
  Chain of Command, 264
  A Civil Action, 99–100
  Cobra II, 90
  The Conscience of a Liberal, 251–52
  Crashing Through, 205
  Deep Economy, 302–3
  Deer Hunting with Jesus, 242
  Dispatches, 71
  The End of America, 256
  Everything Is Miscellaneous, 306
  Fast Food Nation, 110
  Field Notes from a Catastrophe, 44
  Flower Confidential, 18
  Freakonomics, 314
  Friday Night Lights, 50
  God Is Not Great, 264
  The Golden Spruce, 132
  Good to Great, 323
  The Great Deluge, 28

  Heat, 162
  Imperial Life in the Emerald City, 68–69
  The Legend of Colton H. Bryant, 194–85
  The Lemon Tree, 34
  The Long Tail, 298
  The Looming Tower, 269–70
  The Making of a Chef, 169–70
  Moneyball, 54–55
  Newjack: Guarding Sing Sing, 163
  Nickel and Dimed, 164
  Nine Parts of Desire, 8–8
  On the Wealth of Nations, 317
  The Orchid Thief, 199
  The Post-American World, 270
  Predictably Irrational, 298–89
  The Progress Paradox, 120
  Random Family, 210
  The Rebels' Hour, 198
  Richistan, 122
  Rigged, 294
  Self-Made Man, 180
  *The Spirit Catches You and You Fall
      Down*, 10–11
  Starbucked, 290
  *Stiff: The Curious Lives of Human
      Cadavers*, 47
  There Is No Me without You, 196
  Under the Banner of Heaven, 63–64
  Word Freak, 153
  The Working Poor, 130
  The World Is Flat, 301
  The Year of Living Biblically, 154
Book Reviews
  American Fictions, 76
  Bound to Please, 75–76
  Due Considerations, 79
  Falling Upwards, 78–79
  Lonesome Rangers, 77
  *Portraits and Observations: The Essays of
      Truman Capote*, 75
  Uncensored: Views & (Re)views, 77–78
Books and Learning
  American Fictions, 76
  The Bookseller of Kabul, 186–87
  Bound to Please, 75–76
  Due Considerations, 79
  On the Wealth of Nations, 317
  The Year of Living Biblically, 154
Books in Translation
  The Bookseller of Kabul, 186–87
  Drinking the Sea at Gaza, 183–84
  Machete Season, 37–38

The Rebels' Hour, 198
A Russian Diary, 142
Voices from Chernobyl, 134
With Their Backs to the World, 222
Bosnia
  "A Problem from Hell," 143
Boston
  Common Ground, 219–20
  Feeding the Monster, 55
Boston Red Sox
  Feeding the Monster, 55
Botany
  *American Green: The Obsessive Quest for
    the Perfect Lawn*, 26
Boxing
  Without Apology, 151–52
Brain
  Brainwash, 131
  Crashing Through, 205
  *The Dangerous Joy of Dr. Sex and Other
    True Stories*, 219
  The Naked Brain, 128
  The Political Brain, 276
  The Science of Fear, 123
Branding
  Made to Stick, 324–25
Brazil
  *A Miracle, A Universe: Settling Accounts
    with Torturers*, 35
Bremer, Paul
  Imperial Life in the Emerald City, 68–69
Bridge
  *The Backwash Squeeze and Other
    Improbable Feats*, 156
British Columbia
  The Golden Spruce, 132
Brokovich, Erin
  Parts Per Million, 100
Bryant, Colton H.
  The Legend of Colton H. Bryant, 194–85
Buffett, Warren
  *The Snowball: Warren Buffett and the
    Business of Life*, 296
Bush, George W.
  Against All Enemies, 279–80
  Armed Madhouse, 253
  The Assassins' Gate, 32
  Bushworld, 245–46
  Cobra II, 90
  *Comeback: Conservatism That Can Win
    Again*, 234
  The Evangelical President, 237–38

The Fall of the House of Bush, 255–56
*Fiasco: The American Military Adventure
  in Iraq*, 267–68
The Greatest Story Ever Sold, 254
How Bush Rules, 242–43
*Hubris: The Inside Story of Spin, Scandal,
  and the Selling of the Iraq War*, 250
The Occupation, 69
The One Percent Doctrine, 269
Pretensions to Empire, 252
State of Denial, 283
Stupid White Men, 252
What Happened, 280–81
Without Precedent, 91
*World War IV: The Long Struggle against
  Islamofascism*, 237
Worse than Watergate, 244–45
Business
  Aftermath, Inc., 168
  The Age of Fallibility, 282–83
  All the Money in the World, 288–89
  The American Way of Death Revisited, 104
  Appetite for Profit, 111
  Applebee's America, 324
  Ashes to Ashes, 103
  Bait and Switch, 164
  Big-Box Swindle, 316
  The Big Squeeze, 312–13
  Biography of the Dollar, 292
  Bitter Chocolate, 105–6
  Blackout, 112
  Blood Diamonds, 134–35
  Blown to Bits, 306–7
  The Body Hunters, 110–11
  Buying In, 132–33
  Candyfreak, 6–7
  Can't Buy My Love, 125
  Can You Trust a Tomato in January?,
    131–32
  Capitalism 3.0, 299–300
  China, Inc., 300
  The China Price, 99
  China Shakes the World, 302
  A Civil Action, 99–100
  Comfortably Numb, 95–86
  Consumed, 308
  The Corporation, 308
  Corporation Nation, 98
  Deep Economy, 302–3
  Diamond, 43
  The Disposable American, 319–20
  The Elephant and the Dragon, 303

Business (*Cont.*)
The End of Food, 106–7
Everything Is Miscellaneous, 306
Exposed: The Toxic Chemistry of Everyday Products, 109
Fast Food Nation, 110
Fighting for Air, 102
First, Break All the Rules, 323
Flower Confidential, 18
Food Politics, 105
The Fortune Cookie Chronicles, 15–16
Freakonomics, 314
Freedonomics, 236–37
Fugitive Denim, 318
Gig, 36–37
Good to Great, 323
Group Genius, 326
Gusher of Lies, 117
Hard News, 104–5
House Lust, 302
It's Not News, It's Fark, 97–88
Javatrekker, 310
Juicing the Game, 52
Last Harvest, 25–26
Liar's Poker, 315
Lost Mountain, 107–8
Made to Break, 48
Made to Stick, 324–25
Manhattan Passions, 220–21
Maxed Out, 318
A Measure of Endurance, 206
Microtrends, 303–4
The Missing Class, 316
Moneyball, 54–55
My City Was Gone, 127–28
The Naked Brain, 128
Natural Causes, 100–101
Nickel and Dimed, 164
The No Asshole Rule, 326–27
Oil on the Brain, 315
One Market under God, 312
The One Minute Manager, 322–23
One Perfect Day, 103–4
One World, Ready or Not, 313
On the Wealth of Nations, 317
Opting Out?, 38–39
Our Daily Meds, 107
The Outlaw Sea, 25
Outrage, 266–67
The Perfect Scent, 289
Pop! Why Bubbles Are Great for the Economy, 301

Punching In, 165–66
Purple Cow, 324
Remember Me, 9–10
Revolt in the Boardroom, 325–26
Revolutionary Wealth, 305–6
Richistan, 122
Rigged, 294
The Rise of the Creative Class, 311
In Sam We Trust, 106
Screwed: The Undeclared War against the Middle Class, 247–48
The Secret History of the American Empire, 141
Self-Made Man, 180
The Selling of "Free Trade," 92
Setting the Table, 325
Shopping for God, 179–80
The Snowball: Warren Buffett and the Business of Life, 296
The Soul of a New Machine, 15
Spychips, 115
The Squandering of America, 265–66
The Starfish and the Spider, 321–22
Superclass, 317
Super Crunchers, 299
The Sushi Economy, 313–14
Swim Against the Current, 248–49
With These Hands, 169
Throwing the Elephant, 322
The Trap, 209
Trump: The Art of the Deal, 327
Under the Big Top, 165
The United States of Arugula, 13–14
Up from Zero, 22–23
A Very Good Year, 19–20
Watch This, Listen Up, Click Here, 101
A Weekend with Warren Buffett, 289–80
The Whistleblower, 108
Who's Your City?, 300
Why We Buy, 320
Wikinomics, 205
Winning, 327–28
The Working Poor, 130
The World Is Flat, 301
Yes You Can!, 161–62
See also Economics
Business Histories
Adland, 297
Alice Waters and Chez Panisse, 292–83
Bill & Dave, 293
Blackwater, 108–8
Blood of the Earth, 138

Boeing versus Airbus, 294
The Cigarette Century, 308–8
Conspiracy of Fools, 310–11
Deluxe: How Luxury Lost Its Luster, 296–87
Dinner at the New Gene Cafe, 127
Display of Power, 291–82
The Kingdom and the Power, 33–34
McIlhenny's Gold, 295–86
Noble Rot: A Bordeaux Wine Revolution, 290
Once You're Lucky, Twice You're Good, 292
Parts Per Million, 100
Piano: The Making of a Steinway Concert Grand, 7–8
The Pixar Touch, 295
Setting the Table, 325
Starbucked, 290
A Weekend with Warren Buffett, 289–80

Caffeine
    Starbucked, 290
California
    Alice Waters and Chez Panisse, 292–83
    Assembling California, 166–67
    Bill & Dave, 293
    Fame Junkies, 12–13
    The Last Season, 202–3
    Mean Justice, 62
    Moneyball, 54–55
    No Matter How Loud I Shout, 62–63
    Parts Per Million, 100
    Revenge of the Donut Boys, 17
    The Ticket Out, 213
    A Very Good Year, 19–20
Canada
    The Selling of "Free Trade," 92
Cancer
    A Civil Action, 99–100
    Parts Per Million, 100
    The Secret History of the War on Cancer, 119
Capitalism
    Capitalism 3.0, 299–300
    Corporation Nation, 98
    Deep Economy, 302–3
    The End of Work, 304
    One Market under God, 312
    One World, Ready or Not, 313
    On the Wealth of Nations, 317

Capital Punishment
    Back from the Dead, 216
Card Games
    The Backwash Squeeze and Other Improbable Feats, 156
    Hunting Fish, 153–54
Careers
    Bait and Switch, 164
Carter, Jimmy
    Palestine: Peace Not Apartheid, 279
Cartoons
    Killed Cartoons, 111–12
Catholicism
    Magnificent Corpses, 221
Causality
    Made to Stick, 324–25
    Microtrends, 303–4
Celebrations
    Once Upon a Quinceañara, 208
Celebrities and Superstars
    All I Did Was Ask, 76
    Character Studies, 222
    Cleopatra's Nose, 200
    Manhattan Passions, 220–21
    The Worst Person in the World, 253
Central Asia
    The Devil and the Disappearing Sea, 183
Chad
    Oil on the Brain, 315
Character Profiles
    All God's Children, 60–61
    All the Money in the World, 288–89
    American Dream, 119–20
    Among Schoolchildren, 14
    Backyard Giants, 19
    Bill & Dave, 293
    Bomb Squad, 165
    Bringing the Heat, 51–52
    Class Matters, 261–62
    Cleopatra's Nose, 200
    Cookoff: Recipe Fever in America, 157–58
    A Country Practice, 20
    Drinking the Sea at Gaza, 183–84
    Fame Junkies, 12–13
    Feeding the Monster, 55
    Here to Stay, 204
    A Home on the Field, 173
    Home Town, 24
    Horsemen of the Esophagus, 11–12
    Human Cargo, 140–41
    Into the Valley, 184–85

Character Profiles (*Cont.*)
  Justice: Crimes, Trials, and Punishments, 61
  The Long Road Home, 73
  Love, Poverty, and War, 71–72
  Many Sleepless Nights, 42–43
  The Men Who Stare at Goats, 94
  The Miracle of St. Anthony, 56–57
  Moneyball, 54–55
  9 Highland Road: Sane Living for the Mentally Ill, 20–21
  The Nine: Inside the Secret World of the Supreme Court, 275–76
  No Matter How Loud I Shout, 62–63
  100 People Who Are Screwing Up America, 235
  102 Minutes: The Untold Story of the Fight to Survive inside the Twin Towers, 29
  One Man's America, 239–40
  Otherwise Normal People, 17–18
  The Overachievers, 128–29
  Paper Trails, 10
  Portraits and Observations: The Essays of Truman Capote, 75
  Rammer, Jammer, Yellow, Hammer, 157
  Revenge of the Donut Boys, 17
  Revolt in the Boardroom, 325–26
  Richistan, 122
  Rigged, 294
  Road Work, 8
  The Season, 173–74
  The Secret Parts of Fortune, 78
  Sick: The Untold Story of America's Health Care Crisis, 97
  The Soul of a New Machine, 15
  Sowbelly, 150–51
  Tales from Q School, 53–54
  Them: Adventures with Extremists, 177
  There Are No Children Here, 125–26
  With These Hands, 169
  Three Nights in August, 50–51
  Thy Neighbor's Wife, 178
  Travels with Dr. Death, 129
  Uncivilized Beasts and Shameless Hellions, 68
  Under the Big Top, 165
  Up in the Old Hotel, 175–76
  A Very Good Year, 19–20
  The Whale Warriors, 13
  Who Are You People?, 9
  The Wild Trees, 156–57
  Winning, 327–28
  Word Freak, 153
  The Worst Person in the World, 253
  Yes You Can!, 161–62
Charity
  Giving: How Each of Us Can Change the World, 280
Chechnya
  A Russian Diary, 142
Cheerleading
  Cheer! Three Teams on a Quest for College Cheerleading's Ultimate Prize, 18–19
Chefs
  Alice Waters and Chez Panisse, 292–83
  Heat, 162
Chemicals
  The End of Food, 106–7
  Exposed: The Toxic Chemistry of Everyday Products, 109
  The Hundred-Year Lie, 121–22
  Juicing the Game, 52
Chemistry
  American Green: The Obsessive Quest for the Perfect Lawn, 26
Cheney, Richard
  Hubris: The Inside Story of Spin, Scandal, and the Selling of the Iraq War, 250
  The One Percent Doctrine, 269
  Worse than Watergate, 244–45
Chernobyl
  Voices from Chernobyl, 134
Chess
  The Kings of New York, 213–14
Chicago
  American Project: The Rise and Fall of a Modern Ghetto, 34–35
  Courtroom 302, 58
  Cubs Nation, 56
  There Are No Children Here, 125–26
Chicago Cubs
  Cubs Nation, 56
Child, Julia
  The United States of Arugula, 13–14
Childbirth
  Pushed: The Painful Truth about Childbirth and Modern Maternity Care, 116
China
  China, Inc., 300
  The China Price, 99
  China Shakes the World, 302

Deluxe: How Luxury Lost Its Luster, 296–87
The Elephant and the Dragon, 303
Oil on the Brain, 315
Showdown: Why China Wants War with the United States, 259
The World Is Flat, 301
Chocolate
   Bitter Chocolate, 105–6
   Candyfreak, 6–7
Choice
   Predictably Irrational, 298–89
Christianity
   American Fascists, 248
   Blackwater, 108–8
   God on Trial, 274
   The Lost Gospel, 30–31
   Magnificent Corpses, 221
   The Marketing of Evil, 236
   A Match Made in Heaven, 260–61
   The Mighty and the Almighty, 277–78
   See also Religion
CIA
   Brainwash, 131
   Ghost Wars, 89–80
Cigarettes
   Ashes to Ashes, 103
   The Cigarette Century, 308–8
Circus
   Under the Big Top, 165
Civil Rights
   America Behind the Color Line, 37
   Civil Wars: A Battle for Gay Marriage, 31
Claiborne, Craig
   The United States of Arugula, 13–14
Classics
   Alice, Let's Eat, 158
   All the President's Men, 87–88
   American Fictions, 76
   The American Way of Death Revisited, 104
   Among Schoolchildren, 14
   The Armies of the Night, 175
   Assembling California, 166–67
   From Beirut to Jerusalem, 29–30
   The Best and the Brightest, 273
   Bobos in Paradise, 310
   The Breaks of the Game, 54
   Bringing the Heat, 51–52
   A Civil Action, 99–100
   Cold New World, 121
   Common Ground, 219–20

Cover-up: The Army's Secret Investigation of the Massacre at My Lai 4, 91
Coyotes, 172
Dispatches, 71
The Face of War, 69–70
Fast Food Nation, 110
Fear and Loathing in Las Vegas, 178–79
First, Break All the Rules, 323
First Light, 46
Freakonomics, 314
Friday Night Lights, 50
God and Man at Yale, 232
Good to Great, 323
Growing Up Fast, 211
Hegemony or Survival, 243–44
Hell's Angels, 179
Here to Stay, 204
Hiroshima, 137
Justice: Crimes, Trials, and Punishments, 61
The Kingdom and the Power, 33–34
Let Us Now Praise Famous Men, 170–71
Liar's Poker, 315
The Long Tail, 298
M, 186
Made to Stick, 324–25
Many Sleepless Nights, 42–43
A Miracle, A Universe: Settling Accounts with Torturers, 35
Moneyball, 54–55
Newjack: Guarding Sing Sing, 163
Nickel and Dimed, 164
The One Minute Manager, 322–23
The Orchid Thief, 199
The Other Side of the River, 63
An Outside Chance, 55
Paper Lion, 167
Purple Cow, 324
Random Family, 210
Remembering Satan, 64–65
The Right Stuff, 214
Rosa Lee, 209–10
The Soul of a New Machine, 15
The Spirit Catches You and You Fall Down, 10–11
Stiff: The Curious Lives of Human Cadavers, 47
The Summer Game, 49–50
There Are No Children Here, 125–26
Thy Neighbor's Wife, 178
Travels with Dr. Death, 129
Trump: The Art of the Deal, 327

Classics (*Cont.*)
Uncommon Carriers, 16
Under the Banner of Heaven, 63–64
Up in the Old Hotel, 175–76
Vengeance, 138
What It Takes: The Way to the White House, 272
Whiteout: Lost in Aspen, 172–73
Why We Buy, 320
Working, 39
The Working Poor, 130
The World Is Flat, 301
Classism
Armed Madhouse, 253
The Big Con, 89
Bobos in Paradise, 310
Class Matters, 261–62
Cold New World, 121
Common Ground, 219–20
The Conscience of a Liberal, 251–52
Deer Hunting with Jesus, 242
Falling Behind, 311–12
Inequality Matters, 314
Let Us Now Praise Famous Men, 170–71
The Missing Class, 316
On Paradise Drive, 232
Screwed: The Undeclared War against the Middle Class, 247–48
The Season, 173–74
Superclass, 317
The Working Poor, 130
Climate
Field Notes from a Catastrophe, 44
The Long Emergency, 126–27
Clinton, Bill
The Clinton Wars, 278–79
Giving: How Each of Us Can Change the World, 280
The Selling of "Free Trade," 92
Clinton, Hillary
The Clinton Wars, 278–79
Cocaine
Killing Pablo, 59
Coffee
Javatrekker, 310
Starbucked, 290
Cold War
The Atomic Bazaar, 139–40
Brainwash, 131
College
Pledged: The Secret Life of Sororities, 176–77

Colombia
Killing Pablo, 59
Colorado
Whiteout: Lost in Aspen, 172–73
Comfort, Alex
The Dangerous Joy of Dr. Sex and Other True Stories, 219
Coming of Age
Once Upon a Quinceañara, 208
Sweet: An Eight-Ball Odyssey, 163
Communications
Made to Break, 48
Communism
Showdown: Why China Wants War with the United States, 259
Community Life
American Project: The Rise and Fall of a Modern Ghetto, 34–35
Animal, Vegetable, Miracle, 174
Big-Box Swindle, 316
Buried in the Bitter Waters, 124
A Civil Action, 99–100
Civil Wars: A Battle for Gay Marriage, 31
Class Matters, 261–62
Cold New World, 121
A Country Practice, 20
Deep Economy, 302–3
Deer Hunting with Jesus, 242
Feeding the Monster, 55
Friday Night Lights, 50
From the Farm to the Table, 38
Going Up the River, 124
A Home on the Field, 172
Home Town, 24
Last Harvest, 25–26
Living Blue in the Red States, 254–55
McIlhenny's Gold, 295–86
The Miracle of Castel di Sangro, 185–86
Monkey Girl, 264–65
Ms. Moffett's First Year, 12
My City Was Gone, 127–28
9 Highland Road: Sane Living for the Mentally Ill, 20–21
Nobodies, 116–17
The Other Side of the River, 63
Parts Per Million, 100
A Prayer for the City, 209
The Progress Paradox, 120
Red River Rising, 32–33
The Season, 173–74
Show Me a Hero, 208–8
The Trap, 209

Up from Zero, 22–23
The Way of Ignorance, 259
Whiteout: Lost in Aspen, 172–73
Wonderland, 171
Companies
    Appetite for Profit, 111
    The Big Squeeze, 312–13
    Blackout, 112
    The Body Hunters, 110–11
    Boeing versus Airbus, 294
    Buying In, 132–33
    Conspiracy of Fools, 310–11
    The Corporation, 308
    Corporation Nation, 98
    First, Break All the Rules, 323
    Game of Shadows, 98–89
    Good to Great, 323
    Group Genius, 326
    Heist, 94
    In Sam We Trust, 106
    Lost Mountain, 107–8
    McIlhenny's Gold, 295–86
    My City Was Gone, 127–28
    Nation of Secrets, 90
    Natural Causes, 100–101
    Our Daily Meds, 107
    The Pixar Touch, 295
    Punching In, 165–66
    Revolt in the Boardroom, 325–26
    The Rise of the Creative Class, 311
    *The Secret History of the American
        Empire,* 141
    *Sick: The Untold Story of America's Health
        Care Crisis,* 97
    Spychips, 115
    Starbucked, 290
    The Starfish and the Spider, 321–22
    Twinkie, Deconstructed, 41
    Watch This, Listen Up, Click Here, 101
    The Whistleblower, 108
    See also Business
Computers
    Bill & Dave, 293
    Blown to Bits, 306–7
    Brave New Ballot, 275
    Dreaming in Code, 16–17
    Once You're Lucky, Twice You're Good,
        292
    The Pixar Touch, 295
    The Soul of a New Machine, 15
    See also Technology

Con Artists
    The Crime of Sheila McGough, 198–89
Condors
    Return of the Condor, 45–46
Conservatism
    *Comeback: Conservatism That Can Win
        Again,* 234
    God and Man at Yale, 232
    Godless: The Church of Liberalism, 233
    The Vast Left Wing Conspiracy, 240
    Welcome to the Homeland, 266
    *World War IV: The Long Struggle against
        Islamofascism,* 237
Constitution
    The Dark Side, 93
    The Revolution: A Manifesto, 282
Consumerism
    All the Money in the World, 288–89
    Big-Box Swindle, 316
    Buying In, 132–33
    Can't Buy My Love, 125
    The China Price, 99
    China Shakes the World, 302
    Consumed, 308
    Deluxe: How Luxury Lost Its Luster,
        296–87
    Don't Get Too Comfortable, 176
    Falling Behind, 311–12
    Living It Up, 319
    The Long Tail, 298
    One Perfect Day, 103–4
    Shopping for God, 179–80
    Why We Buy, 320
Conway, Eustace
    The Last American Man, 195
Cooking
    Alice Waters and Chez Panisse, 292–83
    Cookoff: Recipe Fever in America, 157–58
    Heat, 162
    The Making of a Chef, 169–70
Corporations
    The Secret History of the War on Cancer,
        119
Corruption
    Blood from Stones, 136–37
    Confessions of a Political Hitman, 92–83
    *Coronary: A True Story of Medicine Gone
        Awry,* 102
    The Corporation, 308
    The Devil and the Disappearing Sea, 183
    Down By the River, 58–59

Corruption (*Cont.*)
Game of Shadows, 98–89
Heist, 94
Mean Justice, 62
The Miracle of Castel di Sangro, 185–86
A Russian Diary, 142
Swim Against the Current, 248–49
The Truth: With Jokes, 247
The Whistleblower, 108
The Wonga Coup, 143–44
Cotton
Fugitive Denim, 318
Cowboys
Blacktop Cowboys, 212
The Legend of Colton H. Bryant, 194–85
Coyle, Joey
Finders Keepers, 203
Creationism
Monkey Girl, 264–65
Creativity
Group Genius, 326
The Rise of the Creative Class, 311
Credit
Maxed Out, 318
Croatia
With Their Backs to the World, 222
Cuba
Guantánamo and the Abuse of Presidential Power, 92
Cults
Under the Banner of Heaven, 63–64
Culture
100 Ways America Is Screwing Up the World, 255
Culture Clash
The Bookseller of Kabul, 186–87
Crossing Over, 140
The Spirit Catches You and You Fall Down, 10–11
Customer Service
Setting the Table, 325
Czechoslovakia
Calamities of Exile, 223

Death and Dying
The American Way of Death Revisited, 104
F5: Devastation, Survival, and the Most Violent Tornado Outbreak of the 20th Century, 31–32
The Legend of Colton H. Bryant, 194–85
Night Draws Near, 187
Remember Me, 9–10

Stiff: The Curious Lives of Human Cadavers, 47
13 Seconds: A Look Back at the Kent State Shootings, 28–29
Debt
Maxed Out, 318
Decisions
Predictably Irrational, 298–89
Declaration of Independence
Blasphemy: How the Religious Right Is Hijacking Our Declaration of Independence, 245
DeLay, Tom
Heist, 94
Democracy
Brave New Ballot, 275
Corporation Nation, 98
Fighting for Air, 102
Democratic Republic of the Congo
The Rebels' Hour, 198
Demographics
The Extreme Future, 118
Future Cast, 304–5
Who's Your City?, 300
Depression
As Nature Made Him, 203–4
Detroit
Paper Lion, 167
Diamonds
Blood Diamonds, 134–35
Blood from Stones, 136–37
Diamond, 43
Dictators
The Wonga Coup, 143–44
Dillon, Michael
The First Man-Made Man, 204–5
Disasters
Breach of Faith, 218
City Adrift: New Orleans Before and After Katrina, 27–28
Disaster: Hurricane Katrina and the Failure of Homeland Security, 88
Red River Rising, 32–33
Voices from Chernobyl, 134
Discrimination
Kabul in Winter, 185
Diseases
The Coming Plague, 41–42
Good Germs, Bad Germs, 47–48
Doctors
Coronary: A True Story of Medicine Gone Awry, 102

Drug Addiction
   Fear and Loathing in Las Vegas, 178–79
   Finders Keepers, 203
   Growing Up Fast, 211
   Random Family, 210
   Rosa Lee, 209–10
Drugs
   Cold New World, 121
   Down By the River, 58–59
   Finders Keepers, 203
   Juicing the Game, 52
   Killing Pablo, 59
   Life on the Outside, 195–86
   Opium Season, 184
   Rosa Lee, 209–10
Dubai
   Rigged, 294
Dunn, Patrick
   Mean Justice, 62
Dysfunctional Families
   Growing Up Fast, 211

Eccentrics
   Character Studies, 222
   *The Dangerous Joy of Dr. Sex and Other
       True Stories*, 219
   The Happiest Man in the World, 200–201
   The Last American Man, 195
   Lone Patriot, 197–88
   The Men Who Stare at Goats, 94
Ecology
   The Man-Eaters of Eden, 22
   The Wild Trees, 156–57
Economics
   The Age of Abundance, 274
   The Age of Fallibility, 282–83
   The Age of Turbulence, 291
   All the Money in the World, 288–89
   American Dream, 119–20
   American Furies, 114
   American Theocracy, 267
   Bait and Switch, 164
   The Big Con, 89
   The Big Squeeze, 312–13
   Biography of the Dollar, 292
   Blood from Stones, 136–37
   Blood of the Earth, 138
   Blown to Bits, 306–7
   Bobos in Paradise, 310
   The Body Hunters, 110–11
   Boeing versus Airbus, 294
   Capitalism 3.0, 299–300

China, Inc., 300
China Shakes the World, 302
Class Matters, 261–62
The Conscience of a Liberal, 251–52
Conspiracy of Fools, 310–11
Consumed, 308
The Corporation, 308
A Crime So Monstrous, 144
Deep Economy, 302–3
Deer Hunting with Jesus, 242
Deluxe: How Luxury Lost Its Luster,
       296–87
The Disposable American, 319–20
Economic Facts and Fallacies, 239
Eight Ways to Run the Country, 274–75
The Elephant and the Dragon, 303
The End of Work, 304
*Exposed: The Toxic Chemistry of Everyday
       Products*, 109
Falling Behind, 311–12
From the Farm to the Table, 38
Flower Confidential, 18
Food Fight, 265
Freakonomics, 314
Freedonomics, 236–37
Fugitive Denim, 318
Future Cast, 304–5
*Giving: How Each of Us Can Change the
       World*, 280
Going Up the River, 124
House Lust, 302
Inequality Matters, 314
Javatrekker, 310
Last Harvest, 25–26
Living It Up, 319
The Long Emergency, 126–27
The Long Tail, 298
Maxed Out, 318
Microtrends, 303–4
The Missing Class, 316
Mission Unaccomplished, 246
Nickel and Dimed, 164
Nobodies, 116–17
Oil on the Brain, 315
One Market under God, 312
One World, Ready or Not, 313
Outrage, 266–67
On Paradise Drive, 232
On the Wealth of Nations, 317
Poor People, 39–40
*Pop! Why Bubbles Are Great for the
       Economy*, 301

Economics (*Cont.*)
The Post-American World, 270
Predictably Irrational, 298–89
The Progress Paradox, 120
Revolt in the Boardroom, 325–26
The Revolution: A Manifesto, 282
Revolutionary Wealth, 305–6
Richistan, 122
Rigged, 294
The Rise of the Creative Class, 311
*Screwed: The Undeclared War against the
    Middle Class*, 247–48
*The Secret History of the American
    Empire*, 141
The Selling of "Free Trade," 92
The Shame of the Nation, 126
*Sick: The Untold Story of America's Health
    Care Crisis*, 97
The Squandering of America, 265–66
Superclass, 317
The Trap, 209
A Weekend with Warren Buffett, 289–80
Wikinomics, 205
With These Hands, 169
The Wonga Coup, 143–44
The Working Poor, 130
The World Is Flat, 301
See also Business
Education
Absolutely American, 211–12
Among Schoolchildren, 14
Fat Envelope Frenzy, 218–19
God and Man at Yale, 232
A Hope in the Unseen, 206–7
The Kings of New York, 213–14
The Making of a Chef, 169–70
The Miracle of St. Anthony, 56–57
Monkey Girl, 264–65
Ms. Moffett's First Year, 12
The Overachievers, 128–29
Pledged: The Secret Life of Sororities,
    176–77
The Shame of the Nation, 126
The Trap, 209
Wonderland, 171
Elections
Confessions of a Political Hitman, 92–83
Political Fictions, 272
Emotion
The Science of Fear, 123
Energy
Blackout, 112

Conspiracy of Fools, 310–11
Feeding the Fire, 120–21
Gusher of Lies, 117
Nuclear Power Is Not the Answer, 96
Engineering
Red River Rising, 32–33
The Soul of a New Machine, 15
Twinkie, Deconstructed, 41
Entertainers
All I Did Was Ask, 76
Environment
Gusher of Lies, 117
Environmental Writing
Animal, Vegetable, Miracle, 174
Assembling California, 166–67
Carnivorous Nights, 182
Deep Economy, 302–3
The Devil and the Disappearing Sea, 183
The End of Food, 106–7
*Exposed: The Toxic Chemistry of Everyday
    Products*, 109
Field Notes from a Catastrophe, 44
Flower Confidential, 18
Fugitive Denim, 318
Garbage Land, 129–30
The Golden Spruce, 132
High Tech Trash, 123
The Hundred-Year Lie, 121–22
The Last American Man, 195
Last Harvest, 25–26
The Last Season, 202–3
The Long Emergency, 126–27
Lost Mountain, 107–8
The Man-Eaters of Eden, 22
My City Was Gone, 127–28
Return of the Condor, 45–46
Selected Essays of John Berger, 75
Suburban Safari, 23
The Way of Ignorance, 259
The Whale Warriors, 13
The Wild Trees, 156–57
Epic Reads
Ashes to Ashes, 103
The Best and the Brightest, 273
The Coming Plague, 41–42
Conspiracy of Fools, 310–11
Ghost Wars, 89–80
The Secret Parts of Fortune, 78
*The Snowball: Warren Buffett and the
    Business of Life*, 296
Up in the Old Hotel, 175–76

What It Takes: The Way to the White House, 272

See also Quick Reads

Epidemiology

The Coming Plague, 41–42

Equatorial Guinea

The Wonga Coup, 143–44

Escobar, Pablo

Killing Pablo, 59

Espionage

Chatter, 139

Ghost Wars, 89–80

Vengeance, 138

Essays

American Fictions, 76

The Angry Right, 251

Bound to Please, 75–76

Bushworld, 245–46

Candyfreak, 6–7

Character Studies, 222

Class Matters, 261–62

Cleopatra's Nose, 200

The Dangerous Joy of Dr. Sex and Other True Stories, 219

Don't Get Too Comfortable, 176

Due Considerations, 79

Falling Upwards, 78–79

Freedom Next Time, 142

From Beirut to Jerusalem, 29–30

Here to Stay, 204

How Bush Rules, 242–43

Inequality Matters, 314

Justice: Crimes, Trials, and Punishments, 61

Living Blue in the Red States, 254–55

Lonesome Rangers, 77

Love, Poverty, and War, 71–72

Manhattan Passions, 220–21

The Nasty Bits, 162

One Man's America, 239–40

An Outside Chance, 55

Paper Trails, 10

The Playboy Book of True Crime, 64

Political Fictions, 272

Portraits and Observations: The Essays of Truman Capote, 75

Pretensions to Empire, 252

Revenge of the Donut Boys, 17

Road Work, 8

The Secret Parts of Fortune, 78

Selected Essays of John Berger, 75

Songbook, 77

Subwayland, 23–24

The Summer Game, 49–50

Travels with Dr. Death, 129

Twilight of the Long-ball Gods, 56

Uncensored: Views & (Re)views, 77–78

Uncommon Carriers, 16

Up in the Old Hotel, 175–76

US Guys, 174–75

The Way of Ignorance, 259

Ethiopia

There Is No Me without You, 196

Ethnicity

The Rebels' Hour, 198

Europe

Exposed: The Toxic Chemistry of Everyday Products, 109

Magnificent Corpses, 221

They Would Never Hurt a Fly, 135–36

European History

With Their Backs to the World, 222

Evolution

Monkey Girl, 264–65

Explicit Sexuality

America Unzipped, 6

Bonk: The Curious Coupling of Science and Sex, 46–47

Random Family, 210

Remembering Satan, 64–65

Skipping towards Gomorrah, 177–78

Thy Neighbor's Wife, 178

Explicit Violence

Aftermath, Inc., 168

All God's Children, 60–61

Buried in the Bitter Waters, 124

Cover-up: The Army's Secret Investigation of the Massacre at My Lai 4, 91

Hell's Angels, 179

Killing Pablo, 59

Machete Season, 37–38

"A Problem from Hell," 143

Random Family, 210

The Rebels' Hour, 198

Remembering Satan, 64–65

The Restless Sleep, 61–62

Where Soldiers Fear to Tread, 181–82

Exposés

Armed Madhouse, 253

Big-Box Swindle, 316

Chain of Command, 264

Conspiracy of Fools, 310–11

Consumed, 308

The Corporation, 308

Exposés (*Cont.*)
   Deluxe: How Luxury Lost Its Luster,
      296–87
   Fiasco: The American Military Adventure
      in Iraq, 267–68
   The Greatest Story Ever Sold, 254
   Juicing the Game, 52
   Maxed Out, 318
   One Market under God, 312
Extremists
   Them: Adventures with Extremists, 177

Fame
   Fame Junkies, 12–13
Family Relationships
   All God's Children, 60–61
   American Dream, 119–20
   Animal, Vegetable, Miracle, 174
   As Nature Made Him, 203–4
   The Blind Side, 205–6
   The Bookseller of Kabul, 186–87
   Civil Wars: A Battle for Gay Marriage, 31
   Class Matters, 261–62
   Cold New World, 121
   Common Ground, 219–20
   Crashing Through, 205
   Crossing Over, 140
   Down By the River, 58–59
   Embryo Culture, 154–55
   F5: Devastation, Survival, and the Most
      Violent Tornado Outbreak of the
      20th Century, 31–32
   The Feminine Mistake, 115–16
   Growing Up Fast, 211
   Justice: Crimes, Trials, and Punishments,
      61
   Kabul in Winter, 185
   Killing Pablo, 59
   The Last American Man, 195
   The Last Season, 202–3
   The Legend of Colton H. Bryant, 194–85
   Life on the Outside, 195–86
   Lone Patriot, 197–88
   The Long Road Home, 73
   McIlhenny's Gold, 295–86
   A Measure of Endurance, 206
   Nine Parts of Desire, 8–8
   Once Upon a Quinceañara, 208
   One Man's America, 239–40
   On Paradise Drive, 232
   Paper Trails, 10
   Random Family, 210

   Rosa Lee, 209–10
   Salvation on Sand Mountain, 152
   Setting the Table, 325
   The Snowball: Warren Buffett and the
      Business of Life, 296
   The Spirit Catches You and You Fall
      Down, 10–11
   There Are No Children Here, 125–26
   There Is No Me without You, 196
   The Town on Beaver Creek, 212–13
   The Underdog, 152–53
   Under the Banner of Heaven, 63–64
   Voices from Chernobyl, 134
   Without Apology, 151–52
   The Working Poor, 130
Fandom
   Cubs Nation, 56
   Fame Junkies, 12–13
   Feeding the Monster, 55
   Rammer, Jammer, Yellow, Hammer, 157
   Who Are You People?, 9
Fascism
   American Fascists, 248
   Liberal Fascism, 235–36
Fashion
   Deluxe: How Luxury Lost Its Luster,
      296–87
   Display of Power, 291–82
   Fugitive Denim, 318
Fear
   The Science of Fear, 123
Female Genital Mutilation
   Nine Parts of Desire, 8–8
Feminism
   Can't Buy My Love, 125
   The Feminine Mistake, 115–16
   Kabul in Winter, 185
   Opting Out?, 38–39
   Pushed: The Painful Truth about
      Childbirth and Modern Maternity
      Care, 116
   Self-Made Man, 180
   The Terror Dream, 246–47
Fertility
   Bonk: The Curious Coupling of Science and
      Sex, 46–47
Film
   Fame Junkies, 12–13
Finance
   The Age of Turbulence, 291
   Liar's Poker, 315
   Maxed Out, 318

Rigged, 294

*The Snowball: Warren Buffett and the
Business of Life*, 296

The Squandering of America, 265–66

The Trap, 209

Trump: The Art of the Deal, 327

A Weekend with Warren Buffett, 289–80

See also Business

Finland

To Air Is Human, 158–59

First Amendment

Killed Cartoons, 111–12

Fishing

Casting a Spell, 51

Sowbelly, 150–51

Flight

Touching History, 33

Floods

Red River Rising, 32–33

The Town on Beaver Creek, 212–13

Florida

Crime Beat, 60

Nobodies, 116–17

The Orchid Thief, 199

The Season, 173–74

Flowers

Flower Confidential, 18

The Orchid Thief, 199

Otherwise Normal People, 17–18

Fly Fishing

Casting a Spell, 51

Flying

Boeing versus Airbus, 294

Food

Alice, Let's Eat, 158

Alice Waters and Chez Panisse, 292–83

Animal, Vegetable, Miracle, 174

Appetite for Profit, 111

Bitter Chocolate, 105–6

Candyfreak, 6–7

Can You Trust a Tomato in January?,
131–32

Cookoff: Recipe Fever in America, 157–58

Dinner at the New Gene Cafe, 127

The End of Food, 106–7

Fast Food Nation, 110

Fat Land, 118–19

Food Fight, 265

Food Politics, 105

The Fortune Cookie Chronicles, 15–16

From the Farm to the Table, 38

Heat, 162

Horsemen of the Esophagus, 11–12

The Hundred-Year Lie, 121–22

Javatrekker, 310

The Making of a Chef, 169–70

McIlhenny's Gold, 295–86

The Nasty Bits, 162

Noble Rot: A Bordeaux Wine Revolution,
290

Setting the Table, 325

The Sushi Economy, 313–14

Twinkie, Deconstructed, 41

The United States of Arugula, 13–14

See also Agriculture

Foodies

Alice, Let's Eat, 158

Alice Waters and Chez Panisse, 292–83

Cookoff: Recipe Fever in America, 157–58

Food Politics, 105

Heat, 162

The Making of a Chef, 169–70

The Nasty Bits, 162

Setting the Table, 325

The United States of Arugula, 13–14

A Very Good Year, 19–20

Football

The Blind Side, 205–6

Bringing the Heat, 51–52

The Education of a Coach, 197

Friday Night Lights, 50

Next Man Up, 53

Paper Lion, 167

Rammer, Jammer, Yellow, Hammer, 157

See also Sports

Foreign Relations

Against All Enemies, 279–80

America at the Crossroads, 263

The Best and the Brightest, 273

Bitter Friends, Bosom Enemies, 268–69

Bushworld, 245–46

Chatter, 139

China Shakes the World, 302

Corporation Nation, 98

The Dark Side, 93

*Fiasco: The American Military Adventure
in Iraq*, 267–68

Hegemony or Survival, 243–44

How Bush Rules, 242–43

How Israel Lost, 262

Imperial Life in the Emerald City, 68–69

Inside Hamas, 135

The Invisible Cure, 136

Killing Pablo, 59

Foreign Relations (*Cont.*)
The Mighty and the Almighty, 277–78
Nemesis: The Last Days of the American Republic, 250–51
Nuclear Terrorism, 258
The Occupation, 69
Opium Season, 184
The Post-American World, 270
"A Problem from Hell," 143
Reconciliation: Islam, Democracy, and the West, 278
The Revolution: A Manifesto, 282
Right Is Wrong, 249
The Selling of "Free Trade," 92
Showdown: Why China Wants War with the United States, 259
Silence of the Rational Center, 261
State of Denial, 283
Target Iran, 268
The Terror Dream, 246–47
The Wonga Coup, 143–44
See also Government
Forensic Science
Stiff: The Curious Lives of Human Cadavers, 47
Forestry
The Golden Spruce, 132
Fossil Fuels
The Long Emergency, 126–27
Founding Fathers
The Revolution: A Manifesto, 282
France
Deluxe: How Luxury Lost Its Luster, 296–87
Hope in Hell, 66–67
Noble Rot: A Bordeaux Wine Revolution, 290
Selected Essays of John Berger, 75
Fraud
Coronary: A True Story of Medicine Gone Awry, 102
Friendships
Absolutely American, 211–12
Blacktop Cowboys, 212
Bomb Squad, 165
Cheer! Three Teams on a Quest for College Cheerleading's Ultimate Prize, 18–19
The Fixer: A Story from Sarajevo, 199–200
The Kings of New York, 213–14
The Last American Man, 195
The Legend of Colton H. Bryant, 194–85

The Lemon Tree, 34
The Long Road Home, 73
The Making of a Chef, 169–70
The Miracle of Castel di Sangro, 185–86
Once Upon a Quinceañara, 208
The Orchid Thief, 199
Pledged: The Secret Life of Sororities, 176–77
Self-Made Man, 180
Setting the Table, 325
The Ticket Out, 213
To Air Is Human, 158–59
Under the Big Top, 165
US Guys, 174–75
Vengeance, 138
We Were One, 72–73
Without Apology, 151–52
Wonderland, 171
Fundamentalism
Kabul in Winter, 185
Them: Adventures with Extremists, 177
Under the Banner of Heaven, 63–64
Futurism
The Extreme Future, 118
Future Cast, 304–5
Revolutionary Wealth, 305–6

Gambling
Bigger Deal, 166
Hunting Fish, 153–54
Games
The Backwash Squeeze and Other Improbable Feats, 156
Word Freak, 153
Gangs
Hell's Angels, 179
Garbage
Garbage Land, 129–30
High Tech Trash, 123
Made to Break, 48
Gardening
American Green: The Obsessive Quest for the Perfect Lawn, 26
Backyard Giants, 19
Otherwise Normal People, 17–18
Suburban Safari, 23
Gaza Strip
Drinking the Sea at Gaza, 183–84
Gender
As Nature Made Him, 203–4
The First Man-Made Man, 204–5
Kabul in Winter, 185

Nine Parts of Desire, 8–8
Peninsula of Lies, 202
Self-Made Man, 180
The Terror Dream, 246–47
US Guys, 174–75
Genetics
   Dinner at the New Gene Cafe, 127
   The End of Medicine, 43–44
Genocide
   Machete Season, 37–38
   "A Problem from Hell," 143
Geography
   Who's Your City?, 300
   The World Is Flat, 301
Geology
   Assembling California, 166–67
   Diamond, 43
Germs
   *Germs: Biological Weapons and America's
      Secret War,* 45
   Good Germs, Bad Germs, 47–48
GLBTQ
   Civil Wars: A Battle for Gay Marriage, 31
   Don't Get Too Comfortable, 176
   Self-Made Man, 180
   Skipping towards Gomorrah, 177–78
Globalization
   The Age of Fallibility, 282–83
   The Big Squeeze, 312–13
   Biography of the Dollar, 292
   Bitter Chocolate, 105–6
   Boeing versus Airbus, 294
   China, Inc., 300
   The China Price, 99
   China Shakes the World, 302
   Consumed, 308
   A Crime So Monstrous, 144
   Crossing Over, 140
   The Disposable American, 319–20
   The Elephant and the Dragon, 303
   The End of Work, 304
   Flower Confidential, 18
   The Fortune Cookie Chronicles, 15–16
   Fugitive Denim, 318
   Future Cast, 304–5
   Gusher of Lies, 117
   Hegemony or Survival, 243–44
   Javatrekker, 310
   Maxed Out, 318
   Nobodies, 116–17
   Oil on the Brain, 315
   One World, Ready or Not, 313

The Post-American World, 270
The Squandering of America, 265–66
Starbucked, 290
Superclass, 317
The Sushi Economy, 313–14
The World Is Flat, 301
God
   God Is Not Great, 264
   See also Religion
Golf
   Tales from Q School, 53–54
Gonzo Journalism
   Fear and Loathing in Las Vegas, 178–79
   Hell's Angels, 179
   Revenge of the Donut Boys, 17
   US Guys, 174–75
Government
   The Age of Turbulence, 291
   Against All Enemies, 279–80
   All the President's Men, 87–88
   America at the Crossroads, 263
   American Dream, 119–20
   *American Ground: Unbuilding the World
      Trade Center,* 24–25
   American Theocracy, 267
   The Angry Right, 251
   Armed Madhouse, 253
   The Assassins' Gate, 32
   The Assault on Reason, 280
   The Atomic Bazaar, 139–40
   The Best and the Brightest, 273
   The Big Con, 89
   Bitter Friends, Bosom Enemies, 268–69
   Blackwater, 108–8
   *Blasphemy: How the Religious Right Is
      Hijacking Our Declaration of
      Independence,* 245
   Brainwash, 131
   Brave New Ballot, 275
   Breach of Faith, 218
   The Bulldozer and the Big Tent, 273
   Bushworld, 245–46
   Calamities of Exile, 223
   Capitalism 3.0, 299–300
   China Shakes the World, 302
   *City Adrift: New Orleans Before and After
      Katrina,* 27–28
   Civil Wars: A Battle for Gay Marriage, 31
   The Clinton Wars, 278–79
   Cobra II, 90
   *Comeback: Conservatism That Can Win
      Again,* 234

Government (*Cont.*)

Confessions of a Political Hitman, 92–83
The Dark Side, 93
The Devil and the Disappearing Sea, 183
Dirty Diplomacy, 281–82
Disaster: Hurricane Katrina and the
    Failure of Homeland Security, 88
The Disposable American, 319–20
Down By the River, 58–59
Eight Ways to Run the Country, 274–75
The End of America, 256
The Evangelical President, 237–38
Exposed: The Toxic Chemistry of Everyday
    Products, 109
Falling Behind, 311–12
The Fall of the House of Bush, 255–56
From Beirut to Jerusalem, 29–30
From the Farm to the Table, 38
Fiasco: The American Military Adventure
    in Iraq, 267–68
Fighting for Air, 102
Food Politics, 105
Freedom Next Time, 142
Freedonomics, 236–37
Future Cast, 304–5
Ghost Wars, 89–80
Godless: The Church of Liberalism, 233
The Greatest Story Ever Sold, 254
Hegemony or Survival, 243–44
Heist, 94
A Home on the Field, 173
How Bush Rules, 242–43
How Israel Lost, 262
Hubris: The Inside Story of Spin, Scandal,
    and the Selling of the Iraq War, 250
If Democrats Had Any Brains, They'd Be
    Republicans, 233
Imperial Grunts, 72
Imperial Life in the Emerald City, 68–69
An Inconvenient Book, 231–32
Independents Day, 262–63
Inequality Matters, 314
Inside Hamas, 135
Inside the Red Zone, 217
It's Getting Ugly Out There, 260
Liberal Fascism, 235–36
Living Blue in the Red States, 254–55
Lone Patriot, 197–88
The Looming Tower, 269–70
A Match Made in Heaven, 260–61
The Men Who Stare at Goats, 94
The Mighty and the Almighty, 277–78

A Miracle, A Universe: Settling Accounts
    with Torturers, 35
Mission Unaccomplished, 246
Ms. Moffett's First Year, 12
Myths, Lies, and Downright Stupidity,
    131
Nation of Secrets, 90
Nemesis: The Last Days of the American
    Republic, 250–51
The Nine: Inside the Secret World of the
    Supreme Court, 275–76
Nuclear Power Is Not the Answer, 96
Nuclear Terrorism, 258
The Occupation, 69
One Market under God, 312
The One Percent Doctrine, 269
The Outlaw Sea, 25
Outrage, 266–67
Palestine: Peace Not Apartheid, 279
A People's History of American Empire,
    257
The Political Zoo, 238
The Post-American World, 270
Power to the People, 236
A Prayer for the City, 209
Pretensions to Empire, 252
"A Problem from Hell," 143
Real Change, 234–35
Reconciliation: Islam, Democracy, and the
    West, 278
The Revolution: A Manifesto, 282
Revolutionary Wealth, 305–6
Right Is Wrong, 249
Screwed: The Undeclared War against the
    Middle Class, 247–48
The Secret History of the War on Cancer,
    119
The Selling of "Free Trade," 92
The Shame of the Nation, 126
Showdown: Why China Wants War with
    the United States, 259
Show Me a Hero, 208–8
Silence of the Rational Center, 261
Spychips, 115
The Squandering of America, 265–66
State of Denial, 283
State of Emergency, 259–60
Stupid White Men, 252
Swim Against the Current, 248–49
Take It Back: Our Party, Our Country,
    Our Future, 243
The Terror Dream, 246–47

13 Seconds: A Look Back at the Kent State Shootings, 28–29
They Would Never Hurt a Fly, 135–36
The Truth: With Jokes, 247
Up from Zero, 22–23
The Vast Left Wing Conspiracy, 240
Voices from Chernobyl, 134
The Way of Ignorance, 259
Welcome to the Homeland, 266
What Happened, 280–81
What It Takes: The Way to the White House, 272
Why We're Liberals, 242
Without Precedent, 91
With Their Backs to the World, 222
The Wonga Coup, 143–44
The World Is Flat, 301
World War IV: The Long Struggle against Islamofascism, 237
Worse than Watergate, 244–45
See also Politics
Grammar
Word Freak, 153
Graphic Novels
The Fixer: A Story from Sarajevo, 199–200
Killed Cartoons, 111–12
A People's History of American Empire, 257
Great Britain
The First Man-Made Man, 204–5
Great Depression
Let Us Now Praise Famous Men, 170–71
The Town on Beaver Creek, 212–13
Greenspan, Alan
The Age of Turbulence, 291
Guantánamo Bay
Guantánamo and the Abuse of Presidential Power, 92
Guatemala
Uncivilized Beasts and Shameless Hellions, 68
Guns
Gun Show Nation, 117–18

Hadwin, Grant
The Golden Spruce, 132
Hall, Gordon Langley
Peninsula of Lies, 202
Hamas
Inside Hamas, 135
Happiness
Makers and Takers, 238
The Progress Paradox, 120

Harvard University
Fat Envelope Frenzy, 218–19
Health Care
City Adrift: New Orleans Before and After Katrina, 27–28
Class Matters, 261–62
Health Issues
Appetite for Profit, 111
Ashes to Ashes, 103
The Body Hunters, 110–11
Bonk: The Curious Coupling of Science and Sex, 46–47
Can You Trust a Tomato in January?, 131–32
The Cigarette Century, 308–8
A Civil Action, 99–100
Comfortably Numb, 95–86
The Coming Plague, 41–42
Coronary: A True Story of Medicine Gone Awry, 102
Crashing Through, 205
Embryo Culture, 154–55
The End of Medicine, 43–44
Fast Food Nation, 110
Fat Land, 118–19
Food Politics, 105
Game of Shadows, 98–89
Good Germs, Bad Germs, 47–48
High Tech Trash, 123
Hiroshima, 137
Hope in Hell, 66–67
The Hundred-Year Lie, 121–22
The Invisible Cure, 136
Junk Science, 114–15
Many Sleepless Nights, 42–43
My City Was Gone, 127–28
Natural Causes, 100–101
9 Highland Road: Sane Living for the Mentally Ill, 20–21
Our Daily Meds, 107
Parts Per Million, 100
Power to the People, 236
Pushed: The Painful Truth about Childbirth and Modern Maternity Care, 116
The Secret History of the War on Cancer, 119
Sick: The Untold Story of America's Health Care Crisis, 97
The Spirit Catches You and You Fall Down, 10–11
The Sun Farmer, 44–45
There Is No Me without You, 196
See also Medicine

Hefner, Hugh
   Thy Neighbor's Wife, 178
Hewlett, Bill
   Bill & Dave, 293
High School
   Fat Envelope Frenzy, 218–19
Hiroshima
   Here to Stay, 204
History
   Killed Cartoons, 111–12
   On the Wealth of Nations, 317
   Political Fictions, 272
   Road Work, 8
Hobbies
   The Backwash Squeeze and Other
      Improbable Feats, 156
   Backyard Giants, 19
   Cookoff: Recipe Fever in America, 157–58
   Fantasyland, 159–60
   Gun Show Nation, 117–18
   Horsemen of the Esophagus, 11–12
   Hunting Fish, 153–54
   The Kings of New York, 213–14
   Rammer, Jammer, Yellow, Hammer, 157
   Saturday Night, 220
   Sowbelly, 150–51
   The Underdog, 152–53
   Under the Big Top, 165
   Who Are You People?, 9
   Word Freak, 153
Holocaust
   Here to Stay, 204
Homeless
   The Happiest Man in the World, 200–201
Homelessness
   All God's Children, 60–61
Homes
   American Green: The Obsessive Quest for
      the Perfect Lawn, 26
   American Project: The Rise and Fall of a
      Modern Ghetto, 34–35
   Falling Behind, 311–12
   House Lust, 302
   Last Harvest, 25–26
   The Lemon Tree, 34
   Suburban Safari, 23
   Who's Your City?, 300
Homicides
   Aftermath, Inc., 168
   All God's Children, 60–61
   Buried in the Bitter Waters, 124

Cover-up: The Army's Secret Investigation
   of the Massacre at My Lai 4, 91
Crime Beat, 60
Down By the River, 58–59
Justice: Crimes, Trials, and Punishments,
   61
Mean Justice, 62
The Other Side of the River, 63
The Playboy Book of True Crime, 64
They Would Never Hurt a Fly, 135–36
Under the Banner of Heaven, 63–64
Horses
   The Race for the Triple Crown, 52–53
Horticulture
   The Orchid Thief, 199
Hospitals
   Coronary: A True Story of Medicine Gone
      Awry, 102
Human Rights
   The China Price, 99
   Dirty Diplomacy, 281–82
   Guantánamo and the Abuse of Presidential
      Power, 92
   Hope in Hell, 66–67
   Human Cargo, 140–41
   Opium Season, 184
   A Russian Diary, 142
   They Would Never Hurt a Fly, 135–36
Humor
   Alice, Let's Eat, 158
   The American Way of Death Revisited, 104
   Armed Madhouse, 253
   The Backwash Squeeze and Other
      Improbable Feats, 156
   Bonk: The Curious Coupling of Science and
      Sex, 46–47
   Bushworld, 245–46
   Candyfreak, 6–7
   Can You Trust a Tomato in January?,
      131–32
   Carnivorous Nights, 182
   Casting a Spell, 51
   Character Studies, 222
   The Dangerous Joy of Dr. Sex and Other
      True Stories, 219
   Deer Hunting with Jesus, 242
   Don't Get Too Comfortable, 176
   The End of Medicine, 43–44
   Fantasyland, 159–60
   Heat, 162
   Helping Me Help Myself, 155–56
   Horsemen of the Esophagus, 11–12

I Am American (and So Can You!), 244
An Inconvenient Book, 231–32
It's Getting Ugly Out There, 260
Magnificent Corpses, 221
The Men Who Stare at Goats, 94
The Nasty Bits, 162
The No Asshole Rule, 326–27
Paper Lion, 167
Paper Trails, 10
The Political Zoo, 238
Remember Me, 9–10
Saturday Night, 220
Skipping towards Gomorrah, 177–78
Songbook, 77
*Stiff: The Curious Lives of Human
    Cadavers*, 47
Stupid White Men, 252
Subwayland, 23–24
Throwing the Elephant, 322
To Air Is Human, 158–59
The Truth: With Jokes, 247
The Underdog, 152–53
Up in the Old Hotel, 175–76
On the Wealth of Nations, 317
A Weekend with Warren Buffett, 289–80
Where in the World Is Osama Bin Laden?,
    187–88
Who Are You People?, 9
The Worst Person in the World, 253
The Year of Living Biblically, 154
Hurley, Bob
    The Miracle of St. Anthony, 56–57
Hurricane Katrina
    Breach of Faith, 218
    *City Adrift: New Orleans Before and After
        Katrina*, 27–28
    *Disaster: Hurricane Katrina and the
        Failure of Homeland Security*, 88
    The Great Deluge, 28
    The Greatest Story Ever Sold, 254
    Uncivilized Beasts and Shameless Hellions,
        68
Hurricanes
    Breach of Faith, 218
    *City Adrift: New Orleans Before and After
        Katrina*, 27–28
    *Disaster: Hurricane Katrina and the
        Failure of Homeland Security*, 88
    The Great Deluge, 28
Hussein, Saddam
    Calamities of Exile, 223

*Hubris: The Inside Story of Spin, Scandal,
    and the Selling of the Iraq War*, 250
Night Draws Near, 187
The Occupation, 69
Road Work, 8
Hutu
    Machete Season, 37–38
Hypnotism
    Brainwash, 131
    Remembering Satan, 64–65

Illinois
    *American Project: The Rise and Fall of a
        Modern Ghetto*, 34–35
    The Sun Farmer, 44–45
Illustrated Books
    *American Green: The Obsessive Quest for
        the Perfect Lawn*, 26
    Carnivorous Nights, 182
    Hope in Hell, 66–67
    Killed Cartoons, 111–12
    Let Us Now Praise Famous Men, 170–71
    Poor People, 39–40
    Rocky Stories, 217–18
Immersion Journalism
    Friday Night Lights, 50
    The Kings of New York, 213–14
    Liar's Poker, 315
    A Weekend with Warren Buffett, 289–80
    The Whale Warriors, 13
Immigrants
    Coyotes, 172–73
    The Fortune Cookie Chronicles, 15–16
    A Home on the Field, 173
    With These Hands, 169
Immigration
    Coyotes, 172
    Crossing Over, 140
    Down By the River, 58–59
    A Home on the Field, 173
    Outrage, 266–67
    State of Emergency, 259–60
    With These Hands, 169
India
    The Elephant and the Dragon, 303
    Freedom Next Time, 142
    The World Is Flat, 301
Industry
    High Tech Trash, 123
    Lost Mountain, 107–8
    Made to Break, 48

Innovation
>   *Once You're Lucky, Twice You're Good*,
>   292
Intelligent Design
>   *Monkey Girl*, 264–65
Internet
>   *Once You're Lucky, Twice You're Good*,
>   292
Interracial Relationships
>   *Peninsula of Lies*, 202
Inventions
>   *The Dangerous Joy of Dr. Sex and Other
>   True Stories*, 219
Iran
>   *Bitter Friends, Bosom Enemies*, 268–69
>   *Target Iran*, 268
Iraq
>   *The Assassins' Gate*, 32
>   *Bitter Friends, Bosom Enemies*, 268–69
>   *Blackwater*, 108–8
>   *Calamities of Exile*, 223
>   *Cobra II*, 90
>   *Fiasco: The American Military Adventure
>   in Iraq*, 267–68
>   *Hubris: The Inside Story of Spin, Scandal,
>   and the Selling of the Iraq War*, 250
>   *Imperial Grunts*, 72
>   *Imperial Life in the Emerald City*, 68–69
>   *Inside the Red Zone*, 217
>   *The Long Road Home*, 73
>   *Night Draws Near*, 187
>   *The Occupation*, 69
>   *The One Percent Doctrine*, 269
>   *On the Road to Kandahar*, 67
>   *Standard Operating Procedure*, 70
>   *State of Denial*, 283
>   *Uncivilized Beasts and Shameless Hellions*, 68
>   *We Were One*, 72–73
>   *World War IV: The Long Struggle against
>   Islamofascism*, 237
Iraq War (2003)
>   *Against All Enemies*, 279–80
>   *America at the Crossroads*, 263
>   *The Assassins' Gate*, 32
>   *Blackwater*, 108–8
>   *Chain of Command*, 264
>   *Cobra II*, 90
>   *The Fall of the House of Bush*, 255–56
>   *Fiasco: The American Military Adventure
>   in Iraq*, 267–68
>   *The Greatest Story Ever Sold*, 254
>   *Gusher of Lies*, 117

*Hubris: The Inside Story of Spin, Scandal,
>   and the Selling of the Iraq War*, 250
Imperial Life in the Emerald City, 68–69
Inside the Red Zone, 217
The Long Road Home, 73
Night Draws Near, 187
The Occupation, 69
Pretensions to Empire, 252
Right Is Wrong, 249
Standard Operating Procedure, 70
State of Denial, 283
We Were One, 72–73
What Happened, 280–81
*World War IV: The Long Struggle against
>   Islamofascism*, 237
Irrationality
>   *The Science of Fear*, 123
Islam
>   *The Bookseller of Kabul*, 186–87
>   *The Enemy at Home*, 233–34
>   *Ghost Wars*, 89–80
>   *Kabul in Winter*, 185
>   *The Looming Tower*, 269–70
>   *Nine Parts of Desire*, 8–8
>   *The Occupation*, 69
>   *On the Road to Kandahar*, 67
>   *Reconciliation: Islam, Democracy, and the
>   West*, 278
>   *Where in the World Is Osama Bin Laden?*,
>   187–88
>   *See also* Religion
Israel
>   *Drinking the Sea at Gaza*, 183–84
>   *Freedom Next Time*, 142
>   *From Beirut to Jerusalem*, 29–30
>   *How Israel Lost*, 262
>   *Inside Hamas*, 135
>   *The Lemon Tree*, 34
>   *Palestine: Peace Not Apartheid*, 279
>   *Vengeance*, 138
Italy
>   *Heat*, 162
>   *The Miracle of Castel di Sangro*, 185–86

Japan
>   *Hiroshima*, 137
>   *Horsemen of the Esophagus*, 11–12
>   *The Sushi Economy*, 313–14
Jefferson, Thomas
>   *Blasphemy: How the Religious Right Is
>   Hijacking Our Declaration of
>   Independence*, 245

Jennings, Cedric
    A Hope in the Unseen, 206–7
Jesus Christ
    The Lost Gospel, 30–31
Jobs, Steve
    The Pixar Touch, 295
Johnson, Lyndon
    the Best and the Brightest, 273
Journalism
    All I Did Was Ask, 76
    All the President's Men, 87–88
    The Argument: Billionaires, Bloggers, and the Battle to Remake Democratic Politics, 271
    Bloodthirsty Bitches and Pious Pimps of Power, 254
    Bushworld, 245–46
    Crime Beat, 60
    The Face of War, 69–70
    The Fixer: A Story from Sarajevo, 199–200
    From Beirut to Jerusalem, 29–30
    The Greatest Story Ever Sold, 254
    Hard News, 104–5
    Hell's Angels, 179
    How Bush Rules, 242–43
    Inside the Red Zone, 217
    It's Getting Ugly Out There, 260
    It's Not News, It's Fark, 97–88
    The Kingdom and the Power, 33–34
    Love, Poverty, and War, 71–72
    One Man's America, 239–40
    Paper Trails, 10
    The Playboy Book of True Crime, 64
    Revenge of the Donut Boys, 17
    Road Work, 8
    13 Seconds: A Look Back at the Kent State Shootings, 28–29
    Twilight of the Long-ball Gods, 56
    Uncivilized Beasts and Shameless Hellions, 68
    War Is a Force that Gives Us Meaning, 70–71
    See also Mass Media
Judaism
    Dead Center, 168–69
    A Match Made in Heaven, 260–61
    The Year of Living Biblically, 154
    See also Religion
Judas Iscariot
    The Lost Gospel, 30–31

Kaplan, Burton
    Good Rat, 59–60

Kennedy, John F.
    The Best and the Brightest, 273
    Here to Stay, 204
Kentucky
    Lost Mountain, 107–8
    The Town on Beaver Creek, 212–13
Kenya
    Ghosts of Tsavo, 151
Khan, A. Q.
    The Atomic Bazaar, 139–40
Kosovo
    Uncivilized Beasts and Shameless Hellions, 68
    With Their Backs to the World, 222

Labor History
    The Big Squeeze, 312–13
    The China Price, 99
    Nickel and Dimed, 164
    Nobodies, 116–17
    Piano: The Making of a Steinway Concert Grand, 7–8
Bin Laden, Osama
    Where in the World Is Osama Bin Laden?, 187–88
La Russa, Tony
    Three Nights in August, 50–51
Las Vegas
    Bigger Deal, 166
    Fear and Loathing in Las Vegas, 178–79
Latin America
    The Secret History of the American Empire, 141
Latinos
    A Home on the Field, 173
Law and Lawyers
    Articles of Faith: A Frontline History of the Abortion Wars, 30
    Capitalism 3.0, 299–300
    Chain of Command, 264
    The Cigarette Century, 308–8
    A Civil Action, 99–100
    The Corporation, 308
    Courtroom 302, 58
    The Crime of Sheila McGough, 198–89
    The End of America, 256
    God on Trial, 274
    Guantánamo and the Abuse of Presidential Power, 92
    Justice: Crimes, Trials, and Punishments, 61
    Mean Justice, 62

Law and Lawyers (*Cont.*)
  A Measure of Endurance, 206
  Monkey Girl, 264–65
  My City Was Gone, 127–28
  Nation of Secrets, 90
  The Nine: Inside the Secret World of the Supreme Court, 275–76
  No Matter How Loud I Shout, 62–63
  Parts Per Million, 100
  Without Precedent, 91
Law Enforcement
  Aftermath, Inc., 168
  American Furies, 114
  Back from the Dead, 216
  Bomb Squad, 165
  Coyotes, 172
  Crime Beat, 60
  Crossing Over, 140
  Down By the River, 58–59
  Fear and Loathing in Las Vegas, 178–79
  Justice: Crimes, Trials, and Punishments, 61
  Killing Pablo, 59
  No Matter How Loud I Shout, 62–63
  The Other Side of the River, 63
  Remembering Satan, 64–65
  The Restless Sleep, 61–62
  13 Seconds: A Look Back at the Kent State Shootings, 28–29
  With These Hands, 169
Leadership
  The No Asshole Rule, 326–27
Lebanon
  From Beirut to Jerusalem, 29–30
Liberalism
  The Conscience of a Liberal, 251–52
  Godless: The Church of Liberalism, 233
  Hegemony or Survival, 243–44
  Take It Back: Our Party, Our Country, Our Future, 243
Lions
  Ghosts of Tsavo, 151
Literary Lives
  All I Did Was Ask, 76
  American Fictions, 76
  The Armies of the Night, 175
  Bound to Please, 75–76
  Due Considerations, 79
  Falling Upwards, 78–79
  Lonesome Rangers, 77
  Portraits and Observations: The Essays of Truman Capote, 75

  Selected Essays of John Berger, 75
  Uncensored: Views & (Re)views, 77–78
Literature
  Love, Poverty, and War, 71–72
London
  The Backwash Squeeze and Other Improbable Feats, 156
Los Angeles
  Crime Beat, 60
  The Ticket Out, 213
Louisiana
  Breach of Faith, 218
  City Adrift: New Orleans Before and After Katrina, 27–28
  The Great Deluge, 28
  McIlhenny's Gold, 295–86
Love Affairs
  The First Man-Made Man, 204–5
  Growing Up Fast, 211
  Thy Neighbor's Wife, 178
Love and Dating
  Random Family, 210
  Wonderland, 171
Luxury
  Don't Get Too Comfortable, 176
  The Perfect Scent, 289

Mafia
  Good Rat, 59–60
  The Playboy Book of True Crime, 64
Mailer, Norman
  Road Work, 8
Maine
  Suburban Safari, 23
Making Sense . . .
  The Age of Abundance, 274
  Blasphemy: How the Religious Right Is Hijacking Our Declaration of Independence, 245
  Bobos in Paradise, 310
  Capitalism 3.0, 299–300
  Eight Ways to Run the Country, 274–75
  The End of America, 256
  The End of Work, 304
  Everything Is Miscellaneous, 306
  God Is Not Great, 264
  Made to Break, 48
  On Paradise Drive, 232
  The Progress Paradox, 120
  Shopping for God, 179–80
  War Is a Force that Gives Us Meaning, 70–71

Who's Afraid of a Large Black Man?,
   215–16
Wikinomics, 205
Management
   Boeing versus Airbus, 294
   First, Break All the Rules, 323
   Group Genius, 326
   The No Asshole Rule, 326–27
   The One Minute Manager, 322–23
   Revolt in the Boardroom, 325–26
   Setting the Table, 325
   The Starfish and the Spider, 321–22
   Winning, 327–28
Manufacturing
   Boeing versus Airbus, 294
Marines
   We Were One, 72–73
Maritime Disasters
   The Outlaw Sea, 25
   The Whale Warriors, 13
Marketing
   Appetite for Profit, 111
   Applebee's America, 324
   Buying In, 132–33
   Food Politics, 105
   Living It Up, 319
   Made to Stick, 324–25
   The Marketing of Evil, 236
   Our Daily Meds, 107
   The Political Brain, 276
   Purple Cow, 324
   Shopping for God, 179–80
   Watch This, Listen Up, Click Here, 101
Marriage
   Alice, Let's Eat, 158
   One Perfect Day, 103–4
   Peninsula of Lies, 202
   Thy Neighbor's Wife, 178
Martha Gellhorn Prize
   The Occupation, 69
Massachusetts
   Among Schoolchildren, 14
   Common Ground, 219–20
   Feeding the Monster, 55
   Growing Up Fast, 211
   Home Town, 24
Mass Media
   The Angry Right, 251
   The Argument: Billionaires, Bloggers, and
     the Battle to Remake Democratic
     Politics, 271

Bloodthirsty Bitches and Pious Pimps of
   Power, 254
Confessions of a Political Hitman, 92–83
Consumed, 308
The Evangelical President, 237–38
Fame Junkies, 12–13
Fighting for Air, 102
Godless: The Church of Liberalism, 233
The Greatest Story Ever Sold, 254
Hard News, 104–5
Hubris: The Inside Story of Spin, Scandal,
   and the Selling of the Iraq War, 250
I Am American (and So Can You!), 244
If Democrats Had Any Brains, They'd Be
   Republicans, 233
An Inconvenient Book, 231–32
Independents Day, 262–63
It's Getting Ugly Out There, 260
It's Not News, It's Fark, 97–88
The Kingdom and the Power, 33–34
Muzzled: From T-Ball to Terrorism, 239
Myths, Lies, and Downright Stupidity,
   131
100 People Who Are Screwing Up
   America, 235
The Political Zoo, 238
Power to the People, 236
Right Is Wrong, 249
The Science of Fear, 123
The Terror Dream, 246–47
The Truth: With Jokes, 247
Uncivilized Beasts and Shameless Hellions,
   68
Watch This, Listen Up, Click Here, 101
The Worst Person in the World, 253
See also Journalism
Mathematics
   Fantasyland, 159–60
   Moneyball, 54–55
   Predictably Irrational, 298–89
   Super Crunchers, 299
May, Michael
   Crashing Through, 205
McGough, Sheila
   The Crime of Sheila McGough, 198–89
Medicine
   As Nature Made Him, 203–4
   The Body Hunters, 110–11
   Comfortably Numb, 95–86
   The Coming Plague, 41–42
   Coronary: A True Story of Medicine Gone
     Awry, 102

Medicine (*Cont.*)
 Crashing Through, 205
 Dead Center, 168–69
 Embryo Culture, 154–55
 The End of Medicine, 43–44
 The First Man-Made Man, 204–5
 Hope in Hell, 66–67
 The Hundred-Year Lie, 121–22
 The Invisible Cure, 136
 Many Sleepless Nights, 42–43
 The Naked Brain, 128
 Natural Causes, 100–101
 Our Daily Meds, 107
 *Pushed: The Painful Truth about
   Childbirth and Modern Maternity
   Care*, 116
 The Secret History of the War on Cancer,
   119
 *Sick: The Untold Story of America's Health
   Care Crisis*, 97
 *The Spirit Catches You and You Fall
   Down*, 10–11
 The Sun Farmer, 44–45
 The Whistleblower, 108
 See also Health Issues
Meir, Golda
 Vengeance, 138
Memoirs
 The Age of Fallibility, 282–83
 Against All Enemies, 279–80
 American Fascists, 248
 Animal, Vegetable, Miracle, 174
 Bigger Deal, 166
 Can't Buy My Love, 125
 Carnivorous Nights, 182
 Confessions of a Political Hitman, 92–83
 The Conscience of a Liberal, 251–52
 Dead Center, 168–69
 The Devil and the Disappearing Sea, 183
 Dirty Diplomacy, 281–82
 Dispatches, 71
 Display of Power, 291–82
 Embryo Culture, 154–55
 The End of Medicine, 43–44
 The Face of War, 69–70
 God and Man at Yale, 232
 Heat, 162
 Hunting Fish, 153–54
 It's Getting Ugly Out There, 260
 Liar's Poker, 315
 The Making of a Chef, 169–70
 An Outside Chance, 55

 Rammer, Jammer, Yellow, Hammer, 157
 *Reconciliation: Islam, Democracy, and the
   West*, 278
 Riding toward Everywhere, 159
 Self-Made Man, 180
 Setting the Table, 325
 Sweet: An Eight-Ball Odyssey, 163
 To Air Is Human, 158–59
 The Underdog, 152–53
 War Is a Force that Gives Us Meaning,
   70–71
 What Happened, 280–81
 Where Soldiers Fear to Tread, 181–82
 The Whistleblower, 108
 Whiteout: Lost in Aspen, 172–73
 Winning, 327–28
 The Year of Living Biblically, 154
 Yes You Can!, 161–62
 See also Biographies
Mental Health
 Comfortably Numb, 95–86
 *9 Highland Road: Sane Living for the
   Mentally Ill*, 20–21
Mexico
 Coyotes, 172
 Crossing Over, 140
 Down By the River, 58–59
 The Selling of "Free Trade," 92
 State of Emergency, 259–60
Michigan
 The Other Side of the River, 63
Micro-histories
 *American Green: The Obsessive Quest for
   the Perfect Lawn*, 26
 Bitter Chocolate, 105–6
 Blood Diamonds, 134–35
 Brainwash, 131
 Casting a Spell, 51
 The Fortune Cookie Chronicles, 15–16
Middle East
 The Assassins' Gate, 32
 Bitter Friends, Bosom Enemies, 268–69
 Blood of the Earth, 138
 Cobra II, 90
 Drinking the Sea at Gaza, 183–84
 From Beirut to Jerusalem, 29–30
 Gusher of Lies, 117
 How Israel Lost, 262
 Imperial Grunts, 72
 Inside Hamas, 135
 The Lemon Tree, 34
 Nine Parts of Desire, 8–8

Palestine: Peace Not Apartheid, 279
On the Road to Kandahar, 67
The Secret History of the American Empire, 141
State of Denial, 283
Target Iran, 268
Vengeance, 138
Where in the World Is Osama Bin Laden?, 187–88
Military
  Absolutely American, 211–12
  Blackwater, 108–8
  Cobra II, 90
  Cover-up: The Army's Secret Investigation of the Massacre at My Lai 4, 91
  Dispatches, 71
  Fiasco: The American Military Adventure in Iraq, 267–68
  Guantánamo and the Abuse of Presidential Power, 92
  Imperial Grunts, 72
  Inside the Red Zone, 217
  Into the Valley, 184–85
  The Long Road Home, 73
  The Men Who Stare at Goats, 94
  Mission Unaccomplished, 246
  My City Was Gone, 127–28
  Nemesis: The Last Days of the American Republic, 250–51
  Nuclear Power Is Not the Answer, 96
  The Occupation, 69
  The Rebels' Hour, 198
  Showdown: Why China Wants War with the United States, 259
  Standard Operating Procedure, 70
  Touching History, 33
  Vengeance, 138
  War Is a Force that Gives Us Meaning, 70–71
  We Were One, 72–73
  Where in the World Is Osama Bin Laden?, 187–88
  The Wonga Coup, 143–44
Mind Body Spirit
  Helping Me Help Myself, 155–56
Mining
  Lost Mountain, 107–8
Money
  Biography of the Dollar, 292
  The Feminine Mistake, 115–16
Money, John
  As Nature Made Him, 203–4

Moores, Eldridge
  Assembling California, 166–67
Morgenson, Randy
  The Last Season, 202–3
Mormonism
  Under the Banner of Heaven, 63–64
  See also Religion
Motivation
  Yes You Can!, 161–62
Motorcycles
  Hell's Angels, 179
Mountains
  The Last Season, 202–3
Movies
  The Pixar Touch, 295
  Rocky Stories, 217–18
Movie Stars
  Portraits and Observations: The Essays of Truman Capote, 75
  Rocky Stories, 217–18
Mozambique
  The Man-Eaters of Eden, 22
Multicultural Issues
  Among Schoolchildren, 14
  The Assassins' Gate, 32
  The Bookseller of Kabul, 186–87
  Coyotes, 172
  Crossing Over, 140
  The Devil and the Disappearing Sea, 183
  Down By the River, 58–59
  Drinking the Sea at Gaza, 183–84
  The Fixer: A Story from Sarajevo, 199–200
  From Beirut to Jerusalem, 29–30
  A Home on the Field, 173
  Hope in Hell, 66–67
  The Invisible Cure, 136
  The Lemon Tree, 34
  Machete Season, 37–38
  Nine Parts of Desire, 8–8
  The Occupation, 69
  Once Upon a Quinceañara, 208
  The Rebels' Hour, 198
  On the Road to Kandahar, 67
  Sahara Unveiled, 155
  The Spirit Catches You and You Fall Down, 10–11
  With Their Backs to the World, 222
  There Is No Me without You, 196
  With These Hands, 169
  Uncivilized Beasts and Shameless Hellions, 68

Music and Musicians
    To Air Is Human, 158–59
    All I Did Was Ask, 76
    *Piano: The Making of a Steinway Concert
        Grand,* 7–8
    Songbook, 77
My Lai
    *Cover-up: The Army's Secret Investigation
        of the Massacre at My Lai 4,* 91

NAFTA
    The Selling of "Free Trade," 92
National Book Award
    A Civil Action, 99–100
    Common Ground, 219–20
    From Beirut to Jerusalem, 29–30
    Newjack: Guarding Sing Sing, 163
    The Right Stuff, 214
    The Soul of a New Machine, 15
National Book Critics Circle
    *The Spirit Catches You and You Fall
        Down,* 10–11
    Voices from Chernobyl, 134
Native Peoples
    The Golden Spruce, 132
Natural Disasters
    The Great Deluge, 28
    Red River Rising, 32–33
Nature
    Casting a Spell, 51
    The Golden Spruce, 132
    The Last American Man, 195
    Return of the Condor, 45–46
    Suburban Safari, 23
    The Whale Warriors, 13
    The Wild Trees, 156–57
    See also Environmental Writing
Nebraska
    *The Snowball: Warren Buffett and the
        Business of Life,* 296
Neoconservatives
    The Fall of the House of Bush, 255–56
Neuroscience
    The Naked Brain, 128
    The Political Brain, 276
Nevada
    Fear and Loathing in Las Vegas, 178–79
New England
    The Education of a Coach, 197
New Jersey
    The Miracle of St. Anthony, 56–57
New Orleans

    Breach of Faith, 218
    *City Adrift: New Orleans Before and After
        Katrina,* 27–28
    *Disaster: Hurricane Katrina and the
        Failure of Homeland Security,* 88
    The Great Deluge, 28
New Perspectives
    Buried in the Bitter Waters, 124
New York
    *9 Highland Road: Sane Living for the
        Mentally Ill,* 20–21
New York City
    *American Ground: Unbuilding the World
        Trade Center,* 24–25
    Bomb Squad, 165
    Cleopatra's Nose, 200
    Dead Center, 168–69
    Display of Power, 291–82
    Good Rat, 59–60
    Hard News, 104–5
    Heat, 162
    The Kings of New York, 213–14
    The Looming Tower, 269–70
    Manhattan Passions, 220–21
    Ms. Moffett's First Year, 12
    *Museum: Behind the Scenes at the
        Metropolitan Museum of Art,* 216
    *102 Minutes: The Untold Story of the
        Fight to Survive inside the Twin
        Towers,* 29
    The Perfect Scent, 289
    *Piano: The Making of a Steinway Concert
        Grand,* 7–8
    The Restless Sleep, 61–62
    Rigged, 294
    Show Me a Hero, 208–8
    Subwayland, 23–24
    Trump: The Art of the Deal, 327
    Up from Zero, 22–23
    Up in the Old Hotel, 175–76
New York Times Notable
    Absolutely American, 211–12
    Against All Enemies, 279–80
    America at the Crossroads, 263
    American Dream, 119–20
    *The Argument: Billionaires, Bloggers, and
        the Battle to Remake Democratic
        Politics,* 271
    The Assassins' Gate, 32
    The Blind Side, 205–6
    Chain of Command, 264
    Cleopatra's Nose, 200

Conspiracy of Fools, 310–11
Down By the River, 58–59
Fat Land, 118–19
Fiasco: The American Military Adventure in Iraq, 267–68
Field Notes from a Catastrophe, 44
Garbage Land, 129–30
The Greatest Story Ever Sold, 254
Heat, 162
Imperial Life in the Emerald City, 68–69
The Invisible Cure, 136
Life on the Outside, 195–86
The Looming Tower, 269–70
Moneyball, 54–55
Night Draws Near, 187
The Nine: Inside the Secret World of the Supreme Court, 275–76
Nuclear Terrorism, 258
102 Minutes: The Untold Story of the Fight to Survive inside the Twin Towers, 29
The Outlaw Sea, 25
The Post-American World, 270
Predictably Irrational, 298–89
Self-Made Man, 180
Songbook, 77
Uncommon Carriers, 16
Under the Banner of Heaven, 63–64
The United States of Arugula, 13–14
Up from Zero, 22–23
Without Apology, 151–52
The Working Poor, 130
Nixon, Richard
   All the President's Men, 87–88
   Worse than Watergate, 244–45
North Carolina
   A Home on the Field, 173
North Dakota
   Red River Rising, 32–33
Nuclear Power
   Nuclear Power Is Not the Answer, 96
   Voices from Chernobyl, 134
Nuclear Weapons
   Bitter Friends, Bosom Enemies, 268–69
   Here to Stay, 204
   Target Iran, 268

Obesity
   Fat Land, 118–19
Obiang, Teodoro
   The Wonga Coup, 143–44

Oceans
   The Outlaw Sea, 25
   The Whale Warriors, 13
Oher, Michael
   The Blind Side, 205–6
Ohio
   13 Seconds: A Look Back at the Kent State Shootings, 28–29
Oil
   American Theocracy, 267
   Blood of the Earth, 138
   Feeding the Fire, 120–21
   Gusher of Lies, 117
   The Long Emergency, 126–27
   Oil on the Brain, 315
   Parts Per Million, 100
   Rigged, 294
   The Wonga Coup, 143–44
Oklahoma
   Nobodies, 116–17
Opium
   Opium Season, 184
Oral Histories
   America Behind the Color Line, 37
   Articles of Faith: A Frontline History of the Abortion Wars, 30
   From the Farm to the Table, 38
   Gig, 36–37
   Machete Season, 37–38
   Museum: Behind the Scenes at the Metropolitan Museum of Art, 216
   Opting Out?, 38–39
   Poor People, 39–40
   Standard Operating Procedure, 70
   Voices from Chernobyl, 134
   We Were One, 72–73
   With Their Backs to the World, 222
   With These Hands, 169
   Working, 39
Oregon
   The Breaks of the Game, 54
Organizations
   A Measure of Endurance, 206
Organized Crime
   Good Rat, 59–60
Orphans
   There Is No Me without You, 196

Packard, Dave
   Bill & Dave, 293

Pakistan
   The Atomic Bazaar, 139–40
   On the Road to Kandahar, 67
   *Reconciliation: Islam, Democracy, and the
      West*, 278
   Uncivilized Beasts and Shameless Hellions,
      68
Palestine
   Drinking the Sea at Gaza, 183–84
   How Israel Lost, 262
   Inside Hamas, 135
   The Lemon Tree, 34
   Palestine: Peace Not Apartheid, 279
   Vengeance, 138
Parapsychology
   The Men Who Stare at Goats, 94
Parenting
   Embryo Culture, 154–55
   The Feminine Mistake, 115–16
   Growing Up Fast, 211
   Opting Out?, 38–39
   *Pushed: The Painful Truth about
      Childbirth and Modern Maternity
      Care*, 116
Paris
   The Perfect Scent, 289
Parker, Sarah Jessica
   The Perfect Scent, 289
Paul, Ron
   The Revolution: A Manifesto, 282
Pearlman, David
   The Happiest Man in the World, 200–201
Pennsylvania
   Bringing the Heat, 51–52
   Finders Keepers, 203
   Monkey Girl, 264–65
   Paper Trails, 10
   A Prayer for the City, 209
   Rocky Stories, 217–18
   Wonderland, 171
Perfume
   The Perfect Scent, 289
Personality
   *The Dangerous Joy of Dr. Sex and Other
      True Stories*, 219
Pharmacology
   The Body Hunters, 110–11
   Brainwash, 131
   Comfortably Numb, 95–86
   The End of Medicine, 43–44
   Good Germs, Bad Germs, 47–48
   Our Daily Meds, 107

   The Whistleblower, 108
Philadelphia
   Bringing the Heat, 51–52
   Finders Keepers, 203
   Paper Trails, 10
   A Prayer for the City, 209
   Rocky Stories, 217–18
Physicians
   The End of Medicine, 43–44
   See also Medicine
Pianos
   *Piano: The Making of a Steinway Concert
      Grand*, 7–8
Pitner, John
   Lone Patriot, 197–88
Plame, Valerie
   What Happened, 280–81
Poker
   Bigger Deal, 166
   Hunting Fish, 153–54
Political Science
   The Angry Right, 251
   *The Argument: Billionaires, Bloggers, and
      the Battle to Remake Democratic
      Politics*, 271
   The Bulldozer and the Big Tent, 273
   *Comeback: Conservatism That Can Win
      Again*, 234
   Food Fight, 265
   *Hubris: The Inside Story of Spin, Scandal,
      and the Selling of the Iraq War*, 250
   Political Fictions, 272
   Why We're Liberals, 242
   See also Government
Politics
   The Age of Abundance, 274
   The Age of Fallibility, 282–83
   The Age of Turbulence, 291
   Against All Enemies, 279–80
   All the President's Men, 87–88
   America at the Crossroads, 263
   American Fascists, 248
   *American Ground: Unbuilding the World
      Trade Center*, 24–25
   American Theocracy, 267
   The Angry Right, 251
   Appetite for Profit, 111
   Applebee's America, 324
   *The Argument: Billionaires, Bloggers, and
      the Battle to Remake Democratic
      Politics*, 271
   Armed Madhouse, 253

The Assassins' Gate, 32
The Assault on Reason, 280
The Atomic Bazaar, 139–40
The Best and the Brightest, 273
The Big Con, 89
Blackout, 112
Blackwater, 108–8
Blasphemy: How the Religious Right Is Hijacking Our Declaration of Independence, 245
Blood from Stones, 136–37
Blood of the Earth, 138
Bloodthirsty Bitches and Pious Pimps of Power, 254
Bobos in Paradise, 310
Brave New Ballot, 275
The Bulldozer and the Big Tent, 273
Bushworld, 245–46
Chatter, 139
China, Inc., 300
City Adrift: New Orleans Before and After Katrina, 27–28
Civil Wars: A Battle for Gay Marriage, 31
Class Matters, 261–62
The Clinton Wars, 278–79
Comeback: Conservatism That Can Win Again, 234
Confessions of a Political Hitman, 92–83
The Conscience of a Liberal, 251–52
Conspiracy of Fools, 310–11
Corporation Nation, 98
Coyotes, 172
The Dark Side, 93
Deep Economy, 302–3
Deer Hunting with Jesus, 242
Dirty Diplomacy, 281–82
Disaster: Hurricane Katrina and the Failure of Homeland Security, 88
Drinking the Sea at Gaza, 183–84
Economic Facts and Fallacies, 239
Eight Ways to Run the Country, 274–75
The End of America, 256
The Enemy at Home, 233–34
The Evangelical President, 237–38
The Fall of the House of Bush, 255–56
Fiasco: The American Military Adventure in Iraq, 267–68
Field Notes from a Catastrophe, 44
Food Fight, 265
Freedom Next Time, 142
Freedonomics, 236–37
From Beirut to Jerusalem, 29–30

Giving: How Each of Us Can Change the World, 280
God and Man at Yale, 232
Godless: The Church of Liberalism, 233
The Great Deluge, 28
The Greatest Story Ever Sold, 254
Guantánamo and the Abuse of Presidential Power, 92
Gusher of Lies, 117
Hegemony or Survival, 243–44
Heist, 94
How Bush Rules, 242–43
Hubris: The Inside Story of Spin, Scandal, and the Selling of the Iraq War, 250
I Am American (and So Can You!), 244
If Democrats Had Any Brains, They'd Be Republicans, 233
Imperial Grunts, 72
Imperial Life in the Emerald City, 68–69
An Inconvenient Book, 231–32
Independents Day, 262–63
Inequality Matters, 314
Inside the Red Zone, 217
It's Getting Ugly Out There, 260
Junk Science, 114–15
Killed Cartoons, 111–12
The Lemon Tree, 34
Liberal Fascism, 235–36
Living Blue in the Red States, 254–55
Lone Patriot, 197–88
The Long Emergency, 126–27
The Looming Tower, 269–70
Makers and Takers, 238
The Marketing of Evil, 236
A Match Made in Heaven, 260–61
Microtrends, 303–4
The Mighty and the Almighty, 277–78
A Miracle, A Universe: Settling Accounts with Torturers, 35
Mission Unaccomplished, 246
Muzzled: From T-Ball to Terrorism, 239
Myths, Lies, and Downright Stupidity, 131
Nemesis: The Last Days of the American Republic, 250–51
Night Draws Near, 187
The Nine: Inside the Secret World of the Supreme Court, 275–76
Nobodies, 116–17
Nuclear Power Is Not the Answer, 96
Nuclear Terrorism, 258
The Occupation, 69

Politics *(Cont.)*
100 People Who Are Screwing Up America, 235
100 Ways America Is Screwing Up the World, 255
One Man's America, 239–40
One Market under God, 312
The One Percent Doctrine, 269
One World, Ready or Not, 313
On Paradise Drive, 232
Outrage, 266–67
Palestine: Peace Not Apartheid, 279
A People's History of American Empire, 257
The Political Brain, 276
Political Fictions, 272
The Political Zoo, 238
The Post-American World, 270
Power to the People, 236
A Prayer for the City, 209
Pretensions to Empire, 252
Real Change, 234–35
Reconciliation: Islam, Democracy, and the West, 278
Revolt in the Boardroom, 325–26
The Revolution: A Manifesto, 282
Right Is Wrong, 249
Road Work, 8
Screwed: The Undeclared War against the Middle Class, 247–48
The Selling of "Free Trade," 92
Showdown: Why China Wants War with the United States, 259
Show Me a Hero, 208–8
Sick: The Untold Story of America's Health Care Crisis, 97
Silence of the Rational Center, 261
Skipping towards Gomorrah, 177–78
The Squandering of America, 265–66
Standard Operating Procedure, 70
State of Denial, 283
State of Emergency, 259–60
Stupid White Men, 252
Swim Against the Current, 248–49
Take It Back: Our Party, Our Country, Our Future, 243
Target Iran, 268
The Terror Dream, 246–47
Them: Adventures with Extremists, 177
The Truth: With Jokes, 247
Up from Zero, 22–23
The Vast Left Wing Conspiracy, 240

Vengeance, 138
War Is a Force that Gives Us Meaning, 70–71
The Way of Ignorance, 259
Welcome to the Homeland, 266
The Whale Warriors, 13
What Happened, 280–81
What It Takes: The Way to the White House, 272
Where in the World Is Osama Bin Laden?, 187–88
Who's Afraid of a Large Black Man?, 215–16
Why We're Liberals, 242
Without Precedent, 91
With Their Backs to the World, 222
The Wonga Coup, 143–44
The Working Poor, 130
The World Is Flat, 301
World War IV: The Long Struggle against Islamofascism, 237
Worse than Watergate, 244–45
The Worst Person in the World, 253
See also Government
Pollution
A Civil Action, 99–100
Junk Science, 114–15
Pool
Sweet: An Eight-Ball Odyssey, 163
Pop Culture
Adland, 297
All I Did Was Ask, 76
America Unzipped, 6
Can't Buy My Love, 125
Cheer! Three Teams on a Quest for College Cheerleading's Ultimate Prize, 18–19
Cleopatra's Nose, 200
Falling Upwards, 78–79
Fame Junkies, 12–13
Freakonomics, 314
Horsemen of the Esophagus, 11–12
I Am American (and So Can You!), 244
It's Not News, It's Fark, 97–88
Lonesome Rangers, 77
Manhattan Passions, 220–21
Muzzled: From T-Ball to Terrorism, 239
Once Upon a Quinceañara, 208
100 Ways America Is Screwing Up the World, 255
Portraits and Observations: The Essays of Truman Capote, 75

Remember Me, 9–10
Revenge of the Donut Boys, 17
The Secret Parts of Fortune, 78
Skipping towards Gomorrah, 177–78
Songbook, 77
To Air Is Human, 158–59
Twinkie, Deconstructed, 41
Uncensored: Views & (Re)views, 77–78
US Guys, 174–75
Who Are You People?, 9
Why We're Liberals, 242
The Year of Living Biblically, 154
Pornography
  America Unzipped, 6
Postmodernism
  The End of Work, 304
Poverty
  American Dream, 119–20
  American Project: The Rise and Fall of a Modern Ghetto, 34–35
  Among Schoolchildren, 14
  The Blind Side, 205–6
  City Adrift: New Orleans Before and After Katrina, 27–28
  Cold New World, 121
  Common Ground, 219–20
  The Disposable American, 319–20
  Growing Up Fast, 211
  A Hope in the Unseen, 206–7
  The Kings of New York, 213–14
  Let Us Now Praise Famous Men, 170–71
  Life on the Outside, 195–86
  The Missing Class, 316
  Nickel and Dimed, 164
  The Other Side of the River, 63
  Poor People, 39–40
  Random Family, 210
  Rosa Lee, 209–10
  Screwed: The Undeclared War against the Middle Class, 247–48
  The Shame of the Nation, 126
  There Are No Children Here, 125–26
  There Is No Me without You, 196
  The Ticket Out, 213
  With These Hands, 169
  The Wonga Coup, 143–44
  The Working Poor, 130
Presidents
  The Clinton Wars, 278–79
  The Evangelical President, 237–38
  State of Denial, 283

What It Takes: The Way to the White House, 272
Prince, Erik
  Blackwater, 108–8
Prisons
  American Furies, 114
  Back from the Dead, 216
  Chain of Command, 264
  Courtroom 302, 58
  Going Up the River, 124
  Guantánamo and the Abuse of Presidential Power, 92
  Life on the Outside, 195–86
  Newjack: Guarding Sing Sing, 163
  Random Family, 210
  Standard Operating Procedure, 70
  They Would Never Hurt a Fly, 135–36
Privacy
  Nation of Secrets, 90
  Spychips, 115
Probability
  Super Crunchers, 299
Profanity
  Blacktop Cowboys, 212
  Deer Hunting with Jesus, 242
  Dispatches, 71
  The Nasty Bits, 162
  The No Asshole Rule, 326–27
  Revenge of the Donut Boys, 17
  What It Takes: The Way to the White House, 272
Professions
  Aftermath, Inc., 168
  Alice Waters and Chez Panisse, 292–83
  All the President's Men, 87–88
  Almost Human: Making Robots Think, 42
  American Ground: Unbuilding the World Trade Center, 24–25
  The American Way of Death Revisited, 104
  Blacktop Cowboys, 212
  Bringing the Heat, 51–52
  Confessions of a Political Hitman, 92–83
  Corporation Nation, 98
  A Country Practice, 20
  Courtroom 302, 58
  Dead Center, 168–69
  Dirty Diplomacy, 281–82
  Display of Power, 291–82
  Dreaming in Code, 16–17
  The Education of a Coach, 197
  The End of Work, 304
  The Feminine Mistake, 115–16

Professions (*Cont.*)
  Garbage Land, 129–30
  Gig, 36–37
  Going Up the River, 124
  Heat, 162
  In Sam We Trust, 106
  Liar's Poker, 315
  The Making of a Chef, 169–70
  Ms. Moffett's First Year, 12
  *Museum: Behind the Scenes at the
      Metropolitan Museum of Art*, 216
  Newjack: Guarding Sing Sing, 163
  Once You're Lucky, Twice You're Good,
      292
  Opting Out?, 38–39
  The Outlaw Sea, 25
  *Piano: The Making of a Steinway Concert
      Grand*, 7–8
  The Restless Sleep, 61–62
  Rigged, 294
  The Rise of the Creative Class, 311
  The Selling of "Free Trade," 92
  Setting the Table, 325
  The Soul of a New Machine, 15
  *Stiff: The Curious Lives of Human
      Cadavers*, 47
  Uncommon Carriers, 16
  What Happened, 280–81
  Why We Buy, 320
  Working, 39
  The Working Poor, 130
  Yes You Can!, 161–62
Programmers
  Once You're Lucky, Twice You're Good,
      292
Progressive
  *Screwed: The Undeclared War against the
      Middle Class*, 247–48
  Swim Against the Current, 248–49
Prostitution
  A Crime So Monstrous, 144
Psychology
  As Nature Made Him, 203–4
  Brainwash, 131
  Buying In, 132–33
  Can't Buy My Love, 125
  Comfortably Numb, 95–86
  *The Dangerous Joy of Dr. Sex and Other
      True Stories*, 219
  The Disposable American, 319–20
  The First Man-Made Man, 204–5
  Group Genius, 326

  House Lust, 302
  Living It Up, 319
  Makers and Takers, 238
  The Men Who Stare at Goats, 94
  The Naked Brain, 128
  Opting Out?, 38–39
  The Progress Paradox, 120
  Remembering Satan, 64–65
  The Science of Fear, 123
  Self-Made Man, 180
  War Is a Force that Gives Us Meaning,
      70–71
  See also Sociology
Public Policy
  Falling Behind, 311–12
Public Safety
  Bomb Squad, 165
Pulitzer Prize
  Ashes to Ashes, 103
  Common Ground, 219–20
  Ghost Wars, 89–80
  The Looming Tower, 269–70
  "A Problem from Hell," 143
  The Soul of a New Machine, 15
Putin, Vladimir
  A Russian Diary, 142

Quick Reads
  Alice, Let's Eat, 158
  *American Ground: Unbuilding the World
      Trade Center*, 24–25
  *Blasphemy: How the Religious Right Is
      Hijacking Our Declaration of
      Independence*, 245
  Can You Trust a Tomato in January?,
      131–32
  Crime Beat, 60
  The Crime of Sheila McGough, 198–89
  *The Dangerous Joy of Dr. Sex and Other
      True Stories*, 219
  Diamond, 43
  Display of Power, 291–82
  The End of America, 256
  The End of Food, 106–7
  The End of Medicine, 43–44
  The Evangelical President, 237–38
  *Exposed: The Toxic Chemistry of Everyday
      Products*, 109
  The Face of War, 69–70
  Fat Land, 118–19
  Fear and Loathing in Las Vegas, 178–79
  Field Notes from a Catastrophe, 44

Finders Keepers, 203
The First Man-Made Man, 204–5
The Fixer: A Story from Sarajevo, 199–200
Freakonomics, 314
Good Rat, 59–60
Gun Show Nation, 117–18
Helping Me Help Myself, 155–56
Hiroshima, 137
How Israel Lost, 262
I Am American (and So Can You!), 244
If Democrats Had Any Brains, They'd Be Republicans, 233
Into the Valley, 184–85
Killed Cartoons, 111–12
The Legend of Colton H. Bryant, 194–85
The Long Tail, 298
Lost Mountain, 107–8
The Men Who Stare at Goats, 94
Ms. Moffett's First Year, 12
Myths, Lies, and Downright Stupidity, 131
100 Ways America Is Screwing Up the World, 255
The One Minute Manager, 322–23
Otherwise Normal People, 17–18
The Outlaw Sea, 25
Punching In, 165–66
Purple Cow, 324
The Revolution: A Manifesto, 282
Rocky Stories, 217–18
Salvation on Sand Mountain, 152
Songbook, 77
Subwayland, 23–24
The Sun Farmer, 44–45
Swim Against the Current, 248–49
They Would Never Hurt a Fly, 135–36
13 Seconds: A Look Back at the Kent State Shootings, 28–29
Throwing the Elephant, 322
Twilight of the Long-ball Gods, 56
Uncommon Carriers, 16
The Underdog, 152–53
Watch This, Listen Up, Click Here, 101
On the Wealth of Nations, 317
A Weekend with Warren Buffett, 289–80
The Whistleblower, 108
Who's Afraid of a Large Black Man?, 215–16
See also Epic Reads

Race Relations
America Behind the Color Line, 37

American Project: The Rise and Fall of a Modern Ghetto, 34–35
Buried in the Bitter Waters, 124
City Adrift: New Orleans Before and After Katrina, 27–28
Cold New World, 121
Common Ground, 219–20
Display of Power, 291–82
Economic Facts and Fallacies, 239
A Hope in the Unseen, 206–7
The Other Side of the River, 63
Peninsula of Lies, 202
Rosa Lee, 209–10
The Shame of the Nation, 126
Show Me a Hero, 208–8
State of Emergency, 259–60
Who's Afraid of a Large Black Man?, 215–16
Racism
America Behind the Color Line, 37
Buried in the Bitter Waters, 124
Gun Show Nation, 117–18
A Hope in the Unseen, 206–7
The Other Side of the River, 63
The Shame of the Nation, 126
Them: Adventures with Extremists, 177
There Are No Children Here, 125–26
Who's Afraid of a Large Black Man?, 215–16
Radiation
The Atomic Bazaar, 139–40
Hiroshima, 137
Radicalism
Lone Patriot, 197–88
Them: Adventures with Extremists, 177
Under the Banner of Heaven, 63–64
Rail Travel
Riding toward Everywhere, 159
Raines, Howell
Hard News, 104–5
Real Estate
House Lust, 302
Trump: The Art of the Deal, 327
Recipes
Cookoff: Recipe Fever in America, 157–58
Recreation
Saturday Night, 220
See also Sports
Recycling
Garbage Land, 129–30
Redwood Trees
The Wild Trees, 156–57

Refugees
Human Cargo, 140–41
Reimer, David
As Nature Made Him, 203–4
Religion
American Fascists, 248
American Theocracy, 267
Applebee's America, 324
Blasphemy: How the Religious Right Is Hijacking Our Declaration of Independence, 245
Dead Center, 168–69
Eight Ways to Run the Country, 274–75
The Enemy at Home, 233–34
The Evangelical President, 237–38
God Is Not Great, 264
Godless: The Church of Liberalism, 233
God on Trial, 274
Gun Show Nation, 117–18
Junk Science, 114–15
Kabul in Winter, 185
The Lost Gospel, 30–31
Magnificent Corpses, 221
The Marketing of Evil, 236
A Match Made in Heaven, 260–61
The Mighty and the Almighty, 277–78
Monkey Girl, 264–65
Nine Parts of Desire, 8–8
Poor People, 39–40
Power to the People, 236
Real Change, 234–35
Reconciliation: Islam, Democracy, and the West, 278
Salvation on Sand Mountain, 152
Shopping for God, 179–80
Skipping towards Gomorrah, 177–78
Under the Banner of Heaven, 63–64
The Year of Living Biblically, 154
Rendell, Edward
A Prayer for the City, 209
Restaurants
Alice Waters and Chez Panisse, 292–83
Appetite for Profit, 111
Setting the Table, 325
Retail
Bait and Switch, 164
Big-Box Swindle, 316
Can You Trust a Tomato in January?, 131–32
Deluxe: How Luxury Lost Its Luster, 296–87
Fast Food Nation, 110

In Sam We Trust, 106
The Long Tail, 298
Nickel and Dimed, 164
One Perfect Day, 103–4
Punching In, 165–66
Why We Buy, 320
Rivers
Casting a Spell, 51
Red River Rising, 32–33
Robotics
Almost Human: Making Robots Think, 42
Rodeos
Blacktop Cowboys, 212
Rural Life
A Country Practice, 20
Let Us Now Praise Famous Men, 170–71
A Measure of Endurance, 206
The Sun Farmer, 44–45
Welcome to the Homeland, 266
Russia
The Atomic Bazaar, 139–40
A Russian Diary, 142
Rwanda
Machete Season, 37–38
The Rebels' Hour, 198

Sahara Desert
Sahara Unveiled, 155
Saints
Magnificent Corpses, 221
Saipan
Nobodies, 116–17
Satire
I Am American (and So Can You!), 244
The Political Zoo, 238
Throwing the Elephant, 322
The Truth: With Jokes, 247
Scholarly
America at the Crossroads, 263
American Furies, 114
American Project: The Rise and Fall of a Modern Ghetto, 34–35
The Angry Right, 251
The Body Hunters, 110–11
The Bulldozer and the Big Tent, 273
Buried in the Bitter Waters, 124
Capitalism 3.0, 299–300
The Coming Plague, 41–42
Economic Facts and Fallacies, 239
Eight Ways to Run the Country, 274–75
The End of Work, 304
From the Farm to the Table, 38

Future Cast, 304–5
Guantánamo and the Abuse of Presidential Power, 92
Living It Up, 319
Made to Break, 48
The Missing Class, 316
One Market under God, 312
Shopping for God, 179–80
Silence of the Rational Center, 261
The Squandering of America, 265–66
Superclass, 317
Who's Your City?, 300
Wikinomics, 205
Schools
The Overachievers, 128–29
The Shame of the Nation, 126
Science
Aftermath, Inc., 168
Almost Human: Making Robots Think, 42
Assembling California, 166–67
Bonk: The Curious Coupling of Science and Sex, 46–47
Carnivorous Nights, 182
The Coming Plague, 41–42
Crashing Through, 205
Diamond, 43
Dinner at the New Gene Cafe, 127
Dreaming in Code, 16–17
Embryo Culture, 154–55
The End of Food, 106–7
The End of Medicine, 43–44
The Extreme Future, 118
Feeding the Fire, 120–21
Field Notes from a Catastrophe, 44
First Light, 46
Food Politics, 105
Germs: Biological Weapons and America's Secret War, 45
Good Germs, Bad Germs, 47–48
The Hundred-Year Lie, 121–22
The Invisible Cure, 136
Junk Science, 114–15
The Long Emergency, 126–27
Made to Break, 48
Many Sleepless Nights, 42–43
Monkey Girl, 264–65
The Naked Brain, 128
Nuclear Power Is Not the Answer, 96
The Political Brain, 276
Red River Rising, 32–33
Return of the Condor, 45–46
The Right Stuff, 214

The Secret History of the War on Cancer, 119
The Sun Farmer, 44–45
Twinkie, Deconstructed, 41
The Wild Trees, 156–57
Scrabble
Word Freak, 153
Seattle
Starbucked, 290
Secret Histories
Ashes to Ashes, 103
Brainwash, 131
Buried in the Bitter Waters, 124
Ghost Wars, 89–80
The Secret History of the American Empire, 141
Travels with Dr. Death, 129
Secret Societies
Worse than Watergate, 244–45
Self-Help
Group Genius, 326
Helping Me Help Myself, 155–56
The Hundred-Year Lie, 121–22
Made to Stick, 324–25
Revolt in the Boardroom, 325–26
Setting the Table, 325
Winning, 327–28
Yes You Can!, 161–62
Serbia
With Their Backs to the World, 222
Sexuality
America Unzipped, 6
As Nature Made Him, 203–4
Bonk: The Curious Coupling of Science and Sex, 46–47
The Dangerous Joy of Dr. Sex and Other True Stories, 219
Shopping
Big-Box Swindle, 316
Consumed, 308
Deluxe: How Luxury Lost Its Luster, 296–87
Living It Up, 319
Why We Buy, 320
See also Retail
Sierra Leone
Blood Diamonds, 134–35
Sierra Nevada Mountains
The Last Season, 202–3
Silicon Valley
Once You're Lucky, Twice You're Good, 292

Slavery
  Bitter Chocolate, 105–6
  A Crime So Monstrous, 144
  McIlhenny's Gold, 295–86
Small Press
  America at the Crossroads, 263
  *American Project: The Rise and Fall of a
      Modern Ghetto*, 34–35
  Blown to Bits, 306–7
  Calamities of Exile, 223
  *City Adrift: New Orleans Before and After
      Katrina*, 27–28
  The End of America, 256
  The End of Food, 106–7
  *Exposed: The Toxic Chemistry of Everyday
      Products*, 109
  Falling Behind, 311–12
  From the Farm to the Table, 38
  The Fixer: A Story from Sarajevo, 199–200
  Food Fight, 265
  Food Politics, 105
  Hope in Hell, 66–67
  How Bush Rules, 242–43
  Javatrekker, 310
  Living Blue in the Red States, 254–55
  Living It Up, 319
  Made to Break, 48
  Opting Out?, 38–39
  Red River Rising, 32–33
  Rocky Stories, 217–18
  Songbook, 77
  Twilight of the Long-ball Gods, 56
  Voices from Chernobyl, 134
  The Way of Ignorance, 259
  The Whistleblower, 108
  Who Are You People?, 9
Small-Town Life
  A Home on the Field, 173
Smith, Adam
  On the Wealth of Nations, 317
Smoking
  Ashes to Ashes, 103
  The Cigarette Century, 308–8
Soccer
  A Home on the Field, 172
  The Miracle of Castel di Sangro, 185–86
Social Action
  *Giving: How Each of Us Can Change the
      World*, 280
Socialism
  Liberal Fascism, 235–36

Society
  The Age of Abundance, 274
  America Behind the Color Line, 37
  American Furies, 114
  The American Way of Death Revisited, 104
  America Unzipped, 6
  Among Schoolchildren, 14
  Applebee's America, 324
  The Armies of the Night, 175
  *Articles of Faith: A Frontline History of the
      Abortion Wars*, 30
  As Nature Made Him, 203–4
  The Assault on Reason, 280
  Bait and Switch, 164
  The Big Con, 89
  *Bloodthirsty Bitches and Pious Pimps of
      Power*, 254
  Blown to Bits, 306–7
  Bobos in Paradise, 310
  Brave New Ballot, 275
  Buying In, 132–33
  Can't Buy My Love, 125
  Capitalism 3.0, 299–300
  Class Matters, 261–62
  *Comeback: Conservatism That Can Win
      Again*, 234
  The Conscience of a Liberal, 251–52
  Consumed, 308
  Corporation Nation, 98
  Deep Economy, 302–3
  Deer Hunting with Jesus, 242
  The Disposable American, 319–20
  Don't Get Too Comfortable, 176
  Economic Facts and Fallacies, 239
  Eight Ways to Run the Country, 274–75
  The End of Food, 106–7
  The End of Work, 304
  The Enemy at Home, 233–34
  Everything Is Miscellaneous, 306
  The Extreme Future, 118
  Fame Junkies, 12–13
  Fat Land, 118–19
  Feeding the Fire, 120–21
  The Feminine Mistake, 115–16
  Food Politics, 105
  The Fortune Cookie Chronicles, 15–16
  Future Cast, 304–5
  *Giving: How Each of Us Can Change the
      World*, 280
  Godless: The Church of Liberalism, 233
  Gun Show Nation, 117–18

Home Town, 24
House Lust, 302
Human Cargo, 140–41
I Am American (and So Can You!), 244
If Democrats Had Any Brains, They'd Be Republicans, 233
An Inconvenient Book, 231–32
Inequality Matters, 314
The Invisible Cure, 136
It's Getting Ugly Out There, 260
It's Not News, It's Fark, 97–88
Junk Science, 114–15
Kabul in Winter, 185
The Kings of New York, 213–14
Liberal Fascism, 235–36
Life on the Outside, 195–86
Living Blue in the Red States, 254–55
The Long Tail, 298
Made to Stick, 324–25
Makers and Takers, 238
Manhattan Passions, 220–21
The Marketing of Evil, 236
A Match Made in Heaven, 260–61
Microtrends, 303–4
The Missing Class, 316
Mission Unaccomplished, 246
Muzzled: From T-Ball to Terrorism, 239
Myths, Lies, and Downright Stupidity, 131
Nation of Secrets, 90
Nemesis: The Last Days of the American Republic, 250–51
Nickel and Dimed, 164
Nine Parts of Desire, 8–8
Once Upon a Quinceañara, 208
One Perfect Day, 103–4
Opting Out?, 38–39
100 People Who Are Screwing Up America, 235
100 Ways America Is Screwing Up the World, 255
On Paradise Drive, 232
The Post-American World, 270
A Prayer for the City, 209
Predictably Irrational, 298–89
The Progress Paradox, 120
Real Change, 234–35
Remember Me, 9–10
Revolutionary Wealth, 305–6
Richistan, 122
Riding toward Everywhere, 159
Sahara Unveiled, 155

The Science of Fear, 123
Screwed: The Undeclared War against the Middle Class, 247–48
The Season, 173–74
The Secret Parts of Fortune, 78
Self-Made Man, 180
The Shame of the Nation, 126
Sick: The Untold Story of America's Health Care Crisis, 97
Skipping towards Gomorrah, 177–78
Spychips, 115
Starbucked, 290
State of Emergency, 259–60
Superclass, 317
Swim Against the Current, 248–49
The Terror Dream, 246–47
There Are No Children Here, 125–26
The Trap, 209
The United States of Arugula, 13–14
US Guys, 174–75
The Vast Left Wing Conspiracy, 240
The Way of Ignorance, 259
Welcome to the Homeland, 266
Whiteout: Lost in Aspen, 172–73
Who's Afraid of a Large Black Man?, 215–16
Who's Your City?, 300
Why We're Liberals, 242
Wikinomics, 205
With Their Backs to the World, 222
The Working Poor, 130
The Year of Living Biblically, 154
See also Sociology
Sociology
Among Schoolchildren, 14
Chatter, 139
Falling Behind, 311–12
Freakonomics, 314
Hell's Angels, 179
Home Town, 24
Life on the Outside, 195–86
Lone Patriot, 197–88
Love, Poverty, and War, 71–72
One Market under God, 312
The Progress Paradox, 120
Revolutionary Wealth, 305–6
The Rise of the Creative Class, 311
The Science of Fear, 123
Self-Made Man, 180
See also Psychology; Society
Software
Dreaming in Code, 16–17

Somalia
  Where Soldiers Fear to Tread, 181–82
Sororities
  Pledged: The Secret Life of Sororities,
    176–77
South Africa
  Calamities of Exile, 223
  Freedom Next Time, 142
South America
  Killing Pablo, 59
South Pacific
  Into the Valley, 184–85
Soviet Union
  Voices from Chernobyl, 134
Space
  First Light, 46
  The Right Stuff, 214
Spirituality
  God Is Not Great, 264
  Salvation on Sand Mountain, 152
Sports
  Bigger Deal, 166
  The Blind Side, 205–6
  The Breaks of the Game, 54
  Bringing the Heat, 51–52
  Casting a Spell, 51
  *Cheer! Three Teams on a Quest for College
    Cheerleading's Ultimate Prize,*
    18–19
  Cubs Nation, 56
  The Education of a Coach, 197
  Fantasyland, 159–60
  Fear and Loathing in Las Vegas, 178–79
  Feeding the Monster, 55
  Friday Night Lights, 50
  Game of Shadows, 98–89
  A Home on the Field, 173
  Horsemen of the Esophagus, 11–12
  Juicing the Game, 52
  The Miracle of Castel di Sangro, 185–86
  The Miracle of St. Anthony, 56–57
  Moneyball, 54–55
  Next Man Up, 53
  An Outside Chance, 55
  Paper Lion, 167
  The Race for the Triple Crown, 52–53
  Rammer, Jammer, Yellow, Hammer, 157
  Road Work, 8
  Sowbelly, 150–51
  The Summer Game, 49–50
  Sweet: An Eight-Ball Odyssey, 163
  Tales from Q School, 53–54

  Three Nights in August, 50–51
  The Ticket Out, 213
  Twilight of the Long-ball Gods, 56
  The Underdog, 152–53
  Who's Afraid of a Large Black Man?,
    215–16
  Without Apology, 151–52
Starbucks
  Starbucked, 290
Statistics
  Fantasyland, 159–60
  Moneyball, 54–55
  Richistan, 122
  The Science of Fear, 123
  Super Crunchers, 299
Steroids
  Game of Shadows, 98–89
Suburb
  Last Harvest, 25–26
Suburbs
  Suburban Safari, 23
Supreme Court
  *Articles of Faith: A Frontline History of the
    Abortion Wars,* 30
  God on Trial, 274
  *The Nine: Inside the Secret World of the
    Supreme Court,* 275–76
Survival Stories
  Breach of Faith, 218
  *F5: Devastation, Survival, and the Most
    Violent Tornado Outbreak of the
    20th Century,* 31–32
  The Great Deluge, 28
  Here to Stay, 204
  Red River Rising, 32–33
  The Sun Farmer, 44–45
  Voices from Chernobyl, 134
Sushi
  The Sushi Economy, 313–14
Sustainability
  Deep Economy, 302–3
  From the Farm to the Table, 38
  Feeding the Fire, 120–21
  Food Politics, 105
  Garbage Land, 129–30
  Nuclear Power Is Not the Answer, 96
  Swim Against the Current, 248–49

Taliban
  Ghost Wars, 89–80
  Kabul in Winter, 185
  Opium Season, 184

Tasmania
   Carnivorous Nights, 182
Taxonomies
   Everything Is Miscellaneous, 306
Teachers
   The Kings of New York, 213–14
Technology
   Adland, 297
   Almost Human: Making Robots Think, 42
   Bigger Deal, 166
   Bill & Dave, 293
   Blackout, 112
   Blown to Bits, 306–7
   Brave New Ballot, 275
   Can You Trust a Tomato in January?, 131–32
   Casting a Spell, 51
   Chatter, 139
   China, Inc., 300
   Dinner at the New Gene Cafe, 127
   Dreaming in Code, 16–17
   The End of Food, 106–7
   The End of Medicine, 43–44
   The End of Work, 304
   Everything Is Miscellaneous, 306
   The Extreme Future, 118
   First Light, 46
   From the Farm to the Table, 38
   Gusher of Lies, 117
   High Tech Trash, 123
   The Long Tail, 298
   Made to Break, 48
   The Naked Brain, 128
   Once You're Lucky, Twice You're Good, 292
   The Pixar Touch, 295
   Pop! Why Bubbles Are Great for the Economy, 301
   The Soul of a New Machine, 15
   Spychips, 115
   The Starfish and the Spider, 321–22
   Super Crunchers, 299
   Wikinomics, 205
   The World Is Flat, 301
Teens
   Growing Up Fast, 211
Teferra, Haregewoin
   There Is No Me without You, 196
Terrorism
   The Age of Fallibility, 282–83
   Against All Enemies, 279–80

   American Ground: Unbuilding the World Trade Center, 24–25
   Blood from Stones, 136–37
   Bomb Squad, 165
   Bushworld, 245–46
   Chain of Command, 264
   The Dark Side, 93
   The Enemy at Home, 233–34
   Germs: Biological Weapons and America's Secret War, 45
   Ghost Wars, 89–80
   The Greatest Story Ever Sold, 254
   Guantánamo and the Abuse of Presidential Power, 92
   Hegemony or Survival, 243–44
   Inside Hamas, 135
   The Looming Tower, 269–70
   Nuclear Terrorism, 258
   102 Minutes: The Untold Story of the Fight to Survive inside the Twin Towers, 29
   The One Percent Doctrine, 269
   Reconciliation: Islam, Democracy, and the West, 278
   The Terror Dream, 246–47
   Touching History, 33
   Vengeance, 138
   Where in the World Is Osama Bin Laden?, 187–88
   Without Precedent, 91
   See also 9/11
Texas
   Down By the River, 58–59
   Friday Night Lights, 50
Tibet
   The First Man-Made Man, 204–5
Tornadoes
   F5: Devastation, Survival, and the Most Violent Tornado Outbreak of the 20th Century, 31–32
Torture
   Brainwash, 131
   The Dark Side, 93
   Dirty Diplomacy, 281–82
   Guantánamo and the Abuse of Presidential Power, 92
   The Men Who Stare at Goats, 94
   A Miracle, A Universe: Settling Accounts with Torturers, 35
   Standard Operating Procedure, 70

Toxins
  *Exposed: The Toxic Chemistry of Everyday
    Products*, 109
  High Tech Trash, 123
  My City Was Gone, 127–28
Trains
  Riding toward Everywhere, 159
Transportation
  Subwayland, 23–24
  Uncommon Carriers, 16
Transsexuals
  The First Man-Made Man, 204–5
  As Nature Made Him, 203–4
  Peninsula of Lies, 202
Travel
  Alice, Let's Eat, 158
  America Unzipped, 6
  Assembling California, 166–67
  Bitter Friends, Bosom Enemies, 268–69
  Blacktop Cowboys, 212
  Blood from Stones, 136–37
  Candyfreak, 6–7
  Carnivorous Nights, 182
  Casting a Spell, 51
  Character Studies, 222
  Cookoff: Recipe Fever in America, 157–58
  Coyotes, 172–73
  A Crime So Monstrous, 144
  Deluxe: How Luxury Lost Its Luster,
    296–87
  The Devil and the Disappearing Sea, 183
  Don't Get Too Comfortable, 176
  Drinking the Sea at Gaza, 183–84
  Fear and Loathing in Las Vegas, 178–79
  Field Notes from a Catastrophe, 44
  Flower Confidential, 18
  From Beirut to Jerusalem, 29–30
  Ghosts of Tsavo, 151
  The Happiest Man in the World, 200–201
  Heat, 162
  Hell's Angels, 179
  Horsemen of the Esophagus, 11–12
  Human Cargo, 140–41
  Hunting Fish, 153–54
  Imperial Grunts, 72
  Javatrekker, 310
  Let Us Now Praise Famous Men, 170–71
  The Lost Gospel, 30–31
  Love, Poverty, and War, 71–72
  Magnificent Corpses, 221
  The Man-Eaters of Eden, 22

  The Miracle of Castel di Sangro, 185–86
  The Nasty Bits, 162
  Noble Rot: A Bordeaux Wine Revolution,
    290
  One Man's America, 239–40
  Opium Season, 184
  The Orchid Thief, 199
  An Outside Chance, 55
  Poor People, 39–40
  Rammer, Jammer, Yellow, Hammer, 157
  Remember Me, 9–10
  Riding toward Everywhere, 159
  On the Road to Kandahar, 67
  Rocky Stories, 217–18
  Sahara Unveiled, 155
  Saturday Night, 220
  Sowbelly, 150–51
  The Sushi Economy, 313–14
  To Air Is Human, 158–59
  Uncivilized Beasts and Shameless Hellions,
    68
  Uncommon Carriers, 16
  The Underdog, 152–53
  Under the Big Top, 165
  US Guys, 174–75
  War Is a Force that Gives Us Meaning,
    70–71
  A Weekend with Warren Buffett, 289–80
  Where in the World Is Osama Bin Laden?,
    187–88
  Where Soldiers Fear to Tread, 181–82
  Whiteout: Lost in Aspen, 172–73
  Who Are You People?, 9
  The Year of Living Biblically, 154
Trials
  A Civil Action, 99–100
  The Crime of Sheila McGough, 198–89
  God on Trial, 274
  Good Rat, 59–60
  Justice: Crimes, Trials, and Punishments,
    61
  Mean Justice, 62
  Monkey Girl, 264–65
  My City Was Gone, 127–28
  No Matter How Loud I Shout, 62–63
  See also Law and Lawyers
Trivia
  All the Money in the World, 288–89
  Can You Trust a Tomato in January?, 131–32
  The Extreme Future, 118
  Microtrends, 303–4

True Adventure
  Bigger Deal, 166
  Carnivorous Nights, 182
  Coyotes, 172
  Dispatches, 71
  *F5: Devastation, Survival, and the Most
      Violent Tornado Outbreak of the
      20th Century*, 31–32
  Ghosts of Tsavo, 151
  Into the Valley, 184–85
  The Last Season, 202–3
  The Lost Gospel, 30–31
  The Man-Eaters of Eden, 22
  Next Man Up, 53
  On the Road to Kandahar, 67
  Opium Season, 184
  The Race for the Triple Crown, 52–53
  Sahara Unveiled, 155
  Sowbelly, 150–51
  Tales from Q School, 53–54
  The Whale Warriors, 13
  Where Soldiers Fear to Tread, 181–82
True Crime
  Aftermath, Inc., 168
  All God's Children, 60–61
  American Furies, 114
  *American Project: The Rise and Fall of a
      Modern Ghetto*, 34–35
  Back from the Dead, 216
  Under the Banner of Heaven, 63–64
  Blood Diamonds, 134–35
  *Coronary: A True Story of Medicine Gone
      Awry*, 102
  Courtroom 302, 58
  Crime Beat, 60
  The Crime of Sheila McGough, 198–89
  A Crime So Monstrous, 144
  Dead Center, 168–69
  Down By the River, 58–59
  Finders Keepers, 203
  Freakonomics, 314
  The Golden Spruce, 132
  Good Rat, 59–60
  Justice: Crimes, Trials, and Punishments,
      61
  Killing Pablo, 59
  The Last Season, 202–3
  Newjack: Guarding Sing Sing, 163
  No Matter How Loud I Shout, 62–63
  The Other Side of the River, 63
  Paper Trails, 10
  The Playboy Book of True Crime, 64

  A Prayer for the City, 209
  Remembering Satan, 64–65
  The Restless Sleep, 61–62
  Road Work, 8
  Show Me a Hero, 208–8
  Travels with Dr. Death, 129
Trump, Donald
  Trump: The Art of the Deal, 327
Tutsi
  Machete Season, 37–38

Uganda
  The Invisible Cure, 136
Ukraine
  Voices from Chernobyl, 134
Underdogs
  The Blind Side, 205–6
  Cubs Nation, 56
  A Home on the Field, 173
  A Hope in the Unseen, 206–7
  The Kings of New York, 213–14
  Life on the Outside, 195–86
  A Measure of Endurance, 206
  The Miracle of Castel di Sangro, 185–86
  Moneyball, 54–55
  Next Man Up, 53
  Poor People, 39–40
  Rocky Stories, 217–18
  Tales from Q School, 53–54
  The Ticket Out, 213
  The Underdog, 152–53
Unions
  The Big Squeeze, 312–13
United Arab Emirates
  Rigged, 294
United Nations
  Outrage, 266–67
Urban Life
  All God's Children, 60–61
  *American Project: The Rise and Fall of a
      Modern Ghetto*, 34–35
  Home Town, 24
  A Hope in the Unseen, 206–7
  Last Harvest, 25–26
  Life on the Outside, 195–86
  The Other Side of the River, 63
  A Prayer for the City, 209
  Random Family, 210
  Rosa Lee, 209–10
  The Shame of the Nation, 126
  Show Me a Hero, 208–8
  There Are No Children Here, 125–26

Urban Life (*Cont.*)
The Ticket Out, 213
Welcome to the Homeland, 266
Who's Your City?, 300
Uruguay
A Miracle, A Universe: Settling Accounts with Torturers, 35
Utah
Under the Banner of Heaven, 63–64
Uzbekistan
The Devil and the Disappearing Sea, 183
Dirty Diplomacy, 281–82

Vermont
Civil Wars: A Battle for Gay Marriage, 31
Field Notes from a Catastrophe, 44
Vietnam War
The Armies of the Night, 175
The Best and the Brightest, 273
Cover-up: The Army's Secret Investigation of the Massacre at My Lai 4, 91
Dispatches, 71
M, 186
13 Seconds: A Look Back at the Kent State Shootings, 28–29
Violence
M, 186
Night Draws Near, 187
13 Seconds: A Look Back at the Kent State Shootings, 28–29
Virginia
Deer Hunting with Jesus, 242

Wal-Mart
Big-Box Swindle, 316
In Sam We Trust, 106
Walton, Sam
In Sam We Trust, 106
War
America at the Crossroads, 263
Bitter Friends, Bosom Enemies, 268–69
Here to Stay, 204
Mission Unaccomplished, 246
The Rebels' Hour, 198
See also War Reporting
War Reporting
Cover-up: The Army's Secret Investigation of the Massacre at My Lai 4, 91
Dispatches, 71
The Face of War, 69–70
The Fixer: A Story from Sarajevo, 199–200
Freedom Next Time, 142

Hiroshima, 137
Hope in Hell, 66–67
How Israel Lost, 262
Human Cargo, 140–41
Imperial Grunts, 72
Imperial Life in the Emerald City, 68–69
Inside the Red Zone, 217
Into the Valley, 184–85
Kabul in Winter, 185
The Long Road Home, 73
Love, Poverty, and War, 71–72
M, 186
Night Draws Near, 187
The Occupation, 69
On the Road to Kandahar, 67
Opium Season, 184
Road Work, 8
Standard Operating Procedure, 70
13 Seconds: A Look Back at the Kent State Shootings, 28–29
Uncivilized Beasts and Shameless Hellions, 68
War Is a Force that Gives Us Meaning, 70–71
We Were One, 72–73
Where Soldiers Fear to Tread, 181–82
With Their Backs to the World, 222
Washington D.C.
The Armies of the Night, 175
The Clinton Wars, 278–79
Rosa Lee, 209–1
Waters, Alice
Alice Waters and Chez Panisse, 292–83
Weapons
The Atomic Bazaar, 139–40
Germs: Biological Weapons and America's Secret War, 45
Gun Show Nation, 117–18
Hiroshima, 137
Nuclear Terrorism, 258
Weather
Breach of Faith, 218
Disaster: Hurricane Katrina and the Failure of Homeland Security, 88
F5: Devastation, Survival, and the Most Violent Tornado Outbreak of the 20th Century, 31–32
The Great Deluge, 28
Red River Rising, 32–33
Weddings
One Perfect Day, 103–4
Welch, Jack
Winning, 327–28

Welfare
   American Dream, 119–20
Whales
   The Whale Warriors, 13
Wilson, Valerie Plame
   *Hubris: The Inside Story of Spin, Scandal,
      and the Selling of the Iraq War*, 250
Wine
   Noble Rot: A Bordeaux Wine Revolution,
      290
   A Very Good Year, 19–20
Wisconsin
   American Dream, 119–20
   The Sun Farmer, 44–45
Women's Contributions
   Alice Waters and Chez Panisse, 292–83
   The Feminine Mistake, 115–16
   Kabul in Winter, 185
   The Mighty and the Almighty, 277–78
   Opting Out?, 38–39
   Pledged: The Secret Life of Sororities,
      176–77
   *Reconciliation: Islam, Democracy, and the
      West*, 278
   The Terror Dream, 246–47
   There Is No Me without You, 196
Women's Nonfiction
   Alice Waters and Chez Panisse, 292–83
   American Dream, 119–20
   *Articles of Faith: A Frontline History of the
      Abortion Wars*, 30
   *Cheer! Three Teams on a Quest for College
      Cheerleading's Ultimate Prize*,
      18–19
   The Crime of Sheila McGough, 198–89
   The Feminine Mistake, 115–16
   Growing Up Fast, 211
   Helping Me Help Myself, 155–56
   Life on the Outside, 195–86
   The Mighty and the Almighty, 277–78
   Ms. Moffett's First Year, 12
   Nine Parts of Desire, 8–8
   Once Upon a Quinceañara, 208
   One Perfect Day, 103–4
   Opting Out?, 38–39
   *Pushed: The Painful Truth about
      Childbirth and Modern Maternity
      Care*, 116
   Random Family, 210
   *Reconciliation: Islam, Democracy, and the
      West*, 278
   Rosa Lee, 209–10

   The Secret History of the War on Cancer,
      119
   Sweet: An Eight-Ball Odyssey, 163
   The Terror Dream, 246–47
   There Is No Me without You, 196
   Without Apology, 151–52
Women's Rights
   *Articles of Faith: A Frontline History of the
      Abortion Wars*, 30
   Can't Buy My Love, 125
   *Pushed: The Painful Truth about
      Childbirth and Modern Maternity
      Care*, 116
Women Travelers
   The Face of War, 69–70
Work Relationships
   Aftermath, Inc., 168
   All the President's Men, 87–88
   *American Ground: Unbuilding the World
      Trade Center*, 24–25
   Bait and Switch, 164
   Blacktop Cowboys, 212
   Bomb Squad, 165
   Bringing the Heat, 51–52
   Carnivorous Nights, 182
   Conspiracy of Fools, 310–11
   A Country Practice, 20
   The Devil and the Disappearing Sea, 183
   Dreaming in Code, 16–17
   The Education of a Coach, 197
   The Feminine Mistake, 115–16
   Gig, 36–37
   Hope in Hell, 66–67
   The Kingdom and the Power, 33–34
   Liar's Poker, 315
   McIlhenny's Gold, 295–86
   The Miracle of Castel di Sangro, 185–86
   Ms. Moffett's First Year, 12
   *Museum: Behind the Scenes at the
      Metropolitan Museum of Art*, 216
   The Nasty Bits, 162
   Newjack: Guarding Sing Sing, 163
   Nickel and Dimed, 164
   The No Asshole Rule, 326–27
   Opting Out?, 38–39
   Paper Lion, 167
   *Piano: The Making of a Steinway Concert
      Grand*, 7–8
   Punching In, 165–66
   The Rise of the Creative Class, 311
   Self-Made Man, 180
   Setting the Table, 325

Work Relationships (*Cont.*)
The Snowball: Warren Buffett and the Business of Life, 296
The Soul of a New Machine, 15
Under the Big Top, 165
We Were One, 72–73
Working, 39
World History
American Fascists, 248
The Assassins' Gate, 32
Bitter Chocolate, 105–6
Bitter Friends, Bosom Enemies, 268–69
Blood of the Earth, 138
Brainwash, 131
Calamities of Exile, 223
Cover-up: The Army's Secret Investigation of the Massacre at My Lai 4, 91
The Devil and the Disappearing Sea, 183
Freedom Next Time, 142
From Beirut to Jerusalem, 29–30
Ghost Wars, 89–80
Hiroshima, 137
Imperial Grunts, 72
Inside Hamas, 135
The Lemon Tree, 34
Liberal Fascism, 235–36
Magnificent Corpses, 221
A Miracle, A Universe: Settling Accounts with Torturers, 35
Night Draws Near, 187
One World, Ready or Not, 313
Palestine: Peace Not Apartheid, 279
"A Problem from Hell," 143
A Russian Diary, 142
War Is a Force that Gives Us Meaning, 70–71
See also American History
World Leaders
They Would Never Hurt a Fly, 135–36
World Travel
Diamond, 43
Fugitive Denim, 318
Oil on the Brain, 315
Them: Adventures with Extremists, 177
World War II
The Face of War, 69–70
Here to Stay, 204
Hiroshima, 137
Into the Valley, 184–85
The Town on Beaver Creek, 212–13
Writers and Writing
Bound to Please, 75–76

Due Considerations, 79
Lonesome Rangers, 77
Portraits and Observations: The Essays of Truman Capote, 75
Uncensored: Views & (Re)views, 77–78
Wyoming
The Legend of Colton H. Bryant, 194–85

YA
Blacktop Cowboys, 212
The Blind Side, 205–6
The Breaks of the Game, 54
Bringing the Heat, 51–52
Cubs Nation, 56
Display of Power, 291–82
Fantasyland, 159–60
Fast Food Nation, 110
Feeding the Monster, 55
Finders Keepers, 203
Friday Night Lights, 50
The Kings of New York, 213–14
The Legend of Colton H. Bryant, 194–85
A Measure of Endurance, 206
The Miracle of St. Anthony, 56–57
Next Man Up, 53
Nickel and Dimed, 164
Once Upon a Quinceañara, 208
A People's History of American Empire, 257
Pledged: The Secret Life of Sororities, 176–77
Rammer, Jammer, Yellow, Hammer, 157
Rocky Stories, 217–18
Stiff: The Curious Lives of Human Cadavers, 47
Sweet: An Eight-Ball Odyssey, 163
Tales from Q School, 53–54
There Are No Children Here, 125–26
Three Nights in August, 50–51
The Ticket Out, 213
To Air Is Human, 158–59
The Whistleblower, 108
Who's Afraid of a Large Black Man?, 215–16
Yale University
God and Man at Yale, 232
Year in the Life
Absolutely American, 211–12
The Backwash Squeeze and Other Improbable Feats, 156
Backyard Giants, 19
Bigger Deal, 166

Blacktop Cowboys, 212
The Blind Side, 205–6
The Breaks of the Game, 54
Bringing the Heat, 51–52
Cheer! Three Teams on a Quest for College Cheerleading's Ultimate Prize, 18–19
Cookoff: Recipe Fever in America, 157–58
A Country Practice, 20
Courtroom 302, 58
Coyotes, 172
Cubs Nation, 56
Dreaming in Code, 16–17
Fantasyland, 159–60
Fat Envelope Frenzy, 218–19
Friday Night Lights, 50
Growing Up Fast, 211
Gun Show Nation, 117–18
Helping Me Help Myself, 155–56
A Home on the Field, 173
The Kings of New York, 213–14
Lost Mountain, 107–8
The Miracle of Castel di Sangro, 185–86
The Miracle of St. Anthony, 56–57
Next Man Up, 53
Noble Rot: A Bordeaux Wine Revolution, 290

No Matter How Loud I Shout, 62–63
Once Upon a Quinceañara, 208
Opium Season, 184
Otherwise Normal People, 17–18
The Overachievers, 128–29
Paper Lion, 167
The Perfect Scent, 289
Pledged: The Secret Life of Sororities, 176–77
A Prayer for the City, 209
Punching In, 165–66
The Race for the Triple Crown, 52–53
Rammer, Jammer, Yellow, Hammer, 157
The Season, 173–74
Suburban Safari, 23
Sweet: An Eight-Ball Odyssey, 163
To Air Is Human, 158–59
The Underdog, 152–53
A Very Good Year, 19–20
The Whale Warriors, 13
Wonderland, 171
Word Freak, 153
Yugoslavia
The Fixer: A Story from Sarajevo, 199–200
They Would Never Hurt a Fly, 135–36

About the Author

SARAH STATZ CORDS has worked for the Madison Public Library and the University of Wisconsin—Madison Engineering Library in Wisconsin. She reviews books for *Library Journal* and Bookslut.com and has taught a course on adult reading interests at the UW—Madison School of Library and Information Studies. She is the author of *The Real Story: A Guide to Nonfiction Reading Interests* (Libraries Unlimited, 2006) and is an associate editor for the Readers' Advisor Online.

Photo by Rich Gassen